THE INTERFACE OF SOCIAL AND CLINICAL PSYCHOLOGY

Key Readings in Social Psychology

General Editor: ARIE W. KRUGLANSKI, University of Maryland at College Park

The aim of this series is to make available to advanced undergraduate and graduate students key articles in each area of social psychology in an attractive, user-friendly format. Many professors want to encourage their students to engage directly with research in their fields, yet this can often be daunting for students coming to detailed study of a topic for the first time. Moreover, declining library budgets mean that articles are not always readily available, and course packs can be expensive and time-consuming to produce. **Key Readings in Social Psychology** aims to address this need by providing comprehensive volumes, each one of which will be edited by a senior and active researcher in the field. Articles will be carefully chosen to illustrate the way the field has developed historically as well as current issues and research directions. Each volume will have a similar structure, which will include:

- an overview chapter, as well as introductions to sections and articles
- questions for class discussion
- annotated bibliographies
- full author and subject indexes

Published Titles

The Self in Social Psychology	Roy F. Baumeister
Stereotypes and Prejudice	Charles Stangor
Motivational Science	E. Tory Higgins and Arie W. Kruglanski
Social Psychology and Human Sexuality	Roy F. Baumeister
Emotions in Social Psychology	W. Gerrod Parrott
Intergroup Relations	Michael A. Hogg and Dominic Abrams
The Social Psychology of Organizational Behavior	Leigh L. Thompson
Social Psychology: A General Reader	Arie W. Kruglanski and E. Tory Higgins
Social Psychology of Health	Peter Salovey and Alexander J. Rothman
The Interface of Social and Clinical Psychology	Robin M. Kowalski and Mark R. Leary

Titles in Preparation

Attitudes	Richard E. Petty and Russell Fazio
Close Relationships	Harry Reis and Caryl Rusbult
Group Processes	John Levine and Richard Moreland
Language and Communication	Gün R. Semin
Persuasion	Richard E. Petty and Russell Fazio
Political Psychology	John T. Jost and Jim Sidanius
Social Cognition	David L. Hamilton
Social Comparison	Diederik Stapel and Hart Blanton
Social Neuroscience	John T. Cacioppo and Gary Berntson

For contiually updated information about published and forthcoming titles in the Key Readings in Social Psychology series, please visit: www.keyreadings.com

THE INTERFACE OF SOCIAL AND CLINICAL PSYCHOLOGY
Key Readings

Edited by

Robin M. Kowalski
Clemson University

Mark R. Leary
Wake Forest University

Psychology Press
Taylor & Francis Group
New York   London

First published in 2004 by
Psychology Press
29 West 35th Street
New York, NY 10001
www.psypress.com

Published in Great Britain by
Psychology Press
27 Church Road
Hove, East Sussex
BN3 2FA
www.psypress.co.uk

This edition published 2012 by Psychology Press

Psychology Press
Taylor & Francis Group
711 Third Avenue
New York, NY 10017

Psychology Press
Taylor & Francis Group
27 Church Road
Hove, East Sussex BN3 2FA

Copyright © 2004 by Taylor & Francis Books, Inc.

Psychology Press is an imprint of the Taylor & Francis Group.

All rights reserved. No part of this book may be reprinted or reproduced or utilized in any form or by any electronic, mechanical, or other means, now known or hereafter invented, including photocopying and recording, or in any information storage or retrieval system, without permission in writing from the publishers.

Library of Congress Cataloging-in-Publication Data

   The interface of social and clinical psychology : key readings / edited by Robin M. Kowalski and Mark R. Leary.— 1st ed.
      p. cm. — (Key readings in social psychology)
   Includes bibliographical references and index.
     ISBN 1-84169-087-2 (hbk) — ISBN 1-84169-088-0 (pbk.)
    1. Social psychiatry. 2. Clinical psychology. 3. Interpersonal relations. 4. Social psychology.
  I. Kowalski, Robin M. II. Leary, Mark
R. III. Series.
    RC455.I536 2003
    362.2—dc21

2003007278

Contents

About the Editors   ix
Acknowledgments   xi

PART 1
Introduction   1

An Introduction to Social-Clinical Psychology   3
Mark R. Leary and Robin M. Kowalski

READING 1
Progress Toward a Viable Interface Between Social and Clinical-Counseling Psychology   11
Mark R. Leary and James E. Maddux

PART 2
Social Psychological Processes in the Development and Maintenance of Emotional and Behavioral Problems   25

READING 2
Behavioral and Characterological Attributional Styles as Predictors of Depression and Loneliness: Review, Refinement, and Test   27
Craig A. Anderson, Rowland S. Miller, Alice L. Riger, Jody C. Dill, and Constantine Sedikides

READING 3
Explanatory Style, Expectations, and Depressive Symptoms   44
Christopher Peterson and Robert S. Vaidya

READING 4

Self-Regulation Failure: An Overview   51

Roy F. Baumeister and Todd F. Heatherton

READING 5

Catastrophizing and Untimely Death   70

Christopher Peterson, Martin E. P. Seligman, Karen H. Yurko, Leslie R. Martin, and Howard S. Friedman

READING 6

Schizophrenic Patients in the Psychiatric Interview: An Experimental Study of Their Effectiveness at Manipulation   78

Benjamin M. Braginsky and Dorothea D. Braginsky

READING 7

Drug Choice as a Self-Handicapping Strategy in Response to Noncontingent Success   85

Steven Berglas and Edward E. Jones

READING 8

Social Contagion of Binge Eating   99

Christian S. Crandall

READING 9

The Role of Low Self-Esteem in Emotional and Behavioral Problems: Why Is Low Self-Esteem Dysfunctional?   116

Mark R. Leary, Lisa S. Schreindorfer, and Alison L. Haupt

READING 10

Marital Satisfaction, Depression, and Attributions: A Longitudinal Analysis   129

Frank D. Fincham and Thomas N. Bradbury

READING 11

Interpersonal Concomitants and Antecedents of Depression Among College Students   147

Jack E. Hokanson, Mark P. Rubert, Richard A. Welker, Glee R. Hollander, and Carla Hedeen

READING 12

Social Confirmation of Dysphoria: Shared and Private Reactions to Depression   162

Stephen Strack and James C. Coyne

READING 13
Implications of Rejection Sensitivity for Intimate Relationships   173
Geraldine Downey and Scott I. Feldman

PART 3
Social Psychological Processes in the Perception and Diagnosis of Psychological Problems   199

READING 14
On Being Sane in Insane Places   201
D. L. Rosenhan

READING 15
A Patient by Any Other Name . . . : Clinician Group Differences in Labeling Bias   216
Ellen J. Langer and Robert P. Abelson

READING 16
When Counselors Confirm: A Functional Analysis   225
John Copeland and Mark Snyder

READING 17
The Mythology of Psychopathology: A Social Cognitive View of Deviance, Difference, and Disorder   240
James E. Maddux

READING 18
Lessons From Social Psychology on Discrediting Psychiatric Stigma   258
Patrick W. Corrigan and David L. Penn

PART 4
Social Psychological Processes in Clinical Treatment and Psychological Change   275

READING 19
American Psychotherapy in Perspective (Excerpt from *Persuasion and Healing*)   277
Jerome Frank

READING 20

The Scientific Study of Counseling and Psychotherapy:
A Unificationist View   290

Donelson R. Forsyth and Stanley R. Strong

READING 21

Disclosure of Traumas and Immune Function:
Health Implications for Psychotherapy   301

James W. Pennebaker, Janice K. Kiecolt-Glaser, and Ronald Glaser

READING 22

Cognitive Dissonance and Psychotherapy: The Role of Effort
Justification in Inducing Weight Loss   313

Danny Axsom and Joel Cooper

READING 23

Reconceptualizing Social Influence in Counseling:
The Elaboration Likelihood Model   324

Brian W. McNeill and Cal D. Stoltenberg

READING 24

The Effects of Choice and Enhanced Personal Responsibility
for the Aged: A Field Experiment in an Institutional Setting   339

Ellen J. Langer and Judith Rodin

READING 25

The Trouble With Change: Self-Verification and
Allegiance to the Self   349

William B. Swann, Jr.

Appendix: How to Read a Journal Article in Social Psychology   357

Christian H. Jordan and Mark P. Zanna

References   367
Author Index   369
Subject Index   381

About the Editors

Robin M. Kowalski is currently a professor of Psychology at Clemson University. She received her PhD in social psychology from the University of North Carolina at Greensboro. Her research interests focus primarily on aversive interpersonal encounters, specifically complaining and teasing. She has published three books on the topic of aversive encounters, including *Aversive Interpersonal Behaviors* (Plenum Press), *Behaving Badly: Aversive Behaviors in Interpersonal Relationships* (American Psychological Association), and *Offensive Encounters: Complaining, Teasing, and Other Annoying Behaviors* (Yale University Press). In addition, she has an edited book (with Mark Leary) entitled *The Social Psychology of Emotional and Behavioral Problems*.

Mark Leary is currently a professor and chair of Psychology at Wake Forest University. He received his PhD in social psychology from the University of Florida. He has written and/or edited eight books—including *Self-Presentation: Impression Management and Interpersonal Behaviors* (Westview), *Interpersonal Rejection* (Oxford), and *Handbook of Self and Identity* (Guilford). Dr. Leary is also the current editor of the journal *Self and Identity*.

Acknowledgments

The editors and publishers are grateful to the following for permission to reproduce the articles in this book:

Reading 1: M. R. Leary and J. E. Maddux, Progress Toward a Viable Interface Between Social and Clinical-Counseling Psychology. *American Psychologist, 42,* 904–911. Copyright © 1987 by the American Psychological Association. Reprinted with permission.

Reading 2: C. A. Anderson, R. S. Miller, A. L. Riger, J. C. Dill, and C. Sedikides, Behavioral and Characterological Attributional Styles as Predictors of Depression and Loneliness: Review, Refinement and Test. *Journal of Personality and Social Psychology, 66,* 549–558. Copyright © 1994 by the American Psychological Association. Reprinted with permission.

Reading 3: C. Peterson and R. S. Vaidya, Explanatory Style, Expectations, and Depressive Symptoms. *Personality and Individual Differences, 31,* 1217–1223. Copyright © 2001 by Elsevier Science. Reprinted by permission of the publisher.

Reading 4: R. F. Baumeister and T. F. Heatherton, Self-Regulation Failure: An Overview. *Psychological Inquiry, 7,* 1–15. Copyright © 1996 by Lawrence Erlbaum Associates. Reprinted with permission.

Reading 5: C. Peterson, M. E. P. Seligman, K. H. Yurko, L. R. Martin, and H. S. Friedman, Catastrophizing and Untimely Death. *Psychological Science, 9,* 127–130. Copyright ©1998 by Blackwell Publishing. Reprinted with permission.

Reading 6: B. M. Braginsky and D. D. Braginsky, Schizophrenic Patients in the Psychiatric Interview: An Experimental Study of Their Effectiveness at Manipulation. *Journal of Consulting Psychology, 31,* 543–547. Copyright ©1967 by the American Psychological Association. Reprinted with permission.

Reading 7: S. Berglas and E. E. Jones, Drug Choice as a Self-Handicapping Strategy in Response to Noncontingent Success. *Journal of Personality and Social Psychology, 36,* 405–417. Copyright © 1978 by the American Psychological Association. Reprinted with permission.

Reading 8: C. S. Crandall, Social Contagion of Binge Eating. *Journal of Personality and Social Psychology, 55,* 588–598. Copyright © 1988 by the American Psychological Association. Reprinted with permission.

Reading 9: M. R. Leary, L. S. Schreindorfer, and A. L. Haupt, The Role of Low Self-Esteem in Emotional and Behavioral Problems: Why Is Low Self-Esteem Dysfunctional? *Journal of Social and Clinical Psychology, 14,* 297–314. Copyright © 1995 by Guilford Publications, Inc. Reprinted with permission of the publisher.

Reading 10: F. D. Fincham and T. N. Bradbury, Marital Satisfaction, Depression, and Attributions: A Longitudinal Analysis. *Journal of Personality and Social Psychology, 64,* 442–452. Copyright © 1993 by the American Psychological Association. Reprinted with permission.

Reading 11: J. E. Hokanson, M. P. Rubert, R. A. Welker, G. R. Hollander, and C. Hedeen, Interpersonal Concomitants and Antecedents of Depression Among College Students. *Journal of Abnormal Psychology, 98,* 209–217. Copyright © 1989 by the American Psychological Association. Reprinted with permission.

Reading 12: S. Strack and J. C. Coyne, Social Confirmation of Dysphoria: Shared and Private Reactions to Depression. *Journal of Personality and Social Psychology, 44,* 798–806. Copyright © 1983 by the American Psychological Association. Reprinted with permission.

Reading 13: G. Downey and S. I. Feldman, Implications of Rejection Sensitivity for Intimate Relationships. *Journal of Personality and Social Psychology, 70,* 1327–1343. Copyright © 1996 by the American Psychological Association. Reprinted with permission.

Reading 14: D. L. Rosenhan, On Being Sane in Insane Places. *Science, 179,* 250–258. Copyright © 1973 American Association for the Advancement of Science. Reprinted with permission.

Reading 15: E. J. Langer and R. P. Abelson, A Patient by Any Other Name . . . : Clinician Group Difference in Labeling Bias. *Journal of Consulting and Clinical Psychology, 42,* 4–9. Copyright © 1974 by the American Psychological Association. Reprinted with permission.

Reading 16: J. Copeland and M. Snyder, When Counselors Confirm: A Functional Analysis. *Personality and Social Psychology Bulletin, 21,* 1210–1220. Copyright © 1995 by the Society for Personality and Social Psychology, Inc. Reprinted by permission of Sage Publications, Inc.

Reading 17: J. E. Maddux, The Mythology of Psychopathology: A Social Cognitive View of Deviance, Difference, and Disorder. *The General Psychologist, 29,* 34–45. Copyright © 1993. Reprinted with permission.

Reading 18: P. W. Corrigan and D. L. Penn, Lessons from Social Psychology on Discrediting Psychiatric Stigma. *American Psychologist, 54,* 765–776. Copyright © 1999 by the American Psychological Association. Reprinted with permission.

Reading 19: Jerome D. Frank, *Persuasion and Healing: A Comparative Study of Psychotherapy,* pp. 312–337. Copyright © 1961, Johns Hopkins University Press. Reprinted/adapted with permission of the The Johns Hopkins University Press.

Reading 20: D. R. Forsyth and S. R. Strong, The Scientific Study of Counseling and Psychotherapy: A Unificationist View. *American Psychologist, 41,* 113–119. Copyright ©1986 by the American Psychological Association. Reprinted with permission.

Reading 21: J. W. Pennebaker, J. K. Kiecolt-Glaser, and R. Glaser, Disclosure of Traumas and Immune Function: Health Implications for Psychotherapy. *Journal of Consulting and Clinical Psychology, 56,* 239–245. Copyright © 1988 by the American Psychological Association. Reprinted with permission.

Reading 22: D. Axsom and J. Cooper, Cognitive Dissonance and Psychotherapy: The Role of Effort Justification in Inducing Weight Loss. *Journal of Experimental Social Psychology, 21,* 149–160. Copyright ©1985 by Elsevier Science. Reprinted with permission of the publisher.

Reading 23: B. W. McNeill and C. D. Stoltenberg, Reconceptualizing Social Influence in Counseling: The Elaboration Likelihood Model. *Journal of Counseling Psychology, 36,* 24–33. Copyright © 1989 by the American Psychological Association. Reprinted with permission.

Reading 24: E. J. Langer and J. Rodin, The Effects of Choice and Enhanced Personal Responsibility for the Aged: A Field Experiment in an Institutional Setting. *Journal of Personality and Social Psychology, 34,* 191–198. Copyright © 1976 by the American Psychological Association. Reprinted with permission.

Reading 25: W. B. Swann, Jr., The Trouble With Change: Self-Verification and Allegiance to the Self. *Psychological Science, 8,* 177–180. Copyright © 1997 by Blackwell Publishing. Reprinted with permission.

PART 1

Introduction

An Introduction to Social-Clinical Psychology

Mark R. Leary and Robin M. Kowalski

Sometime shortly after human beings attained a sufficient degree of self-awareness to reflect about their condition in life, probably within the last 60,000 to 100,000 years, people presumably began to wonder why some individuals in their social groups seemed unusually peculiar, difficult to deal with, dangerous, unhappy, or maladjusted. Certainly, by the time that ancient civilizations flourished in Greece, India, Mesopotamia, and the Far East, many writers were pondering the sources of human problems and ways to deal with them. Plato, Aristotle, and Galen, for example, grappled with the mysteries of the human psyche in Greece, as did Gautama Buddha in India, Lao Tzu in China, and the writers of the Old Testament in the Middle East. Why do people hurt others, and sometimes themselves? Why do smart people often do stupid, self-defeating things? Why are people unhappy? What causes selfishness, greed, anger, violence, and other sources of human misery? Why do some people have strange thoughts, hear voices, or otherwise "act crazy"? For most of history, such questions fell to philosophers, theologians, shamen, and other individuals recognized for their wisdom, and only in the late 1800s did professions arise in medicine and psychology that specialized in studying psychological problems.

The Rise and Fall and Rise of Social-Clinical Psychology

In the early days of psychology, in the late 19th and early 20th centuries, most psychologists were generalists. The discipline was so new and the base of knowledge so small that one person could become familiar with virtually all of it and move among various topics easily. For example, William James, who established the first psychological laboratory in the United States in 1875, had a clear command of many topics that today constitute quite separate subfields of psychology—psychophysiology, sensation, perception, attention, cognition, consciousness, learning, memory, imagination, reasoning, instinct, the self, emotion, and so on. As the research literature grew, however, it became increasingly difficult for one person to become familiar with, much less master, the entire field.

As a result of the burgeoning research literature, psychologists began to specialize. During the early 20th century, many of the major domains of modern psychology were demarcated. Developmental psychology, social psychology, clinical psychology, experimental psychology, and industrial psychology, for example, were each identified as a separate subfield of the growing discipline. The lines between these areas were somewhat arbitrary, spurred by the dual needs to manage the growing mass of knowledge and to organize university psychology departments for administrative purposes. In reality, almost any particular topic could be studied by specialists in a number of fields, and it was largely a matter of preference whether a particular topic became aligned with one specialty or another. To give just one example, the ways in which one person's behavior can be influenced by other people could be studied by social psychologists, developmental psychologists, industrial psychologists, learning psychologists, clinical psychologists, or any number of fields.

The increasing specialization in psychology had an unfortunate consequence. Psychologists began to act as if the divisions among subspecialties of psychology were real barriers rather than convenient organizational categories. As a result, researchers in different specializations often did not communicate with each other even when they were working on similar problems, and the various subfields of psychology grew increasingly further apart. This schism was particularly pronounced between social psychology and clinical psychology. Although social and clinical psychology developed at about the same time, and early social and clinical psychologists shared similar backgrounds and interests, the fields did not view one another as particularly relevant.

Social psychology was only a small segment of psychology during its earliest years. A few researchers examined the influence of social factors on behavior (such as Triplett's [1898] classic study of group competition), but psychologists initially left the study of social behavior to sociologists and social anthropologists. As social psychology began to attract attention following the publication of McDougall's (1908) *An Introduction to Social Psychology*, researchers in the new field generally gravitated toward studying normal patterns of social behavior and paid little attention to abnormality. Thus, despite the fact that the same social influences that affect normal behavior may contribute to psychological problems, social psychologists showed little inclination to study the development or treatment of psychological difficulties.

At about the same time, clinical psychology developed as a subspecialty through the efforts of Lightner Witmer. Although Witmer was trained as an experimental psychologist, he became convinced that a new psychological profession was needed, separate from medicine and education, that applied the findings of experimental psychology to help people with their problems (Benjamin, 1996). Witmer founded the first psychological clinic in 1896, and in 1907 published an article in which he described the operations of his clinic and proposed establishment of a new profession of what he called "clinical psychology." This was a radical idea at the time. Most psychologists viewed psychology as a science whose function was to develop theory and conduct research, not as a profession that provided clinical services. Yet the idea caught on, and clinical psychology grew quickly.

Spurred by the idea that psychologists should devote greater attention to understanding and treating psychological problems, many researchers turned their attention to emotional and behavioral problems. Partly in response to this movement, Morton Prince founded the *Journal of Abnormal Psychology* in 1907, to publish research dealing with "abnormal mental phenomena" from both medical and psychological scientists. Initially, the *Journal of Abnormal Psychology* focused primarily on clinical phenomena such as hallucinations, delusions, obsessions, neuroses, multiple personality, depression, hypnosis, and "deliria." However, in 1921, Prince broadened the scope of the journal to include topics in social psychology. Prince argued that social psychology and abnormal psychology were interested in many of the same phenomena, such as attitudes, communication, group influence, personality traits, the relationship between individuals and the groups to which they belong, and the behavior of crowds. Social psychology may focus on these phenomena primarily among "normal" individuals, whereas abnormal psychology examines them in people with various problems, but Prince was convinced that the basic processes were often the same. Thus, he changed the name of the journal to the *Journal of Abnormal and Social Psychology* and encouraged researchers to submit papers that made explicit connections between social psychological processes and psychological problems.

Despite the efforts of Prince and others, social and clinical psychology moved in different directions during the 1930s, and this separation was fueled by the roles that the two fields played during and after World War II. During the war, social psychologists focused on topics that were of importance to the war effort, such as morale (of both soldiers overseas and the civilians back home), attitudes, persuasion, propaganda, group behavior, and international relations (Hilgard, 1989). The influence of the war molded social psychologists' interests well into the 1960s as popular areas of research continued to involve groups, attitudes, and obedience. For clinical psychologists, World War II brought heightened attention to the two areas that became the core of modern clinical psychology—assessment and psychotherapy. Clinical psychologists became involved in developing tests to measure recruits' aptitudes and psychological adjustment, and in helping soldiers deal with the psychological effects of war. When the war ended, the need for mental health professionals overwhelmed psychiatrists working in Veterans Administration hospitals, so clinical psychologists became increasingly involved in psychotherapy.

The result of these diverging paths was that, by 1960, social and clinical psychology were having little to do with one another. As Goldstein (1966) noted at the time, "researchers interested in psychotherapy and their colleagues studying social psychological phenomena have gone their separate ways, making scant reference to one another's work and, in general, ignoring what appear to be real opportunities for mutual feedback and stimulation" (p. 39). Not only were social and clinical psychologists generally interested in different topics, but their professional worldviews had diverged as well. In particular, where social psychologists stressed the importance of external, interpersonal factors in influencing behavior, clinical psychologists tended to focus on internal, psychogenic determinants. As a result, neither camp saw the other's work as particularly useful or relevant.

The growing schism was unfortunate for both sides. Clearly, many psychological problems can be traced to the kinds of interpersonal processes that are studied by social psychologists, and the effectiveness of psychotherapy depends to a large extent on the social psychological processes that occur in the clinical setting. Yet clinical psychologists virtually ignored the wealth of information on these processes coming from social psychology. At the same time, social psychologists would have benefited from studying the processes of interest to them among psychologically disordered as well as among adjusted individuals. Yet social psychology focused narrowly on normal social behavior, and anything that smacked of psychopathology was left to the clinicians. The split between social and clinical psychology is perhaps best exemplified by the decision to split the *Journal of Abnormal and Social Psychology* into two journals—the *Journal of Abnormal Psychology* and the *Journal of Personality and Social Psychology*—in 1965.

Ironically, at about the same time that the separation between social and clinical psychology peaked, several writers began suggesting again that social and clinical psychology might have something important to say to each other. One of the first was Jerome Frank, who, in *Persuasion and Healing* (1961), proposed that all instances of psychological change are the result of the same social and cognitive processes. Drawing upon research in experimental social psychology, Frank showed that psychological changes—not only the changes that occur as the result of psychotherapy, but also those that occur from experiences such as faith healing and religious conversion—result from social psychological processes. (Reading 18 in this book is a selection from Frank's influential work.) Likewise, Goldstein (1966; Goldstein, Heller, & Sechrest, 1966) discussed the social psychological processes involved in psychotherapy and Strong (1968) suggested that counseling was essentially a process of social influence that could be understood with reference to social psychological perspectives. Little research was being conducted at the time on the social psychology of psychological disorders or clinical treatment, but these writers could see the applicability of even basic theory and research in social psychology.

During the 1970s, one began to glimpse a small but steady increase of interest in the social psychology of emotional and behavioral problems, much of it involving the role that attributions play in creating and sustaining problems such as anxiety and depression (e.g., Abramson, Seligman, & Teasdale, 1978; Valins & Nisbett, 1972). However, the only major effort to bridge the gap between social and clinical psychology on a large scale was provided by Sharon Brehm in *The Application of Social Psychology to Clinical Practice* (1976). In this book, Brehm showed how major theories in social psychology, such as cognitive dissonance theory and reactance theory, could be used to understand and improve the practice of clinical psychology.

The Social-Clinical Interface Comes of Age

By the early 1980s, it was no longer unusual to see psychologists on both sides of the social–clinical fence using social psychological concepts to understand emotional and behavioral problems. Although topics such as shyness, social anxiety, loneliness, depression, hypochondriasis, test anxiety, drug abuse, self-defeating behavior, narcissism, and marital difficulties were once considered the sole domain of clinical and counseling psychologists, mainline social psychologists now waded into the area. Along with this growing interest came efforts to delineate this new subfield of social-clinical psychology (Harvey, 1983; Harvey & Weary, 1979; Hendrick, 1983; Leary & Maddux, 1987), as well as books that examined topics at the interface of the fields (Leary & Miller, 1986; Maddux, Stoltenberg, & Rosenwein, 1987; Weary & Mirels, 1982). Perhaps most importantly, in 1983 John Harvey founded a new journal, the *Journal of Social and Clinical Psychology*, to provide an outlet for research that integrates social and clinical psychology.

Today, researchers move easily across a wide bridge that spans what was once a nearly impassible ravine between social and clinical psychology. Many social psychologists study the origin, diagnosis, or treatment of psychological problems, and many clinical and counseling psychologists borrow constructs, theories, and research from social psychology in their efforts to understand, diagnose, and treat those problems. Of course, most social psychologists continue to focus on normal patterns of behavior, as well they should, and most clinical psychologists recognize that social psychological factors are but one source of psychological dysfunction. The point of social-clinical psychology is not to merge the two subdisciplines into a single field, but rather to facilitate communication and cross-fertilization between them.

Social Psychological Factors in the Development of Dysfunctional Behavior

Theory and research at the interface of social and clinical psychology fall roughly into three categories that focus on the (1) development, (2) diagnosis, and (3) treatment of psychological difficulties. By far the largest body of work focuses on social psychological processes involved in the development and maintenance of emotional and behavioral problems. Basic social psychological processes involving social cognition and perception, self and identity, attitudes, social influence, interpersonal interaction, personal relationships, and group behavior have all been examined as sources of psychological difficulties. Table 1 lists several of the topics for which social psychological perspectives have been applied to understanding how and why psychological problems develop.

TABLE 1. Social Psychological Processes in the Development and Maintenance of Emotional and Behavioral Problems

Social psychological area	Topics
Social perception and cognition	Effects of attributions on emotion (e.g., depression, anxiety)
	Interpretations of negative life events
	Perceptions of control (and lack of control)
	Beliefs about mental illness
Self and identity	Self-focused attention
	Self-concept; self-evaluation; self-esteem
	Self-efficacy
	Dysfunctional identities
	Self-handicapping
	Social comparison
	Self-regulation
	Self-focused emotions (e.g., shame, guilt)
Attitudes	Maladaptive attitudes
	Stigmatization
Social influence	Media influences
	Dysfunctional conformity
	Social contagion of psychological problems
Interpersonal interaction	Self-disclosure
	Maladaptive self-presentations
	Social skills
	Stigmatization
	Nonverbal communication
	Antisocial behavior (including aggression)
Personal relationships	Dysfunctional relationships
	Relationships with troubled individuals
	Conflict
	Relationship break-ups
	Interpersonal rejection
	Social support
	Loneliness
	Jealousy
Group processes	Dysfunctional groups (e.g., gangs, cults)

The topics shown in Table 1 have been studied using three different research approaches. The first involves experimental studies in which basic processes that produce emotional and behavioral problems are examined, usually under controlled laboratory conditions. The participants in this kind of social-clinical research are usually not troubled by any clinical problem and, in most instances, they do not have even mild, "subclinical" disorders. In fact, more often than not, the participants are typical college students. The point of this research is to understand the factors that lead even seemingly "normal" individuals to feel and behave in ways that are analogous, albeit in a less extreme fashion, to the kinds of problems for which people seek professional help. For example, by experimentally manipulating the amount of control participants believe they have over events in the research setting, researchers have found that mild levels of helplessness and depression arise that are similar to the more extreme reactions of many depressed clients. Similarly, research on self-handicapping has examined the conditions under which people behave in self-defeating ways to protect their self-esteem, a phenomenon that underlies many problems in the "real world" outside the lab. Likewise, experiments have been conducted to understand people's reactions following social rejection, the effects of being stigmatized, and the conditions that make people lose self-control.

A second type of study focuses on personality variables that moderate the effects of situational factors on dysfunctional behavior. We can learn a great deal about a behavioral or emotional phenomenon by understanding the kinds of people who do and do not manifest it. So, for example, people with low self-esteem may respond dysfunctionally to certain kinds of situations, whereas people with high self-esteem react dysfunctionally in other kinds of situations. Or, people who are highly sensitive to rejection may actually increase their chances of being rejected by behaving badly when they feel others do not like them. Many of the topics listed in Table 1 have been investigated, in part, by studying personality variables that predispose people to react in a maladaptive fashion.

Third, some research on the effects of social psychological processes on psychological problems has involved field studies that attempt to examine factors that promote problems in everyday life. For example, studies of the negative effects of peer rejection in childhood, the self-handicapping strategies of alcoholics, the social contagion of eating disorders, and the trajectory of troubled relationships that end in divorce have been conducted in the "real world" outside of the psychology laboratory.

Social Psychological Factors in the Perception and Diagnosis of Dysfunctional Behavior

The second major category of theory and research at the interface of social and clinical psychology involves processes that are involved in the perception and diagnosis of emotional and behavioral problems—by therapists, other people, and clients themselves. The same factors that influence everyday social perception and cognition also play a role in the clinical setting. Table 2 lists many of the topics involving perceptions of mental disorder that have been studied.

Much of this work examines factors that affect practicing psychologists' diagnoses and judgments. Psychological diagnosis can be viewed as a process of collecting and interpreting information about other people that bears a great deal of resemblance to the processes by which people form impressions of and think about others in everyday life. Thus, research has examined the social psychology of clinical diagnosis. Other studies have examined how ordinary people perceive, interpret, and react to disordered behavior in other people—for example, the impressions that people have of those who appear depressed, stereotypes

TABLE 2. Social Psychological Processes in the Diagnosis of Emotional and Behavioral Problems

Social psychological area	Topics
Social perception and cognition	Forming impressions of clients
	Diagnostic and judgmental processes
	Therapist biases
	Attributions regarding causes of clients' problems
	Stigmatization of psychological disorders
Self and identity	Self-perceptions of psychological difficulties
	Internalization of clinical labels
Attitudes	Stereotypes of particular disorders
Social influence	Persuading clients of diagnosis
	Effects of diagnostic labels
Interpersonal interaction	Assessment interviews
	Therapist empathy
	Clients' self-presentations to therapists
Personal relationships	Role of relationship partners in seeking professional help
Group processes	Norms regarding the acceptability of testing and therapy

of the "mentally ill," and the conditions under which people judge those who behave in unusual ways to be psychologically disturbed as opposed to merely eccentric.

Of course, people also assess their own psychological well-being, and researchers have studied how people perceive, interpret, and explain their own problematic behaviors. The very extensive social psychological literature on how people perceive and evaluate themselves is obviously quite relevant to understanding how people draw conclusions about their problems.

Social Psychological Factors in the Treatment of Dysfunctional Behavior

Finally, a great deal of work has examined social psychological processes in the treatment of emotional and behavioral problems (see Table 3). Some of this research has been conducted in controlled laboratory studies using samples of college students who have some minor psychological complaint (such as mild test anxiety, shyness, or an over concern with their weight). Other studies in this category have been conducted during the course of real counseling or psychotherapy on actual clients in an effort to understand how these processes operate in vivo. Both approaches have their advantages and disadvantages (Forsyth & Strong, 1986). Laboratory experiments allow researchers to control the setting to study particular variables in isolation, but the participants are typically not real psychotherapy clients. Field investigations in clinical settings study real clients with real problems, but their results are sometimes clouded by the complexities of actual clinical practice. Together, however, these approaches may converge to provide a clear picture of the social psychological processes that facilitate and hamper psychological change.

Recently, many clinical psychologists have embraced a health-promotion or positive psychology perspective. The traditional approach within clinical psychology has been to help people with their problems, whereas many psychologists have suggested that we should also be concerned with promoting adjustment and well-being among people who would not be regarded as psychologically troubled and, thus, not ordinary candidates for counseling

TABLE 3. Social Psychological Processes in the Treatment of Emotional and Behavioral Problems

Social psychological area	Topics
Social perception and cognition	Attributional therapies
	Expectancy effects
Self and identity	Self-concept change
	Client self-efficacy
	Perceived control
	Self-regulation
Attitudes	Changing clients' dysfunctional attitudes
	Cognitive dissonance in therapy
	Effort justification
Social influence	Persuasion in counseling and psychotherapy
	Therapist credibility
	Client compliance, resistance, and reactance
Interpersonal interaction	Interactions between therapists and clients
	Client self-disclosure
	Role-playing therapies
Personal relationships	Therapist–client relationship
	Transference
	Client's social support network
Group processes	Group therapy

or psychotherapy. After all, virtually everyone, no matter how well adjusted, could improve their ability to relate to other people, cope more effectively with life, respond more cooperatively and compassionately, and function more effectively. Parts of counseling psychology have operated out of such a model for many years (starting with the humanistic movement of the 1950s), but the focus of traditional clinical psychology has been on solving problems rather than enhancing well-being. Positive psychology is a growing area of social-clinical psychology devoted to understanding and promoting behaviors such as forgiveness, hope, trust, equanimity, compassion, cooperation, and other positive states.

The Readings

The articles in this book were selected to provide a broad overview of work at the interface of social and clinical psychology. In selecting articles, we tried to include both theoretical and empirical pieces, as well as a mix of classic and recent articles. Given space limitations, we were forced to be selective, and many leading scholars and outstanding articles could not be included. Just because a particular article does not appear in this book does not indicate that it is not a key reading in this area!

Following an article that provides a general introduction to the assumptions that underlie social-clinical psychology, the readings in this book are divided into the three categories described earlier, dealing with social psychological processes involved in the development, diagnosis, and treatment of psychological problems. Each article is preceded by a brief introduction that provides a context for understanding the article, and is followed by a list of discussion questions and suggested readings on the topic of the article.

REFERENCES

Abramson, L. Y., Seligman, M. E. P., & Teasdale, J. D. (1978). Learned helplessness: Critique and reformulation. *Journal of Abnormal Psychology, 87*, 49–74.

Benjamin, L.T. (1996). Lightner Witmer's legacy to American psychology. *American Psychologist, 51*, 235–236.

Brehm, S. (1976). *Applications of social psychology to clinical practice*. Washington, DC: Hemisphere.

Forsyth, D. R., & Strong, S. R. (1986). The scientific study of counseling and psychotherapy: A unificationist view. *American Psychologist, 41*, 113–119.

Goldstein, A. P. (1966). Psychotherapy research by extrapolation from social psychology. *Journal of Counseling Psychology, 13*, 38–45.

Goldstein, A. P., Heller, K., & Sechrest, L. B. (1966). *Psychotherapy and the psychology of behavior change*. New York: Wiley.

Harvey, J. H. (1983). The founding of the *Journal of Social and Clinical Psychology*. *Journal of Social and Clinical Psychology, 1*, 1–13.

Harvey, J. H., & Weary, G. (1979). The integration of social and clinical psychology training programs. *Personality and Social Psychology Bulletin, 5*, 511–515.

Hendrick, C. (1983). Clinical social psychology: A birthright reclaimed. *Journal of Social and Clinical Psychology, 1*, 66–87.

Hilgard, E. R. (1989). *Psychology in America: A historical survey*. New York: Harcourt Brace Jovanovich.

Leary, M. R., & Miller, R. S. (1986). *Social psychology and dysfunctional behavior: Origins, diagnosis, and treatment*. New York: Spring-Verlag.

Leary, M. R., & Maddux, J. E. (1987). Progress toward a viable interface between social and clinical psychology. *American Psychologist, 42*, 904–911.

Maddux, J. E., Stoltenberg, C. D., & Rosenwein, R. (Eds.). (1987). *Social processes in clinical and counseling psychology*. New York: Plenum.

McDougall, W. (1908). *An introduction to social psychology*. London: Methuen.

Reisman, J. M. (1991). *A history of clinical psychology* (2nd ed.). New York: Hemisphere.

Strong, S. R. (1968). Counseling: An interpersonal influence process. *Journal of Counseling Psychology, 15*, 215–224.

Triplett, N. (1898). The dynamogenic factors in pacemaking and competition. *American Journal of Psychology, 9*, 507–533.

Valins, S., & Nisbett, R. E. (1972). Attribution processes in the development and treatment of emotional disorders. In E. E. Jones, D. E. Kanouse, H. H. Kelley, R. E. Nisbett, S. Valins, & B. Weiner (Eds.), *Attribution: Perceiving the causes of behavior* (pp. 137–150). Morristown, NJ: General Learning Press.

Weary, G., & Mirels, H. L. (Eds.). (1982). *Integrations of clinical and social psychology*. New York: Oxford University Press.

READING 1

Progress Toward a Viable Interface Between Social and Clinical-Counseling Psychology

Mark R. Leary and James E. Maddux
• Wake Forest University and George Mason University

Editors' Introduction

As interest in the interface between social and clinical psychology blossomed in the mid-1980s, several articles appeared that charted this new territory, providing intellectual maps of where the field came from, where it currently was, and where it should go. In this article, published in 1987, Mark Leary and James Maddux provide a brief history of the relationship between social and clinical psychology, identify barriers that impede cross-fertilization between the fields, discuss the assumptions underlying the social-clinical interface, examine the impact of the interface on both scientific and professional psychology, and offer suggestions regarding how connections between social and clinical psychology might be improved. The article itself was a collaboration between a social psychologist interested in clinical topics (Leary) and a clinical psychologist interested in social psychology (Maddux).

In the article, Leary and Maddux articulate eight assumptions that underlie work that integrates social and clinical psychology, assumptions showing that psychologists can not ignore the social nature of emotional and behavioral problems. Although these assumptions may appear self-evident, not all psychologists, either today or in 1987, agree with all of them. Even the fundamental assumption—that all psychological problems are, in some way, interpersonal—runs counter to theories of behavior that stress internal, intrapsychic determinants of psychological problems.

Leary and Maddux point out that theory and research that span social and clinical psychology fall into three distinct areas. The largest of these areas involves work that examines social psychological factors in the development of emotional and behavioral problems (what they call *social-dysgenic psychology*). Even at the time this article was published, a great deal of research had examined how interpersonal processes are involved in precipitating and maintaining psychological problems as diverse as marital discord, shyness, eating disorders, underachievement, depression, schizophrenic symptomology, and hypochondriasis. Since then, interest in social-dysgenic processes has literally exploded.

The second area at which social and clinical psychology meet is *social-diagnostic psychology*—involving the study of "interpersonal processes involved in the identification, classification, and assessment of psychological and behavioral problems." When trying to understand a client's problems, clinical and counseling psychologists are in much the same position as people in everyday life when they are trying to learn about a new acquaintance. Psychotherapists and counselors may have specialized measuring instruments at their disposal, but they still must draw inferences about other people from vague, fragmented, and sometimes contradictory information. Applying what we know about the processes involved in perceiving and thinking about other people, including the biases to which person perception is susceptible, should help us develop better means of assessing clients' difficulties.

The third area of the social-clinical interface involves the study of interpersonal processes in the prevention and treatment of psychological difficulties—*social-therapeutic psychology*. Leary and Maddux point out that counseling and psychotherapy are, at their foundation, interpersonal interactions and that whatever happens during therapy to help clients improve resides in those interactions between the psychologist and his or her client. Thus, studying the social psychology of the therapeutic encounter will help us understand why therapy works and how to improve its effectiveness.

Abstract

This article examines the history of the relation between social psychology and clinical-counseling psychology. The authors discuss the barriers that traditionally have impeded close collaboration between the fields and the ways in which these barriers have eroded recently to allow for the emergence of a viable interface between social and clinical-counseling psychology. They describe the current social–clinical-counseling domain, discuss the implicit assumptions underlying the interface, assess the impact of this movement on academic and professional psychology, and make suggestions for further improving the working relations among these fields.

In a provocative analysis of contemporary behavioral science, Staats (1983) argued that psychology suffers from a "crisis of disunity." Overburdened by an immense body of disconnected and often conflicting knowledge, contemporary psychologists tend to specialize narrowly and ignore work in other areas, even areas that are related intimately to their own. Although the problems of disunity and factionalism plague virtually all of psychology, our focus in this article is on the long-standing schism between social psychology on one hand and clinical, counseling, and abnormal psychology on the other.[1]

Theorists of virtually every persuasion have long acknowledged the role of social factors in the development and treatment of behavioral and emotional problems. Furthermore, most contemporary social, clinical, and counseling psychologists share the assumption that many maladaptive behaviors are caused, maintained, and exacerbated by interpersonal factors, and most models of psychopathology and treatment include general consideration of interpersonal factors. Yet few attempts have been made to integrate *specific* perspectives from social psychology into the study of psychological problems and their treatment. Not only have clinical and counseling psychologists been uninformed regarding clinically relevant work in social psychology, but social psychologists have seemed reluctant to study clinical phenomena. As a result, social and clinical-counseling psychologists have often worked in ignorance of relevant aspects of one another's fields.

The commonalities between social and clinical-counseling psychology have been recognized and discussed by several authors over the past few decades (e.g., Brehm, 1976; Carson, 1969; Frank, 1961; Goldstein, 1966). However, recent years have seen a pronounced surge of interest in the "interface" between these fields, accompanied by widespread attempts to promote cross-fertilization between them. In this article, we examine the relation between social and clinical-counseling psychology. We discuss the barriers that have impeded close collaboration between the fields, present the implicit assumptions underlying this interface, describe the social-clinical domain as it currently exists, assess the impact of the interface on both academic and professional psychology, and offer suggestions for improving collaboration between these areas.

Reasons for the Schism

Although professional clinical and counseling psychology as we know them today did not exist in the early 20th century, models of abnormal behavior developed within personality theory and psychiatry. Early social psychologists borrowed freely from these "clinical" theories, but were little concerned with the study of psychological problems or their treatment. Even after bona fide social psychological theories emerged, few psychologists attempted to apply them to clinically relevant phenomena, and social psychology turned away even further from the study of "abnormal" behavior. As a result, by the 1950s, psychologists interested in interpersonal behavior and those interested in dysfunctional processes were scarcely communicating. Shoben observed in 1953 that "the 'applied' *science of psychotherapy* has been essentially divorced from the 'pure' science that presumably should most nourishingly feed it" (p. 121).

This schism arose from a confluence of events in social and clinical psychology. After World War II, clinical psychologists initially were trained in and worked in Veterans Administration hospitals under the direction of psychiatrists. As a result, they adopted the intrapsychic and medical orientations of psychiatry and deemphasized interpersonal theories and interventions in favor of individualistic, intrapsychic, and biological ones (Sarason, 1981). Second, many, if not most, emerging clinical psychology training programs came to emphasize professional practitioner training (e.g., assessment and treatment) rather than research.

In contrast, in the postwar years social psychology increasingly emphasized basic research and showed little interest in clinically relevant topics. With the heightened use of laboratory paradigms and undergraduate subjects, social psychology was viewed as essentially irrelevant to understanding and treating psychological problems in clinical settings.

These differences in purpose and identity were compounded by philosophical and conceptual differences. For example, although practicing clinical and counseling psychologists tended to adopt a holistic perspective that included consideration of many interacting forces on problem behavior, social psychologists conducted research that tended to be atomistic and involved the search for elementary principles regarding specific behaviors. In practice, clinical and counseling psychologists dealt with the subjective experiences of individuals, whereas experimental social psychologists attempted the objective study of aggregated group data. Clinical psychologists' descriptions were largely qualitative, whereas social psychologists stressed quantification. Finally, clinical and counseling psychologists preferred naturalistic research with high external and ecological validity, whereas experimental social psychologists emphasized internal validity. These descriptions are, of course, highly general and do not apply to all clinical, counseling, or social psychologists. Yet these conceptual differences made it difficult for these groups to see the relevance of one another's work for the other field.

The Rapprochement

The 1960s saw several explicit attempts to stimulate connections between basic social psychology and clinical and counseling practice. In *Persuasion and Healing*, Frank (1961) demonstrated the importance of basic social psychological work to understanding psychological and behavioral change. Frank's central thesis was that similar interpersonal and cognitive processes underlie all instances of psychological change, whether they involve faith healing, religious conversion, or psychotherapy.

Goldstein (1966) explicitly called for applying social psychology to clinical practice, by showing how basic social psychological research on expectancy, attraction, authoritarianism, cognitive dissonance, norm setting, and role theory was relevant to psychotherapy. Goldstein, Heller, and Sechrest (1966) offered a social psychological analysis of the therapist–client relationship, reactance in therapy, and group dynamics in therapeutic settings. Goldstein (1971) later pioneered a line of research on psychotherapeutic attraction that drew on work in both social and clinical psychology.

Strong (1968) echoed Goldstein's call for an alliance between social psychologists and practitioners in a landmark article that portrayed psychological counseling as a social influence process. He discussed the relevance to counseling of social psychological literatures on attitude change and subsequently conducted a great deal of research on interpersonal processes in counseling (see Strong, 1982; Strong & Claiborn, 1982, for reviews).

Although Frank, Goldstein, Strong, and their colleagues directed therapists' attention to social psychological approaches during the 1960s, a primary stimulant to social psychologists' interest in such issues was provided by Carson (1969), who applied transactional approaches to the study of personality. Carson argued that deviant behavior emerges from disordered social interactions and that psychological difficulties are best explained by interpersonal rather than intrapersonal processes. This theme was central also in Ullman and Krasner's (1969) influential abnormal psychology text.

Two movements during the 1960s and 1970s converged to improve further the professional relationships between social and clinical-counseling psychologists. First, counseling psychology established itself as a field specializing in normal adjustment problems. Counseling psychology emerged from the guidance movement during the 1950s, but only slowly shifted from intrapsychic models toward social models of behavior (Tyler, 1972). By adopting interpersonal models of relatively "normal" difficulties, counseling psychologists found many concepts and models in social psychology directly relevant to their work.

A second influence was the so-called "crisis of confidence" in social psychology and the accompanying stimulation of interest in "applied" areas (e.g., McGuire, 1973). Disillusioned by a field founded primarily on laboratory studies of microcosmic phenomena, social psychologists became increasingly interested during the 1970s in problems of "real-world" relevance, setting the stage for social psychologists' entry into clinically relevant areas.

Two publications during the 1970s focused additional attention on the emerging interface of social and clinical-counseling psychology and helped to define the area. First, Brehm's (1976) *The Application of Social Psychology to Clinical Practice* dealt with the clinical relevance of reactance, dissonance, and attribution theories. Second, Strong's (1978) chapter in the *Handbook of Psychotherapy and Behavior Change: An Empirical Analysis* offered a theory of psychotherapy based on modifying clients' attributions in ways that result in greater self-control.

The wave of interest sparked by these and other publications in the late 1970s was carried forward by Weary and Mirels's (1982) edited volume that brought together the research of social, clinical, and counseling psychologists working at the interface of these fields. The inauguration of the *Journal of Social and Clinical Psychology* in 1983 (Harvey, 1983) helped legitimize the field by providing an outlet specifically for research at the borders of social and clinical-counseling psychology.

Assumptions Underlying the Interface

As a result of these events and seminal publications, "social-clinical" psychology has emerged as an identifiable subspecialty focusing on the interpersonal aspects of psychological problems and their treatment, and a large corps of researchers and theorists now identify with this area. The rapid growth of the area is reflected in recent books, symposia, issue-oriented articles, discussions of graduate training, and numerous empirical and theoretical articles that integrate constructs from social and clinical-counseling psychology (see Brehm & Smith, 1986; Leary & Miller, 1986; Maddux, Stoltenberg, & Rosenwein, 1987; McGlynn, Maddux, Stoltenberg, & Harvey, 1984; Weary & Mirels, 1982).

A set of implicit assumptions regarding the nature of psychological problems and their treatment provides a foundation for this work at the interface of social, counseling, and clinical psychology, offering a worldview that compels us to consider seriously the potential connections between social and clinical-counseling psychology. We make no claim to originality in elucidating these assumptions; they may be gleaned from the work of numerous theoreticians and researchers over the past three decades.

Assumption 1: Psychological Problems Are Interpersonal

Behavioral and emotional problems are essentially interpersonal problems. The majority of people who seek psychological services do so because they are concerned with their relationships with other people, and most such difficulties arise from people's relationships with others. Common adjustment problems such as depression, anxiety, marital discord, loneliness, and hostility consist primarily of interpersonal beliefs and behaviors that are expressed in interpersonal settings and make little sense when examined outside an interpersonal context. This assumption does not deny that some psychological problems may have strong biological roots but affirms that even biologically based problems are influenced by interpersonal forces.

Assumption 2: "Normal" Behavior Is Sometimes Dysfunctional

Because much of social psychological research and theory deals with how people misperceive, misattribute, and subsequently "misbehave" in their relations with other people, much of social *psychology involves the study of* what Freud (1901/1960) called "the psychopathology of everyday life." Cognitive dissonance theory, reactance theory, and attribution theories, for example, each describe cognitive and motivational processes of normal people, processes that are often illogical, unreasonable, or biased and that lead to poorly reasoned decisions. Therefore, even "normal" social cognitions and their affective and behavioral consequences are sometimes dysfunctional. The clinical or counseling psychologist with an in-depth knowledge of the social cognition literature, especially the errors made by normal people in social perception and judgment, is likely to have a greater awareness of the normality of seemingly pathological thought and behavior. Because the terminology in social psychology is less pathological and less dispositional in connotation, such an awareness should lead to a decreased tendency to overpathologize.

Assumption 3: Social Norms Determine the Distinction Between Normality and Abnormality

The distinction between normality and abnormality is essentially arbitrary and is the product of social norms that are derived and enforced in social settings. Thus, understanding how attitudes and beliefs become norms, how they change, and how they are acquired and enforced is essential to understanding how and why certain behaviors (including those with biological etiologies) are viewed as abnormal and others are not.

Assumption 4: Many Abnormal Social Behaviors Are Distortions of Normal Behaviors

A great number of so-called abnormal social behaviors are essentially distortions or exaggerations of normal patterns of behavior or normal patterns that are displayed at times and in places considered by others to be inappropriate. Thus, the rules that govern normal social interactions and behavior can be used to explain many behaviors that become identified as abnormal, and many behaviors given pathological labels are governed by the same interpersonal processes that determine behaviors that escape the stigma of being labeled as deviant.

Assumption 5: Clinical Judgment Involves the Same Processes as Everyday Social Interaction

Clinical judgment is a process of social cognition and person perception that involves the same processes as everyday social and person perception. Most important, clinicians make errors in clinical judgment that are similar to errors made by nonclinicians in nonclinical judgment (Leary & Miller, 1986). Thus, the study of social inference, problem solving, and decision making is crucial to understanding clinical assessment and diagnosis.

Assumption 6: Most Clinical and Counseling Interventions Focus on Social Cognitions

Most, and possibly all, clinical and counseling interventions, regardless of theoretical foundation, focus on changing what people think about, how people feel, and how people behave toward other people. Marital therapy, family therapy, parenting skills training, assertiveness training, social skills training, interpersonal and cognitive therapies, and other interventions are concerned primarily with helping people get along with other people and feel better about their interpersonal relationships. Indeed, most clinical and counseling psychologists trained in the last 10 years or so (i.e., those trained in social learning or cognitive behavioral models) are essentially "applied social psychologists" in the sense that they are concerned with the effects of social cognitions—attitudes, beliefs, self-statements, attributions, and expectancies—on emotion and behavior.

Assumption 7: Psychotherapy Is a Social Encounter

Psychotherapy, counseling, and other behavior change strategies, either dyadic or group, are, first and foremost, interpersonal encounters, albeit social encounters with a specific goal—one person trying to help another. This assumption dictates that the foundation for psychological intervention is an understanding of interpersonal behavior, particularly relationship development and interpersonal influence processes (e.g., Brehm & Smith, 1986; Strong & Claiborn, 1982).

Assumption 8: Social Psychological Theories Provide a Basis for Models of Behavior Change

Successful psychotherapy and behavior change strategies, regardless of theoretical foundation, have in common a relatively small number of features that explain their effectiveness (Frank, 1961). Because they propose general explanations for a broad range of human behavior, social psychological theories can provide the foundation on which to build an inclusive and comprehensive model of therapeutic behavior change.

The Social–Clinical-Counseling Domain

Work at the interface of social and clinical-counseling psychology can be viewed as composed of three subareas that cut across social, clinical, and counseling psychology. We suggest three labels—social-dysgenic, social-diagnostic, and social-therapeutic psychology—to describe work that examines the development, diagnosis, and treatment of emotional and behavioral problems (see Leary, 1987).

Social-Dysgenic Psychology

Social-dysgenic psychology is the study of interpersonal processes involved in the *development* of dysfunctional behavior. Not only do many psychological problems arise from interpersonal processes, but most such problems involve people's relationships with others. This assumption does not deny the role of genetic and biochemical processes in psychopathology, but it does affirm that even disorders caused primarily by biological factors may be sustained or exacerbated by interpersonal processes.

Work in social-dysgenic psychology has examined topics such as (a) attributional models of shyness, loneliness, spouse abuse, depression, stuttering, insomnia, stress, obesity, and a variety of other disorders; (b) self-presentational models of social anxiety, schizophrenic behavior, and aggression; (c) troubled relationships; (d) the role of social support in adjustment; (e) dysfunctional consequences of attempts to maintain self-esteem; (f) the application of self-awareness theory to problem drinking; and (g) self-efficacy models of fear and avoidance. These literatures share a common emphasis on the role of social processes in the development, maintenance, and exacerbation of dysfunctional behavior.

The goal of social-dysgenic psychology is to understand the interpersonal processes involved in problem behaviors. Thus, psychologists interested in this area need not be trained as clinicians or counselors and need not be interested in clinical or counseling interventions.

Social-Diagnostic Psychology

Social-diagnostic psychology is the study of interpersonal processes involved in the identification, classification, and assessment of psychological and behavioral problems. This work assumes that the basic inferential processes and the errors inherent in these processes are the same as those involved in all social inference. Thus, the social psychological literatures on attribution, person perception, judgmental heuristics, inferential biases, and labeling can shed light on how clinical and counseling psychologists draw conclusions about clients.

Topics in social-diagnostic psychology include the effects of labeling clients on subsequent diagnoses, primacy and recency effects in how clinicians form impressions of clients, illusory correlation in the interpretation of psychological tests, effects of psychologists' theoretical orientations on their perceptions and evaluations of client information, effects of disconfirming evidence on diagnoses, and the cognitive strategies clinicians use to test their preconceptions about clients. (See Leary & Miller, 1986, chap. 8, for a review of this literature.)

Another topic in social-diagnostic psychology is the development of interpersonal diagnostic system as alternatives to traditional psychiatric schemes such as the *Diagnostic and Statistical Manual of Mental Disorders* (*DSM–III;* American Psychiatric Association, 1980). McLemore and

Benjamin (1979) argued that "rigorous and systematic description of social behavior is uniquely critical to effective definition and treatment of the problems that bring most individuals for psychiatric or psychological consultation" (p. 18). They proposed that psychology should develop an interpersonal behavior taxonomy for use in clinical diagnosis and basic research. Such a taxonomy would be, at heart, social psychological.

Social-Therapeutic Psychology

Social-therapeutic psychology is the study of interpersonal processes in the prevention and treatment of dysfunctional behavior. The underlying assumption of social–therapeutic psychology is that the foundation for intervention is an understanding of interpersonal behavior (Maddux, 1987; Strong, 1982). As Kanfer (1984a) stated, "If changes in clinical settings are to be obtained primarily by altering a person's perceptions, cognitions, and attitudes in interviews, cognitive processes and the many concepts of social and personality theory are indispensable" (pp. 2–3).

Examples of research in this vein include the effects of counselor characteristics and behavior on therapeutic outcomes, nonverbal aspects of therapy, attitude change models of counseling, self-efficacy processes in behavior change, socially based treatments for social anxiety, the effects of role-playing in therapy, the usefulness of matching clients and counselors on various characteristics, social support in clinical practice, and impression management processes in psychotherapy. A recent chapter by Brehm and Smith (1986) provides an integrative review of this area.

Current Status and Future Directions

Relative to even 10 years ago, work at the interface between social and clinical-counseling psychology is thriving. A content analysis of articles in major social psychological journals from 1965 through 1983 showed a marked increase in clinically relevant work (Leary, Jenkins, & Sheppard, 1984). However, the general impact of this work on the science and profession of psychology is unclear.

Impact on Research in Clinical and Counseling Psychology

The impetus for applying social psychology to counseling and clinical practice came from a handful of clinical and counseling psychologists who recognized the relevance of social psychology for understanding psychological problems and their remediation. The response to their call has been notable; each year, an increasing number of clinical and counseling studies are conducted that use social psychological concepts and theories.

Attributional approaches have been popular recently. Clinical and counseling researchers have examined the role of attributions in the development and maintenance of psychological problems, as well as the attributional aspects of psychotherapy and counseling (see Harvey & Galvin, 1984). Also of note are counseling studies based on social psychological models of attitude change, work on learned helplessness and depression, and expectancy theories of behavior change. Thus, at the level of scholarly inquiry, clinical and counseling psychologists who work in academic settings appear to be familiar with and generally responsive to social psychological perspectives (see Maddux et al., 1987). In fact, clinical and counseling psychologist researchers who work in the broad area of social learning and cognitive behavior theories may have more in common with contemporary social psychologists—such as an appreciation of empiricism and skepticism regarding intrapsychic models of behavior—than with their clinical and counseling colleagues who adhere to more traditional psychodynamic theories.

Impact on the Practice of Clinical and Counseling Psychology

For several reasons, social psychology has had less impact on the practice of clinical and counseling psychology than on research. First, graduate training programs in clinical and counseling psychology do not emphasize sufficiently the social psychological aspects of dysfunction and treatment. As Strupp (1984) observed, "Therapists are still learning a great deal more from the clinical experience of their preceptors and clinical writings in general than from the research literature" (p. 13). Although clinical and counseling psychologists receive training in research, we believe they could profit from more extensive exposure to the literatures in social-dysgenic, social-diagnostic, and social-therapeutic psychology. Furthermore, graduate training of counseling and clinical psychologists seldom stresses "research consumerism" (Cohen, Sargent, & Sechrest, 1986); thus, the typical practitioner sees little use for psychotherapy research (Morrow-Bradley & Elliott, 1986).

Graduate programs in clinical and counseling psychology require a basic course in social psychology, but our knowledge of such courses indicates that they typically include little material directly relevant to clinical and counseling psychology practice. Fortunately, a number of departments now offer courses that emphasize the social psychology of dysfunctional behavior and its treatment (see Leary, 1985).

We do not claim that current social psychological theory and research can provide specific instructions regarding what practitioners should say or do with any particular client. Even the best theories of psychotherapy do not provide such guidelines. Social psychology can, however, "provide the practitioner . . . with a conceptual framework that serves as a heuristic, a general guide about what to look for in each situation" (Kanfer, 1984b, p. 143). Such a practitioner will be "armed with reasonable hypotheses [but] will need to examine anew each situation to ascertain the relative importance of such variables as the setting, the timing, the specified task, and the available options for action" (Kanfer, 1984b, p. 143).

Another barrier to the integration of social psychology into practice is the modus operandi of experimental social psychology: Such research often involves laboratory studies of highly specific social phenomena and employs deception, artificial paradigms, and hordes of college undergraduates. Each of these practices can be justified in basic research, but they lead practitioners to question the relevance of social psychology to their work. Furthermore, in their writings, social psychologists rarely discuss the clinical implications of basic research. Many recent advances in social-dysgenic, social-diagnostic, and social-therapeutic psychology involve straightforward extensions of basic social psychological principles to clinically relevant areas, but the relevance of social psychological research for clinical practice may not be immediately obvious to many practitioners. In short, social psychologists usually do not make obvious the clinical relevance of their work, and clinical-counseling psychologists do not usually pause to consider whether basic work in social psychology has anything to say to practitioners. Even basic clinical and counseling research is often viewed by practitioners as irrelevant to their work (Cohen et al., 1986; Morrow-Bradley & Elliott, 1986).

Some clinicians and counselors may resist the idea that counseling and psychotherapy involve the same social influence processes that occur in more mundane settings. Others may argue that explaining psychotherapy in terms of everyday social influence processes trivializes the therapeutic encounters by rendering them no more than a social hour or coffee klatch. None of these objections are warranted. Counselors and clinicians are people and presumably do not cease to behave like people when with clients. Thus, their interactions are guided by the same processes that occur in other interpersonal contexts, and such interactions may be understood in terms of social psychological principles.

Impact on Social Psychology

Psychologists of 50 years ago viewed the primary flow of knowledge as moving from abnormal psychology to social psychology (Prince, 1921). Today, most psychologists probably view the flow of information in the opposite direction. Writers often refer to "applications of social psychology to clinical and counseling practice," but seldom, if ever, address the contributions of clinical and counseling psychology to the understanding of everyday interpersonal processes. However, the path between social and clinical-counseling psychology is a two-way street, and clinical and counseling psychology have much to offer social psychologists (see Gerstein, White, & Barke, in press).

Although dysfunctional behaviors were never explicitly excluded from social psychology, they seldom attracted much attention from mainstream social psychologists in the past. The most obvious effect of the interface movement on social psychology is the growing number of social psychologists studying clinically relevant phenomena. Some of this research is explicitly clinical (such as treatment studies based on social psychological models), and some of it is basic research relevant to the development, diagnosis, or treatment of some psychological problem (see Leary & Miller, 1986). Social psychologists today may be more knowledgeable about psychological problems and their treatment than at any previous time. This understanding of and appreciation for clinical and counseling psychology may enhance their own research and theorizing. Indeed, many topics that are currently popular in social psychology attracted interest because of their dysfunctional consequences (e.g., self-handicapping, social anxiety, loneliness, relationship difficulties).[2]

In a recent article, Gerstein et al. (in press) discussed the potential impact of counseling psychology on social psychology. They stated that counseling psychology can influence and enhance the work of social psychologists by offering (a) a new set of contexts and settings for the study of interpersonal behavior (i.e., significant life events across the life span); (b) new populations other than college students (i.e., clients); and (c) new methodologies such as content analysis of verbal behavior and single-case designs. To this we would add that much work in counseling and clinical psychology emphasizes the impact of family and community systems on behavior—factors that have been relatively ignored by social psychologists. In addition, attention to the literature in clinical and counseling psychology can alert social psychologists to phenomena and processes that have been neglected in basic research.

The movement of social psychologists into clinically relevant research has raised the question of whether social psychologists should seek opportunities to practice counseling and psychotherapy. Some argue that, by virtue of their knowledge of the social bases of psychological difficulties, social psychologists have a right to practice counseling and/or psychotherapy (C. Hendrick, 1983). Others argue that social psychologists are not typically trained in the direct application of psychological knowledge to resolving human problems in living and, therefore, may not be qualified to engage in clinical or counseling activities (Maddux & Stoltenberg, 1983). This seemingly logical argument, however, can be countered by research that has failed consistently to demonstrate the superior effectiveness of trained psychotherapists over untrained or paraprofessional counselors (Berman & Norton, 1985).

Given their areas of expertise and their training experiences, some social psychologists are qualified to offer psychological services that may not be regarded as traditional counseling or psychotherapy. For example, social psychologists who are experts in stress may be qualified to give stress management workshops, and those knowledgeable in interaction dysfunctions (e.g., interaction difficulties, loneliness, social anxiety) may be qualified to provide interpersonal training of various sorts. Industrial and organizational psychologists have been involved in such "nonclinical" interventions for many years. The "practice" controversy will not be settled soon, and we offer no easy answers here. The best we can provide is an answer through an example—that of health psychology, a field in which social, clinical, counseling and other psychologists are collaborating effectively with minimal "turf" concerns (S. Hendrick, 1983; Matarazzo, Miller, Weiss, Herd, & Weiss, 1984).

Conclusion

As recently as 1983, writers were wondering whether the surge of interest in the social–clinical–counseling interface represented the emergence of a bona fide subspecialty or another scholarly fad. Today it seems certain that this subspecialty is on a solid foundation supported by a large number of researchers and practitioners in all three component fields. In fact, many psychologists now identify their primary area of interest and expertise as the intersection of these fields. We conclude with a few suggestions for further improving and encouraging collaboration and cooperation. None of these suggestions are original, and few if any should arouse much debate. Yet they bear repeating because they are so often ignored.

1. Clinical and counseling psychology training programs should emphasize more strongly the relevance of social psychological theory and research for understanding emotional and behavioral problems and their treatment. Social psychological perspectives can be increasingly incorporated into coursework, research, and practicum experiences (see Leary, 1985; Leary, Kowalski, Maddux, & Stoltenberg, in press, for course syllabi and reading lists). This is a specific example of the more general need to encourage greater "research consumerism" in clini-

cal and counseling psychology training programs.
2. Graduate programs in social psychology should emphasize more explicitly the possible applications of social psychology to understanding and resolving human problems in living. Furthermore, students in social psychology should receive greater exposure to the literatures in clinical and counseling psychology and should not be discouraged from conducting research on basic interpersonal processes in clinical-counseling phenomena. This need not be done at the expense of scientific training or of "traditional" experimental social psychology. Increased education in the interpersonal aspects of dysfunctional behavior is not incompatible with training in mainstream social psychology and may, in fact, enhance it.
3. Graduate training programs should more actively teach the importance of respect for the work of colleagues in other fields. Professional territorialism and factionalism are among the greatest enemies of scientific progress, particularly progress that requires the integration of disparate fields.
4. Psychologists should become more familiar with work in other fields that is related to their own and integrate such work into their research and writing. Specifically, clinical and counseling psychology researchers should actively search for social psychological models that might explain clinical phenomena, and social psychological researchers should actively attempt to relate their research findings to clinical-counseling issues.

Furthermore, social, counseling, and clinical psychologists—researchers and practitioners—might adopt a "unificationist" view of research in clinical and counseling psychology, as proposed by Forsyth and Strong (1986). This view proposes that "(a) psychotherapy research is science; (b) psychotherapy research is part of a unified effort to understand human behavior; and (c) all scientific tools are acceptable in the effort to understand the process of psychotherapy" (p. 113).
5. Psychologists interested in areas that fall at the nexus of social and clinical-counseling psychology should seek collaborative and consultative relationships with psychologists in other areas. Not only does such collaboration enrich research projects, but presubmission reviews by colleagues in other areas may enhance the chances that a paper will influence both social and clinical-counseling psychology.
6. Formal channels of information exchange should facilitate cross-fertilization among these fields. For example, *Contemporary Social Psychology*, the bulletin of the Society for the Advancement of Social Psychology, regularly publishes articles dealing with the interface of social and clinical-counseling psychology. Other possible avenues of dialogue might include abstracting selected social psychological journals (such as *Journal of Personality and Social Psychology* and *Journal of Social and Clinical Psychology*) in *PsycSCAN: Clinical;* inviting journal articles by persons who are outside the speciality served by a particular journal; including more social psychologists on the editorial review boards of clinical and counseling journals, and vice versa; and increasing the number of convention symposia that include participants from diverse areas.

Many barriers to the interface still exist, and given differences in professional objectives, training, and identity, they will remain with us for some time to come. But the walls between these areas are crumbling, and the beneficiaries of change will be social, clinical, and counseling psychologists and the consumers of psychological services.

ACKNOWLEGMENTS

We extend our sincerest appreciation to Elizabeth Altmaier, John Harvey, Irving Kirsch, Ronald Rogers, Sharon Brehm, and two anonymous reviewers for their helpful suggestions on an earlier version of this article.

NOTES

1. In this article, we generally will not distinguish between clinical and counseling psychology. This is not meant to imply that no differences exist between these fields (see Osipow, Cohen, Jenkins, & Dostal, 1979), but the differences are not relevant to most of the issues we address.
2. Interestingly, we detect a degree of ambivalence to the social–clinical-counseling area among some factions of social psychology. Some experimental social psychologists appear to regard research on dysfunctional behavior as inherently "clinical" even though it emerges from social psychological perspectives and is conducted by social psychologists to enhance the understanding of social behavior. We argue that behavior does not cease to be "social" simply because it is dysfunctional or occurs within the context of a clinical intervention.

REFERENCES

American Psychiatric Association (1980). *Diagnostic and statistical manual of mental disorders* (3rd ed.). Washington, DC: Author.
Berman, J. S., & Norton, N. C. (1985). Does professional training make a therapist more effective? *Psychological Bulletin, 98,* 401–407.
Brehm, S. S. (1976). *The application of social psychology to clinical practice.* Washington, DC: Hemisphere.
Brehm, S. S., & Smith, T. W. (1986). Social psychological approaches to psychotherapy and behavioral change. In S. L. Garfield & A. E. Bergin (Eds.), *Handbook of psychotherapy and behavior change* (3rd ed., pp. 69–115). New York: Wiley.
Carson, R. C. (1969). *Interaction concepts of personality.* Chicago: Aldine.
Cohen, L. H., Sargent, M. M., & Sechrest, L. B. (1986). Use of psychotherapy research by professional psychologists. *American Psychologist, 41,* 198–206.
Forsyth, D. R., & Strong, S. R. (1986). The scientific study of counseling and psychotherapy: A unificationist view. *American Psychologist, 41,* 113–119.
Frank, J. D. (1961). *Persuasion and healing* (1st ed.). Baltimore, MD: Johns Hopkins University Press.
Freud, S. (1960). *The psychopathology of everyday life.* London: Hogarth. (Original work published 1901.)
Gerstein, L. H., White, M. J., & Barke, C. R. (in press). A well-kept secret: What counseling psychology can offer social psychology. *Journal of Applied Social Psychology.*
Goldstein, A. P. (1966). Psychotherapy research by extrapolation from social psychology. *Journal of Counseling Psychology, 13,* 38–45.
Goldstein, A. P. (1971). *Psychotherapeutic attraction.* Elmsford, NY: Pergamon Press.
Goldstein, A. P., Heller, K., & Sechrest, L. B. (1966). *Psychotherapy and the psychology of behavior change.* New York: Wiley.
Harvey, J. H. (1983). The founding of the *Journal of Social and Clinical Psychology. Journal of Social and Clinical Psychology, 1,* 1–13.
Harvey, J. H., & Galvin, K. S. (1984). Clinical implications of attribution theory and research. *Clinical Psychology Review, 4,* 15–33.
Hendrick, C. (1983). Clinical social psychology: A birthright reclaimed. *Journal of Social and Clinical Psychology, 1,* 66–78.
Hendrick, S. (1983). Ecumenical (social and clinical and x, y, z . . .) psychology. *Journal of Social and Clinical Psychology, 1,* 79–87.
Kanfer, F. (1984a). Introduction. In R. P. McGlynn, J. E. Maddux, C. D. Stoltenberg, & J. H. Harvey (Eds.), *Social perception in clinical and counseling psychology* (pp. 1–6). Lubbock, TX: Texas Tech Press.
Kanfer, F. (1984b). Self-management in clinical and social interventions. In R. P. McGlynn, J. E. Maddux, C. D. Stoltenberg, & J. H. Harvey (Eds.), *Social perception in clinical and counseling psychology* (pp. 141–166). Lubbock, TX: Texas Tech Press.
Leary, M. R. (1985). Teaching a course at the interface of social and clinical-counseling psychology. *Contemporary Social Psychology, 11,* 120–123.
Leary, M. R. (1987). The three faces of social–clinical-counseling psychology. *Journal of Social and Clinical Psychology, 5,* 168–175.
Leary, M. R., Jenkins, T. B., & Sheppard, J. A. (1984). The growth of interest in clinically relevant research in social psychology. *Journal of Social and Clinical Psychology, 2,* 333–338.
Leary, M. R., Kowalski, R. M., Maddux, J. E., & Stoltenberg, C. D. (in press). Required reading at the interface of social, clinical, and counseling psychology. *Contemporary Social Psychology.*
Leary, M. R., & Miller, R. S. (1986). *Social psychology and dysfunctional behavior.* New York: Springer-Verlag.
Maddux, J. E. (1987). The interface of social, clinical, and counseling psychology: Why bother and what is it anyway? *Journal of Social and Clinical Psychology, 5,* 27–33.
Maddux, J. E., & Stoltenberg, C. D. (1983). Clinical social psychology and social clinical psychology: A proposal for peaceful coexistence. *Journal of Social and Clinical Psychology, 1,* 289–299.
Maddux, J. E., Stoltenberg, C. D., & Rosenwein, R. (1987). *Social processes in clinical and counseling psychology.* New York: Springer-Verlag.
Matarazzo, J. D., Weiss, S. M., Miller, N. W., Herd, J. A., & Weiss, S. M. (Eds.). (1984). *Behavioral health: A handbook of health enhancement and disease prevention.* New York: Wiley.
McGlynn, R. P., Maddux, J. E., Stoltenberg, C. D., & Harvey, J. H. (Eds.). (1984). *Social perception in clinical and counseling psychology.* Lubbock, TX: Texas Tech Press.
McGuire, W. J. (1973). The yin and yang of progress in social psychology: Seven Koan. *Journal of Personality and Social Psychology, 26,* 446–456.
McLemore, C. W., & Benjamin, L. S. (1979). Whatever happened to interpersonal diagnosis? A psychosocial alternative to DSM–III. *American Psychologist, 34,* 17–34.
Morrow-Bradley, C., & Elliott, R. (1986). Utilization of psychotherapy research by practicing psychologists. *American Psychologist, 41,* 188–197.
Osipow, S. H., Cohen, W., Jenkins, J., & Dostal, J. (1979). Clinical versus counseling psychology: Is there a difference? *Professional Psychology, 10,* 148–153.
Prince, M. (1921). Editorial announcement. *Journal of Abnormal and Social Psychology, 16,* 1–5.
Sarason, I. G. (1981). An asocial psychology and a misdirected clinical psychology. *American Psychologist, 36,* 827–836.
Shoben, E. J. (1953). Some observations on psychotherapy and the learning process. In O. H. Mowrer (Ed.), *Psychotherapy, theory and research* (pp. 120–139). New York: Ronald.
Staats, A. W. (1983). *Psychology's crisis of disunity.* New York: Praeger.
Strong, S. R. (1968). Counseling: An interpersonal influence process. *Journal of Counseling Psychology, 15,* 215–224.
Strong, S. R. (1978). Social psychological approach to psychotherapy research. In S. L. Garfield & A. E. Bergin (Eds.), *Handbook of psychotherapy and behavior change: An empirical analysis* (2nd ed., pp. 101–135). New York: Wiley.
Strong, S. R. (1982). Emerging integrations of clinical and social psychology: A clinician's perspective. In G. Weary

& H. Mirels (Eds.), *Integrations of clinical and social psychology* (pp. 181–213). New York: Oxford.

Strong, S. R., & Claiborn, C. D. (1982). *Change through interaction.* New York: Wiley-Interscience.

Strupp, H. H. (1984). Psychotherapy research: Reflections on my career and the state of the art. *Journal of Social and Clinical Psychology, 2,* 3–24.

Tyler, L. (1972). Reflecting on counseling psychology. *The Counseling Psychologist, 3*(4), 6–11.

Ullman, L. P., & Krasner, L. (1969). *A psychological approach to abnormal behavior.* Englewood Cliffs, NJ: Prentice-Hall.

Weary, G., & Mirels, H. L. (Eds.). (1982). *Integrations of clinical and social psychology.* New York: Oxford.

Discussion Questions

1. Are there any of the eight assumptions underlying the social-clinical interface that you have difficulty accepting? If so, why do you disagree with those assumptions?
2. If Leary and Maddux are correct that the development, diagnosis, and treatment of psychological problems involve social psychological processes, do you think that social psychologists (who are experts regarding these processes) ought to be licensed to practice psychology? Why or why not?
3. Most clinical and counseling psychologists are required, as part of their training, to take a single graduate course in social psychology, often a general one with no explicit connections to psychological problems or their treatment. Would you recommend requiring students in clinical and counseling psychology to take courses in social-clinical psychology? What should such courses cover?
4. Pick a psychological problem and speculate about the social psychological processes that may be involved in its onset, maintenance, diagnosis, and treatment.

Suggested Readings

Journal of Social and Clinical Psychology, New York: Guilford. This journal, published since 1983, publishes research that bridges social and clinical psychology.

Kowalski, R. M., & Leary, M. R. (Eds.) (1999). *The social psychology of emotional and behavioral problems.* Washington, DC: American Psychological Association. The 13 chapters in this book examine processes involving social cognition, the self, interpersonal processes, and personal relationships as they apply to psychological difficulties.

Segrin, C. (2001). *Interpersonal processes in psychological problems.* New York: Guilford. This book examines the role of interpersonal processes in an array of psychological problems, including depression, social anxiety, schizophrenia, bipolar disorder, eating disorders, substance abuse, and personality disorders.

Snyder, C. R., & Forsyth, D. R. (Eds.). (1991). *Handbook of social and clinical psychology: The health perspective.* New York: Pergamon Press. This comprehensive volume covers a broad range of topics that span social and clinical psychology.

PART 2

Social Psychological Processes in the Development and Maintenance of Emotional and Behavioral Problems

READING 2

Behavioral and Characterological Attributional Styles as Predictors of Depression and Loneliness: Review, Refinement, and Test

Craig A. Anderson and Jody C. Dill • University of Missouri, Columbia
Rowland S. Miller • Sam Houston State University
Alice L. Riger • West Virginia University
Constantine Sedikides • University of North Carolina, Chapel Hill

Editors' Introduction

One of the most influential books in social psychology in the 1970s was *Attribution: Perceiving the Causes of Behavior*, an edited volume that explored the important role that people's attributions play in thought, emotion, and behavior. In one chapter of this book, Valins and Nisbett (1972) discussed how emotional disorders may be created and maintained by the attributions that people make for the events that happen in their lives. This chapter not only fostered interest in the link between attributions and emotion, but also provided an impetus for social psychologists to turn their attention to clinically relevant phenomena and for clinical psychologists to draw upon theory and research from social psychology.

The most influential article of the many that followed was Abramson, Seligman, and Teasdale's (1978) reformulation of learned helplessness theory. Abramson et al. proposed that depression and learned helplessness are mediated by the attributions that people make in the face of negative, uncontrollable life events. For example, attributing uncontrollable outcomes (i.e., "helplessness") to unchangeable, internal factors—such as one's stable personal characteristics—results in deeper depression and lower self-esteem than attributing the same outcomes to changeable factors such as a lack of effort or bad luck. Thus, the degree to which people feel depressed depends on how they explain what happens to themselves.

Abramson et al. (1978) speculated that certain people may be more likely to become depressed because they have a "depressive attributional style" in which they attribute negative events in their lives to internal, stable, and global factors. To investigate this hypothesis, researchers set about to design measures of attributional style and to explore how attributional style relates to depression and other problematic reactions such as anxiety, loneliness, hypochondriasis, and jealousy. Although most research supported the idea that attributions relate to depression and other reactions, the picture was clouded by unclear conceptualizations and questionable measures.

In the article reprinted here, Craig Anderson, Rowland Miller, Alice Riger, Jody Dill, and Constantine Sedikides discuss problems in the literature on attributional style, critique various measures of attributional style, then describe a study that examined the relationship between attributional style, depression, and loneliness. Much of this article is based on Janoff-Bulman's (1979) distinction between behavioral and characterological self-blame. According to Janoff-Bulman, when people make internal attributions for a negative event in their lives, they may either attribute the event to a behavioral shortcoming or miscalculation (*I failed the test because I didn't study; My partner is upset with me because I was rude*) or to a characterological flaw (*I failed the test because I'm stupid; My partner is upset with me because I'm a loser*). Janoff-Bulman showed that depressed individuals are more likely to make characterological attributions for bad events. Not all studies found these patterns, however, which prompted Anderson and his colleagues to determine whether inconsistencies in the literature may have something to do with the particular measures used by researchers.

In addition to providing support for Janoff-Bulman's distinction between behavioral and characterological self-blame and the role of attributions more generally, this article demonstrates two important features of all scientific research. First, the findings obtained by a particular researcher are always affected by the methods and measures used in a particular study. Thus, researchers must consider whether their results might be influenced by how they conducted their research and whether inconsistencies between their findings and those of other researchers may be due to methodological differences. Second, this article demonstrates that scientific knowledge is cumulative. We can draw only tentative conclusions from any particular study, but by standing back and looking at the research literature as a whole, seeing the general patterns allows us to be more confident in our conclusions. Anderson and his colleagues made a contribution to the study of attributional style when they looked back at more than a decade of research.

The literature on self-blame and depression reveals two interrelated problems. First, although R. Janoff-Bulman's (1979) conceptualizations of self-blame are clear, empirical operationalization is difficult and has resulted in approaches that do not capture the richness of the constructs. Second, past research has produced inconsistent findings. A comprehensive literature review revealed that the inconsistencies are related to the method of assessing attributions. A correlational study designed to more accurately represent the self-blame conceptualization revealed that both behavioral and characterological self-blame contribute uniquely to depression and loneliness. Supplementary results regarding circumstantial attributions and regarding attributional styles for success were presented. Empirical issues regarding possible methodological refinements and effect size, as well as the value of categorical approaches to the study of attributional style were discussed.

Pete recently received his PhD in structural engineering from a highly respected university. He is the first in his family to go to college. On being asked to name the most important factor in this success he replied, "I worked so very hard to do the best that I could in school."

After years of training and competition, Meredith won a position on the Olympic diving team. In an interview with her hometown newspaper she reported, "I have no real secret to success. I was simply born with the necessary athletic ability and have used this gift."

Jonathan's marriage lasted 2 years, 4 months, and 5 days. He did much soul-searching in the final months. After it was all over he confided to a friend that "It must have been my fault; I'm really not very good at getting along with women."

Julie is a college junior. After a party, she and her boyfriend went to her room, where he physically forced her to have sexual intercourse with him. She explained to the rape crisis counselor that "I guess it was really my fault for getting into that situation. We had been drinking and necking a lot. I shouldn't have invited him to my room."

These kinds of events and the explanations of them are the basic units of all attribution theory. The two most basic questions concern how people go about making a particular attribution for a particular event (the attribution process) and what the effects of a particular attribution are likely to be on a person's emotional, motivational, and behavioral reactions to the event (the attributional process). This distinction has proved useful in thinking about the voluminous attribution literature, as well as in dividing up the sequence of processes involved in attributions and action (e.g., Anderson & Weiner, 1992; Kelley & Michela, 1980).

Attributional Style Effects

This article is mainly concerned with the attributional process, and specifically, with the effects of different types of attributions for good and bad events. Pete's effort attribution for his academic success should produce positive affect as well as high motivation in similar future endeavors. Jonathan's trait attribution for his failed marriage may exacerbate his already negative affective state and could induce self-defeating behaviors in future interpersonal relationships. The other two cases are less clear. Meredith's ability attribution for her diving success may produce generally positive reactions. However, a few well-placed failures in this or related domains, in conjunction with this "ability" view of the task, could lead her to give up too easily. Julie's strategy attribution for the date rape also has mixed implications. Blaming a strategic mistake in judgment might increase her shame and anger in the immediate situation. But, it may also increase her feelings of optimism about the future and about her ability to predict and control the future.

Much research has addressed these types of attributional questions. Of particular interest has been the notion that people differ in the types of attributions they consistently make for events in their lives. Such a consistent pattern of attributions across events is known as a person's *attributional style*. Attributional style differences may play a major role in the development and maintenance of problems in living characterized by negative affect and motivational deficits. The two most widely researched problems are depression and loneliness (for reviews see Anderson & Arnoult, 1985a; Anderson, Jennings, & Arnoult, 1988;

Sweeney, Anderson, & Bailey, 1986). It is clear from these reviews and more recent research that individual differences in attributional style are associated with problems in living.

Process Assumptions and Measurement Technique

Although this research primarily concerns attributional processes (i.e., the effects of attributions), implicit in any particular attributional style study are assumptions about attribution processes (e.g., how people make attributions). For example, do people think about causes in terms of certain dimensions, such as stability and locus? Or, do people think about causes in terms of categories or types, such as effort and ability?

The most popular technique for assessing attributional style has people generate causes for hypothetical events and then rate the causes on key attribution dimensions (controllability, stability, locus, and globality). Recent work (e.g., Anderson, 1991) suggests that such dimensional thinking may be relatively rare, although it is clear that with proper instruction, people can do it acceptably well. The alternative is to develop categorical procedures for assessing attributional style. That is, attributional style can be defined as the relative frequency with which particular types of attributions are made.

The dimensional approach to attributional style research has produced many advances in recent years. There are major issues yet to be resolved, such as which dimensions are truly primary and how to combine various dimensions (Anderson & Deuser, 1991, 1993; Anderson & Riger, 1991; Carver, 1989; Carver & Scheier, 1991). Nonetheless, this approach has been productive and will continue to yield important insights.

Impediments to Progress

The categorical approach to attributional style has also proved fruitful, especially Janoff-Bulman's categories of behavioral and characterological self-blame (Janoff-Bulman, 1979). However, this approach has not caught on nearly so well despite the promise of assessing attributions at the same conceptual level that people use when making attributions. Two interrelated problems may account for this. First, there are definitional problems in creating appropriate attributional style measures of self-blame. Second, the empirical results from the few directly relevant studies have been mixed. We believe that the empirical anomalies are the result of the definitional problems.

DEFINITIONAL PROBLEMS

Janoff-Bulman's (1979) original discussion of characterological and behavioral self-blame attributions still seems quite apt.

> Behavioral self-blame is control related, involves attributions to a modifiable source (one's behavior), and is associated with a belief in the future avoidability of a negative outcome. Characterological self-blame is esteem related, involves attributions to a relatively nonmodifiable source (one's character), and is associated with a belief in personal deservingness for past negative outcomes. (p. 1798)

Both are types of self-blame that are, in standard dimensional terms, internal causes. The primary distinction between the two types is in terms of controllability. Behavioral causes are potentially controllable, whereas characterological ones are not. The stability dimension also captures this distinction to some extent, with behavioral causes being unstable, and characterological ones being stable. Stability is not in itself sufficient, though, because some unstable causes are not controllable (e.g., mood).

Janoff-Bulman (1979) also noted that the two types of self-blame differ in terms of the time orientation of the attributor. Specifically, she wrote the following:

> In blaming one's behavior, an individual is concerned with the future, particularly the future avoidability of the negative outcome. . . . In blaming himself or herself characterologically, the individual is not concerned with control in the future, but rather with the past, particularly deservingness for past outcomes. (p. 1800)

The key elements in this theory can be linked to standard attribution dimensions. These are the locus of the attributed cause (internal for both), the stability of the cause (behavioral are unstable, characterological are stable), and the controllability of the cause (behavioral are controllable, characterological are uncontrollable). The time-orientation distinction may be linked to the controllability element as well; if the controllability question is framed with a future orientation, then controllable causes will also have the intended future orientation.

Three methods have been used to assess characterological and behavioral attributional styles. Each method has subjects imagine themselves in various hypothetical situations. The methods differ in how subjects' attributional reactions to the situations are assessed.

In the *direct rating* method, subjects rate how much they blame various factors for each of the described situations. The rated factors include characterological and behavioral blame. Janoff-Bulman's (1979) characterological blame question was the following (p. 1803): "Given what happened, how much do you blame yourself for the kind of person you are," with specific information relating to the situation included (e.g., "the kind of person who is in an accident," for her accident scenario). The parallel behavioral blame question was, "Given what happened, how much do you blame yourself for what you did?" A number of researchers have used these same questions, or very similar ones, to assess characterological and behavioral blame with the direct rating method (see Table 2.1). Although the questions do seem to tap into the constructs described by Janoff-Bulman, they do not capture the full richness of those constructs. The main problem is that the questions only subtly capture the distinction between controllable and uncontrollable causes. The subtlety may very well elude subjects, especially those who are intent on getting their extra credit and leaving the lab. Similarly, the time-orientation distinction may be too weakly present to capture subjects' attention.

We have labeled the second method *open-ended coding*. Subjects generate open-ended attributions for the hypothetical situations. Then, expert raters

TABLE 2.1. Studies of Characterological and Behavioral Attributional Style and Depression

Study	Stressor	N	Method	Depression	Characterological		Behavioral	
					Failure	Success	Failure	Success
General depression and attributional style studies								
Anderson, Horowitz, & French, 1983, No. 1		304	FC	BDI	.32***	−.04	−.27***	−.12*
Anderson, Horowitz, & French, 1983, No. 2		121	FC	BDI	.41***	.00	−.41***	.00
Peterson et al., 1981		84	OC	BDI	.72***	−.15	−.44***	−.13
Stoltz & Galassi, 1989		334	OC	BDI	.37***		−.10	
Tennen & Herzberger, 1987		87	OC	BDI	.13	.15	.09	−.19
Janoff-Bulman, 1979, No. 1		120	DR	Zung[a]	.19*		ns	
Feather, 1983		248	DR	BDI	.10	−.11	.06	−.07
Carver, Ganellen, & Behar-Mitrani, 1985		101	DR	BDI	.29**		.19*	
Flett, Blankstein, & Holowaty, 1990		201	DR	BDI	.36***		.31***	
Specific stressor, depression, and attributional style studies								
Frazier, 1990	Rape	30/31	DR	BDI	.47**		.40*	
Major, Mueller, & Hildebrandt, 1985								
Immediate	Abortion	243	DR	BDI[a]	.14*	ns		
3 weeks	Abortion	96	DR	BDI[a]	.25*	ns		
Meyer & Taylor, 1986	Rape	58	DR	Own	.46***	.28*		

Note. Method: FC = forced choice attributions; DR = direct ratings of blame; OC = open-ended attributions coded by expert raters. Depression: BDI = Beck Depression Inventory; Zung = Zung Self-Rating Depression Scale; Own = created or modified depression scale.
[a]Original article used a median split procedure; present point biserial correlations were computed from the reported F values.
*p < .05. **p < .01. ***p < .001.

code the attributions. Peterson, Schwartz, and Seligman (1981) were the first to use this procedure. In their study,

> Behavioral codes were made when the attribution referred to some action by the subject—either an overt motor behavior or "internal" behaviors, such as wants, preferences, and intentions. Characterological attributions referred to personality dispositions of the subject, such as stupidity, immaturity, ability, and so on. (pp. 255–256)

Peterson et al. also created an external category. A couple of more recent studies have used this same coding scheme (see Table 2.1). As with the direct rating method, this open-ended coding method captures much of the complexity in the characterological and behavioral constructs. However, it too does not seem to adequately emphasize the controllability feature, which plays so major a role in Janoff-Bulman's distinction between characterological and behavioral blame.

The third method, *forced choice*, presents several attributional choices with each to-be-imagined situation. Subjects then choose the attribution that best fits them. Only one article (two studies) has used this method (Anderson, Horowitz, & French, 1983). In one study, six alternatives were available for each situation: ability, personality, effort, strategy, mood, and circumstances. The first two are characterological; the next two are behavioral. In the other study, only three choices were available: ability, strategy, and effort. Ability and personality are internal, uncontrollable, stable causes that tend to reflect a past orientation. Strategy and effort are internal, controllable, unstable causes that reflect a future orientation. Thus, this method has the controllability distinction built into it. However, this method introduces a different problem. In the forced-choice method, choosing one cause precludes choosing another. A person who makes many characterological choices necessarily makes few behavioral ones. The procedure forces fairly substantial negative correlations between the characterological and behavioral measures of attributional style. Thus, the technique is useful in testing the general proposition that attributional styles along a characterological–behavioral continuum correlate with depression and other problems, but it does not allow precise testing of which component (characterological, behavioral, or both) is contributing to the correlation.

A similar perspective on the definitional-measurement problem arises from the fact that characterological self-blame typically implies behavioral self-blame as well.[1] In the failed marriage example, the characterological attribution, "I'm not very good at getting along with women," implies that the attributor behaved in ways that drove his wife away. The key distinction for classifying that attribution as characterological or behavioral is the presumed modifiability of the behavior. In other words, did the attributor expect it to be unstable and controllable in the future? Or did he truly mean that something about his character, which is relatively stable and uncontrollable, was at fault? The direct rating questions obscure these issues, rather than highlighting them. The expert raters used in open-ended coding procedures are more likely to be sensitive to this distinction, but without knowing what the subject meant, the distinction may be hard to apply. The forced-choice method reduces this confusion by making the subject choose among attributions that differ in precisely the ways that the theory suggests are important.

It is important to note that we are not faulting the various researchers (including ourselves) for this earlier work. Indeed, all the studies and techniques have importantly contributed to the understanding of attributional phenomena. But every study has limitations; the limitations we have highlighted may help explain the inconsistent findings reported in the next section.

EMPIRICAL PROBLEMS

Two main predictions have guided research in this area. First, characterological blame for failure or bad events should correlate positively with depression and similar problems in living. Second, behavioral blame for failure or bad events should correlate negatively with depression and similar problems in living. Characterological and behavioral attributions for success (or positive) events have not received as much theoretical or empirical attention.

Table 2.1 presents the results of all the studies we located (using PsycLit, American Psychological Association, 1990–1992) that met the following criteria: (a) Both characterological and behavioral self-blame were assessed; (b) depression was assessed. The top half presents the main studies of interest, namely, those in which general depression and attributional styles were assessed. The bottom half presents studies in which depression as a reaction to a specific stressor was related to characterological and behavioral blame.

The studies are organized by their attributional style assessment method. This highlights the inconsistencies in results. Frequency of characterological attributions for failure and bad events correlates positively with depression. There is not a single reversal in this pattern. In contrast, frequency of behavioral attributions for failure events shows marked inconsistency. The inconsistencies, however, are almost perfectly related to the method of measuring characterological and behavioral blame. The forced choice and the open-ended coding studies show the expected negative relation between frequency of behavioral attributions for failure and level of depression. The direct rating studies all show the opposite relation.

This pattern suggests that the direct rating method may obscure the controllability implications of behavioral attributions that were intended in the original conceptualization. The other assessment methods may make this dimension more salient and thereby may produce the more predictable pattern. This is speculative, however, and the bottom line is that there is no clear answer to the question of whether behavioral blame is related to depression and other problems in living. The empirical inconsistencies as well as the definitional problems preclude any strong conclusion. Furthermore, there is too little research on characterological and behavioral attributions for success events to draw any conclusions about their relation to depression. And of course, the same definitional problems apply to those few success studies that have been done. Thus, we conducted a study to further examine these issues.

Overview

Goals

The present study had three goals. The first was to assess the attributional style categories of behavioral and characterological self-blame in a manner that avoids the definitional and methodological problems found in the direct rating, open-ended coding, and forced-choice methods *discussed earlier.* The second was to provide comparable attributional style measures for success situations.

The third was a bit more exploratory; it was to assess a third type of attribution that has occasionally been assessed in this domain, *external circumstances* (Anderson et al., 1983; Peterson et al., 1981). Although there has been less theoretical and empirical attention devoted to this attributional category, the work that does exist suggests that the frequency of attributions to circumstances for success should positively relate to problems in living (e.g., depression and loneliness). The data are weaker for circumstantial attributions for failure, but it is reasonable to expect negative correlations with problems in living.

The overriding goal was to provide a cleaner test of the theories relating characterological self-blame positively and behavioral self-blame negatively to problems in living (depression and loneliness). This overriding goal required us to maximize interpretational clarity, so we devised a conservative attributional style assessment procedure. Note that the cost of interpretational clarity was an expected reduction in effect size. For two very different reasons, we expected that the magnitude of the attributional style/problems in living correlations would be considerably lower than those typically found in this area. First, our conservative criteria (described in a later section) guaranteed that many of the attributions generated by subjects would be unclassified because of possible ambiguities. Second, the new attributional style assessment procedure involved translating subjects' dimensional ratings into categorical frequency counts. Some loss of "meaning" or "signal" was expected in the translation process.

Translating From Dimensions to Categories

Characterological, behavioral, and circumstantial attributional styles were assessed for success and failure events. These categorical attributional style measures were derived with a new assessment method designed to circumvent the definitional and interpretational problems discussed earlier. In our dimensional/categorical translation method, subjects generated open-ended attributions for a set of hypothetical events. They then rated their own attributions on the key defining dimensions: locus (internality), controllability, and stability. Individual attributions were then assigned to categories (characterological, behavioral, and circumstantial) on the basis of these ratings. The frequency of each type was used as the measure of that attributional style and was correlated with depression and loneliness. We gathered these data on two different samples, using different versions of the various scales. The two samples were combined for all reported analyses.[2] Multiple regression analyses were used to assess the independent contributions of various predictors.

To meet the goal of creating unambiguous measures of the three categories, we used stringent counting rules for each attributional style category. For instance, an attribution for a failure event was counted as a characterological one only if it was rated as internal and stable and uncontrollable. Although this procedure undoubtedly decreased the frequency of each attribution type and was expected to yield relatively low correlations, our goal of fairly testing the basic theoretical propositions could still be met by using a large sample size. That is, in this context, effect size is not an important consideration, although power to detect a weak effect is. In brief, our conservative translation procedure got us the pure measures we needed; a large sample size got us the necessary statistical power.

Method

Subjects

SAMPLE 1

Six hundred and eighty undergraduates at a large Midwestern university participated for course credit. Students who were not native speakers of English, those who were not United States citizens, and those who were older than 26 were dropped from the sample. Some subjects did not correctly complete all measures relevant to this study. Therefore, the final sample size for analyses involving depression was 614; for loneliness, the final sample size was 625.[3]

SAMPLE 2

Three hundred and twenty-one undergraduates at four different universities (one large Midwestern university and two large and one small Southwestern universities) participated for course credit. Subjects with missing data on any of the measures relevant to this study were dropped from the sample. The final sample size was 282 for both the depression and the loneliness analyses. Table 2.2 shows the distribution of men and women in both samples. There were approximately equal numbers of men and women. Preliminary analyses yielded no sex effects, so all reported analyses combine across sex.

Instruments

DEPRESSION

Sample 1. The full 21-item Beck Depression Inventory (Beck, Ward, Mendelson, Mock, & Erbaugh, 1961) was administered. This scale is a widely used measure of intensity of depression and is the most common measure of depression used in studies of attributional style. Each item describes a specific behavioral manifestation of depression. Scores on each item can range from 0, indicating no depressive symptomatology, to 3, indicating a

TABLE 2.2. Sample Characteristics

Characteristic	Depression		Loneliness	
	Sample 1	Sample 2	Sample 1	Sample 2
No. women	281	155	288	155
No. men	333	127	337	127
No. items in scale	21	13	20	20
Lowest possible	0	0	20	20
Highest possible	63	39	80	80
90th percentile	16	9	52	55
75th percentile	11	6	43	46
50th percentile	6	3	34	37.5
25th percentile	2	1	29	31
10th percentile	0	0	25	26

severe level of symptomatology. Total scale scores can thus range from 0 to 63.

Sample 2. The 13-item short-form of the Beck Depression Inventory (Beck & Beck, 1972) was administered. Because it has fewer items, total scale scores are much lower; the possible range is from 0 to 39.

LONELINESS

Subjects in both samples completed the Revised UCLA Loneliness Scale (Russell, Peplau, & Cutrona, 1980). The scale is based on the assumption that loneliness is a unidimensional construct that varies primarily on experienced intensity or frequency. Each of the 20 items is scored such that a 1 indicates lack of loneliness and a 4 indicates a high level of loneliness. Thus, total scale scores can range from 20 to 80.

ATTRIBUTIONAL STYLE

Sample 1. The 20-item dimensional version of the Attributional Style Assessment Test (ASAT–III; Anderson et al., 1988) was used. This scale presents the subject with five hypothetical situations of each of four types: interpersonal success, noninterpersonal success, interpersonal failure, and noninterpersonal failure. Because the distinction between interpersonal and noninterpersonal situations is irrelevant to the main thrust of this article, all reported analyses combine across this dimension so that there are 10 success and 10 failure situations. Subjects imagine themselves in the situations, write down the most likely major cause of the specified outcome, and rate that cause on several standard attribution dimensions (stability, locus, controllability, and globality).

In the present sample, there was one modification to the wording of the stability dimension. In the ASAT–III, stability of a cause refers to "the degree to which the cause can be expected to be present at the same level every time the same situation arises." In this study, *stability* referred to the extent that the cause was expected to be present again in the future, but did not mention the cause being at the same level. The dimensional definitions for locus, controllability, and globality were the same as in the ASAT–III (see Anderson & Arnoult, 1985b, p. 22).

Subjects rated the causes on 9-point scales, with 9s representing more controllable, internal, unstable, and global causes. For this study of frequency of specific attribution types, it was necessary to translate these dimension ratings into appropriate attribution types. The characterological type was defined as any attribution that was rated as uncontrollable (<5), internal (>5), and stable (<5). The behavioral type was defined as any attribution that was rated as controllable (>5), internal (>5), and unstable (>5). These were the two main attribution types of interest. We also assessed a third type. The circumstances type was defined as any attribution that was rated as uncontrollable (<5), external (<5), and unstable (>5). Because globality is not theoretically a part of these attribution types, it was not used.

The number of characterological, behavioral, and circumstantial attributions was counted separately for success and failure items. Because there were 10 success and 10 failure items, a subject could have from 0 to 10 characterological, behavioral, and circumstantial attributions within each outcome.

Sample 2. The same basic materials and definitions were used to assess the frequency of attribution types, with the following exceptions. First, the original ASAT–III definition of stability was used. Second, items were taken from the ASAT–III (as in Sample 1) and from two other attributional style scales, the Attributional Style Questionnaire (Seligman, Abramson, Semmel, & von Baeyer, 1979) and the Balanced Attributional Style Questionnaire (Feather & Tiggemann, 1984). Because a number of hypothetical situations appear on more than one of the scales, the total number of success and failure items was 20 and 18, respectively. Third, the self-generated causes were rated on 5-point scales, with 3 as the midpoint. Thus, the operationalization of characterological, behavioral, and circumstantial attributions used 3 as the cutoff point.

Procedure

SAMPLE 1

The depression, loneliness, and attributional style instruments were administered in random orders. Testing was done in groups. Within each instrument, the order of items was the same for all subjects. Informed consent was obtained at the start of the testing session. Then the booklets were distributed, with an instruction sheet explaining the tasks. On completion of the tasks, subjects returned their materials to the experimenter and indicated whether they wished to receive further information about the study. Those who requested such information were mailed a thorough debriefing.

SAMPLE 2

The same basic procedures were used, with the following exceptions. First, there were four different versions of the attributional style questionnaire, in which item order and attribution dimension order were varied. Second, a brief written debriefing was administered to all subjects on completion of the questionnaires. A more detailed debriefing was mailed to those who requested it.

Results

Descriptive Summaries

Table 2.2 presents the sample characteristics on depression and loneliness. The two samples were quite comparable. Sample 1 was slightly less lonely than Sample 2 ($Ms = 36.69$ and 39.07, respectively). This difference was reliable, $t(915) = 3.13$, $p < .005$. Sample 1 appeared to be slightly more depressed than Sample 2, after adjusting for the different number of depression items, but a direct statistical comparison of the two groups was not appropriate. The distributional shapes were comparable in the two samples for both depression and loneliness. On the full-scale measure of depression, the sample contained an appreciable number of mildly and moderately depressed individuals. The standard definition of mild depression on this scale is a total score of 10 to 15. Fully 29% of the sample displayed scores of 10 or greater. Moderate depression is defined as a score of 16–23. Fully 10% had scores of 16 or greater.

Table 2.3 presents the frequency of characterological, behavioral, and circumstantial attributions for success and failure situations. The most frequent attribution was the behavioral type for failure situations.

As expected, the relative frequencies were low. Indeed, they were small enough that we should expect some attenuation of attributional style correlations with depression and loneliness. This could be a problem if our goal were to produce a new attributional style technique designed to maximize correlations with depression and loneliness. Our goal, however, was to create a measurement technique that would allow us to test theoretically important issues in as clean a fashion as possible. The expected attenuation in correlation size is relevant to those issues only in that it forced us to use larger sample sizes than normal in this area in order to have some power to detect the theoretical effects under consideration. We turn next to those theoretical tests.

Correlational Summaries

PREDICTIONS

The main questions of interest are whether the frequencies of characterological and behavioral attributions correlated with measures of depression and loneliness. Theoretically, the frequency of characterological attributions for failure should correlate positively with depression and loneliness, whereas the frequency of behavioral attributions for failure should correlate negatively with depres-

TABLE 2.3. Relative Frequency (% of Total) of Characterological, Behavioral, and Circumstantial Attributions by Type of Situation

	Characterological		Behavioral		Circumstantial		Total	
	Failure	Success	Failure	Success	Failure	Success	Failure	Success
Sample 1								
No. attribution items	10	10	10	10	10	10	10	10
Relative frequency	4.8%	3.1%	12.3%	6.1%	3.1%	1.9%	20.2%	11.1%
Sample 2								
No. attribution items	18	20	18	20	18	20	18	20
Relative frequency	2.0%	1.8%	8.0%	0.9%	3.2%	1.1%	13.3%	3.8%

sion and loneliness. Blaming stable uncontrollable aspects of oneself for failure is clearly self-defeating. Blaming unstable controllable aspects of oneself for failure, however, allows for a more optimistic view of the future and may energize behavioral attempts to overcome initial setbacks.

Theoretical predictions for characterological and behavioral attributions in success situations are less clear. The internal and stable aspects of characterological attributions seem adaptive when applied to successes; however, the uncontrollable aspect is generally less positive. Similarly, the internal and controllable aspects of behavioral attributions seem adaptive when applied to successes, but the unstable aspect is troubling.

Circumstantial attributions for successes are obviously maladaptive for both affective and motivational reasons, as one is essentially denying credit and viewing the success as unlikely to be repeatable (i.e., it is uncontrollable) or repeated (i.e., the cause is unstable). The consequences of circumstance attributions for failure are less clear. The external and unstable aspects seem adaptive, but the uncontrollable aspect is maladaptive.

ANALYSIS STRATEGY

The analysis strategy we used is quite straightforward. We computed the correlations between the various attribution frequency measures and depression and loneliness for each sample separately. Then we averaged the corresponding correlations using a weighted r-to-z transformation process. Multiple regression analyses were also used to give a better idea of how well (or poorly) these attribution frequency measures predict depression and loneliness.

FINDINGS

Zero-order correlations. Table 2.4 presents the correlations between the attribution frequency measures and depression and loneliness for success and failure situations. As can be seen by these results, the main theoretical predictions were supported. Subjects who attributed imagined failures to characterological causes were more depressed and more lonely than those who did not ($ps < .001$). Similarly, subjects who attributed failures to behavioral causes were less depressed and less lonely than those who did not ($ps < .005$). Subjects who attributed successes to circumstances were more depressed and lonely than those who did not ($ps < .001$). Overall, these three sets of findings confirm the theoretical work of Janoff-Bulman (1979) and replicate the forced choice and the open-ended coding findings summarized in Table 2.1.

The only empirical anomaly concerned the finding that subjects who attributed successes to characterological causes were more depressed and lonely than those who did not ($ps < .05$). Neither depression nor loneliness correlated significantly with characterological attributions for success in Anderson et al. (1983). This discrepancy may be the result of the very different approaches used to assess attributional tendencies. The present finding also suggests that the negative implications of the uncontrollable aspect of characterological attributions for success outweigh the positive implications of the internal and stable aspects of such attributions.

Finally, depression and loneliness were both negatively correlated with circumstantial attributions for failure, although only the depression correlation was significant ($p < .05$). Subjects who attributed failures to circumstances were less depressed than those who did not.

Two remaining questions concern (a) the overall magnitude of the correlation of attributional style and problems in living when the different measures of attributional style are jointly considered and (b) the independent contributions of the different attributional style categories. The forced-choice methodology of previous categorical stud-

Table 2.4. Correlations Between Attribution Style (Success and Failure) and Loneliness and Depression, Combined Across Samples

Criterion problem	Characterological		Behavioral		Circumstantial	
	Failure	Success	Failure	Success	Failure	Success
Depression ($n = 896$)	.178***	.108***	−.107**	.014	−.072**	.114***
Loneliness ($n = 907$)	.144***	.071*	−.174***	.006	−.032	.119***

*$p < .05$. **$p < .005$. ***$p < .001$.

ies (Anderson et al., 1983) precludes meaningful use of multiple regression techniques, because the predictors are necessarily correlated at high levels. The present method does not force such high (negative) correlations between types of attributions, so a better idea of how well and in what way attributional style categories predict depression and loneliness may be gained by examining the multiple regression results.

Multiple correlations and regression. We first examined the correlations among the attributional style measures. Interestingly, the strongest correlations demonstrated that people tended to use a particular type of attribution across different outcomes. For example, people who made relatively frequent characterological attributions for success also tended to make characterological attributions for failure ($r = .34$, $p < .001$) for both the depression sample and the loneliness sample. Frequency of behavioral success and behavioral failure attributions yielded the next highest correlations ($rs = .32$ and $.31$, $ps < .001$, for the depression and loneliness samples, respectively). Finally, frequency of circumstantial success and circumstantial failure attributions yielded the third highest set of correlations among attributional style measures ($rs = .19$, $p < .001$, for both the depression and loneliness samples).

All six attribution frequencies (number of characterological success attributions, number of characterological failure attributions, etc.) were entered simultaneously as predictors of depression and loneliness. In both cases, highly significant ($ps < .001$) correlations resulted. The magnitude was also respectable in both cases, although still smaller than most correlations reported in the forced choice and open-ended coding studies. The depression and the loneliness Rs (across samples) were both .25. Table 2.5 presents these results.

Do the different types of attributional styles contribute independently to the prediction of depression and loneliness? As noted in the literature review, it could be that one type of attribution (characterological) is particularly maladaptive, but that other types (e.g., behavioral) correlate with depression and loneliness only because of methodological quirks of the forced choice method. The results presented in Table 2.5 rule out this description. The reported t-tests examined the unique variance in the criterion associated with each predictor. It can be seen that characterological, behavioral, and circumstantial attributions for failure, and circumstantial attributions for success, all significantly and uniquely predicted depression ($ps < .01$). Similarly, characterological and behavioral failure attributions and behavioral and circumstantial success attributions all predicted loneliness ($ps < .03$). These results further confirm the original conceptualization that characterological and behavioral attributional styles independently contribute to problems in living.

TABLE 2.5. Multiple Regression Results for the Combined Samples

Predictor	Partial slope	t[a]	$p<$
Depression: $R = .25$, $F(6,889) = 9.68$, $p < .001$			
Characterological failure	.138	3.96	.001
Characterological success	.055	1.59	.112
Behavioral failure	−.101	−2.91	.004
Behavioral success	.065	1.90	.058
Circumstances failure	−.089	−2.69	.008
Circumstances success	.111	3.33	.001
Loneliness: $R = .25$, $F(6,900) = 10.09$, $p < .001$			
Characterological failure	.108	3.10	.002
Characterological success	.025	0.74	.463
Behavioral failure	−.177	−5.18	.001
Behavioral success	.075	2.20	.028
Circumstances failure	−.047	−1.44	.151
Circumstances success	.109	3.30	.001

[a]For depression, $df = 889$; for loneliness, $df = 900$.

Discussion

Summary

Janoff-Bulman's (1979) theoretical insights into characterological and behavioral self-blame have not been consistently matched by the methods used to assess these attributional styles. The direct rating method in particular does not sufficiently highlight the importance of the control aspects of these attribution types. Our literature review confirmed that the varying results of past studies on self-blame and depression are almost perfectly correlated with the methods used to assess selfblame. Our new dimensional–categorical translation method was designed to test theoretical derivations from Janoff-Bulman in a way that accurately captured the locus, stability, and controllability features of her conceptions while avoiding the methodological confounding problems inherent in our earlier forced choice method (Anderson et al., 1983). Specifically, our methodology was designed to more precisely test Janoff-Bulman's original predictions that characterological attributions for negative events (failure) would be positively associated with depression and that behavioral attributions for negative events would be negatively associated with depression. In addition, we provided tests of a third category of attributions, circumstances, and tested all three types of attribution frequencies for both success and failure situations. The results confirmed that (a) all three types of attributions correlate with depression and loneliness; (b) each type contributes uniquely to the prediction of depression and loneliness; and (c) attributional styles for both success and failure situations contribute uniquely to the prediction of depression and loneliness.

Empirical Issues

LOW FREQUENCY OF ATTRIBUTIONAL CATEGORIES

As expected, the relative frequencies of the three attributional categories were low. There are at least two reasons for this. First, most attributions that most people generate are likely to be depression-neutral. That is, no theoretician in this area expects that even a majority of attributions will fit the ideal depressogenic or nondepressogenic categories. Indeed, it seems unlikely that even truly depressed people will generate a majority of depressogenic attributions. Attribution theory merely asserts that on average, depressed (and lonely) people will generate relatively more maladaptive attributions than nondepressed (and nonlonely) people.

Second, the new dimensional–categorical translation procedure produces many attributions that do not fit the conservative definitions of any of the attribution categories. Any attribution that contained at least one dimensional rating at the scale midpoint was necessarily defined as irrelevant to the categories of interest. We know that people frequently use dimensional midpoints when rating ambiguous stimuli. We also know that open-ended attributions are frequently ambiguous with respect to at least one attribution dimension. Thus, it should come as no surprise that many of the generated attributions did not "count" in the categorical scheme.

This rational analysis suggested two empirical predictions: (a) The frequency of attributions with at least one midpoint rating (out of the three dimensions of locus, stability, and controllability) should be fairly high. (b) This frequency should be higher in Sample 2 than in Sample 1 because the former had fewer nonmidpoint choices available (5-point rather than 9-point rating scales). Our results produced exactly this pattern. In Sample 1, 45% of the failure attributions and 35% of the success attributions had at least one midpoint rating. In Sample 2, the corresponding figures increased to 67% and 52%. Thus, the low frequencies of the attribution types derived from our translation method were neither unexpected nor unreasonable.

SMALL EFFECT SIZE

The correlations reported in Table 2.4 are generally quite small. Indeed, these correlations are considerably smaller than those reported in Anderson et al. (1983). The multiple correlations reported in Table 2.5 are certainly respectable, but still are somewhat smaller than the forced-choice correlations obtained in that earlier study of categorical attributional styles. As discussed earlier, one reason has to do with the methodological differences between the forced-choice procedure and the present rating scale translation procedure. The relative frequencies of attributions meeting the present criteria are much smaller than comparable relative frequencies in the forced-choice procedure. For instance, in Study 1 of Anderson et al. (1983), 23% of the failure attributions were to characterological factors (ability and trait). In the present study, only 5% of the failure attributions in Sample 1 and 2% in Sample 2 met the criteria for being defined as characterological. This is a function of the fact that in a forced-choice methodology, each attribution must fit a predetermined attribution category. This is most obvious in Study 2 of Anderson et al. (1983), where all attributions had to be either characterological or behavioral. The present translation methodology does not do this, resulting in many attributions essentially having no impact on the analyses.

Thus, the low correlations were expected and do not detract from the importance of the results in any way, because the theoretical insights gained from the translation procedure remain wholly valid. However, the low correlations do suggest that practical use of the translation procedure in applied settings may be limited.

Three modifications to our translation method may allow higher correlations to emerge. First, increasing the number of hypothetical situations examined should increase the absolute frequencies of the different types of attributions even if the low relative (%) frequencies remain the same. This increase in absolute frequencies should allow better discrimination between depressed and nondepressed people. Second, increasing the number of scale points (say from 9-point to 15-point rating scales) might further increase both the relative and absolute frequencies of relevant attributions. Third, using even-numbered rating scales (e.g., with 10 points) might further reduce the midpoint ambiguity problem discussed earlier.

These three methodological refinements are likely to improve the correlations somewhat, but we have a theoretical notion suggesting an additional limit to the translation procedure. If people typically make categorical attributions and translate them into dimensions only when forced to do so, then dimensional approaches to the study of attributional style may produce artificially low relations. In essence, there may be something lost in the translation from attribution category to attribution dimension. In the present study there was yet an additional translation, essentially a back translation from the dimensional back to the categorical. Some recent work (Anderson, 1991; Anderson & Deuser, 1993) does suggest that people typically think about attributions in categorical rather than dimensional terms. In the present context, this suggests that additional work on attributional style models of depression and other problems in living may best be done using attributional style measures that focus on attribution types. Such research would nicely complement the dimensional approach that so heavily dominates most current work. Prospective designs using a categorical (type) approach, as well as similar intervention studies, would seem especially valuable. This may very well involve using a forced-choice methodology for assessing attributional style. Because psychologists now know that both characterological and behavioral self-blame contribute uniquely to depression and loneliness, future studies can assess both using a forced choice methodology without concern over the confounding problem inherent in this procedure. Alternatively, an open-ended coding method that is explicitly sensitive to all three dimensional features of the key attribution types could be refined and used to test additional categorical attributional style developments.

Finally, it is important to remember that what psychologists typically bemoan as "small" effects are often larger than effects that in other contexts are acknowledged as of immense practical importance. Rosenthal (1990) noted that a major study on aspirin and heart attacks was stopped early, because the effect of aspirin on reducing heart attacks was so great that the researchers felt it would be unethical to continue giving the control group placebos. The effect size in terms of a correlation coefficient was .034, considerably smaller than the effect sizes seen in the present study. Other scholars have noted a variety of contextual conditions in which seemingly small effect sizes are judged as important or impressive (e.g., Abelson, 1985; Prentice & Miller, 1992). Two such conditions apply to the present study. First, when one is primarily interested in testing the validity of specific theoretical propositions, effect size is largely irrelevant except for the purposes of estimating the statistical power of various possible sample sizes. Second, when the methodology is known to produce conditions likely to minimize an effect, the discovery of a reliable effect—no matter how small—is impressive.

Conclusions

The categorical approach, best exemplified by Janoff-Bulman's (1979) theoretical analysis, seems to have been pronounced "dead" prematurely. The vast majority of attributional style studies have used a strictly dimensional approach (but see Schoeneman, Stevens, Hollis, Cheek, & Fischer, 1988, for an innovative categorical approach to attributions for smoking cessation). Perhaps the inconsistencies found in early categorical studies led researchers to conclude that the categorical approach was unworkable. We believe that the approach is a valuable one and that it nicely complements the dimensional approach. We hope that our results help revive this most worthy patient.

NOTES

We thank Lyn Abramson, Ronnie Janoff-Bulman, and the various reviewers for their many helpful comments on a draft of this article.
1. We thank an anonymous reviewer for bringing this perspective to our attention.
2. For each sample, 12 correlations resulted from the design: 3 attribution types (characterological, behavioral, and circumstantial) × 2 outcomes (success and failure) × 2 criteria (depression and loneliness). To ensure that combining correlations across the two samples was appropriate, we tested the differences between each of the 12 pairs of correlations, using a Bonferroni correction against Type I errors. None of the tests approached significance, indicating that the results from the two samples were comparable.
3. Portions of this data set were analyzed by way of more traditional dimensional procedures and reported in Anderson and Riger (1991).

REFERENCES

Abelson, R. P. (1985). A variance explanation paradox: When a little is a lot. *Psychological Bulletin, 97,* 129–133.
American Psychological Association. (1990–1992). *The PsycLIT database.* Washington, DC: Author.
Anderson, C. A. (1991). How people think about causes: Examination of the typical phenomenal organization of attributions for success and failure. *Social Cognition, 9,* 295–329.
Anderson, C. A., & Arnoult, L. H. (1985a). Attributional models of depression, loneliness, and shyness. In J. Harvey & G. Weary (Eds.), *Attribution: Basic issues and applications* (pp. 235–279). San Diego, CA: Academic Press.
Anderson, C. A., & Arnoult, L. H. (1985b). Attributional style and everyday problems in living: Depression, loneliness, and shyness. *Social Cognition, 3,* 16–35.
Anderson, C. A., & Deuser, W. E. (1991). Science and the reformulated learned helplessness model of depression. *Psychological Inquiry, 2,* 14–19.
Anderson, C. A., & Deuser, W. E. (1993). The primacy of control in causal thinking and attributional style: An attributional functionalism perspective. In G. Weary, F. Gleicher, & K. Marsh (Eds.), *Control motivation and social cognition* (pp. 94–121). New York: Springer-Verlag.
Anderson, C. A., Horowitz, L. M., & French, R. (1983). Attributional style of lonely and depressed people. *Journal of Personality and Social Psychology, 45,* 127–136.
Anderson, C. A., Jennings, D. L., & Arnoult, L. H. (1988). Validity and utility of the attributional style construct at a moderate level of specificity. *Journal of Personality and Social Psychology, 55,* 979–990.
Anderson, C. A., & Riger, A. L. (1991). A controllability attributional model of problems in living: Dimensional and situational interactions in the prediction of depression and loneliness. *Social Cognition, 9,* 149–181.
Anderson, C. A., & Weiner, B. (1992). Attribution and attributional processes in personality. In G. Caprara & G. Heck (Eds.), *Modern personality psychology: Critical reviews and new directions* (pp. 295–324). New York: Harvester Wheatsheaf.
Beck, A. T., & Beck, R. W. (1972). Screening depressed patients in family practice: A rapid technic. *Postgraduate Medicine, 52,* 81–85.
Beck, A. T., Ward, C. H., Mendelson, M., Mock, J., & Erbaugh, J. (1961). An inventory for measuring depression. *Archives of General Psychiatry, 4,* 561–571.
Carver, C. S. (1989). How should multifaceted personality constructs be tested? Issues illustrated by self-monitoring, attributional style, and hardiness. *Journal of Personality and Social Psychology, 56,* 577–585.
Carver, C. S., Ganellen, R. J., & Behar-Mitrani, V. (1985). Depression and cognitive style: Comparisons between measures. *Journal of Personality and Social Psychology, 49,* 722–728.
Carver, C. S., & Scheier, M. F. (1991). Unresolved issues regarding the meaning and measurement of explanatory style. *Psychological Inquiry, 2,* 21–24.
Feather, N. T. (1983). Some correlates of attributional stye: Depressive symptoms, self-esteem, and Protestant ethic values. *Personality and Social Psychology Bulletin, 9,* 125–135.
Feather, N. T., & Tiggemann, M. (1984). A balanced measure of attributional style. *Australian Journal of Psychology, 36,* 267–283.
Flett, G. L., Blankstein, K. R., & Holowaty, L. S. (1990). Depression and complex attributions of blame in self and others. *Journal of Social Behavior and Personality, 5,* 175–188.
Frazier, P. A. (1990). Victim attributions and post-rape trauma. *Journal of Personality and Social Psychology, 59,* 298–304.
Janoff-Bulman, R. (1979). Characterological versus behavioral self-blame: Inquiries into depression and rape. *Journal of Personality and Social Psychology, 37,* 1798–1809.
Kelley, H. H., & Michela, J. L. (1980). Attribution theory and research. *Annual Review of Psychology, 31,* 457–501.
Major, B., Mueller, P., & Hildebrandt, K. (1985). Attributions, expectations, and coping with abortions. *Journal of Personality and Social Psychology, 48,* 585–599.
Meyer, C. B., & Taylor, S. E. (1986). Adjustment to rape. *Journal of Personality and Social Psychology, 50,* 1226–1234.

Peterson, C., Schwartz, S. M., & Seligman, M. E. P. (1981). Self-blame and depressive symptoms. *Journal of Personality and Social Psychology, 41,* 253–259.

Prentice, D. A., & Miller, D. T. (1992). When small effects are impressive. *Psychological Bulletin, 112,* 160–164.

Rosenthal, R. (1990). How are we doing in soft psychology? *American Psychologist, 45,* 775–777.

Russell, D., Peplau, L. A., & Cutrona, C. E. (1980). The revised UCLA Loneliness Scale: Concurrent and discriminant validity evidence. *Journal of Personality and Social Psychology, 39,* 472–480.

Schoeneman, T. J., Stevens, V. J., Hollis, J. F., Cheek, P. R., & Fischer, K. (1988). Attribution, affects, and expectancy following smoking cessation treatment. *Basic and Applied Social Psychology, 9,* 173–184.

Seligman, M. E. P., Abramson, L. Y., Semmel, A., & von Baeyer, C. (1979). Depressive attributional style. *Journal of Abnormal Psychology, 88,* 242–247.

Stoltz, R. F., & Galassi, J. P. (1989). Internal attributions and types of depression in college students: The learned helplessness model revisited. *Journal of Counseling Psychology, 36,* 316–321.

Sweeney, P. D., Anderson, K., & Bailey, S. (1986). Attributional style in depression: A meta-analytic review. *Journal of Personality and Social Psychology, 50,* 974–991.

Tennen, H., & Herzberger, S. (1987). Depression, self-esteem, and the absence of self-protective attributional biases. *Journal of Personality and Social Psychology, 52,* 72–80.

Discussion Questions

1. What other emotional reactions besides depression and loneliness might be related to the attributions that people make?
2. What do you see as the advantages and disadvantages of the "dimensional" and "categorical" approaches to attribution that Anderson et al. described?
3. What are the implications of this study for the clinical treatment of people who are troubled by depression or loneliness?

Suggested Readings

Abramson, L. Y. (Ed.) (1988). *Social cognition and clinical psychology: A synthesis.* New York: Guilford. The chapters in this edited book cover not only implications of attribution theory for clinical psychology but also a number of other topics from social psychological research on social cognition.

Abramson, L. Y., Seligman, M. E., & Teasdale, J. D. (1978). Learned helplessness in humans: Critique and reformation. *Journal of Abnormal Psychology, 87,* 49–74. This article examines the role that attribution for negative life events plays in depression and learned helplessness.

Bell-Dolan, D., & Anderson, C. A. (1999). Attributional processes: An integration of social and clinical psychology. In R. M. Kowalski & M. R. Leary (Eds.), *The social psychology of emotional and behavioral problems* (pp. 37–67). Washington, DC: American Psychological Association. This chapter provides a model of the relationship between attributions and emotional/behavioral problems.

Janoff-Bulman, R. (1979). Characterological versus behavioral self-blame: Inquiries into depression and rape. *Journal of Personality and Social Psychology, 37,* 1798–1809. This is the article that first made the distinction between behavioral and characterological self-blame on which the Anderson et al. research was based.

Storms, M. D., & McCaul, K. D. (1976). Attribution processes and the exacerbation of dysfunctional behavior. In J. H. Harvey, W. J. Ickes, & R. F. Kidd (Eds.), *New directions in attribution research* (Vol. 1, pp. 143–164). Hillsdale, NJ: Erlbaum. This chapter discusses how attributions can create and maintain problems, such as insomnia and impotence, in which emotion and arousal play a role.

Valins, S., & Nisbett, K. E. (1972). Attributional processes in the development and treatment of emotional disorder. In E. E. Jones, D. E. Kanouse, H. H. Kelley, R. E. Nisbett, S. Valins, & B. Weiner (Eds.), *Attribution: Perceiving the causes of behavior* (pp. 137–150). Morristown, NJ: General Learning Press. This chapter discusses the link between attributions and emotional disorders.

READING 3

Explanatory Style, Expectations, and Depressive Symptoms

Christopher Peterson and Robert S. Vaidya • University of Michigan

Editors' Introduction

A great deal of research, including the previous reading (Reading 2), has supported Abramson, Seligman, and Teasdale's (1978) attributional reformulation of learned helplessness theory by showing that certain kinds of attributions predispose people to become depressed. In particular, attributing negative events to internal, stable, and global causes is reliably associated with depression. Not only do scores on measures of attributional or explanatory style (different researchers use different labels) correlate with depression, but changes in people's attributions over time predict subsequent changes in how depressed they are. Such findings have been obtained using various measures of attributions across a variety of samples, including children, pregnant women, prisoners, patients hospitalized for depression, and college students.

Christopher Peterson and Robert Vaidya extended this research by examining the role that people's expectations play in mediating the relationship between attributions and depression. The attributional reformulation of learned helplessness theory (Abramson et al., 1978) suggests that people's attributions affect depression by influencing their expectations about the future. For example, believing that one was personally responsible for a negative event (an internal attribution), that the negative effects are long-lasting (a stable attribution), or that it pervades many areas of life (a global attribution) may lead people to develop pessimistic expectations about the future that promote depression. If so, attributions are affecting depression indirectly through the expectations that those attributions create.

To test whether expectations mediate the relationship between attributions and depression, Peterson and Vaidya had a sample of university students complete measures of explanatory style, expectations, and depression. As previous research shows, explanatory style correlated with depression. To examine whether this relationship was mediated by expectations, the authors used structural equations modeling (SEM), an analysis designed to test the statistical plausibility of mediational explanations. This analysis showed that, as predicted, expectations mediated the relationship between explanatory style and depressive symptoms. That is, explanatory style significantly predicted expectations, which then significantly predicted depressive symptoms. To put it differently, people's explanations (i.e., attributions) appear to affect their level of depression by influencing their expectations about the future.

Abstract

One hundred and fifty-five college students completed questionnaires measuring explanatory style, general expectations for future good and bad events, specific expectations for future good and bad events, and depressive symptoms. Structural equation modeling confirmed the prediction of the attributional reformulation of learned helplessness theory that the link between stability and globality of explanatory style and depression is mediated by expectations. Implications of these results were discussed.

Keywords: explanatory style; expectations; depression; learned helplessness reformulation

According to the attributional reformulation of learned helplessness theory, people encountering uncontrollable aversive events ask themselves why these events happened (Abramson, Seligman & Teasdale, 1978). The nature of their answer sets the parameters for the helplessness that can follow in the wake of such events. If their causal attribution is stable ("it is going to last forever"), then induced helplessness is long-lasting; if unstable, then it is transient. If their causal attribution is global ("it is going to undermine everything"), then subsequent helplessness is manifest across a variety of situations; if specific, then it is correspondingly circumscribed. Finally, if the causal attribution is internal ("it is all my fault"), the individual's self-esteem drops following uncontrollability; if external, self-esteem is left intact.

In some cases, the situation itself provides the explanation made by the person. In other cases, the person relies on his or her habitual way of making sense of events that occur, what is called one's explanatory style (Peterson & Seligman, 1984). All things being equal, people tend to offer similar sorts of explanations for disparate bad events. Accordingly, explanatory style is a distal influence on helplessness and failures of adaptation that involve helplessness (Peterson, Maier, & Seligman, 1993).

Explanatory style has been extensively studied as a correlate and risk factor for depressive symptoms. Literally hundreds of studies have supported the hypothesized link between a stable, global, and internal explanatory style for bad events and depression (Sweeney, Anderson, & Bailey, 1986). Other claims of the attributional reformulation have not received nearly as much research attention (Peterson, 1991). For example, few studies have looked at the hypothesized role of expectations as a mediator between explanatory style and depressive symptoms (Buchanan & Seligman, 1995). This neglect is ironic given that the attributional reformulation is an elaboration of a theory—the original helplessness model—in which expectations are regarded as a sufficient condition for maladaptive passivity following aversive events (Maier & Seligman, 1976; Peterson, Maier, & Seligman, 1993; Peterson & Seligman, 1984; Seligman, 1975).

The studies that have looked jointly at explanatory style, expectations, and depression provide only mixed support for the reformulation. Some investigations are consistent with the model (e.g. Dowd, Claiborn, & Milne, 1985; Hull & Mendolia, 1991; Lynd-Stevenson, 1996; McKean, 1994; Riskind, Rholes, Brannon, & Burdick, 1987), whereas others are not (e.g. Ahrens & Haaga, 1993; Covington & Omelich, 1979; DeVellis & Blalock, 1992; Hammen & Cochran, 1981; Tripp, Catano, & Sullivan, 1997). These inconsistent results may be due to the different measures of expectations used by investigators. The specificity and reliability of these measures vary and thereby might introduce unmeasured error into analyses.

The study reported here addressed the role of expectations in the hypothesized link between explanatory style and depressive symptoms by measuring expectations in several ways and using structural equation modeling (SEM) to test the mediational hypothesis. One of the benefits of SEM for this purpose is that it takes into account measurement error.

College students completed a version of the Attributional Style Questionnaire (ASQ; Dykema, Bergbower, Doctora, & Peterson, 1996; Peterson & Villanova, 1988; Peterson et al., 1982) and at the same time reported on the extent of depressive symptoms they were experiencing. Expectations of two sorts were assessed as well. First, research participants completed a measure of dispositional optimism, the Life Orientation Test (LOT; Scheier & Carver, 1985). This questionnaire taps the degree to which a respondent expects generally good versus generally bad events to occur in the future. A representative item, with which respondents express their degree of agreement, is "In uncertain times, I usually expect the best." Second, participants completed a measure of specific expectations for good and bad events relevant to college students that was designed for the present study. They were asked to estimate the likelihood in the next year of such good events as receiving a scholarship that pays all tuition and fees and such bad events as developing an eating disorder.

We expected explanatory style to correlate with the extent of depressive symptoms, and further that expectations would mediate this association. More specifically, stability and globality of explanatory style, as opposed to internality, would begin this cascade because the reformulation proposes that these two dimensions, but not internality, influence expectations (cf. Abramson, Metalsky, & Alloy, 1989).

Method

Research Participants and Procedure

The research participants were 155 first-year college students from the University of Michigan introductory psychology subject pool whose participation satisfied a course requirement. (One additional research participant was dropped because of substantial missing data.) The sample was mainly female (79%) and mainly white (76%). Mean age was 18.1 years, with a range from 17 to 20 years. Gender, ethnicity, and age did not influence the results to be reported here and are not again mentioned. In small groups of 3 to 10 individuals, research participants completed the questionnaires described next. They did so in single sessions.

Questionnaires

After providing written consent, research participants completed, in order, the following self-report measures. First, they provided demographic information. Next, they completed the LOT, a measure of dispositional optimism versus pessimism (Scheier & Carver, 1985). Four items reflect an optimistic orientation to the future, and four items reflect a pessimistic orientation; respondents express their degree of agreement with these items on a 5-point (0–4) scale. Scores are averaged across the appropriate items. In the present sample, internal consistencies of the LOT, estimated by Cronbach's (1951) coefficient alpha, were .70 for the optimism subscale (mean = 2.58, SD = 0.63) and .82 for the pessimism subscale (mean = 1.37, SD = 0.70). These subscales were negatively correlated ($r = -.50, p < .001$).

Respondents were next presented with a list of 16 good events and the instructions to place a mark in each case along a 90-cm line anchored by 0 and 100% (with the intermediate points of 25, 50, and 75% also indicated) to estimate the chances, compared to other first-year students at the university, that the given event would happen to them during the next year. Events were drawn from both the psychosocial ("you will meet the true love of your life") and academic ("you will receive A grades in your courses") domains. Responses were coded by measuring to the nearest 5% where they fell along the line. Internal consistency of this measure of specific expectations for good events was 0.79 (mean = 63%, SD = 12).

The next questionnaire was an analogous measure of specific expectations for bad events. Fourteen bad events were used, again drawn from both the psychosocial ("you will end up in a terrible living situation") and academic ("you will wind up on academic probation") domains. Internal consistency of this measure of specific expectations for bad events was 0.79 (mean = 15%, SD = 9). Expectations for bad events were negatively correlated with expectations for good events ($r = -.31, p < .01$).

Respondents next completed the brief version of the Beck Depression Inventory (BDI; Beck, Rial, & Rickels, 1974). This self-report measure presents respondents with 13 common symptoms and asks them to use 0–3 scales to indicate the degree to which they have experienced each during the past week. Scores are summed. In the present sample, the internal consistency of this measure was .83.

Finally, the version of the ASQ created by Dykema et al. (1996) was completed. This questionnaire presents respondents with 10 bad events (e.g., "you have financial problems") and asks them in each case to imagine the event happening to them. They write down in their words the "one main cause" of this event happening to them and then use 7-point scales in each case to rate the cause in terms of its internality ("it is completely due to me"), its stability ("it will always affect me"), and its globality ("it affects all areas of my life"). These ratings are averaged across events, separately for the three attributional dimensions. Internal consistencies in the present sample for internality (mean = 4.80, SD = 0.92), stability (mean = 4.75, SD = 0.89), and globality (mean = 4.69, SD = 0.96) were, respectively, .62, .77, and .79. Stability and globality scores were entwined ($r = .50, p < .001$), and they were combined into a composite with an internal consistency of .82. Internality scores were only modestly correlated with this stability + globality composite ($r = .23, p < .05$).

Results

As expected, stability + globality of explanatory style was positively correlated with the extent of depressive symptoms ($r = .20, p < .05$), replicating previous studies (Sweeney et al., 1986). Internality of explanatory style was not associated with depression ($r = .03$, ns) and was therefore not used in tests of the mediational hypothesis.

The different measures of expectations appeared to be substantially intercorrelated (median $r = .35$), an impression confirmed by a factor analysis using SPSS for Windows 6.0 software (Norusis, 1993) of the four expectation measures (optimism subscale of the LOT; pessimism subscale of the LOT; specific expectations for good events; and specific expectations for bad events). A principal components factor analysis with varimax rotation revealed only one factor with an eigenvalue greater than 1.00. This factor (eigenvalue = 2.14) accounted for 53% of the variance in the expectation scores. A composite of the four expectation measures was formed by normalizing the scores and summing them (after reverse-scoring the pessimism subscale and the specific expectations for bad events). This composite had an alpha of .71 and was used as the single measure of expectations in the subsequent analyses.

Table 3.1 shows the intercorrelations among the variables of interest. The mediating role of expectations was tested with SEM, using AMOS 4.0 software (Arbuckle, 1994). Because the sample size (n = 155) was relatively small for this sort of analysis, the summary scores (stability + globality of explanatory style; composite expectations; and BDI total) were used rather than the individual items. The reliabilities of these summaries were used to estimate error variances in the model. The

TABLE 3.1. Intercorrelations ($n = 155$)[a]

	1	2	3
1. Stability + globaility (ASQ)			
2. Expectations	−0.17*		
3. Depressive symptoms (BDI)	0.20*	−0.55*	
Mean	4.72	0.00	4.57
SD	0.80	2.92	4.22

[a]ASQ, Attributional Style Questionnaire; BDI, Beck Depression Inventory.
*$p < 0.05$.

resulting model is shown in Fig. 3.1. The hypothesized paths, between explanatory style and expectations and between expectations and depressive symptoms, were both significant. The overall fit of the model was good ($\chi^2 = 0.86$, $df = 1$, $p < .35$; NFI = 0.99; RMSEA = 0.00; PCLOSE = 0.44) and what would be expected given its single degree of freedom. In an additional model (not shown), where a direct path was added between explanatory style and depressive symptoms, this path proved not significant. Also, as suggested by the intercorrelations in Table 3.1, an additional SEM analysis (not shown) showed that the actual data were not at all well described by the alternative model: expectations → explanatory style → depressive symptoms.

Discussion

The present results show that expectations indeed mediate the often-reported association between explanatory style and depressive symptoms. This is an important finding vis-à-vis the helplessness reformulation, given the empirical neglect of the mediational hypothesis for two decades. Researchers working in the helplessness tradition should measure not only explanatory style and helplessness outcomes like depression but also expectations. Indeed, given the strong relationship between expectations and depressive symptoms, it seems particularly important for helplessness researchers to include this construct. Also consistent with theory, the internality dimension did not enter into the model (cf. Peterson, 1991).

On a methodological level, the present results underscore the important of taking into account measurement error when testing the process hypothesized by the helplessness reformulation. The ASQ, in its various incarnations, has been the subject of frequent criticism on grounds of reliability (e.g. Peterson, 1991; Reivich, 1995; Tennen & Herzberger, 1986). Until a highly reliable measure of explanatory style is available, it behooves researchers to adjust for the less-than-ideal consistency of available questionnaires. SEM provides one way to make this adjustment. Previously inconsistent results may thus be resolved.

When the present study was first planned, we wondered whether the level of abstraction of the expectation measure mattered. In other words, would the link between explanatory style and depressive symptoms be differentially mediated by general expectations versus specific expectations? We further wondered if it mattered whether the expectation measure tapped expectations about positive versus negative outcomes. There is a research literature suggesting that optimism and pessimism can be somewhat independent constructs (Chang, 1998; Lai, 1994; Robinson-Whelen, Kim, MacCallum, & Kiecolt-Glaser, 1997). At least in the present study, these distinctions among types of expectations were not pertinent; indeed, all reflected a common factor. The learned helplessness reformulation does not make these sorts of distinctions among expectations, and perhaps it is unnecessary to do so. Recent theoretical discussions of learned helplessness have recast theory and research in terms of optimism

FIGURE 3.1 ■ AMOS Results of structural equation modeling. To simplify presentation, only significant paths are shown (*$p < .01$).

(e.g. Peterson & Bossio, 1991; Seligman, 1991; Seligman, Reivich, Jaycox, & Gillham, 1995), that is, positive expectations, but the present results imply that a more general expectational framework is sufficient (cf. Peterson, 2000).

ACKNOWLEDGMENTS

The statistical consultation of Hannah D'Arcy and Laura Klem is gratefully acknowledged.

REFERENCES

Abramson, L. Y., Metalsky, G. I., & Alloy, L. B. (1989). Hopelessness depression: A theory-based subtype of depression. *Psychological Review, 96*, 358–372.

Abramson, L. Y., Seligman, M. E. P., & Teasdale, J. D. (1978). Learned helplessness in humans: Critique and reformulation. *Journal of Abnormal Psychology, 87*, 49–74.

Ahrens, A. H., & Haaga, D. A. (1993). The specificity of attributional style and expectations to positive and negative affectivity, depression, and anxiety. *Cognitive Therapy and Research, 17*, 83–98.

Arbuckle, J. L. (1994). *AMOS: A structural equations modeling program.* Chicago: SmallWaters.

Beck, A. T., Rial, W. Y., & Rickels, K. (1974). Short form of Depression Inventory: Cross-validation. *Psychological Reports, 34*, 1184–1186.

Buchanan, G. M., & Seligman, M. E. P. (1995). *Explanatory style.* Hillsdale, NJ: Lawrence Erlbaum Associates.

Chang, E. C. (1998). Distinguishing between optimism and pessimism: A second look at the optimism-neuroticism hypothesis. In R. R. Hoffman, M. F. Sherrik, & J. S. Warm, *Viewing psychology as a whole: The integrative science of William N. Dember* (pp. 415–432). Washington, DC: American Psychological Association.

Covington, M. V., & Omelich, C. L. (1979). Are causal attributions causal? A path analysis of the cognitive model of achievement motivation. *Journal of Personality and Social Psychology, 37*, 1487–1504.

Cronbach, L. J. (1951). Coefficient alpha and the internal structure of tests. *Psychometrika, 16*, 297–334.

DeVellis, B. M., & Blalock, S. J. (1992). Illness attributions and hopelessness depression: The role of hopelessness expectancy. *Journal of Abnormal Psychology, 101*, 257–264.

Dowd, E. T., Claiborn, C. D., & Milne, C. R. (1985). Anxiety, attributional style, and perceived coping ability. *Cognitive Therapy and Research, 9*, 575–582.

Dykema, K., Bergbower, K., Doctora, J. D., & Peterson, C. (1996). An Attributional Style Questionnaire for general use. *Journal of Psychoeducational Assessment, 14*, 100–108.

Hammen, C. L., & Cochran, S. D. (1981). Cognitive correlates of life stress and depression in college students. *Journal of Abnormal Psychology, 90*, 23–27.

Hull, J. G., & Mendolia, M. (1991). Modeling the relations of attributional style, expectancies, and depression. *Journal of Personality and Social Psychology, 61*, 85–97.

Lai, J. C. (1994). Differential predictive power of the positively versus the negatively worded items of the Life Orientation Test. *Psychological Reports, 75*, 1507–1515.

Lynd-Stevenson, R. M. (1996). A test of the hopelessness theory of depression in unemployed young adults. *British Journal of Clinical Psychology, 35*, 117–132.

Maier, S. F., & Seligman, M. E. P. (1976). Learned helplessness: Theory and evidence. *Journal of Experimental Psychology: General, 105*, 3–46.

McKean, K. J. (1994). Using multiple risk factors to assess the behavioral, cognitive, and affective effects of learned helplessness. *Journal of Psychology, 128*, 177–183.

Norusis, M. J. (1993). *SPSS for Windows base system user's guide.* Chicago: SPSS.

Peterson, C. (1991). Meaning and measurement of explanatory style. *Psychological Inquiry, 2*, 1–10.

Peterson, C. (2000). The future of optimism. *American Psychologist, 5*, 5544–5555.

Peterson, C., & Bossio, L. M. (1991). *Health and optimism.* New York: Free Press.

Peterson, C., Maier, S. F., & Seligman, M. E. P. (1993). *Learned helplessness: A theory for the age of personal control.* New York: Oxford University Press.

Peterson, C., & Seligman, M. E. P. (1984). Causal explanations as a risk factor for depression: Theory and evidence. *Psychological Review, 91*, 347–374.

Peterson, C., Semmel, A., von Baeyer, C., Abramson, L. Y., Metalsky, G. I., & Seligman, M. E. P. (1982). The Attributional Style Questionnaire. *Cognitive Therapy and Research, 6*, 287–299.

Peterson, C., & Villanova, P. (1988). An Expanded Attributional Style Questionnaire. *Journal of Abnormal Psychology, 97*, 87–89.

Reivich, K. (1995). The measurement of explanatory style. In G. M. Buchanan & M. E. P. Seligman, *Explanatory style* (pp. 21–47). Hillsdale, NJ: Lawrence Erlbaum Associates.

Riskind, J. H., Rholes, W. S., Brannon, A. M., & Burdick, C. A. (1987). Attributions and expectations: A confluence of vulnerabilities in mild depression in a college student population. *Journal of Personality and Social Psychology, 53*, 349–354.

Robinson-Whelen, S., Kim, C., MacCallum, R. C., & Kiecolt-Glaser, J. K. (1997). Distinguishing optimism from pessimism in older adults: Is it more important to be optimistic or not to be pessimistic? *Journal of Personality and Social Psychology, 73*, 1345–1353.

Scheier, M. F., & Carver, C. S. (1985). Optimism, coping, and health: Assessment and implications of generalized outcome expectancies. *Health Psychology, 4*, 219–247.

Seligman, M. E. P. (1975). *Helplessness: On depression, development, and death.* San Francisco: Freeman.

Seligman, M. E. P. (1991). *Learned optimism.* New York: Knopf.

Seligman, M. E. P., Reivich, K., Jaycox, L., & Gillham, J. (1995). *The optimistic child.* New York: Houghton Mifflin.

Sweeney, P. D., Anderson, K., & Bailey, S. (1986). Attributional style in depression: A meta-analytic review. *Journal of Personality and Social Psychology, 50*, 974–991.

Tennen, H., & Herzberger, S. (1986). Attributional Style Questionnaire. In D. J. Keyser & R. C. Sweetland, *Test critiques* (Vol. 4, pp. 20–30). Kansas City, KS: Test Corporation of America.

Tripp, D. A., Catano, V., & Sullivan, M. J. L. (1997). The contributions of attributional style, expectancies, depression, and self-esteem in a cognition-based depression model. *Canadian Journal of Behavioural Science, 29*, 101–111.

Discussion Questions

1. Depression was related to the stability and globality dimensions of explanatory style, but not to the internality dimension. Given the role that pessimistic expectations play in depression, can you explain why?
2. Can we conclude from this study that explanatory style and expectations *cause* depression?
3. What are the possible implications of this study for the treatment of depression in clinical settings?

Suggested Readings

Abramson, L. Y., Metalsky, G. I., & Alloy, L. B. (1989). Hopelessness depression: A theory-based subtype of depression. *Psychological Review, 96,* 358–372. This article describes the nature of the relationships between attributions, hopelessness, and depression, and proposes a new subtype of depression.

Abramson, L. Y., Seligman, M. E., & Teasdale, J. D. (1978). Learned helplessness in humans: Critique and reformulation. *Journal of Abnormal Psychology, 87,* 49–74. This article examines the role that attributions for negative life events play in depression and learned helplessness.

Burns, M. O., & Seligman, M. E. P. (1991). Explanatory style, helplessness, and depression. In C. R. Snyder & D. R. Forsyth (Eds.), *Handbook of social and clinical psychology: The health perspective* (pp. 267–284). New York: Pergamon. This chapter co-authored by Martin Seligman, whose earlier work stimulated interest in the link between learned helplessness and depression, provides a review of the relationship between explanatory style and depression.

Dykema, K., Bergbower, K., Doctora, J. D., & Peterson, C. (1996). An Attributional Style Questionnaire for general use. *Journal of Psychoeducational Assessment, 14,* 100–108. This article describes a recent measure of attributional (or explanatory) style, one that is designed for use with noncollege samples.

READING 4

Self-Regulation Failure: An Overview

Roy F. Baumeister • Department of Psychology, Case Western Reserve University
Todd F. Heatherton • Department of Psychology, Dartmouth College

Editors' Introduction

Many of the problems for which people seek help from psychologists involve difficulties with self-regulation. People who cannot stop smoking, overeating, abusing drugs, losing their temper, worrying, having extramarital affairs, procrastinating, or abusing their children clearly have problems controlling their emotions or behaviors. People sometimes have great difficulty controlling themselves, even when their actions harm themselves or others and create havoc with their lives.

Questions regarding consciousness, will, and self-control have plagued philosophers and scientists for centuries, and self-regulation remains one of the big mysteries of psychology. Although scientists understand a great deal about automatic regulatory mechanisms that control bodily processes, they know relatively little about how people intentionally control themselves. How does a walking mass of cytoplasm (i.e., a human being) consciously decide to change itself, then intentionally carry out those changes?

Despite the fact that we do not understand precisely how self-regulation occurs, we know a great deal about the factors that increase and diminish people's ability to control themselves. In this article, Roy Baumeister and

Todd Heatherton offer an integrative overview of this topic, in which they pull together many fragments of research to provide a compelling picture of why self-regulation often fails. They start with the assumption that three things are required in order for a person to successfully self-regulate. The person must (1) have clear and consistent standards regarding the outcome he or she desires (such as to stop smoking or to exercise more), (2) monitor his or her behavior carefully so that undesired thoughts, emotions, or behaviors will be detected, and desired actions will be maintained, and (3) act to change his or her thoughts, emotions, or behaviors when needed to achieve the desired outcomes. Self-regulation is only as effective as the weakest link in this chain.

Because it has received the least attention previously, Baumeister and Heatherton focus primarily on the third of these ingredients of self-regulation, the stage at which people instigate processes that operate to change their own thoughts, feelings, or actions. They suggest that self-regulation at this stage typically involves the person causing one process to override another so that the desired outcome is achieved. So, for example, a man who is trying to control his temper must react in such a way that a more desirable response (such as calmness) overrides the impulse to become angry. This way of thinking about self-regulation is useful because it focuses on the question of what makes a person able to override one impulse with another and, conversely, what causes people to fail to override those undesired impulses.

Abstract

The major patterns of self-regulatory failure are reviewed. Underregulation occurs because of deficient standards, inadequate monitoring, or inadequate strength. Misregulation occurs because of false assumptions or misdirected efforts, especially an unwarranted emphasis on emotion. The evidence supports a strength (limited-resource) model of self-regulation and suggests that people often acquiesce in losing control. Loss of control of attention, failure of transcendence, and various lapse-activated causes all contribute to regulatory failure.

Modern American society suffers from a broad range of problems that have self-regulation failure as a common core. Crime, teen pregnancy, alcoholism, drug addiction, venereal disease, educational underachievement, gambling, and domestic violence are among the social problems that revolve around the apparent inability of many individuals to discipline and control themselves. Although economic, political, and sociological causes may be relevant to such issues, the proximal importance of self-regulation failure to many cases is undeniable. Moreover, there are many additional problems with self-regulation that cause considerable suffering to individuals even if they do not menace society at large (e.g., eating binges, spending sprees, procrastination, and inappropriate goal setting).

Researchers in the psychology of the self have recently begun to recognize that one of the most elusive, important, and distinctively human traits is the capacity of human beings to alter their own responses and thus remove them from the direct effects of immediate, situational stimuli. An understanding of self-regulation failure would therefore have considerable value not only for its applications to widespread social and personal problems, but also to basic research and the construction of an adequate theoretical account of human selfhood.

Although conceptions of volition and self-control have long been of philosophical, religious, and legal interest, only recently have psychologists focused on the extent to which people influence, modify, or control their own behavior. Pioneers such as Mischel (1974) and Bandura (1977) proposed and demonstrated that human beings do seem to have the unique capacity to alter their own responses. Over the past two decades, theory and research have advanced the understanding of self-regulation considerably (Carver & Scheier, 1981; Kanfer & Karoly, 1972) and models of self-regulation have been applied in diverse areas (e.g., education, drug treatment, emotional control, and task performance). Despite the substantial progress in studying how self-regulation can function, however, relatively little effort has been devoted to direct examination of failures at self-regulation (cf. Kirschenbaum, 1987).

The purpose of this article is to offer a theoretical treatment of self-regulation failure. We have recently reviewed the multiple literatures dealing with the many specific spheres of self-regulation failure (Baumeister, Heatherton, & Tice, 1994), and in this article we articulate some of our main conclusions. Because the empirical literature on these topics is extensive, we cite evidence here only to illustrate key points. A comprehensive review of current research knowledge is beyond the scope of this article, and interested readers are referred to the book.

Self-regulation is a complex, multifaceted process, so it can break down in several different ways. Therefore, it is not possible to identify a single cause or causal sequence that will explain all instances of self-regulation failure. Instead, there are several main patterns, any one of which can produce self-regulation failure independently.

The most basic distinction is between *underregulation* and *misregulation* (e.g., Carver & Scheier, 1981). Underregulation entails a failure to exert self-control; often, the person does not bother or does not manage to control the self. In contrast, misregulation involves the exertion of control over oneself, but this control is done in a misguided or counterproductive fashion, so the desired result is not achieved. At present, there is more research available on underregulation than on misregulation, and it also appears that underregulation is the more common sort of problem. After a brief discussion of the nature of self-regulation, we examine underregulation first and then proceed to misregulation.

Three Ingredients of Self-Regulation

Feedback-loop models of self-regulation, such as the one elaborated by Carver and Scheier (1981, 1982; also Carver, 1979), indicate three main ingredients of self-regulation, and these suggest three main possible pathways for self-regulation failure. The first ingredient is *standards*, which are ideals, goals, or other conceptions of possible states. Without clear and consistent standards, self-regulation will be hampered. Therefore, either a lack of standards or a dilemma of conflicting, incompatible standards can prevent effective self-regulation. There is indeed evidence that such inner conflicts can impair action and undercut efforts at self-regulation (e.g., Emmons & King, 1988; Van Hook & Higgins, 1988). Moreover, inappropriate standards (i.e., those that are too high or too low) can also hamper and thwart self-regulation (Heatherton & Ambady, 1993).

The second ingredient is *monitoring*. The "test" phase of feedback-loop models involves comparing the actual state of the self to the standards, and to do that the person must monitor him- or herself. Keeping close track of one's actions and states is often vital to successful self-regulation, and so when people cease to monitor themselves they tend to lose control. Eating binges, for example, seem to occur when the person ceases to keep track of what he or she is eating (for a review, see Heatherton & Baumeister, 1991; Polivy, 1976). A particularly important factor is alcohol consumption, which reduces self-attention and therefore makes people less able or less willing to monitor themselves (Hull, 1981). Alcohol consumption has been found to promote self-regulatory failure in many different spheres (Baumeister et al., 1994; Steele & Southwick, 1985). The failure to judge one's abilities accurately may also impede successful self-regulation. For instance, people who underestimate their abilities may fail to initiate attempts to achieve their goals.

The third ingredient of self-regulation is contained in the *operate* phase of the feedback loop.

The idea is that when the test phase reveals that the current state falls short of the standards, some process is set in motion to change the current state. Past theories have not devoted a great deal of attention to how these processes actually function to bring about change, partly because they may have seemed complex and heterogeneous. Still, it is clear that self-regulation failure can occur despite clear standards and effective monitoring, simply because the person is unable to bring about the desired change.

We have found it useful to conceptualize such operate changes in terms of one internal process overriding another. Certain responses are set in motion, either by innate programming, learning, habit, or motivation—and self-regulation involves overriding them. In other words, a great many instances of self-regulation involve a response that is initiated by a combination of latent motivations and activating stimuli; self-regulation is a matter of interrupting that response and preventing it from running to its normal, typical outcome. For example, a beer commercial (an activating stimulus) may bring to the fore one's liking for alcohol (a latent motivation) and create an *impulse* to consume alcohol; however, the person who is trying to reduce his or her drinking will seek to override the response sequence and prevent it from leading to the consumption of such a beverage.[1]

In many cases, impulses are automatic in the sense of being beyond a person's volitional control. Thus, the term *impulse control* is misleading. Self-regulation is a controlled process that overrides the usual consequences of an impulse rather than preventing the impulse from occurring. The problem is not that people have impulses; rather, it is that they act on them.

Self-Regulatory Strength: A Limited Resource

We turn now to the issue of what enables a person to override a habitual or motivated response sequence. How does the pacifist turn the other cheek and how does the dieter refrain from eating his or her fill? It is clear that impulses and motivations vary according to strength, and the weaker ones are those that are easier to control and stifle. If the impulses have strength, then whatever stifles them must presumably consist of some greater strength.

Our own research (Baumeister et al., 1994) led us to concur with other scholars such as Mischel (in press) who have suggested that strength models are apt and useful for self-regulation theory. Underregulation is thus often a matter of the inadequacy of one's strength to override the unwanted thought, feeling, or impulse. More precisely, our overview of the self-regulation literature suggests that each person's capacity for self-regulation appears to be a limited resource, which is renewable over time and can be increased or decreased as a result of gradual developments or practice. One cannot regulate everything at once.

Adopting a strength model of self-regulation has several important corollaries for understanding self-regulation failure. There will be important individual differences in self-regulatory strength, which should be consistent across a variety of spheres. There is some evidence to support this view. Thus, individual differences in the capacity to delay gratification predict a variety of interpersonal traits and behaviors that reflect self-control (Funder, Block, & Block, 1983) and can even predict academic performance over a decade later (Mischel, Shoda, & Peake, 1988; Shoda, Mischel, & Peake, 1990). Also, the same individuals show self-regulatory deficits across a broad spectrum of both legal and illegal behavior. A typical criminal, for example, will not specialize in one particular kind of illegal activity, but rather will commit a variety of crimes, and he or she will also be prone to smoke cigarettes, spend impulsively (thereby dissipating any financial gains from crime), become involved in unwanted pregnancies, fail at marriage, abuse alcohol and drugs, have high absenteeism at work or school, and engage in other behaviors indicative of poor self-regulation (Gottfredson & Hirschi, 1990).

The second implication of a strength model is that a person can become exhausted from many simultaneous demands and so will sometimes fail at self-control even regarding things at which he or she would otherwise succeed. As a limited resource, self-regulatory strength can be temporarily depleted. At any given time, a given person will only be able to regulate so much of his or her behavior, so when strength is depleted by demands in one sphere, self-regulatory breakdowns may occur in others. In particular, fatigue or overexertion will deplete the person's strength and hence undermine some patterns of self-control.

The evidence regarding such short-term depletions is not extensive but it is broad and consistent. In particular, many patterns of self-regulation break down when people are under stress, presumably because the stress depletes their self-regulatory capacities. People become more emotional and irritable and they are more likely to increase smoking, break diets or overeat, abuse alcohol or other drugs, and so forth when under stress. Glass, Singer, and Friedman (1969) found that coping with stress seemed to have a "psychic cost" that took the form of lowered self-regulatory capacity, as measured by subsequent capacities to make oneself persist in the face of frustration and to concentrate on a difficult task.

Likewise, if we assume that people are generally fatigued late in the evening, then self-regulation should break down more at such times than at others. Evidence about the timing of such self-regulatory failures is consistent with the fatigue hypothesis (although some of these effects are confounded by the fact that people are more likely to have consumed alcohol late in the day and alcohol impairs monitoring, thereby also weakening self-regulation). Diets are most often broken late in the evening; sexual acts that one will later regret are likewise most common then; people smoke and drink most heavily late in the day; most violent and impulsive crimes are committed between 1:00 and 2:00 a.m.

These first two implications of the strength model furnish a basis for predicting the intercorrelations among indications of self-control in multiple spheres. If there are individual differences in self-regulatory strength, then over the long run there will be positive correlations because strong people will tend to have relatively high levels of self-control in all spheres. On the other hand, in the short run the correlations will be negative because devoting one's self-regulatory efforts to one sphere will take away what is available for controlling oneself in other spheres. Researchers interested in overlaps between self-regulatory effectiveness in different spheres may need to be alert to these opposing empirical tendencies.

The third implication is just as it is possible to increase strength by regular exercise, so self-regulation should become easier the more one does it. This has been asserted by James (1890/1950) and many other observers of human behavior, but we do not know of strong empirical tests of the hypothesis. In this connection, it is of considerable relevance that new programs for prisoners (e.g., "boot camps") involve military-style training, in which an attempt is made to instill self-discipline by means of enforcing external discipline. Although the effectiveness of these programs has yet to be decided, we predict that their success at rehabilitating prisoners will be in proportion to their success at strengthening self-regulatory capacities.

One implication of the notion of increasing strength is that people may become better at practicing self-denial or impulse control over time. Ironically, this could mean that people who repeatedly quit smoking or go on diets may gradually become more effective and successful. Schachter (1982) contended that people improve at quitting smoking with practice. Prochaska and DiClemente (1984, 1986) argued that people become better at quitting a variety of addictions when they do it multiple times. Of course, the fact that they are quitting again means that the prior effort to quit was not a permanent success, but it may be the case that one learns to quit through successive approximations. There could be several reasons for progressive improvement at impulse control, but one of them clearly is the possibility of increasing strength.

Inertia and Attention

A fair amount of evidence suggests that psychological responses are marked by something akin to inertia, which makes them difficult to interrupt. The term *inertia* is borrowed from physics, in which it referred to the (now discredited) theory that bodies in motion acquired a force that sustained them in motion.

We propose that psychological processes do acquire a kind of inertia (unlike physical processes). Indeed, the longer a response has gone on, the more inertia it seems to have and hence the more difficult it is to override. This theoretical principle is not new (indeed, the Zeigarnik effect involved the principle that interrupting an activity becomes more strenuous as it nears its completion), but its importance for understanding self-regulation has been neglected.

Effective self-regulation often seems to involve intervening as early as possible. For example, if the goal of self-regulation is the preservation of chastity, it is often more effective to interrupt sexual activities at the first kiss rather than after an hour's worth of escalating physical contact. The effectiveness of early intervention may well reflect the operation of inertia: To minimize inertia, self-regulatory efforts may be most profitably focused on the very first stages of all response sequences.

Most models of the cognitive control of behavior begin with attention because noticing something is by definition the first stage in information processing. As a result, one would expect that managing attention would be important in many or all spheres of self-regulation, and, as a corollary, the loss of attentional control will be a common first harbinger of self-regulatory failure. Our review of multiple, empirical literatures confirmed these hypotheses. Over and over, we found that managing attention was the most common and often the most effective form of self-regulation and that attentional problems presaged a great many varieties of self-regulation failure. With controlling thoughts, emotions and moods, task-performance processes, and appetites and impulses, the effective management of attention was a powerful and decisive step, and self-regulatory failure ensued when attention could not be managed (Baumeister et al., 1994; see also Kirschenbaum, 1987; Wegner, 1994).

For our purposes, the key point is that the importance of attention is at least partly attributable to the inertia principle. Effective management of attention can prevent the unwanted response sequence from starting, which makes it relatively easy to prevent the unacceptable outcome. In contrast, if attention escapes control it can set the unwanted responses in motion, and once they acquire inertia they are more difficult to control. In simple terms, it is easier to avoid temptation than to overcome it.

Transcendence

One particularly important form of attention control is *transcendence*. Transcendence is a matter of focusing awareness beyond the immediate stimuli (i.e., transcending the immediate situation). This does not necessarily mean ignoring the immediate present so much as seeing it in the context of more distal concerns (e.g., values, goals, and motivations). Phenomenologists have emphasized transcendence as a particularly important capability of human consciousness.

Dieting offers a clear example of transcendence. Human beings may be the only species on the planet in which hungry individuals will voluntarily refuse to consume readily available, appealing food. Effective dieting does, however, require the person to transcend the effects of the immediate stimuli. By contemplating long-range goals and concerns, such as how one will look in a bathing suit next summer, people are available to frame the attractive food as a problematic or dangerous obstacle rather than as an appealing morsel.

Therefore, one proximal cause of self-regulation failure is the failure of transcendence. When attention slips off of long-range goals and high ideals and instead becomes immersed in the immediate situation, self-regulation is in jeopardy. Whatever functions to direct attention to the here and now will tend to weaken the capacity for self-regulation. This may include both situational and dispositional factors. Situational factors include those that promote deindividuation. There are also individual differences in the extent to which people are influenced by environmental cues. Schachter's (1971) influential externality theory of obesity argued that some individuals (i.e., the overweight) were especially prone to be influenced by external cues about eating.

The capacity to delay gratification is one of the important roots of self-regulation theory. A successful delay of gratification requires the person to forego immediately available rewards in favor of larger but remoter ones, and keeping oneself from thinking about the immediate rewards is often a vital part of that success (Mischel, 1974; Rodriguez, Mischel, & Shoda, 1989). Karniol and Miller (1983) showed that self-regulatory failure (in this case, the failure to choose the delayed gratification) is often preceded by shifts in attention to the immediate reward. This shift in attention to the immediate situation is a form of transcendence failure.

Transcendence is often a vital aspect of emotion regulation. People overcome anger, frustration, or disappointment by looking beyond the immediate situation. They imagine how things could have been worse, conjure up possible positive outcomes that may derive from the current setback, or speculate about possibly beneficial motives that the other (offending) person may have had. Emotion is typically linked to a particular value judgment about a particular event or situation; by transcending the situation, one can escape from the emotion that is linked to that value judgment.

Indeed, it is plausible that the contribution of emotional distress to self-regulation failure is often mediated by effects on transcendence. The interrelations among emotion, attention, and self-regulation are not well understood so comments must be speculative, but we propose the following: Emotion increase the salience of whatever produces the emotion, so attention will tend to focus on whatever has prompted the emotion. Most commonly, something in the immediate situation is the cause, so emotion tends to have the effect of concentrating attention in the here and now—thereby thwarting transcendence and making self-regulation more difficult. Violent behavior provides an important illustration of such effects of emotion. Violence typically results because the person becomes angry at some pressing stimulus—a rival who insults one, a child who cries excessively, a spouse who frustrates one's wishes (e.g., Berkowitz, 1989). The anger keeps attention confined to the immediate, provoking situation, so efforts to restrain one's violent impulses are made more difficult. In their discussion of the role of self-control failure in causing crime, Gottfredson and Hirschi (1990) pointed out that long-range considerations would often militate against violence. Thus, most murders bring far more harm than benefit to the perpetrators themselves, and indeed many murderers can hardly recall even the next day what made them so violent. However, in the heat of the moment (i.e., the short-term attentional focus caused by high emotion), people fail to consider long-range implications and act in response to short-term concerns, which may include winning the dispute at all costs and by violent means.

A second mechanism by which emotional distress may thwart transcendence and impair self-regulation occurs when the source of emotional distress is not present in the immediate situation but is highly available in memory (e.g., just after one has received a major rejection or failure experience). Under such circumstances, people will seek to distract themselves to prevent themselves from thinking about the upsetting event; immersion in powerful, short-term stimuli may be an effective means. Unfortunately, some of the most compelling short-term stimuli are precisely the things that the person is otherwise trying to control (e.g., alcohol, sweet foods, or drugs). A great deal of binge behavior, whether it be shopping, gambling, eating, drinking, or having sex, seems to result when people are seeking to keep their attention focused on immediate, concrete stimuli as a means of keeping it away from some threatening or upsetting thoughts.

To be sure, emotion is not invariably bad for self-regulation. Some emotions, such as guilt, may even help self-control (e.g., Baumeister, 1995; Baumeister, Stillwell, & Heatherton, 1995). Still, these instances are consistent with the general arguments about transcendence because they refer to cases in which the emotion facilitates self-regulation by actually promoting transcendence. A dose of anticipatory guilt may help the person realize that what he or she is about to do may cause damage to important, desired relationships or have other unwanted consequences, so the person may interrupt the pursuit of some short-term goal or reward. By calling attention to distal outcomes and meaningful implications, guilt helps the individual transcend the immediate situation and its temptations, thereby aiding self-control.

Transcendence is even relevant to some aspects of task performance, which is an important sphere for self-regulation. In particular, persistence at difficult, boring, and unpleasant tasks is a challenge that is endemic to many forms of work, and such persistence often requires the person to transcend the immediate situation, which on its own merits would seemingly favor quitting. Sansone, Weir, Harpster, and Morgan (1992) showed that persistence on boring tasks is facilitated by mentally transforming them into more interesting processes. Indeed, studies of blue-collar manufacturing workers have shown that such workers tend to restructure their tedious, repetitive tasks into elaborate games; when they are successful, they become totally engrossed in these games to the extent that they continue to talk about them even during breaks and lunch hours (Burawoy, 1979). By extension, when people are unable to effect such transcendent reconceptions of these tasks, they are more likely to quit, which can be a severely problematic form of self-regulation failure.

We noted earlier that alcohol was implicated as one cause of a great many varieties of self-regulation failure. Although we suggested that alcohol's impairment of self-monitoring may be one mechanism by which alcohol has these effects, it is plausible that another one is through the impairment of transcendence. Steele and Josephs (1990) coined the term *alcohol myopia* to describe the way alcohol limits attention and restrains it to a few proximal stimuli. Their argument can readily be extended to say that alcohol impairs the sort of long-range, abstract, meaningful, or mentally flexible thinking involved in transcendence (and, in fact, alcohol does seem to increase the responsivity to immediate stimuli ranging from violent to sexual to appetitive).

Thus, self-control often involves seeing the immediate situation in terms of long-range concerns, values, and goals (see also Carver & Scheier, 1981; Rachlin, 1995; Vallacher & Wegner, 1985). The ability to maintain attention and focus on these long-term issues is one ingredient of self-regulatory strength. In general, factors that bind attention to the immediate situation and pressing stimuli will tend to contribute to self-regulation failure.

Acquiescence and Overriding

One of the most important yet controversial aspects of self-regulation failure is the question of the extent to which people acquiesce in it. The question can be appreciated by considering two contrary images of self-regulation failure. Both of them depict a person who feels an impulse to act in a way that runs contrary to his or her normal standards of proper, desirable behavior. Self-regulation failure means acting out that impulse and thus violating the person's standards. In one image, the well-intentioned person is overwhelmed by an irresistible impulse that no normal person could restrain. In the other, the person simply decides to give in to the impulse rather than go through the exertion and frustration that would accompany self-restraint. Thus, is self-regulation failure a matter of lazy self-indulgence (i.e., heedlessly giving in to temptation) or is it a matter of being overcome by powerful, unstoppable forces?

This question has important implications. One set concerns basic theoretical questions of conscious control and intrapsychic conflict. Another concerns legal issues: Are violent crimes the product of irresistible impulses or deliberate choices? Political issues such as whether addicts, alcoholics, spouse abusers, and others should be treated as needy victims or as criminal degenerates also revolve around this question. Given the sweep of these implications, it is not surprising that there are ample arguments on both sides in both the professional journals and in the popular and mass media. We think that an additional reason for the existence of both sides of the argument is that there is in fact a large gray area. In our view, self-regulation failure is rarely a matter of deliberate, premeditated choice, but then again it is not often a matter of irresistible impulses either.

During the period we spent reading about and studying self-regulation, we grew increasingly skeptical of the irresistible impulse notion. By definition, such impulses cannot be resisted, so they refer to things people would do even if someone were holding a gun to their heads and threatening to kill them if they did the forbidden acts. Despite the popularity of the notion of irresistible impulses in courtroom settings, it is readily apparent that people could and would refrain from most behaviors if their lives depended on it. The vast majority of impulses are resistible.

Thus, the popular image of the passive victim overcome by powerful, irresistible impulses cannot be accepted except in a few rare and extreme cases (e.g., the fact that people cannot indefinitely postpone certain biological functions such as falling asleep, urinating, or breathing—all things that people will eventually do even despite a gun to the head). In reviewing the empirical literature on self-regulation failure, we found over and over that there was significant evidence of deliberate, volitional participation by the individual in the forbidden activity. These findings and patterns do not rule out the possibility that there are points at which people feel helpless and passive and are overcome by strong impulses. They do, however, suggest that the full episode of self-regulation failure usually involves at least some elements of active acquiescence.

Let us consider some examples in which there is evidence of acquiescence in self-regulation failure (Baumeister et al., 1994). Cigarette smoking is a good example because in the contemporary United States it is typically inconvenient, if not outright difficult, to smoke. The would-be smoker must obtain cigarettes and then find a time and place where smoking is still allowed. The person must then go through the motions of lighting up and inhaling. Smoking is well recognized as a powerful addiction and as a source of strong cravings and unpleasant withdrawal symptoms, all of which may be beyond the smoker's control; however, smoking is not a matter of simply going limp, becoming passive, and letting it happen.

Consuming alcohol (or taking other drugs) is subject to a similar analysis. Despite the undeniable addictiveness of alcohol, and despite popular images that many people cannot control their drinking, it is clear that most people who drink alcohol are actively acquiescing in the process. Ordering or pouring a drink and raising a glass to one's lips are deliberate, volitional acts. Binge eaters likewise often describe their eating as out of control, yet in many cases the person must acquiesce to the extent of ordering or preparing food, putting it into his or her mouth, and chewing and swallowing it.

Procrastination is another common self-regulation problem, and procrastinators may often feel like passive, helpless victims, especially during the eventual crisis when the deadline looms and the remaining time is inadequate for the task. Procrastination, however, often involves actively doing other things instead of the deferred activity. Back when there was ample time to begin work on the task, the person was hardly overcome by an irresistible impulse to go out for a beer or watch television instead. Rather, the person actively participated in these other activities.

If procrastination involves a failure to get started, performance is also affected by whether people persist or quit, so the matter of deciding when to quit can be an important aspect of the self-regulation of performance. Although there are occasionally cases in which sheer exhaustion forces the person to stop (e.g., when marathon runners collapse and are carried away on stretchers), usually the decision to quit is much more fluid and negotiable and the person could have gone on a little longer. Quitting during task performance usually occurs well before the point of full exhaustion. The person somehow selects a point at which to quit and then goes and does something else.

Delay of gratification is one of the prototypes of impulse control; yet, in many studies of delay of gratification, the participant must make some active response to obtain the immediate reward. Making that response is often a matter of deliberate action. Outside the laboratory, failures to delay gratification may often involve even more extensive and obvious forms of active acquiescence (e.g., when the person drops out of college or empties a savings account).

There are of course instances in which the person's acquiescence is even more extreme. People do sometimes seem to arrange to lose control. Marlatt (1985) described the case of a compulsive gambler who was planning a trip from San Francisco to Seattle and at the last minute (and following an argument with his wife) changed the planned route to pass through Reno, Nevada, which he claimed would be more scenic. (Seattle is north of San Francisco; Reno is east of it.) In Reno, he needed change for a parking meter and so entered the nearest building, which just happened to be a casino. While in the casino, he decided to place a single bet to test his luck. The ensuing 3-day gambling binge was perhaps not deliberately planned in advance, but the decisions that brought him there seem disingenuous. In similar fashion, people do pick fights in which they lose control, manufacture reasons for consuming alcohol, place themselves in tempting situations, and engage in other patterns that seem as if they were conspiring to thwart their own self-regulatory programs.

Apart from such extreme cases, it would usually be inappropriate to say that the person planned and engineered the entire scenario in advance; in fact, the person may often be quite chagrined by the eventual outcome. To simply say that the self-regulation failures reflect deliberate free choice would therefore be somewhat misleading. On the other hand, the stereotype of the helpless, passive victim overwhelmed against his or her will by uncontrollable impulses is not accurate either. The person did participate, more or less freely and deliberately, in the actions that constituted the self-regulation failure.

In order to resolve the issue of acquiescence, it is first necessary to appreciate that there are often costs and disadvantages to self-control. Foregoing an immediate, desired pleasure is only one of them. Frustration, withdrawal, and feelings of deprivation may be acute. Moreover, if our hypothesis of self-regulatory strength is correct, then maintaining self-control and resisting temptation can be a tiring and draining experience that can even consume resources that may be needed for other acts of self-control.

Resisting temptation is thus, in many cases, an

ongoing (or perennial) and unpleasant exertion. Its difficulty is likely to fluctuate as a function of the strength and salience of the competing impulse and of the self-regulatory capacity. An irresistible impulse is hardly necessary for self-regulation failure; rather, a moment during which the impulse is especially strong or attractive, while the self-regulatory strength is temporarily depleted, may be sufficient. At some point, perhaps, the costs of exerting control may simply seem too high, whereas the anticipated benefits may seem too remote or uncertain or simply too small and so the person gives in.

We are thus portraying the abrogation of self-control as a deliberate choice, but it is one that is made in a very narrow sphere and is strongly influenced by internal and external factors, to which we shall return in a moment. Apparently, however, people often regard the decision as a single event that is not to be reconsidered, at least not until much later. Once the person decides to start eating, drinking, smoking, having sex, venting emotion, spending money, or assaulting someone, the person will often go ahead and participate actively in the process.

There is thus an important asymmetry in the way many people confront internal conflicts surrounding self-regulation. Maintaining self-control is treated as an ongoing process of negotiation and the fact that one resisted temptation a few minutes ago does not necessarily free one from facing a similar decision again. However, abandoning self-control is treated as if it were a single decision that is not subject to further reconsideration.

Why do people fail to reconsider a decision to go ahead and indulge themselves, abandoning restraint? Several reasons can be suggested. The period of indecision is likely to have been one of anxiety and uncertainty and, in contrast, the decision to go ahead is likely to be marked by relief (and often pleasure). To return voluntarily from a state of relief and pleasure to one of anxiety and uncertainty would certainly be an unappealing transition. Moreover, the unpleasantness of the state of denial and inner debate would be enhanced by guilt or other forms of anxiety resulting from the initial indulgence.

As an example, one may consider a hypothetical case of a dieter tempted to enjoy an appealing dessert. The phase of confronting and resisting temptation is probably an unpleasant one, marked by the internal effort of self-denial and salient thoughts of the foregone pleasure, as well as an ongoing inner debate. Finally the person decides to go ahead and have the dessert after all, possibly under the influence of some available excuse (e.g., so as not to offend the hostess). This decision most likely brings pleasure and relief, and as the person enjoys the first few bites, the idea of reconsidering—of returning to self-denial or even of just renewing the inner debate about whether one ought to be eating this—would be most unappealing. To resume self-denial while halfway through the dessert would be unpleasant in several respects: It would mean abandoning a very salient pleasure in order to return to the state of deprivation, it would require a strenuous act of self-regulation, and even if one succeeded in putting down the spoon one would already have earned some remorse (e.g., guilt or shame) because of the portion one had already eaten.

Self-regulation failure can thus occur whenever the person experiences even a very brief period in which the costs seem to outweigh the benefits. The popular image in which a moment of weakness can undermine months or years of virtuous self-denial is somewhat accurate because people tend to treat the decision to abandon control and indulge themselves as irrevocable.

The evidence that people acquiesce in self-regulation failure, as well as the analysis of self-control as an ongoing inner debate that is shaped by perceived costs and benefits, has one more important implication: Cultural and situational factors can exert considerable subtle influence on self-regulation. To put it another way, the point at which people lose (or abandon) self-control is one that can be moved around within a wide gray area, and thus many factors can influence self-control by moving that point.

The self-regulation of violent, aggressive behavior is a good example. Many violent acts are experienced and described by perpetrators as episodes of losing control. Consistent with this, it is clear that most people are usually able to prevent anger from resulting in physical violence. The very high contribution of alcohol to intensifying violent responses to provocations is partly due to the fact that it undermines people's capacity to regulate their behavior, so they act out violent impulses more frequently and extremely (Bushman & Cooper, 1990; Steele & Southwick, 1985).

Despite the appearance that violent behavior involves loss of control, there is evidence of acquiescence: People could control their behavior if they wanted to do so. Most people do stop short of lethal violence even when they are extremely angry (Tavris, 1989). Among the Malays, the pattern of *running amok* institutionalized a general belief that provocations produced anger that led to uncontrollable aggression, but when the British took over and instituted severe penalties for running amok, the practice diminished substantially, indicating that the young men could control it after all (Carr & Tan, 1976). Berkowitz's (1978) study of men in prison for violent assault in Great Britain contained the same mixed message. These men did apparently lose control (often under the influence of alcohol) and beat someone else up to their own disadvantage (hence their imprisonment), but they had managed to restrain themselves from going even farther. In one memorable anecdote, one of Berkowitz's participants described a violent attack on his wife's lover during which he was totally enraged and seemingly out of control. At one point in the attack, he took hold of a bottle by the neck and broke it off to use as a weapon—but then he reconsidered that if he used that weapon he would most likely have killed the other man, which would have had serious consequences for him. As a result, he put down the broken bottle and resumed the attack with his fists, beating the other man senseless but not killing him.

There is thus an undercurrent of control in the loss of control of violent behavior. At some point, people allow themselves to lose control. The determination of that point is subject to a great many subtle influences.

Theories about aggression once explored the notion of a "subculture of violence." According to that theory, certain subcultures placed a positive value on aggressive behavior, so people sought to gain esteem and prestige by acting aggressively. This view was largely discredited by accumulating evidence that violent people did not apparently seek to win approval or esteem by violent acts (e.g., Berkowitz, 1978) and that members of the supposedly violent subcultures did not report that they placed positive values on violent acts (see Tedeschi & Felson, 1994).

We think, however, that the notion of a subculture of violence may deserve to be reconsidered in another form: Subcultures (or indeed cultures) can influence the point at which people believe it is appropriate to lose control over aggressive impulses. Such collective beliefs can exert considerable influence over the point at which people believe it is appropriate, reasonable, or even desirable to abandon self-control. Thus, many assaults and homicides occur in direct response to verbal insults, but most insults do not lead to physical violence. It takes cultural norms to prescribe which insults, in which settings, will cause the person to retaliate with physical aggression. Studies and interviews with teen gang members, for example, often report that the young men and women say that violent retaliation is appropriate and even necessary in response to certain insults (e.g., Anderson, 1994; Bing, 1991; Currie, 1991; Jankowski, 1991). Likewise, the American South has higher homicide rates than other parts of the country, but only for homicides related to arguments, which suggests that Southern culture supports the view that certain provocations require one to lose control of violent, retaliatory impulses (Nisbett, 1993).

Indeed, moving the point at which one loses control may be a major way that a culture can influence self-regulation. From our perspective, various forces in modern American culture have exerted a broad influence to shift this point in ways that make people more likely to abandon self-control. The pervasiveness of self-regulation problems in modern America may be less a result of character flaws or deficiencies than a result of a social climate that encourages people to regard many situations as ones in which an average, reasonable person would supposedly lose control. The notion of irresistible impulses may be weak and dubious as a scientific hypothesis but as a social doctrine (and as a legal defense strategy) it may be powerful and influential. Once it becomes widely accepted, it is likely to operate as a self-fulfilling prophecy.

Misregulation

We turn now to examine a very different type of self-regulation failure, namely, misregulation. Although underregulation may provide the most familiar and vivid instances of self-regulatory failure, not all instances fit in that category. In underregulation, people end up being unable or unwilling to exert the requisite control over themselves. In misregulation, however, the cause of failure lies in the use to which the efforts are directed. The person may even be quite successful at exerting control over him- or herself, but the end result is failure because the efforts are misguided or are wasted in other ways.

Our review of the empirical literature yielded three main causes of misregulation: (a) misunderstood contingencies, (b) quixotic efforts to control the uncontrollable, and (c) giving too much priority to affect regulation. Let us examine each of these in turn.

The first cause involves false beliefs about the self and the world (particularly about the contingencies between them). Well-intentioned and well-executed efforts at self-regulation may end in futility because they were based on false assumptions about what would yield desirable results. Thus, under the influence of inflated egotism and emotional distress, people may set unrealistically high goals that will increase the likelihood or costliness of failure (Baumeister, Heatherton, & Tice, 1993; Ward & Eisler, 1987; Wright & Mischel, 1982). As Heatherton and Ambady (1993) argued, people who are prone to overly optimistic self-views may be especially vulnerable to this form of self-regulation failure.

Unwarranted optimism may also cause excessive persistence in futile endeavors and although the chances of success were minimal all along, the persistence increases the costs (e.g., time, effort, and money) that accompany the failure (Rubin & Brockner, 1975; Staw, 1976). Increased frustration and other emotional costs may result from such failures due to excessive persistence; indeed, in unrequited love, people often persist past the point of rational or optimal hope and the results of such persistence include considerable distress and inconvenience for both the aspiring lover and the target (Baumeister, Wotman, & Stillwell, 1993). One study showed that futile persistence is often mediated by false expectations; when people were educated about common patterns of excessive, fruitless persistence, they were less likely to make the same mistake themselves (Nathanson et al., 1982). Another showed that if people are encouraged to make careful calculations about the probabilities, contingencies, and likely payoffs, they are less likely to fall into the trap of excessive persistence (Conlon & Wolf, 1980), which also indicates that false assumptions and misguided expectations play a crucial role in this form of misregulation.

False assumptions contribute to another pattern of misregulation in the task-performance realm involving speed-accuracy tradeoffs. On many tasks, speed is increased at the expense of accuracy and vice versa, but the relation is far from linear and there are many cases in which reducing speed will fail to yield greater accuracy. Moreover, people may assume falsely that they can increase speed without substantial losses of accuracy. Heckhausen and Strang (1988) showed that athletes attempting to achieve a record performance on an experimental task tended to increase speed dramatically but the loss of accuracy outweighed the gains brought by the increased speed. The role of false assumptions was evident: The athletes in that study believed that they could maintain high accuracy at higher speeds.

Misregulation can also result from false assumptions about emotions. Many people believe that it is helpful to vent their anger or other forms of emotional distress, but they find that such acts often make them more rather than less upset (e.g., Tavris, 1989). Affect misregulation is marked by many patterns of misregulation in which people incorrectly assume that what works once or with one emotion will work with others too. Thus, consuming alcohol often makes people feel good and so they may drink as a way of self-medicating for their own depression; however, they often find that intoxication makes the depression worse rather than better (Doweiko, 1990). Likewise, because socializing with friends is often effective at curing a sad or depressed mood, people may try it to cure angry moods, but in many cases they end up reciting their grievances or problems to these friends and rekindling their own anger (Tice & Baumeister, 1993).

The second general pattern of misregulation involves the quixotic effort to control things that are beyond the scope of potential control. There are many automatic or innately prepared processes that people simply cannot alter and their efforts to control them directly are likely to backfire. One rather clear example is that most emotional and mood states cannot be altered directly by sheer act of will (hence the pervasiveness of indirect strategies for affect regulation). If people try to alter their moods directly, they are likely to be unsuccessful, and indeed the failure of their efforts may make them feel worse.

Thought suppression is a good example of such quixotic misregulation. People often seem to believe that they can directly control their thoughts, so they believe that unwanted thoughts can be driven out of their minds. Research has shown that such efforts at thought suppression are at best only partly successful and they create strong vulnerabilities to resurgences of the unwanted thought (Wegner, Schneider, Carter, & White, 1987); indeed, efforts to suppress undesired thoughts may ironically create a "synthetic obsession" with those thoughts (Wegner, 1992, 1994).

Performance can be impaired by this form of misregulation too, and indeed one of the most familiar and frustrating kinds of performance failure—choking under pressure—is a classic case of it. Choking, which is defined as performing below the level of one's ability despite situational incentives and subjective wishes and efforts to do one's best, arises because the person consciously overrides well-learned patterns of skilled response in the hope of maximizing performance—but then finds that the deliberate, controlled processes cannot perform as efficiently and effectively as the overlearned, automatic ones (Baumeister, 1984). In a typical case, the person has achieved a level of overlearning (i.e., skill) so that performance can flow with a minimum of conscious direction. However, on a particularly important occasion, the pressure and desire to do well cause the person to want to pay special attention and therefore to oversee the performance process consciously. This conscious oversight overrides the automatic quality of skilled performance; sadly, controlled processes cannot match the automatic skills for either speed or accuracy. For example, the typist or pianist who under pressure seeks to consciously monitor every finger movement quickly discovers that both speed and accuracy suffer.

Choking is thus a paradigmatic instance of this second form of misregulation. The person successfully overrides the normal, habitual, overlearned or automatic response, but the person cannot make him- or herself perform effectively without using those skills. The result is that the person ends up performing worse than usual as a direct result of efforts to perform better than usual.

The third broad pattern of misregulation involves aiming one's self-regulatory efforts at a tangential, peripheral, or irrelevant part of the problem. Many problems that confront people have multiple aspects, and self-regulatory efforts can be focused on any part of them. If the person selects the wrong aspect of his or her behavior to regulate, the problem will not be solved and may even get worse.

The most common pattern of misregulation involves emphasizing (short-term) affect regulation at the expense of some other, more lasting and substantive aspect. Often a particular problem consists of both practical obstacles or difficulties and subjective, emotional distress, and when people respond by focusing their efforts on emotional regulation they neglect the more fundamental, practical aspects, thereby leaving the problem unsolved or even compounding it. By giving priority to affect regulation, they allow the cause of the problem to get worse, so in the long run they end up worse off. Often they end up feeling worse even though affect regulation was their top priority.

This form of misregulation can be seen in some patterns of procrastination. A person may have a project deadline but working on the project causes anxiety, possibly because the project is important and because the person wants to do very well. Putting off working on the project thus becomes an effective means of affect regulation in the short run because one escapes from anxiety each time one elects not to work on the task; the cumulative effect of such decisions makes the problem considerably worse because the time until the deadline grows shorter, making it ever harder to do a good job. As the deadline looms, the panic response becomes ever better justified.

Giving top priority to affect regulation may also be a factor behind many destructive patterns of failed impulse control. Many consummatory responses are affectively pleasant, so people will indulge in them as a way of regulating their emotions. People may smoke cigarettes, abuse alcohol, take drugs, go on shopping sprees, engage in promiscuous sex, or gamble away their money as a way of escaping from a bad mood, but the consequences of such actions can be even worse than what caused the bad mood in the first place. Thus, eating or drinking binges may occur because the person thinks that eating or drinking will remedy the emotional distress. Shilts (1987) cited some survey evidence that when the AIDS epidemic was first spreading, many gay men became distraught and upset over the danger and responded by going out to engage in promiscuous, unprotected male–male sex to get their minds off those stressful thoughts. Although that response may have been effective as self-distraction, it tended to increase the underlying problem.

Thus, the category of misregulation encompasses several forms of the misuse or ineffective use of self-control. People may fail at self-regulation because they are trying to control the wrong aspect of the process or because they are trying to control something that is essentially immune to control. False beliefs and assumptions about the contingencies between one's own acts and one's outcomes often play an important role.

Lapse-Activated Responses

Although considerable research has focused on what causes people to violate their standards or other self-regulatory patterns, it is important to realize that the majority of such violations are inherently trivial. A single cookie may violate a weight-loss plan, but the impact of that cookie on the diet is probably minimal. The socially important instances of self-regulation failure tend to involve large-scale breakdowns such as binges. To be sure, a binge may begin with a single lapse, but to understand the lapse is not sufficient to explain the binge.

Our review concluded that in many cases a second and important set of causes of self-regulation failure only enters the picture after an initial lapse, and indeed as a result of that lapse. We use the term *lapse-activated causes* to describe these factors. This concept was anticipated in addiction research by Marlatt (1985), whose term *abstinence violation effect* referred to the tendency for people to respond to an initial indulgence in alcohol or other addictive but forbidden substance by consuming more. The category of lapse-activated responses includes abstinence violation effects as well as other, conceptually similar patterns that are not concerned with abstinence.

An early clear demonstration of lapse-activated misregulation was by Herman and Mack (1985), who termed their effects *counterregulatory eating*. In their study, dieters who had been preloaded with food actually went on to eat more than dieters who had not had such a preload, contrary to what nondieters do (and what common sense would prescribe). Subsequent research has demonstrated that a person's beliefs are the primary determinants of this disinhibited eating. For instance, dieters will engage in counterregulatory eating when they have eaten very small amounts of perceived high-calorie foods (e.g., a small bite of chocolate) but will be able to maintain their diets if they believe they have not broken their diets (even if they have consumed an incredibly fatty Caesar salad). The dieter's initial minor transgression leads to such thoughts as, "What the hell, I have blown it, so I may as well eat the whole darn thing." The irony is that the small amount of fattening food in the initial lapse does not constitute a serious threat to the dieter's goal of weight loss—but the subsequent binge eating does sabotage that goal.

Marlatt (1985) documented this lapse-activated pattern across a number of addictive and problematic behaviors, including smoking, alcoholism, and heroin addiction. Marlatt's model suggests that lapses often arise in high-risk situations in which a person has difficulty coping. Marlatt argued that a lapse becomes a relapse largely because of the person's commitment to complete and absolute abstinence. Performing the forbidden behavior leads to unpleasant dissonance and self-attributions of weakness and failure. The attribution of failure to the self diminishes the person's sense of self-control and he or she abandons attempts to rein in subsequent behavior. Thus, a minor transgression is seen as a catastrophe rather than a small slip, and this perception induces the person to abdicate all self-control. Marlatt's research has led to a therapy known as *relapse prevention*, which consists primarily of cognitive restructuring to help the addict cope with high-risk situations and with lapses.

For our purposes, the key point is that several causal factors come into play as a result of an initial lapse in self-control and these can undermine self-control subsequently. Moreover, it is often the subsequent breakdown in self-control that has the most severe and disastrous results. There are several mechanisms of lapse-activated patterns, as follows.

One important mechanism is that people may cease monitoring themselves after an initial lapse, possibly because it would be distressing to attend to their behavior when they have already failed to live up to standards, and possibly because the initial lapse may provide such pleasure or intense sensation that they focus narrowly on it (i.e., loss of transcendence). Polivy (1976) showed that dieters who had been preloaded with food apparently ceased to keep track of how much they ate, as indicated by errors in retrospective self-reports of subsequent consumption. More generally, eating binges seem to be marked by an immersion in sensation and a cessation of monitoring one's own behavior (Heatherton & Baumeister, 1991).

Spiraling patterns of distress may also be a form of lapse-activated causes of misregulation. An initial lapse may occur because the person was suffering from some form of distress. The lapse may, however, generate guilt, fear, anxiety, or other forms of distress, thereby making the person feel worse. The escalating distress may contribute to a further abandonment of self-control.

Distress is of course not the only emotion that can be activated by a lapse and contribute to further breakdowns in self-regulation. Lawson (1988) noted that many people will initially engage in extramarital sex on the assumption that it will be a casual, isolated episode that will not affect or threaten their marriage. Some find, however, that they begin to experience love or other forms of intimate attachment to their illicit partner, and these feelings may cause the extramarital involvement to escalate, even to the point at which it does become a threat to the marriage.

As we noted, some lapse-activated patterns have little to do with abstinence violations. Performance effects may provide one instance. Under pressure to perform well, people may experience some impairment of skilled performance (i.e., they may choke). The result of this impairment may be to increase the pressure on them to perform well so as to overcome the problems caused by the initial choking. As the pressure increases, they may choke even more. Schlenker, Phillips, Boniecki, and Schlenker (1995) showed that home teams in championship final baseball games tend to make errors when they fall behind, presumably in part because they are trying to overcome their initial deficit. Although more systematic data are needed, the recent Super Bowl games have provided vivid illustrations of such spiraling failures, as the Buffalo teams have made more and more mistakes once they began to fall behind. Likewise, test anxiety seems to conform to the pattern in which the person becomes preoccupied by ruminating over an initial failure (to know an answer) and because of this preoccupation becomes unable to concentrate on subsequent questions (see Wine, 1971).

Destructive patterns of persistence also have elements of lapse-activated causality. In many cases, people must invest time and energy as well as other resources (e.g., money or prestige) in some decision. If it goes bad, people are reluctant to cut their losses, and indeed the more they invest the more difficult it becomes for them to accept that course of action is futile, so the eventual losses continue to mount (e.g., Bazerman, Giuliano, & Appelman, 1984; Staw, 1976). In Teger's (1980) phrase, people become "too much invested to quit," so they invest—and lose—considerably more.

There are of course also interpersonal aspects to many self-control situations, and these can be activated by lapses so as to contribute to escalating failures of self-regulation. The most obvious example would probably involve violent episodes. An initial aggressive outburst may be a momentary lapse in self-control, but it may have lasting effects if someone else is harmed or provoked. An aggressive response by others (or even the formation by others of an expectation that the individual is prone to violent outbursts) may lead to further violence.

Ironically, some factors that aid self-regulation up to the point of an initial lapse may turn into factors that produce misregulation as the result of such a lapse. Most prominent among these are zero-tolerance beliefs. Such beliefs, which are common in some spheres, catastrophize the initial lapse as a way of preventing it. People are encouraged to believe that having a single drink, committing a single sexual indiscretion, or taking a single dose of a drug on one occasion will lead to disaster (see also Marlatt, 1985). Undoubtedly such beliefs discourage people from allowing a lapse to happen. If a lapse does occur, however, such beliefs may help produce lapse-activated increases in the unwanted behavior. The person may feel that a catastrophe has occurred and that there is no use in making further efforts at self-control. Alternatively, the person may find that the predicted catastrophic consequences have not materialized and conclude that the fears and warnings were entirely unfounded. Zero-tolerance beliefs can be compared to a military strategy of putting all troops in the front line, which will indeed strengthen the front line but will leave the army with no reserves to use if the front line is breached.

Conclusion

Self-regulation is a complex mechanism that can break down in many different ways. Underregulation occurs because people lack stable, clear, consistent standards, because they fail to monitor their actions, or because they lack the strength to override the responses they wish to control. Misregulation occurs because they operate on the basis of false assumptions about themselves and about the world, because they try to control things that cannot be directly controlled, or because they give priority to emotions while neglecting more important and fundamental problems.

We have proposed that the evidence about self-regulatory failures conforms to a strength model; that is, the capacity to regulate oneself is a limited, renewable resource. When stress or fatigue depletes an individual's strength, self-regulatory failures become more likely. Capacities for self-control are an important realm of stable, long-term individual differences.

The control of attention is central to self-regulation and loss of attentional control is a decisive precursor of many forms of self-regulation failure. In particular, effective self-regulation often requires the individual to be able to transcend the immediate situation by considering long-term consequences and implications. When transcendence is weakened by anything that binds attention to the here and now, the chances of self-regulation failure are increased.

Many spheres of self-regulation failure show signs of lapse-activated causes. That is, an initial and seemingly minor breakdown in self-control may set off other causes and factors that prevent the reassertion of self-control and cause the breakdown to snowball. Indeed, the initial lapse may often be trivial, whereas the binge is catastrophic, so these lapse-activated factors that produce a snowballing effect are what deserve emphasis in theory, research, and intervention.

The degree of volition and acquiescence in self-regulatory failure is a controversial issue with implications that go far beyond psychology. Our review has led us to reject the model that self-regulatory failure is typically the result of irresistible impulses. Although it would be excessive to say that people freely choose to lose control, they do seem to show considerable active participation and acquiescence in the behaviors that constitute self-regulatory failure. We suggested that self-regulation often involves an unpleasant inner conflict marked by competing wishes and uncertainty. If the person decides even briefly to relax self-control, typically he or she will not consider reinstating it, so a brief abdication of self-regulatory effort can lead to a serious, protracted breakdown. In colloquial terms, the popular image of a moment of weakness is more accurate than the image of the irresistible impulse. Moreover, culture can exert considerable influence by teaching people which circumstances make it appropriate to abandon control.

Unfortunately, the norms and forces that currently dominate modern Western culture seem generally conducive to weakening self-control. As long as this is the case, it seems likely that our society will continue to suffer from widespread and even epidemic problems that have self-regulatory failure as a common core.

NOTES

1. We use the term *impulse* to refer to an inclination to perform a particular action on a particular occasion. Thus, impulses are highly specific, in contrast to motivations, which may be general or abstract. Impulses arise when motivations encounter specific, activating stimuli in a particular situation. For example, hunger is a motivation, whereas the wish to devour one of those fragrant, sizzling cheeseburgers on the grill is an impulse.

REFERENCES

Anderson, E. (1994). The code of the streets. *Atlantic Monthly, 273*(5), 81–94.

Bandura, A. (1977). Self-efficacy: Toward a unifying theory of behavioral change. *Psychological Review, 84*, 191–215.

Baumeister, R. F. (1984). Choking under pressure: Self-consciousness and paradoxical effects of incentives on skillful performance. *Journal of Personality and Social Psychology, 46*, 610–620.

Baumeister, R. F. (1995). Transcendence, guilt, and self-control. *Behavioral and Brain Sciences, 18*, 122–123.

Baumeister, R. F., Heatherton, T. F., & Tice, D. M. (1993). When ego threats lead to self-regulation failure: Negative consequences of high self-esteem. *Journal of Personality and Social Psychology, 64*, 141–156.

Baumeister, R. F., Heatherton, T. F., & Tice, D. M. (1994). *Losing control: How and why people fail at self-regulation.* San Diego: Academic.

Baumeister, R. F., Stillwell, A. M., & Heatherton, T. F. (1995). Personal narratives about guilt: Role in action control and interpersonal relationships. *Basic and Applied Social Psychology, 17,* 173–198.

Baumeister, R. F., Wotman, S. R., & Stillwell, A. M. (1993). Unrequited love: On heartbreak, anger, guilt, scriptlessness, and humiliation. *Journal of Personality and Social Psychology, 64,* 377–394.

Bazerman, M. H., Giuliano, T., & Appelman, A. (1984). Escalation of commitment in individual and group decision making. *Organizational Behavior and Human Performance, 33,* 141–152.

Berkowitz, L. (1978). Is criminal violence normative behavior? Hostile and instrumental aggression in violent incidents. *Journal of Research in Crime and Delinquency, 15,* 148–161.

Berkowitz, L. (1989). Frustration-aggression hypothesis: Examination and reformulation. *American Psychologist, 106,* 59–73.

Bing, L. (1991). *Do or die.* New York: HarperCollins.

Burawoy, M. (1979). *Manufacturing consent.* Chicago: University of Chicago Press.

Bushman, B. J., & Cooper, H. M. (1990). Effects of alcohol on human aggression: An integrative research review. *Psychological Bulletin, 107,* 341–354.

Carr, J. E., & Tan, E. K. (1976). In search of the true Amok: Amok as viewed within the Malay culture. *American Journal of Psychiatry, 133,* 1295–1299.

Carver, C. S. (1979). A cybernetic model of self-attention processes. *Journal of Personality and Social Psychology, 37,* 1251–1281.

Carver, C. S., & Scheier, M. F. (1981). *Attention and self-regulation: A control theory approach to human behavior.* New York: Springer-Verlag.

Carver, C. S., & Scheier, M. F. (1982). Control theory: A useful conceptual framework for personality-social, clinical and health psychology. *Psychological Bulletin, 92,* 111–135.

Conlon, E. J., & Wolf, G. (1980). The moderating effects of strategy, visibility, and involvement on allocation behavior: An extension of Staw's escalation paradigm. *Organizational Behavior and Human Performance, 26,* 172–192.

Currie, E. (1991). *Dope and trouble: Portraits of delinquent youth.* New York: Pantheon.

Doweiko, H. E. (1990). *Concepts of chemical dependency.* Pacific Grove, CA: Brooks/Cole.

Emmons, R. A., & King, L. A. (1988). Conflict among personal strivings: Immediate and long-term implications for psychological and physical well-being. *Journal of Personality and Social Psychology, 54,* 1040–1048.

Funder, D. C., Block, J. H., & Block, J. (1983). Delay of gratification: Some longitudinal personality correlates. *Journal of Personality and Social Psychology, 44,* 1198–1213.

Glass, D. C., Singer, J. E., & Friedman, L. N. (1969). Psychic cost of adaptation to an environmental stressor. *Journal of Personality and Social Psychology, 12,* 200–210.

Gottfredson, M. R., & Hirschi, T. (1990). *A general theory of crime.* Stanford, CA: Stanford University Press.

Heatherton, T. F., & Ambady, N. (1993). Self-esteem, self-prediction, and living up to commitments. In R. Baumeister (Ed.), *Self-esteem: The puzzle of low self-regard* (pp. 131–145). New York: Plenum.

Heatherton, T. F., & Baumeister, R. F. (1991). Binge eating as escape from self-awareness. *Psychological Bulletin, 110,* 86–108.

Heckhausen, H., & Strang, H. (1988). Efficiency under record performance demands: Exertion control—An individual difference variable? *Journal of Personality and Social Psychology, 55,* 489–498.

Herman, C. P., & Mack, D. (1975). Restrained and unrestrained eating. *Journal of Personality, 43,* 647–660.

Hull, J. G. (1981). A self-awareness model of the causes and effects of alcohol consumption. *Journal of Abnormal Psychology, 90,* 586–600.

James, W. (1950). *The principles of psychology* (Vol 2). New York: Dover. (Original work published 1890)

Jankowski, M. S. (1991). *Islands in the street: Gangs and American urban society.* Berkeley: University of California Press.

Kanfer, F. H., & Karoly, P. (1972). Self-control: A behavioristic excursion into the lion's den. *Behavior Therapy, 3,* 398–416.

Karniol, R., & Miller, D. T. (1983). Why not wait?: A cognitive model of self-imposed delay termination. *Journal of Personality and Social Psychology, 45,* 935–942.

Kirschenbaum, D. S. (1987). Self-regulatory failure: A review with clinical implications. *Clinical Psychology Review, 7,* 77–104.

Lawson, A. (1988). *Adultery: An analysis of love and betrayal.* New York: Basic.

Marlatt, G. A. (1985). Relapse prevention: Theoretical rationale and overview of the model. In G. A. Marlatt & J. R. Gordon (Eds.), *Relapse prevention* (pp. 3–70). New York: Guilford.

Mischel, W. (1974). Processes in delay of gratification. In L. Berkowitz (Ed.), *Advances in experimental social psychology* (Vol. 7, pp. 249–292). San Diego: Academic.

Mischel, W. (in press). From good intentions to willpower. In P. Gollwitzer & J. Bargh (Eds.), *The psychology of action.* New York: Guilford.

Mischel, W., Shoda, Y., & Peake, P. K. (1988). The nature of adolescent competencies predicted by preschool delay of gratification. *Journal of Personality and Social Psychology, 54,* 687–696.

Nathanson, S., Brockner, J., Brenner, D., Samuelson, C., Countryman, M., Lloyd, M., & Rubin, J. Z. (1982). Toward the reduction of entrapment. *Journal of Applied Social Psychology, 12,* 193–208.

Nisbett, R. E. (1993). Violence and U.S. regional culture. *American Psychologist, 48,* 441–449.

Polivy, J. (1976). Perception of calories and regulation of intake in restrained and unrestrained subjects. *Addictive Behaviors, 1,* 237–243.

Prochaska, J. O., & DiClemente, C. C. (1984). *The transtheoretical approach: Crossing traditional boundaries of change.* Homewood, IL: Irwin.

Prochaska, J. O., & DiClemente, C. C. (1986). Toward a comprehensive model of change. In W. Miller & N. Heather (Eds.), *Treating addictive behaviors: Processes of change* (pp. 3–27). New York: Plenum.

Rachlin, H. (1995). Self-control: Beyond commitment. *Behavioral and Brain Sciences, 18,* 109–121.

Rodriguez, M. L., Mischel, W., & Shoda, Y. (1989). Cognitive person variables in the delay of gratification of older children at risk. *Journal of Personality and Social Psychol-*

ogy, 57, 358–367.

Rubin, J. Z., & Brockner, J. (1975). Factors affecting entrapment in waiting situations: The Rosencrantz and Guildenstern effect. *Journal of Personality and Social Psychology, 31*, 1054–1063.

Sansone, C., Weir, C., Harpster, L., & Morgan, C. (1992). Once a boring task, always a boring task? Interest as a self-regulatory mechanism. *Journal of Personality and Social Psychology, 63*, 379–390.

Schachter, S. (1971). Some extraordinary facts about obese humans and rats. *American Psychologist, 26*, 129–144.

Schachter, S. (1982). Recidivism and self-cure of smoking and obesity. *American Psychologist, 37*, 436–444.

Schlenker, B. R., Phillips, S. T., Boniecki, K. A., & Schlenker, D. R. (1995). Championship pressures: Choking or triumphing in one's own territory? *Journal of Personality and Social Psychology, 68*, 623–643.

Shilts, R. (1987). *And the band played on: Politics, people, and the AIDS epidemic.* New York: Viking.

Shoda, Y., Mischel, W., & Peake, P. K. (1990). Predicting adolescent cognitive and self-regulatory competencies from preschool delay of gratification: Identifying diagnostic conditions. *Developmental Psychology, 26*, 978–986.

Staw, B. M. (1976). Knee-deep in the big muddy: A study of escalating commitment to a chosen course of action. *Organizational Behavior and Human Performance, 16*, 27–44.

Steele, C. M., & Josephs, R. A. (1990). Alcohol myopia: Its prized and dangerous effects. *American Psychologist, 45*, 921–933.

Steele, C. M., & Southwick, L. (1985). Alcohol and social behavior I: The psychology of drunken excess. *Journal of Personality and Social Psychology, 48*, 18–34.

Tavris, C. (1989). *Anger: The misunderstood emotion.* New York: Simon & Schuster.

Tedeschi, J. T., & Felson, R. B. (1994). *Violence, aggression, and coercive actions.* Washington, DC: American Psychological Association.

Teger, A. I. (1980) *Too much invested to quit.* New York: Pergamon.

Tice, D. M., & Baumeister, R. F. (1993). Controlling anger: Self-induced emotion change. In D. M. Wegner & J. W. Pennebaker (Eds.), *Handbook of mental control* (pp. 393–409). Englewood Cliffs, NJ: Prentice Hall.

Vallacher, R. R., & Wegner, D. M. (1985). *A theory of action identification.* Hillsdale, NJ: Lawrence Erlbaum Associates.

Van Hook, E., & Higgins, E. T. (1988). Self-related problems beyond the self-concept: Motivational consequences of discrepant self-guides. *Journal of Personality and Social Psychology, 55*, 625–633.

Ward, C. H., & Eisler, R. M. (1987). Type A behavior, achievement striving, and a dysfunctional self-evaluation system. *Journal of Personality and Social Psychology, 53*, 318–326.

Wegner, D. M. (1992). You can't always think what you want: Problems in the suppression of unwanted thoughts. In M. Zanna (Ed.), *Advances in experimental social psychology* (Vol. 25, pp. 193–225). San Diego, CA: Academic.

Wegner, D. M. (1994). Ironic processes of mental control. *Psychological Review, 101*, 34–52.

Wegner, D. M., Schneider, D. J., Carter, S. R., & White, T. L. (1987). Paradoxical effects of thought suppression. *Journal of Personality and Social Psychology, 53*, 5–13.

Wine, J. (1971). Test anxiety and direction of attention. *Psychological Bulletin, 76*, 92–104.

Wright, J., & Mischel, W. (1982). Influence of affect on cognitive social learning person variables. *Journal of Personality and Social Psychology, 43*, 901–914.

Discussion Questions

1. Pick two behaviors that sometimes cause trouble for you and that you have had difficulty controlling in the past. Analyze these two problems from the standpoint of this article.
2. For each of these two problems, make a list of three recommendations, based on the article, that might help increase your self-control.
3. On the surface, an article such as this may not seem to involve *social* psychology because it deals with processes that occur in the individual's head and do not appear to involve other people. Yet Baumeister and Heatherton are social psychologists, and many social psychologists have studied self-regulation and related phenomena (such as thought suppression). In what ways is self-regulation a social psychological phenomenon?

Suggested Readings

Baumeister, R. F., Bratalavsky, E., Muraven, M., & Tice, D. M. (1998). Ego depletion: Is the active self a limited resource? *Journal of Personality and Social Psychology, 74,* 1252–1265. To many psychologists' surprise, this research demonstrated that self-control can be "used up," at least temporarily, when people self-regulate.

Dale, K. L., & Baumeister, R. F. (1999). Self-regulation and psychopathology. In R. M. Kowalski & M. R. Leary (Eds.), *The social psychology of emotional and behavioral problems* (pp. 139–166). Washington, DC: American Psychological Association. This chapter applies research on self-regulation to understanding psychological problems such as mood disorders, obsessive-compulsive disorder, eating disorders, and substance abuse.

Mischel, W., Shoda, Y., & Rodriguez, M. (1989). Delay of gratification in children. *Science, 244,* 933–938. This article summarizes over 20 years of Mischel's ground-breaking research on self-control.

Muraven, M., Tice, D. M., & Baumeister, R. F. (1998). Self-control as a limited resource: Regulatory depletion patterns. *Journal of Personality and Social Psychology, 74,* 774–789. This article describes research on factors that lead to self-control failure.

READING 5

Catastrophizing and Untimely Death

Christopher Peterson • University of Michigan
Martin E. P. Seligman • University of Pennsylvania
Karen H. Yurko • Children's Hospital of Michigan
Leslie R. Martin • La Sierra University
Howard S. Friedman • University of California, Riverside

Editors' Introduction

Over the past three decades, researchers have investigated the role that people's attributions for negative events play in the onset and maintenance of depression (Burns & Seligman, 1991). Early research on learned helplessness demonstrated that exposure to uncontrollable stimuli causes people to become passive and leads to other cognitive, motivational, and emotional deficits. Once researchers realized that people differ in the attributions they make for the negative, uncontrollable events in their lives, they began to study how these individual differences in explanatory style may account for differences in people's experience of depression and their ability to cope with negative events.

An individual's explanatory style is a function of the kinds of attributions he or she makes along three dimensions: internal/external, stable/unstable, and global/specific. People who make internal attributions for events attribute events to something about themselves, whereas those who make external attributions attribute events to something in the situation. Stable attributions are explanations to causes that are not likely to change over time. Unstable attributions are much more variable. The globality of people's attributions refers to the degree to which they believe that negative events affect many aspects of their life (i.e., global) versus the degree to which negative effects are compartmentalized (i.e., specific). People who make internal, stable, and global attributions for negative events are said to have a pessimistic explanatory style.

In this investigation of the relationship between explanatory style and death, Peterson et al. studied participants who were part of the Terman Life-Cycle Study (Terman & Oden, 1947). The Terman study began in the early 1920s to examine the lives of bright children who lived in California. In 1936 and 1940, 1,500 participants, most of whom were preadolescents, completed a series of open-ended questionnaires about bad events in their lives. Peterson et al. were able to content analyze the responses to these questions to determine participants' explanatory styles. Specifically, each bad event that was mentioned was coded by eight raters for attributions regarding internality, stability, and globality. Causes of death for those participants who had died since 1940 were then obtained from death certificates or from their next-of-kin. The results showed that making global attributions for negative events was a risk factor for untimely death, particularly among men, and that global attributions showed the strongest relationship with dying due to accidents or violence.

Abstract

Participants in the Terman Life-Cycle Study completed open-ended questionnaires in 1936 and 1940, and these responses were blindly scored for explanatory style by content analysis. Catastrophizing (attributing bad events to global causes) predicted mortality as of 1991, especially among males, and predicted accidental or violent deaths especially well. These results are the first to show that a dimension of explanatory style is a risk factor for mortality in a large sample of initially healthy individuals, and they imply that one of the mechanisms linking explanatory style and death involves lifestyle.

Explanatory style is a cognitive personality variable that reflects how people habitually explain the causes of bad events (Peterson & Seligman, 1984). Among the dimensions of explanatory style are

- Internality ("it's me") versus externality.
- Stability ("it's going to last forever") versus instability.
- Globality ("it's going to undermine everything") versus specificity.

These dimensions capture tendencies toward self-blame, fatalism, and catastrophizing, respectively. Explanatory style was introduced in the attributional reformulation of helplessness theory to explain individual differences in response to bad events (Abramson, Seligman, & Teasdale, 1978). Individuals who entertain internal, stable, and global explanations for bad events show emotional, motivational, and cognitive disturbances in their wake.

Explanatory style has been examined mainly with regard to depression, and all three dimensions are consistent correlates of depressive symptoms (Sweeney, Anderson, & Bailey, 1986). More recent studies have looked at other outcomes (notably, physical well-being), and researchers have also begun to examine the dimensions separately. Stability and globality—but not internality—predict poor health (Peterson & Bossio, 1991). This is an intriguing finding, but questions remain.

First, do these correlations mean that explanatory styles are risk factors for early death? Previous studies are equivocal either because of small samples or because research participants were already seriously ill.

Second, is the link between explanatory style and health the same or different for males versus females? Again, previous studies are equivocal because they often included only male or only female research participants.

Third, what mediates the link between ways of explaining bad events and poor health? The path is probably overdetermined, but one can ask if fatalism and catastrophizing predict differentially to particular illnesses. These explanatory styles, as cognates of hopelessness, may place one at special risk for cancer, implying an immunological pathway (Eysenck, 1988). Alternatively, these explanatory tendencies, because of their link with stress, may place one at special risk for heart disease, suggesting a cardiovascular pathway (Dykema, Bergbower, & Peterson, 1995). Or perhaps fatalism and catastrophizing predispose one to accidents and injuries and thus point to an uncautious lifestyle as a mediator. Once again, previous studies are equivocal either because illness was deliberately operationalized in nonspecific terms or because only one type of illness was studied.

We attempted to answer these questions by investigating explanatory style and mortality among participants in the Terman Life-Cycle Study (Terman & Oden, 1947). The original sample of more than 1,500 preadolescents has been followed from the 1920s to the present, with attrition (except by death) of less than 10% (Friedman et al., 1995). For most of those who have died (about 50% of males and 35% of females as of 1991), year of death and cause of death are known. In 1936 and 1940, the participants completed open-ended questionnaires about difficult life events, which we content-analyzed for explanatory style. We determined the associations between dimensions of explanatory style on the one hand and time of death and cause of death on the other.

Method

Sample

The Terman Life-Cycle Study began in 1921–1922, when most of the 1,528 participants were in public school. Terman's original objective was to obtain a reasonably representative sample of bright California children (IQs of 135 or greater) and to examine their lives. Almost every public school in the San Francisco and Los Angeles areas was searched for intelligent children. The average birth date for children in the sample was 1910 ($SD = 4$ years). Most of the children were preadolescents when first studied; those still living are now in their 80s. Data were collected prospectively, without any knowledge of eventual health or longevity.

In young adulthood, the participants were generally healthy and successful. In middle age, they were productive citizens, but none was identifiable as a genius. The sample is homogeneous on dimensions of intelligence (above average), race (mostly White), and social class (little poverty).

Content Analysis of Causal Explanations

We scored explanatory style of the responses to the 1936 and 1940 questionnaires using the CAVE (content analysis of verbatim explanations) technique (Peterson, Schulman, Castellon, & Seligman, 1992). A single researcher read through all responses in which bad events were described. Examples of questions that elicited such responses include

> (From 1936): Have any disappointments, failures, bereavements, uncongenial relationships with others, etc., exerted a prolonged influence upon you?
> (From 1940): What do you regard as your most serious fault of personality or character?

When a bad event was accompanied by a causal explanation, the event and the attribution were written down. These events, each with its accompanying attribution, were then presented in a nonsystematic order to eight judges who blindly and independently rated each explanation on a 7-point scale according to its stability, its globality, and its internality. The researchers (supervised by Peterson) who identified and rated attributions were independent of the researchers (supervised by Friedman) who collected and coded mortality information (see the next section).

A total of 3,394 attributions was obtained from 1,182 different individuals, an average of 2.87 attributions per person, with a range of 1 to 13. Each of these attributions was rated by each of the eight judges along the three attributional dimensions. We estimated coding reliability by treating the judges as "items" and calculating Cronbach's (1951) alpha for each dimension; alphas were satisfactory: .82, .73, and .94, for stability, globality, and internality, respectively. Ratings were averaged across raters and across different attributions for the same participant. These scores were intercorrelated (mean $r = .52$), as previous research has typically found (Peterson et al., 1982). The means (and standard deviations) were 4.52 (0.86) for stability, 4.46 (0.64) for globality, and 4.49 (1.29) for internality.

Cause of Death

Death certificates for deceased participants were obtained from the relevant state bureaus and coded for underlying cause of death by a physician-supervised certified nosologist using the criteria of the ninth edition of the International Classification of Diseases (U.S. Department of Health and Human Services, 1980) to distinguish among deaths by cancer, cardiovascular disease, accidents or violence, and other causes. For approximately 20% of the deceased, death certificates were unavailable; whenever possible, cause of death was assigned from information provided by next-of-kin. Among the 1,182 participants for whom explanatory style scores were available, mortality information was known for 1,179. The numbers of deaths as of 1991 were 148 from cancer (85 men, 63 women), 159 from cardiovascular disease (109 men, 50 women), 57 from accidents or violence (40 men, 17 women), 87 from other (known) causes (50 men, 37 women), and 38 from unknown causes (24 men, 14 women).

Results

Explanatory Styles and Mortality

To investigate the association between explanatory styles and mortality (through 1991), we used Cox proportional hazards regressions and checked them with logistic regressions. The Cox approach is nonparametric and assumes that the ratio of hazard functions for individuals with differing values of the covariates (stability, globality, and internality) is invariant over time. We used Tuma's (1980) RATE program for the Cox models, and LOGIST of SAS for the logistic regressions. When all three attributional dimensions were examined simultaneously for the entire sample, only globality was associated with mortality, with a risk hazard (rh) of 1.26 ($p < .01$). Results from the logistic regression analyses (predicting to a dichotomous variable of survival to at least age 65 vs. not) were consistent with this finding; only the odds ratio associated with globality was significant ($rh = 1.25, p < .05$).

Figure 5.1 depicts the probability of a 20-year-old in this sample dying by a given age as a function of sex and globality (top vs. bottom quartiles of scores). The point at which each curve crosses the .50 probability line represents the "average" age of death of individuals in the group. As can be seen, males with a global explanatory style were at the highest risk for early death.

To test whether the effects of globality were due to individuals being seriously ill or suicidal at the time of assessment, we conducted additional survival analyses that excluded individuals who died before 1945. The effects of globality remained for males.

Globality of Explanatory Style and Cause of Death

Next we investigated whether globality was differentially related to causes of death (cancer, cardiovascular disease, accidents or violence, other, and unknown) by comparing Gompertz models (see Table 5.1). When comparing a model with both sex and globality as predictors but constraining the effects of globality to predict equally across all causes of death (Model 2) with an unconstrained model in which globality was allowed to predict differentially to separate causes of death (Model 3), we found that the unconstrained model fit the data better than did the constrained model. This finding was also obtained when participants who did not survive until at least 1945 were excluded, $\Delta\chi^2(4, N = 1,157) = 13.29, p < .01$.

Globality best predicted deaths by accident or violence ($rh = 1.98, p < .01$) and deaths from unknown causes ($rh = 2.08, p < .01$). The risk ratios associated with other causes were 1.03 for cardiovascular disease (n.s.), 1.18 for cancer (n.s.), and 1.22 for other (known) causes (n.s.).

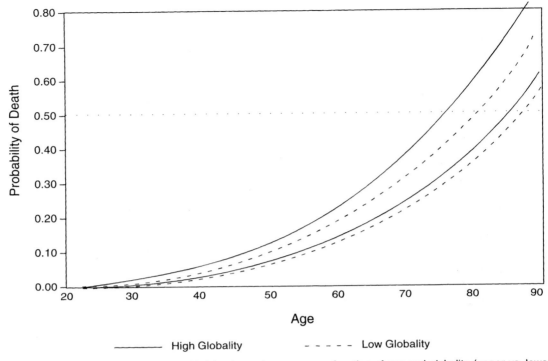

Figure 5.1 ■ Probability of a 20-year-old dying by a given age as a function of sex and globality (upper vs. lower quartiles).

Finally, we computed a Cox model for prediction from globality specifically to suicide (which had been included in the accident–violence group). The result was marginally significant ($rh = 1.84$, $p < .06$), but only 25 individuals in the sample with globality scores available were known to have committed suicide. When these 25 individuals were excluded, along with individuals who died of accidents (some of which may have been suicides), and the analyses already described were repeated, the same results were obtained: Globality predicted mortality for the entire sample ($rh = 1.20$, $p < .05$), especially for males ($rh = 1.31, p < .05$).

Additional Analyses

How might we explain the finding that globality of explanatory style predicted untimely death? In

TABLE 5.1. Goodness of Fit for Gompertz Models Predicting (Age-Adjusted) Cause of Death From Sex and Globality of Explanatory Style ($n = 1,179$)

Model	$\Delta\chi^2$	df
Model 1: predicting mortality from sex	705.44**	10
Model 2: predicting mortality from sex and globality, constraining the effect of globality to be equal across all causes of death	715.83**	11
Model 3: predicting mortality from sex and globality, not constraining the effects of globality to be equal across all causes of death	726.62**	15
Model 2 vs. Model 1	10.39**	1
Model 3 vs. Model 1	21.18**	5
Model 3 vs. Model 2	10.79*	4

*$p < .05$. **$p < .001$.

terms of simple correlations, men who had years earlier made global attributions experienced more mental health problems in 1950 ($r = .14, p < .001$), had lower levels of adjustment at this time ($r = -.11, p < .02$), and reported that they drank slightly more ($r = .07, p < .08$) than men who had made more specific attributions (see Martin et al., 1995). We examined other variables such as education, risky hobbies, and physical activity from 1940 through 1977, but none of the simple associations with globality was significant. The subsample of individuals for whom we had smoking data available was substantially smaller than the original sample because these data were collected in 1990–1991; however, within this group, no associations with globality were found.

Additional survival analyses were conducted, controlling for mental health and psychological adjustment. In these analyses, the association between globality and mortality risk remained stable and significant. When mental health was controlled, the relative hazard associated with globality was 1.27 ($p < .05$). When level of adjustment was controlled, the relative hazard was 1.29 ($p < .01$). A final model controlling for both mental health and adjustment resulted in a relative hazard of 1.24 ($p < .05$). Globality, although related to these aspects of psychological well-being, was distinct, and its association with mortality was not substantially mediated by these other factors.

Finally, globality of explanatory style was inversely related to a measure of neuroticism constructed from 1940 data ($r = -.15, p < .001$) (Martin, 1996). This finding seems to rule out confounding of our measures by response sets involving complaints or exaggeration.

Discussion

The present results extend past investigations of explanatory style and physical well-being. They represent the first evidence from a large sample of initially healthy individuals that a dimension of explanatory style—globality—is a risk factor for early death, especially among males. Because globality scores were the least reliably coded of the three attributional dimensions and had the most restricted range, the present results may underestimate the actual association between globality and mortality. In any event, our findings were not due to confounding by neuroticism, suicide, or psychological maladjustment. Stability per se did not predict mortality, perhaps because it involves a belief that is circumscribed, that is, relevant in certain situations but not others.

In contrast, globality taps a pervasive style of catastrophizing about bad events, expecting them to occur across diverse situations. Such a style can be hazardous because of its link with poor problem solving, social estrangement, and risky decision making across diverse settings (Peterson, Maier, & Seligman, 1993). Supporting this interpretation is the link between globality and deaths due to accident or violence. Deaths like these are often not random. "Being in the wrong place at the wrong time" may be the result of a pessimistic lifestyle, one more likely among males than females. Perhaps deaths due to causes classified as unknown may similarly reflect an incautious lifestyle.

Explanatory style, at least as measured in this study, showed no specific link to death by cancer or cardiovascular disease. Speculation concerning explanatory style and poor health has often centered on physiological mechanisms, but behavioral and lifestyle mechanisms are probably more typical and more robust. We were unable to identify a single behavioral mediator, however, which implies that there is no simple set of health mediators set into operation by globality.

Previous reports on the health of the Terman Life-Cycle Study participants found that childhood personality variables predicted mortality (Friedman et al., 1993). Specifically, a variable identified as "cheerfulness" was inversely related to longevity. Its components involved parental judgments of a participant's "optimism" and "sense of humor." Because a hopeless explanatory style is sometimes described as pessimistic and its converse as optimistic, these previous reports appear to contradict the present results. However, in this sample, cheerfulness in childhood was unrelated to explanatory style in adulthood. If cheerfulness and explanatory style tap the same sense of optimism, then this characteristic is discontinuous from childhood to adulthood. It is also possible, perhaps likely, that these two variables measure different things. An optimistic explanatory style is infused with agency, the belief that the future will be pleasant because one can control important outcomes.

In summary, a cognitive style in which people catastrophize about bad events, projecting them across many realms of their lives, foreshadows untimely death decades later. We suggest that a lifestyle in which an individual is less likely to avoid or escape potentially hazardous situations is one route leading from pessimism to an untimely death.

ACKNOWLEDGMENTS

This research was supported by Research Grants AG-05590 and AG-08825 from the National Institute on Aging, by Research Grant MH-19604 from the U.S. Public Health Service, and by the Health and Behavior Network of the MacArthur Foundation. Some of these data were made available from the Terman Life-Cycle Study, begun by Lewis Terman. Further assistance was provided by Eleanor Walker, Albert Hastorf, and Robert Sears at Stanford University. Help in identifying, transcribing, and rating causal attributions was provided by Laura Brauninger, Julie Brody, Debbie Dormont, Rikki Feinstein, Eric Franz, Elissa Gartenberg, Denise Glenn, Karen Kantor, Margot Morrison, Madhuri Nannapaneni, Elysa Saldrigas, Kristin Shook, and Lynn (Hannah) Smitterberg at the University of Michigan.

NOTE

This article is one of a series developed from a large-scale, multiyear, multidisciplinary project on psychosocial predictors of health and longevity. The data are derived from thousands of variables in the 70-year Terman Life-Cycle Study archives or follow-ups. Relevant findings are included to the extent feasible in each report, but multiple publication is necessitated because of the complexity and scope of the project. Care should be taken not to include overlapping findings in meta-analyses or other reviews.

REFERENCES

Abramson, L. Y., Seligman, M. E. P., & Teasdale, J. D. (1978). Learned helplessness in humans: Critique and reformulation. *Journal of Abnormal Psychology, 87,* 49–74.

Cronbach, L. J. (1951). Coefficient alpha and the internal structure of tests. *Psychometrika, 16,* 297–334.

Dykema, J., Bergbower, K., & Peterson, C. (1995). Pessimistic explanatory style, stress, and illness. *Journal of Social and Clinical Psychology, 14,* 357–371.

Eysenck, H. J. (1988). Personality and stress as causal factors in cancer and heart disease. In M.P. Janisse (Ed.), *Individual differences, stress, and health psychology* (pp. 129–145). New York: Springer-Verlag.

Friedman, H. S., Tucker, J. S., Schwartz, J. E., Tomlinson-Keasey, C., Martin, L. R., Wingard, D. L., & Criqui, M. H. (1995). Psychosocial and behavioral predictors of longevity: The aging and death of the "Termites." *American Psychologist, 50,* 69–78.

Friedman, H. S., Tucker, J. S., Tomlinson-Keasey, C., Schwartz, J. E., Wingard, D. L., & Criqui, M. H. (1993). Does childhood personality predict longevity? *Journal of Personality and Social Psychology, 65,* 176–185.

Martin, L. R. (1996). *Consonance of archival and contemporary data: A comparison of personality scales constructed from the Terman data set with modern personality scales.* Unpublished doctoral dissertation, University of California, Riverside.

Martin, L. R., Friedman, H. S., Tucker, J. S., Schwartz, J. E., Criqui, M. H., Wingard, D. L., & Tomlinson-Keasey, C. (1995). An archival prospective study of mental health and longevity. *Health Psychology, 14,* 381–387.

Peterson, C., & Bossio, L. M. (1991). *Health and optimism.* New York: Free Press.

Peterson, C., Maier, S. F., & Seligman, M. E. P. (1993). *Learned helplessness: A theory for the age of personal control.* New York: Oxford University Press.

Peterson, C., Schulman, P., Castellon, C., & Seligman, M. E. P. (1992). CAVE: Content analysis of verbatim explanations. In C. P. Smith (Ed.), *Motivation and personality: Handbook of thematic content analysis* (pp. 383–392). New York: Cambridge University Press.

Peterson, C., & Seligman, M. E. P. (1984). Causal explanations as a risk factor for depression: Theory and evidence. *Psychological Review, 91,* 347–374.

Peterson, C., Semmel, A., von Baeyer, C., Abramson, L. Y., Metalsky, G. I., & Seligman, M. E. P. (1982). The Attributional Style Questionnaire. *Cognitive Therapy and Research, 6,* 287–299.

Sweeney, P. D., Anderson, K., & Bailey, S. (1986). Attributional style in depression: A meta-analytic review. *Journal of Personality and Social Psychology, 50,* 974–991.

Terman, L. M., & Oden, M. H. (1947). *Genetic studies of genius: IV. The gifted child grows up: Twenty-five years follow-up of a superior group.* Stanford, CA: Stanford University Press.

Tuma, N. (1980). *Invoking RATE.* Unpublished manuscript, Stanford University, Stanford, CA.

U.S. Department of Health and Human Services. (1980). *International classification of diseases* (9th rev., clinical modification, 2nd ed., DHHS Publication No. PHS 80–1260). Washington, DC: U.S. Government Printing Office.

Discussion Questions

1. This article focused on the relationship between explanatory style and untimely death. What implications do you think a pessimistic explanatory style would have for other life outcomes, such as academic or job performance, substance abuse, or marital problems?
2. If a pessimistic explanatory style is related to untimely death and poor health outcomes, would an optimistic explanatory style be related to longer life and improved health?
3. What kinds of attributions would characterize an optimistic explanatory style? Would they be the exact opposite of a pessimistic explanatory style?
4. How do you think people come to acquire a particular explanatory style? Are they born with it or is it learned?

Suggested Readings

Alloy, L. B., Abramson, L. Y., Metalsky, G. I., & Hartlage, S. (1988). The hopelessness theory of depression: Attributional aspects. *British Journal of Clinical Psychology, 27,* 5–21. This article expands upon the hopelessness theory of depression with a focus on the research that has been conducted testing this theory.

Burns, M. O., & Seligman, M. E. P. (1991). Explanatory style, helplessness, and depression. In C. R. Snyder & D. R. Forsyth (Eds.), *Handbook of social and clinical psychology: The health perspective* (pp. 267–284). New York: Pergamon. This chapter provides a review of the literature on the reformulated learned helplessness model of depression.

Peterson, C., Bishop, M. P., Fletcher, C. W., Kaplan, M. R., Yesko, E. S., Moon, C. H., Smith, J. S., Michaels, C. E., & Michaels, A. J. (2001). Explanatory style as a risk factor for traumatic mishaps. *Cognitive Therapy and Research, 25,* 633–649. This article describes a series of studies examining the relationship between explanatory style and risk of traumatic mishaps.

Terman, L. M., & Oden, M. H. (1947). *Genetic studies of genius: IV. The gifted child grows up: Twenty-five years follow-up of a superior group.* Stanford, CA: Stanford University Press. This article examines the lives of bright children who lived in California during the 1920s, and includes follow-up information on 1,500 of these individuals.

READING 6

Schizophrenic Patients in the Psychiatric Interview: An Experimental Study of Their Effectiveness at Manipulation

Benjamin M. Braginsky • Yale University
Dorothea D. Braginsky[1] • Veterans Administration Hospital, West Haven, Connecticut

Editors' Introduction

Schizophrenia has traditionally been viewed as a disorder that compromises the cognitive and social abilities of the individual. According to this view, the symptoms of schizophrenia, as well as many other mental disorders, are largely beyond the person's control. Beginning in the 1960s, however, some researchers and theorists suggested that psychiatric symptoms sometimes reflect intentional, self-presentational behaviors designed to accomplish desired outcomes for the troubled patient. In essence, some mental patients, even those diagnosed with schizophrenia, may use symptoms of mental illness to obtain things that they desire. If so, psychiatric symptoms are sometimes intentional social behaviors and schizophrenics may have more control over themselves than has been suspected. In support of this idea, an early study by Braginsky and Braginsky (1967) found that schizophrenic patients answered a psychological questionnaire in self-protective ways. Patients who wanted to be released from the mental hospital responded in a manner that made them appear healthy, whereas those who wanted to remain within the institution responded in a manner that made them appear "sick."

Although psychologically healthy people may find it difficult to understand why someone would want to appear maladjusted, the answer may lie in the fact that psychological dysfunction frees an individual from normal personal and social responsibilities. Many individuals who reside in psychiatric institutions are poor and uneducated. As opposed to being homeless and unemployed, the option of living in a mental hospital might seem a welcome respite from the hardships of life.

In this study, Braginsky and Braginsky examined whether schizophrenics engage in impression management in a face-to-face interview when doing so has benefits for them. Thirty male schizophrenics who were living on an open hospital ward were randomly assigned to either a discharge condition (i.e., believed the interviewer was interested in determining if they were ready to be discharged), an open ward condition (i.e., believed the interviewer was interested in determining whether they should be sent to a less desirable closed ward), or a mental status condition (i.e., believed the interviewer was interested in how they were getting along in the hospital). The results of the study revealed that patients in the open ward condition presented themselves as less disturbed than participants in either of the other two conditions. Relative to patients in the discharge or mental status condition, patients in the open ward condition presented themselves more positively. In fact, no patient who thought that his or her suitability for an open ward was being assessed made any reference to psychotic symptoms. Thus, the patients effectively engaged in impression management in order to obtain desired outcomes and to avoid undesired outcomes.

This finding does not suggest that schizophrenics do not really have problems. Schizophrenia is a devastating illness that affects all aspects of a person's psychological functioning. What the finding does show, however, is that mental patients may strategically use their symptoms, within limits, to obtain what they want from other people.

Abstract

This study attempted to examine whether chronic schizophrenic patients could effectively engage in the manipulative strategy of impression management in an evaluative interview situation. The data supported the expectation that schizophrenic mental patients can effectively present themselves as "sick" or "healthy," whichever is more suited to their needs and goals. Thus, when the patients' open ward status was questioned, they convincingly presented themselves in the interview as "healthy" and eligible for open ward living; when their residency status was questioned, they convincingly presented themselves as "sick" and ineligible for discharge. These findings were interpreted as supporting assumptions of patient effectiveness in implementing goals.

The present investigation is concerned with the manipulative behavior of hospitalized schizophrenics in evaluative interview situations. More specifically, the study attempts to answer the question: Can schizophrenic patients effectively control the impressions (impression management; Goffman, 1959) they make on the professional hospital staff?

Typically, the mental patient has been viewed as an extremely ineffectual and helpless individual (e.g., Arieti, 1959; Becker, 1964; Bellak, 1958; Joint Commission on Mental Illness and Health, 1961; Redlich & Freedman, 1966; Schooler & Parkel, 1966; Searles, 1965). For example, Redlich and Freedman (1966) described the mental patient and his pathological status in the following manner: "There is a concomitant loss of focus and coherence and a profound shift in the meaning and value of social relationships and goal directed behavior. This is evident in the inability realistically to implement future goals and present satisfactions; they are achieved magically or through fantasy and delusion" (p. 463). Schooler and Parkel (1966) similarly underline the mental patients' ineffectual status in this description: "The chronic schizophrenic is not Seneca's 'reasoning animal,' or Spinoza's 'social animal,' or even a reasonably efficient version of Cassirer's 'symbol using animal.' . . . Since he violates so many functional definitions of man, there is heuristic value in studying him with an approach like that which would be used to study an alien creature" (p. 67).

Thus, the most commonly held assumptions concerning the nature of the schizophrenic patient stress their ineffectuality and impotency. In this context one would expect schizophrenics to perform less than adequately in interpersonal situations, to be unable to initiate manipulative tactics, and, certainly, to be incapable of successful manipulation of other people.[2]

In contrast to the above view of the schizophrenic, a less popular orientation has been expressed by Artiss (1959), Braginsky, Grosse, and Ring (1966), Goffman (1961), Levinson and Gallagher (1964), Rakusin and Fierman (1963), Szasz (1961, 1965), and Towbin (1966). Here schizophrenics are portrayed in terms usually reserved for neurotics and normal persons. Simply, these authors subscribe to the beliefs that: (a) the typical schizophrenic patient, as compared to normals, is not deficient, defective, or dissimilar in intrapsychic functioning; (b) the typical schizophrenic patient is not a victim of his illness; that is, it is assumed that he is not helpless and unable to control his behavior or significantly determine life outcomes; (c) the differences that some schizophrenic patients manifest (as compared to normals) are assumed to be more accurately understood in terms of differences in belief systems, goals, hierarchy of needs, and interpersonal strategies, rather than in terms of illness, helplessness, and deficient intrapsychic functioning. This orientation leads to the expectation that schizophrenic patients do try to achieve particular goals and, in the process, effectively manipulate other people.

There is some evidence in support of this viewpoint (e.g., Artiss, 1959; Braginsky, Holzberg, Finison, & Ring, 1967; Levinson & Gallagher, 1964). Furthermore, a recent study (Braginsky et al., 1966) demonstrated that schizophrenic patients responded, on a paper-and-pencil "mental status" test, in a manner that would protect their self-interests. Those who wanted to remain in the hospital (chronic patients) presented themselves as "sick," whereas those who desired to be discharged (first admissions) presented themselves as "healthy." That is, they effectively controlled the impressions they wished to make on others. Their manipulative performance, however, was mediated by an impersonal test.

Therefore, the following question is asked: Can schizophrenics engage in similar manipulative behaviors in a "face-to-face" interview with a psychologist? That is, will chronic schizophrenics who desire to remain in the hospital and live on open wards present themselves in an interview situation when they perceive that their open ward status is being questioned as (a) "healthy" and, therefore, eligible for open ward living, and in another interview situation when their residential status is being questioned as (b) "sick" and, therefore, ineligible for discharge? If so, are their performances convincing to a professional audience (i.e., psychiatrists)?

Method

A sample of 30 long-term (more than 2 continuous years of hospitalization) male schizophrenics living on open wards was randomly selected from ward rosters. Two days prior to the experiment, the patients were told that they were scheduled for an interview with a staff psychologist. Although each patient was to be interviewed individually, all 30 were brought simultaneously to a waiting room. Each patient interviewed was not allowed to return to this room, to insure that patients who had participated would not communicate with those who had not.

Each patient was escorted to the interview room

by an assistant, who casually informed the patient in a tone of confidentiality about the purpose of the interview (preinterview induction). Patients were randomly assigned by the assistant to one of three induction conditions (10 to each condition). The interviewer was unaware of the induction to which the patients were assigned, thereby eliminating interviewer bias.

Induction Conditions

Discharge induction. Patients were told: "I think the person you are going to see is interested in examining patients to see whether they might be ready for discharge."

Open ward induction.[3] Patients were told: "I think that the person you are going to see is interested in examining patients to see whether they should be on open or closed wards."

Mental status induction.[4] Patients were told: "I think the person you are going to see is interested in how you are feeling and getting along in the hospital."

After greeting each patient the interviewer asked: "How are you feeling?" Patients who responded only with physical descriptions were also asked: "How do you feel mentally?" whereas those who only gave descriptions of their mental state were asked: "How are you feeling physically?" The patients' responses were tape-recorded. The interview was terminated after 2 minutes,[5] whereupon the purpose of the experiment was disclosed.

Three staff psychiatrists from the same hospital separately rated each of the 30 tape-recorded interviews during two 40-minute sessions. The psychiatrists had no knowledge of the experiment, and they were unfamiliar with the patients; they were told by the experimenter that these were mental patients residing in the hospital and that as a group they represented a wide range of diagnostic categories.

The psychiatrists rated the patients on the following dimensions: (a) the patient's degree of psychopathology, using a 5-point scale ranging from "not at all ill" to "extremely ill"; (b) the amount of hospital control a patient needed, ranging on an 8-point scale from complete freedom ("discharge") to maximum *control* ("closed ward, continual observation"); and (c) the structural or qualitative aspects of the patient's speech, such as pressure of speech, affect, volume, etc. The score for each patient's speech characteristic was based on the sum of the psychiatrist's rating of 14 Lorr scale items (Lorr, 1953). Each item was rated on an 8-point scale ranging from not at all atypical to extremely atypical verbal behavior.

Predictions

If long-term patients are both motivated to live on open wards and to remain in the hospital and if, in addition, they effectively engage in impression management in order to realize these desires, then the following would be expected:

1. Psychiatrists will rate patients in the discharge and the mental status conditions as being similar with respect to psychopathology and need for hospital control. Mental status interviews are generally used by the hospital to evaluate patients for discharge; therefore, the mental status and discharge conditions offer the same potential consequences for patients. Thus, patients in both conditions will give the impression of being "sick" and in need of hospital control in order to decrease the probability of discharge. The purpose of including the discharge induction was to present the consequences of the interview as explicitly as in the open ward induction.
2. Psychiatrists will rate the patients in the open ward condition significantly less mentally ill and less in need of hospital control than patients in the discharge and mental status conditions. That is, patients in the open ward condition will give the impression of being "healthy" in order to maximize their chances of remaining on an open ward.

Subjects

The mean age of the patients was 47.4 years ($SD = 8.36$). The mean educational level of the group was 8.05 years of schooling ($SD = 3.44$). The median length of hospitalization was 10 years. In terms of diagnostic categories, 43% of the sample was diagnosed as chronic undifferentiated schizophrenic, 37% as paranoid schizophrenic, 10% as catatonic, and the remaining 10% as simple schizophrenic. There were no differences between the three experimental groups on any of the above variables.

Results and Discussion

The reliability coefficients of the three psychiatrists' combined ratings of the patient interviews were as follows: (a) ratings of psychopathology—$r = .89$, $p < .01$; (b) need for hospital control—$r = .74$, $p < .01$; (c) normality of speech characteristics—$r = .65$, $p < .01$. Thus, it was concluded that there was significant agreement between the three psychiatrists.

The means of the psychopathology ratings by experimental condition are presented in Table 6.1. The ratings ranged from 1 to 5. The analysis of variance of the data yielded a significant condition effect ($F = 9.38$, $p < .01$). The difference between the open ward and discharge conditions was statistically significant ($p < .01$; Tukey multiple-range test). In addition, the difference between the open ward and the mental status condition was significant ($p < .01$). As predicted, there was no significant difference between the discharge and mental status conditions.

The means of the ratings of need for hospital control are presented in Table 6.1. These ratings ranged from 1 to 8. The analysis of these data indicated a significant difference between the means ($F = 3.85$, $p < .05$). Again, significant differences (beyond the .05 level) were obtained between the open ward and the discharge conditions, as well as between the open ward and mental status conditions. No difference was found between the discharge and mental status conditions.

On the basis of these analyses, it is clear that patients in the open ward condition appear significantly less mentally ill and in less need of hospital control than patients in either the discharge or mental status conditions. Obviously the patients in these conditions convey different impressions in the interview situation. In order to ascertain the manner by which the patients conveyed these different impressions, the following three manipulative tactics were examined: (a) number of positive statements patients made about themselves, (b) number of negative statements made about themselves (these include both physical and mental referents), and (c) normality of speech characteristics (i.e., how "sick" they sounded, independent of the content of speech). The first two indexes were obtained by counting the number of positive or negative self-referent statements a patient made during the interview. These counts were done by three judges independently, and the reliability coefficient was .95. The third index was based on the psychiatrists' ratings on 14 Lorr scale items of the speech characteristics of patients. A score was obtained for each patient by summing the ratings for the 14 scales.

Ratings of psychopathology and need for hospital control were, in part, determined by the frequency of positive and negative self-referent statements. The greater the frequency of positive statements made by a patient, the less ill he was perceived ($r = -.58$, $p < .01$) and the less in need of hospital control ($r = -41$, $p < .05$). Conversely, the greater the frequency of negative statements, the more ill a patient was perceived ($r = .53$, $p < .01$) and the more in need of hospital control ($r = .37$, $p < .05$). It is note-worthy that patients were consistent in their performances; that is, those who tended to say positive things about themselves tended not to say negative things ($r = -.55$, $p < .01$).

When self-referent statements were compared by condition, it was found that patients in the open ward condition presented themselves in a significantly more positive fashion than patients in the discharge and mental status conditions. Only 2 patients in the open ward condition reported having physical or mental problems, whereas 13 patients in the mental status and discharge conditions presented such complaints ($\chi^2 = 5.40$, $p < .05$).

The frequency of positive and negative self-referent statements, however, cannot account for important qualitative components of the impressions the patients attempted to convey. For example, a patient may give only one complaint, but it may be serious (e.g., he reports hallucinations),

TABLE 6.1. Mean Psychopathology and Need-for-Hospital-Control Ratings by Experimental Condition

Rating	Open ward		Mental status		Discharge	
	M	SD	M	SD	M	SD
Psychopathology	2.63	0.58	3.66	0.65	3.70	0.67
Need for hospital control	2.83	1.15	4.10	1.31	4.20	1.42

whereas another patient may state five complaints, all of which are relatively benign. In order to examine the severity of symptoms or complaints reported by patients, the number of "psychotic" complaints, namely, reports of hallucinations or bizzare delusions, was tallied. None of the patients in the open ward condition made reference to having had hallucinations or delusions, while nine patients in the discharge and mental status conditions spontaneously made such reference ($\chi^2 = 4.46$, $p < .05$).

In comparing the structural or qualitative aspects of patient speech, no significant differences were obtained between experimental conditions. Patients "sounded" about the same in all three conditions. The majority of patients (80%) were rated as having relatively normal speech characteristics. Although there were no differences by condition, there was a significant inverse relationship ($r = -.35$, $p < .05$) between quality of speech and the number of positive statements made. That is, patients were consistent to the extent that those who sounded ill tended not to make positive self-referent statements.

In summary then, the hypotheses were confirmed. It is clear that patients responded to the inductions in a manner which maximized the chances of fulfilling their needs and goals. When their self-interests were at stake, patients could present themselves in a face-to-face interaction as either "sick" or "healthy," whichever was more appropriate to the situation. In the context of this experiment, "sick" impressions were conveyed when the patients were faced with the possibility of discharge. On the other hand, impressions of "health" were conveyed when the patients' open ward status was questioned. Moreover, the impressions they conveyed were convincing to an audience of experienced psychiatrists.

One may argue, however, that the differences between the groups were a function of differential anxiety generated by the inductions rather than a function of the patients' needs, goals, and manipulative strategies. More specifically, the discharge and the mental status conditions would generate more anxiety and, therefore, more pathological behavior than the open ward condition. As a result, the psychiatrists rated the patients in the discharge and mental status conditions as "sicker" than patients in the open ward condition. According to this argument, then, the patients who were rated as sick were, in fact, more disturbed, and those rated healthy were, in fact, less disturbed.

No differences, however, were found between conditions in terms of the amount of disturbed behavior during the interview. As was previously mentioned, the psychiatrists did not perceive any differences by condition in atypicality of verbal behavior. On the contrary, the patients were judged as sounding relatively normal. Thus, the psychiatrists' judgments of psychopathology were based primarily on the symptoms patients reported rather than on symptoms manifested. Patients did not behave in a disturbed manner; rather, they told the interviewer how disturbed they were.

The traditional set of assumptions concerning schizophrenics, which stresses their irrationality and interpersonal ineffectuality, would not only preclude the predictions made in this study, but would fail to explain parsimoniously the present observations. It is quite plausible and simple to view these findings in terms of the assumptions held about people in general; that is, schizophrenics, like normal persons, are goal-oriented and are able to control the outcomes of their social encounters in a manner that satisfies their goals.

NOTES

1. The authors would like to express their appreciation to Doris Seiler and Dennis Ridley for assisting with the data collection.
2. This statement is explicitly derived from formal theories of schizophrenia and not from clinical observations. It is obvious to some observers, however, that schizophrenics do attempt to manipulate others. The discrepancy between these observations and traditional theoretical assumptions about the nature of schizophrenics is rarely, if ever, reconciled.
3. It may be suggested that the open ward induction was meaningless, since no patient enjoying open ward status would believe that he could be put on a closed ward on the basis of an interview. At the time this experiment was being conducted, however, this hospital was in the process of recognization, and open and closed ward status was a salient and relevant issue.
4. Mental status evaluation interviews are typically conducted yearly. Thus, patients who have been in the hospital for more than a year expect to be interviewed for the purposes of determining their residency status.
5. Although, admittedly, psychiatrists would never base decisions concerning mental status and discharge on a 2-minute interview, it was adequate for the purposes of this study (namely, to determine if mental patients effectively engage in impression management). The 2-minute response to the single question provided sufficient information for psychiatrists to form reliable impressions of the patients. Interestingly, the typical mental status interview conducted by these psychiatrists is rarely longer than 30 minutes.

REFERENCES

Arieti, S. (1959). *American handbook of psychiatry.* New York: Basic Books.
Artiss, K. L. (1959). *The symptom as communication in schizophrenia.* New York: Grune & Stratton.
Becker, E. (1964). *The revolution in psychiatry.* London: Collier-Macmillan.
Bellak, C. (1958). *Schizophrenia: A review of the syndrome.* New York: Logos Press.
Braginsky, B., Grosse, M., & Ring, K. (1966). Controlling outcomes through impression-management: An experimental study of the manipulative tactics of mental patients. *Journal of Consulting Psychology, 30,* 295–300.
Braginsky, B., Holzberg, J., Finison, L., & Ring, K. (1967). Correlates of the mental patient's acquisition of hospital information. *Journal of Personality, 35,* 323–342.
Goffman, E. (1959). *The presentation of self in everyday life.* New York: Doubleday.
Goffman, E. (1961). *Asylums.* New York: Doubleday.
Joint Commission on Mental Illness and Health. (1961). *Action for mental health.* New York: Basic Books.
Levinson, D. S., & Gallagher, E. B. (1964). *Patienthood in the mental hospital.* Boston: Houghton-Mifflin.
Lorr, M. (1953). Multidimensional scale for rating psychiatric patients. *Veterans Administration Technical Bulletin, 51,* 119–127.
Rakusin, J. M., & Fierman, L. B. (1963). Five assumptions for treating chronic psychotics. *Mental Hospitals, 14,* 140–148.
Redlich, F. C., & Freedman, D. T. (1966). *The theory and practice of psychiatry.* New York: Basic Book.
Schooler, C., & Parkel, D. (1966). The overt behavior of chronic schizophrenics and its relationship to their internal state and personal history. *Psychiatry, 29,* 67–77.
Searles, H. F. (1965). *Collected papers on schizophrenia and related subjects.* New York: International Universities Press.
Szasz, T. S. (1961). *The myth of mental illness.* New York: Hoeber-Harper.
Szasz, T. S. (1965). *Psychiatric justice.* New York: Macmillan.
Towbin, A. P. (1966). Understanding the mentally deranged. *Journal of Existentialism, 7,* 63–83.

Discussion Questions

1. What psychological problems other than schizophrenia may involve self-presentational efforts to show people that the person is disturbed?
2. Have you ever portrayed yourself to other people as more anxious, depressed, distraught, or otherwise upset than you really felt? Why? What goals were you attempting to achieve?
3. The study by Braginsky and Braginsky also suggests that people may not be able to tell when others are manipulating them through their self-presentations. In general, how good do you think people are at detecting false self-presentations?

Suggested Readings

Braginsky, B. M., Braginsky, D. D., & Ring, K. (1982). *Methods of madness: The mental hospital as a last resort.* Lanham, MD: University Press of America. This provocative book presents the idea that mental institutions may serve as a "resort" for many troubled individuals.
Fontana, A. F., Klein, E. B., Lewis, E., & Levine, L. (1968). Presentation of self in mental illness. *Journal of Consulting and Clinical Psychology, 32,* 110–119. This article reports the results of research comparing "healthy presenters" with "sick presenters" in a mental hospital.
Kowalski, R. M., & Leary, M. R. (1990). Strategic self-presentation and the avoidance of aversive events: Antecedents and consequences of self-enhancement and self-depreciation. *Journal of Experimental Social Psychology, 26,* 322–336. This study found that otherwise normal people will strategically manage their impressions, even if it portrays them in an unfavorable light, in order to avoid aversive, undesired events.
Sadow, L., & Suslick, A. (1961). Simulation of previous psychotic state. *Archives of General Psychiatry, 4,* 452–458. The authors describe case studies of former mental patients who simulate previous psychoses when they are experiencing adversity.

READING 7

Drug Choice as a Self-Handicapping Strategy in Response to Noncontingent Success

Steven Berglas • Harvard Medical School
Edward E. Jones • Princeton University

Editors' Introduction

Often, people's difficulties in life are the result of them "shooting themselves in the foot," and it is difficult to understand why people would intentionally do things that undermine their performance on a test or other important activity. However, many examples of self-defeating behavior can be found: a student drinking too much the night before a major exam, an athlete missing several practices before an important competition, or a job candidate staying up the night before an interview. This article explores one source of these kinds of self-defeating behaviors.

Although people often want accurate information about their abilities, they understandably do not like receiving information that casts them in a negative light. In an effort to deflect the implications of undesirable feedback, people may self-handicap. Berglas and Jones define self-handicapping as "any action or choice of performance setting that enhances the opportunity to externalize (or excuse) failure and to internalize (reasonably accept credit for) success." By setting up a situation so that it causes them to fail, people who self-handicap can blame the situation for their shortcomings, allowing them to maintain their self-esteem.

The two studies reported in this article by Berglas and Jones were the first experimental studies conducted on self-handicapping. In an effort to understand when people are likely to self-handicap, Berglas and Jones created two experimental conditions. In the noncontingent success condition, participants worked on a series of unsolvable anagrams, believing that the anagrams provided an index of their intellectual ability, and were then told that they had performed very well on the test. In the contingent success condition, participants worked on a series of solvable anagrams, followed by feedback that they had performed very well on the test. The researchers hypothesized that participants would be more likely to self-handicap after noncontingent success (i.e., a condition in which participants are unsure of whether they were responsible for their success or whether it was merely an accident) than contingent success (i.e., participants knew that their success was due to their own ability). Unsure of their likelihood of success on future tasks, participants in the noncontingent success condition should want to create a situation that would allow them to externalize any future failure. Should they succeed in spite of the handicap, then they could internalize their success.

To test this idea, Berglas and Jones provided participants in the contingent and noncontingent success conditions the opportunity to take either a performance-enhancing drug or a performance-inhibiting drug before completing a second test of intellectual ability. The results showed that men in the noncontingent success group tended to choose the performance-inhibiting drug, one that would make them perform worse on the second test! Because they were uncertain regarding the source of their success on the initial test (and whether they could repeat their success in the future), these participants could provide themselves with an excuse for possible failure by taking a drug that interfered with performance. If they failed, they could then blame the drug rather than their lack of ability. Berglas and Jones discuss possible implications of this finding for people's problems in everyday life.

Abstract

In two closely related experiments, college student subjects were instructed to choose between a drug that allegedly interfered with performance and a drug that allegedly enhanced performance. This choice was the main dependent measure of the experiment. The drug choice intervened between work on soluble or insoluble problems and a promised retest on similar problems. In Experiment 1, all subjects received success feedback after their initial problem-solving attempts, thus creating one condition in which the success appeared to be accidental (noncontingent on performance) and one in which the success appeared to be contingent on appropriate knowledge. Males in the noncontingent-success condition were alone in preferring the performance-inhibiting drug, presumably because they wished to externalize probable failure on the retest. The predicted effect, however, did not hold for female subjects. Experiment 2 replicated the unique preference shown by males after noncontingent success and showed the critical importance of success feedback.

The present research is concerned with one kind of attempt to control the esteem implications of performance feedback by the choice of setting in which performance occurs. Specifically, we present two experiments designed to show an important set of conditions under which people will choose to take a drug *because* it is authoritatively alleged to interfere with performance. We cautiously suggest that such conditions commonly exist in socialization and may serve as an important precursor of the appeal of alcohol and other substances with performance-inhibiting reputations.

A ubiquitous assumption in psychology is that persons are generally eager to receive accurate information about the nature of their environment and reliable diagnostic feedback about their capacities to act on that environment. Such an assumption is the starting point for Festinger's (1954) theory of social comparison processes. It is also a widely accepted premise of attribution theory (Heider, 1958) that people are typically motivated to penetrate accurately the causal structure of the social world and to gain control through adequate understanding (cf. Kelley, 1971).

A separate tradition, anchored in the theory of achievement motivation, emphasizes individual differences in the tendency to seek unequivocal information regarding one's own competence. Atkinson (1957) proposed that individuals high in achievement motivation prefer tasks of moderate difficulty. Weiner et al. (1971) have argued that this tendency stems from the interest among high-need achievers in obtaining accurate feedback concerning their abilities. Trope (1975; Trope & Brickman, 1975) showed that it is indeed the diagnostic informational value of a task that makes it appealing to those high in achievement motivation. But it is also true that subjects high in fear of failure show a tendency to prefer either very simple or very difficult tasks, tasks typically low in diagnosticity. As early as 1961, McClelland noted that not everyone wants to have "concrete knowledge of results of their choices of actions" (p. 231).

The present experiments attempt to capitalize on this insight and to point to one set of antecedent conditions that promote the desire to avoid diagnostic information. The search for such conditions begins with the hunch that diagnostic information will be avoided when the chances are good that such information will indicate inferior competence. Ideally, performers should seek out those settings in which only success can be internally attributed—linked to the self-esteem of the performer. *Self-handicapping* strategies serve this goal. We define such strategies as any action or choice of performance setting that enhances the opportunity to externalize (or excuse) failure and to internalize (reasonably accept credit for) success. Self-handicapping exploits the performer's understanding of Kelley's (1971) augmentation principle.

This principle may be seen with the example of alcohol use. Alcohol may be viewed as an inhibitory cause of successful performance, whereas ability is a facilitative cause. The inference that ability is the most likely potential cause of a successful performance is augmented by the presence of alcohol. Regardless of what the performance outcome is, then, the self-handicapper cannot lose. Some other examples of self-handicapping are getting too little sleep or underpreparing before an examination, exaggerating the effects of illness or injury, or in general embracing impediments and plausible performance handicaps. (The concept of self-handicapping and its determinants is more fully discussed in Jones & Berglas, in press.)

Any use of self-handicapping that involves more than cognitive distortion presumably decreases the chances of success. Mettee (1971) has explored some of the conditions under which people deliberately choose failure over success, tying this choice primarily to the desire to avoid raising unfulfillable expectations for future performance. Marecek and Mettee (1972) have shown that those who are low in self-esteem and certain of it are especially prone to avoid success when it is most likely to be attributed to their ability. Our present reasoning is that self-handicapping strategists do not primarily set out to insure failure; they are willing to accept (probable) failure if it can be explained away *and* if (possible) success will have augmented value for self-esteem.

No doubt some persons are more prone to adopt self-handicapping strategies than are others. We propose that there is probably a modest correlation between such strategic preferences and the appeal of performance-affecting substances like drugs and alcohol. Our present interest, however, is in isolating, in the laboratory, at least one set of conditions that should promote self-handicapping, in this case the choice of performance-inhibiting drugs. The hope is that this will provide an analogue to comparable conditions in the prior socialization environment of the alcohol- or drug-prone adult.

We speculate that self-handicapping tendencies reflect a basic uncertainty concerning how competent one is. People who know they have the talent and resources to master life's challenges are not likely to hide behind the attributional shield of self-handicapping. Such persons have, presumably, learned the close relationship between their goal-directed actions and the desirable effects these actions are designed to bring about. They have also presumably learned that the better their information is about the tasks at hand, the better their control can be over effective performance.

At the other extreme are individuals who rarely enjoy success at anything and who have been forced to scale down their expectations about the effects of their actions. They are "klutzes," and they know it. They have learned to avoid chronic failure by tackling only the most attainable objectives and, perhaps, by aligning themselves with others more capable of control and mastery over the environment. But they do not succumb to the ready self-delusion implicit in self-handicapping because they are also dependent on an accurate reading of "task difficulty." They need to know on a given occasion whether there is any point in trying, and to find out they must monitor environmental demands and challenges with a certain detached realism.

We now propose that self-handicappers fall between these two extremes and that their strategic orientation stems from a capricious, chaotic reinforcement history. It is not that their histories are pocked with repeated failure; they have been amply rewarded, but in ways and on occasions that leave them deeply uncertain about what the reward was for. These individuals may feel, for example, that they have been rewarded for extraneous reasons such as beauty, some unrelated past success, or the ascribed status of simply being a family member. This description is reminiscent of Seligman's (1975) theory of helplessness and depression as conditions growing out of noncontingent-reward histories. Of particular present relevance is the "success depression" (pp. 98–99), in which rewards have been ample but uninformative regarding one's competence image.

To the extent that individuals have passed through a history of noncontingent reward, they may have a strong sense of being impostors or pretenders. They do not deserve their rewards because they did not really do anything to earn them. They were just lucky, they happened to be in the right place at the right time, the evaluation standards were lax—any of these subjective hypotheses are consistent with the underlying fear that (a) successful performance cannot be repeated or sustained and (b) impostors must eventually pay for their inequitable current receipts.

We suggest that the victims of noncontingent success are never clearly reconciled to the fact that their success is something arbitrarily bequeathed to them and out of their control. There is almost always sufficient ambiguity to feed the processes of self-deception and wishful thinking about competence. It is true that the anticipation of accurate future performance evaluation inhibits the more obvious kinds of autistic thinking. People are willing to settle for modest appraisals of their own competence in the face of upcoming further assessments (Eagly & Acksen, 1971; Jones, 1973; Wortman, Costanzo, & Witt, 1973). But strategies of self-handicapping can preserve the ambiguity of such further assessments. As long as people can avoid clearly diagnostic feedback settings, they may maintain the precarious illusion of control. They may, paradoxically, deliberately run the risk of being out of control—through drug abuse, or inadequate preparation, or not trying—to protect their belief in ultimately being capable of control when it is really necessary, when the chips are down. Among other things, this strategy fits in with the mañana fantasies so commonly observed in budding alcoholics and in the early stages of drug addiction. These fantasies involve thoughts about how successful they will be *when* they break the drinking habit or could be *if* they did.

One question remains before we turn to a description of experimental procedures. The notion of a strategy may suggest that self-handicapping is directed only to a public effect, that we are talking essentially about the self-presentational control of *others'* attributions concerning our basic, underlying competence. Although the possible effects on an audience, including an experimenter or test administrator, may augment the tendency to choose performance settings that obscure the drawing of correspondent inferences about competence (cf. Jones & Davis, 1965), we propose that the basic purpose behind such strategic choices is the control of the actor's *self*-attributions of competence and control. The choice of self-handicapping settings should occur, therefore, even if the susceptible person were being tested under conditions of total privacy.

Experiment 1 was designed to test the proposition linking self-handicapping strategies—in this case, the choice of a performance-inhibiting drug—to a recent history of noncontingent success. Noncontingent success refers specifically to an operation where success feedback follows a performer's attempt to offer solutions to insoluble problems. More conceptually, the performers do not see that the outcome is appropriate to their performance. They feel that they lack the knowledge or control that success feedback implies. This lack generates the anxious uncertainty that an effective performance cannot be repeated at will because the degree of control may have been misjudged or incorrectly indexed in the first place—that luck or measurement error may have been involved.

In addition, the experiment provided for an evaluation of whether such self-handicapping is exclusively a maneuver designed to influence the attributions of an audience or serves purely self-protective functions as well. To this end, subjects were recruited for an experiment allegedly designed to measure the effects of drugs on intellectual performance. Some subjects were exposed to insoluble problems and others to readily soluble problems before being given enthusiastic success feedback. Subjects were then allowed to choose between performance-facilitating and performance-inhibiting drugs whose effect would be active during a retest on comparable problems. In half of the cases, the experimenter administering the drugs was clearly unaware of the subject's prior intellectual performance; in the remaining cases, he was obviously aware. The main prediction was that noncontingent-success subjects, in both the private and public knowledge conditions, would choose the performance-inhibiting drug more than contingent-success subjects.

Experiment 1

Method

Subjects. Introductory psychology students (68 males and 43 females) volunteered for an experiment entitled "Drugs and Intellectual Performance" as part of a research participation requirement. Thus, there was initial selection of subjects willing to take drugs as part of a psychology experiment. After 15 subjects were excluded because of heavy drug usage, procedural errors, or suspicion, the finally analyzed sample consisted of 60 males and 36 females.

Procedure. Each subject was greeted at the lab by a male experimenter. After preliminary probing of drug-usage history and establishing that subjects were of majority age, the experimenter explained that the present experiment had been designed to determine if either of two (actually bogus) drugs used to treat metabolic disorders had an effect on intellectual performance. To make this determination, the subject was to take two parallel forms of a difficult intellectual performance test, separated by the ingestion of one of the two drugs. The purpose of this procedure was to compare the subject's initial test score, achieved while free from the influence of a drug, with the test score achieved while under its influence.

The subject was told that one of the two drugs being tested, Actavil, was expected to facilitate intellectual performance, whereas the other drug, Pandocrin, was expected to inhibit or disrupt intellectual performance. The experimenter added that the predicted performance effects were not certain to occur, and thus the present experiment was necessary in order to gather more reliable data.

The experimenter then described the nature of the intellectual performance test. Subjects were told that they would be taking two 20-question tests, each of which contained a randomly selected group of analogies and progressions borrowed from two nationally used aptitude tests. It was further explained that the tests were "designed to discriminate the uppermost levels of intellectual potential." Subjects were told to expect scores no higher than "between the 60th and 70th percentiles" and then shown two relatively easy examples of the questions that would follow. After each subject solved the sample questions, the experimenter called his testing assistant (a female) to the room. After introductions, the experimenter left the room.

Contingency manipulation. The testing assistant administered a 20-question test of analogies and progressions, and their difficulty level plus the subsequently announced success defined the contingency manipulation. In the noncontingent conditions, the problems were largely insoluble; in the contingent conditions, they were largely soluble. All subjects then received success feedback.

In administering the test, the testing assistant handed the subjects individual multiple-choice questions printed on index cards. Subjects were told to respond orally to each item within 15 seconds. Furthermore, their answer on each trial was to be accompanied by a subjective probability estimate of its accuracy, expressed in terms of a percentage between 0 and 100.

The testing assistant randomly assigned subjects to either contingent- or noncontingent-success conditions. Subjects in the noncontingent conditions were given 16 insoluble questions and 4 questions that were easily solved. In spite of this, noncontingent-success subjects were given feedback to the effect that they had successfully solved 16 out of 20 problems. The contingent-success outcome was achieved by tailoring the problems given to subjects in such a way as to tax them but nevertheless insure that they would perform quite well. This was accomplished by having the assistant sift through a variety of (presealed) question-difficulty levels so that if a subject began to solve too many problems, the assistant moved to a more difficult level, and if the subject began to have difficulty with the questions, an easier question was selected for the following trial. The actual number of problems solved in the contingent-success condition ranged from 9 to 16, but the vast majority of the scores were between 12 and 14 correct. Subjects in the contingent-success conditions were always provided with their actual scores following the test. Regardless of what condition subjects were in, upon completion of the test they were congratulated by the testing assistant and told that they had done exceptionally well: "Yours was one of the best scores seen to date!"

It may be noted that the subjective probability estimates were included to strengthen the manipulation of feedback contingency. During pretesting it became apparent that it was quite difficult to establish a noncontingent-success condition. Subjects proved to be very facile in explaining to themselves and to the testing assistant how they managed to get a correct answer on an insoluble problem. Thus, the confidence ratings were introduced to anchor the noncontingent-success subject's realization that he did not have good control over the test. It was predicted that the subjective probability ratings would be quite low in the noncontingent conditions, making it difficult for those subjects to conclude later that they really understood the contingency between their responses and the success feedback.

Publicity manipulation. When the testing session was completed, the experimenter was signaled to return and either was or was not told about the subject's performance. In the public feedback condition, the experimenter asked how the subject had done, and when he was told by the assistant that the subject attained one of the highest scores recorded, he expressed his congratulations. In the private feedback conditions, the experimenter specifically admonished subjects not to say anything about their performance so that he could remain blind in order to maintain experimental control. Subjects in this condition were given a "subject record sheet" with a subject number to protect their anonymity and told that their data would be turned in to a secretary who would code their responses for computer analysis. Following this manipulation, the testing assistant left the room.

At this point, both independent treatments had been established. It is important to note that the experimenter was kept blind as to which contingency condition the subject was in. Furthermore, the testing assistant was kept blind as to the publicity treatment until the end of the testing session.

The experimenter then prepared the subject for the drug ingestion part of the experiment. However, prior to this procedure, the experimenter informed the subject of a modification in scoring the post-drug-ingestion intellectual performance test. After providing an appropriate rationale for the change in procedures on the posttest, the experimenter informed subjects that an incorrect response to a question would be penalized, that is, subtracted from the total score, whereas simply choosing to "pass" on an item would produce neither a credit nor a debit. This penalty for guessing, which increased the likelihood of a lower score on the posttest, should have exacerbated the concern of subjects in the noncontingent condition with "being discovered."

Following a brief "medical" examination consisting of a pulse count, blood pressure measurement, and pupillary dilation check—intended to entrench more firmly the cover story—the experimenter provided subjects with "all necessary and pertinent" information about the two drugs. This information was intended to make salient the probable consequences for future performance of taking each drug. Subjects were first presented with a pair of line graphs depicting some pilot data collected on the effects of Actavil and Pandocrin. The graphs clearly illustrated that for the most part, subjects who had taken Actavil showed improvement in their intellectual performance between the first and second tests, whereas those subjects who had taken Pandocrin tended to have poorer performances on their postdrug test. However, subjects were cautioned that these pilot data were not conclusive, since an insufficient number of cases were considered and because there were several reversals in the two trends.

Subjects were next given a "preliminary" PDR (*Physicians' Desk Reference*) report for both Pandocrin and Actavil. These (actually bogus) reports provided information about the chemistry and benign side effects of each drug and the critical information about each drug's influence on intellectual performance. One report noted that Actavil should facilitate intellectual performance through "stimulation of associative processes and a general heightening of cognitive acuity." The report for Pandocrin indicated that this drug should disrupt intellectual performance as a result of decrements in "cognitive association, . . . attention, and powers of concentration," as well as "information retrieval processes." Following the presentation of the two PDR reports, the experimenter repeated his assurances that no previous subject had experienced any unpleasant side effects from either drug and that although there would probably be performance effects, they would most probably occur without the subject's awareness. Furthermore, subjects were assured that if the drugs did in fact affect their performance, this effect would be transitory.

Dependent measures. The major dependent measure in this study was the drug and dosage level selected by the subject. Following the presentation of the PDR reports, subjects were shown a lucite tray on which drugs and dosages were arrayed as if in a scale, from the maximum 10-mg dosage of Actavil on the left to the maximum 10-mg dosage of Pandocrin on the right. Intermediate dosages of 2.5, 5, and 7.5 mg of each drug were clearly marked along the tray, as well as a blank space in the center of the tray labeled "Control."

Subjects were instructed to choose which drug and which dosage level they wished to take. Though they had the option of taking neither drug ("since control subjects were needed"), some pressure was exerted to take one of the larger dosages of either Actavil or Pandocrin. However, the experimenter clearly stated, "I don't want you to take either drug at any particular dosage level to please me. . . . Select either drug or no drug at all according to your own personal preference, according to what you will find most interesting."

After indicating which drug and dosage level they would be taking, subjects were asked to complete a series of manipulation checks disguised as a "Mid-point Questionnaire." In addition to standard questions probing for suspicion or an awareness of the hypothesis being tested, subjects were asked to indicate how they felt the chosen drug would affect both the average individual's and their own intellectual performance. In addition, subjects were asked to indicate how difficult they felt the intellectual performance test was and to indicate the extent to which luck versus ability accounted for their test scores. The experiment was then terminated, and the subject was completely debriefed.

Results

Validation of manipulations. Because of the differences in problem solubility that constituted the contingency manipulation, subjects in the noncontingent-success condition should have registered lower confidence scores after each problem solution than contingent-success subjects. Each subject's confidence scores were totaled. The contingent-success subjects ($M = 64.40$) indeed expressed greater confidence in the accuracy of each problem solution than the noncontingent-success subjects ($M = 45.32$); $F(1, 88) = 102.72$, $p < .001$. As Table 7.1 shows, both males and females also saw the test version used in the noncontingent condition as greater in difficulty, $F(1, 88) = 12.89$, $p < .001$. This is especially true in the private condition, as reflected in a significant Contingency × Publicity interaction, $F(1, 88) = 6.31$, $p < .01$.

Of somewhat greater theoretical interest, subjects in the contingent-success condition attributed their intellectual performance more to ability (versus luck) than noncontingent-success subjects, $F(1, 88) = 34.43$, $p < .001$. It seems abundantly clear that the contingency manipulation was successful in the expected direction and that subjects who were "successful" on problems that actually had no correct solution acknowledged a certain amount of luck, their overall mean being slightly on the "luck-only" side of the mid-point.

The *public–private variable* entered into two significant effects for the male subjects. When rating the difficulty level of the test, male subjects in the public conditions did not distinguish between the soluble and insoluble items. Those in the private condition, however, distinguished sharply between them, a difference between differences that is reflected in the highly significant interaction effect, $F(1, 56) = 15.83$, $p < .001$, involving contingency and publicity (see Table 7.1). Subjects in the public condition may have let their ratings be slightly affected by self-presentational concerns. Since the experimenter collecting the questionnaires knew they had done well, it was important for subjects not to claim that the problems were very easy (which puts down the other subjects who did not do as well and which may seem to contradict the congratulating experimenter) or very difficult (which suggests boastfulness).

In addition, public subjects attributed their successful performance to ability more than private subjects did, $F(1, 88) = 5.97$, $p < .05$. Although this effect is small compared to the contingency effect, we may speculate that public subjects hesitated to claim too much luck in front of an experimenter who knew that they did very well, since this would tend to impugn the reliability of the test.

These speculations are only that, however, and though we can point to significant statistical effects to support the claim that the public–private manipulation had an impact, it is difficult to articulate the precise nature of that impact. All we should argue, perhaps, is that the link of knowledge between the two experimenters was less salient in the private than in the public conditions, and this differential saliency had a detectable effect on subjects' experiential reports.

As for our success in conveying potential drug effects, the information was clearly accepted. Subjects responded that most people do better after Actavil and worse after Pandocrin, $t(93) = 30.96$, $p < .001$, and their expectancies concerning their own intellectual performance were also significantly affected by the anticipated drug choice, $t(93) = 13.54$, $p < .001$. Since subjects were told that the pretest data were not firm or highly reliable (thus the present study) and that a few previous subjects had done better under Pandocrin and worse under Actavil, it is quite appropriate that their own expectations were less affected by the choice of drug than their general expectations about "most people."

Drug choice. The last three columns of Table 7.1 indicate the effects of the cross-cutting conditions (and sex of subject) on drug choice. The overall effect of performance contingency on drug choice using the scale value measure is highly significant, $F(1, 88) = 18.28$, $p < .001$, but it is clear from the Contingency × Sex interaction, $F(1, 88)$

TABLE 7.1. Experiment 1: Mean Difficulty Estimates, Ability Attributions, and Drug Choice

	Difficulty[a]			Ability[b]			Drug choice[c]					
							Male ($n = 60$)		Female ($n = 36$)		Total ($n = 96$)	
Condition	Male ($n = 60$)	Female ($n = 36$)	Total ($n = 96$)	Male ($n = 60$)	Female ($n = 36$)	Total ($n = 96$)	Scale value	% Pandocrin	Scale value	% Pandocrin	Scale value	% Pandocrin
Contingent success												
Private	9.13	9.60	9.32	10.87	9.80	10.44	2.2	13	5.0	40	3.5	24
Public	10.87	9.44	10.33	11.27	10.33	10.92	2.3	13	2.8	11	2.5	13
Noncontingent success												
Private	12.73	12.00	12.50	7.20	6.29	6.91	6.1	73	4.4	29[d]	5.5	59[d]
Public	10.67	10.70	10.68	9.53	7.80	8.84	6.3	67	5.4	50	5.9	60

[a] Question 5: How difficult did you feel the intellectual performance test was? (1 = extremely easy; 15 = extremely difficult).
[b] Question 6: To what factors do you attribute your intellectual performance score? (1 = luck only; 8 = ability and luck; 15 = ability only).
[c] Scale values run from 1, the highest dosage of Actavil, to 9, the highest dosage of Pandocrin. % Pandocrin indicates the percentage of subjects choosing Pandocrin in that condition.
[d] One subject in this condition chose "no drug."

$= 6.51$, $p < .05$, and the separate analyses for male and female, that the effect is attributable largely to the male subjects, $F(1, 56) = 33.93$, $p < .001$. Overall, 70% of the males following a noncontingent-success experience chose Pandocrin; only 13% of those males whose success was contingent on performance chose Pandocrin. For females, the percentages were, respectively, 40% and 26%.

In line with prediction, the publicity of the subject's success was not a significant factor in this drug choice. With the more robust male sample, the public and private conditions produced almost identical drug-choice distributions. With the female sample, there is the hint of an interaction between contingency and publicity, $F(1, 32) = 2.66$, the females tending to follow the drug-choice predictions only in the public conditions.

As for the possible bases of this sex difference, there is some evidence that the entire experimental situation had less impact on the females than on the males. As Table 7.1 shows, females were less inclined than males to attribute their performance to ability, $F(1, 88) = 5.67$, $p < .05$. Since their attributions to luck were thus more generous, the need for strategic handicapping through Pandocrin choice may have been reduced.

In the confidence data, there was a significant interaction between contingency and sex, $F(1,88) = 5.05$, $p < .05$. The males were more confident than the females in the contingent conditions and less confident than the females in the noncontingent condition. In this respect, then, the contingency manipulation had more impact on the males' crucial subjective feelings of control than on the females' feelings. Also, in the private conditions, male subjects thought the contingent problems were easier and the noncontingent problems harder than the female subjects did. This feeling contributes to the highly significant interaction between contingency and publicity for males on ratings of task difficulty; this interaction does not approach significance for females.

Discussion

The male data are clearly consistent with the underlying assumption of attributional control as well as the more particular derivation concerning drug choice. However, the data by no means compel agreement concerning the processes involved. There are two sources of evidence regarding such processes: (a) the subjects' own verbalized accounts of the reasons behind their choice and (b) evidence inherent in the comparisons provided by the research design itself.

Turning first to the self-report data collected just prior to debriefing, only 2 out of 30 noncontingent-success Pandocrin takers explained their choice in defensive terms. The remaining Pandocrin choosers either claimed that the choice was completely arbitrary or that they were helping to make the experiment "work" because, having scored 16 out of 20 on the first test, they had more room for downward than upward movement. Thus, the effects of the drug could be easier to see with

Pandocrin than with Actavil. The self-report data, then, are of little help in confirming the theoretical reasoning about self-handicapping.

The design of the present experiment was limited to the crucial contingency variable and an attempt to manipulate whether the knowledge about performance was shared by the two experimenters. For males, at least, the public-private variation had no effect on drug choice, though it did have effects on attributions to ability and problem difficulty. This result is intriguing because it suggests that under the proper circumstances, people will choose to avoid diagnostic information about themselves that cannot be discounted, even when only they will know the significance of the information. To stretch rather widely for an analogy in the natural environment, the concept of self-handicapping helps to explain the solitary as well as the social drinker.

Although the design yields information concerning the self-knowledge implications of self-handicapping, it is not sufficiently complex or differentiated to rule out some of the available alternatives. Several alternative explanations question the importance of success on the first test items. Is it the fact that subjects succeeded on the insoluble items that is important or just that they knew the items were, and would be, very difficult?

It is possible that emotional factors took precedence over the attributional implications of success and failure in the choice of Pandocrin. Perhaps subjects became so frustrated with trying to solve the insoluble problems that they wanted to take the Pandocrin in order to "drop out" of the situation psychologically. The only evidence we have that frustration reduction was not the key factor in taking Pandocrin comes from noncontingent-success pretest subjects prior to the institution of the confidence ratings and restructured scoring of the second task. These subjects took Actavil almost without exception, and yet they had been exposed to the same insoluble problems. Also, one might imagine that the success feedback would go a long way toward removing the emotional residue of struggling with insoluble problems. Nevertheless, the frustration-reduction hypothesis remains a possibility that cannot entirely be dismissed.

Especially if we take seriously the Pandocrin subjects' own comments, another possibility looms as an alternative explanation of the findings. A few Pandocrin choosers in the noncontingent conditions clearly stated that they took Pandocrin to help the experimenter. Since they scored so high that there was not much room to improve with Actavil, the best way to test for drug effectiveness (and therefore make it a useful experiment) was to take Pandocrin. It will be recalled that on the average, contingent-success subjects did not score as high as the alleged score of 16 out of 20 in the noncontingent-success conditions. Their average score was 12.5. There are two bits of evidence arguing against this plausible alternative. First, contingent-success Pandocrin takers were as likely as noncontingent-success Pandocrin takers to mention helping the experimenter. Second, within the combined contingent-success conditions, the correlation between actual test score and drug preference score was $-.381$ ($n = 50, p < .01$). In other words, within the limited range of actual scores, the better the contingent-success subject did, the *less* likely he or she was to choose Pandocrin. This is precisely the opposite from what would be predicted if the "help-the-experimenter" alternative were of importance in the present results.

Nevertheless, because of these interpretive loose ends, a second experiment was planned with three purposes in mind. First, and most important, the role of problem solubility was examined by varying whether success feedback was provided. Second, when feedback was given, both contingent- and noncontingent-success subjects received the identical feedback count—16 out of 20 correct. This means that feedback in the contingent-success condition was only approximately accurate. Finally, we wished to see if the sex differences observed in Experiment 1 would be replicated. Thus, the design of Experiment 2 varied sex of subject, whether the problems were soluble, and whether subjects received feedback (which was always "success").

Experiment 2

Method

A total of 87 subjects were assigned to the eight-condition design. Assignment was random except that approximately twice as many subjects were assigned to each of the two critical conditions: male, insoluble problems, success feedback, and male, insoluble problems, no feedback. An additional 9 volunteers were dismissed prior to drug choice. Five subjects were dismissed at the outset of the experiment for medical reasons or strong suspicion. The remaining 4 subjects were dismissed when it was clear that they did not accept the experimenter's final drug-choice spiel.

The procedural details were precisely the same in Experiment 2 as in the public conditions of Experiment 1 except that (a) conditions were added so that exposure to either soluble or insoluble problems was not followed by feedback of any kind, (b) subjects in the success feedback conditions were told that they had solved 16 out of 20 problems and that this was exceptionally good, and (c) the experimenter neither asked about the subjects' performance nor stressed the importance of his not knowing about it.

The same two experimenters played the same two roles, and the subjects were recruited from a comparable subject pool approximately 1 year after those participating in Experiment 1. Again, the testing assistant was blind until the last moment to the feedback condition, and the drug administrator was blind to problem solubility.

Results

Validation of manipulations. Again, subjects in the soluble-problems conditions were on the average more confident in their solutions ($M = 65.52$) than subjects exposed to insoluble problems ($M = 57.08$); $F(1, 79) = 46.20, p < .001$. No other effects approached significance on this measure.

Also, as expected, the insoluble problems were seen as more difficult than the soluble ones, $F(1, 79) = 26.60, p < .001$. There were, however, main effects of sex and feedback on this measure. Males rated the task as more difficult than females, $F(1, 79) = 5.23, p < .05$, and success-feedback subjects rated the task as less difficult than subjects receiving no feedback, $F(1, 79) = 4.34, p < .05$. The condition means for this measure are provided in Table 7.2. Not surprisingly, it is especially clear that task difficulty is rated highest when the subject is exposed to insoluble problems without subsequent feedback.

Subjects who worked on the soluble problems were more likely than those who worked with insoluble problems to attribute their performance to ability, $F(1, 79) = 10.03, p < .01$. In Experiment 1, males were significantly more likely than females to attribute their performance to ability. The same tendency held in Experiment 2, though the difference was not quite significant, $F(1, 79) = 3.85$, $p < .10$. In any event, the results on the confidence, difficulty, and ability indices all strongly validate the manipulation of problem solubility or difficulty, and the major results to follow also make clear that subjects were very cognizant of the feedback in assessing their performance.

As in Experiment 1, subjects clearly comprehended that most people do better after Actavil and most people do worse after Pandocrin,

TABLE 7.2. Experiment 2: Mean Difficulty Estimates, Ability Attributions, and Drug Choice

	Difficulty[a]			Ability[b]			Drug choice[c]					
							Male ($n = 53$)		Female ($n = 34$)		Total ($n = 87$)	
Condition	Male ($n = 53$)	Female ($n = 34$)	Total ($n = 87$)	Male ($n = 53$)	Female ($n = 34$)	Total ($n = 87$)	Scale value	% Pandocrin	Scale value	% Pandocrin	Scale value	% Pandocrin
Soluble problem												
Success	10.10	8.78	9.44	10.67	10.44	10.56	2.11	11	3.56	22	2.84	17
No feedback	10.13	9.22	9.68	9.75	9.00	9.38	3.13	25	2.78	11[d]	2.96	18
Insoluble problem												
Success	11.67	10.25	10.96	9.56	8.00	8.78	5.72	61	3.38	25	4.55	50
No feedback	12.56	12.38	12.47	8.78	7.75	8.27	2.50	11	4.75	25[e]	3.63	15

[a] Question 5: How difficult did you feel the intellectual performance test was? (1 = extremely easy; 15 = extremely difficult).
[b] Question 6: To what factors do you attribute your intellectual performance score? (1 = luck only; 8 = ability and luck; 15 = ability only).
[c] Scale values run from 1, the highest dosage of Actavil, to 9, the highest dosage of Pandocrin. % Pandocrin indicates the percentage of subjects choosing Pandocrin in that condition.
[d] One subject in this condition chose "no drug."
[e] Three subjects in this condition chose "no drug."

$t(85) = 25.91, p < .001$. Also, once again subjects thought their own performance would be somewhat less affected by the drug taken, but it still would be clearly affected, $t(85) = 14.20, p < .001$.

Drug choice. Experiment 2 was designed to answer three basic questions: (a) Do the sex differences replicate? (b) Is success feedback important? And (c) could the results of Experiment 1 have been affected by differential information concerning the number of problems solved? The prediction was that subjects would prefer the performance-inhibiting drug only in the condition in which the problems were insoluble and they had received success feedback. The last three columns of Table 7.2 show that this prediction was clearly confirmed, and again this result was true for males only. An unweighted-means analysis of variance produces a significant triple order interaction, $F(1, 79) = 6.80, p < .05$, indicating that solubility, feedback, and sex all play a role as determinants of drug choice. Examination of the means makes clear that this interaction reflects the uniqueness of the male noncontingent-success condition. Though the mean scale score of the female insoluble-problem-no-feedback condition appears close to the mean of this crucial cell, 3 out of 8 subjects in this condition chose not to take either drug. Thus, the percentages choosing Pandocrin in two conditions are substantially different.

Since the design was intended to emphasize the comparison of the success versus no-feedback, insoluble-problems conditions for males, and twice the number of subjects were assigned to these conditions, the unweighted-means analysis is highly conservative in this case. A direct comparison between the two crucial conditions shows a much higher level of Pandocrin choice when male subjects have received success feedback after working on insoluble problems than after no feedback, $t(51) = 4.63, p < .001$. There is no hint of this difference among female subjects.

Basis of sex differences. In the report of Experiment 1, we cited evidence that the experimental situation had less impact on the female than on the male subjects. In both experiments, females were less inclined than males to attribute their performance to ability, though the tendency only approached significance ($p < .10$) in the present case. We earlier noted that greater attribution to luck in the crucial noncontingent-success cell may have reduced the need for self-handicapping through Pandocrin choice.

Differences on the confidence ratings did not replicate. In Experiment 1, males were significantly more confident than females in the contingent-success condition and less confident than females in noncontingent-success condition. There was a nonsignificant trend for males in Experiment 2 to be more confident in both success feedback conditions.

General Discussion

The basic assumption underlying the present experiments is that people arrange their environments to influence the dispositions that can be attributed to them—by themselves as well as by others. In the particular case of the present experiments, people are shown to select the available environment best designed to protect their image of self-competence in the event of poor performance. Male subjects choose a performance-inhibiting drug in a condition in which they have just experienced a success apparently based substantially on luck. In this way, their claim on this success cannot be rudely challenged by a subsequent failure. At least their choice has provided them with a ready external attribution for any downward change in performance.

The results of Experiment 1 permitted a plausible alternative explanation: It could have been the insolubility of the problems rather than the noncontingency of the success that prompted the choice of a performance-inhibiting drug. The results of Experiment 2, however, clearly rule out this alternative. When an insoluble-problems—no-feedback condition is compared to an insoluble-problems condition with success feedback, there is no tendency for subjects in the former condition to prefer the performance-inhibiting drug. The contribution of success feedback, so important for the theoretical argument, is emphasized by this final set of results.

Sex differences. Quite surprisingly, in view of the reliability of these results among male subjects, the female subjects do not show the predicted response to noncontingent success in either experiment. Even the directional trend in Experiment 1, under public feedback conditions, did not replicate in Experiment 2, where the experimenter did not mention the importance of his not knowing the test results. It is conceivable that the experimenter's public congratulations stimulated self-handicapping among the female subjects in Experiment 1.

There is some evidence in both experiments that the female subjects attributed their performance to luck more than the male subjects did. This tendency has been noted in numerous other studies comparing the attributions of male and female subjects after success feedback (e.g., Deaux & Farris, 1977; cf. Frieze, Fisher, Hanusa, McHugh, & Valle, in press). It might be that females chose this attributional option (luck) to blunt the impact of experimental conditions. Females may have seen less reason to protect a success readily acknowledged to be based on luck. One might wonder whether those females who did attribute their success to ability tended to choose Pandocrin in the noncontingent-success or insoluble-problem condition. There is strong support for the relation between ability attribution and Pandocrin choice in only one condition: the female public condition of Experiment 1. Here the correlation ($r = .76$, $n = 10$) shows that those females who attributed to ability also tended to choose Pandocrin. However, females in the private condition of Experiment 1 and in Experiment 2, which was essentially public, showed no such relationship. It is difficult to know what conclusion to draw about the females, given the discrepancy between experiments and the public-private conditions of Experiment 1. Our general caution concerning the meaning of the female results is further increased by the realization that the results might have been different with a female experimenter.

Although any conclusions must be restricted to male subjects at this point, the present results make more tenable the proposition that alcohol and certain forms of drug usage may be facilitated by prior experiences of success unaccompanied by subjective feelings of mastery and control. Such experiences promote strategies designed to protect "ill-gotten" performance gains and a fragile but positive competence image.

NOTE

This research was supported by National Science Foundation Grant G1114X and by Grant 1 F32 AA05072-01 from the Alcohol, Drug Abuse, and Mental Health Administration. We are very indebted to Karen Hardin Fedor for her skillful performance in the role of testing assistant in both experiments and for her aid in the overall conduct of the study.

REFERENCES

Atkinson, J. W. (1957). Motivational determinants of risk-taking behavior. *Psychological Review, 64,* 359–372.

Deaux, K., & Farris, E.) (1977). Attributing causes of one's own performance: The effects of sex, norms, and outcome. *Journal of Research in Personality, 11,* 59–72.

Eagly, A. H., & Acksen, B. A. (1971). The effect of expectancy to be evaluated on change toward favorable and unfavorable information about oneself. *Sociometry, 34,* 411–422.

Festinger, L. A. (1954). Theory of social comparison processes. *Human Relations, 7,* 117–140.

Frieze, I. H., Fisher, J., Hanusa, B., McHugh, M. C., & Valle, V. A. (in press) Attributions of the causes of success and failure as internal and external barriers to achievement in women. In J. Sherman & F. Denmark (Eds.), *Psychology of women: Future dimensions of research.* Psychological Dimensions.

Heider, F. (1958). *The psychology of interpersonal relations.* New York: Wiley.

Jones, E. E., & Berglas, S. (in press). Control of attributions about the self through self-handicapping strategies: The appeal of alcohol and the role of under-achievement. *Personality and Social Psychology Bulletin.*

Jones, E. E., & Davis, K. E. (1965). From acts to dispositions: The attribution process in person perception. In L. Berkowitz (Ed.), *Advances in experimental social psychology* (Vol. 2, pp. 219–266). New York: Academic Press.

Jones, S. C. (1973). Self and interpersonal evaluations: Esteem theory versus consistency theories. *Psychological Bulletin, 79,* 185–199.

Kelley, H. H. (1971). *Attribution in social interaction.* Morristown, NJ: General Learning Press.

Marecek, J., & Mettee, D. R. (1972). Avoidance of continued success as a function of self-esteem, level of esteem certainty, and responsibility for success. *Journal of Personality and Social Psychology, 22,* 98–107.

McClelland, D. C. (1961). *The achieving society.* Princeton, NJ: Van Nostrand.

Mettee, D. R. (1971). Rejection of unexpected success as a function of the negative consequences of accepting success. *Journal of Personality and Social Psychology, 17,* 332–341.

Seligman, M. P. (1975). *Helplessness.* San Francisco: Freeman.

Trope, Y. (1975). Seeking information about one's own ability as a determinant of choice among tasks. *Journal of Personality and Social Psychology, 32,* 1004–1013.

Trope, Y., & Brickman, P. (1975). Difficulty and diagnosticity as determinants of choice among tasks. *Journal of Personality and Social Psychology, 31,* 918–925.

Weiner, B., Frieze, I., Kukla, A., Reed, L., Rest, S., & Rosenbaum, R. (1971). *Perceiving the causes of success and failure.* Morristown, NJ: General Learning Press.

Wortman, C. B., Costanzo, P. R., & Witt, T. R. (1973). Effect of anticipated performance on the attributions of causality to self and others. *Journal of Personality and Social Psychology, 27,* 372–381.

Discussion Questions

1. Do you think that some people are more likely to self-handicap than others? If so, what personality characteristics might characterize people who are prone to self-handicap?
2. Berglas and Jones found that the results of their study applied to males but not to females (and later research confirmed this pattern). They suggested that females had a greater tendency than males to attribute their success to luck. Would you expect a similar pattern of results to be obtained today or has society changed the attributions that females are likely to make for their performance?
3. The use of self-handicapping can be reinforcing because it helps people avoid the self-relevant implications of failure. If you were a clinical or counseling psychologist, what techniques would you use to discourage a client from self-handicapping?
4. How might you use the construct of self-handicapping to explain other maladaptive behavior patterns, such as underachievement, alcohol abuse, overeating, and drug abuse?

Suggested Readings

Berglas, D., & Baumeister, R. (1993). *Your own worst enemy: Understanding the paradox of self-defeating behavior.* New York: Basic Books. This book examines the types of self-defeating behavior, including self-handicapping.

Leary, M. R., & Shepperd, J. A. (1986). Behavioral self-handicaps versus self-reported handicaps: A conceptual note. *Journal of Personality and Social Psychology, 51,* 1265–1268. This article suggests an important distinction between true self-defeating behavior (behavioral self-handicaps) and mere reports of factors that may adversely affect performance (self-reported handicaps).

Rhodewalt, F., Saltzman, A. T., & Wittmer, J. (1984). Self-handicapping among competitive athletes: The role of practice in self-esteem protection. *Basic and Applied Social Psychology, 5,* 197–209. This article reports the results of a study on self-handicapping among competitive swimmers and golfers.

Snyder, C. R., Smith, T. W., Augelli, R. W., & Ingram, R. E. (1985). On the self-serving function of social anxiety: Shyness as a self-handicapping strategy. *Journal of Personality and Social Psychology, 48,* 970–980. This study found that male participants who were socially anxious reported more symptoms of social anxiety when those symptoms could be used as an excuse for unfavorable performance evaluations.

READING 8

Social Contagion of Binge Eating

Christian S. Crandall • Yale University

Editors' Introduction

Although the causes of binge eating are not fully understood, three theories have been proposed. The sociocultural approach suggests that social norms lead many women to pursue unattainable standards of thinness. However, this explanation is not complete because all women are exposed to societal norms, yet only a small percentage develop eating disorders or become binge eaters. The clinical approach tries to explain bulimia in light of existing clinical diagnoses, such as depression. The idea is that women who are experiencing psychological problems are at risk for bulimia, but again psychological problems are not always accompanied by bulimia. The epidemiological approach focuses on factors that predict bulimia, such as body image, stress, and genetics. The result of this approach has been a large compendium of variables that show some relationship to bulimia, but with no overarching structure or process explaining why these variables might actually lead to disordered eating. Thus, although informative, none of the three existing approaches completely explains binge eating.

According to Christian Crandall, what is needed is a theory that includes social processes, particularly those involving social influence. Specifically, he argues that social pressures within social groups, particularly groups of women, are central to the acquisition and spread of binge eating. Much research shows that people conform to the attitudes and behaviors that are central to their groups, so perhaps some binge eating occurs when women conform to groups that support binging.

To examine the social contagion of binge eating, Crandall conducted two studies of women who were members of college sororities. Participants completed a questionnaire examining personal risk factors for eating disorders (e.g., self-esteem, height, weight, and psychological health), binge eating behavior patterns, and social networks. The measure of social networks was used to assess each woman's popularity and the degree to which social norms toward binge eating were present in her social groups.

The results of the study documented a social norm for binge eating. In one of the two sororities studied, women who deviated from the normative level of binge eating in either direction were perceived to be less popular. In the second sorority, however, the more an individual binged, the more popular she was. Participants' levels of binge eating were also correlated with the binging levels of their friends, which suggested that social influence processes were responsible for the similarity.

The benefits of this study are twofold. First, the social influence model of binge eating provides an overarching theoretical framework that encompasses the three theories that had previously been used to explain bulimia. Second, the study provides evidence for the role of social factors in the onset and maintenance of binge eating.

Abstract

A social psychological account of the acquisition of binge eating, analogous to the classic social psychological work, *Social Pressures in Informal Groups* (Festinger, Schachter, & Back, 1950), is suggested and tested in two college sororities. In these sororities, clear evidence of group norms about appropriate binge-eating behavior was found; in one sorority, the more one binged, the more popular one was. In the other, popularity was associated with binging the right amount: Those who binged too much or too little were less popular than those who binged at the mean. Evidence of social pressures to binge eat were found as well. By the end of the academic year, a sorority member's binge eating could be predicted from the binge-eating level of her friends (average $r = .31$). As friendship groups grew more cohesive, a sorority member's binge eating grew more and more like that of her friends (average $r = .35$). The parsimony of a social psychological account of the acquisition of binge eating behavior is shown. I argue that there is no great mystery to how bulimia has become such a serious problem for today's women. Binge eating seems to be an acquired pattern of behavior, perhaps through modeling, and appears to be learned much like any other set of behaviors. Like other behaviors, it is under substantial social control.

Bulimia is rapidly becoming *the* women's psychological disease of our time, rivaling depression in its prevalence. It is receiving a great deal of attention in both the scientific community (Gandour, 1984; Schlesier-Stropp, 1984; Striegel-Moore, Silberstein, & Rodin, 1986) and the popular press (Boskind-Lodahl & Sirlin, 1977). Bulimia is an eating pattern characterized by periodic episodes of uncontrolled binge eating alternating with periods of fasting, strict dieting, or purging via vomiting, diuretics, or laxatives. The uncontrolled eating is usually accompanied by negative affect, a sense of loss of control, and guilt. Nearly all of those affected are women (Gandour, 1984).

The evidence is that bulimia is indeed quite prevalent; estimates suggest 4–15% of college women have serious problems with bulimia (Halmi, Falk, & Schwartz, 1981; Sinoway, Raupp, & Newman, 1985; Strangler & Printz, 1980). In contrast, there is little evidence to suggest that bulimia afflicated any more than a handful of people prior to the late 1960s and early 1970s (Rosenzweig & Spruill, 1986).

The sudden and dramatic appearance of bulimia as a set of clinical symptoms has prompted a great deal of psychological and psychiatric theorizing about the roots of the syndrome. Surprisingly little is known about the causes of bulimia. Bulimics seem to be virtually indistinguishable from non-bulimic controls on a surprising number of variables, such as height, weight (Gandour, 1984), sex role orientation (Srikameswaran, Leichner, & Harper, 1984), and even ego involvement with food and eating (Crandall, 1987). There have been three general classes of explanations put forward: a sociohistorical/cultural approach, a clinical/psychiatric approach, and an epidemiological/risk factors approach.

Sociocultural Approach

Sociocultural theorists argue that changing norms in our society, especially those toward thinness for women, have created a cult of dieting (Dwyer, Feldman, & Mayer, 1970; Orbach, 1978). For example, Garner, Garfinkel, Schwartz, and Thompson (1980) have shown that body sizes of the winners of the Miss America Pageant and the *Playboy* centerfolds have been steadily decreasing over the past 20 years. Apparently, now more than ever, thin is in.

Women have internalized the message that they should care a great deal about how they look and at the same time internalize a thinness norm that is virtually unattainable for most of them (Rodin, Silberstein, & Striegel-Moore, 1984). Initial and subsequent attempts to reach this social rather than biological norm (i.e., dieting) are disruptive to the body's natural balance (Nisbett, 1972), making weight reduction extremely difficult (Bennett & Gurin, 1982; Garrow, 1978). At the same time, because there is a heavy psychological investment in dieting, the success or failure of behaviors related to weight loss attempts are very self-relevant, and strongly affectively tinged.

There is undoubtedly a sociocultural component to bulimia, because severe binge eating accompanied by an emotional roller coaster among women is a new problem, but social history certainly does not contain a complete account of the phenomenon. Thinness norms have come and gone in the past few centuries, and social roles have gone through dramatic changes as well, both apparently without concomitant increases in bulimia. During the Roaring Twenties, for example, although the flappers were as thin as plastic drinking straws, there is no indication that bulimia was a problem then (Bennett & Gurin, 1982). (The exact data to establish this are very difficult to collect; see Rosenzweig & Spruill, 1986, for one attempt.)

More important, however, is that these social pressures operate on all women in the middle-class subculture. Thus, the most difficult problem for the sociocultural perspective is that it fails to specify who is at risk for bulimia and who is not at risk. Although thinness norms and the fear of fatness are everywhere in our society, not all women are in trouble with dieting, binging, and body image. Why beauty norms for thinness work their destruction on only a relative minority of the population is a question that this perspective has a great deal of difficulty in answering.

Clinical/Psychiatric Approach

A wide variety of researchers and clinicians have proposed models of bulimia based on existing psychiatric/clinical models, for example, impulsiveness (Dunn & Ondercin, 1981), feelings of inadequacy or low self-efficacy (Garfinkel & Garner, 1982), borderline personality disorder (Radant, 1986), or parents' psychological health and family structure (Strober, Morell, Burroughs, Salkin, & Jacobs, 1985). One approach claims that bulimia is simply a variant of major affective disorder (Pope & Hudson, 1984).

The clinical approach provides an answer to the "Why this person?" question, which the sociocultural perspective does not: Women experiencing psychological distress are at risk. However, a serious problem for the clinical perspective is the vagueness with which it specifies predisposing factors. The personality and family predisposing factors that have been linked to bulimia can separate bulimics from the normal population, but they cannot successfully discriminate bulimics from other globally defined kinds of psychological disorders such as depression (Cantwell, 1985). Also, it is not clear how feelings of inadequacy or low self-efficacy, for example, should lead to problems with binge eating. In their 240-page book, Pope and Hudson (1984) made a reasonable case for the role of depression in bulimia, but they fail to say anything about why depression should lead to problems with binge eating in particular, or whether depression is a cause or a consequence of the disorder.

Most important, problems such as feelings of inadequacy and impulsiveness have been around for some time, long before bulimia became a major health problem. Unless one is willing to argue that such things as clinical levels of inadequacy or impulsiveness are exhibiting a huge growth, it is hard to claim that they are the cause of bulimia. The crucial issues are, why should such things as depression, impulsiveness, or inadequacy be linked to binge eating, and why now?

Epidemiological/Risk Factors Approach

An epidemiological approach to bulimia focuses on the various factors that can be expected to predict bulimia (Johnson, Lewis, & Hagman, 1984). It is a statistical approach: What are the independent variables one can use to predict the dependent variable of bulimia?

Rodin and her colleagues (Rodin et al., 1984; Striegel-Moore et al., 1986) have reviewed an impressive amount of literature relating to binge eating and bulimia and have outlined the various factors that put a person at risk for bulimia. The list is long and diverse, including body image, affective instability, family factors, hormones, sex roles, stress, exercise, genetic factors, coping skills, developmental factors, and so forth. It seems certain that a number of the factors on this list can be used to predict bulimia, using as they do factors from the entire range of theoretical perspectives.

Though practical, the approach is not parsimonious; the focus for this group of theorists has been on inclusion rather than exclusion. The result has been a large compendium of likely risk factors for bulimia. It is both descriptive and predictive, but the process of acquiring bulimic behavior remains obscure.

A useful tool at this point would be an account of bulimia that is both plausible and parsimonious. It should be plausible in that it fits the known facts about bulimia, and it should be parsimonious in that the phenomenon is not overexplained by many concomitant, nonindependent forces. An appropriate theory should define the people at risk for the disorder as well as those not at risk. A good theory should also describe the process of acquiring the symptoms themselves.

None of the existing theories can do all of these things. Although the sociocultural approach can define who is at risk, it neither effectively defines who is not at risk nor how bulimics acquire the binge-eating behavior. The clinical perspective is well suited to defining who is at risk and who is not at risk but has not carefully spelled out how it is that the symptoms are acquired. The epidemiological approach, like the clinical approach, is better suited to defining risk factors than to describing processes of symptom acquisition. I wish to propose a model that is well suited to describing the symptom acquisition process, based on social psychological processes.

Social Psychological Factors

There is good reason to think that social processes are implicated in various ways with respect to bulimia and binge eating. Anecdotal evidence suggests that bulimia tends to run in social groups, such as cheerleading squads (Squire, 1983), athletic teams (Crago, Yates, Beutler, & Arizmendi, 1985), and dance camps (Garner & Garfinkel, 1980). There is also indication that the onset of eating disorders follows entrance into the group (e.g., Crago et al., 1985), suggesting that social pressure might be involved.

There is a great deal of speculation about social psychological factors of bulimia by clinicians and the popular press. In *The Slender Balance*, Squire (1983) tells the story of a cheerleader, Laura, who

> explains matter-of-factly "everyone on the [cheerleading] squad binges and vomits. That's how I learned." . . . Laura considers her behavior frightening and awful, except in one context: be-

fore cheerleading a game. "Everybody does it then, so it doesn't seem like the same thing." (p. 48)

One of the most interesting and yet underexamined processes in bulimia is the acquisition of bulimic behavior, particularly binge eating. The few studies that have looked at this problem have focused almost exclusively on particular social groups, for example, dance camps (Garner & Garfinkel, 1980) and athletic teams (Crago et al., 1985).

This focus is not an accident. I wish to argue that social groups are at the very heart of the issue of symptom acquisition. Symptoms are spread from one member to another in these groups, and group membership is at the heart of the transmission. Groups that are most likely to transmit the symptoms of bulimia, most notably binge eating, are groups that are made up almost entirely of women of the same age. This includes dance camps and athletic teams as well as sororities, all-women dormitories, or workplaces comprising mostly women.

Social groups are important to us. They serve to tell us who we are (McGuire & Padawer-Singer, 1976), what to think (Cantril, 1941), and how to behave (Sherif, 1936). The more we value the social group, the more we are willing to be influenced by it.

> The power of a group may be measured by the attractiveness of the group for its members. If a person wants to stay in a group, he will be susceptible to influences coming from the group, and he will be willing to conform to the rules which the group sets up. (Festinger, Schachter, & Back, 1950, p. 91)

Members of the same social group tend to be relatively uniform in the attitudes and behaviors that are important to the group (Festinger, 1954). When a particular individual deviates from the group, social pressures are brought to bear to bring the prodigal back into the fold via direct communication, emotional support, or disapproval. Ultimately, the deviate is rejected if he or she fails to conform (Schachter, 1951).

I wish to argue that social pressures in friendship groups are important mechanisms by which binge eating is acquired and spread. Social groups such as athletic teams, cheerleading squads, dormitories, and sororities develop social norms about what is appropriate behavior for their members. If eating, dieting, and losing weight are important to the members, then norms will arise in the group defining how much, when, and with whom. Deviation from these norms will result in rejection from the group, as evidenced by a reduction in the person's popularity (Schachter, 1951). Thus, not only is there likely to be modeling of the behaviors and attitudes associated with bulimia, but there are likely to be sanctions for counternormative behavior.

People are very motivated to imitate or model attitudes or behaviors that are important, characteristic, or definitional to the social group. The more important the social group, and the more central a behavior is to the group, the greater the pressure toward uniformity and the more likely that members of the group will imitate each others' behavior (Festinger, 1950). Friends should become more like each other as they spend time together and grow closer. If binge eating is an important or meaningful behavior to a social group, then over time within groups, people's binge-eating patterns should grow more similar.

Social Pressures in Informal Groups

A classic investigation of the effects of social norms on group life is the study *Social Pressures in Informal Groups* by Festinger et al. (1950). Their study provides a template to examine how social influence affects binge eating. Festinger et al. were interested in how social norms about attitudes toward a tenant organization were related to popularity and communication patterns within a housing project. Two housing arrangements were studied, Westgate and Westgate West, which were adjoining but physically and architecturally distinct. In Westgate, social groups were defined by courts of grouped houses, ranging from 7 to 13 homes. In Westgate West, social groups were apartment buildings with ten apartments in each.

In Westgate, Festinger et al. (1950) found that the different groups had different norms about the attitudes to take toward the tenant organization; some courts were strongly in favor of the organization, and some were strongly against it. When the court's prevailing attitude toward the tenant organization was positive, those who had negative attitudes toward the organization were less well liked, and when the court's prevailing attitude was negative, those who had a positive attitude were less popular than others.

In Westgate West, the normative pattern was different. Tenants of all of the apartment buildings had primarily favorable attitudes toward the tenant organization. (Westgate West was occupied after the tenant organization had already been established, so that the more controversial aspects of the organization were less salient to the occupants of Westgate West.) There was no correlation between attitude and popularity in Westgate West; those who did not share the generally positive attitude toward the organization did not suffer in terms of popularity. Festinger et al. (1950) interpreted this to mean that, although the overarching group norm was a positive attitude, local group norms were neither salient nor particularly strong.

Festinger et al. (1950) studied existing social groups at one point in time (although the comparison between Westgate and Westgate West is implicitly temporal). But social groups have a dynamic life cycle: Groups form, exert pressures on their members, go up and down in cohesion and uniformity, and eventually disband (Moreland & Levine, 1982). Groups usually do not form with ready-made cohesion; when groups are new, one should not expect pressures toward uniformity to have taken effect. It is only after some amount of time that individuals should become more like the other group members. As more information is shared among members, and as the groups become more cohesive, similarity among group members on binge eating should increase.

Festinger et al. (1950) also reasoned that as group pressures increase in strength, characteristics of the person should decrease in importance. They argued that the amount of time one expected to stay in the housing project should be correlated with how much one is concerned with the quality of life there, so one's expected length of stay would normally be associated with a positive attitude toward the organization. This was true for the Westgate West complex, where norms were weak. However, at Westgate, in the presence of strong local norms about the tenant organization, anticipated length of stay was uncorrelated with attitude.

With respect to binge eating, however, social pressures are not likely to remove completely the importance of personal characteristics, because, in addition to social psychological factors, other psychobiological and psychiatrically relevant variables are likely to affect the behavior. A variety of factors might be important (Striegel-Moore et al., 1986). A woman's weight puts her at risk; the heavier she is, the more likely she is to feel pressure to diet, which puts her at risk for binge eating (Polivy & Herman, 1985). Her general psychological health is also likely to be a factor; the poorer her mental health, the more likely she is to acquire binging. Furthermore, the lower her self-esteem, the more likely she is to be open to social influence (Janis, 1954).

One social group that is ideally suited for studying such questions as they apply to binge eating is the college sorority. There is anecdotal evidence that sororities are breeding grounds for eating disorders (Squire, 1983), so that one is likely to find a range of binging severity in such a group. Second, women in a sorority are, on average, very interested in physical appearance, weight, and body shape (Rose, 1985), which is a risk factor for bulimia (Johnson et al., 1984; Striegel-Moore et al., 1986).

But most important, sorority membership is a very powerful source of social influence. Much of a sorority woman's social and academic life revolves around the living group, in addition to the more mundane aspects of life, such as sleeping, eating, laundry, and so forth.

From the point of view of social impact theory (Latane & Wolf, 1981), a sorority will have a dramatic impact on its members' lives. It is large enough to generate a strong consensus, the strength of the group is high due to its high degree of attractiveness to members, and the continuing closeness of other members in the sorority ensures the immediacy of their impact.

Finally, a sorority has the distinct advantage of being a well-defined social group with clearly discernible boundaries. With such a social group, one can obtain a fairly clear picture of the social influence patterns in a substantial portion of these women's lives.

If social pressures in friendship groups play a role in the acquisition of binge eating, a variety of research questions present themselves. To what extent are there group norms about binge eating? What role does binging play in determining social acceptance or rejection? To what extent are there social pressures toward uniformity in binge eating? Do women come to have binge eating behavior that resembles that of their friends over time? These questions were looked at in two consecutive studies of 163 women living in sororities.

Method

Overview

Two different sororities were investigated during two different academic years. In Study 1, one sorority was studied in the spring only. In Study 2, two sororities were studied in both the fall and spring. Subjects responded to questions of three general sorts: social ties, personal factors, and binge eating. Social ties were measured by having subjects list their friends within the sorority; this served as information to distinguish subgroups or cliques, as well as popularity. Personal factors were used to some extent to help define those women most at risk for binge eating. These included, among other things, self-esteem as a rough measure of a woman's general psychological health, and height and weight.

In Study 1, Sorority Alpha was contacted. The sorority members filled out questionnaires anonymously, 3 weeks before the summer break. In Study 2, both Sorority Alpha and a second house, Sorority Beta, filled out a modified version of the questionnaire. They filled out the questionnaires both in the fall, shortly after "rush" (when new members are selected by the sorority to move in during the following year) and again the spring (as in Study 1). Because social influence takes some time to operate, it was expected that there would be relatively little evidence of social pressures operating in the fall data collection, after only 6 weeks of contact.[1] In the spring, however, after 7 months of steady and intense contact, ample opportunity for pressures toward uniformity to operate was expected. This two-wave design of Study 2 also allowed for comparison over time. If social pressures were operating, then the individual sorority member's levels of binge eating should change over time, and these changes should be predicted by those social influences. In the presence of social influence, whether it is active social pressure or simply modeling, friends should grow more alike.

Subjects were active members of two different college sororities (all female). The sororities were both popular and highly sought-after houses at the campus of a large state university. The sororities were paid $150 for each wave of the study.

Subjects were given questionnaires, characterized as "a study of community and sorority life." The questionnaires were given out only to those women actually residing in the sorority house (made up of mostly sophomores and juniors). The pledge class (new recruits) and inactives (mostly seniors living outside the house and relatively removed from sorority life) were not included in these analyses. Responses to the questionnaire were completely anonymous. A code sheet was prepared by a member of the sorority's executive council; code numbers were used instead of names to investigate the social networks within the sororities.

Design

In Study 1, women from Sorority Alpha filled out a nine-page questionnaire in the spring ($n = 46$), a few weeks before the sorority closed down for the end of the term. In Study 2, members of both Sorority Alpha ($n = 51$) and Sorority Beta ($n = 66$) filled out questionnaires of seven pages in the fall and five pages in the spring, at the same time of year as in Study 1.[2]

SUBJECTS

A general description of the subjects can be found in Table 8.1. Height, weight, and age were included in all forms of the questionnaire. Parents' educational status, as a proxy for social class, was included in Study 2 only on the fall questionnaire. The body-mass index found in Table 8.1 is a measure of overweight, or "fatness" (Sjostrom, 1978), and is calculated by the formula: weight (kg)/height^2 (m). The body-mass index correlates highly (>.90) with other common measures of overweight, such as the ponderal index and deviation from the Metropolitan Life Insurance tabled norms for height and weight.

Questionnaire

The three versions of the questionnaire from the three waves differed slightly from each other, but

TABLE 8.1. Demographic Description and Design Overview

Variable	Sorority Alpha		Sorority Beta		
	Spring_1	Fall_2	Spring_2	Fall_2	Spring_2
Sorority size	46	52	44	66	61
Percent response rate	100	98	82	100	92
Mean age (years)	19.8	19.5	19.7	20.4	20.6
Weight (kg)					
M	55.8	54.3	55.8	58.2	58.6
SD	5.8	6.3	6.4	6.9	6.5
Body-mass index					
M	21.0	20.6	21.0	20.9	21.3
SD	1.6	1.7	1.9	2.0	2.7
BES scores					
M	13.9	13.7	11.5	11.8	10.1
SD	6.1	6.9	5.8	8.2	7.1
Height (m)					
M	1.63	1.62	1.62	1.69	1.68
SD	0.05	0.06	0.06	0.06	0.07
Percent fathers with graduate or professional degree	54	58	—	43	—
Percent mothers with graduate or professional degree	22	32	—	23	—

Note. Subjects were measured in the spring and fall. Subscripts on seasons indicate either Study 1 or Study 2. Dashes indicate that parents' educational data were not collected for the second wave of Study 2. BES = Binge Eating Scale.

there was a central, invariant core to all of them. (Across sororities all questionnaires were identical at any given time. Only the core questions are discussed in this article.)

Binge eating. Bulimia was measured by the Binge Eating Scale (BES; Gormally, Black, Daston, & Rardin, 1982). The 16-item BES was designed to assess the criteria for bulimia defined by the *Diagnostic and Statistical Manual (DSM–III)* of the American Psychiatric Association (1980), but has the advantage of providing a continuous measure rather than a classification of bulimic versus not bulimic. All of the *DSM–III* aspects of bulimia were measured: binge eating, purging (either by vomiting or by restrictive dieting), the emotional consequences of binging, inconspicuous eating during a binge, and so forth. Previous research at the same university has found the BES to have a one-factor solution; all items load substantially on the first factor. It has a 2-month test–retest reliability of .84. Further validation materials are available (Gormally, 1984; Gormally et al., 1982).

How severe was binge eating in the sororities? Only a handful of the nearly 160 different subjects had high enough scores on the BES to be worthy of professional attention; almost all of the binge eating described here is at subclinical levels. However, binge eating was significantly higher in the sororities than subjects in two all-women dormitories ($n = 86$) measured at the same time as Study 1, $t(131) = 2.47, p < .01$.[3] Women with low BES scores reported that they were able to stop eating when they wanted to; they did not feel they had trouble controlling eating urges, and did not think a great deal about food. Women with high BES scores reported frequent uncontrollable eating urges, they spent a lot of time trying not to eat any more food, and had days where they could not seem to think about anything else but food. Women with moderate BES scores reported a *compulsion* to eat "every so often"; they spent some of their time trying to control eating urges and had brief periods of total occupation with thoughts of food.

Social networks. To uncover the pattern of social ties within the houses, respondents were asked to list their "ten best friends (within the house), in order." Popularity was defined as the number of times one was chosen by other people on their lists of friends. These data were also used to form friendship clusters or cliques, via cluster analyses. Membership in clusters was nonoverlapping; no woman was assigned membership in more than one social group.

The cluster analyses were performed on a square n by n matrix of friendship choices (the "top ten"). In this matrix, rows represented a subject's friendship choices, and columns represented subjects being chosen. Choices were weighted from 10 (*top choice*) to 1 (*10th choice*), and then divided by the weighted sum of all of the choices, $n(n + 1)/2$, so that the weighted choices summed to unity for each set. The diagonal of the matrix, which represents self-choice (all zeros, as no one chose herself from her list of friends), was replaced with ones. The result of this is that being chosen by others in the friendship groups was more important to cluster assignment than sharing choices of other people in common. Thus, friends who chose each other and had similar patterns of friendship choices were put into the same cliques by the cluster analysis. Euclidean distances were used as a measure of similarity, and an average linkage criterion was used to join cases to clusters. Using different measures of similarity, different linkage criteria, a different weighting of the variables, or different values along the diagonal had little effect on the solutions. Separate cluster analyses were performed for each sorority at each time period, so that friendship cliques were determined for each wave of the study. These analyses resulted in an average of 10.0 ($SD = 2.9$) friendship clusters in each sorority at each time period, with an average of 5.1 ($SD = 2.3$) persons in each cluster.

The Festinger et al. (1950) study differs from ours in that they were fortunate enough to have relatively equal-sized groups of individuals, whose members were randomly assigned to membership. In this study, groups were uncovered on the basis of friendship choices rather than being independent of them. The drawback to this is that friendship clusters were almost uniformly cohesive, based as they were on the similarity of their friendship choices. No friendship cluster contains a true isolate. Because groups were based in large part on reciprocated friendship choices (mutual popularity), finding group members particularly low in within-group popularity was relatively difficult.

SELF-ESTEEM

As a brief global measure of psychological health, a six item version of the Rosenberg Self-Esteem Scale (RSE; Rosenberg, 1965) was included. Among college students at the same university, the RSE correlated with the Eysenck Neuroticism Scale at $r = -.55$, with the Beck Depression Inventory at $r = -.62$, and with the Spielberger Trait Anxiety Scale at $r = -.69$.[4] Self-esteem is also likely to be an important factor in that those low in self-esteem are more likely to be open to the influence of their peers, compared with those high in self-esteem (Janis, 1954).

Results

Social Norms

The first issue for understanding how social norms work is to uncover their existence and patterns. To look for social norms, we traced the patterns of popularity within each of the social groups. If there are indeed norms about binge eating within a group, then deviation from those norms should be associated with a reduction in popularity. The less conforming to a binge eating norm one is, the more one is likely to be sanctioned through a reduction in popularity.

By the same token, whatever the most popular people do in any group is defined as normative. If the norm for binge eating is at the mean level of binging in the sorority, with absolute deviations from the mean representing deviations from the norm, then distance from the mean represents social deviance. In Sorority Alpha, this measure of social deviance correlated with popularity at .30 in Study 1, and -.25 in Study 2, for spring. In this sorority, the highest levels of popularity were among moderate bingers; binging both too little as well as too much were associated with reductions in popularity. These data are summarized in Table 8.2.

In Sorority Beta, a different pattern emerged. Surprisingly, in this group there was apparently a social norm that promoted binge eating; the more a woman binged, the more popular she was ($rs = .28$ for fall and .32 for spring). (The actual data

TABLE 8.2. Patterns of Popularity and Binge Eating

Variable	Sorority Alpha		Sorority Beta		
	Spring$_1$	Fall$_2$	Spring$_2$	Fall$_2$	Spring$_2$
Popularity and deviation from mean of binging	−.30†	.12	−.25	−.02	−.12
Popularity and binging	−.02	−.04	−.06	.28†	.32†
Prestige of group and group's normative binge level (aggregate)	−.80‡	.33	−.53	.61†	.60†
Popularity within-group and within-group level of binge eating	−.10	.16	−.04	.22*	.36‡

Note. Correlations are based on ns of 46, 51, 36, 66, and 55, respectively. Correlations between prestige and group's normative binge level were calculated with groups as the unit of analysis; the numbers of groups were 7, 9, 8, 12, and 14, respectively. Subscripts on seasons indicate either Study 1 or Study 2.
*p < .05, one-tailed. † p < .05, two-tailed. ‡ p < .01, two-tailed.

peak in popularity was empirically determined to be not at the top of the binging severity distribution, but about 1.3 *SD*s above the mean; or about 1.2 *SD*s below the highest end.) Thus, there was evidence for social norms in support of some level of binge eating in both Sorority Alpha and Sorority Beta. The norms appeared to be somewhat different. In Sorority Alpha, a moderate level was associated with greater popularity. In Sorority Beta more binge eating was associated with more popularity.

It is somewhat surprising to find in Sorority Beta that more binging and more popularity went hand in hand. It is possible that the popularity of binge eaters was inflated if those women who binged the most in Sorority Beta all chose each other exclusively, whereas the women who did not binge as much spread their choices out among bingers and nonbingers alike. On the other hand, if a higher degree of binge eating was actually associated with greater popularity, then groups with high levels of binging should have been more prestigious within the entire sorority. To test this, average levels of binge eating in the cliques were calculated and correlated with a measure of group prestige: the percentage of out-group members who chose people within that group (i.e., the average amount of times in-group members were chosen by the out-group). This calculation is presented in the third line of Table 8.2. The prediction was borne out the groups that binged the most were the most prestigious in Sorority Beta. The companion effect is also shown for Sorority Alpha. The more deviant the group was from the mean level of binge eating, the more it suffered from a reduction in prestige.

Not only were high-binging groups more popular in Sorority Beta; but also within social groups, those who binged more were better liked. In the bottom row of Table 8.2, the correlations between within-group popularity[5] and level of binging (adjusted for each group mean) are described; again, Sorority Beta demonstrated a norm in support of greater binge eating.

Festinger et al. (1950) found that, within groups, those who deviated from the local group norm were less popular than those who followed the norm. This suggests that, within friendship clusters, the more a woman deviates from her group mean, the less popular she should be. The patterns of correlations between within-group popularity and within-group deviance did not support this prediction, however; in the spring they ranged from −.15 to .16, and averaged .03 (all *p*s were *ns*). The inability to find the effect was largely due to the manner in which social groups were defined in this study. Because mutual choice and reciprocity were used in the cluster analysis, no social groups could have had true isolates, and thus the variability among group members was likely to be greatly attenuated.

Pressures Toward Uniformity

In the presence of social norms in a valued social group there will be pressures toward uniformity. If a woman's friends are binge eaters, then the likelihood that she is also a binge eater increases. This is the crux of the social psychological account of the acquisition of bulimic behavior, and it is represented as the contagion coefficient in the top line of Table 8.3.

TABLE 8.3. Pressure Toward Uniformity in Social Groups

Variable	Sorority Alpha			Sorority Beta	
	Spring$_1$	Fall$_2$	Spring$_2$	Fall$_2$	Spring$_2$
Contagion coefficient	.30†	.00	.21*	−.15	.40‡
% choices made in-group	81.6	87.2	89.4†	82.3	85.4‡
Deviation from friends in fall with how binging changed over time	—		−.36†		−.34‡

Note. Correlations are based on *n*s of 46, 51, 36, 66, and 55, respectively. Subscripts on seasons indicate either Study 1 or Study 2.
*Different from −.08 at $p < .05$, one-tailed. † $p < .05$, two-tailed. ‡ $p < .01$, two-tailed.

The contagion coefficient is a calculation based on the social networks analysis previously described. Subjects were sorted into social friendship clusters (cliques) by means of a cluster analysis. The contagion coefficient is the Pearson *r* between a woman's binge-eating level and the average binge-eating level of her closest friends in the sorority (statistically, this is the correlation between her own BES score and the average BES score of her cluster-mates, not including the target subject). The contagion coefficient is a behavior-to-behavior model of influence; it asks the question, To what extent is a woman's binge eating like that of her friends?

The answer, apparent from Table 8.3, is "considerably." In the fall, after only 6 weeks of interaction within the friendship cliques, there was no indication that friends were more like each other than any other sorority member (*r*s = .00 and −.15, for Alpha and Beta, respectively). However, after 7 months of interaction, friends had become more uniform (*r*s ranged from .21 to .40).

It is important to note that the expected value for the contagion coefficient under the null hypothesis is not in fact .00, because when a woman is removed from the population, the mean of that population, and hence the expected value of the sample of friends, is shifted slightly in the opposite direction. To ascertain exactly what size correlation to expect by chance, a Monte Carlo study based on 200 randomly generated data sets was performed for each of the sororities.[6] These analyses yielded, under the null hypothesis, expected contagion coefficients of −.09 for Sorority Alpha in Study 1, −.08 for Sorority Alpha in Study 2, and −.07 for Sorority Beta.

The time difference is probably due to two effects. First, social influence probably would require more than 6 weeks to have any appreciable effect on a woman's binge eating. Second, the more cohesive the group, the more influence it should have over its members.

The second row of Table 8.3 indicates that, in fact, cohesion increased over time. "Percentage choices made within group" is the total number of in-group choices made, divided by the total number of in-group choices possible. Because the subjects made 10 friendship choices, and the average cluster size was 5.1 members (and the members did not choose themselves), 41% of all possible choices could have been made to the in-group. Across all studies, of the possible 4.1 choices, approximately 3.5, or 85% of possible choices, were made in-group. In spite of the relatively high cohesion even in the fall, cohesion did increase over time (daggers represent the significance levels of pairwise *t*-tests). Thus, it is likely that time and increased cohesion worked together to bring friends' binging levels into agreement.

In fact, at the entire group level, there was a decrease in variability on binge eating over the course of the year. The standard deviation shrank from 6.9 to 5.8 in Sorority Alpha, and from 8.2 to 7.1 in Sorority Beta (see Table 8.1). This difference across both sororities was significant at $p < .05$ (test of equality of variances, one-tailed).

Apparently, at both the group level (whole sorority) and the friendship level (within clusters), friends became more similar over time. The central question to ask at this point is, Do we have evidence here of social pressure, or is this evidence of assortative friendships (birds of a feather flock together)? Is the behavior-to-behavior correlation found in Table 8.3 evidence of contagion or of assortment? If sorority members were making friends on the basis of how much they binged, then a similar pattern of within-group results would obtain in the absence of any actual social pressures or movement toward uniformity. Several converging lines of evidence suggest that this is a pattern of social influence and not merely differential assortment.

Evidence of Social Influence

First, if the phenomenon observed is merely assortment, then personality-type variables other than binge eating should also correlate among friends. This, however, does not seem to be the case; for example, self-esteem (RSE) correlates were .01, .00, and .04 in the spring for Alpha 1, Alpha 2, and Beta, respectively. Such problems, however, are best handled by data collected over time, and Study 2 provided us with just these sorts of data.

If binge eaters were simply reassorting to be with "birds of a feather," the social cliques uncovered in the spring (which differed significantly on binging) should have differed from each other in their past binging level as well; their fall BES scores should have been significantly different by cluster. However, in neither Sorority Alpha nor Sorority Beta were these differences significant. In fact, friendship choices were quite stable. Because friendship patterns are not continuous but nominal variables, a class measure of association, the *contingency coefficient*, was used to describe stability of friendship patterns.[7] From fall to spring, choices were stable, with contingency coefficients of .87 and .94 in Alpha and Beta, respectively.

If the contagion coefficient were due merely to self-selection into similar groups, then one would expect this correlation to be significant in the fall. Six weeks is probably enough time to learn something about one another's eating habits; however, there is no evidence of contagion in the fall, indicating that 6 weeks was not enough time for social influence to take place.

If one allows the necessary passage of time and the increased group cohesion that accompanies it, then we would expect that pressures toward uniformity should, across the two waves, pressure women to become more like their immediate social groups. To test this, we calculated the distance a woman was from her friends at Time 1 by subtracting her binge-eating level from the average binge-eating level of her friends. This number was then correlated with how her binging level moved over the academic year. If there were social pressures toward uniform levels of binging, then the distance a woman was from her friends at Time 1 should have correlated negatively with the change in her binging level. If she binged much less than her friends, she should have increased her binging level; if she binged much more, she should have decreased.

This is exactly what happened. The bottom row of Table 8.3 describes these correlations. In both sororities Alpha and Beta, women became more like their friends over time. The less each woman was like her friends in the fall, the more she moved toward them over the academic year. Thus, the contagion coefficient seems to be, in sum, a measure of social influence.

One possible interpretation of this finding is that it is regression toward the mean. Certainly, regression toward the mean is likely to take place. But what is the size of correlations that we would expect to find based merely on chance, and are these correlations significantly larger? To test this, a Monte Carlo study based on the same parameters, but using 325 randomly generated data sets, generated expected correlations of −.079 for Sorority Alpha and −.091 for Sorority Beta, significantly smaller than the correlations found in Table 8.3 (both $ps < .05$, two-tailed).[8]

Festinger et al. (1950) found that in Westgate, social norms overrode personal factors, so that the potential value of the tenants organization to a person was entirely independent of his or her attitude toward it. This does not seem to be the case in the present study. Because the personal factors are essentially risk factors in the epidemiological model, standardized regressions on binge eating by risk factors were computed. Both psychological health, as measured by the RSE, and degree of fatness, as measured by the body-mass index, were independently predictive of binge eating in almost all groups at all times (see Table 8.4). Even as social pressures grew over the course of the year, the correlations between binge eating and the risk factors of fatness and low self-esteem remained relatively stable (no beta weights were significantly different from each other between fall and spring).

To demonstrate the simplicity of this account of the acquisition of the behavior of binge eating, Table 8.5 shows the regressions within each sorority of an overall regression testing the social

TABLE 8.4. **Risk Factors for Binge Eating in Studies 1 and 2 Expressed as Standardized Beta Weights**

Sorority and wave	Body-mass index	Self-esteem
Alpha		
Spring$_1$	.28*	−.46***
Alpha		
Fall$_2$	.41***	−.37**
Spring$_2$	.42**	−.50***
Beta		
Fall$_2$	.37***	−.37***
Spring$_2$	.20	−.46***

Note. Beta weights are based on ns of 46, 51, 36, 66, and 55, for each row respectively. Subscripts on seasons indicate either Study 1 or Study 2.
*$p < .05$. **$p < .01$. ***$p < .005$.

contagion model of binge eating. Using only the RSE as a measure of general psychological well-being, the average binging level of a woman's friends, and her body-mass index, one can predict a woman's binge-eating score with a multiple correlation of .48 to .57. Although this is a fairly parsimonious account of binge eating, it nonetheless appears to be fairly useful for explaining patterns of binge eating in these sororities.

Discussion

To demonstrate social norms, popularity patterns were traced with respect to binge eating. In Sorority Alpha, deviations from the normative level of binge eating were associated with reductions in popularity. In Sorority Beta, a different normative pattern emerged; the more a woman binged, the more popular she was.

TABLE 8.5. **Social Influence, Body Mass, and Self-Esteem: The Social Contagion Model of Binge Eating**

Study	Adjusted R	Adjusted R^2
Sorority Alpha		
Study 1	.51*	.26
Study 2	.57*	.32
Sorority Beta		
Study 2	.48*	.23

Note. Multiple correlations are based on ns of 46, 36, and 55 for each row, respectively. The regression model includes social influence, self-esteem, and the body-mass index as predictors, and are based on spring data.
*$p < .005$.

To demonstrate behavior-to-behavior influence on binge eating, sorority members' binge-eating levels were correlated with the binge-eating levels of their friends. This correlation was found in the spring for both sororities. This finding was most likely due to social influence rather than assortment, based on data including the stability of friendship ties, the lack of friend-to-friend correlation of self-esteem and other person variables, and the lack of difference among spring groups in their prior fall binging levels. Most important, however, is the correlation that directly indicates social influence: Women became more like their friends over time.

I have suggested that when a woman experiences distress, she is open to social influence. When the influence she is receiving in terms of social information and approval is in support of binging, she is more likely to become a binge eater. Some sort of interaction between social influence and susceptibility is necessary to explain the problem of binge eating. For example, there is no reason to expect that the significant negative correlations between binge eating and self-esteem reflect a fact of nature. Prior to the sociocultural development of binge eating as a symptom related to psychological distress, binge eating and self-esteem had to be uncorrelated; there was such a low incidence of problem binging prior to the early 1970s that little variability existed in binge eating (Rosenzweig & Spruill, 1986). It is only in the presence of models for and information about binge eating that low self-esteem is likely to lead to binge eating. Because both of these sororities had prescriptive norms about binge eating, the appropriate social group with which to compare the self-esteem to binge-eating correlation—no backdrop of social norms—could not be included here. If it is true that an interaction between social influence and susceptibility is necessary, then individuals who are susceptible to influence (e.g., are low in self-esteem), but are not in groups where there are norms about binge eating, should not binge eat any more than average.

A Social Psychological Integration

The social influence account of binge eating provides a parsimonious bridge among the three accounts of bulimia discussed in the introduction. From the sociocultural perspective, one can discern which kinds of influence are likely to be found among social groups. Currently, one kind of influence is toward binge eating, and a college sorority is likely to reflect current concerns of this sort. From the clinical perspective, one can discern who is at risk for this social influence. In fact, many of the personality characteristics that clinicians have uncovered can be characterized as indicators of susceptibility to social influence: low self-esteem, depression, impulsivity, poor family environment, poorly developed sense of self, etc. For the epidemiological perspective, the social influence model provides a mechanism by which we can describe how symptoms are acquired and spread.

The social influence model works together with the other three approaches to meet the necessary theoretical criteria specified in the introduction. Who is and who is not at risk for binge eating is a function of both the immediate social influence and one's susceptibility to that influence. Influence and susceptibility will be affected by group cohesion, consensus on norms, and the attractiveness of the group, as well as the individuals' general susceptibility to influence based on depression, self-esteem, and so forth.

The sorority milieu is likely to be a breeding ground for eating disorders (Squire, 1983); it is a powerful setting for translating cultural influence into direct social influence. The extreme social importance of body size and shape for this population most likely serves to increase the risk of beginning dieting and hence binge eating. It is likely that in other social groups where physical attractiveness and body shape are not weighed so heavily, the sorts of findings reported here would be greatly attenuated or even nonexistent.

It is important to note that a social influence model of binge eating explicitly predicts this possibility. If the group norm is entirely against dieting and binging but rather for, vegetarianism, for example, the correlation between psychological distress and binging should approach zero. Instead, the correlation between distress and vegetarianism should be high. For this reason, the size and direction of correlations should differ between groups, depending on what the norms are for handling personal distress (e.g., Garner & Garfinkel, 1980). The content portion of the social influence model (in this case, binge eating) is a relatively open slot. Distress may be handled in a number of ways, and social pressures could as easily result in smoking, delinquency, heavy drinking, loss of virginity, drug use, or depression (Jessor & Jessor, 1977; Orford, 1985). It may be in this way that bulimia has replaced depressive symptoms as a primary pathway of expressing psychological distress among younger women. If cultural norms move away from the current overconcern with dieting and thinness, then bulimia and binge eating will disappear with them. The expression of psychological distress will continue to follow cultural norms, wherever they may wander.

These results indicate that a social psychological analysis of eating disorders is warranted and likely to bear fruit. The spread of one important symptom of bulimia—binge eating—through a population is likely to be the result of social influence. Further research in this social psychological vein is necessary to delineate the interrelationship of the variables in the model. The role and development of social norms about binge eating and their importance to friendship ties, the nature of the transfer of behavior from friend to friend, and, especially, whether and how social pressures are applied among friends, are important issues that now face us. What is necessary are longitudinal studies of women at risk for binge eating and bulimia that are begun prior to the development of disordered eating habits. This may mean beginning longitudinal studies as early as junior high school, or even before.

The question remains, What form does social influence take in these sororities? A variety of possibilities exist. It may be that the women are directly teaching each other appropriate binging levels, although several informants indicated that they felt this was unlikely. It may be a case of leadership, where the most popular women set the tone for the rest of the sorority. This would be consistent with an account based on simple imitation or modeling: The high status members' level of binging is transmitted via imitation to the rest of the group. Or members of social groups may be coerced into conforming to a clique's standard. Presumably, the coercion could be based on the giving or withholding of popularity. However, the exact process of acquisition cannot be determined in this study.

Nonetheless, these data do appear to fit the model of behavioral contagion proposed by Wheeler (1966). Wheeler, following Redl (1949), proposed that in cases where a behavior has both some sort of prior restraint to it (as excessive binge eating certainly does) and at the same time has some other strong impulse or urge toward fulfillment of a need, the presence of a model acting out the conflictual behavior increases the likelihood of the behavior being performed (Wheeler, 1966). In a sense, the avoidance gradient in an approach-avoidance conflict is lowered, making approach more likely. The social norms of the sorority, in combination with the presence of models, are likely to make the costs associated with binge eating appear less severe and increase the likelihood of higher levels of binge eating. In this way, observation of binge eating, motivated (or released) in part by social pressures based on popularity, may account for how binge eating as a behavior is acquired and expressed.

A general model of the social influence patterns in psychological distress could be derived from the social psychological model proposed here. It would involve changing the content of the social influence but not its pattern. In general, the pattern of influence is likely to follow the outline described by Kerckhoff and Back (1968) in their study of contagion in a North Carolina garment factory. Whichever symptom is being spread, it still should appear among people experiencing distress, it should spread out along sociometric and communication: networks, and the norms about the behavior should change toward acceptance as the behavior becomes more widespread. Thus, the social influence model could apply to as diverse phenomena as the hysterical fainting found in Freud's day, depression, or bulimia. All one would need to change in the model is the type of data made socially available in terms of social norms and modeling of the behavior, and one can predict fainting, rashes, vomiting, depression, or binge eating.

Indeed, the social influence processes described here look strikingly like those described by Newcomb (1943) in his famous Bennington study. A strong social norm in favor of left-wing politics emerged at Bennington College, first among the faculty, and increasingly with age, the students. New students who did not follow the norm, that is, did not espouse left-wing politics, were sanctioned with a reduction in popularity. Newcomb (1943) argued that the process of social influence and attitude change was not specific to political attitudes, but could generalize to almost any expressible attitude or set of behaviors, and these results with respect to binge eating seem to bear out his claim.

An important task remains. Peer influence may account for how behaviors such as binge eating or alcohol use begin (Orford, 1985), but an account of the sort outlined here does not describe how these behaviors can escalate into full-blown bulimia or alcoholism. Although some social factors have been studied, the role of social influence in this process as yet remains far too unexamined.

ACKNOWLEDGMENTS

This article is based on my dissertation at the University of Michigan. Financial support came from an NIMH training grant in health and social behavior to the University of Michigan, the Michigan Alumni Fund, University of Michigan Continuing Education for Women, a Society for the Psychological Study of Social Issues Grant-in-Aid, and NSF Grant SES85–07342 to Richard Nisbett.

Special thanks are due to my committee for their helpful comments and encouragement: Eugene Burnstein, Hazel Markus, Andre Modigliani, and especially to the chairman, Richard Nisbett, whose guiding hand can be seen throughout. This version also profited from discussions with and knowledgeable comments from Monica Biernat, Steve Cardoze, Adam Drewnowski, Martin Gold, Norbert Kerr, Adam Lehman, Judith Rodin, Lisa Silberstein, David Smith, and three anonymous reviewers.

NOTES

1. Presumably, a substantial portion of the social impact of the sorority on its members dissipates over the summer.
2. There is, of course, no one who is in both Sorority Alpha and Sorority Beta. However, there is some degree of overlap (40%) within Sorority Alpha over the two studies.
3. I collected data from two all-women dormitories with a very similar questionnaire at the same time as Sorority Alpha, Study 1, hoping to compare the dormitories to the sororities. Unfortunately, the response rate was much too low in the dormitories (42%) to study social networks, so the data are not discussed further here.
4. I am grateful to Jonathan Shedler for making these data available.
5. Within-group popularity is based on the percentage of people within a person's group choosing her. Because smaller clusters are likely to have more reciprocal choices just by chance (a group of two is sure to have 100% reciprocation), each person's percentage choice was divided by the group's average percentage within choice. Each group's mean thus becomes 1.00; numbers above that indicate higher within-group popularity, numbers below it, lower popularity.
6. For the Monte Carlo analyses, random data were generated with the same mean, standard deviation, and size of cliques

for each sorority separately. All other calculations were made as in the actual data set. Observed correlations were in the 99th, 97th, and 99th percentile of their respective null hypothesis distributions.
7. The contingency coefficient is calculated as

$$c = \sqrt{\frac{x^2}{x^2 + N}}$$

where the minimum value of C is for .00, and the maximum value is never greater than 1.00.

8. The same procedure for Monte Carlo analyses was followed as before. Random data were generated with the same mean, standard deviation, and size of cliques for each sorority separately. Furthermore, the randomly generated variables representing fall and spring Binge Eating Scale scores were correlated to the same extent as the observed data. All other calculations were made as in the actual data set. Observed correlations were in the 98th and 99th percentile of their respective null hypothesis distributions.

REFERENCES

American Psychiatric Association. (1980). *Diagnostic and statistical manual of mental disorders* (3rd ed.). Washington, DC: Author.

Boskind-Lodahl, M., & Sirlin, J. (1977, March). The gorging-purging syndrome. *Psychology Today*, pp. 50–52, 82, 85.

Bennett, W., & Gurin, J. (1982). *The dieter's dilemma*. New York: Basic Books.

Cantril, H. (1941). *The psychology of social movements*. New York: Wiley.

Cantwell, P. (1985). Understanding bulimia. *Contemporary Psychology, 30*, 196–198.

Crago, M., Yates, A., Beutler, L. E., & Arizmendi, T. G. (1985). Height-weight ratios among female athletes: Are collegiate athletics the precursors to an anorexic syndrome? *International Journal of Eating Disorders, 4*, 79–87.

Crandall, C. S. (1987). Do men and women differ in emotional and ego involvement with food? *Journal of Nutrition Education, 19*, 229–236.

Dunn, O. K., & Ondercin, P. (1981). Personality variables related to compulsive eating in college women. *Journal of Clinical Psychology, 37*, 43–49.

Dwyer, J., Feldman, J. J., & Mayer, J. (1970). The social psychology of dieting. *Journal of Health and Social Behavior, 11*, 269–287.

Festinger, L. (1950). Informal social communication. *Psychological Review, 57*, 271–292.

Festinger, L. (1954). A theory of social comparison processes. *Human Relations, 7*, 117–140.

Festinger, L., Schachter, S., & Back, K. W. (1950). *Social pressures in informal groups*. New York: Harper.

Gandour, M. J. (1984). Bulimia: Clinical description, assessment, etiology, and treatment. *International Journal of Eating Disorders, 3*, 3–38.

Garfinkel, P. E., & Garner, D. M. (1982). *Anorexia nervosa: A multidimensional perspective*. New York: Brunner/Mazel.

Garner, D. M., & Garfinkel, P. E. (1980). Socio-cultural factors in the development of anorexia nervosa. *Psychological Medicine, 10*, 647–656.

Garner, D. M., Garfinkel, P. E., Schwartz, D., & Thompson, M. (1980). Cultural expectations of thinness in women. *Psychological Reports, 47*, 483–491.

Garrow, J. (1978). The regulation of energy expenditure. In G. A. Bray (Ed.), *Recent advances in obesity research* (Vol. 2). London: Newman.

Gormally, J. (1984). The obese binge eater: Diagnosis, etiology and clinical issues. In R. C. Hawkins II, W. J. Fremouw, & P. F. Clement (Eds.), *The binge-purge syndrome*. New York: Springer.

Gormally, J., Black, S., Daston, S., & Rardin, D. (1982). The assessment of binge eating severity among obese persons. *Addictive Behaviors, 7*, 47–55.

Halmi, K. A., Falk, J. R., & Schwartz, E. (1981). Binge-eating and vomiting: A survey of a college population. *Psychological Medicine, 11*, 697–706.

Janis, I. L. (1954). Personality correlates of susceptibility to persuasion. *Journal of Personality, 22*, 504–518.

Jessor, R., & Jessor, S. (1977). *Problem behavior and psychosocial development: A longitudinal study of youth*. New York: Academic Press.

Johnson, C., Lewis, C., & Hagman, L. (1984). The syndrome of bulimia. *Psychiatric Clinics of America, 7*, 247–274.

Kerckhoff, A. C., & Back, K. W. (1968). *The june bug: A study of hysterical contagion*. Englewood Cliffs, NJ: Prentice-Hall.

Latane, B., & Wolf, S. (1981). The social impact of majorities and minorities. *Psychological Review, 88*, 438–454.

McGuire, W. J., & Padawer-Singer, A. (1976). Trait salience in the spontaneous self-concept. *Journal of Personality and Social Psychology, 33*, 743–754.

Moreland, R. L., & Levine, J. M. (1982). Socialization in small groups: Temporal changes in individual-group relations. In L. Berkowitz (Ed.), *Advances in experimental social psychology* (Vol. 15, pp. 137–189). New York: Academic Press.

Newcomb, T. M. (1943). *Personality and social change*. New York: Dryden.

Nisbett, R. E. (1972). Hunger, obesity and the ventromedial hypothalamus. *Psychological Review, 79*, 433–453.

Orbach, S. (1978). *Fat is a feminist issue*. New York: Berkeley Press.

Orford, J. (1985). *Excessive appetites*. London: Wiley.

Polivy, J., & Herman, C. P. (1985). Dieting and binging: A causal analysis. *American Psychologist, 40*, 193–204.

Pope, H. G., & Hudson, J. I. (1984). *New hope for binge eaters: Advances in the understanding and treatment of bulimia*. New York: Harper & Row.

Radant, S. (1986, May). *Bulimia as a subtype of borderline personality disorder: A comparison study*. Paper presented at the meeting of the Western Psychological Association, Seattle, WA.

Redl, F. (1949). The phenomenon of contagion and "shock effect" in group therapy. In K. R. Eissler (Ed.), *Searchlights on delinquency*. New York: International Universities Press.

Rodin, J., Silberstein, L., & Striegel-Moore, R. (1984). Women and weight: A normative discontent. *Nebraska symposium on motivation* (Vol. 27, pp. 267–307). Lincoln: University of Nebraska Press.

Rose, M. A. (1985). *Rush: The girl's guide to sorority success*. New York: Villard.

Rosenberg, M. (1965). *Society and adolescent self-image*. Princeton, NJ: Princeton University Press.

Rosenzweig, M., & Spruill, J. (1986). Twenty years after Twiggy: A retrospective investigation of bulimic-like behaviors. *International Journal of Eating Disorders, 6*, 24–31.
Schachter, S. (1951). Deviation, rejection, and communication. *Journal of Abnormal and Social Psychology, 46*, 190–207.
Schlesier-Stropp, B. (1984). Bulimia: A review of the literature. *Psychological Bulletin, 95*, 247–257.
Sherif, M. (1936). *The psychology of social norms.* New York: Harper.
Sinoway, C. G., Raupp, C. D., & Newman, J. (1985, August). *Binge eating and bulimia: Comparing incidence and characteristics across universities.* Paper presented at the meeting of the 93rd Annual Convention of the American Psychological Association, Los Angeles, CA.
Sjostrom, L. (1978). The contribution of fat cells to the determination of body weight. In G. A. Bray (Ed.), *Recent advances in obesity research* (Vol. 2). London: Newman.
Squire, S. (1983). *The slender balance.* New York: Pinnacle.
Srikameswaran, S., Leichner, P., & Harper, D. (1984). Sex role ideology among women with anorexia nervosa and bulimia. *International Journal of Eating Disorders, 3*, 39–43.
Strangler, R. S., & Printz, A. M. (1980). DSM-III: Psychiatric diagnoses in a university population. *American Journal of Psychiatry, 137*, 937–940.
Striegel-Moore, R. H., Silberstein, L., & Rodin, J. (1986). Toward an understanding of risk factors for bulimia. *American Psychologist, 41*, 246–263.
Strober, M., Morell, W., Burroughs, J., Salkin, B., & Jacobs, C. (1985). A controlled family study of anorexia nervosa. *Journal of Psychiatric Research, 19*, 239–246.
Wheeler, L. (1966). Toward a theory of behavioral contagion. *Psychological Review, 73*, 179–192.

Discussion Questions

1. Given the evidence obtained by Crandall for social processes involved in the onset and maintenance of a psychological problem, what approach do think a clinical psychologist should adopt in treating a client who shows signs of binge eating and bulimia?
2. To what degree might social contagion be useful in *decreasing* the incidence of binge eating?
3. What other social psychological processes besides social influence might be involved in the development of disordered eating?
4. Why do you think social influence encourages binge eating today whereas, in times past, such social norms did not appear to operate to the same degree even though similar norms for thinness among women existed?

Suggested Readings

Festinger, L., Schachter, S., & Back, K. W. (1950). *Social pressures in informal groups.* New York: Harper. This classic book examines the role that social norms play in determining life within social groups.
Paxton, S. J., Schutz, H. K., Wertheim, E. H., & Muir, S. L. (1999). Friendship clique and peer influences on body image concerns, dietary restraint, extreme weight-loss behaviors, and binge eating in adolescent girls. *Journal of Abnormal Psychology, 108*, 255–266. This article discusses the influence that friendship attitudes and friendship cliques have on body image concerns and binge eating.
Stice, E., Presnell, K., & Spangler, D. (2002). Risk factors for binge eating onset in adolescent girls: A 2-year prospective investigation. *Health Psychology, 21*, 131–138. This article examines a host of different variables thought to predict the onset of binge eating.

READING 9

The Role of Low Self-Esteem in Emotional and Behavioral Problems: Why Is Low Self-Esteem Dysfunctional?

Mark R. Leary, Lisa S. Schreindorfer, and Alison L. Haupt
• Wake Forest University

Editors' Introduction

Social and clinical psychologists alike have been interested in the construct of self-esteem for many years. Social psychologists have been intrigued by the fact that people's level of self-esteem is related to how they behave in social situations. Research has shown that self-esteem predicts how people perceive other individuals, interpret events that happen to them, approach difficult academic and interpersonal situations, interact with other people, react to failure and rejection, and deal with relationship problems. Clinical and counseling psychologists have been interested in self-esteem because low self-esteem appears to be associated with poorer psychological well-being than high self-esteem. Almost every psychological difficulty—depression, anxiety, loneliness, eating disorders, alcohol abuse, and so on—is more common among people with low rather than high self-esteem. In light of this relationship, many writers have suggested that low self-esteem is a risk factor for psychological problems.

In this article, Mark R. Leary, Lisa Schreindorfer, and Alison L. Haupt offer an explanation regarding why low self-esteem is usually more problematic than high self-esteem. This explanation, which is based on sociometer theory, suggests that the dysfunctional effects of low self-esteem are not actually due to self-esteem per se. (In fact, they argue that self-esteem itself has no causal effects on emotion or behavior.) Rather, the relationship between low self-esteem and emotional and behavioral problems is due to the fact that people with low self-esteem feel less accepted by other people than those with high self-esteem. Not only does social rejection create a variety of psychological problems, but people who feel rejected are likely to resort to dysfunctional ways of seeking acceptance. Together, these two processes account for the relationship between low self-esteem and psychological problems.

More recent research has suggested another side to the story. Although the behaviors that Leary and his colleagues discuss in this article are indeed related to low self-esteem, research has shown that high self-esteem can sometimes be problematic as well. Having exceptionally high self-esteem is sometimes related to self-centeredness, narcissism, prejudice, violence when one's ego is threatened, and a lack of concern for other people. Presumably, sociometer theory would explain these negative effects by pointing out that assuming that one is highly accepted by other people sometimes leads people to act in undesirable ways.

Abstract

Low self-esteem has been linked to a number of emotional and behavioral problems. This article examines the relationship between low self-esteem and a variety of psychological difficulties from the standpoint of the sociometer model of self-esteem. According to this model, the behavioral concomitants of low self-esteem are best viewed as reactions to real, anticipated, or imagined rejection rather than as consequences of low self-esteem per se. Evidence relevant to this hypothesis is reviewed as it relates to dysphoric emotions, substance abuse, irresponsible sexual behavior, aggression, membership in deviant groups, and eating disorders. Implications of this approach for treating certain psychological problems are also discussed.

Low self-esteem ranks among the strongest predictors of emotional and behavioral problems. Compared to people with high self-esteem, people with low self-esteem tend to be more anxious, depressed, lonely, jealous, shy, and generally unhappy. They are also less assertive, less likely to enjoy close friendships, and more likely to drop out of school. Furthermore, they are more inclined to behave in ways that pose a danger to themselves or others: Low self-esteem is associated with unsafe sex, teenage pregnancy, aggression, criminal behavior, the abuse of alcohol and other drugs, and membership in deviant groups (for reviews, see Baumeister, 1993; Bednar, Wells, & Peterson, 1989; Mecca, Smelser, & Vasconcellos, 1989). Given that research strongly implicates low self-esteem as a risk factor for psychological distress and behavioral problems, some have recommended raising self-esteem as a way to remediate a variety of personal and social problems (e.g., Mecca et al., 1989).

However, despite thousands of studies on the antecedents, concomitants, and consequences of self-esteem, we do not have an adequate understanding of *why* low self-esteem lies at the root of so many psychological difficulties, or even whether the culprit is, in fact, self-esteem. The purpose of this article is to explore this question. We begin by describing a theory of self-esteem that will provide the framework for our discussion. We then examine various maladaptive concomitants of low self-esteem within this perspective, and conclude with a discussion of the clinical implications of this approach.

The Sociometer Model

In a discussion of the functions of self-esteem, Leary and Downs (1995) proposed that the universality and potency of the self-esteem motive suggests that it serves an important function, possibly one that evolved because it conferred survival value for primitive humans. Rather than viewing the need for self-esteem as a free-standing motive, Leary and Downs suggested that subjective self-esteem might best be regarded as a psychological gauge or indicator that allows people to efficiently monitor others' reactions to them.

Other people's reactions, particularly the degree to which they accept and include versus reject and exclude the individual, are vital to the individual's physical and psychological well-being. In light of this, the self-esteem system may have developed to monitor the social environment in an automatic and preattentive fashion for cues that connote rejection and exclusion. When this *sociometer* detects real or potential rejection, it alerts the individual via negative affect (subjectively experienced as an aversive "loss" of state self-esteem) and motivates behavior that restores the individual's standing in others' eyes.

From the perspective of the sociometer model (and contrary to what many theorists have supposed), people do not possess an inherent motive to maintain their self-esteem for its own sake. Rather, people are motivated to maintain connections with other significant people in their lives (Baumeister & Leary, 1995); subjective self-esteem is the internal gauge that monitors the likelihood that one will be included and excluded. Recent research supports the notion that self-esteem is particularly sensitive to perceived rejection. Events that lower self-esteem are those that have undesired implications for the individual's inclusion by other people (Leary, Tambor, Terdal, & Downs, 1995).

According to the sociometer model, feelings of state self-esteem—transient feelings about oneself that fluctuate as a function of the immediate situation—are the backbone of this monitoring system. State self-esteem may involve situated thoughts about oneself as well—for example, thoughts that one has succeeded on a task, behaved inappropriately, made a particular impression on others who are present, or that other events have occurred that have implications for one's inclusion or exclusion by others, yet state self-esteem, at heart, involves how people *feel* about themselves (Brown, 1993; Leary et al., 1995). Losses of self-esteem are invariably associated with negative affect.

Although the sociometer model posits that people monitor their inclusionary status via changes in *state* self-esteem, a corollary of the model is that individual differences in *trait* self-esteem reflect the cumulative effects of perceived inclusion and exclusion over time. Considerable evidence shows that people who have received large doses of acceptance and social inclusion tend to develop higher trait self-esteem than those who are frequently ignored or rejected (Harter, 1993). For example, among children and adolescents, perceptions of parental acceptance correlate significantly with self-esteem (Litovsky & Dusek, 1985; Morvitz & Motta, 1992). Not surprisingly, then, trait self-esteem correlates strongly with the belief that one is generally accepted and included by other people (Leary et al., 1995). The fact that acceptance by other people appears essential for the maintenance of self-esteem (Eskilson, Wiley, Meuhlhauer, & Dodder, 1986; Harter, 1993) is easily explained by a model in which self-esteem operates as a gauge of social acceptance and rejection.

Taking this link between perceived rejection and low self-esteem one step further leads to the suggestion that the dysfunctional concomitants of low self-esteem are effects not of low self-esteem per se, but of social exclusion. According to this view, low self-esteem does not cause emotional and behavioral problems as many have supposed. Rather, low self-esteem is associated with dysphoria and maladaptive behavior because it is linked to rejection in two ways.

First, social rejection is an antecedent both of

certain psychological difficulties and of low self-esteem. For example, research shows that peer rejection is a strong predictor of both psychological maladjustment and low self-esteem (Asher, Parkhurst, Hymel, & Williams, 1990; Kupersmidt & Patterson, 1991). Because of the importance of social inclusion to the individual, people experience a variety of ill effects when their need to belong is thwarted. (Baumeister and Leary [1995] discuss in detail the deleterious consequences of unfulfilled needs for inclusion.) The source of these problems, however, is not low self-esteem, but interpersonal rejection.

In addition, some dysfunctional behaviors that are associated with low self-esteem reflect maladaptive attempts to increase one's acceptance by other people. Much of social life can be construed as efforts to establish and maintain a "minimum quantity of lasting, positive, and impactful interpersonal relationships" (Baumeister & Leary, 1995). People usually pursue inclusion in these relationships through adaptive means—for example, by achieving at socially sanctioned pursuits, increasing their interpersonal appeal, abiding by social standards, and engaging in socially valued behaviors.[1] However, when people do not believe that they will be accepted and included via socially sanctioned routes, they may try to enhance their social inclusion through maladaptive actions such as joining a gang or behaving promiscuously. Because people with low trait self-esteem perceive that their interpersonal relationships are more tenuous than people with high trait self-esteem (Leary et al., 1995), they are more prone to pursue acceptance through whatever means are available, even if their behaviors are, in the long run, detrimental to their well-being.

In the sections that follow, we examine the links between rejection, self-esteem, and psychological difficulties from the standpoint of the sociometer model. As will be seen, the research evidence is consistent with the view that, rather than being a consequence of low self-esteem, these difficulties, like low self-esteem, are effects of perceived rejection or exclusion.

Dysphoric Emotions

As noted earlier, low self-esteem is associated with dysphoric reactions of many kinds. Compared with people high in self-esteem, low-self-esteem people are more depressed, anxious, lonely, jealous, and otherwise dysphoric (see Leary, 1990). In our view, self-esteem is not the cause of these reactions. Rather, these emotional problems reflect the effects of social exclusion.

Because inclusion in supportive groups and relationships provides a wealth of social, material, psychological, and physical benefits, people strive to establish and maintain supportive relationships with others (Barash, 1977; Baumeister & Leary, 1995; Cohen & Wills, 1985). To the extent that people need and desire social inclusion, the perception that one is inadequately integrated into important social groups or relationships results in negative affect. Such reactions may provide an affective-motivational "warning system" that alerts individuals to threats to their social standing and that motivates remediative behavior (Averill, 1968; Baumeister & Tice, 1990; Leary & Downs, 1995; Scheff, 1990). In addition, because most rewards are obtained through interpersonal relationships, people may believe they will lose positive outcomes and/or experience negative outcomes when they perceive themselves as excluded (Izard, 1977).

Depression is one emotion that is strongly related to low self-esteem (Battle, Jarratt, Smit, & Precht, 1988; Hammen, 1988; Quellet & Joshi, 1986; Rawson, 1992; Smart & Walsh, 1993). Although depression may be precipitated by a wide variety of events, both social and nonsocial, feeling excluded is certainly one such event. Depression is a common response to events such as divorce, unrequited love, failing to be admitted to an organization, moving to a new city, or not receiving an invitation to an important social event, all of which involve elements of exclusion (Brown & Harris, 1978; Stokes & McKirnan, 1989). Among preadolescent girls in one study, low peer acceptance was the sole predictor of depression (Kupersmidt & Patterson, 1991).

Similarly, a study of children who moved to a new school found that "children's perceptions of their social acceptance significantly predicted their level of self-reported depressive symptoms one year later" (Panak & Garber, 1992, p. 161). The actual loss of a person evokes perhaps the deepest depression—grief—which may be regarded as a response to permanent "exclusion" from a valued relationship (Baumeister & Tice, 1990; Bowlby,

1973, 1980; Lofland, 1982). Snyder's (1994) analysis of hope suggested that the failure to establish and maintain connections with other people is a primary source of hopelessness and depression. We are not claiming that all depression involves perceived exclusion, only that perceived exclusion is a common cause of depression.

In our view, low self-esteem and depression are linked because they both result from real, potential, or imagined social exclusion. This does not preclude the possibility that people with low self-esteem may feel incapable of achieving desired goals and thus feel helpless and depressed, but the sociometer model contributes another perspective to the link.

Self-esteem is also among the strongest predictors of anxiety (Battle et al., 1988; Rawson, 1992). As Coopersmith (1967) noted, "subjective self-esteem and anxiety are closely and negatively related" (p. 132). Trait self-esteem correlates negatively with measures of trait anxiety and neuroticism, and persons with low self-esteem are more likely to experience anxiety in response to specific events (Bednar et al., 1989; French, 1968; Strauss, Frame, & Forehand, 1987). Baumeister and Tice (1990) offered a persuasive case for the hypothesis that much, if not most, anxiety results from social exclusion. In their view, human beings are innately prepared to experience anxiety at the prospect of exclusion. Anxiety deters people from behaving in ways that might lead to rejection, alerts them to threats to their inclusionary status, and motivates remedial action when they have committed social infractions. (See Miller & Leary, 1992, for a similar analysis of embarrassment.)

The case is perhaps clearest with social anxiety. The proximal cause of social anxiety is a concern with how one is being perceived and evaluated by others (Leary & Kowalski, 1995; Schlenker & Leary, 1982). One reason that people worry about their public images is that making desired impressions on others is, to some extent, a prerequisite for acceptance and social support (Leary & Kowalski, 1990; Schlenker, 1980). As a result, people become apprehensive at the prospect of making unsatisfactory impressions because they are concerned about social acceptance and inclusion (Leary, 1995). Not surprisingly, we find that people with low self-esteem experience greater social anxiety than those with high self-esteem (Leary, 1983).

Loneliness—the subjective experience that one's social relationships are deficient (Peplau & Perlman, 1982)—reflects, at its heart, feelings that one is not adequately included in supportive relationships (Jones, 1990; Russell, Cutrona, Rose, & Yurko, 1984). Although lonely people do not necessarily think others have overtly excluded them, the primary antecedent of loneliness is the sense that one is not included in psychologically intimate relationships. For example, rejected children report greater loneliness than nonrejected children (Asher et al., 1990). However, research shows that loneliness is more strongly related to individuals' perceptions of social isolation than to objective indices of their actual social networks, such as their number of friends (Williams & Solano, 1983). Not surprisingly, then, loneliness is also associated with low self-esteem (Haines, Scalise, & Ginter, 1993; Quellet & Joshi, 1986, Vaux, 1988). In one study, adolescents who scored low in self-esteem more commonly reported feeling dejected and isolated. Furthermore, the intensity of these emotions correlated inversely with self-esteem (Haines et al., 1993).

The notion that perceived exclusion or rejection results in negative emotional states such as those just described is not new. Several personality theorists have proposed that feelings of anxiety, insecurity, isolation, and helplessness stem from events that disturb the security of one's interpersonal relationships, particularly with parents and other intimates (Horney, 1937; Maslow, 1970; Rogers, 1959). Similarly, Bowlby (1973) proposed that anxiety and grief are responses to the disruption of social attachments, and Watson and Clark (1984) noted that negative affectivity includes "a sense of rejection" (p. 465). Along the same lines, Baumeister and Tice (1990) proposed that perceived exclusion from important social groups and relationships is a primary cause of anxiety. Furthermore, several theorists have traced loneliness, grief, and depression to the dissolution of social bonds (Lofland, 1982; Peplau & Perlman, 1982; Stokes & McKirnan, 1989). Although others have discussed the effects of disrupted relationships on emotional distress, the sociometer model helps to explain why low self-esteem is also associated with these reactions.

Substance Abuse

People who abuse alcohol and other drugs tend to have lower self-esteem than those who do not abuse drugs (Cookson, 1994; Griffin-Shelley, Sandler, & Lees, 1990; Macdonald & Czechowicz, 1986; Vega, Zimmerman, Warheit, & Apospori, 1993). At least three explanations of the relationship between self-esteem and substance abuse have been suggested, all of which are consistent with the sociometer model.

First, some people with low self-esteem may use drugs to increase the likelihood of inclusion into certain groups. Adolescents and young adults sometimes believe, often correctly, that using alcohol and other drugs will faciliate their acceptance by peers (Kandel, 1980; Shute, 1975). Farber, Khavari, and Douglass (1980) found that one primary factor that promoted drinking was the belief that alcohol consumption helps one to achieve interpersonal goals such as approval and peer acceptance. Similarly, adolescents who smoke often start because of peer influence and their desire to fit in and be accepted (Botvin, Baker, Botvin, & Dusenbury, 1993). Boys who smoke indicated that smoking "makes you feel part of the gang" (Clayton, 1991, p. 119). People who feel inadequately accepted (and, thus, who have lower self-esteem) are more prone to do whatever it takes to be included than those who already feel accepted.

Second, people with low self-esteem may use alcohol and drugs to blunt the negative emotions associated with real or imagined interpersonal rejection. As we have seen, feeling excluded results in negative feelings, particularly depression and anxiety. Understandably, people wish to reduce such feelings, and alcohol and drug use offers one way to escape aversive self-relevant thought and affect (Baumeister, 1991; Hull, 1981).

Third, the habitual use of alcohol and drugs may lower self-esteem directly because the person is excluded by significant others for using drugs or indirectly because drug use interferes with successful performance in work, academic, and interpersonal settings. People who use alcohol and other drugs may be ostracized because they are often in an altered state or because their drug use leads to repeated failure. In both instances, low self-esteem is a consequence rather than an antecedent of substance abuse.

In brief, rather than emerging from low self-esteem per se, excessive drug and alcohol abuse may reflect attempts to increase social acceptance, escape aversive self-related affect, or deflect the negative impact of rejection.

Sexual Behavior

Sexual union is, among other things, a mode of social inclusion. The fact that someone else wishes to have sex with us can induce a sense of bonding or belonging. In addition, agreeing to have sex is sometimes a tactic for enhancing one's acceptance by another person. In light of this, we might expect that persons with lower self-esteem (who feel less included) would be more indiscriminately sexual.

The evidence on this point is inconclusive, however. By and large, studies show little or no relationship between self-esteem and sexual activity among adolescents (Cvetkovich & Grote, 1981; Plotnick & Butler, 1991). However, such data do not bear directly on our hypothesis because low self-esteem should not be related to sexual activity per se, but rather to indiscriminate sexuality or promiscuity. To our knowledge, no research exists regarding the link between low self-esteem and the tendency to use one's sexuality to enhance social acceptance.

However, indirect evidence for a link between self-esteem and sexual behavior is provided by the finding that women who have sex with their therapists not only tend to have low self-esteem, but often have just gone through divorce or separation—an exclusionary experience. Solursh, Solursh, and Williams (1993) explicitly acknowledged the link with rejection by referring to these clients as "lonely women searching for acceptance" (p. 443). Furthermore, prostitutes tend to have notably low self-esteem (Bagley & Young, 1987), and increases in prostitutes' self-esteem are associated with lowered prostitution (Wuzhacher, Evans, & Moore, 1991).

Although the relationship between self-esteem and sexual activity is equivocal, low self-esteem is clearly associated with the failure to use contraception and practice safe sex (Tashakkori & Thompson, 1992). Crokenberg and Soby (1989) suggested that adolescents with high self-esteem are more likely than those with low self-esteem to have personal goals that would be compromised by an unplanned pregnancy. Although this may be true, another possibility is that people, particularly women, may forego safe sex to please their partners. Among adolescents, responsibility for contraception often falls on the female (Herz & Reis, 1987); those who are more highly motivated to be accepted or to avoid rejection may be more willing to have sex without a condom to please their partners. If our analysis is correct, we would expect to find a stronger relationship between self-esteem and contraceptive use for female than male adolescents. Just such an effect was obtained by Holmbeck, Crossman, Wandrei, and Gasiewski (1994). Along the same lines, research shows that gay men who engage in unprotected anal intercourse often do so to avoid rejection for being a "wimp" (Gold, Skinner, Grant, & Plummer, 1991).

Aggression

Violence has many causes, many of which have little to do with either self-esteem or rejection. Even so, two facts are well established: (1) people with low self-esteem are particularly prone to aggression, including domestic violence (Paulson, Coombs, & Landsverk, 1990; Russell & Hulson, 1992; see, however, Hurlbert, Whittaker, & Munoz, 1991), child abuse (Culp, Culp, Soulis, & Letts, 1989), homicide (Lowenstein, 1989), and other forms of harmful behavior; and (2) they are particularly likely to aggress when their sense of inclusion or acceptance has been threatened (Goldstein & Rosenbaum, 1985).

Although evidence on this point is not conclusive, data suggest that perceived rejection, rather than low self-esteem per se, may underlie much aggression. For example, children who are ostracized tend to be more hostile, aggressive, and disruptive than those who are accepted (Bullock, 1992; Coie & Dodge, 1988; Hymel, Rubin, Rowden, & LeMare, 1990). In a study of popular, rejected, and neglected elementary school children, French and Waas (1987) found that rejected children were significantly more aggressive and hostile than the other groups. Similarly, aggressive conduct disorder is associated with rejection by peers and, not surprisingly, by low self-esteem (Stewart, 1985). Although aggressive people are undoubtedly rejected because they are violent, their aggressiveness may stem from prior rejection. In his study of violence, Toch (1992) identified a subclass of violent men who behave aggressively when others cast aspersions on their image—that is, when others behave in a rejecting or dismissive manner toward them. Similarly, research on domestic violence suggests that abusive husbands tend to feel that their wives often threaten their self-concept by treating them in critical, rejecting ways (Goldstein & Rosenbaum, 1985).

Another category of violent men identified by Toch (1992) consisted of "rep-defenders" whose social identities are based on their aggressiveness. Such individuals behave violently to obtain acceptance by other members of their groups. Violent men typically have low self-esteem, but perceived slights and potential rejection rather than low self-esteem appear to underlie their aggressiveness.

Interestingly, one common form of aggression—bullying among children—has not been found to be related to self-esteem (Hoover & Hazler, 1991; Rigby & Slee, 1993). This may be because bullies are often integrated into their social groups and may, in fact, use bullying to maintain their acceptance by the group. In contrast, chronic *victims* of bullies tend to be socially isolated and, not surprisingly, have low self-esteem (Hoover & Hazler, 1991).

Membership in Deviant Groups

Studies have shown that low self-esteem predicts membership in socially deviant groups such as gangs and cults (Tennant-Clark, Fritz, & Beauvais, 1989; Wheeler, Wood, & Hatch, 1988). Such a link is consistent with the sociometer model. To the extent that low self-esteem reflects a sense of low perceived inclusion, persons with low self-esteem will be more likely to seek membership in groups that offer them a sense of belonging. As one gang member remarked about his membership in a gang, "It was fun and I belonged" (Vigil, 1988, p. 154).

Wheeler and colleagues (1988) suggested that adolescents become involved in satanism as an escape from feelings of alienation and isolation. Early research showed that deliquent boys tended to come from families characterized by severe punitiveness and parental rejection (Bandura & Walters, 1959; Glueck & Glueck, 1950). Parental rejection has been identified as a causal factor in adolescent deviance, even when other family factors, such as control, organization, conflict, and religiosity, are controlled (Simons, Robertson, & Downs, 1989).

Interestingly, although low self-esteem is associated with joining deviant groups, members who are integrated into such groups often have self-esteem that is as high as anyone else (Latkin, 1990). This suggests that, as the sociometer model suggests, membership in such groups raises self-esteem by providing a sense of belonging. As Vigil (1988) observed, "often youths feel loved, respected, and supported for the first time as a result of joining a gang" (p. 88).

Eating Disorders

Women with eating disorders tend to have lower self-esteem than those who do not (Gross & Rosen, 1988; Katzman & Wolchik, 1984; Shisslak, Pazda, & Crago, 1990; Wagner, Halmi, & Maguire, 1987). Furthermore, among women with eating disorders, the severity of the disorder correlates negatively with self-esteem (Mintz & Betz, 1988). Several researchers have also noted a link between eating disorders and an intense fear of disapproval and rejection (Dunn & Ondercin, 1981; Katzman & Wolchik, 1984; Weinstein & Richman, 1984). However, unlike the problems discussed thus far, the reason for the link between rejection and eating disorders is not clear.

One possibility is that some people (particular women in the contemporary United States), may become obsessed with their weight because being thin is seen as a route to social acceptance (Leary, Tchividjian, & Kraxberger, 1994; Rodin, Silberstein, & Striegel-Moore, 1985). Although this seems to be part of the explanation, the link between rejection and eating disorders appears to reflect more than a simple desire to make favorable impressions or to increase one's chances of approval or acceptance.

In an experimental study by Rezek and Leary (1991), women who scored low or high in anorexic tendencies spoke over an intercom to another participant while receiving bogus feedback regarding how interested the other participant was in what they were saying. (Presumably, this feedback connoted acceptance versus rejection). Results showed that women with anorexic tendencies subsequently ate significantly less during a food-tasting study when they had been unsuccessful at holding the other participant's attention than when the other person had seemed interested in what they were saying. Given that the other participant could not see the woman during the conversation and was not privy to how much she ate during the food test, it seems unlikely that eating was an interpersonal tactic intended to either control one's weight or to convey the image of being a light eater. Even so, the fact that women with anorexic tendencies reduced their food intake only when they received rejecting feedback implicates perceived exclusion in the link between low self-esteem and eating disorders.

Clinical Implications

Given that low self-esteem has long been recognized as a predictor of maladaptive behavior, many psychologists have suggested ameliorating certain emotional and behavioral problems by raising self-esteem.[2] However, in our view, the effectiveness of these psychotherapeutic approaches derives from modifying the ways in which clients deal with issues involving interpersonal acceptance and rejection rather than from enhancing self-esteem per se. As we have seen, many of the problems that have been attributed to low self-esteem are parsimoniously explained in terms of social rejection. People do not experience these sorts of difficulties because their self-esteem is low, but rather because their need for belonging and acceptance is not being met (Baumeister & Leary, 1995). We regard it as more plausible that unmet needs for social inclusion lead to dysphoria and to maladaptive efforts to be included rather than that low self-esteem inherently causes dysfunctional behavior.

One implication of this view is that interventions that raise self-esteem may alleviate certain problems not because they raise self-esteem, but because they increase individuals' perceptions that they are socially included. Some programs—such as social support groups, recreation programs, and Outward Bound experiences—may do this directly by creating a social context that fosters a sense of inclusion and belonging (Fashimpar & Harris, 1987; Forsyth, 1991; Tutty, Ridgood, & Rothery, 1993). For example, programs such as Outward

Bound and "mini-hike" programs (probation combined with group recreational activities for juvenile offenders) have successfully reduced gang membership (Berland, Homlish, & Blotcky, 1989; Fashimpar, 1991; Fashimpar, & Harris, 1987). Not surprisingly, these interventions, which promote a sense of belonging to a supportive group, not only reduce maladaptive behavior but raise self-esteem as well. Similarly, treatments designed to extricate people from the grasp of fanatical groups and cults emphasize increasing self-esteem and showing the person that he or she is loved by friends and family outside of the cult. Social support groups also help to raise the self-esteem of victims of rape, domestic violence, and sexual abuse (e.g., Resnick, 1993).

Other programs have their effects by helping individuals acquire knowledge, skills, or other characteristics that increase their sense of includability. Developing social skills, learning to read, obtaining one's G.E.D., or developing other competencies increases both the real and perceived probability of social acceptance, often by increasing the person's job opportunities. For example, programs that encourage gang members to pursue education and job training lowers gang membership and drug abuse (Bell & Jenkins, 1991). Similarly, prostitutes who attended an alternative "street school" showed increased self-esteem and lower rates of prostitution after only 2 months. Riggio, Throckmorton, and DePaola (1990) noted that social skills facilitate the "initiation, development, and maintenance of human relationships" (p. 799). Not surprisingly, then, social-skills training raises self-esteem as it reduces a variety of problems. Although such interventions increase self-esteem, we maintain that their effects on behavior and affect result from increased includability rather than heightened self-esteem.

In addition to treatments that explicitly focus on increasing self-esteem and a sense of includability, many common psychotherapies include features that would be expected to provide benefits by increasing the client's perceived inclusionary status. Rogers's (1959) focus on unconditional positive regard, for example, can be reinterpreted within the sociometer perspective as a means of enhancing clients' sense of inclusion and decreasing their fear of rejection. Rational-emotive therapy (e.g., Ellis & Harper, 1975) attempts to rid clients of their irrational beliefs, many of which involve beliefs regarding the importance of acceptance and the criteria for which people are accepted. For example, clients are urged to reconsider their beliefs regarding the importance of being accepted by everyone and the necessity of being perfect in order to be loved. Even Freudian therapy can be reconceptualized as dealing with issues involving social inclusion, specifically how clients can satisfy their id impulses in a manner that does not lead to rejection.

Conclusion

Psychologists of many theoretical persuasions have implicated low self-esteem as a factor in behavioral and emotional problems. The sociometer theory offers a tentative explanation for the link between self-esteem and maladaptive behavior by suggesting that, rather than causing psychological difficulties, low self-esteem is a co-effect of perceived social exclusion. Interpersonal rejection appears to us a more likely cause of these difficulties than low self-esteem per se. Furthermore, interventions designed to remediate these problems may well have their effects by enhancing the client's real or perceived acceptance rather than by simply raising self-esteem.

Although humans and their prehominid ancestors have always faced the possibility of rejection and exclusion, people today may experience more difficulty establishing and maintaining their connections with one another than they did in the past. Our ancestors tended to live out their lives in a single social group, surrounded by large extended families and a wider community of familiar others whose support could be counted on in times of need. In contrast, people in Western societies today are not only more mobile but tend to be included and excluded largely on the basis of their personal attributes and ability, rather than on ascribed characteristics. As a result, members of modern, mobile societies may face the possibility of social exclusion more frequently than those of previous generations (see Baumeister, 1987). As a result, rejection and its dysfunctional consequences—including low self-esteem—may be more common today than they were during earlier times.

NOTES

[1] Terror management theory (e.g., Solomon, Greenberg, & Pyszczynski, 1991) also proposes that people strive to behave in socially valued ways that maintain their self-esteem. However, terror management theory and sociometer theory diverge regarding the underlying motive for doing so. Terror management theory posits that people behave according to cultural standards because their resulting sense of self-esteem buffers them from the anxiety caused by awareness of their own fragility and mortality. In contrast, the sociometer theory maintains that people generally act in esteem-enhancing ways because socially desirable behavior increases the likelihood of social inclusion.

[2] In one particularly ambitious effort of this type, the California State Assembly created in 1986 the California Task Force to Promote Self-Esteem and Personal and Social Responsibility. They hoped to reduce not only personal difficulties, but also societal problems such as delinquency and academic failure (Mecca et al., 1989).

REFERENCES

Asher, S. R., Parkhurst, J. T., Hymel, S., & Williams, G. A. (1990). Peer rejection and loneliness in childhood. In S. R. Asher & J. D. Coie (Eds.), *Peer rejection in childhood* (pp. 253–273). New York: Cambridge University Press.

Averill, J. R. (1968). Grief: Its nature and significance. *Psychological Bulletin, 70*, 721–748.

Bagley, C., & Young, L. (1987). Juvenile prostitution and child sexual abuse: A controlled study. *Canadian Journal of Community Mental Health, 6*, 5–26.

Bandura, A., & Walters, R. (1959). *Adolescent aggression.* New York: Ronald Press.

Barash, D. P. (1977). *Sociobiology and behavior.* New York: Elsevier.

Battle, J., Jarratt, L., Smit, S., & Precht, D. (1988). Relations among self-esteem, depression, and anxiety of children. *Psychological Reports, 62*, 999–1005.

Baumeister, R. F. (1987). How the self became a problem: A psychological review of historical research. *Journal of Personality and Social Psychology, 52*, 163–176.

Baumeister, R. F. (1991). *Escaping the self.* New York: Basic Books.

Baumeister, R. F. (Ed.). (1993). *Self-esteem: The puzzle of low self-regard.* New York: Plenum.

Baumeister, R. F., & Leary, M. R. (1995). The need to belong: Desire for interpersonal attachments as a fundamental human motivation. *Psychological Bulletin,* 497–529.

Baumeister, R. F., & Tice, D. M. (1990). Anxiety and social exclusion. *Journal of Social and Clinical Psychology, 9*, 165–195.

Bednar, R. L., Wells, M. G., & Peterson, S. R. (1989). *Self-esteem: Paradoxes and innovations in clinical theory and practice.* Washington, DC: American Psychological Association.

Bell, C. C., & Jenkins, E. J. (1991). Traumatic stress and children. Third national conference: Health care for the poor and underserved "children at risk." *Journal of Health Care for the Poor and Underserved, 2*, 175–185.

Berland, D. T., Homlish, J. S., & Blotcky, M. J. (1989). Adolescent gangs in the hospital. *Bulletin of the Menniger Clinic, 53*, 31–43.

Botvin, G. J., Baker, E., Botvin, E. M., & Dusenbury, L. (1993). Factors promoting cigarette smoking among Black youth: A causal modeling approach. *Addictive Behaviors, 18*, 397–405.

Bowlby, J. (1973). *Attachment and loss, Vol. 2: Separation.* New York: Basic Books.

Bowlby, J. (1980). *Attachment and loss, Vol. 3: Loss.* New York: Basic Books.

Brown, G. W., & Harris, T. (1978). *Social origins of depression: A study of psychiatric disorder in women.* New York: Free Press.

Brown, J. D. (1993). Self-esteem and self-evaluations: Feeling is believing. In J. Suls (Ed.), *Psychological perspectives on the self* (Vol. 4, pp. 27–58). Hillsdale, NJ: Lawrence Erlbaum Associates.

Bullock, J. R. (1992). Children without friends: Who are they and how can teachers help? *Childhood Education, 69*, 92–96.

Clayton, S. (1991). Gender differences in psychosocial determinants of adolescent smoking. *Journal of School Health, 61*, 115–120.

Cohen, S., & Wills, T. A. (1985). The stress buffering hypothesis of social support. *Psychological Bulletin, 98*, 310–357.

Coie, J., & Dodge, K. (1988). Multiple sources of data on social behavior and social status in the school: A cross-age comparison. *Child Development, 59*, 815–829.

Cookson, H. (1994). Personality variables associated with alcohol use in young offenders. *Personality and Individual Differences, 16*, 179–182.

Coopersmith, S. (1967). *The antecedents of self-esteem.* San Francisco: W. H. Freeman.

Crokenberg, S. B., & Soby, B. A. (1989). Self-esteem and teenage pregnancy. In A. M. Mecca, N. J. Smelser, & J. Vasconcellos (Eds.), *The social importance of self-esteem* (pp. 125–164). Berkeley: University of California Press.

Culp, R., Culp, A. M., Soulis, J., & Letts, D. (1989). Self-esteem and depression in abusive, neglecting, and nonmaltreating mothers. *Infant Mental Health Journal, 10*, 243–251.

Cvetkovich, G., & Grote, B. (1981). Psychological maturity and teenage contraception use: An investigation of decision-making and communication skills. *Population and Environment, 4*, 211–226.

Dunn, P. K., & Ondercin, P. (1981). Personality variables related to compulsive eating in college women. *Journal of Clinical Psychology, 37*, 43–49.

Ellis, A., & Harper, R. (1975). *A new guide to rational living.* Englewood Cliffs, NJ: Prentice-Hall.

Eskilson, A., Wiley, M. G., Meuhlhauer, G., & Dodder, L. (1986). Parental pressure, self-esteem and adolescent reported deviance: Bending the twig too far. *Adolescence, 21*, 501–515.

Farber, P. D., Khavari, K. A., & Douglass, F. M. (1980). A factor analytic study of reasons for drinking: Empirical validation of positive and negative reinforcement dimensions. *Journal of Consulting and Clinical Psychology, 48*, 780–781.

Fashimpar, G. A. (1991). From probation to mini-hikes: A comparison of traditional and innovative programs for community treatment of delinquent adolescents. *Social Work with Groups, 14*, 105–118.

Fashimpar, G. A., & Harris, L. T. (1987). Social work at 30 MPH: Mini-hike rehabilitation groups for juvenile delinquents. *Social Work with Groups, 10,* 33–48.

Forsyth, D. R. (1991). Change in therapeutic groups. In C. R. Snyder & D. R. Forsyth (Eds.), *Handbook of social and clinical psychology* (pp. 664–680). New York: Pergamon.

French, D. C., & Waas, G. A. (1987). Social-cognitive and behavioral characteristics of peer-rejected boys. *Professional School Psychology, 2,* 103–112.

French, J. R. P. (1968). The conceptualization and measurement of mental health in terms of self-identity theory. In S. B. Bells (Ed.), *The definition and measurement of mental health.* Washington, DC: U. S. Department of Health, Education, and Welfare.

Glueck, S., & Glueck, E. (1950). *Unraveling junenile delinquency.* New York: Commonwealth Fund.

Gold, R. S., Skinner, M. J., Grant, P. J., & Plummer, D. C. (1991). Situational factors and thought processes associated with unprotected intercourse in gay men. *Psychology and Health, 5,* 259–278.

Goldstein, D., & Rosenbaum, A. (1985). An evaluation of the self-esteem of maritally violent men. *Family Relations Journal of Applied Family and Child Studies, 34,* 425–428.

Griffin-Shelley, E., Sandler, K. R., & Lees, C. (1990). Sex-role perceptions in chemically dependent subjects: Adults versus adolescents. *International Journal of the Addictions, 25,* 1383–1391.

Gross, J., & Rosen, J. C. (1988). Bulimia in adolescents: Prevalence and psychological correlates. *International Journal of Eating Disorders, 7,* 51–61.

Haines, D. A., Scalise, J. J., & Ginter, E. J. (1993). Relationship of loneliness and its affective elements to self-esteem. *Psychological Reports, 73,* 479–482.

Hammen, C. (1988). Self-cognitions, stressful events, and the prediction of depression in children of depressed mothers. *Journal of Abnormal Child Psychology, 16,* 347–360.

Harter, S. (1993). Causes and consequences of low self-esteem in children and adolescents. In R. F. Baumeister (Ed.), *Self-esteem: The puzzle of low self-regard* (pp. 87–116). New York: Plenum.

Herz, E. J., & Reis, J. S. (1987). Family life education for young inner-city teens: Identifying needs. *Journal of Youth and Adolescence, 16,* 361–377.

Holmbeck, G. N., Crossman, R. E., Wandrei, M. L., & Gasiewski, E. (1994). Cognitive development, egocentrism, self-esteem, and adolescent contraceptive knowledge, attitudes, and behavior. *Journal of Youth and Adolescence, 23,* 169–193.

Hoover, J. H., & Hazler, R. J. (1991). Bullies and victims. *Elementary School Guidance and Counseling, 25,* 212–219.

Horney, K. (1937). *Neurotic personality of our times.* New York: Norton.

Hull, J. G. (1981). A self-awareness model of the causes and effects of alcohol consumption. *Journal of Abnormal Psychology, 90,* 586–600.

Hurlbert, D., Whittaker, K., & Munoz, C. J. (1991). Etiological characteristics of abusive husbands. *Military Medicine, 156,* 670–675.

Hymel, S., Rubin, K. H., Rowden, L., & LeMare, L. (1990). Children's peer relationships: Longitudinal prediction of internalizing and externalizing problems from middle to late childhood. *Child Development, 61,* 2004–2021.

Izard, C. E. (1977). *Human emotions.* New York: Plenum.

Jones, W. H. (1990). Loneliness and social exclusion. *Journal of Social and Clinical Psychology, 9,* 214–220.

Kandel, D. B. (1980). Drug and drinking behavior among youth. *Annual Review of Sociology, 6,* 235–285.

Katzman, M. A., & Wolchik, S. A. (1984). Bulimia and binge eating in college women: A comparison of personality and behavioral characteristics. *Journal of Consulting and Clinical Psychology, 52,* 423–428.

Kupersmidt, J. B., & Patterson, C. J. (1991). Childhood peer rejection, aggression, withdrawal, and perceived competence as predictors of self-reported behavior problems in preadolescence. *Journal of Abnormal Child Psychology, 19,* 427–449.

Latkin, C. A. (1990). The self-concept of Rajneeshpuram commune members. *Journal for the Scientific Study of Religion, 29,* 91–98.

Leary, M. R. (1983). Social anxiousness: The construct and its measurement. *Journal of Personality Assessment, 47,* 66–75.

Leary, M. R. (1990). Responses to social exclusion: Social anxiety, jealousy, loneliness, depression, and low self-esteem. *Journal of Social and Clinical Psychology, 9,* 221–229.

Leary, M. R. (1995). *Self-presentation: Impression management and interpersonal behavior.* Dubuque, IA: Brown & Benchmark.

Leary, M. R., & Downs, D. L. (1995). Interpersonal functions of the self-esteem motive: The self-esteem system as a sociometer. In M. Kernis (Ed.), *Efficacy, agency, and self-esteem* (pp. 123–144). New York: Plenum.

Leary, M. R., & Kowalski, R. M. (1990). Impression management: A literature review and two-component model. *Psychological Bulletin, 107,* 34–47.

Leary, M. R., & Kowalski, R. M. (1995). *Social anxiety.* New York: Guilford Press.

Leary, M. R., Tambor, E., Terdal, S., & Downs, D. L. (1995). Self-esteem as an interpersonal monitor: The sociometer hypothesis. *Journal of Personality and Social Psychology, 68,* 518–530.

Leary, M. R., Tchividjian, L. R., & Kraxberger, B. E. (1994). Self-presentation can be hazardous to your health: Impression management and health risk. *Health Psychology, 13,* 461–470.

Litovsky, V. G., & Dusek, J. B. (1985). Perceptions of child rearing and self-concept development during the early adolescent years. *Journal of Youth and Adolescence, 14,* 373–387.

Lofland, L. H. (1982). Loss and human connection: An exploration into the nature of the social bond. In W. Ickes & E. S. Knowles (Eds.), *Personality, roles, and social behavior* (pp. 219–242). New York: Springer-Verlag.

Lowenstein, L. F. (1989). Homicide: A review of recent research (1975–1985). *Criminologist, 13,* 74–89.

Macdonald, D. T., & Czechowicz, D. (1986). Marijuana: A pediatric overview. *Psychiatric Annals, 16,* 215–218.

Maslow, A. H. (1970). *Motivation and personality* (2nd ed). New York: Harper & Row.

Mecca, A. M., Smelser, N. J., & Vasconcellos, J. (1989). *The social importance of self-esteem.* Berkeley: University of California Press.

Miller, R. S., & Leary, M. R. (1992). Social sources and interactive functions of emotion: The case of embarrassment. In M. Clark (Ed.), *Emotion and social behavior* (pp. 202–221). Beverly Hills, CA: Sage.

Mintz, L., & Betz, N. (1988). Prevalence and correlates of eating disordered behaviors among undergraduate women. *Journal of Counseling Psychology, 35*, 463–471.

Morvitz, E. & Motta, R. W. (1992). Predictors of self-esteem: The roles of parent-child perceptions, achievement, and class placement. *Journal of Learning Disabilities, 25*, 72–80.

Panak, W. F., & Garber, J. (1992). Role of aggression, rejection, and attributions in the prediction of depression in children. *Development and Psychopathology, 4*, 145–165.

Paulson, M. J., Coombs, R. H. & Landsverk, J. (1990). Youth who physically assault their parents. *Journal of Family Violence, 5*, 121–133.

Peplau, L. A., & Perlman, D. (Eds.). (1982). *Loneliness: A sourcebook of current theory, research, and therapy.* New York: John Wiley & Sons.

Plotnick, R. D., & Butler, S. S. (1991). Attitudes and adolescent nonmarital childbearing: Evidence from the National Longitudinal Survey of Youth. *Journal of Adolescent Research, 6*, 470–497.

Quellet, R., & Joshi, P. (1986). Loneliness in relation to depression and self-esteem. *Psychological Reports, 58*, 821–822.

Rawson, H. E. (1992). The interrelationship of measures of manifest anxiety, self-esteem, locus of control, and depression in children with behavior problems. *Journal of Psychoeducational Assessment, 10*, 319–329.

Resnick, P. A. (1993). The psychological impact of rape. *Journal of Interpersonal Violence, 8*, 223–255.

Rezek, P. J., & Leary, M. R. (1991). Perceived control, drive for thinness, and food consumption: Anorexic tendencies as a displaced reactance. *Journal of Personality, 59*, 129–142.

Rigby, K., & Slee, P. T. (1993). Dimensions of interpersonal relation among Australian children and implications for psychological well-being. *Journal of Social Psychology, 133*, 33–42.

Riggio, R. E., Throckmorton, B., & DePaola, S. (1990). Social skills and self-esteem. *Personality and Individual Differences, 11*, 799–804.

Rodin, J., Silberstein, L., & Striegel-Moore, R. (1985). Women and weight: A normative discontent? In T. B. Sonderregger (Ed.), *Nebraska symposium on motivation: Psychology and gender* (pp. 267–307). Lincoln: University of Nebraska Press.

Rogers, C. R. (1959). A theory of therapy, personality, and interpersonal relationships, as developed in the client-centered framework. In S. Koch (Ed.), *Psychology: A study of a science* (Vol. 3, pp. 184–256). New York: McGraw-Hill.

Russell, D., Cutrona, C., Rose, J., & Yurko, K. (1984). Social and emotional loneliness: An examination of Weiss' typology of loneliness. *Journal of Personality and Social Psychology, 46*, 1313–1321.

Russell, R. J., & Hulson, R. (1992). Physical and psychological abuse of heterosexual partners. *Personality and Individual Differences, 13*, 457–473.

Scheff, T. J. (1990). *Microsociology: Discourse, emotion, and social structure.* Chicago: University of Chicago Press.

Schlenker, B. R. (1980). *Impression management: The self-concept, social identity, and interpersonal relations.* Monterey, CA: Brooks/Cole.

Schlenker, B. R., & Leary, M. R. (1982). Social anxiety and self-presentation: A conceptualization and model. *Psychological Bulletin, 92*, 641–669.

Shisslak, C. M., Pazda, S., & Crago, M. (1990). Body weight and bulimia as discriminators of psychological characteristics among anorexic, bulimic, and obese women. *Journal of Abnormal Psychology, 99*, 380–384.

Shute, R. E. (1975). The impact of peer pressure on the verbally expressed drug attitudes of male college students. *American Journal of Drug and Alcohol Abuse, 2*, 231–243.

Simons, R. J., Robertson, J. F., & Downs, W. R. (1989). The nature of the association between parental rejection and delinquent behavior. *Journal of Youth and Adolescence, 18*, 297–310.

Solomon, S., Greenberg, J., & Pyszcynski, T. (1991). A terror management theory of social behavior: The psychological functions of self-esteem and cultural worldview. In M. P. Zanna (Ed.), *Advances in experimental social psychology* (Vol. 24, pp. 93–159). San Diego: Academic Press.

Smart, R. G., & Walsh, G. W. (1993). Predictors of depression in street youth. *Adolescence, 28*, 41–53.

Snyder, C. R. (1994). *The psychology of hope.* New York: Free Press.

Solursh, D. S., Solursh, L. P., & Williams, N. R. (1993). Patient–therapist sex: "Just say no" isn't enough. *Medicine and Law, 12*, 431–438.

Stewart, M. A. (1985). Aggressive conduct disorder: A brief Review. Sixth Biennial Meeting of the International Society for Research on Aggression (1984, Turku, Finland). *Aggressive Behavior, 11*, 323–331.

Stokes, J. P., & McKirnan, D. J. (1989). Affect and the social environment: The role of social support in depression and anxiety. In P. C. Kendall & D. Watson (Eds.), *Anxiety and depression: Distinctive and overlapping features* (pp. 253–283). New York: Academic Press.

Strauss, C., Frame, C., & Forehand, R. (1987). Psychosocial impairment associated with anxiety in children. *Journal of Clinical Child Psychology, 16*, 235–239.

Tashakkori, A., & Thompson, V. D. (1992). Predictors of intention to take precautions against AIDS among Black college students. *Journal of Applied Social Psychology, 22*, 736–753.

Tennant-Clark, C. M., Fritz, J. J., & Beauvais, F. (1989). Occult participation: Its impact on adolescent development. *Adolescence, 24*, 757–772.

Toch, H. (1992). *Violent men.* Washington, DC: American Psychological Association.

Tutty, L. M., Ridgood, B. A., & Rothery, M. A. (1993). Support groups for battered women: Research on their efficacy. *Journal of Family Violence, 8*, 325–343.

Vaux, A. (1988). Social and emotional loneliness: The role of social and personal characteristics. *Personality and Social Psychology Bulletin, 14*, 722–734.

Vega, W. A., Zimmerman, R. S., Warheit, G. J., & Apospori, E. (1993). Risk factors for early adolescent drug use in four ethnic and racial groups. *American Journal of Public Health, 83*, 185–189.

Vigil, J. D. (1988). *Barrio gangs: Street life and identity in southern California.* Austin: University of Texas Press.

Wagner, S., Halmi, K. A., & Maguire, T. V. (1987). The sense of personal ineffectiveness in patients with eating disorders: One construct or several? *International Journal of Eating Disorders, 6,* 495–505.

Watson, D. & Clark, L. A. (1984). Negative affectivity: The disposition to experience aversive emotional states. *Psychological Bulletin, 96,* 465–490.

Weinstein, H. M., & Richman, A. (1984). The group treatment of bulimia. *Journal of American College Health, 32,* 208–215.

Wheeler, B. R., Wood, S., & Hatch, R. J. (1988). Assessment and intervention with adolescents involved in satanism. *Social Work, 33,* 547–550.

Williams, J. G., & Solano, C. H. (1983). The social reality of feeling lonely: Friendship and reciprocation. *Personality and Social Psychology Bulletin, 9,* 237–242.

Wuzhacher, K. V., Evans, E. D., & Moore, E. J. (1991). Effects of alternative street school on youth involved in prostitution. Special Issue: Homeless youth. *Journal of Adolescent Health, 12,* 549–554.

Discussion Questions

1. The fact that all of the psychological difficulties discussed in the article are related to perceptions of social rejection (or at least low acceptance) suggests that being accepted must be exceptionally important to human well-being. Identify several possible benefits of being accepted by other people.
2. The article ties low self-esteem to several negative emotions—depression, anxiety (especially social anxiety), loneliness, and so on. If all of these emotions are reactions to real or potential rejection, why do we need so many? Why isn't there just one rejection emotion?
3. Thinking about the "normal" analogues of clinically relevant behaviors often makes them easier to understand. List and discuss at least three dangerous or dysfunctional things that you have done in order to be accepted by other people. Similarly, list and discuss at least three occasions on which you experienced dysphoric emotions because you felt inadequately accepted.
4. According to the authors, why do clinical interventions that raise clients' self-esteem often result in psychological improvement?

Suggested Readings

Baumeister, R. F., Smart. L. & Boden, J. M. (1996). Relation of threatened egotism to violence and aggression: The dark side of high self-esteem. *Psychological Review, 103,* 5–33. Although Reading 9 focused on the dysfunctional features of low self-esteem, high self-esteem can have its downside as well.

Leary, M. R. (1999). The social and psychological importance of self-esteem. In R. M. Kowalski & M. R. Leary (Eds.), *The social psychology of emotional and behavioral problems* (pp. 197–221). Washington, DC: American Psychological Association. This chapter delves more deeply into the question of why self-esteem is important to human well-being.

Murray, S. L., Holmes, J. G., MacDonald, G., & Ellsworth, P. (1998). Through the looking glass darkly? When self-doubts turn into relationship insecurities. *Journal of Personality and Social Psychology, 75,* 1459–1480. This research investigated how low self-esteem may undermine the quality of people's romantic relationships.

READING 10

Marital Satisfaction, Depression, and Attributions: A Longitudinal Analysis

Frank D. Finchman • University of Illinois
Thomas N. Bradbury • University of California

Editors' Introduction

Although the study of attributions has a long history within social psychology, their application to close relationships is relatively recent. Their importance to relationships is reflected in Harvey's (1987) observation that attributions are a barometer of the health of a relationship. When negative or positive things happen in a relationship, each partner searches for explanations for those events. Not only do the people's attributions reflect something about the quality of the relationship, but they can also affect the relationship itself. The fact that two partners are interdependent suggests that both are probably, at least in part, to blame for problems that arise, yet when they make attributions that lead them to blame one another, the relationship is likely to be affected.

As discussed by Leary and Miller (1986), three themes surface in research on attributions in close relationships. First, partners fall prey to the actor–observer bias in which they easily see the effects of situational influences on their own behavior but fail to see the role of situational influences in determining their partner's behavior. Relatedly, relational partners often do not see that their partner's actions are often in response to their own behavior. Second, self-serving biases occur when relational partners make attributions for events. In marriages, for example, each partner tends to claim a disproportionate share of the credit for positive events and levies a disproportionate share of the blame for negative events on the partner. Third, the attributions that relationship partners make appear to be linked to their satisfaction with the relationship. People who are satisfied with their relationships give their partners credit for positive events and give them the benefit of the doubt for negative events. People in unsatisfying relationships, on the other hand, take personal credit for positive events and blame the partner for the negative things that happen.

Fincham and Bradbury address the latter of these three themes, focusing on the relationship between people's attributions for negative events and marital satisfaction. The purpose of the study was twofold. First, the researchers wanted to replicate and extend previous research that found a relationship between satisfaction and relational attributions. Second, they wanted to eliminate alternative explanations for the observed relationship between satisfaction and attributions. Specifically, they wanted to determine whether attributions made for relationship events account for unique variance in satisfaction above and beyond that accounted for by depression (which has been shown to be related both to attributions, Robins, 1988, and marital satisfaction, Beach, Sandeen, & O'Leary, 1990) or by self-esteem (which has also been shown to be related to both attributions, Ickes, 1988, and satisfaction, Vanfossen, 1986).

In this research, husbands and wives completed measures of marital satisfaction, depression, self-esteem, and attributions. Results of the study supported previous research by finding relationships between marital satisfaction and attributions, depression, and self-esteem. In addition, the attributions made by husbands and wives accounted for unique variance in marital satisfaction above and beyond the variance accounted for by depression and self-esteem. In fact, attributions made by relationship partners at the outset of the study significantly predicted marital satisfaction 12 months later. Furthermore, among husbands, marital satisfaction at the beginning of the study predicted the kinds of attributions they made 12 months later, suggesting that the relationship between attributions and marital satisfaction may be cyclical and self-perpetuating.

Abstract

This study examined the longitudinal relation between causal attributions and marital satisfaction and tested rival hypotheses that might account for any longitudinal association found between these variables. Data on attributions for negative partner behaviors, marital satisfaction, depression, and self-esteem were provided by 130 couples at 2 points separated by 12 months. To the extent that spouses made nonbenign attributions for negative partner behavior, their marital satisfaction was lower a year later. This finding was not due to depression, self-esteem, or initial level of marital satisfaction, and also emerged when persons reporting chronic individual or marital disorder were removed. Results support a possible causal relation between attributions and marital satisfaction.

In the past decade, researchers have expended considerable effort in trying to understand the role of attributions in close relationships. Numerous studies now document an association between relationship satisfaction and attributions for relationship events (for reviews, see Bradbury & Fincham, 1990; Harvey, 1987; Weiss & Heyman, 1990). Compared to happy partners, distressed partners tend to locate the causes of negative relationship events in the other person and to see the causes of those events as stable and global; the inverse pattern of findings is obtained for positive events. Although this research was largely motivated by conceptual analyses that emphasized the effects of attributions on marital satisfaction (e.g., Baucom, 1987; Epstein, 1982), surprisingly few studies have addressed the causal status of attributions in close relationships. In addition, little attempt has been made to investigate rival explanations for the attribution–satisfaction link, leaving open the possibility that this association is an artifact of unmeasured variables. To address the causal status of attributions, we investigated the longitudinal association between attributions and marital satisfaction. A second purpose of this study is to examine factors that might account for any concurrent and longitudinal associations found between these two variables.

Are Attributions Causally Related to Marital Satisfaction?

It is widely assumed that causal attributions for marital events maintain, and perhaps initiate, marital distress. This effect may be direct or it may be mediated by the assumed effects of causal inferences for partner behavior on subsequent responses to the behavior (for an integrative model relating attributions, behavior, and satisfaction, see Bradbury & Fincham, 1990). Few data have been collected to examine the effect of attributions on satisfaction, a circumstance that may be due, in part, to constraints on conducting experiments in this area.

In one of the few experimental studies conducted, Seligman, Fazio, and Zanna (1980) used dating couples to show that making salient the extrinsic causes for being in the relationship resulted in lower scores on Rubin's (1970) Love Scale. However, the attribution manipulation did not affect scores on Rubin's Liking Scale or global ratings of love and liking. These findings are promising but need to be interpreted cautiously in view of their inconsistency and a failure to replicate them (Rempel, Holmes, & Zanna, 1985). In addition, they contrast with the results of marital therapy outcome research showing that supplementing standard treatments with attributionally oriented interventions does not enhance marital satisfaction more than standard interventions (e.g., Baucom, Sayers, & Sher, 1990; for a review see Fincham, Bradbury, & Beach, 1990).[1]

As Olson and Ross (1985) noted, perhaps the most viable means of investigating a possible causal relation between attributions and marital satisfaction is to collect longitudinal data. The two longitudinal studies conducted to date suggest that attributions may indeed influence relationship satisfaction. Fletcher, Fincham, Cramer, and Heron (1987) found that the extent to which dating partners (76% of the sample were women) attributed the maintenance of the relationship to themselves versus their partner predicted happiness with the relationship 2 months later after initial happiness had been statistically controlled. In a similar vein, Fincham and Bradbury (1987) assessed marriages at two points separated by a 12-month interval and found that initial attributions predicted later marital satisfaction. Nonetheless, these findings must also be viewed with caution because only one of two relevant analyses revealed a significant longitudinal relation in the Fletcher et al. study and the longitudinal association in Fincham and Bradbury's study was obtained for wives but not husbands. The latter finding is consistent with the hypothesis that women are barometers of relationship well-being (Ickes, 1985).

Available data relevant to assessing the indirect effects of attributions on satisfaction (e.g., by demonstrating the effect of attributions on behavior) are similarly limited. Experimental (Fincham & Bradbury, 1988) and correlational data document an association between attributions and observed behavior (Bradbury & Fincham, 1991; Doherty, 1982; Miller, Lefcourt, Holmes, Ware, & Saleh, 1986; Sillars, 1985). However, in Doherty's study the attribution–behavior link was found only for women. Although a reliable association appears to exist between attributions and behavior, additional data are needed to understand more precisely the causal nature of this relation.

In summary, several lines of evidence are consistent with the hypothesis that attributions influence relationship satisfaction. However, both within and across studies, the results are not uniformly supportive of this hypothesis. Even if these studies did show a consistent effect, it might be artifactual because of unconsidered variables. This points to the importance of rival hypotheses for the attribution-satisfaction link, a topic to which we now turn.

Is the Attribution–Satisfaction Association an Artifact?

In the discussion here, we consider two important threats to the validity of past research on attributions in relationships. First, the consistent relation obtained between attributions and satisfaction may simply reflect their joint association with some third variable. Second, the longitudinal association could result from the failure to exclude from the sample persons with chronic disorders.

Depression and Self-Esteem

In view of the association between attributions and depression (see Robins, 1988) and between depression and marital distress (see Beach, Sandeen, & O'Leary, 1990), it is possible that depression accounts for the attribution–satisfaction link. Three studies have addressed this possibility. Fincham, Beach, and Bradbury (1989) conducted two studies that investigated wives' responsibility attributions. Unlike causal attributions, which pertain to who or what produced an outcome or event, responsibility attributions concern accountability for the outcome and determine liability for sanctions (for further discussion see Bradbury & Fincham, 1990; Shaver, 1985). In their first study, Fincham et al. (1989) examined a community sample and found that when depression scores and responsibility attributions (indices comprising judgments of blame, motivation, and intent) were simultaneously entered into a regression equation, only the latter predicted marital satisfaction. The second study included wives with clinically diagnosed levels of depression and showed that the attributions of depressed and nondepressed wives who were maritally distressed did not differ but that both groups differed from happily married wives. Fletcher, Fitness, and Blampied (1990) found that in dating couples, relationship happiness accounted for unique variance in spontaneous and elicited attributions when depression scores were statistically controlled.

Several factors need to be considered in evaluating the studies just described. First, none addressed the role of depression in the longitudinal relation between attributions and satisfaction. Second, the need to study both husbands and wives is self-evident. Third, because attributional models of depression pertain to causal attributions, this type of attribution requires further study; although Fletcher et al. (1990) examined causal attributions, they combined them with responsibility attribution dimensions to form an overall attribution index, and they omitted ratings of the self as causal locus from the index. The significance of this omission is addressed later.

Although attributional models of depression and of relationship satisfaction are similar in their predictions for stable and global attributions, they differ in the predictions they make for causal locus. According to these models, depressed spouses should view themselves as the cause of negative relationship events, whereas maritally distressed spouses should see their partners as the cause of such events. In each case the spouse makes nonbenign attributions that apply either to the self or to the partner and are likely to accentuate the impact of the negative event.

These differential predictions highlight a fundamental problem with the analysis of the locus dimension in prior relationship research. Specifically, self and partner have been used as endpoints in assessments of the locus dimension. This implies an inverse relation between the two loci that runs counter to data on this issue (e.g., Fincham, 1985; Taylor & Koivumaki, 1976). Independent assessments that have been obtained typically have been analyzed separately. The problem with this practice is that spouses' responses are likely to be guided by the extent to which the partner is seen as the cause relative to the self. For example, a husband who locates the cause in his partner and does not see himself as a causal locus is likely to react differently to the partner's behavior than is a husband who similarly locates the cause in the partner but also sees himself as a cause of the behavior. In the latter case, the discounting principle should lead him to moderate his reactions to the partner's behavior. Alternatively, he may be more tolerant of such behavior to avoid possible censure for his own role in producing it. In light of such observations, Bradbury and Fincham (1990) have argued that future research must examine separate locus dimensions relative to one another. Therefore, in the present study we examine the utility of this comparative conception of causal locus.

A second variable that may account for the attribution–satisfaction link is self-esteem. The attribution pattern associated with depression has also been related to self-esteem (Ickes, 1988; Ickes & Layden, 1978). Self-esteem, in turn, is widely thought to be influenced by marital quality, a viewpoint that has gained some empirical support. For example, receiving affirmation in a marital relationship has been related to higher levels of self-esteem (Vanfossen, 1986). To date, no data have been collected to test the hypothesis that self-esteem accounts for the attribution-satisfaction link.

Because loss of self-esteem is often a symptom of depression, it seems reasonable to ask whether the findings just outlined for studies of depression and attributions in marriage can be generalized to self-esteem. At least two factors caution against such generalizations. First, loss of self-esteem can occur independently of depression, suggesting that the correlation between the two constructs is likely to be moderate. Second, positive aspects of well-being, such as self-esteem, may have different correlates than negative aspects, such as depression (cf. Zautra & Reich, 1983). Zautra, Guenther, and Chartier (1985) provided empirical support for this view that is particularly germane in the present context; they found that causal attribution dimensions relating to positive events correlated significantly with self-esteem but not with depression. In view of these observations, depression and self-esteem should not be considered to have equivalent relations with attributions, and as a consequence, we examine them separately in the present study.

Finally, several considerations point to a possible sex difference in the magnitude of the correlations involving depression, self-esteem, and marital satisfaction, including the higher incidence of depression among wives than husbands (Gotlib & McCabe, 1990) and the widespread belief that women value intimate relationships more than men (e.g., Fitzpatrick, 1988), that wives more commonly feel unappreciated by their spouses than do husbands (Noller, 1987), and that wives tend to be more self-critical than their husbands (Carver & Ganellen, 1983). These considerations, together with the growing literature on gender differences in marriage (see Baucom, Notarius, Burnett, & Haefner, 1990) and the studies noted earlier in which attribution findings obtained only for wives (Doherty, 1982; Fincham & Bradbury, 1987), emphasize the importance of examining relations separately for husbands and wives.

Chronic Disorder

Depue and Monroe (1986) noted that in life stress research the most powerful predictor of subsequent disorder is prior disorder. Furthermore, they showed that most people who score high on measures of psychological distress in general population samples have stable disturbances and that this can lead to artifactual longitudinal relations between distress and its correlates. One means of addressing this problem is to statistically control for initial distress. However, this solution is less than optimal because longitudinal relations and the underlying processes that give rise to the relations may differ for chronic and acute psychological distress. For example, attributions may play different roles in the initiation of disorder than they do in the maintenance of disorder. A more desirable means of addressing such problems is to increase the homogeneity of the sample studied. Accordingly, in the present study we examined the effect of excluding persons with high disorder scores on the longitudinal relations studied.

Overview

The primary goal of our study was to examine the longitudinal relation between causal attributions and marital satisfaction. Such information is crucial for addressing the assumed causal relation between these two variables that is basic to theoretical analyses in this area and to attributionally oriented treatment outcome research. A second goal was to test rival hypotheses for any concurrent and longitudinal associations found between these two variables. Ruling out rival hypotheses is critical to understanding existing data that document a link between attributions and marital satisfaction. A final goal was to replicate findings concerning the correlates of marital satisfaction and to examine the longitudinal relation between depression and marital satisfaction. To address these goals, we collected data from married couples at two points 12 months apart.

Method

Subjects

We initially recruited 130 married couples through advertisements in local newspapers. Couples had been married an average of 9.4 ($SD = 9.9$) years and averaged 1.5 ($SD = 1.6$) children. Gross family income was $25,000–$30,000. Of the wives, 97% were White and 55% chose Protestant as their religious preference (Catholic = 19%; other = 17%; no religious preference = 9%). Wives averaged 32.0 ($SD = 9.8$) years of age, 14.3 ($SD = 2.2$) years of education, and obtained a mean score of 111.1 ($SD = 22.9$) on the Marital Adjustment Test (MAT; Locke & Wallace, 1959). Husbands were also predominantly White (97%) and Protestant (54%; Catholic = 14%; other = 17%; no religious preference = 15%). Husbands averaged 34.0 ($SD = 10.2$) years of age, 14.5 ($SD = 2.6$) years of education, and a score of 110.4 ($SD = 21.7$) on the MAT.

At 12 months after the first phase of the study, we attempted to recontact couples, and obtained data from 106 couples. We conducted multivariate t-tests to examine whether spouses who provided data for the first phase of the data collection differed from those who provided data for both phases of the study. The two groups did not differ in terms of demographics or any of the variables investigated in the study, indicating that attrition did not bias the sample providing longitudinal data.

Procedure

At both phases of the project, couples received two sets of materials by mail, together with separate postage-paid return envelopes and a cover letter that thanked them for their participation in the project and instructed them on their task. They were asked to complete the materials independently and to seal the completed materials in separate envelopes before talking about the project. Couples were paid $15.00 upon receipt of the completed materials.

Measures

Marital satisfaction. The MAT (Locke & Wallace, 1959) is a widely used measure of marital satisfaction that yields a score ranging from 2 to 158. It has adequate reliability (split half = .90) and discriminates between nondistressed spouses and spouses who have documented marital problems (Locke & Wallace, 1959). Scores on this instrument also correlate with clinicians' judgments of marital discord (Crowther, 1985).

Depressive symptoms. We assessed depressive symptoms using the Beck Depression Inventory (BDI; Beck & Beamesderfer, 1974). This scale reliably measures the severity of affective, cognitive, motivational, and physical (vegetative) symptoms of depression in nonpsychiatric samples (mean level of internal consistency over 15 samples = .81, range = .73 to .92). The BDI correlates highly with clinical ratings and other measures of depression and differentiates depression from anxiety (Beck, Steer, & Garbin, 1988).

Self-esteem. The Rosenberg (1965) Self-

Esteem Scale is a 10-item measure that reliably assesses self-esteem (2-week test–retest reliability is .85). This scale also correlates (.56 to .83) with other similar measures and with clinical assessments of self-concept problems (Silber & Tippett, 1965).

Attributions. We assessed attributions for negative events because they appear to be related more consistently and more strongly to marital satisfaction than attributions for positive events (e.g., Fincham, Beach, & Nelson, 1987; Baucom, Sayers, & Duhe, 1989), they have been implicated in theoretical attempts to understand the negative behavior exchanges that are the hallmark of marital distress (Fincham & Bradbury, 1991), and they are most relevant in the clinical context. The decision to focus on attributions for negative events was also guided by two well-established findings in the broader marital literature—that negative behaviors have a far greater impact on the marriage than positive behaviors, and that this impact occurs independently of positive events (see Weiss & Heyman, 1990).

We used four common partner behaviors as stimuli to obtain attribution judgments ("Your wife/husband criticizes something you say," "Your wife/husband begins to spend less time with you," "Your wife/husband does not pay attention to what you are saying," "Your wife/husband is cool and distant"). We used hypothetical behaviors because of the advantages conferred by standard stimuli across spouses and because the pattern of responses to such behaviors is similar to that found for attributions for marital difficulties (Fincham & Beach, 1988). The behaviors used as stimuli were selected to be common enough to permit virtually all spouses to imagine them occurring in their relationship.

For each partner behavior, we asked respondents to rate their agreement with attribution statements about three causal attribution dimensions. Two statements assessed causal locus and inquired about the extent to which the cause rested in the partner ("My husband's behavior was due to something about him [e.g., the type of person he is, the mood he was in]"), and rested in themselves ("My husband's behavior was due to something about me [e.g., what I said or did, the kind of person I am]"). The remaining two questions assessed the stability and globality of causal dimensions, respectively. The stability item inquired about the extent to which the cause was likely to change ("The reason my husband criticized me is something that is *not* likely to change") and the globality item assessed the extent to which the cause affected other areas of the marriage. ("The reason my husband criticized me is something that affects other areas of our marriage"). Spouses rated the statements after imagining that the stimulus behavior had just occurred in their marriage.

Ratings were made using a 6-point scale on which each scale point was labeled (ranging from *disagree strongly* to *agree strongly*) to make the task as concrete as possible. We summed responses to corresponding statements across the four stimulus events and computed coefficient alpha for each attribution dimension (partner locus: husbands = .70, wives = .63; self locus: husbands = .58, wives = .63; stability: husbands = .65, wives = .76; globality: husbands = .78, wives = .75). For the two locus dimension items, higher scores indicated that the respondent was more likely to locate the cause in the partner and in the self, respectively. Higher stability scores indicated that the cause was seen as more stable and higher globality scores reflected the perception that the cause was more global.

To examine partner attributions relative to self-attributions, we combined the responses to the two causal locus questions to obtain a single locus score by subtracting self-ratings from partner ratings (coefficient alpha, husbands = .64, wives = .63). Higher scores indicated that the spouse was more likely than the self to be viewed as the locus of the cause.

In the marital literature, hypotheses specific to individual attribution dimensions are rare (cf. Bradbury & Fincham, 1990). Instead, the theoretical focus has been on responses across causal dimensions leading some investigators to use an overall composite index of attributions (e.g., Fincham & Bradbury, 1987). Because there is some debate regarding the use of individual attribution dimension scores instead of a composite attribution index that sums across individual dimensions (Carver, 1989; Fincham & Bradbury, 1992), we examined both in the present study. As all three attribution dimension indices were scored in the same direction (with higher scores reflecting attributions that are likely to be negatively related to satisfaction), a composite attribution index was computed by simply summing the locus, stability, and globality scores (α for wives = .73, for husbands = .71). This score therefore constitutes an index of relationship negative attributions.

Results

Consistent with past research and the rationale outlined in the introduction, separate analyses are reported for husbands and wives. Unless otherwise specified, the results reported pertain to the husbands ($n = 96$) and wives ($n = 94$) who provided complete data on all the variables investigated.

Attributions, Depression, Self-Esteem, and Concurrent Marital Satisfaction

Table 10.1 shows the concurrent correlations among the variables at Time 1 and Time 2. Several prior findings were replicated, including the association between marital satisfaction and depressive symptoms, self-esteem, and attributions. However, the depression–attribution association was inconsistent and varied across attribution dimensions and gender. As anticipated, the magnitude of the correlation between depression scores and self-esteem was moderate, supporting the decision to measure these two constructs independently.

We conducted regression analyses for husbands and for wives to determine whether depressive symptoms and self-esteem might account for the concurrent relation between marital satisfaction and attributions. Marital satisfaction served as the dependent variable and the three attribution dimensions, depression scores, and self-esteem served as predictor variables that were entered simultaneously into the regression equation. To test the hypothesis that the "third variables" (depression and self-esteem) account for the attribution-marital satisfaction relation, we computed the unique variance associated with the attribution dimensions. This variance is the amount R^2 would drop if the attribution dimensions were omitted and the regression equation was recomputed. We also computed the unique variance associated with depression and self-esteem.

Table 10.2 shows the R^2 associated with the regression equations for wives and husbands at Time 1 and Time 2 as well as the unique variance associated with the attribution dimensions and the variables of depression and self-esteem. The results are consistent across time and gender. Overall, the predictor variables accounted for a significant por-

TABLE 10.1. Concurrent Correlations Among Measures for Wives (Above Diagonal) and Husbands (Below Diagonal) at Time 1 and Time 2

Measure	1	2	3	4	5	6	7
				Time 1			
1. MAT	—	−.41**	.22	−.18	−.44**	−.49**	−.51**
2. BDI	−.38**	—	−.56**	.04	.20	.46**	.32**
3. RSES	.31*	−.56**	—	.09	−.01	−.22	−.06
4. Locus	−.10	−.01	.08	—	.10	.17	.60**
5. Stability	−.38**	.18	−.15	.05	—	.55**	.75**
6. Globality	−.33**	.15	−.24	.05	.63**	—	.80**
7. Composite	−.37**	.15	−.14	.56**	.77**	.79**	—
				Time 2			
1. MAT	—	−.37**	.29*	−.16	−.32**	−.45**	−.45**
2. BDI	−.37**	—	−.66**	−.07	.16	.29*	.18
3. RSES	.34**	−.55**	—	.17	−.17	−.35**	−.16
4. Locus	−.02	−.21	.14	—	.23	.01	.64**
5. Stability	−.45**	.28*	−.33**	.01	—	.41**	.74**
6. Globality	−.35**	.31*	−.32**	−.14	.61**	—	.70**
7. Composite	−.41**	.19	−.26*	.44**	.81**	.74**	—

Note. MAT = Marital Adjustment Test (Locke & Wallace, 1959); BDI = Beck Depression Inventory (Beck & Beamesderfer, 1974); RSES = Rosenberg Self-Esteem Scale (Rosenberg, 1965).
*$p < .01$ one-tailed. ** $p < .001$ one-tailed.

TABLE 10.2. Variance in Marital Satisfaction Accounted for Overall and Unique Variance Associated With Attribution Dimensions and With Depression and Self-Esteem at Time 1 and Time 2

Predictors	Time 1		Time 2	
	R^2	F	R^2	F
Wives				
Overall	.34	9.2***	.30	7.7***
Attribution dimensions	.17	7.8***	.16	6.9***
Locus	.01	1.7	.02	2.7
Stability	.05	6.8**	.01	1.0
Globality	.02	2.9*	.08	10.3***
BDI and RSES	.06	3.7**	.06	4.0**
BDI	.03	3.8*	.04	4.7**
RSES	.00	<1	.00	<1
Husbands				
Overall	.27	6.6***	.28	7.1***
Attribution dimensions	.11	4.6***	.12	4.9***
Locus	.01	1.0	.01	<1
Stability	.04	4.7***	.06	6.9***
Globality	.01	<1	.00	<1
BDI and RSES	.10	6.4***	.07	4.6**
BDI	.04	5.4**	.03	4.2**
RSES	.01	<1	.01	<1

Note. BDI = Beck Depression Inventory (Beck & Beamesderfer, 1974); RSES = Rosenberg Self-Esteem Scale (Rosenberg, 1965).
* $p < .10$. ** $p < .05$. *** $p < .01$.

tion of the variance in marital satisfaction ($M = 29.7\%$). In each equation, the attribution dimensions accounted for a significant portion of unique variance in satisfaction; hence the attribution-satisfaction relation does not simply reflect level of depressive symptoms or self-esteem.

Because it has been recommended that research reports include findings for both individual attribution dimensions and the attribution indices used in prior research (Carver, 1989; Fincham & Bradbury, 1992), we computed an identical set of regression equations using the composite measure of causal attributions in place of the three individual attribution dimensions. We obtained the same pattern of results, and percentages of variance accounted for were very close to those reported in Table 10.2 (in no case was the difference greater than 3%).

Attributions, Depression, Self-Esteem, and Future Marital Satisfaction

We conducted longitudinal analyses with the complete sample and with a subset of the sample that excluded persons who initially reported depression or marital distress. Spouses were excluded if they met either of two criteria: a score below 100 on the MAT or a score above 10 on the BDI in the initial phase of the study. These criteria are widely used to distinguish distressed from nondistressed spouses (Locke & Wallace, 1959) and to differentiate nondepressed persons from those who are depressed (Beck et al., 1988). Using these criteria, we excluded 13 husbands and 21 wives from the sample available for analysis. The restricted sample therefore consisted of wives ($n = 73$; depression scores, $M = 4.91$, $SD = 3.01$; satisfaction scores, $M = 118.13$, $SD = 17.14$) and husbands ($n = 83$; depression scores, $M = 4.0$, $SD = 2.59$; satisfaction scores, $M = 114.94$, $SD = 18.91$) who were neither maritally distressed nor depressed at Time 1.

Table 10.3 shows the correlations between the variables at Time 1 and Time 2. As anticipated, we found longitudinal relations between depression and self-esteem and later satisfaction. Therefore, we computed regression analyses to examine whether these longitudinal relations for depression and self-esteem might account for the

TABLE 10.3. Longitudinal Correlations Between Measures at Time 1 and Time 2 for Wives and Husbands

Time 1	Time 2						
	1	2	3	4	5	6	7
Wives							
Full sample							
1. MAT	.70**	−.10	.14	−.20	−.30*	−.29*	−.38**
2. BDI	−.42**	.54**	−.48**	.02	.16	.25*	.20
3. RSES	.30*	−.40**	.64**	.03	−.06	−.20	−.11
4. Locus	−.30*	.06	.14	.44**	.15	.19	.39**
5. Stability	−.20	-.07	−.03	.16	.44*	.24	.38**
6. Globality	−.29*	.15	-.25*	.12	.26*	.48**	.42**
7. Composite	−.37**	.07	-.06	.33*	.39**	.42**	.55**
Restricted sample							
1. MAT	.67**	−.07	.18	−.16	−.22	−.25	−.32*
2. BDI	−.11	.43**	−.31*	.02	.16	.15	.16
3. RSES	.12	−.08	.44**	−.04	.02	−.12	−.08
4. Locus	−.39**	.23	.02	.44**	.08	.21	.39**
5. Stability	−.19	-.02	−.07	.09	.44**	.20**	.35*
6. Globality	−.15	.16	−.19	.14	.21	.44**	.41**
7. Composite	−.35*	.17	−.11	.32*	.35*	.40**	.54**
Husbands							
Full sample							
1. MAT	.72**	−.39**	.27*	.17	−.35**	−.33**	−.26*
2. BDI	−.38**	.67**	−.41**	−.12	.15	.20	.11
3. RSES	.27*	−.46**	.54**	.13	−.15	−.19	−.10
4. Locus	−.28*	.02	.08	.49**	−.01	−.05	.22
5. Stability	−.26	.21	−.11	−.20	.37**	.42**	.29*
6. Globality	−.28*	.18	−.17	−.07	.32**	.46**	.35**
7. Composite	−.39**	.19	−.09	.13	.31*	.38**	.41**
Restricted sample							
1. MAT	.63**	−.24	.15	.19	−.34**	−.30*	−.21
2. BDI	−.04	.40**	−.18	−.18	.14	.12	.04
3. RSES	.05	−.27*	.45**	.15	−.20	−.15	−.09
4. Locus	−.23	−.01	.14	.48**	−.01	−.04	.21
5. Stability	−.28	.06	−.06	−.18	.36**	.40**	.28*
6. Globality	−.31*	.09	−.17	−.09	.34**	.43**	.34**
7. Composite	−.39**	.06	−.04	.12	.32*	.36**	.39**

Note. MAT = Marital Adjustment Test (Locke & Wallace, 1959); BDI = Beck Depression Inventory (Beck & Beamesderfer, 1974); RSES = Rosenberg Self-Esteem Scale (Rosenberg, 1965).
* *p* < .01 one-tailed. ** *p* < .001 one-tailed.

longitudinal relations found for the attribution variables. Marital satisfaction at Time 2 served as the dependent variable and predictor variables were Time 1 measures of satisfaction, depression, self-esteem, and attributions. To examine whether attributions account for variance in the Time 2 satisfaction beyond that associated with initial satisfaction, depression, and self-esteem, we computed the unique variance associated with the predictor variables.

As shown in Table 10.4, for wives and husbands the Time 1 attribution dimensions accounted for a significant portion of unique variance in Time 2 satisfaction. This finding also obtained for wives in the restricted sample, but husbands' initial attributions were only marginally significant predic-

TABLE 10.4. Variance in Time 2 Satisfaction Accounted for Overall and Unique Variance Associated With Time 1 Satisfaction, Depression and Self-Esteem, and Attribution Dimensions

	Marital satisfaction (Time 2)							
	Full sample				Restricted sample			
	Husbands		Wives		Husbands		Wives	
Time 1 predictors	R^2	F	R^2	F	R^2	F	R^2	F
Overall	.57	19.8***	.58	19.9***	.46	10.7***	.54	12.8***
Marital satisfaction	.30	62.2***	.30	60.9***	.30	42.7***	.32	44.9***
BDI and RSES	.02	1.7	.04	4.1*	.01	<1	.00	<1
BDI	.01	2.3	.01	2.6	.00	<1	.00	<1
RSES	.00	<1	.01	1.6	.00	<1	.00	<1
Attribution dimensions	.05	3.6**	.06	4.1**	.05	2.4*	.08	3.9**
Locus	.04	9.3***	.04	8.8***	.03	4.5**	.07	10.4***
Stability	.00	<1	.00	<1	.00	<1	.00	<1
Globality	.01	1.1	.01	1.7	.00	<1	.02	2.2

Note. BDI = Beck Depression Inventory (Beck & Beamesderfer, 1974); RSES = Rosenberg Self-Esteem Scale (Rosenberg, 1965).
* $p < .10$. ** $p < .05$. *** $p < .01$.

tors of later satisfaction in the restricted sample. However, the magnitude of the relation between husbands' attributions and later satisfaction did not differ significantly in the two samples. These findings are particularly noteworthy in view of the high correlation found between satisfaction scores in the two phases of the project, which greatly reduced the proportion of variance for which attribution dimensions could account. In sum, it appears that the set of attribution dimensions predicts later satisfaction for husbands and wives and that these longitudinal relations are not due to depression, self-esteem, or the presence of chronic disorder.[2]

To investigate the role of individual attribution dimensions, we examined the unique variance associated with each. For husbands and wives and full versus restricted samples, the locus dimension alone accounted for unique variance in later satisfaction, a finding that most likely reflects the high correlation between stability and globality and the low correlation between these two dimensions and causal locus. As the locus dimension combined two separate ratings, we computed the unique variance associated with partner and self causal loci by substituting these two measures for the composite locus measure used in the regression equations. There was no change in the significance levels shown in Table 10.4. For husbands, both partner, $F(1, 88) = 4.4$, $p < .05$, and self, $F(1, 88) = 4.9$, $p < .05$, attribution loci predicted later satisfaction. Locating the cause in the partner was negatively associated with later satisfaction, whereas self-attributions for partner behavior were positively related to later satisfaction. For wives, only the self-attribution locus significantly predicted later satisfaction, $F(1, 86) = 6.2$, $p < .05$; self-attributions were again positively associated with later satisfaction.

Before interpreting these findings, it is important to consider whether marital satisfaction predicts later attributions. If this were the case, the data would be consistent with the view that marital satisfaction influences attributions. To examine this possibility, we adopted the same strategy used in the analyses described earlier. That is, we computed a regression equation for each of the three attribution dimensions. In each case, the Time 2 attribution dimension served as the dependent variable and the corresponding dimension score at Time 1 was entered into the equation together with the depression, self-esteem, and marital satisfaction scores.

Table 10.5 shows that husbands' satisfaction accounted for significant unique variance in the equations used to predict later locus and stability attribution dimensions and a marginally significant amount of variance in the equation predicting the globality dimension. Although the level of significance changed for the stability and globality

TABLE 10.5. *Unique Variance in Prediction of Time 2 Attribution Dimensions From Corresponding Time 1 Dimension, Depression and Self-Esteem, and Martial Satisfaction*

	Attribution dimensions							
	Full sample				Restricted sample			
	Husbands		Wives		Husbands		Wives	
Time 1 predictors	R^2	F	R^2	F	R^2	F	R^2	F
Locus (Time 2)								
Locus	.25	32.3***	.16	17.8***	.22	23.5***	.18	15.2***
BDI and RSES	.00	<1	.00	<1	.01	<1	.01	<1
Marital satisfaction	.04	4.6**	.02	2.1	.04	4.0***	.00	<1
Stability (Time 2)								
Stability	.06	6.7**	.12	13.0***	.06	5.6**	.14	12.1***
BDI and RSES	.00	<1	.01	<1	.02	<1	.01	<1
Marital satisfaction	.04	4.9**	.01	1.2	.04	3.7*	.00	<1
Globality (Time 2)								
Globality	.13	15.6***	.13	15.3***	.12	11.9***	.14	12.1***
BDI and RSES	.00	<1	.01	<1	.00	<1	.01	<
Marital satisfaction	.03	3.1*	.00	<1	.03	2.6	.01	<1

Note. BDI = Beck Depression Inventory (Beck & Beamesderfer, 1974); RSES = Rosenberg Self-Esteem Scale (Rosenberg, 1965).
* $p < .10$. ** $p < .05$. *** $p < .01$.

attributions in the restricted sample, the relations did not differ significantly for husbands in the two samples. In contrast, Time 1 satisfaction did not predict later attributions for wives in either the full or restricted samples. The differing patterns of results obtained for husbands and wives suggest that the nature of the causal relation between attributions and satisfaction may differ across gender. Specifically, the data for wives are consistent with the view that attributions influence later satisfaction, whereas the husbands' data are consistent with a bidirectional causal relation between attributions and marital satisfaction.

Following Carver's (1989) and Fincham and Bradbury's (1992) recommendations, we also investigated the longitudinal relations between attributions and satisfaction using the composite index of attribution. We computed a similar set of regression equations substituting the composite score for the three individual attribution dimensions. Unlike the results concerning concurrent correlations, we obtained a different pattern of findings. Specifically, the wives' attribution composite did not predict their later satisfaction in either the complete or restricted samples. Initial marital satisfaction did not predict wives' later attributions in either sample. In contrast, husbands' initial attributions tended to increase the variance accounted for in later satisfaction in the complete, $\Delta R^2 = .02$, $F(1, 95) = 3.5$, $p < .07$, and restricted, $\Delta R^2 = .04$, $F(1, 82) = 5.0$, $p < .05$, samples. However, initial satisfaction did not predict the husbands' later attributions.

Finally, we found limited evidence that was consistent with a causal relation between depression and marital satisfaction. To investigate this issue, we conducted regression analyses in which we used Time 1 depression to predict Time 2 satisfaction with initial satisfaction entered into the regression equation. We computed analogous regressions using Time 2 depression as a dependent variable. For wives, earlier depression increased the variance accounted for in later satisfaction, $\Delta R^2 = .02$, $F(1, 93) = 3.98$, $p < .05$, a finding that did not obtain for the restricted sample. However, initial satisfaction did not predict later depression. In contrast, husbands' initial depression did not predict Time 2 satisfaction, whereas initial satisfaction increased the variance accounted for in later depression in the full sample, $\Delta R^2 = .02$, $F(1, 95) = 3.93$, $p < .05$, and was a marginally significant predictor in the restricted sample, $\Delta R^2 = .03$, $F(1$,

82) = 3.1, $p < .09$. When attribution dimensions were entered into the regression equation, none of the findings just discussed remained significant.

Discussion

Replication of Prior Findings

Although the primary purpose of the present study was to examine the longitudinal relation between attributions and marital satisfaction, the study also provided the opportunity to replicate concurrent correlates of marital satisfaction. Consistent with prior findings, higher levels of depressive symptoms were inversely related to marital satisfaction and self-esteem was positively related to marital satisfaction. With the exception of wives' self-esteem at Time 1, the correlations were statistically significant for husbands and for wives at both assessment periods. Although gender differences might have been expected in view of such factors as differential rates of depression, degree of self-criticism, and valuing of intimate relationships across husbands and wives, we found no such differences in the relation between depression and marital satisfaction or in the relation between self-esteem and satisfaction.

Attributions Vary as a Function of Concurrent Marital Satisfaction

As expected, the inverse relation between attributions for partner behavior and marital satisfaction emerged for husbands and wives at both assessments. In view of the finding that attribution dimensions accounted for a significant portion of unique variance in wives' and husbands' marital satisfaction when depression and self-esteem were included along with the attribution dimensions in regression analyses that predicted satisfaction, the attribution–satisfaction link does not appear to be an artifact of depression or self-esteem.

Our results extend prior findings in two important respects. First, they build on the Fletcher et al. (1990) findings for dating couples by showing that depression does not account for the attribution–relationship happiness link in married couples. In a similar vein, they extend the Fincham et al. (1989) results by demonstrating that they apply to causal attributions and to husbands. Second, these are the first data to rule out self-esteem as a variable that might account for the association between attributions and concurrent marital satisfaction.

Before turning to the longitudinal findings, it is worth noting that the data on concurrent relations among the variables also address an issue of increasing importance to marital researchers, namely, the relation between depression and marital satisfaction. Because "it is not yet clear to what extent . . . attributions mediate the association between depression and marital distress" (Gotlib & Hooley, 1988, p. 565), it should be noted that depression accounted for statistically significant proportions of unique variance in the regression equations predicting concurrent satisfaction for husbands and wives at both assessments (see Table 10.2). These findings suggest that in a community sample, causal attributions do not play a mediating role in the link between depression and concurrent marital distress, although they clearly play a moderating role in this relation.

The importance of these concurrent findings is emphasized by their theoretical and applied significance. At the theoretical level, they answer the critical question of whether the attribution patterns documented in the marital literature constitute a marital phenomenon per se. By ruling out depression and self-esteem as factors that might account for the attribution–satisfaction link, the present findings provide support for the role accorded to attributions in recent theoretical analyses of marital dysfunction. At the applied level, the results suggest that interventions designed to alleviate spousal depression may not be sufficient to reverse the maladaptive attributions associated with marital distress.

Causal Attributions Are Likely to Influence Marital Satisfaction

The longitudinal relations between attributions and satisfaction also replicate and extend prior findings. As in Fincham and Bradbury's (1987) study, wives' initial attributions predicted their marital satisfaction 12 months later. Thus, we have obtained consistent evidence to suggest that causal attributions may influence wives' marital satisfaction. The present findings indicate further that this relation cannot be attributed to depression, self-esteem, or chronic individual or marital distress.

The present study provides the first data documenting a longitudinal relation between attributions and husbands' satisfaction. Husbands' attributions, similar to their wives', predicted later satisfaction independently of depression, self-esteem, or initial disorder. The positive finding regarding husbands' attributions contrasts with Fincham and Bradbury's (1987) results. The reason for this discrepancy is unclear, although it could be due to a number of factors, including the use of a far larger sample in the present study. In any event, for both wives and husbands, this study provides data consistent with a central assumption of recent theoretical analyses of marital dysfunction, namely, that attributions influence marital satisfaction. The significance of these findings is emphasized by the relative stability of the variables studied, a circumstance that most likely reflects the investigation of couples married for some time (mean length of marriage = 9.4 years).

However, the data are also consistent with a causal relation in which husbands' marital satisfaction influences later attributions. It is therefore quite possible that a reciprocal causal relation exists between attributions and marital satisfaction. In view of this possibility, it is important to note that the power of attributions at time n to predict satisfaction at time $n + 1$ may result from the fact that these attributions are simply a reflection of marital satisfaction at time $n - 1$.[3] Data from a longitudinal study that includes at least three assessment phases are therefore needed before stronger conclusions can be drawn about the longitudinal relation, and possible causal nature of the relation, between attributions and marital satisfaction. The importance of multiwave, longitudinal data are also emphasized by the need to investigate the temporal relation between attributions and satisfaction using different time lags. It is quite possible that any effects these variables have on each other might occur over longer or shorter intervals. Thus, the absence of any information pertaining to the optimal lag for attributions and satisfaction to influence each other renders the present findings all the more noteworthy.

Two intriguing patterns emerge when the concurrent and longitudinal relations between attributions and satisfaction are compared. First, analysis of individual attribution dimensions and the composite attribution index yields the same pattern of findings in relation to concurrent satisfaction. However, we found fewer longitudinal relations using the composite attribution index. These findings emphasize the importance of avoiding premature use of composite indices in the investigation of attribution dimensions (Bradbury & Fincham, 1990).

Second, the locus dimension was not significantly related to concurrent satisfaction for either husbands or wives but correlated significantly with later marital satisfaction. Moreover, locus accounted for unique variance in later satisfaction. These findings are consistent with recent behavioral research showing that changes in marital satisfaction are best predicted by behaviors that are not related to concurrent satisfaction (Gottman & Krokoff, 1989). The present results suggest that perceived causal locus may be a risk factor for marital discord. Specifically, the locus dimension may play a role in initiating marital discord but not necessarily in maintaining the discord. Although intriguing, the findings regarding causal locus should be interpreted with caution, as the magnitude of concurrent and longitudinal correlations involving causal dimensions and satisfaction did not differ statistically.

Because attributional models of depression and of marital distress both predict a correlation with causal locus, the absence of concurrent relations involving this dimension seems surprising. As regards depression, it is important to recall that the attribution pattern associated with this disorder tends to occur only when the person makes attributions concerning his or her own behavior and not the behavior of others (e.g., Garber & Hollon, 1980). In the present study, the stimuli for which attribution judgments were made consisted of partner behaviors, a circumstance that might account for the lack of association between this dimension and depression scores. It is still possible that attributions for relationship events that clearly result from the attributor's behavior are related to depression. An important task for future research is to examine the relations among depression, marital satisfaction, the self-attributions typically studied in depression research, and the attributions assessed in marital studies that usually involve partner behavior.

The lack of a concurrent relation between causal locus and marital satisfaction is more puzzling. However, this causal dimension has yielded the least robust association with marital satisfaction, leading to inconsistent results across and within studies. Such inconsistency most likely reflects difficulties in conceptualizing the nature of this dimension in both basic attribution research (cf. Ross, 1977) and marital research (cf. Fincham, 1985). Nonetheless, our attempt to investigate partner and self loci relative to each other was useful in predicting later marital satisfaction and therefore deserves further study.

Although not central to the present study, the data also speak to a possible causal relation between depression and marital satisfaction, a topic that is gaining increasing attention (e.g., Beach et al., 1990; Gotlib & Hooley, 1988). Again an interesting pattern of findings emerged that differed across gender; wives' initial depression predicted later satisfaction whereas husbands' initial satisfaction predicted later depression. Thus, some evidence was obtained that is consistent with a bidirectional causal relation between depression and marital satisfaction. However, these findings should be interpreted cautiously because the finding for wives did not occur in the restricted sample and the relation found for husbands was only marginally significant in this sample. The significance of these findings also assumes continuity between mild forms of depressive symptoms and depression as a clinical syndrome, an assumption that remains controversial.

Final Comments

We have noted several cautions in discussing the results of this study. However, two additional factors require emphasis when interpreting the present findings. First, longitudinal data are correlational and therefore can only provide data consistent with a particular causal interpretation. Ideally, attributions and marital satisfaction should be manipulated to determine their effects on each other. However, ethical and practical restraints make such manipulations extremely difficult in this domain. Second, the collection of data by mail is a potential threat to the integrity of the data. It assumes that spouses answer questions sincerely and follow instructions in the absence of supervision. Although the sincerity of self-report cannot be guaranteed under any conditions, the replication of several prior findings provides some support for these assumptions. In view of their limitations, the present results are best view as suggestive findings that need to be replicated in a multiwave longitudinal study that spans a period when significant things happen in the marriage (e.g., the first few years of marriage, the birth of a child).

Notwithstanding these cautionary notes, the present study is among the first to provide data consistent with recent theoretical analyses of cognition in close relationships in which attributions are accorded a central role. Specifically, it shows that the attributions studied in the marital literature are not simply the function of a general pattern of attributions that result from depression or self-esteem and provides data that are consistent with the widely assumed effects of attributions on marital satisfaction. It therefore provides some support for the more difficult task of investigating the processes whereby attributions influence satisfaction, an endeavor that emphasizes the need for data relating attributions to marital behavior.

ACKNOWLEDGMENT

Preparation of this article was supported by a Faculty Scholar Award from the William T. Grant Foundation and Grant R01 MH 44078-01 from the National Institute of Mental Health awarded to Frank D. Fincham, and by Grant F31 MH 09740-01 from the National Institute of Mental Health awarded to Thomas N. Bradbury. We thank Susan Campbell and Ben Karney for their helpful comments on an earlier version of this article.

NOTES

1. The results of intervention studies are perhaps not surprising in view of their limitations. These include the failure to document the manipulation of attributions, the limited nature of the attribution interventions, and, most importantly, the power of the studies to detect differences between treatments (see Fincham, Bradbury, & Beach, 1990).
2. Regression analyses using the combined data from husbands and wives yielded similar results. However, husbands and wives do not provide independent data points and therefore combining their data in this manner can artificially inflate correlations. Consequently, the results are reported separately for husbands and wives.
3. In view of this observation, it is worth noting that husbands' satisfaction accounted for a significant increase in $R2$ in the equations used to predict later locus and stability attribution dimensions and a marginally significant increase in R^2 in the equation predicting the globality dimension. In contrast, Time 1 satisfaction did not predict later attributions for wives in either the full or restricted samples. The differing patterns of results obtained for husbands and wives suggest that the nature of the longitudinal relation between attributions and satisfaction may differ across gender.

REFERENCES

Baucom, D. H. (1987). Attributions in distressed relations: How can we explain them? In S. Duck & D. Perlman (Eds.), *Heterosexual relations, marriage, and divorce* (pp. 177–206). London: Sage.

Baucom, D. H., Notarius, C. I., Burnett, C. K., & Haefner, P. (1990). Gender differences and sex-role identity in marriage. In F. D. Fincham & T. N. Bradbury (Eds.), *The psychology of marriage* (pp. 150–171). New York: Guilford Press.

Baucom, D. H., Sayers, S. L., & Duhe, A. (1989). Attributional style and attributional patterns among married couples. *Journal of Personality and Social Psychology, 56*, 596–607.

Baucom, D. H., Sayers, S. L., & Sher, T. G. (1990). Supplementing behavioral marital therapy with cognitive restructuring and emotional expressiveness training: An outcome investigation. *Journal of Consulting and Clinical Psychology, 58*, 636–645.

Beach, S. R. H., Sandeen, E., & O'Leary, K. D. (1990). *Depression in marriage*. New York: Guilford Press.

Beck, A. T., & Beamesderfer, A. (1974). Assessment of depression: The depression inventory. In P. Pichot (Ed.), *Modern problems in pharmacopsychiatry* (pp. 151–169). Basel, Switzerland: Karger.

Beck, A. T., Steer, R. A., & Garbin, M. G. (1988). Psychometric properties of the Beck Depression Inventory: Twenty-five years of evaluation. *Clinical Psychology Review, 8*, 77–100.

Bradbury, T. N., & Fincham, F. D. (1990). Attributions in marriage: Review and critique. *Psychological Bulletin, 107*, 3–33.

Bradbury, T. N., & Fincham, F. D. (1992). Attributions and behavior in marital interaction. *Journal of Personality and Social Psychology, 63*, 613–628.

Carver, C. S. (1989). How should multifaceted constructs be tested? Issues illustrated by self-monitoring, attributional style, and hardiness. *Journal of Personality and Social Psychology, 56*, 577–585.

Carver, C. S., & Gannellen, R. J. (1983). Depression and components of self-punitiveness: High standards, self-criticism, and over-generalization. *Journal of Abnormal Psychology, 92*, 330–337.

Crowther, J. H. (1985). The relationship between depression and marital adjustment: A descriptive study. *The Journal of Nervous and Mental Disease, 173*, 227–231.

Depue, R. A., & Monroe, S. M. (1986). Conceptualization and measurement of human disorder in life stress research: The problem of chronic disturbance. *Psychological Bulletin, 99*, 36–51.

Doherty, W. J. (1982). Attribution style and negative problem solving in marriage. *Family Relations, 31*, 201–205.

Epstein, N. (1982). Cognitive therapy with couples. *American Journal of Family Therapy, 10*, 5–16.

Fincham, F. D. (1985). Attributional processes in distressed and non-distressed couples: 2. Responsibility for marital problems. *Journal of Abnormal Psychology, 94*, 183–190.

Fincham, F. D., & Beach, S. R. (1988). Attribution processes in distressed and nondistressed couples: 5. Real versus hypothetical events. *Cognitive Therapy and Research, 5*, 505–514.

Fincham, F. D., & Beach, S. R. H., & Bradbury, T. N. (1989). Marital distress, depression, and attributions: Is the marital distress–attribution association an artifact of depression? *Journal of Consulting and Clinical Psychology, 57*, 768–771.

Fincham, F. D., Beach, S. R., & Nelson, G. (1987). Attributional processes in distressed and nondistressed couples: 3. Causal and responsibility attributions for spouse behavior. *Cognitive Therapy and Research, 11*, 71–86.

Fincham, F. D., & Bradbury, T. N. (1987). The impact of attributions in marriage: A longitudinal analysis. *Journal of Personality and Social Psychology, 53*, 481–489.

Fincham, F. D., & Bradbury, T. N. (1988). The impact of attributions in marriage: An experimental analysis. *Journal of Social and Clinical Psychology, 7*, 147–162.

Fincham, F. D., & Bradbury, T. N. (1991). Cognition in marriage: A program of research on attributions. *Advances in Personal Relationships, 2*, 159–203.

Fincham, F. D., & Bradbury, T. N. (1992). Assessing attributions in marriage: The Relationship Attribution Measure. *Journal of Personality and Social Psychology, 62*, 457–468.

Fincham, F. D., Bradbury, T. N., & Beach, S. R. (1990). To arrive where we began: Cognition in marital therapy. *Journal of Family Psychology, 4*, 167–184.

Fitzpatrick, M. A. (1988). *Between husband and wife: Communication in marriage*. Beverly Hills, CA: Sage.

Fletcher, G. J. O., Fincham, F. D., Cramer, L., & Heron, N. (1987). The role of attributions in the development of dating relationships. *Journal of Personality and Social Psychology, 53*, 510–517.

Fletcher, G. J. O., Fitness, J., & Blampied, N. M. (1990). The link between attributions and happiness in close relationships: The roles of depression and explanatory style. *Journal of Social and Clinical Psychology, 9*, 243–255.

Garber, J., & Hollon, S. D. (1980). Universal versus personal helplessness: Belief in uncontrollability or incompetence. *Journal of Abnormal Psychology, 89*, 56–66.

Gotlib, I. H., & Hooley, J. M. (1988). Depression and marital functioning. In S. Duck (Ed.), *Handbook of personal relationships: Theory, research and interventions* (pp. 543–570). Chichester, England: Wiley.

Gotlib, I. H., & McCabe, S. B. (1990). Marriage and psychopathology. In F. D. Fincham & T. N. Bradbury (Eds.), *The psychology of marriage* (pp. 226–257). New York: Guilford Press.

Gottman, J. M., & Krokoff, L. J. (1989). Marital interaction and marital satisfaction: A longitudinal view. *Journal of Consulting and Clinical Psychology, 57*, 47–52.

Harvey, J. H. (1987). Attributions in close relationships: Research and theoretical developments. *Journal of Social and Clinical Psychology, 5*, 420–434.

Ickes, W. (1985). Sex-role influences on compatibility in relationships. In W. Ickes (Ed.), *Compatible and incompatible relationships* (pp. 187–208). New York: Springer-Verlag.

Ickes, W. (1988). Attributional styles and the self-concept. In L. Y. Abramson (Ed.), *Social cognition and clinical psychology* (pp. 66–97). New York: Guilford Press.

Ickes, W., & Layden, M. A. (1978). Attributional styles. In J. H. Harvey, W. Ickes, & R. F. Kidd (Eds.), *New directions in attribution research* (Vol. 2, pp. 121–157). Hillsdale, NJ: Lawrence Erlbaum Associates.

Locke, H. J., & Wallace, K. M. (1959). Short marital adjustment and prediction tests: Their reliability and validity. *Marriage and Family Living, 21*, 251–255.

Miller, P. C., Lefcourt, H. M., Holmes, J. G., Ware, E. E., & Saleh, W. E. (1986). Marital locus of control and marital problem solving. *Journal of Personality and Social Psychology, 51*, 161–169.

Noller, P. (1987). Nonverbal communication in marriage. In D. Perlman & S. Duck (Eds.), *Intimate relationships: Development, dynamics, and deterioration* (pp. 123–147). Beverly Hills, CA: Sage.

Olson, J. M., & Ross, M. (1985). Attribution: Past, present and future. In J. H. Harvey & G. Weary (Eds.), *Attribution: Basic issues and applications* (pp. 282–311). San Diego, CA: Academic Press.

Rempel, J. K., Holmes, J. G., & Zanna, M. P. (1985). Trust in close relationships. *Journal of Personality and Social Psychology, 49*, 95–112.

Robins, C. J. (1988). Attributions and depression: Why is the literature so inconsistent? *Journal of Personality and Social Psychology, 54*, 880–889.

Rosenberg, M. (1965). *Society and adolescent self-image*. Princeton, NJ: Princeton University Press.

Ross, L. (1977). The intuitive psychologist and his shortcomings. In L. Berkowitz (Ed.), *Advances in experimental social psychology* (Vol. 10, pp. 173–220). San Diego, CA: Academic Press.

Rubin, Z. (1970). Measurement of romantic love. *Journal of Personality and Social Psychology, 16*, 265–273.

Seligman, C., Fazio, R. H., & Zanna, M. P. (1980). Effects of salience of extrinsic rewards on liking and loving. *Journal of Personality and Social Psychology, 38*, 453–460.

Shaver, K. G. (1985). *The attribution of blame: Causality, responsibility, and blameworthiness*. New York: Springer-Verlag.

Silber, E., & Tippett, J. (1965). Self-esteem: Clinical assessment and measurement validation. *Psychological Reports, 16*, 1017–1071.

Sillars, A. L. (1985). Interpersonal perception in relationships. In W. Ickes (Ed.), *Compatible and incompatible relationships* (pp. 277–305). New York: Springer-Verlag.

Taylor, S. E., & Koivumaki, J. H. (1976). The perception of self and others: Acquaintanceship, affect, and actor-observer differences. *Journal of Personality and Social Psychology, 33*, 403–406.

Vanfossen, B. E. (1986). Sex differences in depression: The role of spouse support. In S. E. Hobfoll (Ed.), *Stress, social support, and women* (pp. 78–89). Washington, DC: Hemisphere.

Weiss, R. L., & Heyman, R. (1990). Marital distress and therapy. In A. S. Bellack, M. Hersen, & A. E. Kazdin (Eds.), *International handbook of behavior modification* (2nd ed., pp. 475–501). New York: Plenum Press.

Zautra, A. J., Guenther, R. T., & Chartier, G. M. (1985). Attributions for real and hypothetical events: Their relation to self-esteem and depression. *Journal of Abnormal Psychology, 94*, 530–540.

Zautra, A. J., & Reich, J. W. (1983). Life events and perceptions of life quality: Developments in a two-factor approach. *Journal of Community Psychology, 11*, 121–132.

Discussion Questions

1. Which do you think comes first: attributions that place the blame for negative events on a relationship partner or dissatisfaction with one's relationship?
2. If you were a marital therapist, what strategies would you use to get relationship partners to stop blaming each other for negative events that occur in the marriage?
3. Why is it that the relationships that we so eagerly seek out when we first meet and begin to date someone become the source of some of our greatest distress?
4. Elaborate on the role that the actor–observer bias and self-serving bias play in facilitating maladaptive attributions in close relationships.

Suggested Readings

Bradbury, T. N., & Fincham, F. D. (1990). Attributions in marriage: Review and critique. *Psychological Bulletin, 107,* 3–33. This article reviews research on the relationship between attributions for a partner's behavior and marital satisfaction.

Bradbury, T. N., & Fincham, F. D. (1991). Clinical and social perspectives on close relationships. In C. R. Snyder & D. R. Forsyth (Eds.), *The handbook of social and clinical psychology: The health perspective* (pp. 309-326). New York: Pergamon. This purpose of this chapter is to encourage collaboration by clinical and social psychologists who study close relationships. Among the topics discussed are attributions and marital satisfaction.

Harvey, J. H. (1987). Attributions in close relationships: Research and theoretical developments. *Journal of Social and Clinical Psychology, 5,* 420–434. This article discusses the pervasiveness of attributions in close relationships, the functions of those attributions, and the effects they have on relationships.

Ickes, W. (1988). Attributional styles and the self-concept. In L. Y. Abramson (Ed.), *Social cognition and clinical psychology* (pp. 66–97). New York: Guilford Press. This chapter examines the implications of one's attributional style for the self-concept and mental health.

Leary, M. A., & Miller, R. S. (1986). *Social psychology and dysfunctional behavior.* New York: Springer-Verlag. This book provides an overview of topics at the interface of social, clinical, and counseling psychology.

READING 11

Interpersonal Concomitants and Antecedents of Depression Among College Students

Jack E. Hokanson, Mark P. Rubert, Richard A. Welker, Glee R. Hollander, and Carla Hedeen • Florida State University

Editors' Introduction

Early research on the concomitants and antecedents of depression examined primarily intrapersonal factors, the characteristics of depressed individuals that precipitate and maintain their depressed state. In the 1970s, the focus shifted to include an examination of interpersonal factors as well (see Coyne, 1976). One idea behind this line of work was that people who are depressed or depression prone tend to interact in ways that cause other people to experience negative emotions such as frustration, anger, and depression. These negative emotions then lead people to avoid or reject the depressed individual, whose depression then worsens.

Two specific hypotheses emerged from this work on interpersonal aspects of depression. The *concomitant hypothesis* of depression suggests that interpersonal problems go along with or accompany depression. According to this approach, interpersonal issues do not necessarily cause depression, but they are instrumental in maintaining it. Alternatively, the *antecedent hypothesis* suggests that interpersonal problems actually cause or facilitate the initial onset of depression. These two theories have not been teased apart because it is difficult to determine whether interpersonal features of depression cause depression or simply go along with it.

Hokanson and his colleagues conducted a study to examine the degree to which interpersonal problems precede depressive episodes or simply co-occur with them. In addition to allowing a test of these competing hypotheses, this study's methodology improved upon weaknesses in previous studies that examined the relationship between interpersonal problems and depression. Specifically, the researchers used a longitudinal research design whereby the interactions of individuals who were classified as depressed, as suffering from some other type of psychopathology, or as normal were studied over time. Participants' diagnostic status was determined by a diagnostic interview that was administered three times during the course of the study. The first interview examined the occurrence of depression and other psychological problems over the course of the person's life up until then, whereas the second and third interviews assessed problems that had arisen since the previous interview. At each of the three interview sessions, participants also completed self-report measures that assessed their interactions with their roommate and participated in a 30-minute video-taped interview in which they discussed their relationship with their roommate. Finally, throughout the course of the study, participants completed a social activities log that was mailed to the researchers each week.

The results revealed more support for the concomitant hypothesis than for the antecedent hypothesis. Specifically, depressed participants differed from individuals with other types of psychopathology and from normal controls on three variables: lower amount of social contact with their roommates, less enjoyment of interactions with roommates, and higher levels of perceived stress. Roommates of depressed individuals, compared to roommates of participants in the other two groups, reported finding interactions with their roommate to be less enjoyable and that they had more aggressive-competitive reactions toward their roommates. However, depressed participants did not differ significantly from participants with other types of psychopathology on other variables. Thus, to the degree that interpersonal problems are involved in the maintenance of depression, they also appear to be involved in other psychological problems as well.

Abstract

Depressed college students were compared with other-psychopathology and normal controls regarding the relationship they developed with dormitory roommates during a 9-month period. Diagnostic status was periodically assessed via SADS interviews, thus also permitting identification of new cases of depression during the year. Psychosocial characteristics found to be uniquely associated with current depression were: (a) low social contact with roommates, (b) low enjoyability of these contacts, and (c) high life-event stress. Roommates of depressives reported low enjoyability of the relationship and high levels of aggressive behavior towards the depressive. No features were found to be uniquely associated with new cases before they became depressed; however, several antecedents of general psychopathology were identified.

The purpose of this article is to evaluate two related hypotheses that are central to interpersonal theories of depression. The first proposes that interpersonal difficulties are likely accompaniments of depression (concomitant hypothesis). When it occurs, interpersonal strife presumably serves to maintain or intensify depressive symptoms (Coyne, 1976a). The second hypothesis, in essence a stronger version of the first, proposes that interpersonal problems precede the onset of depression (antecedent hypothesis). Here, problematic social relations are thought to play a contributory role in the development of the disorder (Brown & Harris, 1978; Lewinsohn, Youngren, & Grosscup, 1979).

The theories underlying these hypotheses appear, either explicitly or implicitly, to adopt an interactional viewpoint. Depressed or depression-prone persons are seen as displaying deficient or problematic social behaviors that elicit negative reactions in others. Interpersonal processes that become increasingly strained are presumed to occur, leading to frustration and withdrawal by family and friends (Coyne, 1976a), low rates of positive reinforcement from others (Lewinsohn et al., 1979), and loss of confiding, intimate relationships (Brown & Harris, 1978). Deteriorating social relations presumably provoke depressive symptoms, or, as proposed by Brown and Harris (1978), render the depression-prone person vulnerable to stressful life events. From this interactional perspective, the specific aims of this study are to identify social behavioral patterns in depressed and depression-prone individuals that are problematic and to investigate others' behaviors as they develop a relationship with the depressed person.

Methodological limitations in the existing research literature on depression make it difficult to garner strong support for either hypothesis at present, or to disentangle concomitant from antecedent effects of the disorder. Much of the work pertaining to the concomitant hypothesis has involved brief laboratory encounters between strangers, exposure to simulated depression, or observations of patients during group therapy sessions—all questionable analogues of the more intimate relationships referred to by theory. Moreover, a majority of studies use subclinical college students selected on the basis of Beck Depression Inventory scores, a procedure that precludes generalizing to the clinical syndrome of depression (Kendall, Hollon, Beck, Hammen, & Ingram, 1987). In addition, most studies in this area fail to include a nondepressed, other-psychopathology control group. Such controls are needed to infer that any observed interpersonal characteristics are specific to depression (Youngren & Lewinsohn, 1980).

Investigations that attempt to study the social antecedents of depression appear to be burdened with some additional methodological difficulties. Most investigations use cross-sectional designs, and they rely on retrospective reports concerning interpersonal problems or life stresses that occurred before the onset of the disorder (Cohen & Wills, 1985). When data regarding the depression itself are gathered at the same time that information about prior events is collected, there is a risk of obtaining spurious correlations between independent and dependent variables due to the operation of subjects' response sets or imprecise recall (Coyne & Gotlib, 1983; Monroe & Steiner, 1986).

More fundamentally, cross-sectional designs do not permit definite conclusions regarding the temporal sequence of the presumed antecedents of a disorder and the onset of the disorder itself (Barnett & Gotlib, 1988; Hammen, Mayol, deMayo, & Marks, 1986; Lewinsohn, Steinmetz, Larson, & Franklin, 1981).

This investigation attempts to overcome some of these difficulties by using a longitudinal design with college student subjects whose diagnostic status was periodically evaluated via the Schedule for Affective Disorders and Schizophrenia (SADS; Endicott & Spitzer, 1978). Only subjects who met the Research Diagnostic Criteria (RDC) for major, minor, or intermittent depression were used, along with SADS/RDC-defined control subjects who displayed either a nondepressive disorder or a "not mentally ill" status. The relationship that these individuals (hereafter designated as "target" subjects) developed with their dormitory roommates over the course of an academic year served as the vehicle by which interpersonal behavior patterns were assessed. The feasability of using roommates was suggested by an earlier pilot project in which it was found that roommate dyads that contained a person with elevated Beck Depression Inventory scores developed a more problematic relationship than did normal control dyads during a 3-month period of study (Hokanson, Loewenstein, Hedeen, & Howes, 1986). As in the earlier project, roommates in this study were strangers at the beginning of the year, thus making it possible to examine the evolving relationship uncontaminated by prior acquaintanceship factors.

Target subjects' diagnostic status was assessed via SADS/RDC at three points in time. The first evaluation occurred in early fall, shortly after roommates started living together. A lifetime SADS (SADS–L) and an interview covering the preceding month were administered at this time. The second and third evaluations took place in winter and in late spring, respectively, and each covered the time interval since the previous assessment. These procedures permitted the identification and tracking of depressed, other-psychopathology, and nonsymptomatic subjects throughout the year. It also allowed identification of "new cases" of depression, that is, subjects who were assessed as "not mentally ill" at the fall evaluation but who later received a diagnosis of depression at the mid-year assessment, the spring assessment, or both.

Our strategy for evaluating hypotheses is a variant of that adopted by Lewinsohn et al. (1981) in their test of cognitive concomitants and antecedents of depression. In this study, the concomitant hypothesis is evaluated by comparing the target-roommate interpersonal behaviors of pairs containing a currently depressed subject with those of other-psychopathology and normal control pairs. Support for the concomitant hypothesis would be derived from finding more problematic social behaviors occurring in roommate pairs containing a currently depressed member, relative to control groups. The antecedent hypothesis is evaluated by comparing interpersonal behaviors in the new case group prior to the time that they received a diagnosis of depression with those of currently depressed, other-psychopathology, and normal controls. The antecedent hypothesis would be supported by a finding of more problematic social behaviors in new case pairs relative to other-psychopathology and normal control pairs during this pre-episodic period.

Method

Participants

Initial screening. During late July and August of 1985, new students (freshmen and transfers) entering Florida State University attended 3-day orientation meetings. With the cooperation of the Dean of Students Office, incoming students were informed that a year-long study of roommate relationships was planned, and that they might be asked to participate. A short form of the Beck Depression Inventory (BDI–SF; Beck & Beck, 1972) and the Brief Symptom Inventory (BSI; Derogatis, 1975) were administered to the 2,900 students attending the orientation. Students also completed a form providing demographic data as well as information regarding campus housing plans and whether or not they were acquainted with their prospective roommates.

The short form of the BDI has been found to have a correlation of .61 with clinicians' severity ratings of depression, and it also correlates highly (.96) with the long form (Beck & Beck, 1972). Although not appropriate for establishing diagnoses, the BDI–SF was considered to be an adequate instrument for assessing current state of dysphoria during this initial phase of screening (Kendall et al., 1987). The BSI is a short form of the SCL–90 (Derogatis, Lipman, & Covi, 1973) and it yields scores on nine symptom dimensions. It also provides a composite general symptom index (BSI–GSI) reflecting overall symptomatic disturbance. The general symptom index was used as another screening measure in this study. A test–retest reliability of .90 has been reported for the BSI–GSI (Derogatis, 1975).

The information collected at the screening sessions was used in the following way. First, subjects who would be living in two-person dormitory rooms and who were unacquainted with their prospective roommates were deemed eligible for the study. Scores on the BDI–SF and the BSI general symptom index were then used to establish a pool of subjects who would be invited for a SADS interview. Individuals who scored above 8 on the BDI–SF were identified as "possibly depressed," and those who scored above a T score of 70 on the BSI–GSI were considered as reflecting possible psychopathology. For a randomly selected group, 200 "normal" subjects were identified by scores on the BDI–SF and BSI–GSI of below 6 and 65, respectively.

Individuals in these preliminary groupings, along with their roommates, were contacted by telephone during the first week of the fall semester, and each was independently given a detailed description of the project. They were asked to volunteer with the understanding that if selected, each would be paid $40 at the conclusion of the study. This procedure resulted in 51% of the roommate pairs agreeing to take part in the study. To assess the possibility of arriving at a biased sample because of self-selection factors, the screening scores of volunteers were compared with those of nonvolunteers. Within the "depressed" and the "general psychopathology" pools, the screening scores (BDI–SF and BSI–GSI) did not significantly differ by t-test (all $ps > .50$). However, in the normal pool, the BSI–GSI scores of volunteers were higher ($p < .01$) than those of nonvolunteers (60.2 vs. 51.0, respectively). Because our research strategy was to compare the social behaviors of depressed subjects with those of normal controls, the finding that our normals had a somewhat elevated GSI will result in conservative tests of our hypotheses.

SADS interview. Target subjects from the depressed, general psychopathology, and normal pools were scheduled for a diagnostic interview during the 1st–4th weeks of the fall semester. The Schedule for Affective Disorders and Schizophrenia–Lifetime version (SADS–L; Endicott & Spitzer, 1978) and a SADS pertaining to current functioning (prior month) were administered. Application of Research Diagnostic Criteria (RDC; Spitzer, Endicott, & Robins, 1978) decision rules to the current SADS data resulted in the following groupings: depression (major, minor, or intermittent), 37; bipolar or cyclothymic disorder, 17; nondepressive-other psychopathology, 19; and not currently ill, 19. Subjects whose symptom ratings were elevated but who did not quite meet the criteria for a diagnosis were not included. Also, for purposes of this study, subjects in the bipolar/cyclothymic category and those displaying uncomplicated bereavement were excluded from subsequent analyses. Subjects in the other-psychopathology group displayed primarily neurotic, anxiety-related disorders (74%), with the remainder representing personality disorders.

Attrition. During the course of this 9-month study, a 26% dropout rate occurred. Exit interviews indicated that 13% of target subjects or their roommates discontinued because they could not devote sufficient time to the project. Another 13% changed roommates during the study, and hence their data could not be used. Attrition in each subgroup was as follows: depressed, 4 (10.8%); other psychopathology, 3 (15.7%); and not currently ill, 39 (32.7%). A chi-square analysis of these data yielded a value of 6.5 ($p < .05$, $df = 2$), indicating that a disproportionate number of normal subjects were lost.

Final sample. The SADS was administered to target subjects on two more occasions (winter and late spring), with each interview assessing the occurrence or continuation of diagnosable disorder since the previous administration. When change in diagnostic status did occur, careful note of the date of change was made. This procedure permitted the post hoc assignment of target subjects to the following subgroups: (a) unremitted depressives ($n = 19$)—those subjects who received a diagnosis of major, minor, or intermittent depression at each assessment; (b) remitted depressives ($n = 14$)—those who received a diagnosis of depression on the fall assessment but were categorized as not currently ill on the second or third SADS; (c) new cases of depression ($n = 27$)—targets who were not currently ill at the fall assessment but who received a diagnosis of depression on the second or third interview; (d) other psychopathology ($n = 16$)—subjects who received a nondepressive diagnosis at all assessments; and (e) normal ($n = 43$)—target subjects who were categorized as not currently ill on all assessments.[1]

The new cases group is an especially important one for evaluating the antecedent hypothesis; thus, some additional details should be noted. Ten of the 27 subjects in this group (37%) reported prior episodes of depression on the lifetime version of the SADS, with all such episodes having occurred more than 6 months prior to the beginning of the study. This subgroup could be more appropriately labeled as "relapsers." In our data analyses, relapsers will be pooled with true new cases only if it can first be demonstrated that subjects with a history of depression display no residual effects on our dependent measures. This is a procedure similar to that used by Lewinsohn et al. (1981) in their study of cognitive antecedents of depression. It is also noteworthy that in the pooled new cases group, the time elapsed from the fall SADS assessment (when these subjects were not clinically depressed) to the onset of the depressive episode was calculated, with a mean time of 2.69 months obtained ($SD = 1.36$). Finally, to evaluate the degree of psychopathology displayed by new cases prior to the onset of the depressive episode, their screening scores were compared to those of normal controls and currently depressed subjects via one-way analyses of variance (ANOVAs). On the short form of the BDI a significant between-groups effect was obtained, $F(2, 100) = 3.51, p < .05$, and subsequent cell comparisons by the Tukey–Kramer procedure revealed that new cases (5.47) scored significantly higher than normals (4.62) and significantly lower than currently depressed subjects (9.02; both $ps < .05$). A similar pattern of results was obtained on the general symptom index of the BSI, $F(2, 100) = 3.79, p < .05$, with new cases (65.7) scoring higher than the normal group (60.2) and lower than the currently depressed subjects (72.8; both $ps < .05$). Although elevated with respect to normals, it should be noted that the mean scores for the new cases group were not at levels generally considered as reflecting psychopathology (BDI–SF = 8, BSI = 70).

The total sample of 119 target subjects and their normal, same-sex roommates ranged in age from 18 to 22, with a high proportion of Caucasians (95%).[2] They were primarily college freshmen (83%), and the sample was composed largely of female subjects. The percentage of female pairs in each group was: unremitted depressives, 89%; remitted depressives, 79%; new cases, 74%; other psychopathology, 44%; and normal, 70%. Statistical analysis of gender distribution across groups was nonsignificant, $\chi^2(4) = 6.22; p > .10$; however, the relatively low proportion of females in the other psychopathology group should be noted. This, coupled with the low number of male subjects in our sample, dictates that gender be used as a covariate in our later statistical analyses. Last, among groups with depressed target subjects (unremitted, remitted, and new cases), there was no significant difference in the distribution of depressive diagnoses, $c^2(2) = .04, p = .97$. The overall proportions were major depression, 38%; minor depression, 57%; and intermittent depression, 5%. At the beginning of the study, none of the participants were in treatment, although later in the year 5 subjects inquired about local mental health facilities, and this information was provided. These requests were equally distributed across groups (unremitted, 2; remitted, 1; new cases, 1; other psychopathology, 1).

Procedure

SADS training. Twelve graduate students in clinical psychology and four advanced undergraduates served as interviewers throughout the study. They underwent a 6-week training period that included didactic work on SADS/RDC methodology using materials supplied by Endicott and Spitzer (1978). Training also involved observation of experienced clinicians, supervised practice in numerous role-played formats, and completion of two interviews with volunteer subjects. Reliability was assessed in the following manner. At the completion of training, pairs of interviewers corated two interviews conducted on patients from local mental health facilities, and a mean percentage agreement of 93% for current primary diagnosis was obtained. During the early fall interviews with subjects, pairs of interviewers corated two additional sets of data, again yielding a 93% agreement for current diagnosis. Using Fleiss's (1971) method, Kappa was calculated on these latter data, and a value of .83 was obtained.

Because target subjects received three SADS interviews during the year, scheduling was arranged so that a different interviewer conducted each session, and they were unaware of prior diagnosis. This procedure was used to minimize any possible carry-over effects on judgments of current diagnostic status. In addition, at the first, early-fall assessment, interviewers were unaware of subjects' screening scores.

Data collection. Target subjects and their roommates came to three data collection sessions in our research offices during the course of the year (October–November, January–February, and April–May). During these meetings each participant independently completed a variety of self-report instruments regarding behaviors and reactions toward their roommates and life events during the prior month. At each meeting roommates also engaged in a 30-minute conversation about their relationship that was videotaped for future analysis. In addition to these sessions, each participant was asked to maintain a daily "social activities log" throughout the course of the study, which, along with other data, recorded the frequency and type of contact roommates had with each other. These logs were mailed to our research offices on a weekly basis. Subjects returned an average of 11.1 logs over the duration of the study, which represents 43% of the time that roommates were actually living together. A one-way ANOVA indicated that there were no significant differences among subject groups as to number of logs returned, $F(4, 115) = .60$, $p = .61$.

Measures

Choice of the types of interpersonal behaviors and perceptions to be measured was guided by theory and prior research. Coyne's (1976a) formulation dictates that specific social interactional patterns between roommates be evaluated. Lewinsohn et al. (1979) indicated that assessments should be made of target subjects' general social skills, conversational behaviors, and perceived positive reinforcement from the social environment. Additionally, Brown and Harris's (1978) conceptualization focuses attention on stressful life events, the amount and quality of contact with friends (social support), and self-esteem among target subjects.

Interpersonal Checklist (ICL). This self-report instrument is based on Leary's (1957) circumplex model of interpersonal behavior, and it provides scores reflecting eight types of social responding: managerial–autocratic, responsible–overgenerous, cooperative–friendly, docile–dependent, modest–self-effacing, skeptical–distrustful, blunt–aggressive, and competitive–exploitive (LaForge & Suczek, 1955). At each data collection session subjects were asked to indicate on the ICL the characteristic ways that they had behaved toward their roommates during the past month. For target subjects, the following scores were used in our analyses: (a) dependency–self-devaluation (a composite of the docile–dependent and modest–self-effacing scales, (b) aggressive–competitive (a composite of the blunt–aggressive and competitive–exploitive scales), and (c) the single score on the skeptical–distrustful scale. Two scores were derived for the roommates of target subjects: (a) friendly–responsible (composite of the cooperative–friendly and the responsible–overgenerous scales), and (b) aggressive–competitive (composite of the blunt–aggressive and competitive–exploitive scales). Each of these sets of scores has previously been found to distinguish pairs of college roommates in which one member was dysphoric from normal control pairs (Hokanson et al., 1986). Overall, the ICL scales appear to have acceptable psychometric properties, with a mean test–retest reliability of .78 and reasonable validity in tapping behavioral characteristics (LaForge & Suczek, 1955; Wiggins, 1982).

Self-esteem inventory. At each of the 3-month data collection sessions, target subjects were administered a 23-item self-esteem scale devised by Flippo and Lewinsohn (1971). Subjects were asked to indicate how they generally felt about themselves during the prior month. This scale has been used previously to discriminate between depressed and nondepressed subjects, and it has a good level of internal consistency with an alpha of .85 (Lewinsohn et al., 1981).

Videotaped conversations. Roommates engaged in a 30-minute conversation at each of the data collection sessions. Instructions to subjects were nondirective except that they were told to focus their discussion on "how their relationship was going." Subjects were aware that their interaction was being recorded from behind a one-way screen.

Two sets of measures were derived. The first was obtained from a content analysis of target subjects and roommates' conversational responses, and the second set was based on global ratings of target subjects' social skills by trained observers.

For the content analysis, a system derived from methods previously used by Howes and Hokanson (1979) was used. A 10-min segment of each conversation was scored, with each discrete phrase or sentence by each participant being tallied. For target subjects two categories of response were used: negative or positive affective communications. The former included expressions of self-criticism, disapproval or negative attitudes toward others, and pessimism or negativity about events in general. The latter category encompassed positive statements about self, others, or events. The two response categories used to score roommates' conversations were more specific and focused on statements of approval/liking, or criticism/dislike, of the target subject.

Six psychology graduate students who were blind to subject diagnostic status coded the conversations. All had undergone 40 hours of training and had achieved 90% agreement for specific response categories with expert coders on practice tapes. Interjudge reliability was assessed using randomly selected 2-minute segments from 10 subject videotapes, and the mean kappa across pairs of coders was .87 (range = .67–1.00). During the 8 weeks of actual coding, biweekly reliability check sessions were held with all coders to prevent reliability drift.

The second set of measures derived from the videotaped conversations were global ratings of target subjects' social skills. These ratings were obtained using a procedure devised by Lewinsohn, Mischel, Chaplin, and Barton (1980). This system uses a set of 12 descriptors, and subjects are rated on 7-point scales as to how characteristic their behaviors are of each descriptor (friendly, popular, assertive, attractive, warm, communicates clearly, socially skillful, interested in other people, understands what others say, humorous, speaks fluently, and open/self-disclosing). A 15-minute segment of each videotape was used to make these ratings, and a mean rating across the 12 items was used as an overall measure of social skill. Ten undergraduate and five graduate psychology students served as raters, and all were unaware of target subjects' diagnostic status. Videotapes from each data session were scored by different persons to prevent carry-over effects. Raters had undergone 30 hours of training on practice materials and, prior to scoring the actual videotapes, had achieved a 90% agreement rate (within 1 scale point) with experts on each of the 12 items. Interrater reliability among all raters was assessed using the overall social skills score from 10 randomly selected subjects, and a mean correlation between pairs of raters of 88 was obtained.

SOCIAL ACTIVITY LOG

These records, which were kept independently by target subjects and by their roommates, were to be mailed to our research office at the end of each week. Subjects had been given a supply of record forms and were instructed in their use at the beginning of the study. The logs were composed of a variety of instruments that permitted assessment of the amount and quality of ongoing social activity as well as pleasant and unpleasant life events. Data from each instrument were subsequently averaged into three phases that corresponded with the three time periods of data collection in the study (fall, winter, and late spring).

Measures of *social contact with others* were obtained in the following way. Subjects were provided with a form that contained a comprehensive list of usual college student activities (e.g., walking to class, studying, eating meals, and various recreational pursuits) on which they could tally the occurrence of activities each day. For each tallied activity subjects were also to indicate whether they engaged in that activity alone, with their roommate, or with other acquaintances. These daily data were subsequently summed across each 7-day period (and converted to percentages of total activities) to provide two "contact" scores: percentage of activities with roommate and percentage of activities with others. The accuracy of subjects' record keeping was a concern; however, with one of these measures a check was available. Because both roommates independently kept these logs, it was possible to compare the "activities with roommate" scores of each participant. A Pearson correlation between target subjects' and roommates' weekly scores yielded an r of .92.

As part of the social activity log, subjects also completed several *event schedules* that are short forms of instruments developed by Lewinsohn and colleagues. These schedules were to be completed at the end of each week. Specifically, two versions of the Interpersonal Events Schedule were used (IES; Youngren, Zeiss, & Lewinsohn, 1975). On one version subjects were to respond so as to reflect social events that occurred with their roommates during the prior week (IES–Roommate); the other version referred to social events with friends and acquaintances (IES–Friends). In addition, short forms of the Pleasant Events Schedule (PES; MacPhillamy & Lewinsohn, 1976) and the Unpleasant Events Schedule (UES; Lewinsohn, Mermelstein, Alexander, & MacPhillamy, 1983) were administered. By taking into account the frequency of various events and the subjectively rated enjoyability of events, these schedules each provide an estimate of the positive reinforcement or aversiveness that a subject experienced that week in each domain being assessed. Thus, these data permit assessment of positive reinforcement (enjoyability) derived from the roommate relationship (IES–Roommate), from other people (IES–Friends), and generally from environmental events (PES). The Unpleasant Events Schedule score is used here as a measure of weekly life-event stress; it is considered suitable for this function because the UES taps major stressors as well as "daily hassles."

Results

Overview

A relatively large number of measures were used with target subjects (13) and with their roommates (7). The measures are grouped into several domains, and these groupings are shown on the left side of Table 11.1.[3] Data with regard to each hypothesis were first subjected to multivariate analyses of covariance (MANCOVAs) within each measurement domain. Because of the relatively few male subjects, gender comparisons were not feasible; hence, gender was used as the covariate in these analyses. Subsequent univariate F-tests and Tukey–Kramer cell comparisons were conducted only when the multivariate analysis achieved significance at the .05 level.

Concomitant Hypothesis

Evaluation of this hypothesis involves comparison of roommate pairs containing a currently depressed subject with those containing other-psychopathology and normal target subjects. The data for currently depressed subjects were drawn from several sources within the design: (a) unremitted depressives at all three assessment periods, (b) remitted depressives at Time 1 (when these subjects were still depressed), and (c) new cases at either the second or third data collection period (after these subjects became depressed). When data were drawn from several time periods, each subject's mean score across periods on each measure was the entry used in the analyses.

Group means for target subjects and their roommates on each measure are presented in Table 11.1. Included in the table are the F-values for MANCOVAs performed on each measurement domain, as well as the results of Tukey–Kramer group comparisons (letter subscripts). As can be seen in Table 11.1, three of the four MANCOVAs pertaining to target subject measures were significant, as well as two of the three analyses on roommate measures. The two domains in which the MANCOVAs failed to show significance involved analyses of verbal behaviors during the videotaped conversations.

It should be noted that in Table 11.1 among the 13 target subject measures, 8 showed differences in expected directions between currently depressed subjects and normal controls (Interpersonal Event Schedules regarding both roommates and friends, Unpleasant Events Schedule, dependency—self-devaluation and skeptical—distrustful behaviors on the Interpersonal Checklist, self-esteem, and percentage of contact with roommate and with friends). It can also be seen, however, that depressives differed in the expected direction from other-psychopathology subjects on only three of these measures (Interpersonal Events Schedule–Roommate, Unpleasant Events Schedule, and contact with roommate). This overlap in responding between depressed and other-psychopathology groups was not apparent in their roommates' data. The partners of currently depressed subjects differed from the roommates of both other-psychopathology and normal targets in the expected direction on the two measures that showed significant group effects (Interpersonal Events

TABLE 11.1. Target Subjects' and Roommates' Mean Scores on Dependent Measures: Concomitant Hypothesis

Measure	Currently depressed ($n = 60$)	Group[a] Other psychopathology ($n = 16$)	Normal ($n = 43$)	MANCOVA F-value (df)
Target event schedules				
IES–Roommate[b]	4.20$_a$	9.50$_b$	7.57$_b$	
IES–Friends[b]	7.02$_a$	6.81$_a$	10.09$_b$	1.85
Pleasant events	33.32	37.85	35.11	$p < .05$
Unpleasant events	16.21$_b$	13.46$_a$	13.69$_a$	(8,226)
Target verbal behavior				
Number of positive statements	8.43	9.44	7.09	1.73
Number of negative statements	13.33	13.47	11.02	$p < .15$
Social skills rating[b]	4.35	4.51	4.37	(6,228)
Target interpersonal checklist				
Dependency–self-devaluation	5.64$_b$	6.22$_c$	5.19$_a$	
Aggressive—competitive	5.96	6.00	5.43	3.72
Skeptical–distrustful	2.81$_b$	2.53$_{a,b}$	2.11$_a$	$p < .01$
Target self-esteem[b]	28.92$_a$	29.66$_a$	38.05$_b$	(8,226)
Target contact with others[c]				
Percentage with roommate	13.8$_a$	29.1$_c$	18.1$_b$	2.12
Percentage with friends	49.1$_a$	52.3$_{a,b}$	55.1$_b$	$p < .05$ (4,230)
Roommate event schedules				
IES—target[b]	6.55$_b$	8.60$_a$	8.63$_a$	1.99
Pleasant events	34.87	36.65	33.95	$p < .05$
Unpleasant events	14.02	11.94	12.92	(6,228)
Roommate verbal behavior				
Number of approval statements	2.63	3.71	2.87	0.51
Number of critical statements	2.80	4.57	2.27	$p < .90$ (4,230)
Roomate interpersonal checklist				
Friendly–responsible	5.82	5.75	5.87	2.81
Aggressive–competitive	5.93$_b$	5.30$_a$	5.41$_a$	$p < .05$ (4,230)

[a] Cell means with different subscripts are significantly different from one another ($p < .05$) by the Tukey–Kramer test.
[b] Higher scores indicate more positive reactions.
[c] Analyses used an arcsin transformation.

Schedule–Target and aggressive–competitive behavior toward the target).

Antecedent Hypothesis

The critical group for evaluating the antecedent hypothesis is composed of subjects who were not depressed at the fall SADS assessment (Time 1) but who received a depressive diagnosis later in the year. Two subgroups fall into this category: (a) subjects who indicated no previous episodes of depression (first-time cases), and (b) subjects who did report prior depression (relapsers). Because the cell sizes were relatively small in each of these subgroups (17 and 10, respectively), it was deemed important to be able to combine them into a new cases group. Before this could be done, however, it was necessary to demonstrate that subjects with a history of depression display no residual effects of prior episodes. To test for such residuals, all subjects who reported previous episodes of depression ($n = 22$) were compared with normal controls on the 13 target measures at Time 1. As in the earlier analyses, MANCOVAs, with gender as the covariate, were performed on each measurement domain, and in all cases the multivariate F-values were nonsignificant (all $ps > .30$). Thus, the apparent absence of residual effects on our measures was used as justification for combining first-time cases with relapsers into a new cases group.

The antecedent hypothesis was tested by comparing the new cases (predepression), currently depressed, other-psychopathology, and normal groups at Time 1. The currently depressed group was composed of unremitted depressed subjects and remitted depressives (who were still depressed at Time 1). The same measures as earlier were used, along with the same strategy for statistical analysis (MANCOVA, ANCOVA, and Tukey–Kramer). Group means for target subjects and their roommates on each measure are presented in Table 11.2. With respect to target subjects' data, two of the four MANCOVAs performed on measurement domains produced significant group effects, and, as can be seen in the lower portion of Table 11.2, none of the MANCOVAs pertaining to roommate responding were significant.

Several between-group comparisons are of importance in Table 11.2. First, the results indicate that the pre-episodic new cases group differed in the expected direction from normal controls on 7 of the 13 target measures (both Interpersonal Event Schedules, Unpleasant Events Schedule, dependency–

TABLE 11.2. Target Subjects' and Roommates' Mean Scores on Dependent Measures at Time 1: Antecedent Hypothesis

Measure	Group[a]				MANCOVA F-value (df)
	New cases before depression (n = 27)	Currently depressed (n = 33)	Other psychopathology (n = 16)	Normal (n = 43)	
Target event schedules					
IES–Roommate[b]	5.38$_a$	5.25$_a$	7.00$_{a,b}$	8.43$_b$	2.86
IES–Friends[b]	6.91$_b$	7.25$_b$	1.32$_a$	11.17$_c$	$p < .05$
Pleasant events	31.33	35.56	33.84	36.23	(12,297)
Unpleasant events	17.35$_b$	13.59$_a$	14.53$_{a,b}$	14.18$_a$	
Target verbal behavior					
Number of positive statements	6.81	6.05	9.75	7.67	1.78
Number of negative statements	13.26	17.15	15.06	10.48	$p < .15$
Social skills rating[b]	4.42	4.63	4.57	4.43	(9,275)
Target interpersonal checklist					
Dependency–self-devaluation	5.89$_b$	6.10$_b$	6.19$_b$	5.33$_a$	
Aggressive–competitive	6.37$_b$	6.41$_b$	6.18$_b$	5.53$_a$	3.76
Skeptical–distrustful	2.89$_b$	2.81$_b$	2.56$_b$	2.07$_a$	$p < .01$
Target self-esteem[b]	30.02$_a$	29.17$_a$	29.35$_a$	38.04$_b$	(12,297)
Target contact with others[c]					
Percentage with roommate	19.6	17.6	29.5	19.3	1.13
Percentage with friends	56.5	55.7	53.3	54.4	$p < .40$
					(6,228)
Roommate event schedules					
IES—Target[b]	7.89	7.82	7.54	8.32	1.27
Pleasant events	35.59	33.35	35.39	35.78	$p < .30$
Unpleasant events	15.19	10.12	11.85	13.78	(9,275)
Roommate verbal behavior					
Number of approval statements	3.15	3.14	3.10	2.25	0.81
Number of critical statements	3.30	3.85	5.90	2.61	$p < .60$
					(6,228)
Roommate interpersonal checklist					
Friendly–responsible	6.53	5.75	6.18	6.03	1.17
Aggressive–competitive	5.35	5.54	5.27	5.79	$p < .40$
					(6,228)

[a] Cell means with different subscripts are significantly different from one another ($p < .05$) by the Tukey–Kramer test.
[b] Higher scores indicate more positive reactions.
[c] Analyses used an arcsine transformation.

self-devaluation, aggressive–competitive, skeptical–distrustful scores on the Interpersonal Checklist, and self-esteem). Second, on 6 of these indices, the new cases group did not differ from the currently depressed group. The one exception was the Unpleasant Events Schedule, and on this measure the pre-episodic subjects reported a more aversive impact of life events than did currently depressed subjects ($p < .05$). Finally, it can be noted in Table 11.2 that the new cases group did not differ from the other-psychopathology group in the expected direction on any of the measures.

Correlation Between Social Behaviors and Partners' Enjoyability

The conceptual rationale underlying our study presupposes that the social behaviors of roommates have a significant impact on each other. To assess this question, a series of partial correlations were performed between target subjects' scores on the Interpersonal Checklist (dependency–self-devaluation, aggression–competition, skepticism–distrust) and their roommates' Interpersonal Events Schedule (enjoyability) score regarding the target (IES–Target). Scores on each of the ICL measures and on the IES–Target were averaged across the three time periods, and correlations were calculated using the entire sample of subjects ($n = 119$ pairs). For each correlation between a particular target ICL measure and their roommates' (IES–Target) scores, the effects of the other two ICL measures were partialled out. Results indicated that all three target ICL measures (dependency–self-devaluation, aggression–competition, and skepticism–distrust) were negatively correlated with the roommate enjoyability score ($-.22$, $-.18$, and $-.20$, respectively; all $ps < .05$). Similar analyses were performed on roommates' ICL measures and targets' IES–Roommate (enjoyability) scores. Here it was found that roommates' friendly–responsible scores were positively related to targets' enjoyability ($r = .19$, $p < .05$), whereas roommates' aggression–competition scores were negatively associated with target enjoyability ($r = -.23, p < .05$).

Discussion

The purpose of this study was to identify psychosocial antecedents and concomitants of a depressive episode in a young adult sample. The theoretical impetus for such an investigation came from formulations of depression that implicate interpersonal processes as playing either a contributory or maintaining role in the disorder (Brown & Harris, 1978; Coyne, 1976a; Lewinsohn et al., 1979). The use of a prospective design with our new cases group was deemed important because it permitted an assessment of psychosocial factors before the onset of a diagnosable episode of depression—a methodology that is relatively rare in this area of exploration (Barnett & Gotlib, 1988). An associated issue concerned the question of whether any psychosocial factors that might be identified were specific to depression or, alternatively, whether they were reflections of general psychopathology in the group under study. This issue was addressed by including a nondepressed psychopathology control group in the design.

Our data regarding psychosocial concomitants of depression present a mixed picture. Although the currently depressed subjects displayed numerous differences with normal controls, they were not significantly distinguished from the other-psychopathology group on a majority of these measures. The features that appeared to be unique to the depressed group were a relatively reduced amount of social contact with their roommates, low enjoyability of such contact, and comparatively high levels of experienced stress. In addition, several roommate characteristics were specific to the depressed group, notably, low ratings of enjoyability and relatively strong aggressive–competitive reactions toward their depressed partners. Taken together, these findings are generally consistent with theory and prior research, in that currently depressed subjects have been shown to have a negative impact on others and to become involved in stressful, problematic interpersonal relations (Billings & Moos, 1985; Coyne, 1976b; Coyne et al., 1987; Gotlib & Robinson, 1982; Howes, Hokanson, & Loewenstein, 1985; Strack & Coyne, 1983). What failed to materialize in our data was a clear picture of social behavioral patterns, specific to depressed subjects, that could be seen as contributing to the problematic roommate relationship. Prior research with depressives suggests that a dependent, self-devaluating, and distrustful interpersonal style might prompt rejection and strife in social relations (Blumberg & Hokanson, 1983; Hirschfeld, Klerman, Clayton,

& Keller, 1983; Hokanson et al., 1986; Youngren & Lewinsohn, 1980). This indeed may be the case, but our data suggest that similar social characteristics are associated with other forms of psychopathology, and, hence, they may not be uniquely associated with depression.

The lack of specificity in the findings is seen more vividly in our evaluation of psychosocial antecedents of depression. The pre-episodic new cases group differed from normal controls on a substantial number of measures at Time 1, but they did not differ from other-psychopathology subjects in the expected direction on any of these variables. Several issues need to be considered in evaluating this overlap in the findings. First, it should be recalled that at Time 1 our pre-episodic subjects were being compared with a group that was displaying a current diagnosable disorder. A more appropriate comparison group would have been one composed of subjects who would develop nondepressive psychopathology in the future. Unfortunately, our subject selection procedures failed to identify such premorbid individuals, and, consequently, we had to rely on a less preferred control group. Despite this difference in diagnostic status, it is noteworthy that our pre-episodic subjects displayed psychosocial deficits comparable to those exhibited by current cases of nondepressive (and depressive) disorders. A second factor to be considered pertains to the composition of the other-psychopathology control group, three-quarters of whom received diagnoses related to anxiety. Gotlib (1984) found moderately strong correlations between measures of anxiety and depression in a college sample, and he reviewed a sizable group of earlier studies that point to similar correlations in clinical populations. These prior findings, coupled with the present results, raise the possibility that disorders involving "negative affective states" may be associated with similar psychosocial antecedents in a young adult population.

In summary, the present new cases data indicate that the search for psychosocial vulnerability factors specific to depression remains an elusive endeavor. The findings do, however, point toward a group of personality–interpersonal features that may represent risk factors for general psychopathology in a college population. Low self-esteem, sensitivity to stressful life events, and a dependent, self-effacing, aggrieved–mistrustful pattern of social behavior appear to be part of such a constellation. Our correlational data suggest that these social behaviors are associated with negative reactions by others, and, hence, they may contribute to the development of psychopathology by fostering interpersonal stress and alienating potential sources of social support.

ACKNOWLEDGMENT

This research was supported by Grant MH40308 from the National Institute of Mental Health to Jack E. Hokanson.

NOTES

1. Our assessment procedures did not identify any "remitters" or "new cases" in the nondepressive–other-psychopathology group. Whether this is due to some unique aspects of our evaluation procedures or the relative stability of nondepressive disorders in this sample is difficult to say.
2. Constraints on time and personnel made it unfeasible to administer SADS interviews to all roommates of target subjects. However, when roommate BDI or BSI scores (administered 3 times during the year) were found to be elevated an SADS was administered, and any roommate found to have a diagnosable disorder was noted. This was relatively rare (8 cases), and such instances were equally distributed across target groups.
3. Because targets' and roommates' measures of weekly contact were highly correlated ($r = .92$), the roommates' contact score is redundant and, hence, not included in our analysis.

REFERENCES

Barnett, P. A., & Gotlib, I. H. (1988). Psychosocial functioning and depression: Distinguishing among antecedents, concomitants, and consequences. *Psychological Bulletin, 104*, 97–126.

Beck, A. T., & Beck, R. W. (1972). Screening depressed patients in family practice: A rapid technique. *Postgraduate Medicine, 52*, 81–85.

Billings, A. G., & Moos, R. H. (1985). Psychosocial processes of remission in unipolar depression: Comparing depressed patients with matched community controls. *Journal of Consulting and Clinical Psychology, 53*, 314–325.

Blumberg, S. R., & Hokanson, J. E. (1983). Effects of response style on behavior in depression. *Journal of Abnormal Psychology, 91*, 196–204.

Brown, G. W., & Harris, T. (1978). *Social origins of depression: A study of psychiatric disorders in women.* London: Tavistock.

Cohen, S., & Wills, T. A. (1985). Stress, social support, and the buffering hypothesis. *Psychological Bulletin, 98*, 310–357.

Coyne, J. C. (1976a). Toward an interactional description of depression *Psychiatry, 39*, 28–40.

Coyne, J. C. (1976b). Depression and the response of others. *Journal of Abnormal Psychology, 85*, 186–193.

Coyne, J. C., & Gotlib, I. H. (1983). The role of cognition in depression. A critical appraisal. *Psychological Bulletin, 94,* 472–505.

Coyne, J. C., Kessler, R. C., Tal, M., Turnbull, J., Wortman, C. B., & Greden, J. (1987). Living with a depressed person: Burden and psychological distress. *Journal of Consulting and Clinical Psychology, 55,* 347–352.

Derogatis, L. R. (1975). *Brief Symptom Inventory.* Baltimore, MD: Clinical Psychometric Research.

Derogatis, L. R., Lipman, R. S., & Covi, L. (1973). SLC-90: An outpatient psychiatric rating scale—Preliminary report. *Psychopharmacology Bulletin, 9,* 13–27.

Endicott, J., & Spitzer, R. L. (1978). A diagnostic interview: The Schedule for Affective Disorders and Schizophrenia. *Archives of General Psychiatry, 35,* 837–844.

Fleiss, J. L. (1971). Measuring nominal scale agreement among many raters. *Psychological Bulletin, 76,* 378–382.

Flippo, J. R., & Lewinsohn, P. M. (1971). Effects of failure on the self-esteem of depressed and non-depressed subjects. *Journal of Consulting and Clinical Psychology, 36,* 151.

Gotlib, I. H. (1984). Depression and general psychopathology in university students. *Journal of Abnormal Psychology, 93,* 19–30.

Gotlib, I. H., & Robinson, L. A. (1982). Responses to depressed individuals: Discrepancies between self-report and observer-rated behavior. *Journal of Abnormal Psychology, 91,* 231–240.

Hammen, C., Mayol, A., deMayo, R., & Marks, T. (1986). Initial symptom levels and the life-event-depression relationship. *Journal of Abnormal Psychology, 95,* 114–122.

Hirschfeld, R. M. A., Klerman, G. L., Clayton, P. J., & Keller, M. B. (1983). Personality and depression: Empirical findings. *Archives of General Psychiatry, 40,* 993–998.

Hokanson, J. E., Loewenstein, D. A., Hedeen, C., & Howes, M. J. (1986). Dysphoric college students and roommates: A study of social behaviors over a three-month period. *Personality and Social Psychology Bulletin, 12,* 311–324.

Howes, M. J., & Hokanson, J. E. (1979). Conversational and social responses to depressive interpersonal behavior. *Journal of Abnormal Psychology, 88,* 625–634.

Howes, M. J., Hokanson, J. E., & Loewenstein, D. A. (1985). Induction of depressive affect after prolonged exposure to a mildly depressed individual. *Journal of Personality and Social Psychology, 49,* 1110–1113.

Kendall, P. C., Hollon, S. D., Beck, A. T., Hammen, C. L., & Ingram, R. E. (1987). Issues and recommendations regarding use of the Beck Depression Inventory. *Cognitive Therapy and Research, 11,* 289–299.

LaForge, R., & Suczek, R. (1955). The interpersonal dimension of personality: III. Interpersonal checklist. *Journal of Personality, 24,* 94–112.

Leary, T. F. (1957). *Interpersonal diagnosis of personality.* New York: Ronald.

Lewinsohn, P. M., Mermelstein, R., Alexander, C., & MacPhillamy, D. (1983). *The unpleasant events schedule: A scale for the measurement of aversive events.* Unpublished manuscript, University of Oregon.

Lewinsohn, P. M., Mischel, W., Chaplin, W., & Barton, R. (1980). Social competence and depression: The role of illusory self-perceptions. *Journal of Abnormal Psychology, 89,* 203–212.

Lewinsohn, P. M., Steinmetz, J. L., Larson, D. W., & Franklin, J. (1981). Depression-related cognitions: Antecedent or consequence? *Journal of Abnormal Psychology, 90,* 213–219.

Lewinsohn, P. M., Youngren, M. A., & Grosscup, S. J. (1979). Reinforcement and depression. In R. A. Depue (Ed.), *The psychobiology of depressive disorders: Implications for the effects of stress* (pp. 291–316). New York: Academic Press.

MacPhillamy, D. J., & Lewinsohn, P. M. (1976). *Manual for the Pleasant Events Schedule.* Unpublished manuscript, University of Oregon.

Monroe, S. M., & Steiner, S. C. (1986). Social support and psychopathology: Interrelations with preexisting disorder, stress, and personality. *Journal of Abnormal Psychology, 95,* 29–39.

Spitzer, R. L., Endicott, J., & Robins, E. (1978). Research diagnostic criteria: Rationale and reliability. *Archives of General Psychiatry, 35,* 773–782.

Strack, S., & Coyne, J. C. (1983). Social confirmation of dysphoria: Shared and private reactions to depression. *Journal of Personality and Social Psychology, 44,* 798–806.

Wiggins, J. S. (1982). Circumplex models of interpersonal behavior in clinical psychology. In P. C. Kendall & J. N. Butcher (Eds.), *Handbook of research methods in clinical psychology* (pp. 183–221). New York: Wiley.

Youngren, M. A., & Lewinsohn, P. M. (1980). The functional relation between depression and problematic interpersonal behavior. *Journal of Abnormal Psychology, 89,* 333–341.

Youngren, M. A., Zeiss, A., & Lewinsohn, P. M. (1975). *Interpersonal events schedule.* Unpublished manuscript, University of Oregon.

Discussion Questions

1. If depressed individuals behave in ways that lead others to reject them, which leads to further depression and even more rejection, how can a person who is depressed break this cycle?
2. Why would people respond to a depressed person with hostility and rejection? Would it matter if people believed that the depressed person did not have control over his or her depression?
3. Which theory do you personally find most convincing—the concomitant hypothesis or the antecedent hypothesis? Why?
4. Do you think that living with a depressed individual leads to depression among other family members? Why?

Suggested Readings

Barnett, P. A., & Gotlib, I. H. (1988). Psychosocial functioning and depression: Distinguishing among antecedents, concomitants, and consequences. *Psychological Bulletin, 104,* 97–126. This article reviews the literature that tries to distinguish psychosocial variables that precede depression from those that are consequences of depression.

Coyne, J. C., Kessler, R. C., Tal, M., Turnball, J., Wortman, C. B., & Greden, J. (1987). Living with a depressed person: Burden and psychological distress. *Journal of Consulting and Clinical Psychology, 55,* 347–352. This study examined the effects of living with a depressed person, which were found to be more serious than those caused by living with someone with problems other than depression.

Howes, M. J., Hokanson, J. E., & Loewenstein, D. A. (1985). Induction of depressive affect after prolonged exposure to a mildly depressed individual. *Journal of Personality and Social Psychology, 49,* 1110–1113. This study examines the effects of living with a depressed person, one of which is an increase in one's own depression.

READING 12

Social Confirmation of Dysphoria: Shared and Private Reactions to Depression

Stephen Strack • University of Miami
James C. Coyne • University of California, Berkeley

Editors' Introduction

Traditional explanations of depression have focused on the psychological characteristics of the depressed individual himself or herself. Self-derogation, pessimistic explanatory styles, and excessive dependency were among the intrapsychic processes believed to perpetuate depression. However, due largely to the work of Coyne (1976), researchers began to explore possible interpersonal factors in depression—processes that occur between individuals that foster and maintain a person's depressed state. In his interactional theory of depression, Coyne proposed that people who are depressed act in ways that lead other people to experience negative emotions and to avoid or reject the depressed person. This rejection then fuels the person's depression, leading to even more rejection, followed by greater depression in a spiraling cycle.

Coyne conducted a study in which nondepressed female students engaged in 20-minute phone conversations with depressed female outpatients. Following the conversations, Coyne examined the mood of the students. As he expected, interacting with a depressed individual made the students feel hostile, depressed, and anxious, and led them to reject the depressed individual. Thus, individuals who are depressed induce negative feelings in other people that lead them to be shunned, creating even more depression.

The following article describes a further test of the interactional theory. Strack and Coyne had undergraduate students interact with a person who either was or was not mildly depressed. (Importantly, the depressed individuals were not experiencing clinical levels of depression but were only mildly depressed or "dysphoric.") Following the interaction, participants answered questions about their mood and rated the other person. Furthermore, participants believed that their ratings either would or would not be seen by the other person.

Participants who interacted with depressed individuals reported more hostility, depression, and anxiety than participants who interacted with nondepressed individuals, and they rated the depressed individuals more negatively. Interestingly, the depressed individuals also rejected the nondepressed participants even though they did not rate them negatively. No differences were obtained as a function of whether participants thought their ratings of the other individual would be shared with that person or remain private.

Although the participants in this study were initially unacquainted with one another, the possible implications of these results for relationships with friends and romantic partners are intriguing. Studies have demonstrated that students whose roommates or romantic partners are depressed similarly experience hostility, depression, and anxiety, and tend to end up rejecting the depressed individual.

Abstract

Social responses to dysphoria were investigated. Subjects conversed for 15 minutes with persons selected on the basis of the presence or absence of depressed mood. Following the conversations, mood measures were administered along with social perception questionnaires that were described as either being confidential or to be shared with the other person. Subjects who interacted with depressed persons were anxious, depressed, and hostile, and the subjects rejected them. Contrary to predictions, subjects were willing to share their negative responses with the depressed persons. The depressed persons correctly anticipated rejection and reciprocated. The authors argue that cognitive models of depression need to be integrated with a conception of the social environment as being active and responsive. Judgments of cognitive distortion cannot be made without an understanding of the feedback typically available from the social environment.

Studies of both depressed mood in normal subjects and clinical depression have tended to assume the sufficiency of cognitive processes in explaining the maintenance of depression (Beck, 1974). Whether negative mood states may have social consequences that feed back and perpetuate them is generally not considered (Coyne, 1976a). The bulk of the current literature examines depressed persons' attributions for experimenter-provided success and failure, their estimates of their performance on impersonal laboratory tasks, and their expectations for future performance when outcomes are governed by skill or by chance (for a review, see Beck & Rush, 1978).

Such studies can tell us something about how

depressed persons process particular kinds of input, but they give only a limited understanding of the role of cognition in depression. Free of the constraints of the laboratory task, depressed persons do some things and leave other things undone, affect the impression that the social environment has of them, and receive feedback. Coyne (in press) has argued that current cognitive models of depression do not give a satisfactory account of depressed persons' ongoing involvement with the environment and that we cannot have an adequate model of depression without an understanding of depressed persons' ecological niches, typical responses, and resulting feedback. Similarly, Coyne, Aldwin, and Lazarus (1981) have suggested the need to examine the cycle in which depressed persons approach situations with negative affect and expectations, cope ineffectively, face distressing circumstances, and in turn are burdened by these outcomes in their next encounters.

The study of social interactions involving depressed persons is critical to the development of cognitive models of depression. One cannot provide an adequate description of the cognitive processes of depressed persons without some reference to the information typically available to them. "It is logically and strategically prior to any detailed proposals about processing to describe the available stimulation" (Mace, 1974, p. 44). In the absence of these data we are likely to localize in the individual's cognitive processes what should more appropriately be seen as the product of the interplay of that person and his or her typical circumstances (Snyder, in press; Wachtel, 1973). For example, rather than being a matter of cognitive distortion (Beck, 1974), depressed persons' complaints of rejection and social ineffectiveness may reflect the feedback available to them in social interactions.

Coyne (1976a) has proposed a model of depression in which the behavior of the depressed person becomes interwoven and concatenated with a depressing response from others. Depression and the response of others thus become mutually maintaining aspects of an interpersonal system. Coyne (1976b) showed that in brief encounters depressed persons induce a negative mood in others and get rejected. Libet and Lewinsohn (1973) had previously shown that depressed persons in a group therapy situation are lower than controls in initiation of interactions, range of contacts, and rate of positive response, and they concluded that these differences were evidence of depressed persons' lack of social skills. However, Coyne (1976b) noted how each of these measures was related to the response from others, and he offered the alternative interpretation that other people are unwilling to interact with depressed persons who lack the special skills necessary to overcome this.

Testing Coyne's (1976a) model, a number of studies have used written and recorded scripts and role-playing confederates to examine subjects' reactions to persons showing indications of depressed mood. The general finding has been that depressed persons have an aversive impact on others (Hammen & Peters, 1978; Robbins, Strack, & Coyne, 1979; Winer, Bonner, Blaney, & Murray, 1981). Howes and Hokanson (1979) used a role-enactment methodology, and they found that depressed persons elicited more direct support from others—but fewer positive and neutral conversation-maintaining responses—as well as more punishing and insulting remarks and expressions of displeasure. Howes and Hokanson interpreted their results as being consistent with Coyne's (1976b) notion that other people give a double message of both reassurance and rejection to depressed persons. Yarkin, Harvey, and Bloxom (1981) provided to subjects a videotape of a woman with and without the information that she was facing depressing circumstances and that she was worried about her mental health. When subjects were given an opportunity to interact with her, those who were told she was depressed sat farther away, made less eye contact, engaged in more negatively valenced conversation, and spoke with her for a shorter period of time.

In summary, the recent literature suggests that depressed people prove aversive and get rejected. However, the evidence for this conclusion generally comes from studies using standardized descriptions of depressed persons or actors playing a depressed role. Such studies may be premature, given our lack of knowledge concerning the salient interpersonal features of depression. Inadvertently, researchers may be merely exploring their and the subjects' preconceived notions about interactions involving depressed persons.

Studies actually using depressed persons have involved designs that limit any generalization from their findings to interactions between depressed persons and their peers in the natural environment.

Thus, the studies of Lewinsohn and his colleagues (Libet & Lewinsohn, 1973; Youngren & Lewinsohn, 1980) examined the interpersonal behavior of depressed persons in therapeutic groups. The severely depressed outpatients in Coyne's (1976a) study spoke on a telephone in a community mental health center to college students who differed considerably from them in age, education, and income. Hokanson, Sacco, Blumberg, and Landrum (1980) examined the communication of depressed persons and their peers, but it was in the context of a highly structured Prisoner's Dilemma Game.

At the present, there has been no direct test of whether persons drawn from a normal population but showing depressed mood are able to elicit an affective reaction from others that is consistent with their negative self-perceptions. It is possible that cognitive factors alone can account for the persistence of dysphoria in such a population and that social confirmation occurs only in response to more severe mood disturbance or to confederates enacting an exaggerated depressive role.

The present study examined whether persons chosen from a normal population on the basis of dysphoria would induce a negative mood in others and get rejected. Additionally, it examined whether others would be willing to provide feedback directly to them. Previously, Robbins et al. (1979) found that subjects indicated less willingness to provide positive responses to depressed persons. Cohen, Baker, Cohen, Fromm-Reichmann, and Weigert (1954), Jacobson (1971), and McLean, Ogston, and Grauer (1973) have suggested that dysphoria frequently elicits sharp criticism and hostility from others. However, Platt (1977) found that as an interpersonal strategy, self-derogation produces a negative private reaction but a positive public reaction in others. To the extent that depressed persons use such a strategy, they may succeed in inhibiting the expression of negative reactions from others and even elicit an ungenuinely positive reaction (see also Coyne, 1976a).

If, as previous research suggests, depressed persons prove aversive and get rejected, direct feedback to this effect may provide at least a partial basis for their negative self-perceptions. Theoretical ascriptions of cognitive distortions to depressed persons would then have to be tempered by a recognition of the depressing feedback that they may frequently face. If, on the other hand, others are inhibited from expressing their negative reactions, depressed persons may face a difficult interpretative task in social interactions. Ambiguous and even positive overt reactions may conceal contradictory impressions. A context is thus established in which depressed persons must risk the future embarrassment or disappointment of having assumed more acceptance by others than is the case or, alternatively, they must risk making overly negative interpretations of the response of others. Any attempts to clarify the reactions of others are likely to prove uncomfortable for everyone involved and to risk further alienation of others.

In the present study it was specifically hypothesized that depressed persons would (a) induce negative affect in others and (b) get rejected. Such results would be consistent with the argument that the social impact of negative mood can serve to perpetuate it. It was additionally hypothesized that (c) there would be an interaction effect between depression and conditions of response (shared vs. private). Specifically, it was anticipated that depressed persons would elicit a positive response when subjects expected it to be shared with them but a negative response when subjects expected it would be confidential.

Method

Subjects interacted with depressed or nondepressed target persons. The designation of target persons was made on the basis of an established measure of dysphoria rather than on a clinical diagnosis. Following their conversations, all subjects and target persons filled out questionnaires concerning their mood, perception of the other person, and their willingness to interact with her. Half of all subject-target pairs were told that their responses would be kept confidential, while half were told that their responses would be provided as feedback to the other person. Thus, the study involved a 2 (depressed or nondepressed target person) × 2 (private vs. shared response) design. Finally, subjects and target persons were asked to guess the response of the other person to them.

Subjects and Target Persons

Female college students from introductory psychology classes served as both subjects and target persons, and they received course credit for their participation in the study. Selection and classification took place in two stages. First, students were administered in groups a battery of tests including the short form of the Beck Depression Inventory (BDI–SF; Beck & Beck, 1972). Students whose scores were 7 or above were selected as the pool from which depressed target persons were to be drawn, while those with scores of 2 or less were selected as the pool from which both nondepressed target persons and subjects were to be drawn.

In the second stage, 147 persons meeting the initial criteria were contacted and given appointments from 1 to 6 weeks later. At that time they again completed the BDI–SF. Persons from the depressed pool whose scores were less than 6 and persons from the nondepressed pool whose scores were greater than 2 were eliminated. The final sample consisted of 30 depressed target persons (BDI–SF $M = 9.73$) and a total of 90 nondepressed target persons and subjects (BDI–SF $M = .58$).

Procedure

Equal numbers of nondepressed persons were randomly chosen to serve as either nondepressed target persons, subjects conversing with a depressed person, or subjects conversing with a nondepressed target person. Each subject—target pair was told that this was a study of the casual acquaintance process. They were told that after the experimenter left the room, they would have 15 minutes to talk about whatever they liked for the purpose of getting to know one another. No other instructions were given except that after the conversation, they would be asked to complete some questionnaires.

Following the conversation, subjects and target persons were taken to separate rooms where they were asked to fill out a mood questionnaire. Then, under one of two instructional sets, they were asked to indicate their perception of the other person and their willingness to interact again under varying conditions. Subjects in the shared condition were told:

> With this ... questionnaire we want you to describe, as honestly and accurately as you can, your impressions of the person you talked to. ... Toward the end of the experiment we are going to let your co-subject read your answers to this questionnaire so that she can see what your impression of her is like. This is the *only* questionnaire of yours she will read. And of course, you will get to read the questionnaire that she filled out about you.

Actually, all questionnaires were kept confidential. Subjects in the private condition were instructed:

> With this ... questionnaire we want you to describe, as honestly and accurately as you can, your impressions of the person you talked to. ... If I haven't mentioned it before, I want you to know that all of the questionnaires you are filling out are confidential. They are for research purposes only and will not be communicated to your co-subject or anyone else.

Subjects and targets were then asked to predict their partner's answers to the questions indicting willingness to interact. Partial instructions went as follows:

> What we'd like you to do now is answer some of the same questions you just finished but this time to guess—as accurately as you can—how your partner answered them about you. Take the next few moments to think about this and then answer the following questions as you believe your partner did when she was asked to describe you.

Subjects and targets in the shared condition then completed a postexperimental questionnaire asking about the effects on their answers of the instructions for the items concerning perception of the other and willingness to interact.

Measures

The Multiple Affect Adjective Check List Today Form (MAACL; Zuckerman & Lubin, 1965) was used to measure postconversation mood in both targets and subjects.

Willingness to engage in future interaction was measured by nine questions answered on a 6-point scale ranging from "definitely yes" to "definitely no." The questions were fashioned after those used by Coyne (1976a) and sampled situations such as meeting with the person, asking her for advice, and admitting her to the respondent's circle of friends (e.g., "Would you like to meet with this person again?"). Predictions of the other's responses to these questions were obtained by having subjects complete the same nine items as they thought their partner had done.

After Coyne (1976a), perception of the other participant was measured using two sets of scales. The first asked "How do you think your partner would prefer that you see her?" and was followed by 11 bipolar adjectives on a 6-point continuum. The adjectives were happy–sad, pleasant–unpleasant, negative–positive, good–bad, comfortable–uncomfortable, weak–strong, cold–warm, attractive–unattractive, high–low, active–passive, and friendly–unfriendly. The second question, "What do you think your partner would be like if you really got to know her?," was followed by the same adjectives.

The postexperimental measure consisted of the question, "Do you feel that being told that your questionnaire would be read by your co-subject affected the way you responded?" Subjects answering "yes" were then asked to indicate how they were affected by checking whether they had rated their partner in "a more positive light," "a more negative light," or in a more or less honest manner. An "other" category was also provided.

Results

Subject Variables

Table 12.1 presents the means and standard deviations for mood measures administered to the subjects immediately following their conversation with the target persons. As predicted, subjects who had conversed with depressed target persons were significantly more depressed, $F(1, 56) = 6.56$, $p < .02$, anxious, $F(1, 56) = 8.40$, $p < .005$, and hostile, $F(1, 56) = 5.84$, $p < .02$, than those who had conversed with nondepressed target persons.

Measures of willingness to engage in future interactions were combined in one overall willingness-to-interact score. Coefficient alpha (Cronbach, 1951) for the 9-item scale was .90. Group means and standard deviations are presented in Table 12.2. Subjects who had conversed with depressed target persons were significantly less willing to interact with them in the future, $F(1, 56) = 5.84$, $p < .02$. Subjects who had been told that their responses would be shared with the target persons indicated significantly more willing-

TABLE 12.1. Subject Mood as Reported on the MAACL

Mood	Spoke with depressed person		Spoke with nondepressed person	
	M	SD	M	SD
Anxiety	5.30	2.76	3.16	2.85
Depression	10.67	4.97	7.20	5.57
Hostility	5.50	2.43	3.93	2.53

Note. MAACL = Multiple Affect Adjective Check List Today Form (Zuckerman & Lubin, 1965).

ness to interact in the future than did subjects who had been told that their responses would remain confidential, $F(1, 56) = 4.55$, $p < .05$. There was no interaction effect ($F < 1$); thus, the combined effects of target status (depressed or nondepressed) and the fate of responses (shared or confidential) were additive, not multiplicative.

The 11 bipolar adjective ratings that subjects completed in answer to the question "How do you think that your partner would prefer that you see her?" were combined into a single positive–negative scale with a coefficient alpha of .89. Group means and standard deviations are presented in Table 12.2. Subjects who conversed with depressed target persons took a much more negative view of them than did subjects conversing with a nondepressed target person, $F(1, 56) = 15.20$, $p < .001$, and subjects who had been told that their responses would remain confidential overall gave a more negative view of the target individuals, $F(1, 56) = 4.80$, $p < .05$. However, there was no Target × Response interaction effect.

The 11 bipolar adjective ratings that subjects completed in answer to the question "what do you think your partner would be like if you really got to know her?" were also combined into a single positive-negative score. Coefficient alpha for the scale was .90, and group data are presented in Table 12.2. Subjects who had conversed with depressed target persons gave a significantly more negative evaluation of what they would be like, $F(1, 56) = 9.75$, $p < .005$, and subjects who believed that their responses would be kept confidential gave more negative evaluations, $F(1, 56) = 9.19$, $p < .005$. Once again, no interaction effect was found ($F < 1$).

Subjects' estimates of how willing the target individuals would be to interact with them were combined into a 9-item scale with a coefficient

TABLE 12.2. Subject Questionnaire Responses

Questionnaire	Spoke with depressed person		Spoke with nondepressed person	
	M	SD	M	SD
Willingness to interact				
Shared condition	19.00	4.16	15.93	6.50
Private condition	24.53	11.18	18.47	7.20
How target prefers to be seen				
Shared condition	19.73	5.40	14.60	4.63
Private condition	23.86	8.41	17.13	4.20
What subject would really be like				
Shared condition	19.67	4.64	14.80	4.09
Private condition	23.93	8.47	19.53	4.70

Note. Higher values indicate more negative responses.

alpha of .91. There were no significant main or interaction effects, but there was a nonsignificant tendency for subjects who had conversed with depressed target persons to predict more rejection from them, $F(1, 56) = 3.18$, $p < .10$. As will be seen later, depressed subjects were actually significantly less willing to interact with the subject with whom they conversed than were the nondepressed target persons.

Postexperimental questionnaire data are presented in Table 12.3. In the shared condition, subjects who had conversed with a depressed person were more likely to indicate that their response had been influenced by being told that their questionnaire would be shared with the other person, $\chi^2(1) = 4.82$, $p < .05$. They also indicated that they felt they were being less honest as a result, $\chi^2(1) = 6.14$, $p < .01$, but their tendency to indicate that they were being more positive was not significant $\chi^2(1) = 1.43$, $p > .1$.

Target Variables

As would be expected, depressed target persons were more depressed, $F(1, 56) = 20.32$, $p < .001$, anxious, $F(1, 56) = 19.51$, $p < .001$, and hostile, $F(1, 56) = 15.16$, $p < .001$, than were nondepressed target persons. There were no main or interaction effects for depressed and nondepressed target person responses to the questions "How do you think your partner would prefer that you see her?" or "What do you think your partner would be like if you really got to know her?" under the shared and private instructional sets (see Table 12.4). However, depressed persons were significantly more rejecting of their partners than were nondepressed

TABLE 12.3. Postexperimental Questionnaire Responses of Subjects in the Shared Condition

Question	Spoke with depressed person	Spoke with nondepressed person
Was affected by being told that partner would see response		
Yes	10	4
No	5	11
Was less honest as a result		
Yes	8	1
No	7	14
Rated partner more positively as a result		
Yes	6	3
No	9	12

TABLE 12.4. Willingness-to-Interact Questionnaire

Actual and estimated responses	Depressed target persons		Nondepressed target persons	
	M	SD	M	SD
Responses to subjects				
Shared condition	16.93	5.06	15.86	4.98
Private condition	23.67	7.30	18.46	5.03
Target persons' estimates of responses to them				
Shared condition	24.60	7.76	19.86	5.51
Private condition	26.80	6.74	20.53	4.80
Subjects' estimates of target persons' responses				
Shared condition	22.40	4.54	21.07	4.95
Private condition	25.67	8.52	21.67	4.06

Note. Higher values indicate more negative scores.

persons, $F(1, 56) = 4.57$, $p < .05$, and target persons under the private instructional set were in general more rejecting, $F(1, 56) = 10.13$, $p < .002$. There was no interaction effect. Depressed persons also correctly anticipated more rejection from the subjects with whom they interacted than did nondepressed target persons, $F(1, 56) = 11.40$, $p < .001$, but there was no main effect for instructional set and no interaction effect.

In the shared condition, depressed target persons were more likely to indicate that they had been influenced by the manipulation, $\chi^2(1) = 5.00$, $p < .05$, and that they were less honest, $\chi^2(1) = 7.78$, $p < .01$, and more positive, $\chi^2(1) = 4.66$, $p < .05$, as a result.

Discussion

In a 15-minute conversation, depressed persons induced hostility, depression, and anxiety in others and got rejected. Their guesses that they were not accepted were not a matter of cognitive distortion, as current models of depression (Beck, 1974) would suggest, but were consistent with the response of others. Although the depressed persons did not indicate negative perceptions of those with whom they conversed, they reciprocated the rejection they received.

Experimental studies have shown that the effects of social reinforcers are mediated by a person's affective state and specifically that negative mood reduces the effectiveness of social reinforcers (Gouaux, 1971; Gouaux, Lamberth, & Friedrich, 1972). Coyne (1976a) reasoned that because the depressed patients in his study induced negative mood in others, it was likely that any nondepressed, prosocial behavior they emitted would have a reduced impact, that is, would be met with less reward. This in turn could lead to less adaptive behavior and further deterioration of their social situation. The results of the present study suggest that a negative mood induction is not limited to severely depressed patients but can also arise in interactions with mildly dysphoric persons. The ease with which such an effect can be obtained in brief encounters between strangers suggest that negative responses to dysphoria may be common. Reactions from others may perpetuate negative mood states and even contribute to the development of more severe mood disturbance.

It is theoretically noteworthy that depressed persons were rejecting even though they did not perceive their partners in negative terms. It is likely that the

mood → reduced reinforcer effectiveness

sequence also holds true for depressed persons. Costello (1976) has previously suggested such a link. One cognitive theorist has rejected it as implausible (Seligman, 1978), and the dominant models of depression tend to treat affect as a consequence of cognitive—perceptual processes rather than a possible antecedent (Beck, 1974). In general, it may be time to reassess dogmatic assertions about the causal priority of cognition over other psychological processes (Lazarus, Coyne, & Folkman, 1982; Zajonc, 1980).

Coyne (1976a) has previously suggested that other people may attempt to reduce the aversiveness of depressed persons by manipulating them with ungenuine positive responses. Platt (1977) produced results consistent with this in an analogue study using self-derogating confederates. However, in the present study, the predicted interaction between depression and condition of response (shared vs. private) was not obtained. Yet, while the willingness-to-interact questionnaire data do not support our hypothesis, postexperimental questionnaire data indicate that persons who conversed with depressed persons admitted less honesty in the shared-feedback condition relative to subjects who conversed with nondepressed persons. Further research is needed to resolve this discrepancy. We did not make any postexperimental inquiry of subjects in the private condition, but it may be that subjects rating depressed persons would admit to less honesty there also. There may be a general reluctance to make explicit negative evaluations of depressed persons, and this reluctance influenced responses in both the private and shared conditions. In future research, it would be useful to include such a postexperimental inquiry but also to examine whether there are discrepancies among the verbal and nonverbal behavior and questionnaire responses of persons interacting with depressed persons.

Alternatively, it may be that the self-derogation studied by Platt (1977) was not a salient behavior among our mildly depressed sample. Instead, self-derogation may be used more sparingly and strategically to elicit support or as a *disclaimer* when demands are made. Hewitt and Stokes (1975) define disclaimer as a "verbal device employed to ward off and defeat in advance doubts and negative typlifications . . . by calling other's attention to possible undesired typlifications and asking forebearance" (p. 3). Self-derogation is generally considered a characteristic and ever-defining feature of depression, but at the present time little is known about the circumstances under which it is displayed.

Clearly, more research is needed to specify exactly what depressed persons do that induces negative mood in others and elicits rejection. Yet attempting to describe this characteristic behavior can be frustrating. When differences are found (Libet & Lewinsohn, 1973), they tend not to be replicated (Youngren & Lewinsohn, 1980). The latter study found that neither verbal nor nonverbal behavioral measures discriminated between depressed and nondepressed persons, even though observers rated the depressed persons more negatively. Jacobson and Anderson (in press) have recently produced data that suggest that sequential analyses of the timing of depressed persons' behavior may be a productive strategy. Currently we are undertaking a study in which we use ratings by the spouses and roommates of persons selected on the basis of the presence or absence of prolonged depressed mood.

Studies such as the present one can document that dysphoria elicits confirmatory negative social responses and they highlight the need to consider dysphoria as a social as well as an intrapersonal phenomenon. However, the present study samples only fleeting contacts between strangers who have minimal responsibilities toward each other, other than maintaining a conversation. It is likely that the various deficiencies and social role impairments of depressed persons (Weissman & Paykel, 1974) have a more profound impact on ongoing relationships that entail extensive mutual responsibilities. Attention needs to be directed to the social feedback available in these contexts.

Identification of potentially depressing responses from the social environment requires a more complex conceptualization of dysphoria than one that explains its persistence by reference to isolated cognitive processes. Purported cognitive distortions may in part be explained by the reasonable expectation that negative responses will be forthcoming. Like other people, depressed persons may form expectations and interpret ambiguous situations in terms of frequent and salient recent experiences. Cognitive conceptions of dysphoria and of psychological phenomena in general tend to ignore the obvious observations that the social environment is composed of other active, thoughtful, and responsive persons and that cognitive and social processes are not readily separable.

Finally, it should be noted that we wish to avoid making any simple statement about the causal priorities in the relationship between dysphoria and social rejection. In the laboratory it is likely that either variable can be isolated and treated as an antecedent condition in order to study its effect on the other. However, we must be careful in how we generalize from artificially delimited sequences to the complexities of social relationships in the naturalistic environment. There, relevant

> events seldom occur only once, but persist, overlap, and recur with maddening complexity, [and therefore] a circular causal model is often more appropriate than a linear one that artificially abstracts events from the intricate sequences in which they occur. (Coyne & Holroyd, 1982, p. 114)

Once either dysphoria or social rejection have occurred, the other is more likely, and the development and persistence of more severe affective disorder may well involve extended sequences in which there is a mutually causative relationship between displays of dysphoria and the response from others.

ACKNOWLEDGMENTS

The authors wish to thank Paul H. Blaney for his consultation and advice. Thanks also go to Renee Dry-foos, Allison Spearman, Betty Diekneit, and Tanya Levina for their help in data collection.

REFERENCES

Beck, A. T. (1974). Cognition, affect and psychopathology. In H. London & R. E. Nisbett (Eds.), *Thought and feeling*. Chicago: Aldine.
Beck, A. T., & Beck, R. W. (1972). Screening depressed patients in family practice: A rapid technique. *Postgraduate Medicine, 52*, 81–85.
Beck, A. T., & Rush, A. J. (1978). Cognitive approaches to depression and suicide. In G. Serban (Ed.), *Cognitive defects in the development of mental illness*. New York: Brunner/Mazel.
Cohen, M. B., Baker, G., Cohen, R. A., Fromm-Reichmann, F., & Weigert, E. A. (1954). An intensive study of twelve cases of manic-depressive psychoses. *Psychiatry, 17*, 103–137.
Costello, C. G. (1976). *Anxiety and depression: The adaptive emotions*. Montreal, Canada: McGill-Queens University.
Coyne, J. C. (1976a). Depression and the response of others. *Journal of Abnormal Psychology, 85*, 186–193.
Coyne, J. C. (1976b). Toward an interactional description of depression. *Psychiatry, 39*, 28–40.
Coyne, J. C. (in press). A critique of cognitions as causal entities with particular reference to depression. *Cognitive Therapy and Research*.

Coyne, J. C., Aldwin, C., & Lazarus, R. S. (1981). Depression and coping in stressful episodes. *Journal of Abnormal Psychology, 90*, 439–447.
Coyne, J. C., & Holroyd, K. (1982). Stress, coping and illness: A transactional perspective. In T. Millon, C. Green, & R. Meagher (Eds.), *Handbook of health care clinical psychology*. New York: Plenum Press.
Cronbach, L. J. (1951). Coefficient alpha and the internal structure of tests. *Psychometrika, 16*, 542–548.
Gouaux, C. (1971). Induced affective states and interpersonal attraction. *Journal of Personality and Social Psychology, 20*, 37–43.
Gouaux, C., Lamberth, J., & Friedrich, G. (1972). Affect and interpersonal attraction: A comparison of trait and state measures. *Journal of Personality and Social Psychology, 24*, 53–58.
Hammen, C. L., & Peters, S. D. (1978). Interpersonal consequences of depression: Responses to men and women enacting a depressed role. *Journal of Abnormal Psychology, 87*, 322–332.
Hewitt, J. P., & Stokes, R. Disclaimers. (1975). *American Sociological Review, 40*, 1–11.
Hokanson, J. E., Sacco, W. P., Blumberg, S. R., & Landrum, G. C. (1980). Interpersonal behavior of depressed individuals in a mixed-motive game. *Journal of Abnormal Psychology, 89*, 320–332.
Howes, M. J., & Hokanson, J. E. (1979). Conversational and social responses to depressive interpersonal behavior. *Journal of Abnormal Psychology, 88*, 625–634.
Jacobson, E. (1971). *Depression: Comparative studies of normal, neurotic, and psychotic conditions*. New York: International Universities Press.
Jacobson, N. S., & Anderson, E. (in press). Interpersonal skill deficits and depression in college students: A sequential analysis of the timing of self-disclosure. *Behavior Therapy*.
Lazarus, R. S., Coyne, J. C., & Folkman, S. (1982). Cognition, emotion and motivation: The doctoring of Humpty-Dumpty. In R. W. J. Neufeld (Ed.), *Psychological stress and psychopathology*. New York: McGraw-Hill.
Libet, J. M., & Lewinsohn, P. M. (1973). Concept of social skill with special reference to the behavior of depressed persons. *Journal of Consulting and Clinical Psychology, 40*, 304–312.
Mace, W. M. (1974). Ecologically stimulating cognitive psychology: Gibsonian perspectives. In W. Weimer & D. Palermo (Eds.), *Cognition and the symbolic processes*. Hillsdale, NJ: Lawrence Erlbaum Associates.
McLean, P. D., Ogston, K., & Grauer, L. (1973). A behavioral approach to the treatment of depression. *Journal of Behavior Therapy and Experimental Psychiatry, 4*, 323–336.
Platt, B. (1977). *Perceived adjustment and positivity of self-presentation as determinants of others' public and private evaluations*. Unpublished doctoral dissertation, Miami University.
Robbins, B. P., Strack, S., & Coyne, J. C. (1979). Willingness to provide feedback to depressed persons. *Social Behavior and Personality, 7*, 199–203.
Seligman, M. E. P. (1978). Comment and integration. *Journal of Abnormal Psychology, 87*, 165–179.
Snyder, M. (in press). On the influence of individuals on situations. In N. Cantor & J. F. Kihlstrom (Eds.), *Cognition:*

Social interaction and personality. Hillsdale, NJ: Lawrence Erlbaum Associates.

Wachtel, P. (1973). Psychodynamics, behavior therapy and the implacable experimenter: An inquiry into the consistency of personality. *Journal of Abnormal Psychology, 82,* 324–334.

Weissman, M. M., & Paykel, E. S. (1974). *The depressed woman.* Chicago: University of Chicago.

Winer, D. L., Bonner, T. O., Blaney, P., & Murray, E. G. (1981). Depression and social interaction. *Motivation and Emotion, 5,* 153–165.

Yarkin, K., Harvey, J. L., & Bloxom, B. M. (1981). Cognitive sets, attribution, and social interaction. *Journal of Personality and Social Psychology, 41,* 243–252.

Youngren, M. A., & Lewinsohn, P. M. (1980). The functional relation between depression and problematic interpersonal behavior. *Journal of Abnormal Psychology, 89,* 333–341.

Zajonc, R. B. (1980). Feeling and thinking: Preferences need no inferences. *American Psychologist, 35,* 151–175.

Zuckerman, M., & Lubin, B. (1965). *Manual for the Multiple Affect Adjective Check List.* San Diego, CA: Educational and Industrial Testing Service.

Discussion Questions

1. How might the results of this study generalize to problems other than depression? In other words, to the degree that other psychological problems also create social difficulties and negative emotions in other people, would you expect the effects to be the same?
2. Exactly what is it about depression or depressed people that leads those who interact with them to feel hostile, depressed, and anxious?
3. How would you teach a depressed client to behave so that he or she is not rejected by other people?
4. Do all depressed individuals induce negative affect in other people, or are certain depressed individuals more or less likely to induce negative affect in others? What might determine the degree to which a depressed person creates depression in others?

Suggested Readings

Coyne, J. C. (1976). Depression and the response of others. *Journal of Abnormal Psychology, 85,* 186–193. This article presents data showing that people respond differently to depressed others and that this effect is determined, in part, by the behaviors of the depressed individuals.

Coyne, J. C. (1976). Toward an interactional description of depression. *Psychiatry, 39,* 28–40. This article discusses the interpersonal nature of depression and how interpersonal processes may make depression self-perpetuating.

Coyne, J. C., Burchill, S. A. L., & Stiles, W. B. (1991). An interactional perspective on depression. In C. R. Snyder & D. R. Forsyth (Eds.), *Handbook of social and clinical psychology: The health perspective* (pp. 327–349). New York: Pergamon. This chapter presents a review of research support for the interactional theory of depression.

Joiner, T., & Coyne, J. C. (Eds.). (1999). *The interactional nature of depression.* Washington, DC: American Psychological Association. This chapters in this edited volume examine interpersonal processes involved in depression and the responses that people offer to those who are depressed.

READING 13

Implications of Rejection Sensitivity for Intimate Relationships

Geraldine Downey • Columbia University
Scott I. Feldman • University of California, Los Angeles

Editors' Introduction

Human beings are highly social animals. Not only do we generally live and work in groups, but our relationships with other people—friends, romantic partners, group members, family, and so on—are exceptionally important to us. Because human beings are rather vulnerable when living on their own, natural selection favored individuals who formed and maintained relationships with others. As a result of the benefits of sociality and group living throughout evolutionary history, modern people possess a strong drive to form lasting, positive relationships with other people (Baumeister & Leary, 1995).

Although everyone desires to be accepted and to avoid rejection, some individuals are more sensitive to rejection than others. In this article, Geraldine Downey and Scott Feldman discuss the concept of rejection sensitivity and describe four studies that examined it. In the first study, Downey and Feldman developed a new self-report measure—the Rejection Sensitivity Questionnaire (RSQ)—to assess differences in people's tendency to "anxiously expect, readily perceive, and overreact to rejection." Study 2 demonstrated that people who score high on the RSQ react more negatively to a stranger's ambiguous behavior that could be interpreted as possibly rejecting than people who score low on the RSQ. Studies 3 and 4 examined the implications of rejection sensitivity for intimate relationships, showing not only that people who are high in rejection sensitivity expect their romantic partners to reject them but also that their anxious preoccupation with rejection (which often manifests as jealousy, dependency, and efforts to control the other person) undermines their partner's satisfaction with the relationship. Paradoxically, then, the overreactions of rejection-sensitive people can lead to precisely the rejection that they fear!

Downey and Feldman's research not only bridges social and clinical psychology, but also draws heavily upon personality and developmental psychology as the authors speculate regarding how the personalities of rejection-sensitive people may develop during childhood. A full understanding of many phenomena require using concepts and theories from several subdisciplines of psychology.

Since this article was published in 1996, rejection sensitivity has been explored in dozens of studies, both by Downey and her colleagues and by other researchers. One study found that rejection-sensitive college men who placed a great deal of importance on romantic relationships were more likely to engage in dating violence (Downey, Feldman, & Ayduk, 2000), and another found that highly rejection-sensitive women became more hostile than lows when they felt rejected (Ayduk, Downey, Testa, Yen, & Shoda, 1999). Other research found that adolescents who scored high in rejection sensitivity became increasingly aggressive over time, presumably because their negative reactions to perceived rejection led to greater rejection, which then led to more negative reactions, then even more rejection in an escalating spiral (Downey, Lebolt, Rincon, & Freitas, 1998). Clearly, an understanding of rejection sensitivity may help clinical and counseling psychologists deal with a variety of relationship problems, including aggression between romantic partners.

Abstract

People who are sensitive to social rejection tend to anxiously expect, readily perceive, and overreact to it. This article shows that this cognitive–affective processing disposition undermines intimate relationships. Study 1 describes a measure that operationalizes the anxious-expectations component of rejection sensitivity. Study 2 provides experimental evidence that people who anxiously expect rejection readily perceive intentional rejection in the ambiguous behavior of others. Study 3 shows that people who enter romantic relationships with anxious expectations of rejection readily perceive intentional rejection in the insensitive behavior of their new partners. Study 4 demonstrates that rejection-sensitive people and their romantic partners are dissatisfied with their relationships. Rejection-sensitive men's jealousy and rejection-sensitive women's hostility and diminished supportiveness help explain their partners' dissatisfaction.

The desire to achieve acceptance and to avoid rejection is widely acknowledged to be a central human motive (Horney, 1937; Maslow, 1987; McClelland, 1987; Rogers, 1959; Sullivan, 1937; see Baumeister & Leary, 1995, for a review). Consistent with this claim, social rejection is known to diminish well-being and disrupt interpersonal functioning. Responses to perceived rejection include hostility, dejection, emotional withdrawal, and jealousy (e.g., Baumeister & Leary, 1995; Coie, Lochman, Terry, & Hyman, 1992; Coyne, 1976; Dodge & Somberg, 1987; Fauber, Forehand, Thomas, & Wierson, 1990; Lefkowitz & Tesiny, 1984; Maccoby & Martin, 1983; Rohner & Rohner, 1980; Salovey & Rodin, 1986).

However, people differ in their readiness to perceive and react to rejection. Some people interpret undesirable interpersonal events benignly and maintain equanimity in their wake. Others readily perceive intentional rejection in the minor or imagined insensitivity of their significant others and overreact in ways that compromise their relationships and well-being. We have proposed that the latter people's readiness to perceive and overreact to rejection is facilitated by a tendency to anxiously expect rejection by the significant people in their lives. We have applied the term *rejection sensitive* to people who anxiously expect, readily perceive, and overreact to rejection (Downey, Feldman, Khuri, & Friedman, 1994; Feldman & Downey, 1994). Our prior research has documented a link between rejection sensitivity and exposure to rejecting parenting in childhood (Feldman & Downey, 1994). In this article, we test the proposition that rejection sensitivity fosters difficulties in intimate adult relationships.

Conceptualizing Rejection Sensitivity

The Psychological Legacy of Rejection

The assertion that rejection sensitivity, originating in childhood rejection, underlies interpersonal difficulties has precedents in classical interpersonal theories of personality (e.g., Bowlby, 1969, 1973, 1980; Erikson, 1950; Horney, 1937; Sullivan, 1953). Horney (1937) attributed maladaptive orientations to relationships to "basic anxiety" about desertion, abuse, humiliation, and betrayal. She viewed this anxiety as underlying a painful sensitivity "to any rejection or rebuff no matter how slight, [for example,] a change in an appointment, having to wait, failure to receive an immediate response" (Horney, 1937, pp. 135–136). Erikson (1950) proposed that a basic mistrust of others would compromise the possibility of personal and interpersonal fulfillment. Sullivan (1953) claimed that generalized expectations or "personifications" of significant others as meeting needs or as punitive, disapproving, or rejecting form the basis for how people perceive and relate to others.

Bowlby's attachment theory is the most elaborated model of the psychological mediators linking early rejection with later interpersonal functioning (Bowlby, 1969, 1973, 1980). Bowlby proposed that children develop mental models of themselves and of relationships that influence their future relationships. At the core of these models are expectations about whether significant others will satisfy their needs or be rejecting. These expectations derive from the reliability with which their primary caretaker meets their needs in early childhood. When caretakers tend to meet children's needs sensitively and consistently, children develop secure working models that incorporate the expectation that others will accept and support them. When caretakers tend to meet children's needs with rejection, children develop insecure working models that incorporate doubts and anxieties about whether others will accept and support them. Insecure working models are thought to underlie mistrustful or ambivalent orientations to adult relationships (Hazan & Shaver, 1994).

As Bretherton, Ridgeway, and Cassidy (1990) have noted, when Bowlby introduced the internal working model "it was little more than a metaphor with useful connotations" (p. 275). The task of clarifying, elaborating, and operationalizing the working model is currently being approached in two ways by researchers interested in applying Bowlby's ideas to adult relationships (Bretherton, 1985; Hazan & Shaver, 1987, 1994; Kobak & Sceery, 1988; Main & Goldwyn, 1984; Main, Kaplan, & Cassidy, 1985). One approach has focused on establishing how the quality of early caretaking is represented in memory. This approach is exemplified in Main's use of the detail, coherence, affective tone, and content of childhood memories as a basis for inferring people's working models (e.g., Main & Goldwyn, 1984). A second approach has been to characterize the interpersonal styles of adults presumed to differ in the security of their working models. This approach is exemplified in Hazan and Shaver's profiles of secure, ambivalent, and avoidant attachment styles (Hazan & Shaver, 1987; see also Bartholomew & Horowitz, 1991).

Conceptualizing Rejection Sensitivity as a Cognitive–Affective Processing Disposition

Although attachment researchers view working models as guiding current information processing, they have paid little attention to directly investigating how early rejection experiences shape the moment-to-moment cognitive and affective processes that generate behavior in specific social situations. These immediate psychological antecedents of behavior have been the focus of much contemporary research from a cognitive–affective information-processing perspective (e.g., Bandura, 1986; Crick & Dodge, 1994; Dweck & Leggett, 1988; Higgins & Bargh, 1987; Higgins & Kruglanski, in press; Mischel, 1973; Mischel & Shoda, 1995). Ready links can be made between the ideas of Bowlby and the other early interpersonal theorists about the psychological legacy of parental rejection and key information-processing variables (Feldman & Downey, 1994). These variables include expectancies about the outcomes of one's actions, the subjective value placed on different outcomes, attributional biases, and scripts for regulating one's affective and behavioral response to various experiences (Bandura, 1986; Mischel, 1973; Mischel & Shoda, 1995).

In our research we have conceptualized the psychological legacy of early rejection in cognitive–affective processing terms. Specifically, we have sought to establish how early rejection experiences shape (a) the expectations, values and concerns, interpretative biases, and self-regulatory strategies that underlie behavior in particular interpersonal contexts and (b) the dynamic relations among these cognitive–affective variables and interpersonal behavior (Downey et al., 1994; Feldman & Downey, 1994).

Drawing on Bowlby (1980), our model proposes that when parents tend to meet children's expressed needs with rejection, children become sensitive to rejection. That is, they develop the expectation that when they seek acceptance and support from significant others they will probably be rejected, and they learn to place a particularly high value on avoiding such rejection. They thus experience anticipatory anxiety when expressing needs or vulnerabilities to significant others.

These anxious expectations of rejection make them hypervigilant for signs of rejection. When they encounter rejection cues, however minimal or ambiguous, they readily perceive intentional rejection and experience feelings of rejection. The perceived rejection is then likely to prompt both affective and behavioral overreactions, which may include anger and hostility, despondency, withdrawal of support, jealousy, and inappropriate attempts to control the significant other's behavior.

In sum, we draw on a rich theoretical tradition to propose that early rejection experiences leave a psychological legacy that emerges in the disposition to be sensitive to rejection by significant others. In support of this claim, we have previously found that childhood exposure to family violence and rejection is associated with heightened sensitivity to rejection (Feldman & Downey, 1994; Downey, Lebolt, & Rincon, 1995). We now consider the potential implications of rejection sensitivity for intimate relationships in adulthood.

Impact of Rejection Sensitivity on Intimate Relationships

Although rejection sensitivity may originally develop as a self-protective reaction to parental rejection, this system may prompt behaviors that are poorly adapted to adult circumstances (see Bowlby, 1973). When activated in a relatively benign social world, rejection sensitivity may lead people to behave in ways that undermine their chances of maintaining a supportive and satisfying close relationship.

Our model suggests that people who enter a relationship disposed to anxiously expect rejection from significant others should be likely to (a) perceive intentional rejection in their partner's insensitive or ambiguous behaviors, (b) feel insecure and unhappy about their relationship, and (c) respond to perceived rejection or threats of rejection by their partner with hostility, diminished support, or jealous, controlling behavior. When unjustified and exaggerated, these behaviors are likely to erode even a committed partner's satisfaction with the relationship.

There is a basis for some of our predictions in prior research. First, the prediction that anxious expectations of rejection underlie a readiness to perceive rejection has general support in findings that people's attributions are driven at least in part by expectations (see Olson, Roese, & Zanna, in press). More specific support is provided by Dodge and Somberg's (1987) finding that experimentally manipulated explicit threats of peer rejection prompted a substantial increase in aggressive children's hostile attributions to their peers' behavior.

Second, the prediction that rejection sensitivity undermines people's relationships finds support in research from both an attachment perspective and an attributional perspective. Adult attachment researchers have shown that insecurely attached people, that is, people who are generally mistrustful of others or who worry about their partner's commitment, find their relationships unsatisfactory, and their romantic partners agree with this assessment (Carnelley, Pietromonaco, & Jaffe, 1994; Collins & Read, 1990; Feeney & Noller, 1990; Hazan & Shaver, 1987; Kobak & Hazan, 1991; Simpson, 1990). There is also some evidence that insecurely attached adults behave toward their partner in ways that may undermine the relationship (Kobak & Hazan, 1991).

Marital attribution researchers have found that spouses who attribute their partners' behaviors to negative intent and, in particular, to lack of love, dislike, or lack of consideration for their needs, are more dissatisfied with their relationship than are spouses who interpret their partners' behavior more benignly (see Bradbury & Fincham, 1990, for a review; Bradbury & Fincham, 1992; Epstein, Pretzer, & Fleming, 1987; Fincham & Beach, 1988; Fincham, Beach, & Baucom, 1987; Fincham, Beach, & Nelson, 1987; Fincham & Bradbury, 1992; Holtzworth-Munroe & Jacobson, 1985). Negative attributions have also been found to predict the type of negative interactions that typify unsatisfactory relationships (for a review, see Fincham, 1994).

Overview

Our two main goals in the research described in this article were (a) to operationalize and validate the construct of rejection sensitivity and (b) to demonstrate its impact on intimate relationships. To accomplish the first of these goals, we began with the development of a measure of rejection sensitivity. This measure is described in Study 1. Because our model proposes that anxious expectations of rejection by significant others are at the core of rejection sensitivity, rejection sensitivity is operationalized as anxious expectations of rejection in situations that afford the possibility of rejection by significant others.

To validate our construct, we tested the proposition that anxious expectations of rejection fuel a readiness to perceive intentional rejection in the ambiguous behavior of others. In Study 2 we tested whether people with anxious expectations of rejection are more likely than others to perceive intentional rejection in the ambiguous behavior of someone with whom they have just finished a friendly conversation. In Study 3 we used longitudinal data to assess whether people who enter romantic relationships with anxious expectations of rejection tend to attribute hurtful intent to their new partner's insensitive behavior. In Study 3 we also assessed whether the impact of anxious expectations of rejection on attributions of hurtful intent can be distinguished from the impact of related constructs, including social anxiety and adult attachment style.

To accomplish the second goal, we investigated the impact of rejection sensitivity on romantic relationships. Specifically, we used data from couples in committed dating relationships to test the hypotheses that rejection-sensitive people and their partners have less satisfying relationships and that rejection-sensitive people's hostile, jealous, and unsupportive behaviors contribute to their partners' dissatisfaction.

Study 1

Study 1 describes the development of the Rejection Sensitivity Questionnaire (RSQ). This measure operationalizes rejection sensitivity as generalized expectations and anxiety about whether significant others will meet one's needs for acceptance or will be rejecting. Thus, situations that involve expressing a need to a significant other should be particularly likely to activate generalized rejection anxieties and expectations, thereby revealing the extent of a person's sensitivity to rejection.

On the basis of this assumption, the RSQ presents respondents with a range of situations in which they must make a request of a significant other. They are asked whether they would be concerned or anxious about the response to their request and whether they would expect the other person to honor or reject the request. Insofar as they are anxious about the outcome and also expect a rejecting outcome, they are considered to be sensitive to rejection. The measure incorporates situations involving parents, friends, teachers, romantic partners, potential romantic partners, and potential friends. We conducted pilot work to identify pertinent situations in the lives of young adults, the target population of this study.

Method

SAMPLE AND PROCEDURE

Participants were 321 female and 263 male undergraduates. Posters seeking participants for a study of interpersonal relationships for pay were placed around a college campus. Participants received $5 for completing a survey that included the RSQ and basic demographic questions. Participants received and returned surveys through the campus mail system.

The participants' mean age was 18.7 years ($SD = 1.6$). The racial and gender composition of the sample was representative of the undergraduate population. Fifty-four percent of the participants were Caucasian, 26% were Asian-American, 7.5% were Hispanic, 6.5% were African-American, and 6% were from other ethnic backgrounds. The majority of participants were in their first or second year of college.

A subsample of 166 women and 127 men completed three additional surveys over the academic year. Participants received $7, $5, and $5, respectively, for completing the surveys, which included measures used to assess the reliability and predictive utility of the RSQ (see Study 3). This subsample did not differ from the original sample in racial composition, age distribution, or mean level of rejection sensitivity.

Measures: RSQ

The RSQ was developed from open-ended interviews with 20 undergraduates. These students were presented with 30 hypothetical interpersonal situations generated by a different group of undergraduates. The 20 undergraduates were asked for detailed descriptions of what they thought would happen and how they would feel in each situation.

The situations were selected to represent a broad cross-section of interpersonal situations that young adults encounter in which rejection is possible. Sample situations included "You ask a friend to do you a big favor"; "You call your boyfriend/girlfriend after a bitter argument and tell him/her you want to see him/her"; and "You ask your parents to come to an occasion important to you."

Answers to the hypothetical situations varied along two dimensions: (a) degree of anxiety and concern about the outcome and (b) expectations of acceptance or rejection. Responses along these two dimensions did not covary systematically. For example, some people would be anxious about asking their parents to come to an important occasion but would not expect them to refuse. Other people with a similar level of anxiety would expect their parents to refuse. Of theoretical interest to us were people who both expected rejection and were concerned about this outcome in various interpersonal situations.

We reduced the initial set of situations by eliminating situations that did not generate variance in responses along both dimensions. The RSQ is based on the remaining 18 situations. (Table 13.1 gives the items.)[1] We developed fixed-choice responses to each situation to assess rejection anxiety and rejection expectations, the two dimensions identified in the pilot interviews. The RSQ first asks people to indicate their degree of concern or anxiety about the outcome of each situation (e.g., "How concerned or anxious would you be over whether or not your friend would want to help you out?") on a 6-point scale ranging from *very unconcerned* (1) to *very concerned* (6). They are then asked to indicate the likelihood that the other person(s) would respond in an accepting fashion (e.g., "I would expect that he/she would willingly agree to help me out.") on a 6-point scale ranging from *very unlikely* (1) to *very likely* (6). High likelihood of this outcome represents expectations of acceptance, and low likelihood represents expectations of rejection.

Reflecting our adoption of an expectancy-value model (Bandura, 1986) of anxious expectations of rejection, computation of the RSQ scores was as follows. First, we obtained a rejection sensitivity score for each situation by weighting the expected likelihood of rejection by the degree of concern over its occurrence. Specifically, we reversed the score on expectancy of acceptance to

TABLE 13.1. Factor Loadings for Rejection Sensitivity Questionnaire (RSQ) Items and Mean RSQ Score for the Sample

Item	Total sample	Men	Women
1. You ask someone in class if you can borrow his/her notes.	.42	.38	.43
2. You ask your boyfriend/girlfriend to move in with you.	.44	.34	.56
3. You ask your parents for help in deciding what programs to apply to.	.33	.34	.35
4. You ask someone you don't know well out on a date.	.54	.50	.54
5. Your boyfriend/girlfriend has plans to go out with friends tonight, but you really want to spend the evening with him/her, and you tell him/her so.	.55	.47	.59
6. You ask your parents for extra money to cover living expenses.	.42	.38	.43
7. After class, you tell your professor that you have been having some trouble with a section of the course and ask if he/she can give you some extra help.	.44	.37	.52
8. You approach a close friend to talk after doing or saying something that seriously upset him/her.	.53	.49	.55
9. You ask someone in one of your classes to coffee.	.62	.57	.66
10. After graduation you can't find a job and you ask your parents if you can live at home for a while.	.42	.44	.39
11. You ask a friend to go on vacation with you over Spring Break.	.68	.68	.68
12. You call your boyfriend/girlfriend after a bitter argument and tell him/her you want to see him/her.	.59	.53	.63
13. You ask a friend if you can borrow something of his/hers.	.54	.47	.61
14. You ask your parents to come to an occasion important to you.	.41	.49	.38
15. You ask a friend to do you a big favor.	.67	.56	.72
16. You ask your boyfriend/girlfriend if he/she really loves you.	.55	.47	.58
17. You go to a party and notice someone on the other side of the room, and then you ask them to dance.	.58	.52	.59
18. You ask your boyfriend/girlfriend to come home to meet your parents.	.50	.41	.56
Mean score on RSQ	9.66	9.73	9.60
Mdn	9.55	9.56	9.44
SD	3.03	2.71	3.28
Minimum score	2.40	2.70	2.40
Maximum score	23.50	18.60	23.50
N	584	263	321

index expectancy of rejection (expectancy of rejection = 7 − expectancy of acceptance). We then multiplied the reversed score by the score for degree of anxiety or concern. Second, we computed a total (cross-situational) rejection sensitivity score for each participant by summing the rejection sensitivity scores for each situation and dividing by 18, the total number of situations.

Results

FACTOR ANALYSIS AND NORMS

We conducted a principal-components factor analysis on the scores for each item (situation) of the RSQ to establish whether a single cross-situational factor could be extracted from the data. The analysis yielded five factors with eigenvalues greater than 1, but only one factor was retained by the scree test. This factor accounted for 27% of the variance, compared with only 10% and 7% for the second and third factors, respectively. The factor loadings of the items on the first factor are given in Table 13.1. Seventeen of the 18 RSQ items loaded at greater than .40, and all 18 loaded at greater than .30. Separate factor analyses were conducted for men and for women. Table 13.1 shows similar factor loadings for the two sexes. Table 13.1 also gives the mean, median, standard deviation, and range of RSQ scores for the total sample and for male and female participants. The mean RSQ scores of men and women did not differ significantly, $t(582) = 0.61$. The distribution of RSQ scores for male participants did not differ significantly from normality (Shapiro–Wilk statistic, $W = .98$, $p > .98$). Because of the presence of a few high-scoring women, the distribution of RSQ scores for women differed significantly from normality (Shapiro–Wilk statistic, $W = .96$, $p < .01$). When the 5 highest scoring women were dropped from the sample, the distribution of the RSQ for women no longer differed significantly from normality. Studies of the distribution of other measures of anxiety have also found that the presence of a few high-scoring women accounted for positively skewed data (e.g., Leary, 1993).

INTERNAL AND TEST–RETEST RELIABILITY OF THE RSQ

The RSQ shows high internal reliability ($a = .83$). All items correlated above .30 with the corrected item total, and we could not improve the reliability by deleting any individual item. The RSQ also shows high test–retest reliability. Two to 3 weeks after the first administration, we readministered the RSQ to a subsample of 104 participants randomly selected from the larger sample to examine the RSQ's short-term test–retest reliability. For this sample, the correlation between Time 1 and Time 2 scores was .83 ($p < .001$). Another nonoverlapping subsample of 223 participants was readministered the RSQ 4 months after the first administration, and for this sample, the correlation was .78 ($p < .001$).

Discussion

This study describes the development of the RSQ and reports its psychometric properties. Principal-components factor analysis supported averaging across the different request-making situations in order to construct an overall rejection-sensitivity score. The factor structure was similar for men and women. This factor structure was also replicated in a sample of high-school students (Downey, Lebolt, & O'Shea, 1995). The RSQ shows good internal consistency and test–retest reliability, which suggests that the RSQ taps a relatively enduring and coherent information-processing disposition. The test–retest correlations compare favorably with those reported for other inventories that assess relationship dispositions (e.g., Berscheid, Snyder, & Omoto, 1989; Fincham & Bradbury, 1992). In sum, these results indicate that the RSQ is a reliable measure of the anxious-expectation-of-rejection component of rejection sensitivity.

Study 2

Study 2 was designed to test the assumption that anxious expectations of rejection predict a readiness to perceive rejection in interpersonal situations. We designed an experiment to assess whether rejection-sensitive people were more likely than others to feel rejected in a situation that was ambiguous but that could be perceived as intentionally rejecting. Participants were introduced to an opposite-sex stranger, a confederate, with whom they were going to converse during two short sessions (of 10 and 5 minutes, respectively). Following a pleasant initial interaction, however, the participant was informed that the confederate did not want to continue with the experiment. No explanation was given for the confederate's decision. We expected that high rejection-sensitive people would be more likely than low rejection-sensitive people to report heightened feelings of rejection in response to the confederate's action.

Half of the sample was exposed to this experimental condition, and the other half was exposed to a control condition in which they were told that the interaction had to end early because of time constraints. The control condition provided participants with an explicit impersonal explanation for the outcome of the interaction. This condition was not expected to induce feelings of rejection in either high or low rejection-sensitive people.

Participants completed self-report assessments of mood before the interaction and after the experimental manipulation. The dependent variables in the study were change in self-reported feelings of rejection from pre- to postinteraction and behaviorally manifest emotional reaction as rated by the experimenter. Pre- and postinteraction assessments of other dimensions of distress were also obtained. These assessments permitted us to test whether the experimental manipulation induced rejection rather than generalized distress in rejection-sensitive people. We expected that in the experimental condition, rejection-sensitive people would report a specific increase in feeling of rejection and would show a more negative emotional reaction to being told that the confederate did not want to continue with the experiment.

Method

SAMPLE

Participants were 23 women and 24 men randomly selected from the Study 1 sample. Their mean rejection sensitivity ($M = 9.93$) and standard deviation ($SD = 3.45$) did not differ significantly from those of the total sample, $t(640) = 0.24$, ns, and $F(46, 594) = 1.30$, ns, respectively. Women and men did not differ significantly on mean rejection sensitivity, $t(45) = 0.63$, ns. Participants were randomly assigned to either the experimental or control group. The two groups did not differ significantly by gender composition, $\chi^2 (1, N = 47) = 0.86$, or mean rejection sensitivity, $t(45) = 0.81$, ns.

EXPERIMENTAL PROCEDURE

On reporting to the laboratory, the participant was brought into a room with a table and two chairs and told that the other participant had not yet arrived. Minutes later, the experimenter reentered the room with the opposite-sex confederate and introduced the participant and confederate by name.

The experimenter and confederate were blind to the participants' level of rejection sensitivity, and the confederate was blind to the experimental condition. The same experimenter and the same male and female confederates were used throughout the study. The participant and confederate were told that this was a study about how people form initial impressions of others. They would have two brief sessions to "get to know one another" that would last 10 and 5 minutes, respectively. After each session, the interaction partners would be asked to complete questionnaires evaluating how the interaction had gone. Both the participant and the confederate were asked to read and sign a consent form describing the purpose and structure of the experiment. The experimenter then verbally summarized the information in the consent form, noting that either person was free to withdraw from the study at any point.

After describing the study, the experimenter asked the participant and confederate to complete a mood scale. When they had both completed the scale, the experimenter explained that she would knock on the door when 10 minutes had elapsed. She then left them alone in the room. To help ensure that the interaction was a positive experience and that its premature termination would not be viewed with relief, the confederate had been instructed to be congenial and to allow the participant to lead the conversation. After the 10 minutes had elapsed, the experimenter knocked and reentered the room with a general questionnaire on how the interaction was going (interaction questionnaire) for each of the interaction partners to complete. She asked the confederate to follow her to a separate room to complete the questionnaire, and they left the participant alone with the door ajar.

Once the participant had completed the questionnaire, the experimenter reentered the room and introduced the manipulation. In the experimental condition, she told the participant, "[The confederate] does not want to continue with the second part of the experiment." In the control condition, she told the participant, "There is not enough time for the second interaction." The experimenter then left the room and recorded the participant's response to this information. On returning to the room, the experimenter assured the participant that he or she would be able to complete the rest of the study as planned and asked the participant to fill out a second mood scale. On finishing this questionnaire, the participant was informed of the confederate's true identity and the nature of the experimental manipulation. The experimenter reassured the participant that the confederate had not known what the experimenter was going to tell the participant after the interaction, and the confederate was reintroduced to the participant. Any remaining concerns were addressed and the participant was thanked and paid $5.

MEASURES

Mood scale. The items used to assess negative mood were drawn from the Anxiety, Anger, and Depression subscales of the Affects Balance Scale (Derogatis, 1975). Additional adjectives descriptive of feelings of rejection (i.e., unaccepted, rejected, hurt, disliked, discouraged) and positive items were added to the scale to make 38 items in total. Participants were asked to circle the number that best described how much they were experiencing each of the feelings right now, on a 4-point scale from 0 (*not at all*) to 3 (*very much*). Besides the standard anxiety, anger, and depression indices, we calculated a rejection index by taking the mean of the relevant rejection items. The internal consistencies, calculated separately for the first and second administrations, were above .8 for each subscale. We calculated change on each negative mood scale by subtracting the score on the first administration from that on the second. Thus, a positive change score indicated an increase in the particular mood subsequent to the interaction and experimental manipulation. The average intercorrelation among the four change-in-negative-mood scores was .48.

Interaction questionnaire. This questionnaire was administered after the interaction and before the experimental manipulation. It consisted of two open-ended questions designed to check that the interaction with the confederate was viewed positively by the participant and to reinforce expectations of a second meeting. The questions were as follows: "Overall, how well do you feel the first interaction period went?" and "Are you looking forward to meeting the other person again?"

Experimenter observation of reaction to manipulation. The experimenter answered the question "Which of the following adjectives is most descriptive of the participant's response to being told the second interaction would not take place?" For each participant, the experimenter circled one of the following answers: *upset, angry, happy, confused,* or *no reaction.* None of the participants were rated as having been angry, and only one (a control) was rated as having been happy. A dichotomous variable was constructed with a value of 0 indicating no emotional reaction and a value of 1 indicating a negative emotional reaction (upset or confused).

Results

INTERACTION CHECK

Participants' ratings of how well they thought the interaction had gone (made before the experimental manipulation) ranged from *fairly well* to *very well.* As expected, interacting with the confederate was generally viewed as a positive experience. Only one person (a control) reported not looking forward to meeting the confederate again; of the remaining participants, five reported being indifferent and the rest reported looking forward to the second interaction. Responses to the two interaction check items did not vary systematically as a function of experimental condition or rejection sensitivity.

SELF-REPORTED CHANGE IN REJECTED MOOD

To assess whether there were preexisting differences in mood as a function of experimental condition or rejection sensitivity, we conducted regressions with experimental condition and rejection sensitivity as independent variables and each of the four preinteraction mood scores derived from the mood questionnaire as dependent variables. Table 13.2 presents these results. None of the initial mood scores, including feelings of rejection, was significantly associated with experimental condition or rejection sensitivity. We also used regression analyses to assess whether initial mood scores differed as a function of the interaction of rejection sensitivity and experimental condition. Experimental Condition × Rejection Sensitivity effects were nonsignificant except for anxiety, $b = -.17$, $t(43) = 2.86$, $p < .01$.

Next, we conducted regression analyses to assess changes in anxiety, anger, depression, and rejection as a function of rejection sensitivity, experimental group, and their interaction (see Table 13.2). The general lack of a significant association between initial mood scores and rejection sensitivity, experimental condition, and their interaction eliminated the need to control for initial mood in the analyses of change in mood. The one exception was the significant Rejection Sensitivity × Experimental Condition interaction for anxiety. Controlling for initial level of anxiety did not alter the results of the regression analyses for change in anxiety.

We were interested specifically in whether changes in mood were restricted to increased feelings of rejection in high rejection-sensitive people in the experimental condition. There was a significant Experimental Condition × Rejection Sensitivity interaction effect for change in rejection, $b = .06$, $t(43) = 2.46$, $p < .02$. As Table 13.2 shows, the interaction term was not significant for any of the other mood measures.

Figure 13.1 plots the predicted values of change in rejected mood for the experimental and control groups as a function of rejection sensitivity. Figure 13.1 shows that members of the control group

TABLE 13.2. Regression of Initial Mood and Change in Mood on Experimental Group and Rejection Sensitivity

Dependent variable	Intercept	Experimental group (= 1) vs. control (= 0)		Experimental group X rejection sensitivity		Rejection sensitivity		F ratio
		b	β	b	β	b	β	
Initial level of anxiety	.58	−.14	−.10	.03	.16	—	0.88	
Initial level of anger	.24	−.09	−.08	.01	.07	—	0.30	
Initial level of depression	.27	−.10	−.09	.02	.13	—	0.63	
Initial level of rejection	.12	−.15	−.13	.03	.17	—	1.15	
Change in anxiety	−.43	−.22	−.26	.007	.05	.02	.30	0.56
Change in anger	−.14	−.15	−.22	.006	.06	.02	.31	0.70
Change in depression	−.08	−.02	−.04	−.003	−.04	.01	.21	0.40
Change in rejection	.16	−.26	−.36	−.002	−.02	.06*	.96	11.36

Note. n = 46; df for initial level analyses = 2,44; df for change analyses = 3, 43. * p < .05.

showed a similar decrease in rejected mood from before the interaction regardless of their level of rejection sensitivity. In the experimental group, those who were highest in sensitivity to rejection showed the greatest increase in feelings of rejection following the manipulation. Thus, being told that the confederate did not want to continue the experiment induced increased feelings of rejection in people to the extent that they were sensitive to rejection.

OBSERVED EMOTIONAL REACTION

Examination of the experimenter's rating of participants' reaction to the manipulation was restricted to members of the experimental group because the experimenter was not blind to whether people were in the experimental or control group when the rating was made. She was, however, unaware of participants' RSQ scores. The observed negativity of the participant's reaction to being told the confederate did not want to continue with the study was significantly associated with rejection sensitivity ($r = .52, p < .02$) and with self-reported increase in rejected mood ($r = .71, p < .001$). Controlling for premanipulation rejected mood did not alter this latter finding (partial $r = .72, p < .001$).

Discussion

Our purpose in Study 2 was to test the hypothesis that a person's RSQ score would predict the extent to which he or she would feel rejected in an ambiguous rejection situation. The results supported the hypothesis: Following the presentation of experimentally manipulated ambiguous rejection feedback after interaction with a confederate, high rejection-sensitive people reported greater feelings of rejection than low rejection-sensitive people. This effect was limited to feelings of rejection, rather than reflecting greater emotional distress in general, and was behaviorally manifest to the experimenter.

Furthermore, the results suggested that the increase in rejected mood experienced by people who were highly sensitive to rejection was contingent specifically on receiving the ambiguous rejection feedback. High and low rejection-sensitive people

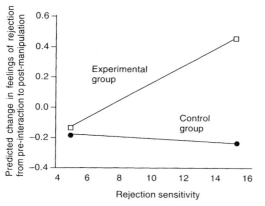

FIGURE 13.1 ■ Predicted changes in feelings of rejection from preinteraction to postmanipulation as a function of rejection sensitivity.

did not differ in level of initial rejected mood. Nor did they differ in change in rejected mood in the control condition, in which the feedback was explicitly nonrejecting. Social interaction in itself, in the absence of any potential rejection cues, did not induce feelings of rejection in rejection-sensitive people. Thus, the results of this study support the theoretical assumption that rejection-sensitive people more readily perceive intentional rejection in the ambiguously rejecting behavior of others.

Qualitative data from the debriefings further support this conclusion. Rejection-sensitive people were likely to ruminate over what they had done to cause the confederate to reject them; for example, some of their comments were "I felt so badly. I wondered what I had done wrong" and "I was worried that I had bored him." People who were low in rejection sensitivity were not concerned with understanding why the confederate did not return. They were also less likely to perceive the confederate's behavior as a rejection, attributing it instead to nonpersonal causes, as in the comment "I thought maybe she was in a rush."

In summary, the results of this study support the proposition that rejection-sensitive people readily construe intentional rejection in the ambiguous or negative behavior of others. This cognitive–affective processing disposition has behavioral consequences: rejection-sensitive people's feelings of rejection in the experimental condition were evident to the experimenter. Because the study was conducted with an initially unacquainted confederate, however, it is unclear whether these findings extend to rejection-sensitive people's thoughts, feelings, and behavior with people they know well. An advantage of observing interaction with a new acquaintance was that we could eliminate characteristics of an ongoing relationship as an explanation for participants' responses during the experiment. Instead, we could conclude that participants' reactions reflected the dispositions that they brought to the situation. Nevertheless, we are ultimately interested in the implications of rejection sensitivity for intimate relationships.

Study 3

Accordingly, our purpose in Study 3 was to investigate the connection between anxious expectations of rejection and perceptions of rejection in the behavior of an intimate partner. We addressed this question in a prospective study of college students. We tested whether a person's RSQ score would predict attributions of hurtful intent to a subsequent romantic partner's insensitive behavior. By assessing an individual's RSQ score before the romantic relationship began, we ensured that any association found between anxious expectations of rejection and perceptions of the partner's behavior could not reflect the impact of dissatisfaction with the relationship or the partner's actual behavior on rejection sensitivity.

We were also interested in establishing whether anxious expectations of rejection could be distinguished from conceptually and empirically related constructs in terms of their effects on attributions of hurtful intent to the partner. Particularly relevant is the construct of social anxiety, which we have previously found to correlate with rejection sensitivity (Feldman & Downey, 1994). Social anxiety refers to the anxiety that people experience when they anticipate being unable to make a positive impression on others (Schlenker & Leary, 1982). Because of the salience of first impressions in social interactions with strangers, especially in public situations, these types of situations are thought to be particularly likely to trigger social anxiety in people so disposed. Thus, social anxiety is typically operationalized as anxiety or distress about encounters with strangers in public settings (e.g., Cheek & Buss, 1981; Leary, 1983; Watson & Friend, 1969). This type of anxiety is believed to motivate the avoidance of social interaction with strangers and, thus, to impede the development of new relationships.

Rather than focusing on anxiety about negative evaluation by strangers, we focused on anxiety about the willingness of significant others to meet an individual's needs in a relationship. Insofar as social anxiety and rejection sensitivity are correlated, there appears to be some overlap in people's anxiety about casual and intimate relationships. However, we expect that anxiety about emotional rejection by significant others should have a stronger influence on how people behave in intimate relationships than anxiety about making a negative impression on strangers.

We have also previously found that young adults with insecure attachment styles are more rejection sensitive than young adults with secure attachment styles (Feldman & Downey, 1994). In theory, we would also expect RSQ scores to be associated with self-esteem, with people who are rejection sensitive showing low self-esteem (Horney, 1937). Thus, we examined whether attachment style or self-esteem might account for any observed relationship between anxious expectations of rejection and perceptions of rejection by the partner.

Finally, it might be argued that sensitivity to rejection is a facet of a broader personality dimension like neuroticism or introversion. Anxious expectations might be subsumed by a general disposition to experience negative affect (i.e., neuroticism). Or, the social anxiety associated with rejection sensitivity might reflect introversion. Thus, it was important to establish whether anxious expectations of rejection had an impact on attributions of hurtful intent independent of the influence of these general personality dispositions.

Method

SAMPLE AND PROCEDURE

The sample consisted of 166 female and 127 male first-year students who participated in the longitudinal component of Study 1. This sample was screened to identify people who had begun a new romantic relationship after completing the RSQ and before completing a questionnaire on their attributions for their current romantic partner's insensitive behavior approximately 4 months later. Thirty-five men and 38 women were identified as meeting this criterion. Eligible people were identified from a record they provided of the start dates of their romantic relationships over the course of the academic year. This record was completed at the end of the academic year. This sample and the larger sample from which it was drawn did not differ from the Study 1 sample in racial composition, age distribution, and mean level of rejection sensitivity.

MEASURES

Besides completing the RSQ, respondents completed the measures described below. The RSQ and the measure of attachment style were completed at the beginning of the academic year, about 4 months before the measure of attributions of hurtful intent. The remaining measures were completed 2 to 3 weeks after the RSQ by a somewhat smaller sample than completed the RSQ.

Attributions of hurtful intent. Participants were asked to indicate on a 6-point scale the extent of their agreement (6 = *agree strongly*; 1 = *disagree strongly*) with the following three statements: "If your boyfriend or girlfriend was being cool and distant, you would feel he or she was being intentionally hurtful to you"; "If your boyfriend or girlfriend was intolerant of something you did, you would feel he or she was being intentionally hurtful to you"; and "If your boyfriend or girlfriend began to spend less time with you, you would feel he or she was being intentionally hurtful to you." These items were adapted from Fincham and Bradbury's (1992) Relationship Attribution Scale to reflect behavior that was insensitive but that could have occurred for a variety of reasons besides the partner's desire to be hurtful. For example, a partner might appear cool and distant because of preoccupation with upcoming examinations. Responses were averaged across the three items ($a = .72$).

Interpersonal Sensitivity subscale (IPS) of the Symptom Distress Checklist (SCL–90–R; Derogatis, 1984). The SCL–90–R is a reliable and valid instrument for assessing several dimensions of psychopathology (Derogatis, 1984). The IPS consists of nine items that assess on a 5-point scale the extent to which people are bothered by feelings of uneasiness in social situations (e.g., "feeling very self-conscious with others"), feelings that others are unfriendly or unsympathetic toward the person (e.g., "feeling that other people are unfriendly or dislike you"), and feelings of inferiority (e.g., "feeling inferior to others"). This measure is frequently included in studies of clinical disorders that have as a core symptom chronic oversensitivity to rejection, defined as extreme reactions to real or imagined rejection (i.e., social phobia, atypical depression; e.g., Liebowitz et al., 1988, 1992).

Social Avoidance and Distress Scale (SADS; Watson & Friend, 1969). The SADS assesses people's distress or anxiety about public social situations and avoidance of social situations. The measure consists of 14 statements about nervousness or anxiety in public social situations or situations involving unfamiliar people (e.g., "I am usually nervous with people unless I know them well") and 14 statements about avoidance of social situations (e.g., "I try to avoid situations that force me to be sociable"). The social distress items are similar in content to those included in Cheek and Buss's (1981) shyness measure and Leary's (1983, 1993) Interaction Anxiousness Scale. The social avoidance items are similar in content to those included to tap lack of sociability in Cheek and Buss's (1981) measure of sociability. The statements used in the SADS are derived from college students' descriptions of interpersonal anxiety. Respondents are asked to indicate whether each statement is true or false of them. We obtained a summary social distress score by taking the mean of the distress items, after correcting for reverse-scored items. A summary social avoidance score was similarly obtained.

Adult Attachment Style Questionnaire–Continuous Version (Levy & Davis, 1988). The continuous Adult Attachment Style Questionnaire (AASQ) was adapted from Hazan and Shaver's (1987) categorical measure of adult attachment style, which requires people to indicate whether their attachment style is secure, anxious-avoidant, or anxious-ambivalent. In common with the original questionnaire, the continuous measure consists of descriptions of three styles of attachment behavior adapted for adults from Ainsworth, Blehar, Waters, and Wall's (1978) descriptions of patterns of infant behavior in the Strange Situation. Participants indicate the degree to which they feel each of the three descriptions is true of them on a 7-point scale from *strongly agree* (1) to *strongly disagree* (7). This approach yields separate scores for attachment security, anxious avoidance, and anxious ambivalence, which are reversed so that higher scores indicate greater agreement with the description. The AASQ scores show moderate test–retest reliability (Hazan & Shaver, 1994; Levy & Davis, 1988). In the present study, avoidance and security were strongly negatively correlated ($r = -.69$, $p < .001$) and ambivalence and security were weakly negatively correlated ($r = -.17$, $p < .01$), whereas avoidance and ambivalence were uncorrelated ($r = .02$, ns). These correlations resemble those obtained in previous research (Levy & Davis, 1988; Shaver & Brennan, 1992). We expected that rejection sensitivity would correlate negatively with security of attachment and positively with both avoidance and ambivalence.

Self-esteem. Self-esteem was measured with a 10-item Likert-format scale (Rosenberg, 1979) consisting of items such as "I take a positive attitude toward myself." Respondents indicate the degree to which each statement reflects their self-attitudes. In this study, a high score indicates high self-esteem.

Eysenck Personality Inventory (EPI; Eysenck & Eysenck, 1964). Introversion was measured with responses to 24 EPI items. Each item used a yes-or-no format; each *yes* was scored 1 and each *no* was scored 0; thus, the total score could range from 0 to 24. A typical introversion item is "Generally, do you prefer reading books to meeting people?" Neuroticism was also measured with 24 EPI items, and the total score could range from 0 to 24. A typical neuroticism item is "Would you call yourself a nervous person?"

Results

DOES THE RSQ PREDICT ATTRIBUTIONS OF HURTFUL INTENT TO A NEW ROMANTIC PARTNER'S BEHAVIOR?

People who anxiously expected rejection by significant others at Time 1 tended to report at Time 2 that they would attribute hurtful intent to a new romantic partner's insensitive behavior ($r = .39$, $p < .001$). As the partial correlations in the first column of numbers in Table 13.3 show, this relationship did not change appreciably when each of the following dispositional variables was statistically controlled: self-esteem, interpersonal sensitivity, social avoidance, social distress, attachment security, anxious avoidance, anxious ambivalence, neuroticism, and introversion. Controlling simultaneously for all eight dispositional variables also did not alter the relationship appreciably (partial $r = .38$, $p < .05$).

All of these dispositional variables were significantly associated with people's RSQ scores in theoretically expected directions. The second column of numbers gives the correlations between the RSQ and these dispositional variables for the subsample of respondents who began a romantic relationship after completing the RSQ. The third column of numbers gives the correlations between the same variables and RSQ for the larger sample from which the subsample of respondents was selected. Although each of the dispositional variables was significantly related to the RSQ, none prospectively predicted attributions of hurtful intent to a

TABLE 13.3. Correlations Between Various Dispositional Variables and Rejection Sensitivity and Attributions of Hurtful Intent for the Behavior of a Subsequent Romantic Partner

Dispositional variable	Correlation of RSQ with attributions of hurtful intent, partialing out the relevant dispositional variable[a]	Correlation of dispositional variable with RSQ for current sample	Correlation of dispositional variable with RSQ for the large longitudinal sample (minimum n = 192)	Correlation of dispositional variable with attributions of hurtful intent
Neuroticism (n = 52)	.34*	.35**	.36***	.06
Introversion (n = 52)	.35*	.46***	.22***	.08
Self-esteem (n = 52)	.34*	−.43**	−.33***	−.13
Social avoidance (n = 52)	.30*	.44***	.26***	.17
Social distress (n = 52)	.31*	.49***	.39***	.16
Interpersonal sensitivity (n = 52)	.35**	.40**	.39***	.06
Secure attachment (n = 73)	.40***	−.30**	−.28***	.04
Resistant attachment (n = 73)	.42***	.24*	.24***	−.12
Avoidant attachment (n = 73)	.43***	.32**	.17**	−.07

Note. RSQ = Rejection Sensitivity Questionnaire.
[a]The zero-order correlation between RSQ and attributions of hurtful intent was .35 for n = 52 and .35 for n = 52 and .39 for n = 73.
* p < .05. ** p < .01. *** p < .001.

new romantic partner, as shown in the last column in Table 13.3.

Discussion

This study demonstrated that anxious expectations of rejection assessed before a romantic relationship began predicted the extent to which people would attribute hurtful intent to their new romantic partner's insensitive behavior. This relation was not an artifact of a variety of possible third variables including social anxiety (SADS social distress items and IPS), social avoidance (SADS social avoidance items), attachment style, self-esteem, neuroticism, and introversion. Although all of these dispositional variables were significantly related with RSQ, none was a significant predictor of attributions of hurtful intent for the insensitive behavior of a romantic partner. Thus, this study provides evidence for the distinctive predictive utility of the RSQ.

Study 4

The previous two studies showed that people who are disposed to anxiously expect rejection also readily perceive intentional rejection in the negative or ambiguous behavior of new acquaintances and romantic partners. This tendency to perceive and feel rejection combined with chronic anxiety about its occurrence are likely to compromise the quality of people's intimate relationships. In Study 4 we investigated this prediction in dating couples.

Specifically, we hypothesized that rejection-sensitive people would experience heightened concern about the possibility of being rejected by their partner and that their insecurity would be evident to their partner. We further hypothesized that their insecurity would compromise their satisfaction with the relationship, as well as that of their partner (Collins & Read, 1990; Feeney & Noller, 1990; Hazan & Shaver, 1987; Kobak & Hazan, 1991; Simpson, 1990). Finally, we hypothesized that they would show a predictable pattern of interactional difficulties with their partner. First, we expected that they would respond with hostility when they perceived hurtful intent in their partner's negative or ambiguous behavior (Bradbury & Fincham, 1992). Second, we expected that they would behave in a jealous and controlling manner toward their partner, which would reflect their insecurities about the future of the relationship. Finally, we expected that they would stop being emotionally supportive to their partner because of their doubts about his or her commitment to the relationship. We examined whether these behavioral patterns would help explain the dissatisfaction of the partners of rejection-sensitive people with their relationships.

Method

SAMPLE AND PROCEDURE

The sample consisted of 80 heterosexual couples recruited through posted announcements on a university campus. The study was limited to couples who were in committed, nonmarital relationships. Couples were invited to come to a psychology laboratory to complete 45-minute questionnaires on their relationship. Each partner received $10 for participating in the study. The questionnaires were completed by 86 couples. However, the data from 6 couples were excluded because of suspicions raised about the veracity of their data by large discrepancies between partners' reports of facts about the relationship. The mean age of the female participants was 20.64 years ($SD = 1.98$), and that of the male participants was 21.30 years ($SD = 2.46$). Fifty-six percent of the women were Caucasian, 26% were Asian-American, 3% were Hispanic, 5% were African-American, and 10% were from other ethnic backgrounds. Fifty-five percent of the men were Caucasian, 23% were Asian-American, 9% were Hispanic, 3% were African-American, and 10% were from other ethnic backgrounds. The couples had been dating an average of 17 months ($SD = 13$).

Measures

Both members of the couple completed the RSQ and, in addition, provided information about themselves and about their partner. In the Results section, data are presented separately for men and women.

Concern about rejection by partner. Four items assessed participants' concerns that their partner might want to leave the relationship: "My partner often thinks of leaving our relationship"; "My partner does not feel very attached to me"; "My partner feels trapped in our relationship"; and "My partner thinks that his/her life would be better if he/she were in a relationship with someone else." These items were selected from a larger pool of items administered to a pilot sample of 113 people who were currently dating. Participants were asked to indicate how true they thought each statement was of their partner's feelings, from 0 (*not at all true of my partner's feelings*) to 8 (*completely true of my partner's feelings*). We computed the mean of these items to derive an overall rejection concern score. The scale was reliable for both men ($\alpha = .82$) and women ($\alpha = .78$).

Perceptions of partner's security with the relationship. Participants were asked to indicate the degree to which they felt that the statement "My partner feels secure in our relationship" was true of their partners' feelings on a 9-point scale from 0 (*not at all true of my partner's feelings*) to 8 (*completely true of my partner's feelings*). For men, $M = 5.50$, $SD = 1.42$; for women, $M = 5.93$, $SD = 1.25$.

Commitment to the relationship. Participants answered the question "How much longer would you like your relationship to last?" They chose one of nine responses ranging from "0 days" (coded as 1) to "several years" (coded as 9).

Satisfaction with the relationship. Participants' satisfaction with the relationship was assessed with the following three items: "I am satisfied with our relationship"; "Our relationship meets my expectations of what a good relationship should be like"; and "I could not be happier in our relationship." Participants indicated the extent to which each statement was true of their feelings on an 8-point scale from 0 (*not at all true of my feelings*) to 7 (*completely true of my feelings*). For men, $\alpha = .86$; for women, $\alpha = .82$. In a pilot sample of 148 people, scores on this scale correlated .73 ($p < .001$) with relationship satisfaction as assessed by the Dyadic Adjustment Scale (Spanier, 1976).

Perception of partner's satisfaction with the relationship. A three-item scale assessed participants' perceptions of their partner's satisfaction with the relationship: "My partner is satisfied with our relationship"; "My partner feels positively about our relationship"; and "My partner feels we communicate well." Participants rated the degree to which they felt each statement was true of their partner's feelings, on an 8-point scale from 0 (*not at all true of my partner's feelings*) to 8 (*completely true of my partner's feelings*). For men, $\alpha = .70$; for women, $\alpha = .71$.

Reports of partner's behavior. Participants were

presented with 37 positive and negative interactional behaviors drawn from a longer list developed by Kasian and Painter (1992) for use with college students. Participants were asked to indicate how often their partner had enacted each behavior toward them during the past month, on a 6-point scale from 0 (*never*) to 5 (*daily/always*). Factor analysis yielded three interpretable factors: Hostile Behavior, Jealous Behavior, and Emotionally Supportive Behavior. Items loading above .40 on only one factor were used to compute means for each of the three behaviors for each participant. Hostile behavior was indexed by the following items: "My partner insulted or shamed me in front of others"; "My partner called me nasty names"; "My partner treated me like I was an inferior"; "My partner sulked or refused to talk about a problem"; "My partner withheld affection from me"; "My partner treated me like his/her servant"; "My partner told me my feelings are irrational or crazy"; "My partner blamed me for causing his or her violent behavior"; "My partner tried to make me feel like I was crazy"; and "My partner blamed me when I had nothing to do with it" (men, α = .86; women, α = .83). Jealous behavior was indexed by the following items: "My partner was jealous of other men/women"; "My partner was jealous and suspicious of my friends"; and "My partner monitored my time and made me account for my whereabouts" (men, α = .70; women, α = .65). Emotionally supportive behavior was indexed by the following items: "My partner treated me as if my feelings were important and worthy of consideration"; "My partner said things to encourage me"; "My partner praised me in front of others"; "My partner told me my feelings were reasonable or normal"; "My partner let me talk about my feelings"; "My partner was affectionate with me"; "My partner was sensitive to my sexual needs and desires"; and "My partner made requests politely" (men, α = .82; women, α = .78). Scores on this scale were reversed so that high scores indicated low emotional support.

Results

RELATIONSHIP SECURITY

To test whether rejection-sensitive people were concerned about being rejected by their partners, we computed correlations between people's rejection sensitivity and their perceptions of their partners' desire to leave the relationship. Rejection sensitivity was significantly related to being concerned about rejection by the partner for both men ($r = .44, p < .001$) and women ($r = .48, p < .001$). We tested whether this might simply be an accurate appraisal of the partners' feelings about the relationship by reestimating the correlations controlling for the partners' self-reported commitment to the relationship. The correlations were essentially unchanged (for men, partial $r = .43, p < .001$; for women, partial $r = .47, p < .001$). Thus, rejection-sensitive people showed heightened concern about being rejected by their partners, irrespective of their partners' commitment to the relationship.

Next, we examined whether participants' self-reported insecurity about the relationship was apparent to their partners. Participants' rejection sensitivity was significantly negatively related to their partners' ratings of participants' security, for both men ($r = -.29, p < .01$) and women ($r = -.29, p < .01$). These correlations confirm participants' self-reports of greater insecurity about the continuity of the relationship. Moreover, they suggest that rejection sensitivity is evident in interpersonal behavior. We return to the second point later in the Results section.

Relationship Satisfaction

To examine whether participants' rejection sensitivity influenced the quality of the relationship, we estimated the correlations between the RSQ and self and partner reports of satisfaction with the relationship. Both rejection-sensitive men and women reported significantly less relationship satisfaction ($r = -.39, p < .001$, and $r = -.45, p < .001$, respectively). Their partners also reported being less satisfied (men, $r = -.28, p < .01$; women, $r = -.39, p < .001$). Moreover, rejection-sensitive men and women perceived that their partners were less satisfied ($r = -.35, p < .001$, and $r = -.45, p < .001$, respectively). Because partners' rejection sensitivity scores were significantly related ($r = .22, p < .05$), we recomputed all of these correlations while controlling for partners' rejection sensitivity. The original correlations were not altered appreciably.

Although rejection-sensitive people's reports that their partners are less satisfied with the relationship are confirmed by partner reports, high rejection-sensitive people might still exaggerate their partners' level of dissatisfaction. To test this hypothesis, we recomputed the correlations between participants' rejection sensitivity and their appraisals of their partners' satisfaction while controlling for their partners' reports of their own satisfaction. The partial correlations remained significant for both men (partial $r = -.25, p < .05$) and women (partial $r = -.35, p < .001$). Thus, rejection-sensitive people appear to magnify their partners' dissatisfaction with the relationship.

Partners' Reports of the Interpersonal Behavior of High Rejection-Sensitive People

Given rejection-sensitive people's insecurity about their relationships, it is not surprising that they were less satisfied with them and perceived their partners to be dissatisfied as well. Their partners' independent reports of being less satisfied, however, suggest that rejection-sensitive people may behave in ways that jeopardize the quality of their relationships. To investigate this possibility, we assessed the correlation between participants' rejection sensitivity and their partners' reports of the participants' behavior in the relationship. Rejection-sensitive men were reported by their partners to show more jealousy ($r = .22, p < .05$). Rejection-sensitive women were reported by their partners to be more hostile ($r = .26, p < .05$) and more emotionally unsupportive ($r = .31, p < .05$). For women, the correlation between rejection sensitivity and jealousy was nonsignificant. For men, the correlations between rejection sensitivity and both hostility and emotional support were nonsignificant. None of these results changed appreciably when we recomputed the correlations while controlling for the partners' own levels of rejection sensitivity.

Next, we conducted a path analysis to assess the extent to which rejection-sensitive people's behavior toward their partners might account for their partners' dissatisfaction with the relationship. For men, we examined the mediational effect of jealousy. For women, we examined the mediational effect of hostile and unsupportive behavior. With a series of regression analyses, the relationship between rejection sensitivity and partner's dissatisfaction with the relationship can be divided into two parts: (a) a part mediated through behavior (the indirect effect of rejection sensitivity on partner's dissatisfaction) and (b) a part unrelated to behavior (the direct effect of rejection sensitivity on partner's dissatisfaction; see Cohen & Cohen, 1983, chap. 9).

To test the mediational role of jealousy for men, we first regressed their female partners' self-reported dissatisfaction on men's rejection sensitivity ($b = .28, p < .01; b = .11$). We then added men's jealousy to the basic regression model. The results are presented in Figure 13.2. The b for men's rejection sensitivity fell from .28 to .20. This latter coefficient is the direct effect of men's rejection sensitivity on their partners' dissatisfaction. The indirect effect of men's rejection sensitivity on their partners' dissatisfaction is .28 − .20, or .08. Thus, jealous behavior accounts for 29% (.08/.28) of the effect of men's rejection sensitivity on their female partners' relationship dissatisfaction.

To test the mediational role of hostile and unsupportive behavior for women, we first regressed their male partners' dissatisfaction on

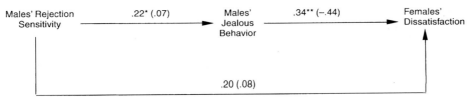

FIGURE 13.2 ■ Test of whether males' jealous behavior mediates the link between their levels of rejection sensitivity and their partners' dissatisfaction with the relationship. The numbers above each arrowed line give the standardized regression coefficients and, in parentheses, the unstandardized regression coefficients for the model. The standardized coefficient for the original association between male rejection sensitivity and female dissatisfaction with the relationship was .28** (.11); *$p < .05$. **$p < .01$.

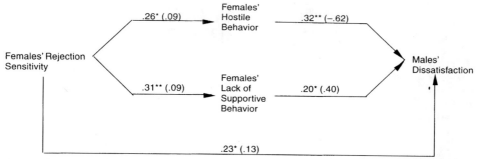

FIGURE 13.3 ■ Test of whether females' hostility and diminished support mediate the link between their levels of rejection sensitivity and their partners' dissatisfaction with the relationship. The numbers above each arrowed line give the standardized regression coefficients and, in parentheses, the unstandardized regression coefficients for the full model. The standardized regression coefficient for the original association between male rejection sensitivity and female dissatisfaction with the relationship was .39*** (.22). *$p < .05$; **$p < .01$; ***$p < .001$.

women's rejection sensitivity ($\beta = .39$, $p < .001$; $b = .22$). We then added women's hostile and unsupportive behavior to the basic regression model. The results are presented in Figure 13.3. The b for women's rejection sensitivity fell from .39 to .23. This latter coefficient is the direct effect of women's rejection sensitivity on their male partners' dissatisfaction. The indirect effect of rejection sensitivity on partner dissatisfaction is .39 − .23, or .16. Thus, hostility and lack of support account for 41% (.16/.39) of the effect of women's rejection sensitivity on their male partners' relationship dissatisfaction. Although not shown in the figure, women's hostile behavior alone accounted for 32% of this association and their lack of support alone accounted for 23% of it.

Discussion

As hypothesized, rejection sensitivity was found to undermine romantic relationships. It led people to feel insecure and dissatisfied with their relationships and to exaggerate their partners' dissatisfaction and desire to leave the relationship. Moreover, the partners of rejection-sensitive individuals found the relationship less satisfying because of rejection-sensitive men's jealous and controlling behavior and rejection-sensitive women's hostility and diminished emotional support. Thus, the specific hypotheses outlined in the introduction to this study were generally supported, with the unexpected finding of gender differences in the behaviors of rejection-sensitive people that undermined partner satisfaction.

General Discussion

In this research we had two goals. The first was to describe and validate the construct of rejection sensitivity, which we defined as the disposition to anxiously expect, readily perceive, and overreact to rejection. The second was to establish whether rejection sensitivity undermined intimate relationships.

Describing and Validating the Construct of Rejection Sensitivity

We operationalized rejection sensitivity in terms of the moment-to-moment cognitive and affective processes that guide social interaction. Study 1 describes the development of a measure of anxious expectations of rejection by significant others, which we view as at the core of rejection sensitivity. We reasoned that the expression of important needs to significant others should trigger anxious expectations of rejection in people so disposed. Thus, the RSQ asks people whether they would (a) be concerned or anxious about a significant other's response to an important request, and (b) expect a significant other to honor their request.

In our efforts to validate our conceptualization of rejection sensitivity, we had two objectives: (a) to document support for operationalizing rejection sensitivity as anxious expectations of rejection by showing that anxious expectations activate perceptions of, and overreactions to, rejection, and (b) to demonstrate that rejection sensitivity captures a distinctive cognitive–affective processing disposition.

Anxious Expectations of Rejection Predict a Readiness to Perceive and Overreact to Rejection

The results of Studies 2 and 3 validate our operationalization of rejection sensitivity as anxious expectations of rejection by demonstrating that individuals' anxious expectations of rejection promote a readiness on their part to perceive and overreact to rejection. Study 2 showed that people who were high in rejection sensitivity felt rejected following experimentally manipulated ambiguous rejection feedback from a new acquaintance. When exposed to the same feedback, people who were low in rejection sensitivity did not feel rejected. Study 3 showed that people who were highly sensitive to rejection when they entered into a romantic relationship were prone to interpret their new partner's negative behavior, such as being distant or inattentive, as motivated by hurtful intent. Besides validating our conceptualization of rejection sensitivity, our findings support calls for greater attention to the expectations and concerns that people bring to relationships in efforts to understand cognitive–affective processes in relationships (Berscheid, 1994; Fincham, 1994). In particular, the findings suggest the importance of extending research on relationship attributions in order to examine how generalized expectations about relationships influence attributions for specific interpersonal events.

Rejection Sensitivity Is a Distinctive Cognitive–Affective Processing Disposition

Study 3 provided evidence that rejection sensitivity has a unique predictive utility. We were particularly interested in whether the impact of rejection sensitivity on attributions of hurtful intent to a new romantic partner's insensitivity could be distinguished from the impact of social anxiety. It could. Social anxiety did not account for the impact of anxious expectations of rejection on attributions of hurtful intent. Moreover, it did not independently predict attributions of hurtful intent to a romantic partner. This was also true of social avoidance.

Rejection sensitivity also is not redundant, in terms of its predictive utility, with established trait personality constructs to which it is conceptually and empirically related. These include trait measures of introversion and neuroticism, general attachment style, and self-esteem. This finding provides further support for claims that the predictive precision of personality measures can be enhanced considerably by attending to people's characteristic behavior in particular situations (Mischel & Shoda, 1995).

Impact of Rejection Sensitivity on Intimate Relationships

Our second goal, to establish the implications of rejection sensitivity for intimate relationships, addressed the following questions: How do rejection-sensitive people think about and behave toward their romantic partners? How does their behavior affect their partners' feelings about the relationship?

Regarding the first question, Study 3 provides clear evidence that people who enter relationships disposed to anxiously expect rejection more readily perceive rejection in their romantic partner's insensitive behavior. Study 4 showed that rejection-sensitive people exaggerated their partner's dissatisfaction with and lack of commitment to the relationship and behaved in ways that reflected their expectations and perceptions of rejection. Rejection-sensitive men were jealous and suspicious and sought to control their partner's contacts with others. Rejection-sensitive women tended to blame their partners unjustly and to be hostile and unsupportive toward them. Regarding the second question, hostile and unsupportive behaviors by rejection-sensitive women and jealous, controlling behaviors by rejection-sensitive men helped explain their partner's dissatisfaction with the relationship.

Issues for Future Research

Besides supporting our conceptualization of rejection sensitivity and demonstrating its unfortunate implications for intimate relationships, our findings raise several questions that warrant consideration in future research.

WHY DO REJECTION-SENSITIVE PEOPLE PURSUE INTIMATE RELATIONSHIPS?

Given that intimate relationships appear to afford rejection-sensitive people considerable opportunities for feeling rejected, why do they continue to pursue them? The clinical literature suggests that they view relationships as opportunities for acceptance and, in the initial stages, work hard to ingratiate themselves with partners (Horney, 1937). Their initial consideration and attentiveness are likely to evoke a positive reaction from their partner. Such a reaction is likely to reinforce the rejection-sensitive person's belief that this relationship will provide the acceptance that is so strongly desired.

Even in relationships that begin well, however, transient negativity, insensitivity, and waning enthusiasm are inevitable as the relationship progresses. Rejection-sensitive people should be particularly adept at interpreting these occurrences as omens of impending rejection, and defensive action may supplant ingratiating behavior. Defensive action may entail giving up on the relationship or engaging in coercive efforts to prevent the partner from leaving the relationship. However, the sense of hopefulness and acceptance that rejection-sensitive people experience early in their relationships may help maintain their belief in the power of relationships to meet their needs: It may simply be a matter of selecting the right partner— someone without the hidden flaws that emerged as the relationship progressed; or, it may be a matter of convincing (or coercing) the partner to remain in the relationship in the belief that the relationship will improve.

WHAT CONDITIONS TRIGGER ANXIOUS EXPECTATIONS OF REJECTION?

To better understand the processes through which the relationships of rejection-sensitive people begin to unravel, it is essential to identify with increasing precision the situations that trigger and reinforce concern about rejection. Conflicts may be particularly good candidates. Rejection-sensitive people are likely to perceive them as opportunities for the partner to reject them rather than as opportunities for resolving difficulties in the relationship. Thus, their anxiety about rejection combined with their tendency to overreact to perceived rejection should promote behaviors that compromise successful conflict resolution (e.g., blaming, threatening *harm, or refusing to discuss* the problem). Arguments will probably end with the instigating issue unresolved and both partners feeling distressed and dissatisfied. Such feelings should fuel further conflict, providing new opportunities for the rejection-sensitive person to feel rejected and for partners to reassess their commitment to the relationship.

These predictions could be tested using daily reports of the thoughts, feelings, and behaviors of rejection-sensitive people and their partners before, during, and after naturally occurring conflict. This approach, of course, is limited by its reliance on the self-reports of couples. A complementary approach would be to use procedures developed by marital interaction researchers (e.g., Gottman, 1979; Weiss & Summers, 1983) to observe couples' behavior as they discuss a topic of ongoing conflict. Such an approach would allow independent assessment of the rejection-sensitive person's reactivity to the partner's behavior during social interaction and of the partner's behavior.

WHAT UNDERLIES GENDER DIFFERENCES IN THE BEHAVIOR OF REJECTION-SENSITIVE PEOPLE?

Study 4 revealed unexpected gender differences in the behavior of rejection-sensitive people toward their romantic partners. The jealous and controlling behavior of rejection-sensitive men may be a manifestation of men's general tendency to cope in active ways with failure and adversity (Nolen-Hoeksema, 1987). The negativity and diminished positivity of rejection-senitive women may be a consequence of women's general tendency to cope with adversity and failure with rumination (Nolen-Hoeksema, 1987). Rumination about perceived rejection is likely to foster the belief that the partner has given up on the relationship and that one is helpless to do anything about it. This belief pattern may promote hostile retaliation against the partner, which may account for the increased negativity of rejection-sensitive women. It may also lead rejection-sensitive women to stop investing in the relationship, which may account for their decreased positivity.

It is noteworthy that the jealous, controlling behavior characteristic of rejection-sensitive men is common in physically abusive relationships (Walker, 1984). Abusers are described as attempting to control and minimize their partners' contacts with perceived rivals in the misguided belief that this approach will prevent their partner from leaving them (Goldner, Penn, Sheinberg, & Walker, 1990; Walker, 1984). Thus, in men, rejection sensitivity may be a risk factor for being physically abusive toward a romantic partner. In fact, there is some evidence that physically abusive men are particularly reactive to perceived threats of rejection (Downey, Feldman, & Fletcher, 1995; Dutton & Browning, 1988; Holtzworth-Munroe & Hutchinson, 1993).

Finding that rejection-sensitive women are hostile and unsupportive because they feel helpless to avert rejection by their partner would suggest that they are at risk for depression. Consistent with this suggestion is the finding that atypical depression, which is characterized by extreme sensitivity and emotional reactivity to perceived rejection, is more common in women than men (American Psychiatric Association, 1994).

ARE ANXIOUS EXPECTATIONS OF REJECTION FULFILLED?

We have shown that people who enter relationships anxiously expecting rejection feel more rejected than other people because of their readiness to perceive intentional rejection in partner behaviors that others would interpret more benignly. Our research did not directly address whether they were also more likely to be rejected by their partners and thus have their expectations fulfilled. However, the finding that their partners are more dissatisfied suggests that this may be the case. There is considerable evidence that dissatisfied partners are more likely to reciprocate negative behavior and to end a relationship (Buehlman, Gottman, & Katz, 1992; Simpson, 1990). Moreover, research from an interpersonal perspective on depression (Coyne, 1976) has shown that excessive concern about rejection tends to elicit rejection (Hokanson & Butler, 1992).

Thus, significant others may provide intentional as well as unintentional opportunities for rejection-sensitive people to experience rejection. In this way, anxious expectations of rejection may be fulfilled and thus sustained (Berscheid, 1994). These observations suggest that rejection sensitivity has a self-perpetuating quality: Expectations of rejection facilitate subjective perceptions of rejection, which cause behaviors that evoke objective rejections, reinforcing expectations of rejection. It will be important to examine evidence for this transactional dynamic in future research.

CAN SUPPORTIVE SOCIAL RELATIONSHIPS HELP BREAK THE CYCLE LINKING REJECTION SENSITIVITY TO REJECTION?

Besides providing a context for the maintenance of rejection sensitivity, social relationships may also provide opportunities for change. Research on people who transcend severe childhood rejection suggests a potential role for significant others in helping people break out of the negative cycle we have described (Egeland, Jacobvitz, & Sroufe, 1988; Patterson, Cohn, & Kao, 1989; Quinton, Rutter, & Liddle, 1984). Supportive relationships, whether with a parent, another adult, a peer, an intimate partner, or a therapist, can fundamentally alter people's expectations and anxieties about rejection and help them to develop less malevolent explanations for others' behavior and more adaptive conflict-resolution skills. Yet rejection sensitivity is deeply ingrained. Thus, change is probably unlikely to occur unless the rejection-sensitive person is highly motivated and the partner can provide effective guidance and encouragement. The role of naturally occurring relationships in modifying rejection sensitivity warrants further investigation.

Conclusions

The belief that concern about acceptance and rejection contributes in crucial ways to interpersonal functioning has a long history in personality psychology. In this article we proposed that rejection sensitivity—a disposition to anxiously expect, readily perceive, and overreact to rejection—describes this concern in cognitive–affective processing terms. Our data substantiate the claim that rejection sensitivity has important implications for how people think, feel, and behave in their intimate relationships and, thus, for their own and their partners' satisfaction.

ACKNOWLEDGMENTS

This research was supported by grants from the National Institute of Mental Health (R29-MH51113) and the Harry Frank Guggenheim Foundation and by a W. T. Grant Faculty Scholar Award.

We thank Rachel Becker, Phyllis Fletcher, Hala Khouri, Paul Marr, Amy McFarland, and Sara Niego for their help with data collection. We thank Niall Bolger, Carol Dweck,

E. Tory Higgins, Walter Mischel, David Shaffer, and Yuichi Shoda for helpful comments on earlier versions of this article.

NOTE

[1] A complete copy of the questionnaire is available at http://www.columbia.edu/~gd20/

REFERENCES

Ainsworth, M., Blehar, M., Waters, E., & Wall, S. (1978). *Patterns of attachment: A psychological study of the strange situation.* Hillsadale, NJ: Lawrence Erlbaum Associates.

American Psychiatric Association (1994). *Diagnostic and statistical manual of mental disorders* (4th ed.). Washington, DC: American Psychiatric Association.

Bandura, A. (1986). *Social foundations of thought and action.* Englewood Cliffs, NJ: Prentice Hall.

Bartholomew, K., & Horowitz, L. M. (1991). Attachment styles among young adults: A test of a four category model. *Journal of Personality and Social Psychology, 61,* 147–178.

Baumeister, R., & Leary, M. (1995). The need to belong: Desire for interpersonal attachments as a fundamental human motivation. *Psychological Bulletin, 117,* 497–529.

Berscheid, E. (1994). Interpersonal relationships. *Annual Review of Psychology, 1,* 79–129.

Berscheid, E., Snyder, M., & Omoto, A. M. (1989). The Relationship Closeness Inventory: Assessing the closeness of interpersonal relationships. *Journal of Personality and Social Psychology, 57,* 792–807.

Bowlby, J. (1969). *Attachment and loss: Vol. 1. Attachment.* New York: Basic Books.

Bowlby, J. (1973). *Attachment and loss: Vol. 2. Separation.* New York: Basic Books.

Bowlby, J. (1980). *Attachment and loss: Vol. 3. Loss, sadness, and depression.* New York: Basic Books.

Bradbury, T. N., & Fincham, F. D. (1990). Attributions in marriage: Review and critique. *Psychological Bulletin, 107,* 3–33.

Bradbury, T. N., & Fincham, F. D. (1992). Attributions and behavior in marital interactions. *Journal of Personality and Social Psychology, 63,* 613–628.

Bretherton, I. (1985). Attachment theory: Retrospect and prospect. In 1. Bretherton & E. Waters (Eds.), Growing points of attachment theory and research. *Monographs of the Society for Research in Child Development, 50*(1–2, Serial No. 209), 3–35.

Bretherton, I., Ridgeway, D., & Cassidy, J. (1990). Assessing internal working models of the attachment relationship: An attachment story completion task for 3-year-olds. In M. Greenberg, D. Cicchetti, & E. M. Cummings (Eds.), *Attachment in the preschool years: Theory, research, and intervention* (pp. 273–308). Chicago: University of Chicago Press.

Buehlman, K. T., Gottman, J. M., & Katz, L. F. (1992). How a couple views their past predicts their future: Predicting divorce from an oral history interview. *Journal of Family Psychology, 5,* 295–318.

Carnelley, K., Pietromonaco, P., & Jaffe, K. (1994). Depression, working models of others, and relationship functioning. *Journal of Personality and Social Psychology, 66,* 127–140.

Cheek, J., & Buss, A. (1981). Shyness and sociability. *Journal of Personality and Social Psychology, 41,* 330–339.

Cohen, J., & Cohen, P. (1983). *Applied multiple regression/correlational analyses for the behavioral sciences.* Hillsdale, NJ: Lawrence Erlbaum Associates.

Coie, J., Lochman, J., Terry, R., & Hyman, C. (1992). Predicting early adolescent disorder from childhood aggression and peer rejection. *Journal of Consulting and Clinical Psychology, 60,* 783–792.

Collins, N. L., & Read, S. J. (1990). Adult attachment, working models, and relationship quality in dating couples. *Journal of Personality and Social Psychology, 58,* 644–663.

Coyne, J. C. (1976). Depression and the response of others. *Journal of Abnormal Psychology, 85,* 186–193.

Crick, N., & Dodge, K. (1994). A review and reformulation of social information-processing mechanisms in children's social adjustment. *Psychological Bulletin, 115,* 74–101.

Derogatis, L. (1975). *Affects Balance Scale.* Towson, MD: Clinical Psychometrics Research Unit.

Derogatis, L. (1984). *SCL-90-R manual—II: Administration, scoring and procedures.* Towson, MD: Clinical Psychometrics Research Unit.

Dodge, K., & Somberg, D. (1987). Hostile attributional biases are exacerbated under conditions of threats to the self. *Child Development, 58,* 213–224.

Downey, G., Feldman, S., & Fletcher, P. (1995, August). *Rejection sensitivity and violence in romantic relationships.* Paper presented at the 103rd Annual Convention of the American Psychological Association, New York.

Downey, G., Feldman, S., Khuri, J., & Friedman, S. (1994). Maltreatment and child depression. In W. M. Reynolds & H. F. Johnson (Eds.), *Handbook of depression in childhood and adolescence* (pp. 481–508). New York: Plenum.

Downey, G., Lebolt, A., & O'Shea, K. (1995, March). *Implications of rejection sensitivity for adolescent peer and dating relationships.* Paper presented at the biennial meeting of the Society for Research on Adolescence, Indianapolis, IN.

Downey, G., Lebolt, A., & Rincon, C. (1995). *Rejection sensitivity: A consequence of rejection and a cause of interpersonal difficulties in adolescence.* Unpublished manuscript, Columbia University.

Dutton, D. G., & Browning, J. J. (1988). Concern for power, fear of intimacy, and aversive stimuli for wife assault. In G. Hotaling, D. Finkelhor, J. T. Kirkpatrick, & M. A. Straus (Eds.), *Family abuse and its consequences: New directions in research* (pp. 130–175). Newbury Park, CA: Sage.

Dweck, C. S., & Leggett, E. L. (1988). A social-cognitive approach to personality and motivation. *Psychological Review, 95,* 256–273.

Egeland, B., Jacobvitz, D., & Sroufe, L. A. (1988). Breaking the cycle of abuse. *Child Development, 59,* 1080–1088.

Epstein, N., Pretzer, J. L., & Fleming, B. (1987). The role of cognitive appraisal in self-reports of marital communication. *Behavior Therapy, 18,* 51–69.

Erikson, E. (1950). *Childhood and society.* New York: Norton.

Eysenck, H. J., & Eysenck, S. B. G. (1964). *Manual of the Eysenck Personality Inventory.* San Diego, CA: Educational and Industrial Testing Service.

Fauber, R., Forehand, R., Thomas, A., & Wierson, M. (1990). A mediational model of the impact of marital conflict on adolescent adjustment in intact and divorced families: The role of disrupted parenting. *Child Development, 61,* 1112–1123.

Feeney, J. A., & Noller, P. (1990). Attachment style as a predictor of adult romantic relationships. *Journal of Personality and Social Psychology, 58,* 281–291.

Feldman, S., & Downey, G. (1994). Rejection sensitivity as a mediator of the impact of childhood exposure to family violence on adult attachment behavior. *Development and Psychopathology, 6,* 231–247.

Fincham, F. (1994). Cognition in marriage: Current status and future challenges. *Applied and Preventative Psychology, 3,* 185–198.

Fincham, F. D., & Beach, S. R. (1988). Attribution processes in distressed and nondistressed couples: 5. Real versus hypothetical events. *Cognitive Therapy and Research, 12,* 505–514.

Fincham, F. D., Beach, S. R., & Baucom, D. H. (1987). Attribution processes in distressed and nondistressed couples: 4. Self–partner attribution differences. *Journal of Personality and Social Psychology, 52,* 739–748.

Fincham, F. D., Beach, S. R., & Nelson, G. (1987). Attribution processes in distressed and nondistressed couples: 3. Causal and responsibility attributions for spouse behavior. *Cognitive Therapy and Research, 11,* 71–86.

Fincham, F. D., & Bradbury, T. N. (1992). Assessing attributions in marriage: The relationship attribution measure. *Journal of Personality and Social Psychology, 62,* 457–468.

Goldner, V., Penn, P., Sheinberg, M., & Walker, G. (1990). Love and violence: Gender paradoxes in volatile attachments. *Family Process, 29,* 343–364.

Gottman, J. M. (1979). *Marital interaction: Experimental investigations.* New York: Academic Press.

Hazan, C., & Shaver, P. (1987). Romantic love conceptualized as an attachment process. *Journal of Personality and Social Psychology, 52,* 511–524.

Hazan, C., & Shaver, P. (1994). Attachment as an organizational framework for research on close relationships. *Psychological Inquiry, 5,* 1–22.

Higgins, E. T., & Bargh, J. (1987). Social cognition and social perception. In M. R. Rosenzweig & L. W. Porter (Eds.), *Annual Review of Psychology* (Vol. 38, pp. 369–425). Palo Alto, CA: Annual Reviews.

Higgins, E. T., & Kruglanski, A. (Eds.). (in press). *Handbook of social psychology: Basic principles.* New York: Guilford Press.

Hokanson, J., & Butler, A. (1992). Cluster analysis of depressed college students' social behaviors. *Journal of Personality and Social Psychology, 62,* 273–280.

Holtzworth-Munroe, A., & Hutchinson, G. (1993). Attributing negative intent to wife behavior: The attributions of maritally violent versus nonviolent men. *Journal of Abnormal Psychology, 102,* 206–211.

Holtzworth-Munroe, A., & Jacobson, N. S. (1985). Causal attributions of married couples: When do they search for causes? What do they conclude when they do? *Journal of Personality and Social Psychology, 48,* 1398–1412.

Horney, K. (1937). *The neurotic personality of our time.* New York: Norton.

Kasian, M., & Painter, S. L. (1992). Frequency and severity of psychological abuse in a dating population. *Journal of International Violence, 7,* 350–364.

Kobak, R., & Hazan, C. (1991). Attachment in marriage: Effects of security and accuracy of working models. *Journal of Personality and Social Psychology, 60,* 861–869.

Kobak, R., & Sceery, A. (1988). Attachment in late adolescence: Working models, affect regulation, and representations of self and others. *Child Development, 59,* 135–146.

Leary, M. R. (1983). Social anxiousness: The construct and its measurement. *Journal of Personality Assessment, 47,* 66–75.

Leary, M. R., & Kowalski, R. M. (1993). The Interaction Anxiousness Scale: Construct and criterion-related validity. *Journal of Personality Assessment, 61,* 136–146.

Lefkowitz, M., & Tesiny, E. (1984). Rejection and depression: Prospective and contemporaneous analyses. *Developmental Psychology, 20,* 776–785.

Levy, M., & Davis, K. (1988). Lovestyles and attachment styles compared: Their relations to each other and to various relationship characteristics. *Journal of Social and Personal Relationships, 5,* 439–471.

Liebowitz, M., Quitkin, F., Stewart, J., McGrath, P., Harrison, W., Markowitz, J., Rabkin, J., Tricamo, E., Goetz, D., & Klein, D. (1988). Antidepressant specificity in atypical depression. *Archives of General Psychiatry, 45,* 129–137.

Liebowitz, M., Schneier, F., Campeas, R., Hollander, E., Hatterer, J., Fyer, A., Gorman, J., Papp, L., Davies, S., Gully, R., & Klein, D. (1992). Phenelzine vs. atenolol in social phobia: A placebo-controlled comparison. *Archives of General Psychiatry, 49,* 290–300.

Maccoby, E. E. & Martin, J. A. (1983). Socialization in the context of the family: Parent–child interaction. In P. H. Mussen (Series Ed.) & E. M. Hetherington (Vol. Ed.), *Handbook of child psychology: Vol. 4. Socialization, personality, and social development* (4th ed., pp. 1–101). New York: Wiley.

Main, M., & Goldwyn, R. (1984). Predicting rejection of her infant from mother's representation of her own experience: Implications for the abused–abusing intergenerational cycle. *Child Abuse and Neglect, 8,* 203–217.

Main, M., Kaplan, K., & Cassidy, J. (1985). Security in infancy, childhood, and adulthood: A move to the level of representation. In I. Bretherton & E. Waters (Eds.), Growing points of attachment theory and research. *Monographs of the Society for Research in Child Development, 50*(1–2, Serial No. 209), 66–104.

Maslow, A. (1987). *Motivation and personality* (3rd ed.). New York: Harper & Row.

McClelland, D. C. (1987). *Human motivation.* Cambridge, England: Cambridge University Press.

Mischel, W. (1973). Toward a cognitive social learning reconceptualization of personality. *Psychological Review, 80,* 252–283.

Mischel, W., & Shoda, Y. (1995). A cognitive–affective system theory of personality: Reconceptualizing situations, dispositions, dynamics, and invariance in personality structures. *Psychological Review, 102,* 246–268.

Nolen-Hoeksema, S. (1987). Sex differences in uni-polar depression. *Psychological Bulletin, 109,* 259–282.

Olson, J., Roese, N., & Zanna, M. (in press). In E. T. Higgins & A. Kruglanski (Eds.), *Handbook of social psychology: Basic principles.* New York: Guilford Press.

Patterson, C., Cohn, D., & Kao, B. (1989). Maternal warmth as a protective factor against risks associated with peer rejection among children. *Development and Psychopathology*, *1*, 21–38.

Quinton, D., Rutter, M., & Liddle, C. (1984). Institutional rearing, parenting difficulties, and marital support. *Psychological Medicine*, *14*, 107–124.

Rogers, C. (1959). A theory of therapy, personality, and interpersonal relationships, as developed in the client-centered framework. In S. Koch (Ed.), *Psychology: A study of a science* (Vol. 3, pp. 184–226). New York: McGraw-Hill.

Rohner, R. P., & Rohner, E. (1980). Antecedents and consequences of parental rejection: A theory of emotional abuse. *Child Abuse and Neglect*, *4*, 189–198.

Rosenberg, M. (1979). *Concerning the self*. New York: Basic Books.

Salovey, P., & Rodin, J. (1986). The differentiation of social-comparison jealousy and romantic jealousy. *Journal of Personality and Social Psychology*, *50*, 1100–1112.

Schlenker, B., & Leary, M. R. (1982). Social anxiety and self-presentation: A conceptualization and model. *Psychological Bulletin*, *92*, 641–669.

Shaver, P., & Brennan, K. (1992). Attachment styles and the "big five" personality traits: Their connections with each other and with romantic relationship outcomes. *Personality and Social Psychology Bulletin*, *18*, 536–545.

Simpson, J. A. (1990). Influence of attachment styles on romantic relationships. *Journal of Personality and Social Psychology*, *59*, 971–980.

Spanier, G. (1976). Measuring dyadic adjustment: New scales for assessing the quality of marriage and similar dyads. *Journal of Marriage and the Family*, *38*, 15–28.

Sullivan, H. S. (1937). A note on the implications of psychiatry, the study of interpersonal relations, for investigation in the social sciences. *American Journal of Sociology*, *43*, 157–164.

Sullivan, H. S. (1953). *The interpersonal theory of psychiatry*. New York: Norton.

Walker, L. E. (1984). *The battered woman syndrome*. New York: Springer.

Watson, P., & Friend, R. (1969). Measurement of social-evaluative anxiety. *Journal of Consulting and Clinical Psychology*, *33*, 448–457.

Weiss, R. L., & Summers, K. (1983). Marital Interaction Coding System III. In E. Filsinger (Ed.), *Marriage and family assessment* (pp. 35–115). Beverly Hills, CA: Sage.

Discussion Questions

1. Think of someone you know who you think would score high on the Rejection Sensitivity Questionnaire. Do they behave as Downey and Feldman suggest?
2. The concept of rejection sensitivity involves both the tendency to be concerned about being rejected and the tendency to expect to be rejected. On the Rejection Sensitivity Questionnaire, respondents indicate both their degree of concern or anxiety and the likelihood of receiving a rejecting reaction. Some researchers have suggested that it may be useful to separate these two components because being concerned about rejection and expecting rejection are not the same thing. What is your opinion? How might these two components of rejection sensitivity manifest themselves differently?
3. Speculate on how rejection sensitivity may be related to people's behavior in areas other than intimate relationships—for example, in the workplace, sports activities, consumer behavior, the political arena, education, medicine, and so on.
4. Imagine that you are a clinical or counseling psychologist who is working with a highly rejection-sensitive client. What approaches might you take to help the client deal with his or her insecurity, tendency to overperceive and overreact to rejection, and relationship problems that are fueled by rejection sensitivity?

Suggested Readings

Ayduk, O., Downey, G., Testa, A., Yen, Y., & Shoda, V. (1999). Does rejection elicit hostility in rejection sensitive women? *Social Cognition*, *17*, 245–271. This study found that women who were high in rejection sensitivity responded with more hostility than women low in rejection sensitivity when they though they were being rejected.

Baumeister, R. F., & Leary, M. R. (1995). The need to belong: Desire for interpersonal attachments as a fundamental human motivation. *Psychological Bulletin, 117,* 497–529. This article discusses the importance of social acceptance to human well-being and argues that the need to belong underlies a great deal of human behavior.

Downey, G., Feldman, S., & Ayduk, O. (2000). Rejection sensitivity and male violence in romantic relationships. *Personal Relationships, 7,* 45–61. This study provides data suggesting that, among men, anxiety about the prospect of being rejected by a close other is related to dating violence.

Downey, G., Freitas, A. L., Michealis, B., & Khouri, H. (1998). The self-fulfilling prophecy in close relationships: Do rejection sensitive women get rejected by their romantic partners? *Journal of Personality and Social Psychology, 75,* 545–560. This fascinating study examines the effects of rejection sensitivity on romantic relationships.

Downey, G., Lebolt, A., Rincon, C., & Freitas, A. L. (1998). Rejection sensitivity and children's interpersonal difficulties. *Child Development, 69,* 1074–1091. This study examines the self-fulfilling nature of rejection sensitivity. Adolescents who were high in rejection sensitivity behaved in ways likely to elicit the rejection they feared.

Levy, S. R., Ayduk, O., & Downey, G. (2001). The role of rejection sensitivity in people's relationships with significant others and valued social groups. In M. R. Leary (Ed.), *Interpersonal rejection* (pp. 251–289). New York: Oxford University Press. This chapter reviews the extensive research literature on rejection sensitivity.

PART 3

Social Psychological Processes in the Perception and Diagnosis of Psychological Problems

READING 14

On Being Sane in Insane Places

D. L. Rosenhan

Editors' Introduction

Historically, psychologists have subscribed to one of two general views about mental illness. One perspective views the source of mental illness as lying entirely within the patient. According to this view, psychologically disturbed individuals can be distinguished from "normal" people because they display certain symptoms (and thus receive a particular diagnosis) that distinguishes them from those who are well adjusted. The alternative perspective suggests that mental illness resides as much in the eyes of observers as within people themselves. Because there is no clear line that demarcates normal from abnormal behavior, almost any behavior can be interpreted as indicating psychopathology. As a result, judgments about normalcy are subject to cultural influences, personal expectations, and an array of biases. Furthermore, once someone is labeled as mentally ill, other people will perceive and treat that person as disturbed, whether the diagnosis is accurate or not. This latter view does not imply that some people are not psychologically troubled. Rather, it suggests that psychopathology is often in the eye of the beholder, and once a person is classified as psychologically disturbed, that label takes on a life of its own.

To examine the effects of labeling on the perception of psychiatric patients, Rosenhan and seven other normal individuals were able to get themselves admitted as patients to psychiatric hospitals across the country. All eight individuals reported to doctors that they were experiencing vague auditory hallucinations, and seven of the eight subsequently received a diagnosis of schizophrenia. Given that they were indeed acting "crazy," the fact that these normal individuals were diagnosed as disturbed is not surprising. However, once admitted, the eight individuals, some of whom were mental health professionals, began behaving completely normally and tried to convince their doctors and the hospital staff that they were no longer "mentally ill." Even still, hospital staff, believing the individuals were mentally ill, continued to interpret the behavior of the "patients" in light of their diagnosis. Thus, even normal behaviors were interpreted as evidence of the patient's schizophrenia. Only when the schizophrenia was believed to be in remission were the eight individuals discharged from their respective hospitals. Ironically, although hospital personnel failed to recognize normalcy in these eight individuals, many of the real patients in the hospital questioned whether or not these eight individuals were, in fact, actually mentally ill.

Rosenhan's conclusion that psychologists and psychiatrists are sometimes unable to distinguish the sane from the insane has met with some criticism. Some (Millon, 1975; Spitzer, 1975; Weiner, 1975) argue that Rosenhan's study was not even effectively designed to test such an idea. Even so, there can be little doubt that psychiatrists, psychologists, counselors, and other mental health professionals may fall victim to the same errors in person perception as everyone else, being influenced by labels and preconceptions. Diagnostic labels may lead them to misinterpret "normal" behaviors as "abnormal." Preconceived notions regarding the source of a person's difficulties may lead them to ignore other possible influences on the person's behavior. Also, they may discount information that contradicts their preconceptions about a patient's mental state or diagnostic classification.

I f sanity and insanity exist, how shall we know them?

The question is neither capricious nor itself insane. However much we may be personally convinced that we can tell the normal from the abnormal, the evidence is simply not compelling. It is commonplace, for example, to read about murder trials wherein eminent psychiatrists for the defense are contradicted by equally eminent psychiatrists for the prosecution on the matter of the defendant's sanity. More generally, there are a great deal of conflicting data on the reliability, utility, and meaning of such terms as "sanity," "insanity," "mental illness," and "schizophrenia".[1] Finally, as early as 1934, Benedict suggested that normality and abnormality are not universal.[2] What is viewed as normal in one culture may be seen as quite aberrant in another. Thus, notions of normality and abnormality may not be quite as accurate as people believe they are.

To raise questions regarding normality and abnormality is in no way to question the fact that some behaviors are deviant or odd. Murder is deviant. So, too, are hallucinations. Nor does raising such questions deny the existence of the personal anguish that is often associated with "mental illness." Anxiety and depression exist. Psychological suffering exists. But normality and abnormality, sanity and insanity, and the diagnoses that flow from them may be less substantive than many believe them to be.

At its heart, the question of whether the sane can be distinguished from the insane (and whether degrees of insanity can be distinguished from each other) is a simple matter: Do the salient characteristics that lead to diagnoses reside in the patients themselves or in the environments and contexts in which observers find them? From Bleuler, through Kretchmer, through the formulators of the recently revised *Diagnostic and Statistical Manual* of the American Psychiatric Association, the belief has been strong that patients present symptoms, that those symptoms can be categorized, and, implicitly, that the sane are distinguishable from the insane. More recently, however, this belief has been questioned. Based in part on theoretical and anthropological considerations, but also on philosophical, legal, and therapeutic ones, the view has grown that psychological categorization of mental illness is useless at best and downright harmful, misleading, and pejorative at worst. Psychiatric diagnoses, in this view, are in the minds of the observers and are not valid summaries of characteristics displayed by the observed.[3-5]

Gains can be made in deciding which of these is more nearly accurate by getting normal people (that is, people who do not have, and have never suffered, symptoms of serious psychiatric disorders) admitted to psychiatric hospitals and then determining whether they were discovered to be sane and, if so, how. If the sanity of such pseudopatients were always detected, there would be prima facie evidence that a sane individual can be distinguished from the insane context in which he is found. Normality (and presumably abnormality) is distinct enough that it can be recognized wherever it occurs, for it is carried within the person. If, on the other hand, the sanity of the pseudopatients were never discovered, serious difficulties would arise for those who support traditional modes of psychiatric diagnosis. Given that the hospital staff was not incompetent, that the pseudopatient had been behaving as sanely as he had been outside of the hospital, and that it had never been previously suggested that he belonged in a psychiatric hospital, such an unlikely outcome would support the view that psychiatric diagnosis betrays little about the patient but much about the environment in which an observer finds him.

This article describes such an experiment. Eight sane people gained secret admission to 12 different hospitals.[6] Their diagnostic experiences constitute the data of the first part of this article; the remainder is devoted to a description of their experiences in psychiatric institutions. Too few psychiatrists and psychologists, even those who have worked in such hospitals, know what the experience is like. They rarely talk about it with former patients, perhaps because they distrust information coming from the previously insane. Those who have worked in psychiatric hospitals are likely to have adapted so thoroughly to the settings that they are insensitive to the impact of that experience. And while there have been occasional reports of researchers who submitted themselves to psychiatric hospitalization,[7] these researchers have commonly remained in the hospitals for short periods of time, often with the knowledge of the hospital staff. It is difficult to know the extent to which they were treated like patients or like research colleagues. Nevertheless, their reports about the inside of the psychiatric hospital have been valuable. This article extends those efforts.

Pseudopatients and Their Settings

The eight pseudopatients were a varied group. One was a psychology graduate student in his 20s. The remaining seven were older and "established." Among them were three psychologists, a pediatrician, a psychiatrist, a painter, and a housewife. Three pseudopatients were women; five were men. All of them employed pseudonyms, lest their alleged diagnoses embarrass them later. Those who were in mental health professions alleged another occupation in order to avoid the special attentions that might be accorded by staff, as a matter of courtesy or caution, to ailing colleagues.[8] With the exception of myself (I was the first pseudopatient and my presence was known to the hospital administrator and chief psychologist and, so far as I can tell, to them alone), the presence of pseudopatients and the nature of the research program was not known to the hospital staffs.[9]

The settings were similarly varied. In order to generalize the findings, admission into a variety of hospitals was sought. The 12 hospitals in the sample were located in five different states on the East and West coasts. Some were old and shabby, some were quite new. Some were research-oriented, others not. Some had good staff–patient ratios, others were quite understaffed. Only one was a strictly private hospital. All of the others were supported by state or federal funds or, in one instance, by university funds.

After calling the hospital for an appointment, the pseudopatient arrived at the admissions office complaining that he had been hearing voices. Asked what the voices said, he replied that they were often unclear, but as far as he could tell they said "empty," "hollow," and "thud." The voices were unfamiliar and were of the same sex as the pseudopatient. The choice of these symptoms was occasioned by their apparent similarity to existential symptoms. Such symptoms are alleged to arise from painful concerns about the perceived meaninglessness of one's life. It is as if the hallucinating person were saying, "My life is empty and hollow." The choice of these symptoms was also determined by the *absence* of a single report of existential psychoses in the literature.

Beyond alleging the symptoms and falsifying name, vocation, and employment, no further alterations of person, history, or circumstances were made. The significant events of the pseudopatient's life history were presented as they had actually occurred. Relationships with parents and siblings, with spouse and children, with people at work and in school, consistent with the aforementioned exceptions, were described as they were or had been. Frustrations and upsets were described along with joys and satisfactions. These facts are important to remember. If anything, they strongly biased the subsequent results in favor of detecting sanity, since none of their histories or current behaviors were seriously pathological in any way.

Immediately upon admission to the psychiatric ward, the pseudopatient ceased simulating *any* symptoms of abnormality. In some cases, there was a brief period of mild nervousness and anxiety, since none of the pseudopatients really believed that they would be admitted so easily. Indeed, their shared fear was that they would be immediately exposed as frauds and greatly embarrassed. Moreover, many of them had never visited a psychiatric ward; even those who had, nevertheless had some genuine fears about what might happen to them. Their nervousness, then, was quite appropriate to the novelty of the hospital setting, and it abated rapidly.

Apart from that short-lived nervousness, the pseudopatient behaved on the ward as he "normally" behaved. The pseudopatient spoke to patients and staff as he might ordinarily. Because there is uncommonly little to do on a psychiatric ward, he attempted to engage others in conversation. When asked by staff how he was feeling, he indicated that he was fine, that he no longer experienced symptoms. He responded to instructions from attendants, to calls for medication (which was not swallowed), and to dining-hall instructions. Beyond such activities as were available to him on the admissions ward, he spent his time writing down his observations about the ward, its patients, and the staff. Initially these notes were written "secretly," but as it soon became clear that no one much cared, they were subsequently written on standard tablets of paper in such public places as the dayroom. No secret was made of these activities.

The pseudopatient, very much as a true psychiatric patient, entered a hospital with no foreknowledge of when he would be discharged. Each was told that he would have to get out by his own devices, essentially by convincing the staff that he was sane. The psychological stresses associated with hospitalization were considerable, and all but one of the pseudopatients desired to be discharged almost immediately after being admitted. They were, therefore, motivated not only to behave sanely, but to be paragons of cooperation. That their behavior was in no way disruptive is confirmed by nursing reports, which have been obtained on most of the patients. These reports uniformly indicate that the patients were "friendly," "cooperative," and "exhibited no abnormal indications."

The Normal Are Not Detectably Sane

Despite their public "show" of sanity, the pseudopatients were never detected. Admitted, except in one case, with a diagnosis of schizophrenia,[10] each was discharged with a diagnosis of schizophrenia "in remission." The label "in remission" should in no way be dismissed as a formality, for at no time during any hospitalization had any question been raised about any pseudopatient's simulation. Nor are there any indications in the hospital records that the pseudopatient's status was suspect. Rather, the evidence is strong that, once labeled schizophrenic, the pseudopatient was stuck with that label. If the pseudopatient was to be discharged, he must naturally be "in remission"; but he was not sane, nor, in the institution's view, had he ever been sane.

The uniform failure to recognize sanity cannot be attributed to the quality of the hospitals, for, although there were considerable variations among them, several are considered excellent. Nor can it be alleged that there was simply not enough time to observe the pseudopatients. Length of hospitalization ranged from 7 to 52 days, with an average of 19 days. The pseudopatients were not, in fact, carefully observed, but this failure clearly speaks more to traditions within psychiatric hospitals than to lack of opportunity.

Finally, it cannot be said that the failure to recognize the pseudopatients' sanity was due to the fact that they were not behaving sanely. While there was clearly some tension present in all of them, their daily visitors could detect no serious behavioral consequences—nor, indeed, could other patients. It was quite common for the patients to "detect" the pseudopatients' sanity. During the first three hospitalizations, when accurate counts were kept, 35 of a total of 118 patients on the admissions ward voiced their suspicions, some vigorously. "You're not crazy. You're a journalist, or a professor [referring to the continual note-taking]. You're checking up on the hospital." While most of the patients were reassured by the pseudopatient's insistence that he had been sick before he came in but was fine now, some continued to believe that the pseudopatient was sane throughout his hospitalization.[11] The fact that the patients often recognized normality when staff did not raises important questions.

Failure to detect sanity during the course of hospitalization may be due to the fact that physicians operate with a strong bias toward what statisticians call the type 2 error.[5] This is to say that physicians are more inclined to call a healthy person sick (a false positive, type 2) than a sick person healthy (a false negative, type 1). The reasons for this are not hard to find: It is clearly more dangerous to misdiagnose illness than health. Better to err on the side of caution, to suspect illness even among the healthy.

But what holds for medicine does not hold equally well for psychiatry. Medical illnesses, while unfortunate, are not commonly pejorative. Psychiatric diagnoses, on the contrary, carry with them personal, legal, and social stigmas.[12] It was therefore important to see whether the tendency toward diagnosing the sane insane could be reversed. The following experiment was arranged at a research and teaching hospital whose staff had heard these findings but doubted that such an error could occur in their hospital. The staff was informed that at some time during the following 3 months, one or more pseudopatients would attempt to be admitted into the psychiatric hospital. Each staff member was asked to rate each patient who presented himself at admissions or on the ward according to the likelihood that the patient was a pseudopatient. A 10-point scale was used, with a 1 and 2 reflecting high confidence that the patient was a pseudopatient.

Judgments were obtained on 193 patients who were admitted for psychiatric treatment. All staff who had had sustained contact with or primary responsibility for the patient—attendants, nurses, psychiatrists, physicians, and psychologists—were asked to make judgments. Forty-one patients were alleged, with high confidence, to be pseudopatients by at least one member of the staff. Twenty-three were considered suspect by at least one psychiatrist. Nineteen were suspected by one psychiatrist *and* one other staff member. Actually, no genuine pseudopatient (at least from my group) presented himself during this period.

The experiment is instructive. It indicates that the tendency to designate sane people as insane can be reversed when the stakes (in this case, prestige and diagnostic acumen) are high. But what can be said of the 19 people who were suspected of being "sane" by one psychiatrist and another staff member? Were these people truly "sane," or was it rather the case that in the course of avoiding the type 2 error the staff tended to make more errors of the first sort—calling the crazy "sane"? There is no way of knowing. But one thing is certain: any diagnostic process that lends itself so readily to massive errors of this sort cannot be a very reliable one.

The Stickiness of Psychodiagnostic Labels

Beyond the tendency to call the healthy sick—a tendency that accounts better for diagnostic behavior on admission than it does for such behavior after a lengthy period of exposure—the data speak to the massive role of labeling in psychiatric assessment. Having once been labeled schizophrenic, there is nothing the pseudopatient can do to overcome the tag. The tag profoundly colors others' perceptions of him and his behavior.

From one viewpoint, these data are hardly surprising, for it has long been known that elements are given meaning by the context in which they occur. Gestalt psychology made this point vigorously, and Asch[13] demonstrated that there are "central" personality traits (such as "warm" vs. "cold") that are so powerful that they markedly color the meaning of other information in forming an impression of a given personality.[14] "Insane," "schizophrenic," "manic-depressive," and "crazy" are probably among the most powerful of such central traits. Once a person is designated abnormal, all of his other behaviors and characteristics are colored by that label. Indeed, that label is so powerful that many of the pseudopatients' normal behaviors were overlooked entirely or profoundly misinterpreted. Some examples may clarify this issue.

Earlier I indicated that there were no changes in the pseudopatient's personal history and current status beyond those of name, employment, and, where necessary, vocation. Otherwise, a veridical description of personal history and circumstances was offered. Those circumstances were not psychotic. How were they made consonant with the diagnosis of psychosis? Or were those diagnoses modified in such a way as to bring them into accord with the circumstances of the pseudopatient's life, as described by him?

As far as I can determine, diagnoses were in no way affected by the relative health of the circumstances of a pseudopatient's life. Rather, the reverse occurred: The perception of his circumstances was shaped entirely by the diagnosis. A clear example of such translation is found in the case of a pseudopatient who had had a close relationship with his mother but was rather remote from his father during his early childhood. During adolescence and beyond, however, his father became a close friend, while his relationship with his mother cooled. His present relationship with his wife was characteristically close and warm. Apart from occasional angry exchanges, friction was minimal. The children had rarely been spanked. Surely there is nothing especially pathological about such a history. Indeed, many readers may see a similar pattern in their own experiences, with no markedly deleterious consequences. Observe, however, how such a history was translated in the psychopathological context, this from the case summary prepared after the patient was discharged.

This white 39-year-old male . . . manifests a long history of considerable ambivalence in close relationships, which begins in early childhood. A warm relationship with his mother cools during his adolescence. A distant relationship to his father is described as becoming very intense. Affective stability is absent. His attempts to control emotionality with his wife and children are punctuated by angry outbursts and, in the case of the children, spankings. And while he says that he has several good friends, one senses considerable ambivalence embedded in those relationships also. . . .

The facts of the case were unintentionally distorted by the staff to achieve consistency with a popular theory of the dynamics of a schizophrenic reaction.[15] Nothing of an ambivalent nature had been described in relations with parents, spouse, or friends. To the extent that ambivalence could be inferred, it was probably not greater than is found in all human relationships. It is true the pseudopatient's relationships with his parents changed over time, but in the ordinary context that would hardly be remarkable—indeed, it might very well be expected. Clearly, the meaning ascribed to his verbalizations (that is, ambivalence, affective instability) was determined by the diagnosis: schizophrenia. An entirely different meaning would have been ascribed if it were known that the man was "normal."

All pseudopatients took extensive notes publicly. Under ordinary circumstances, such behavior would have raised questions in the minds of observers, as, in fact, it did among patients. Indeed, it seemed so certain that the notes would elicit suspicion that elaborate precautions were taken to remove them from the ward each day. But the precautions proved needless. The closest any staff member came to questioning these notes occurred when one pseudopatient asked his physician what kind of medication he was receiving and began to write down the response. "You needn't write it," he was told gently. "If you have trouble remembering, just ask me again."

If no questions were asked of the pseudopatients, how was their writing interpreted? Nursing records for three patients indicate that the writing was seen as an aspect of their pathological behavior. "Patient engages in writing behavior" was the daily nursing comment on one of the pseudopatients who was never questioned about his writing. Given that the patient is in the hospital, he must be psychologically disturbed. And given that he is disturbed, continuous writing must be a behavioral manifestation of that disturbance, perhaps a subset of the compulsive behaviors that are sometimes correlated with schizophrenia.

One tacit characteristic of psychiatric diagnosis is that it locates the sources of aberration within the individual and only rarely within the complex of stimuli that surrounds him. Consequently, behaviors that are stimulated by the environment are commonly misattributed to the patient's disorder. For example, one kindly nurse found a pseudopatient pacing the long hospital corridors. "Nervous, Mr. X?" she asked. "No, bored," he said.

The notes kept by pseudopatients are full of patient behaviors that were misinterpreted by well-intentioned staff. Often enough, a patient would go "berserk" because he had, wittingly or unwittingly, been mistreated by, say, an attendant. A nurse coming upon the scene would rarely inquire even cursorily into the environmental stimuli of the patient's behavior. Rather, she assumed that his upset derived from his pathology, not from his present interactions with other staff members. Occasionally, the staff might assume that the patient's family (especially when they had recently visited) or other patients had stimulated the outburst. But never were the staff found to assume that one of themselves or the structure of the hospital had anything to do with a patient's behavior. One psychiatrist pointed to a group of patients who were sitting outside the cafeteria entrance half an hour before lunchtime. To a group of young residents he indicated that such behavior was characteristic of the oral-acquisitive nature of the syndrome. It seemed not to occur to him that there were very few things to anticipate in a psychiatric hospital besides eating.

A psychiatric label has a life and an influence of its own. Once the impression has been formed that the patient is schizophrenic, the expectation is that he will continue to be schizophrenic. When a sufficient amount of time has passed, during which the patient has done nothing bizarre, he is considered to be in remission and available for discharge. But the label endures beyond discharge, with the unconfirmed expectation that he will behave as a schizophrenic again. Such labels, conferred by mental health professionals, are as influential on the patient as they are on his relatives and friends, and it should not surprise anyone that the diagnosis acts on all of them as a self-fulfilling prophecy. Eventually, the patient himself accepts the diagnosis, with all of its surplus meanings and expectations, and behaves accordingly.[5]

The inferences to be made from these matters are quite simple. Much as Zigler and Phillips have demonstrated that there is enormous overlap in the symptoms presented by patients who have been variously diagnosed,[16] so there is enormous overlap in the behaviors of the sane and the insane. The sane are not "sane" all of the time. We lose our tempers "for no good reason." We are occasionally depressed or anxious, again for no good reason. And we may find it difficult to get along with one or another person—again for no reason that we can specify. Similarly, the insane are not always insane. Indeed, it was the impression of the pseudopatients while living with them that they were sane for long periods of time—that the bizarre behaviors upon which their diagnoses were allegedly predicated constituted only a small fraction of their total behavior. If it makes no sense to label ourselves permanently depressed on the basis of an occasional depression, then it takes better evidence than is presently available to label all patients insane or schizophrenic on the basis of bizarre behaviors or cognitions. It seems more useful, as Mischel[17] has pointed out, to limit our discussions to *behaviors*, the stimuli that provoke them, and their correlates.

It is not known why powerful impressions of personality traits, such as "crazy" or "insane," arise. Conceivably, when the origins of and stimuli that give rise to a behavior are remote or unknown, or when the behavior strikes us as immutable, trait labels regarding the *behaver* arise. When, on the other hand, the origins and stimuli are known and available, discourse is limited to the behavior itself. Thus, I may hallucinate because I am sleeping, or I may hallucinate because I have ingested a peculiar drug. These are termed sleep-induced hallucinations, or dreams, and drug-induced hallucinations, respectively. But when the stimuli to my hallucinations are unknown, that is called craziness, or schizophrenia—as if that inference were somehow as illuminating as the others.

The Experience of Psychiatric Hospitalization

The term "mental illness" is of recent origin. It was coined by people who were humane in their inclinations and who wanted very much to raise the station of (and the public's sympathies toward) the psychologically disturbed from that of witches and "crazies" to one that was akin to the physically ill. And they were at least partially successful, for the treatment of the mentally ill *has* improved considerably over the years. But while treatment has improved, it is doubtful that people really regard the mentally ill in the same way that they view the physically ill. A broken leg is something one recovers from, but mental illness allegedly endures forever.[18] A broken leg does not threaten the observer, but a crazy schizophrenic? There is by now a host of evidence that attitudes toward the mentally ill are characterized by fear, hostility, aloofness, suspicion, and dread.[19] The mentally ill are society's lepers.

That such attitudes infect the general population is perhaps not surprising, only upsetting. But that they affect the professionals—attendants, nurses, physicians, psychologists, and social workers—who treat and deal with the mentally ill is more disconcerting, both because such attitudes are self-evidently pernicious and because they are unwitting. Most mental health professionals would insist that they are sympathetic toward the mentally ill, that they are neither avoidant nor hostile. But it is more likely that an exquisite ambivalence characterizes their relations with psychiatric patients, such that their avowed impulses are only part of their entire attitude. Negative attitudes are there too and can easily be detected. Such attitudes should not surprise us. They are the natural offspring of the labels patients wear and the places in which they are found.

Consider the structure of the typical psychiatric hospital. Staff and patients are strictly segregated. Staff have their own living space, including their dining facilities, bathrooms, and assembly places. The glassed quarters that contain the professional staff, which the pseudopatients came to call "the cage," sit out on every dayroom. The staff emerge primarily for caretaking purposes—to give medication, to conduct a therapy or group meeting, to instruct or reprimand a patient. Otherwise, staff keep to themselves, almost as if the disorder that afflicts their charges is somehow catching.

So much is patient–staff segregation the rule that for four public hospitals in which an attempt was made to measure the degree to which staff and patients mingle, it was necessary to use "time out of the staff cage" as the operational measure. While it was not the case that all time spent out of the cage was spent mingling with patients (attendants, for example, would occasionally emerge to watch television in the dayroom), it was the only way in which one could gather reliable data on time for measuring.

The average amount of time spent by attendants outside of the cage was 11.3% (range, 3 to 52%). This figure does not represent only time spent mingling with patients, but also includes time spent on such chores as folding laundry, supervising patients while they shave, directing ward cleanup, and sending patients to off-ward activities. It was the relatively rare attendant who spent time talking with patients or playing games with them. It proved impossible to obtain a "percent mingling time" for nurses, since the amount of time they spent out of the cage was too brief. Rather, we counted instances of emergence from the cage. On the average, daytime nurses emerged from the cage 11.5 times per shift, including instances when they left the ward entirely (range, 4 to 39 times). Late-afternoon and night nurses were even less available, emerging on the average 9.4 times per shift (range, 4 to 41 times). Data on early-morning nurses, who arrived usually after midnight and departed at 8 a.m., are not available because patients were asleep during most of this period.

Physicians, especially psychiatrists, were even less available. They were rarely seen on the wards. Quite commonly, they would be seen only when they arrived and departed, with the remaining time being spent in their offices or in the cage. On the average, physicians emerged on the ward 6.7 times per day (range, 1 to 17 times). It proved difficult to make an accurate estimate in this regard, because physicians often maintained hours that allowed them to come and go at different times.

The hierarchical organization of the psychiatric hospital has been commented on before,[20] but the latent meaning of that kind of organization is worth noting again. Those with the most power have least to do with patients, and those with the least power are most involved with them. Recall, however, that the acquisition of role-appropriate behaviors occurs mainly through the observation of others, with the most powerful having the most influence. Consequently, it is understandable that attendants not only spend more time with patients than do any other members of the staff—that is required by their station in the hierarchy—but also, insofar as they learn from their superiors' behavior, spend as little time with patients as they can. Attendants are seen mainly in the cage, which is where the models, the action, and the power are.

I turn now to a different set of studies, these dealing with staff response to patient-initiated contact. It has long been known that the amount of time a person spends with you can be an index of your significance to him. If he initiates and maintains eye contact, there is reason to believe that he is considering your requests and needs. If he pauses to chat or actually stops and talks, there is added reason to infer that he is individuating you. In four hospitals, the pseudopatient approached the staff member with a request which took the following form: "Pardon me, Mr. [or Dr. or Mrs.] X, could you tell me when I will be eligible for grounds privileges?" (or ". . . when I will be presented at the staff meeting?" or ". . . when I am likely to be discharged?"). While the content of the question varied according to the appropriateness of the target and the pseudopatient's (apparent) current needs, the form was always a courteous and relevant request for information. Care was taken never to approach a particular member of the staff more than once a day, lest the staff member become suspicious or irritated. In examining these data, remember that the behavior of the pseudopatients was neither bizarre nor disruptive. One could indeed engage in good conversation with them.

The data for these experiments are shown in Table 14.1, separately for physicians (column 1) and for nurses and attendants (column 2). Minor differences between these four institutions were overwhelmed by the degree to which staff avoided continuing contacts that patients had initiated. By far, their most common response consisted of either a brief response to the question, offered while they were "on the move" and with head averted, or no response at all.

The encounter frequently took the following bizarre form: (pseudopatient) "Pardon me, Dr. X. Could you tell me when I am eligible for grounds privileges?" (physician) "Good morning, Dave. How are you today?" (moves off without waiting for a response).

It is instructive to compare these data with data recently obtained at Stanford University. It has been alleged that large and eminent universities are characterized by faculty who are so busy that they have no time for students. For this comparison, a young lady approached individual faculty members who seemed to be walking purposefully

TABLE 14.1. Self-Initiated Contact by Pseudopatients With Psychiatrists and Nurses and Attendants, Compared to Contact With Other Groups

Contact	Psychiatric hospitals		University campus (nonmedical)		University medical center Physicians	
	(1) Psychiatrists	(2) Nurses and attendants	(3) Faculty	(4) "Looking for a psychiatrist"	(5) "Looking for an internist"	(6) No additional comment
Responses						
Moves on, head averted (%)	71	88	0	0	0	0
Makes eye contact (%)	23	10	0	11	0	0
Pauses and chats (%)	2	2	0	11	0	10
Stops and talks (%)	4	0.5	100	78	100	90
Mean number of questions answered (out of 6)	*	*	6	3.8	4.8	4.5
Respondents (number)	13	47	14	18	15	10
Attempts (number)	185	1283	14	18	15	10

* Not applicable.

to some meeting or teaching engagement and asked *them the following* six questions.

1. "Pardon me, could you direct me to Encina Hall?" (at the medical school: ". . . to the Clinical Research Center?").
2. "Do you know where Fish Annex is?" (there is no Fish Annex at Stanford).
3. "Do you teach here?"
4. "How does one apply for admission to the college?" (at the medical school: ". . . to the medical school?").
5. "Is it difficult to get in?"
6. "Is there financial aid?"

Without exception, as can be seen in Table 14.1 (column 3), all of the questions were answered. No matter how rushed they were, all respondents not only maintained eye contact, but stopped to talk. Indeed, many of the respondents went out of their way to direct or take the questioner to the office she was seeking, to try to locate "Fish Annex," or to discuss with her the possibilities of being admitted to the university.

Similar data, also shown in Table 14.1 (columns 4, 5, and 6), were obtained in the hospital. Here too, the young lady came prepared with six questions. After the first question, however, she remarked to 18 of her respondents (column 4), "I'm looking for a psychiatrist," and to 15 others (column 5), "I'm looking for an internist." Ten other respondents received no inserted comment (column 6). The general degree of cooperative responses is considerably higher for these university groups than it was for pseudopatients in psychiatric hospitals. Even so, differences are apparent within the medical school setting. Once having indicated that she was looking for a psychiatrist, the degree of cooperation elicited was less than when she sought an internist.

Powerlessness and Depersonalization

Eye contact and verbal contact reflect concern and individuation; their absence, avoidance and depersonalization. The data I have presented do not do justice to the rich daily encounters that grew up around matters of depersonalization and avoidance. I have records of patients who were beaten by staff for the sin of having initiated verbal contact. During my own experience, for example, one patient was beaten in the presence of other patients for having approached an attendant and told him, "I like you." Occasionally, punishment meted out to patients for misdemeanors seemed so excessive that it could not be justified by the most radical interpretations of psychiatric canon. Nevertheless, they appeared to go unquestioned. Tempers were often short. A patient who had not heard a call for medication would be roundly excoriated, and the morning attendants would often wake patients with, "Come on, you m———f———s, out of bed!"

Neither anecdotal nor "hard" data can convey the overwhelming sense of powerlessness that invades the individual as he is continually exposed to the depersonalization of the psychiatric hospital. It hardly matters *which* psychiatric hospital—the excellent public ones and the very plush private hospital were better than the rural and shabby ones in this regard, but, again, the features that psychiatric hospitals had in common overwhelmed by far their apparent differences.

Powerlessness was evident everywhere. The patient is deprived of many of his legal rights by dint of his psychiatric commitment.[21] He is shorn of credibility by virtue of his psychiatric label. His freedom of movement is restricted. He cannot initiate contact with the staff, but may only respond to such overtures as they make. Personal privacy is minimal. Patient quarters and possessions can be entered and examined by any staff member, for whatever reason. His personal history and anguish is available to any staff member (often including the "gray lady" and "candy striper" volunteer) who chooses to read his folder, regardless of their therapeutic relationship to him. His personal hygiene and waste evacuation are often monitored. The water closets may have no doors.

At times, depersonalization reached such proportions that pseudopatients had the sense that they were invisible, or at least unworthy of account. Upon being admitted, I and other pseudopatients took the initial physical examinations in a semi-public room, where staff members went about their own business as if we were not there.

On the ward, attendants delivered verbal and occasionally serious physical abuse to patients in the presence of other observing patients, some of whom (the pseudopatients) were writing it all down. Abusive behavior, on the other hand, terminated quite abruptly when other staff members were known to be coming. Staff are credible witnesses. Patients are not.

A nurse unbuttoned her uniform to adjust her brassiere in the presence of an entire ward of viewing men. One did not have the sense that she was being seductive. Rather, she didn't notice us. A group of staff persons might point to a patient in the dayroom and discuss him animatedly, as if he were not there.

One illuminating instance of depersonalization and invisibility occurred with regard to medications. All told, the pseudopatients were administered nearly 2,100 pills, including Elavil, Stelazine, Compazine, and Thorazine, to name but a few. (That such a variety of medications should have been administered to patients presenting identical symptoms is itself worthy of note.) Only two were swallowed. The rest were either pocketed or deposited in the toilet. The pseudopatients were not alone in this. Although I have no precise records on how many patients rejected their medications, the pseudopatients frequently found the medications of other patients in the toilet before they deposited their own. As long as they were cooperative, their behavior and the pseudopatients' own in this matter, as in other important matters, went unnoticed throughout.

Reactions to such depersonalization among pseudopatients were intense. Although they had come to the hospital as participant observers and were fully aware that they did not "belong," they nevertheless found themselves caught up in and fighting the process of depersonalization. Some examples: A graduate student in psychology asked his wife to bring his textbooks to the hospital so he could "catch up on his homework"—this despite the elaborate precautions taken to conceal his professional association. The same student, who had trained for quite some time to get into the hospital, and who had looked forward to the experience, "remembered" some drag races that he had wanted to see on the weekend and insisted that he be discharged by that time. Another pseudopatient attempted a romance with a nurse. Subsequently, he informed the staff that he was applying for admission to graduate school in psychology and was very likely to be admitted, since a graduate professor was one of his regular hospital visitors. The same person began to engage in psychotherapy with other patients—all of this as a way of becoming a person in an impersonal environment.

The Sources of Depersonalization

What are the origins of depersonalization? I have already mentioned two. First are attitudes held by all of us toward the mentally ill—including those who treat them—attitudes characterized by fear, distrust, and horrible expectations on the one hand, and benevolent intentions on the other. Our ambivalence leads, in this instance as in others, to avoidance.

Second, and not entirely separate, the hierarchical structure of the psychiatric hospital facilitates depersonalization. Those who are at the top have least to do with patients, and their behavior inspires the rest of the staff. Average daily contact with psychiatrists, psychologists, residents, and physicians combined ranged from 3.9 to 25.1 minutes, with an overall mean of 6.8 (6 pseudopatients over a total of 129 days of hospitalization). Included in this average are time spent in the admissions interview, ward meetings in the presence of a senior staff member, group and individual psychotherapy contacts, case presentation conferences, and discharge meetings. Clearly, patients do not spend much time in interpersonal contact with doctoral staff. And doctoral staff serve as models for nurses and attendants.

There are probably other sources. Psychiatric installations are presently in serious financial straits. Staff shortages are pervasive, staff time at a premium. Something has to give, and that something is patient contact. Yet, although financial stresses are realities, too much can be made of them. I have the impression that the psychological forces that result in depersonalization are much stronger than the fiscal ones and that the addition of more staff would not correspondingly improve patient care in this regard. The incidence of staff meetings and the enormous amount of record-keeping on patients, for example, have not been as substantially reduced as has patient contact. Priorities exist, even during hard times. Patient contact is not a significant priority in the traditional psychiatric hospital, and fiscal pressures do not account for this. Avoidance and depersonalization may.

Heavy reliance on psychotropic medication tacitly contributes to depersonalization by convincing staff that treatment is indeed being conducted and that further patient contact may not be necessary. Even here, however, caution needs to be exercised in understanding the role of psychotropic drugs. If patients were powerful rather than powerless, if they were viewed as interesting individuals rather than diagnostic entities, if they were socially significant rather than social lepers, if their anguish truly and wholly compelled our sympathies and concerns, would we not *seek* contact with them, despite the availability of medications? Perhaps for the pleasure of it all?

The Consequences of Labeling and Depersonalization

Whenever the ratio of what is known to what needs to be known approaches zero, we tend to invent "knowledge" and assume that we understand more than we actually do. We seem unable to acknowledge that we simply don't know. The needs for diagnosis and remediation of behavioral and emotional problems are enormous. But rather than acknowledge that we are just embarking on understanding, we continue to label patients "schizophrenic," "manic-depressive," and "insane," as if in those words we had captured the essence of understanding. The facts of the matter are that we have known for a long time that diagnoses are often not useful or reliable, but we have nevertheless continued to use them. We now know that we cannot distinguish insanity from sanity. It is depressing to consider how that information will be used.

Not merely depressing, but frightening. How many people, one wonders, are sane but not recognized as such in our psychiatric institutions? How many have been needlessly stripped of their privileges of citizenship, from the right to vote and drive to that of handling their own accounts? How many have feigned insanity in order to avoid the criminal consequences of their behavior, and, conversely, how many would rather stand trial than live interminably in a psychiatric hospital—but are wrongly thought to be mentally ill? How many have been stigmatized by well-intentioned, but nevertheless erroneous, diagnoses? On the last point, recall again that a "type 2 error" in psychiatric diagnosis does not have the same consequences it does in medical diagnosis. A diagnosis of cancer that has been found to be in error is cause for celebration. But psychiatric diagnoses are rarely found to be in error. The label sticks, a mark of inadequacy forever.

Finally, how many patients might be "sane" outside the psychiatric hospital but seem insane in it—not because craziness resides in them, as it were, but because they are responding to a bizarre setting, one that may be unique to institutions that harbor nether people? Goffman[4] calls the process of socialization to such institutions "mortification"—an apt metaphor that includes the processes of depersonalization that have been described here. And although it is impossible to know whether the pseudopatients' responses to these processes are characteristic of all inmates—they were, after all, not real patients—it is difficult to believe that these processes of socialization to a psychiatric hospital provide useful attitudes or habits of response for living in the "real world."

Summary and Conclusions

It is clear that we cannot distinguish the sane from the insane in psychiatric hospitals. The hospital itself imposes a special environment in which the meanings of behavior can easily be misunderstood. The consequences to patients hospitalized in such an environment—the powerlessness, depersonalization, segregation, mortification, and self-labeling—seem undoubtedly countertherapeutic.

I do not, even now, understand this problem well enough to perceive solutions. But two matters seem to have some promise. The first concerns the proliferation of community mental health facilities, of crisis intervention centers, of the human potential movement, and of behavior therapies that, for all of their own problems, tend to avoid psychiatric labels, to focus on specific problems and behaviors, and to retain the individual in a relatively nonpejorative environment. Clearly, to the extent that we refrain from sending the distressed to insane places, our impressions of them are less likely to be distorted. (The risk of distorted perceptions, it seems to me, is always present, since we are much more sensitive to an individual's behaviors and verbalizations than we are to the subtle contextual stimuli that often promote them. At issue here is a matter of magnitude. And, as I have shown, the magnitude of distortion is exceedingly high in the extreme context that is a psychiatric hospital.)

The second matter that might prove promising speaks to the need to increase the sensitivity of mental health workers and researchers to the "Catch 22" position of psychiatric patients. Simply reading materials in this area will be of help to some such workers and researchers. For others, directly experiencing the impact of psychiatric hospitalization will be of enormous use. Clearly, further research into the social psychology of such total institutions will both facilitate treatment and deepen understanding.

I and the other pseudopatients in the psychiatric setting had distinctly negative reactions. We do not pretend to describe the subjective experiences of true patients. Theirs may be different from ours, particularly with the passage of time and the necessary process of adaptation to one's environment. But we can and do speak to the relatively more objective indices of treatment within the hospital. It could be a mistake, and a very unfortunate one, to consider that what happened to us derived from malice or stupidity on the part of the staff. Quite the contrary, our overwhelming impression of them was of people who really cared, who were committed and who were uncommonly intelligent. Where they failed, as they sometimes did painfully, it would be more accurate to attribute those failures to the environment in which they, too, found themselves than to personal callousness. Their perceptions and behavior were controlled by the situation, rather than being motivated by a malicious disposition. In a more benign environment, one that was less attached to global diagnosis, their behaviors and judgments might have been more benign and effective.

NOTES

1. P. Ash, *J. Abnorm. Soc. Psychol.* **44**, 272 (1949); A. T. Beck, *Amer. J. Psychiat.* **119**, 210 (1962); A. T. Boisen, *Psychiatry* **2**, 233 (1938); N. Kreitman, *J. Ment. Sci.* **107**, 876 (1961); N. Kreitman, P. Sainsbury, J. Morrisey, J. Towers, J. Scrivener, *ibid.*, p. 887; H. O. Schmitt and C. P. Fonda, *J. Abnorm. Soc. Psychol.* **52**, 262 (1956); W. Seeman, *J. Nerv. Ment. Dis.* **118**, 541 (1953). For an analysis of these artifacts and summaries of the disputes, see J. Zubin, *Annu. Rev. Psychol.* **18**, 373 (1967); L. Phillips and J. G. Draguns, *ibid.* **22**, 447 (1971).
2. R. Benedict, *J. Gen. Psychol.* **10**, 59 (1934).
3. See in this regard H. Becker, *Outsiders: Studies in the Sociology of Deviance* (Free Press, New York, 1963); B. M. Braginsky, D. D. Braginsky, K. Ring, *Methods of Madness: The Mental Hospital as a Last Resort* (Holt, Rinehart & Winston, New York, 1969); G. M. Crocetti and P. V. Lemkau, *Amer. Sociol. Rev.* **30**, 577 (1965); E. Goffman, *Behavior in Public Places* (Free Press, New York, 1964); R. D. Laing, *The Divided Self: A Study of Sanity and Madness* (Quadrangle, Chicago, 1960); D. L. Phillips, *Amer. Sociol. Rev.* **28**, 963 (1963); T. R. Sarbin, *Psychol. Today* **6**, 18 (1972); E. Schur, *Amer. J. Sociol.* **75**, 309 (1969); T. Szasz, *Law, Liberty and Psychiatry* (Macmillan, New York, 1963); *The Myth of Mental Illness: Foundations of a Theory of Mental Illness* (Hoeber-Harper, New York, 1963). For a critique of some of these views, see W. R. Gove, *Amer. Sociol. Rev.* **35**, 873 (1970).
4. E. Goffman, *Asylums* (Doubleday, Garden City, NY, 1961).
5. T. J. Scheff, *Being Mentally Ill: A Sociological Theory* (Aldine, Chicago, 1966).
6. Data from a ninth pseudopatient are not incorporated in this report because although his sanity went undetected, he falsified aspects of his personal history, including his marital status and parental relationships. His experimental behaviors therefore were not identical to those of the other pseudopatients.
7. A. Barry, *Bellevue Is a State of Mind* (Harcourt Brace Jovanovich, New York, 1971); I. Belknap, *Human Problems of a State Mental Hospital* (McGraw-Hill, New York, 1956); W. Caudill, F. C. Redlich, H. R. Gilmore, E. B. Brody, *Amer. J. Orthopsychiat.* **22**, 314 (1952); A. R. Goldman, R. H. Bohr, T. A. Steinberg, *Prof. Psychol.* **1**, 427 (1970); unauthored, *Roche Report* **1** (No. 13), 8 (1971).
8. Beyond the personal difficulties that the pseudopatient is likely to experience in the hospital, there are legal and social ones that, combined, require considerable attention before entry. For example, once admitted to a psychiatric institution, it is difficult, if not impossible, to be discharged on short notice, state law to the contrary notwithstanding. I was not sensitive to these difficulties at the outset of the project, nor to the personal and situational emergencies that can arise, but later a writ of habeas corpus was prepared for each of the entering pseudopatients and an attorney was kept "on call" during every hospitalization. I am grateful to John Kaplan and Robert Bartels for legal advice and assistance in these matters.
9. However distasteful such concealment is, it was a necessary first step to examining these questions. Without concealment, there would have been no way to know how valid these experiences were; nor was there any way of knowing whether whatever detections occurred were a tribute to the diagnostic acumen of the staff or to the hospital's rumor network. Obviously, since my concerns are general ones that cut across individual hospitals and staffs, I have respected their anonymity and have eliminated clues that might lead to their identification.
10. Interestingly, of the 12 admissions, 11 were diagnosed as schizophrenic and one, with the identical symptomatology, as manic-depressive psychosis. This diagnosis has a more favorable prognosis, and it was given by the only private hospital in our sample. On the relations between social class and psychiatric diagnosis, see A. deB.

Hollingshead and F. C. Redlich, *Social Class and Mental Illness: A Community Study* (Wiley, New York, 1958).
11. It is possible, of course, that patients have quite broad latitudes in diagnosis and therefore are inclined to call many people sane, even those whose behavior is patently aberrant. However, although we have no hard data on this matter, it was our distinct impression that this was not the case. In many instances, patients not only singled us out for attention, but came to imitate our behaviors and styles.
12. J. Cumming and E. Cumming, *Community Ment. Health* **1**, 135 (1965); A. Farina and K. Ring, *J. Abnorm. Psychol.* **70**, 47 (1965): H. E. Freeman and O. G. Simmons, *The Mental Patient Comes Home* (Wiley, New York, 1963); W J. Johannsen, *Ment. Hygiene* **53**, 218 (1969); A. S. Linsky, *Soc. Psychiat.* **5**, 166 (1970).
13. S. E. Asch, *J. Abnorm. Soc. Psychol.* **41**, 258 (1946); *Social Psychology* (Prentice Hall, New York, 1952).
14. See also I. N. Mensh and J. Wishner, *J. Personality* **16**, 188 (1947); J. Wishner, *Psychol. Rev.* **67**, 96 (1960); J. S. Bruner and R. Tagiuri, in *Handbook of Social Psychology*, G. Lindzey, Ed. (Addison-Wesley, Cambridge, Mass., 1954), vol. 2, pp. 634–654; J. S. Bruner, D. Shapiro, R. Tagiuri, in *Person Perception and Interpersonal Behavior*, R. Tagiuri and L. Petrullo, Eds. (Stanford University Press, Stanford, CA, 1958), pp. 277–288.
15. For an example of a similar self-fulfilling prophecy, in this instance dealing with the "central" trait of intelligence,
see R. Rosenthal and L. Jacobson, *Pygmalion in the Classroom* (Holt, Rinehart & Winston, New York, 1968).
16. E. Zigler and L. Phillips, *J. Abnorm. Soc. Psychol.* **63**, 69 (1961). See also R. K. Freudenberg and J. P. Robertson, *A.M.A. Arch. Neurol. Psychiatr.* **76**, 14 (1956).
17. W. Mischel, *Personality and Assessment* (Wiley, New York, 1968).
18. The most recent and unfortunate instance of this tenet is that of Senator Thomas Eagleton.
19. T. R. Sarbin and J. C. Mancuso, *J. Clin. Consult. Psychol.* **35**, 159 (1970); T. R. Sarbin, *ibid.* **31**, 447 (1967); J. C. Nunnally, Jr., *Popular Conceptions of Mental Health* (Holt, Rinehart & Winston, New York, 1961).
20. A. H. Stanton and M. S. Schwartz, *The Mental Hospital: A Study of Institutional Participation in Psychiatric Illness and Treatment* (Basic, New York, 1954).
21. D. B. Wexler and S. E. Scoville, *Ariz. Law Rev.* **13**, 1 (1971).
22. I thank W. Mischel, E. Orne, and M. S. Rosenhan for comments on an earlier draft of this manuscript.

The author is professor of psychology and law at Stanford University, Stanford, California. Portions of these data were presented to colloquiums of the psychology departments at the University of California at Berkeley and at Santa Barbara; University of Arizona, Tucson; and Harvard University, Cambridge, Massachusetts.

Discussion Questions

1. Do you think it is possible to train clinicians and counselors to overcome errors and biases in their judgment? If so, how would you go about doing so?
2. Is it possible that the misperceptions that occurred in the Rosenhan study on the part of psychiatrists could also occur in other settings, such as courtrooms? What implications would such misconceptions have?
3. In the Rosenhan study, psychiatrists continued to interpret the behavior of normal individuals as consistent with the diagnosis that had been given to the patients. Do you think that real patients, once given a diagnosis, might do the same thing? Would they also interpret their behaviors in light of their diagnosis, even if that diagnosis was wrong?
4. Can you think of times when you have behaved in much the same way as the medical practitioners in the Rosenhan study? Have there been times when you have continued to believe something about another person even though (in retrospect) you had evidence to the contrary?

Suggested Readings

Dawes, R. (1994). *House of cards: Psychology and psychotherapy built on myth.* New York: Free Press. In this interesting book, Dawes critiques many of the assumptions of psychotherapy as well as the methods and expertise of clinicians.

Garb, H. N. (1994). Judgment research: Implications for clinical practice and testimony in court. *Applied and Preventive Psychology, 3,* 173–183. This article suggests that clinicians be cognizant of the way in which they make judgments and decisions and that they be aware of biases that might influence their judgment.

Millon, T. (1975). Reflections on Rosenhan's "On being sane in insane places." *Journal of Abnormal Psychology, 84,* 456–461. This article critiques the Rosenhan study, suggesting that the methodology and design of the study are flawed.

READING 15

A Patient by Any Other Name . . . : Clinician Group Differences in Labeling Bias[1]

Ellen J. Langer and Robert P. Abelson[2] • Yale University

Editors' Introduction

People often label other individuals to help them deal with the volume of information that they must process each day. Labels are essentially cognitive shortcuts that summarize information about other people in just a few words. For example, these labels may reflect a person's membership in particular groups (female, African-American, gay), personality characteristics (extraverted, lazy, intelligent), or social roles (mother, professor, unemployed). Psychologists also use labels, classifying their clients into diagnostic categories such as schizophrenic, narcissistic, or passive-aggressive. Although labels may be useful in summarizing information about a person, they can also be harmful. As Rappaport and Cleary (1980, p. 77) noted, mental health professionals "who label people may often create as much harm as good by the very process of practicing their trade."

A number of studies have examined the consequences of labeling, and many of these have focused on the effects of labeling people as "mentally ill." Most of these studies show that attaching a descriptive label to a person influences other people's perceptions of that individual. For example, in Kelley's (1950) classic study, participants who were informed beforehand that a guest lecturer was "warm" formed a more positive impression of that individual during his lecture than those informed that the instructor was "cold." Participants also interpreted particular behaviors in ways that were consistent with the initial label they had received. In essence, starting with different labels led to different impressions and inferences.

One might think that, because of their training, clinical and counseling psychologists may be relatively immune to the effects of labeling on their perceptions of other people, clients in this case. However, it is not clear that psychologists can fully escape the normal labeling biases that characterize all normal human beings. In fact, Temerlin (1968) found that labeling a person as "psychotic" led psychologists to actually perceive that individual as psychotic.

Furthermore, not all clinicians are trained to avoid the use of labeling to the same degree. Whereas psychologists working from a behaviorist background tend to shy away from classifying patients according to particular diagnostic categories (preferring instead to simply describe their behavior), other therapists, such as those who adopt a psychodynamic approach, use diagnostic labels more extensively.

To study labeling among psychologists, Langer and Abelson used as participants graduate and postgraduate clinicians from programs that were either behaviorally oriented or psychodynamically oriented. Participants in both groups were told that they would watch a segment of a videotaped interview between one of the researchers and a man who had recently interviewed for a job or who was a patient. In fact, all participants watched exactly the same videotape. They then completed a questionnaire examining their perceptions of the person on the videotape. All participants, regardless of their theoretical orientation, evaluated the job interviewee in much the same way. When the videotaped individual was described as a patient, however, ratings differed as a function of participants' clinical orientation. Relative to behaviorally oriented clinicians, psychodynamically oriented clinicians viewed the "patient" as more disturbed. Thus, for the participants with a psychodynamic orientation, thinking that the interviewee was a patient created a cognitive set that influenced how they perceived and evaluated that individual.

The results of this study are both encouraging and discouraging. On one hand, certain types of clinical training do seem to discourage the use of diagnostic categories and labels in forming impressions of patients, as in the case of the behaviorally oriented clinicians. On the other hand, the fact that the judgments of psychodynamically oriented clinicians were affected by the labels suggests that not all biases are automatically eliminated with professional training.

Abstract

The effect of labels on clinicians' judgments was assessed in a 2 × 2 factorial design. Clinicians representing two different schools of thought, behavioral and analytic, viewed a single videotaped interview between a man who had recently applied for a new job and one of the authors. Half of each group was told that the interviewee was a "job applicant," and the remaining half was told that he was a "patient." At the end of the videotape, all clinicians were asked to complete a questionnaire evaluating the interviewee. The interviewee was described as fairly well adjusted by the behavioral therapists regardless of the label supplied. This was not the case, however, for the more traditional therapists. When the interviewee was labeled "patient," he was described as significantly more disturbed than he was when he was labeled "job applicant."

The fact that labels create sets that influence subsequent perception has long been established. Researchers have generally studied these effects by providing different labels and observing the reactions they occasion in their subjects.

Kelley (1950), extending Asch's (1946) work, has shown that by assigning the label warm/cold to a lecturer, one could significantly affect another's perceptions of that person. A more recent study (Huguenard, Sager, & Ferguson, 1970) demonstrated the same result in simulated employment interviews. Along with varying the interviewer's initial set (warm/cold), they also varied the length of the interview (10, 20, or 30 minutes). While the interviewer's initial set significantly affected his after-interview ratings, the length of the interview did not. Thus, the effect of labels is pervasive and not readily overridden by the additional information that may be provided by a prolonged interaction. In another study of this kind (Rapp, 1965), the researcher had pairs of subjects describe a child's behavior. One member of each pair was informed that the child was feeling "under par," while the other was given the opposite label. Their written descriptions of the child's behavior were significantly different in the predicted direction.

Because of its implication in the institutional and social ostracism of a large group of individuals, one of the labels most widely studied is that of the "mental patient" (Braginsky, Braginsky, & Ring, 1969). In a provocative study, Rosenhan (1972) and some of his colleagues entered psychiatric hospitals as pseudopatients. Upon admission under assumed names, they complained of hearing voices. All of the additional information they supplied was veridical. All but one of these pseudopatients was diagnosed as schizophrenic—the exception was labeled manic-depressive. Right after their admission their symptoms ceased, but they were not immediately discharged. Although they were trying to behave as sanely as possible in order to obtain release, the initial label was apparently still influential. When they were finally discharged, the diagnosis was schizophrenia "in remission."

Rothaus, Hanson, Cleveland, and Johnson (1963) asked employment placement interviewers to conduct a typical placement interview with a patient. Prior to the interview, they were given forms regarding the patient's background. Half of these forms were couched in problem-centered terms, and half were couched in mental illness terms. Those interviewers who were set to view the patient in terms of interpersonal problems gave much more positive after-interview ratings. Temerlin (1968) had psychiatrists, clinical psychologists, and graduate students in clinical psychology diagnose a sound-recorded interview after hearing the interviewee described by a prestigious confederate to be "a very interesting man because he looks neurotic, but actually is quite psychotic." Among the different control groups, one diagnosed the tape without prior suggestions and one diagnosed it with the suggestion reversed. The experimental group rated the interviewee as mentally ill significantly more often than did the controls. In addition, 60% of the psychiatrists diagnosed psychosis.

In most of the experiments just described, the investigators provided the different labels and observed the effects on the subjects' behavior, presumably taking precautions to assure that the groups differed only in the label that they were given. Although individual differences in the utilization of labels were not examined, it is reasonable to assume that the prior beliefs or attitudes that one brings to the experimental situation will affect the use of labels. In addition, the explicit training that one has received in regard to the use of labels should also be relevant. Clinicians are supposed to be trained to withhold diagnosis until many cues are utilized. However, Temerlin (1968) has shown that clinicians' judgments are also susceptible to labeling bias effects. Because labels make information processing manageable, their use is certainly adaptive. However, there are times, as in the case of the therapeutic interview, when labels may have the deleterious effect of preventing a relatively objective evaluation. It is therefore of interest to know whether explicit training to avoid the use of such labels would be successful in overcoming this tendency.

In the present experiment, it was hypothesized that the therapeutic orientations of clinicians would influence the effect that labels had on their clinical judgments. In particular, a behavioral orientation toward clinical practice typically includes severe skepticism about the utility of diagnostic categories and labels. Yates (1970), for example, stated:

> One important consequence of the application of the medical model to abnormal behavior was the attempt to derive a diagnostic or classificatory system for the pigeonholing of patients. There are at least three serious objections which can be brought against any such system: it is unreliable; it is invalid; and even if it were both reliable and valid, it would serve no useful purpose. (p. 5)

If clinicians adopt the ideology associated with their training, it would seem likely that behavior therapists would tend not to display labeling effects characterizing the judgments of clinicians who had received more traditional training.

Two groups of therapists with appropriately contrasting training were shown a videotaped interview with a man who had recently applied for a new job. Before viewing the tape, half of the subjects were told that the interviewee was a job applicant, and the other half were told that he was a patient. It was predicted that (a) when the interviewee was labeled "patient" he would in general be perceived as a more disturbed individual than when he was labeled "job applicant," and (b) this labeling bias would be less for the behavior therapists than for the traditional therapists.

Method

Subjects

Forty clinicians associated with university departments known to be either behaviorally or psychodynamically oriented served as subjects. These clinicians were either graduate or postdoctoral clinical students, residents, or faculty members. Twenty-one clinicians from the State University of New York at Stony Brook represented the behavioral bent, and 9 clinicians affiliated with New York University and 10 clinicians affiliated with the School of Psychiatry at Yale University represented the more traditional view. The institutional differences in orientation are clear. The descriptive printed handout given to all Stony Brook applicants states that

> the program ... finds expression in the behavioral point of view toward Clinical Psychology, in general, and the behavior modification approach to therapy in particular. Students seeking training in other orientations would be ill-advised to enter our program.

By contrast, the comparable New York University document makes no mention whatever of the terms "behavioral" or "behavior modification" and gives as a prime objective of the training program, "To familiarize the student with the theories and practice of dynamic psychotherapy." The Yale Psychiatry (not Psychology) Course Bulletin likewise makes no mention of behavior therapy, and in rather eclectic terms speaks of "personality dynamics" and the "treatment of [the] ill person." The question of the conformance of individual subjects to the dominant orientations of their institutions is addressed later. Subjects were randomly assigned to one of two conditions. Ten therapists from Stony Brook, five from New York University, and five from Yale were in the "patient" condition. The remainder were in the "job applicant" condition. The mean age was 28.47 years for the behavior therapists and 29.21 years for the analytic therapists.

Materials

The subjects were recruited for a study designed to evaluate a videotaped interview. The videotape was of an interview by a bearded professor (the second author) of a younger man of about 26 years. The young man was one of several individuals recruited through a newspaper ad offering $10 to someone who had recently applied for a new job and was willing to be interviewed. The interview itself was unstructured, but it centered around the interviewees' feelings and experience relating to his past work. Because clinical interviews very often concern the patient's reactions to or interpretations of his life situation, his occupation in particular (Howard, Orlinsky, & Hill, 1969), it seemed likely that a work-oriented interview between a patient and therapist would not be seen as unusual.

Our stated interest was in the evaluation of the young man, and not in the nature of the interview probes. Therefore, the interviewer's voice was eliminated from the videotape as much as possible. The tape was cut down to the most interesting 15-minute segment, and the result was an authentic, rambling, and autobiographical monologue by the young man describing a number of jobs he had held and dwelling particularly on his conflicts with bureaucratic authorities in his job as a youth worker and during an abortive business enterprise. The life situations described were complex and ambiguous, and the man's style intense, but uncertain, so that he could easily be seen either as sincere and struggling or as confused and troubled.

Procedure

The subjects entered a room in the school with which they were affiliated, were seated, and were read one of the following sets of instructions:

> [Job applicant condition.] Thank you for coming. Lately I've been studying job interviewing. All that I'm going to ask you to do is to view part of a videotaped interview with a man who has recently applied for a new job and then fill out a short questionnaire evaluating the job applicant. The interviewer's voice has been eliminated as much as possible so as not to distract you from focusing on the job applicant.

> [Patient condition.] Thank you for coming. Lately I've been studying patient interviewing. All that I'm going to ask you to do is to view part of a videotaped interview with a patient and then fill out a short questionnaire evaluating the patient. The interviewer's voice has been eliminated as much as possible so as not to distract you from focusing on the patient.

The label assigned to the interviewee constituted the independent variable. The experimenter made the label salient once again at the end of the tape: "Here is the job applicant [patient] evaluation form."

Dependent Measure

The evaluation form was a questionnaire asking for a brief free-response description of the interviewee, his gestures, attitudes, and the factors that probably explained his outlook on life. It also asked what kind of job subjects would recommend for him. Open-ended rather than multiple-choice questions were used so as to make the task most natural and congenial to the clinicians.

These descriptive replies were later quantified by having five graduate student raters, blind to the experimental hypotheses and conditions, rate each of the 40 randomly ordered clinicians' questionnaires on a scale from 1 (very disturbed) to 10 (very well-adjusted) for the clinician's beliefs about the interviewee. The mean interrater correlation over the 40 judgments was .76. The five ratings were averaged to yield a mean adjustment rating for each clinician questionnaire. By Spearman–Brown formula, the reliability of this mean adjustment rating is .94.

Clinician Groupings

To make sure that the therapists affiliated with the different schools indeed held different theoretical orientations, a biographical questionnaire was administered after the completion of the session. Along with questions about the amount of clinical experience they had had to date, the clinicians were asked the label that they would give to the kind of psychotherapy they themselves practiced. All 21 Stony Brook clinicians called themselves behavior therapists, and 17 of the 19 subjects from traditional programs chose an analytic label. (Two from Yale said they practiced behavior therapy as well.)

In addition, the clinicians were asked how strongly they agreed or disagreed with four statements that touch issues of disagreement between schools of therapy. It was presumed that the majority of behavior therapists would agree with the first statement and disagree with the rest,[3] while the reverse would tend to be true for the analytic therapists: (a) If you have cured the symptom you have usually solved the problem; (b) the examination of childhood experience is essential to effective psychotherapy; (c) the official APA Diagnostic Nomenclature for Psychiatric Disorders is helpful to both patient and clinician; (d) most people need some kind of psychotherapeutic help.

By scoring each item on a scale from 0 to 4 (with Item 1 reversed), a 4-item Likert scale score from 0 to 16 was assigned to each clinician. The median score for the 40 subjects was 4.5. Sixteen of the 21 Stony Brook subjects had scores below the median, whereas 15 of the 19 presumed traditionalists had scores above the median. The four exceptions were all in the Yale group, which had a score distribution intermediate between the "classical" New York University group and the "radical" Stony Brook group.

These large group differences in individual attitudes and self-designations (albeit with a few stray cases), combined with the clear institutional differences in theoretical orientation, provide assurance that a group comparison in assessment of the interviewee is a meaningful test of our second hypothesis.

Results

The mean adjustment ratings for all cells are shown in Table 15.1. The New York University and Yale subgroups of traditional therapists are shown separately because it is of interest to know to what extent they were differentially susceptible to a labeling effect.

One evident tendency in the table is that when the interviewee is labeled job applicant, there is not much difference in mean adjustment ratings by clinicians at the three schools. However, the patient label seems to produce sharp differential effects. For both traditional groups, the means are on the "disturbed" side of the midpoint of the 1–10 adjustment scale: the Yale mean of 4.80 slightly so and the New York University mean of 2.40 very much so.

The complete analysis of variance of the data for Table 15.1 is shown in Table 15.2. The five degrees of freedom between cells are decomposed into five single degrees of freedom contrasts—one for label, one for the main effect of training (behavioral vs. traditional), one for subgroup within traditional (Yale vs. New York University), one for the Label × Training interaction, and one for the Label × Subgroup interaction. From the standpoint of our hypotheses, the crucial contrast is the Label × Training interaction: Do the traditional clinicians generate a significantly bigger adjustment difference between job applicant and patient than do the behavioral clinicians? The answer is yes ($F = 4.75, p < .05$). The differential in labeling effect between Yale and New York University subgroups of traditionalists is, on the other hand, not significant ($F = 1.29, p > .25$).

TABLE 15.1. Mean Adjustment Rating by Interviewee Label and Clinician Group

	Interviewee label	
Clinical group	Job applicant	Patient
Behavior therapist		
Stony Brook	6.26	5.98
n	10	11
Traditional		
Yale	6.52	4.80
n	5	4
NYU	5.88	2.40
n	5	5

TABLE 15.2. Analysis of Variance of Mean Adjustment Ratings

Source	df	MS	F
Label (A)	1	28.85	10.26***
Clinicians (B)			
Behavioral vs. traditional (B1)	1	14.76	5.25**
Subgroup of traditionals (B2)	1	10.87	3.87*
A × B			
A × B1	1	13.34	4.75**
A × B2	1	3.64	1.29
Within cells	34	2.81	

*$p < .10$.
**$p < .05$.
***$p < .01$.

A slightly different way of looking at labeling bias is to take the difference in mean adjustment ratings for job applicant and patient in each of the three schools in the study (Stony Brook, .28; Yale, 1.72; New York University, 3.48). It is possible, taking appropriate account of the different Ns in the six cells, to apply a Tukey multiple-comparisons test (Winer, 1962) to these differences. The outcome of this test is that the New York University subgroup was significantly more susceptible to labeling bias than the Stony Brook group ($q = 3.51$; $df = 3/34$, $p < .05$). The Yale subgroup, intermediate to the other two, cannot be declared significantly different from either on these small sample sizes.

Discussion

There is far too much information surrounding any situation for any individual to process more than a small fraction of it. Labels provide one vehicle through which the input may be organized. They serve as categories or sets that, in addition to structuring the previous input, determine what further information is attended to. Thus, by assigning different labels (in this case "job applicant" or "patient"), different people may be led to view this same event in vastly disparate ways.

In the study just described, all of the subjects saw the same videotaped interview. Yet when asked to describe the interviewee, the behavior therapists said he was "realistic"; "unassertive"; "fairly sincere, enthusiastic, attractive appearance"; "pleasant, easy manner of speaking"; "relatively bright, but unable to assert himself"; "appeared responsible in interview." The analytic therapists who saw a job applicant called him "attractive and conventional looking"; "candid and innovative"; "ordinary, straightforward"; "upstanding, middle-class citizen type, but more like a hard hat"; "probably of lower- or blue-collar class origins"; "middle-class protestant ethic orientation; fairly open—somewhat ingenious." The analytic therapists that saw a patient described him as a "tight, defensive person . . . conflict over homosexuality"; "dependent, passive-aggressive"; "frightened of his own aggressive impulses"; "fairly bright, but tries to seem brighter than he is . . . impulsivity shows through his rigidity"; "passive, dependent type"; "considerable hostility, repressed or channeled."

The fact that the different labels set the analytic therapists to look for very different behaviors may be further exemplified by reviewing typical responses to the question, "What do you think might explain Mr. Smith's outlook on life? Do you think he is realistic?"

Analytic therapists viewing a patient said: "Doesn't seem to be realistic because he seems to use denial (and rationalization and intellectualization) to center his problems in situations and other people," "seems afraid of his own drives, motives . . . outlook not based on realities of 'objective world,' " "anxiety about his ability and adequacy," "basically fear of his aggressive drives and in particular as they are related to his fear of women."

Those analytic therapists viewing a job applicant said: "His attitudes are consistent with a large subculture in the U.S. . . . the silent majority"; "he seems fairly realistic," "fairly reality oriented; recognizes injustices of large systems but doesn't seem to think he can individually do anything to change them"; "realistic to some degree, he knows how to conform but finds it difficult"; "he seems to be perceptive and realistic about politicians"; "values capitalist system."

Behavior therapists given either label respond very much like the latter group of analytic therapists: "His previous experience working in bureaucratic organizations might account for his distrust of authority. . . . He is probably realistic"; "his desire to be a successful businessman may have been partly a function of the business orientation of his friends and family"; "his negative attitudes probably result from the frustrations of working in backward correctional or educational institutions"; "he seems fairly realistic and apparently wants to do something to help the kids he's working with"; "his pessimism is realistic"; "don't know what his outlook on life is, except that he thinks people should be more involved in their work, and that is realistic."

The present research does not tell us why the behavior therapists were apparently immune to the biasing effects of the mere label patient versus job applicant. Perhaps they tended to focus so heavily on the manifest behaviors in the interview that they barely even attended to background information such as labels; more likely, they actively noted the label patient but consciously discounted its relevance because their training explicitly encourages such discounting. Likewise, we do not know how the analytic therapists succumbed to the labeling effect, whether by using the patient label to filter differentially the variety of cues on the tape or simply by superimposing their general concept of a sick person on the particular concept of this person gleaned from the tape. Whichever the case, it is interesting that the New York University group, trained (or self-selected) to subscribe more completely to the classical doctrine of mental illness than the Yale group, is more extreme in its susceptibility to the labeling effect. Our results are apparently sensitive to the particulars of different university training programs, although our sample of three programs is obviously quite limited.

In practical terms, the labeling bias may have unfortunate consequences whatever the specific details of its operation. Once an individual enters a therapist's office for consultation, he has labeled himself "patient." From the very start of the session, the orientation of the conversation may be quite negative. The patient discusses all the negative things he said, did, thought, and felt. The therapist then discusses or thinks about what is wrong with the patient's behavior, cognitions, and feelings. The therapist's negative expectations in turn may affect the patient's view of his own difficulties, thereby possibly locking the interaction into a self-fulfilling gloomy prophecy. As in the study presented here, if the therapist were not given the label "patient," he would see a very different range of behaviors or attribute the given behaviors to factors other than the patient's "illness." He might, for example, attribute the loss of a prior job by the interviewee to economic conditions on a national or state level, rather than to the interviewee's emotional problems. This factor was indeed often taken into account when "Mr. Smith" was described as a job applicant rather than as a patient.

Another way of viewing the present results, of course, is that the person on the tape did indeed bare deep underlying problems to which the behavior therapists were not sensitive and that the traditional therapists only looked for when there was good reason, that is, when the individual was presumably a patient. Because the person being discussed was able to cope with his environment and was in fact not a patient, this alternative seems to the present authors not too satisfactory.

Despite the questionable light in which the analytic therapist group was cast in the present study, one strongly suspects that conditions might be arranged wherein the behavior therapists would fall into some kind of error, as much as the traditionalists. No single type of orientation toward clinical training is likely to avoid all types of biases or blind spots. In any case, all we can claim to have shown is that the behavior therapists avoid the particular kind of bias in which the superficial cue "patient" produces drastically negative interpretations, even when an extended visual and verbal segment filled with personal cues is available.

NOTES

1. This research was conducted while the first author was a National Institute of Mental Health predoctoral fellow (1 FO1 MH 54544-01).
2. The authors are very grateful to those persons who made the necessary arrangements for us to conduct the present study. Our thanks are also extended to Barry Cook for his technical advice.
3. As it turned out, Item 2 on childhood experiences was by far the most discriminating of the four items, although all yielded results in the anticipated direction.

REFERENCES

Asch, S. E. (1946). Forming impressions of personality. *Journal of Abnormal and Social Psychology, 41,* 258–290.

Braginsky, B., Braginsky, D., & Ring, K. L. (1969). *Methods of madness: The mental hospital as a last resort.* New York: Holt, Rinehart & Winston.

Kelley, H. H. (1950). The warm-cold variable in first impressions of persons. *Journal of Personality, 18,* 431–439.

Howard, K. I., Orlinsky, D. E., & Hill, J. A. (1969). Context of dialogue in psychotherapy. *Journal of Counseling Psychology, 16,* 396–404.

Huguenard, T., Sager, E. B., & Ferguson, L. W. (1970). Interview time, interview set, and interview outcome. *Perceptual and Motor Skills, 31,* 831–836.

Rapp, D. W. (1965). *Detection of observer bias in the written record.* Unpublished manuscript, University of Georgia. Cited in Rosenthal, R. (1966). *Experimenter effects in behavioral research* (p. 21). New York: Appleton-Century-Crofts.

Rosenhan, D. L. (1973). On being sane in insane places. *Science, 179,* 250–257.

Rothaus, P., Hanson, P. G., Cleveland, S. E., & Johnson, D. L. (1963). Describing hospitalization: A dilemma. *American Psychologist, 18,* 85–89.

Temerlin, M. K. (1968). Suggestion effects in psychiatric diagnosis. *Journal of Nervous and Mental Disease, 147,* 349–359.

Winer, B. J. (1962). *Statistical principles in experimental design.* New York: McGraw-Hill.

Yates, A. J. (1970). *Behavior therapy.* New York: Wiley.

Discussion Questions

1. This study looked at the effects of labeling someone as mentally ill. What effects do you think labeling has within the educational system? For example, what, if any, effects would there be of labeling a kid as "delayed" or "learning disabled"?
2. Why do labels affect how people interpret all other information they received about another person? What social psychological processes are involved in the labeling bias?
3. What do you think it was about the training of behaviorally oriented clinicians in the present study that made them less susceptible to the effects of labeling?
4. What role do you think being labeled as "mentally ill" has on the patient himself or herself?

Suggested Readings

Kelley, H. H. (1950). The warm–cold variable in first impressions of persons. *Journal of Personality, 18,* 431–439. This classic study shows how the effects of receiving information about another person prior to meeting them can influence how one perceives that person upon actually meeting them.

Penn, D. L., & Nowlin-Drummond, A. (2001). Politically correct labels and schizophrenia: A rose by any other name? *Schizophrenia Bulletin, 27,* 197–203. This article discusses the ways in which information can influence people's attitudes toward and reactions to particular individuals.

Temerlin, M. K. (1968). Suggestion effects in psychiatric diagnosis. *Journal of Nervous and Mental Disease, 147,* 349–359. This interesting study illustrates that diagnosing patients is merely an act of labeling.

Wright, B. A. (1991). Labeling: The need for greater person–environment individuation. In C. R. Snyder & D. R. Forsyth (Eds.), *Handbook of social and clinical psychology: The health perspective* (pp. 469–487). New York: Pergamon. This chapter reviews the literature on labeling and argues for a new perspective in clinical psychology that emphasizes positive features of the client and focuses on environmental factors involved in diagnosis and treatment.

READING 16

When Counselors Confirm: A Functional Analysis

John Copeland • Information Resources
Mark Snyder • University of Minnesota, Twin Cities

Editors' Introduction

Readings 14 and 15 focus on the fact that psychologists' professional judgments may be biased by their preconceptions about a particular individual. Such findings raise two important questions: Why do psychologists' initial perceptions of a client exert such a strong influence on their later perceptions and diagnoses, and what effect do these initial perceptions have on the client? The article by John Copeland and Mark Snyder addresses these two questions.

One reason that initial impressions affect later judgments is that people interpret information they receive about a person in light of the impressions they already have of him or her. For example, if you learned that John teased Mary, you would interpret John's behavior differently if your impression was that John was a kind and playful person than if you thought he was cold and cruel. Furthermore, when people seek information about another person, they search in a manner that is biased toward supporting their initial impression. If you were trying to find out if John was kind and playful, you might ask other people whether they had ever seen John kid around, but if you thought he was cruel, you might ask others if John was ever mean. The way in which you asked for information would probably affect the answers that you obtained. Research by Wilson Dallas and Baron (1985) showed that therapists demonstrate this same hypothesis-confirming bias when they try to learn about other people. They seek information that biases what they learn in the direction of their initial perceptions.

These initial expectations may then become a self-fulfilling prophecy through the process of behavioral confirmation. Research shows that people sometimes come to behave consistently with another person's perceptions of them (even if they don't know what that person's perceptions are). Behavioral confirmation occurs because the person's initial perception leads him or her to treat the individual in a particular way, which then elicits behavior that is consistent with the person's initial perception. If you thought John was kind and playful, your behavior would probably lead him to respond pleasantly, thereby confirming your impression. If, however, you thought he was cold and cruel, you might act more aloof, thus leading him to respond more coolly toward you.

Copeland and Snyder studied these processes in the context of a peer counseling session. Their study showed that when participants were instructed to form a diagnosis of a client, they perceived these clients in a way that was consistent with the initial expectation they had received. Furthermore, they inadvertently led the clients to behave in ways that confirmed their initial impression.

Some practitioners dismiss the results of studies such as this one in which the participants are students rather than actual practitioners. Although we must always question the generalizability of results obtained in analogue studies such as this, we should not be too quick to dismiss them. Conducting studies under controlled laboratory conditions can eliminate the effects of variables that might contaminate a study that was run during real counseling sessions. When we find that certain processes occur in controlled experiments, we must consider the possibility that they also occur outside the laboratory.

Abstract

To investigate the motivational moderators of behavioral confirmation in a psychotherapeutic environment, the authors performed a functional analysis on counselors' behavior. Counselors' concerns with diagnosis and rapport building were identified as possible functions that might lead to expectation-confirming client behavior. Students randomly assigned to the role of either counselor or client engaged in a face-to-face, videotaped discussion. Prior to the discussion, counselors received an expectation suggesting that the client was either characteristically extroverted or introverted. Orthogonal to the expectation, counselors received either no specific discussion instructions, instructions to form a diagnosis, or instructions to establish rapport. Results indicated that only counselors motivated by diagnostic concerns elicited behavioral confirmation. Implications of therapeutic motivations are discussed, as is the usefulness of a functional approach to social psychological phenomena.

As an important prerequisite for productive psychotherapy, counselors generally attempt to achieve an accurate assessment of a client's psychological status. As social information processors, however, therapists can find themselves prone to some of the same social perception and inferential errors as laypersons—errors that have been a popular topic of study in social psychology for some time (Asch, 1946; Bruner & Tagiuri, 1954). Research on clinical inference processes reveals that impressions of clients can be formed very rapidly (Gauron & Dickinson, 1969; Meehl, 1960; Rubin & Shontz, 1960) and can be influenced by variables of which therapists are unaware (Gauron & Dickinson, 1966). This is not to say that therapists' impressions of clients are likely to be incorrect, but simply that therapists—as social information processors—must come to grips with the same sorts of judgmental errors that affect all individuals (for a review of inferential processes in psychotherapy, see Murray & Abramson, 1983).

One potentially deleterious consequence of therapists' inferential errors occurs when clients actually come to behave in ways consistent with therapists' erroneous impressions. This *behavioral confirmation* effect can frequently result to at least some degree, and it has been the focus of a great deal of nonclinical research in psychology (Jussim, 1986; Miller & Turnbull, 1986; Rosenthal, 1974; Snyder, 1984). Although important boundary conditions to the phenomenon exist (Jussim, 1991), persons with expectations (often called perceivers) often behave toward the targets of those expectations in ways that bolster perceivers' expectation-consistent impressions (perceptual confirmation) and elicit expectation-confirming behavior from targets (behavioral confirmation).

In one study, Snyder, Tanke, and Berscheid (1977) gave men one of two types of photographs before a conversation with female partners. The men believed the women in the photos were their conversation partners when, in fact, the pictures were randomly assigned and portrayed the women as either physically attractive or unattractive. Snyder, Tanke, and Berscheid wondered whether a "what is beautiful is good" stereotype would influence participants' behavior during the conversations. At the conclusions of the conversations, not only did the men given an attractive photograph form more positive impressions than men given an unattractive photograph (perceptual confirmation), but the women labeled as attractive also behaved in a more warm and friendly manner than the women labeled as unattractive (behavioral confirmation). Independent judges' ratings indicated that behavioral confirmation was effected through the differential behavior of the men in the two experimental conditions. Men given an attractive photograph, expecting to interact with friendly women, were friendly themselves, more so than men given an unattractive photo, and the women reciprocated this behavior.

The extent to which such confirmatory processes occur in psychotherapeutic environments has been a question of interest to social psychologists and therapists alike (Harris & Rosenthal, 1986; Leary & Miller, 1986; Snyder & Thomsen, 1988; Wilson Dallas & Baron, 1985). Snyder and Thomsen (1988), in their review, pointed out that therapeutic environments are particularly ripe for expectation-confirming interactions. First, as therapists test their hypotheses about the diagnostic categories that might be appropriate for their clients' problems, the manner in which they test those hypotheses may guide the outcome in a hypothesis-consistent direction. Then, after these assessments have been made, as the therapists seek to understand the origins of the disorder, they may preferentially look for evidence in clients' life histories that reinforce therapists' etiologic beliefs. Finally, expectation confirmation may occur during treatment, as therapists monitor the effectiveness of the particular interventions they believe to be most beneficial and selectively attend to any evidence supporting those beliefs.

Evidence of confirmatory effects in therapeutic encounters comes from a number of studies. Wilson Dallas and Baron (1985) asked therapists to interview college students to test hypotheses about them. Therapists received information prior to their interviews indicating that the students were either introverted or extroverted. Therapists chose to ask questions that preferentially probed for expectation-confirming evidence from their clients; when evaluating an ostensibly introverted client, therapists sought evidence of introversion and when evaluating an ostensibly extroverted client, therapists sought evidence of extroversion. Results further indicated that the college students provided behavioral confirmation of therapists' hypotheses during the interviews; students labeled as introverts behaved in a more introverted manner than students labeled as extroverts.

Harris and Rosenthal (1986) examined personality characteristics of counselors and clients as moderators of behavioral confirmation. In their study, students completed a battery of personality measures prior to a 20-minute role-playing session in which they were randomly assigned the role of either peer counselor or client. Student counselors received information before the session indicating that their clients were either introverted or extroverted. Results indicated that female counselors were more likely to produce a confirming effect in their clients than male counselors, as were counselors who scored higher on a measure of dogmatism.

Although these studies provide evidence of an expectation-confirming tendency in counselors' behavior, other studies have failed to produce such an effect. Strohmer and his colleagues (Strohmer & Chiodo, 1984; Strohmer & Newman, 1983) found that counselors do not always seek to confirm their impressions of clients. In their studies, counselors did not seek to preferentially confirm the experimental expectations given to them. However, the extent to which counselors formed expectation-confirming impressions of their clients and the extent of clients' behavioral confirmation were not assessed, prohibiting an actual assessment of either perceptual or behavioral confirmation.

Understanding when and why counselors are likely to elicit behavioral confirmation from their clients might be facilitated, we suggest, through a functional analysis of counselors' behavior in therapeutic settings. A functional analysis focuses on the purposes, reasons, and motivations that underlie psychological phenomena; additionally, a functional analysis deals with how individuals' needs, plans, and goals are served by their beliefs and actions based on those beliefs (e.g., Snyder, 1993). Functionally oriented theoretical analyses of behavioral confirmation have suggested motives that may serve as important moderators of the phenomenon (Snyder, 1992); accordingly, in the current setting, a functional analysis would examine the needs, plans, and goals being served for counselors when they interact with clients.

One function that might be served by counselors' behavior, especially during initial encounters with clients, is the assessment or diagnosis of clients' mental status. For example, counselors must account for one client's chronic depression or understand why another client abhors social interaction. Although some psychotherapists downplay the importance of client assessment (e.g., those adopting the humanistic-existential traditions), most therapeutic relationships begin with at least some attempts at determining the client's state of mind (Burke, 1989). These beliefs are very influential in determining the type of intervention to be employed and its probability of success (Berman, 1979; Berman & Wenzlaff, 1983). From this perspective, counselors may act as if their expectations are true because of the sense of client predictability and intervention direction such functional behaviors give them. If behavioral confirmation of counselors' expectations occurs, it then serves to bolster counselors' beliefs about their clients and possible interventions.

A second function that may be served by counselors' behavior is the establishment of rapport with their clients. At a minimal level, rapport exists when clients feel comfortable with their counselors, and in most therapeutic traditions, the achievement of rapport is a necessary first step toward effective treatment (Burke, 1989; MacKinnon & Yudofsky, 1991). From this perspective, counselors may behave as if their expectations are true because they believe that doing so will facilitate the establishment of rapport with their clients. By trying to get along well with the type of people they believe their clients to be, counselors may attempt to make clients feel at ease and open to discussion, intervention, and, unfortunately, behavioral confirmation.

Although efforts at diagnosis and rapport establishment may both occur in the interview process, they are conceptually distinct objectives. Additionally, there may be situations in which the two functions are at odds with each other. Sometimes, effecting a comfortable, open relationship with a client may not allow for much in the way of an assessment. Similarly, understanding a client's personal problems may necessitate a less-than-pleasant interaction. For these reasons, we decided to investigate the role of each function independently in the interview process.

To determine whether these motivational functions affect a counselor's tendency to elicit behavioral confirmation from a client, college students randomly assigned to the role of either counselor-perceivers or client-targets participated in a face-to-face peer counseling interview. We employed a *strategy of addition*, wherein we began with a minimally defined setting in which students were randomly assigned the roles of either peer counselors or clients; without being given any additional specific motivational instructions, counselors were asked to interview clients. To this setting, we then systematically added elements designed to engage motivations related to diagnosis or rapport-building functions (cf. Snyder & Haugen, in press). Prior to the interview, counselors were given ostensible personality information about their clients, leading them to expect that their clients were either extroverts or introverts. Independent of the personality information, counselors were also given a set of instructions designed to engage either a diagnostic function, a rapport function, or neither of the two functions (no special instructions were given here). Clients always received the same basic instructions and no expectation-inducing information was delivered to them.

Videotapes were made of the participants' interactions and were coded for evidence of behavioral confirmation. In this case, behavioral confirmation would be evident if clients who were believed to be introverted in fact acted in a more quiet, withdrawn, and passive manner relative to their ostensibly extroverted counterparts. To the extent that counselor motivations are functionally linked to expectation confirmation, we expected to find evidence of the phenomenon only in those conditions in which perceivers' behavior served the relevant functions. Thus, in the basic situation, in which specific motivations were not made salient to our perceiver-counselors, we did not expect to find evidence of expectation confirmation (cf. Snyder & Haugen, in press).

Although this examination was largely exploratory in nature, we did predict that, insofar as the diagnosis and rapport motivations might facilitate counselors' tendencies to elicit behavioral confirmation from their clients, we would see relatively more behavioral confirmation in those conditions than in the basic condition. That is, if counselors' diagnosis motivations indeed lead to expectation-confirming outcomes, then we should see behavioral confirmation when we arouse counselors' concerns with arriving at a diagnosis of their clients. On the other hand, if counselors preoccupied with establishing rapport are likely to elicit behavioral confirmation, we should see behavioral confirmation when we make rapport-building salient. To the extent that both types of motives lead to confirmatory outcomes independent of each other, we should see behavioral confirmation in both functional conditions. If neither of the two functions is related to counselors' tendencies to engage in expectation-confirming interactions with clients, behavioral confirmation should not occur in either of the two functional conditions.

Method

Participants

A total of 118 undergraduates from the University of Minnesota, Twin Cities (68 women and 50 men), agreed to participate in what was billed as a peer counseling study; they received either $6.00 or extra credit for their introductory psychology course. Participants were scheduled in same-sex pairs. The data from one dyad of women were discarded when it was discovered that the participants knew each other before the experiment.[1]

Materials and Procedure

Participants arrived at staggered times to two experimental rooms. Briefed separately, the participants were informed by two experimenters that the purpose of the research was to study the "kinds of discussions that occur in peer counseling situations" and that each participant would be involved in a peer counseling discussion with another student.[2]

One participant in each dyad, randomly assigned to the role of client, spent the remaining time before the discussion contemplating "some current concerns or problems" for the discussion. Additionally, clients completed a demographic questionnaire during this time.

The participants randomly assigned to the role of peer counselors received further instructions designed to engage a particular psychological function for their discussions. Experimenters informed them that peer counselors sometimes have expectations of clients even before they meet them. Additionally, peer counselors randomly assigned to the diagnosis condition learned that although many strategies can be employed when talking with clients, in the current discussion, they were to "find out the ways the client is and is not like what they expected them to be." Experimenters asked these counselors to "form a diagnosis of the client, finding out what personality traits [their clients possessed]," and to "form a stable and predictable impression of the client." Discussions following such a strategy, peer counselors learned, were often very effective.

Peer counselors randomly assigned to the rapport condition received instructions emphasizing a coordinated, enjoyable interaction between the counselor and the client. These participants learned that their expectations of their clients should be employed "to get along with the type of person the client might be . . . even taking your cues from the client to allow the client to be more like herself or himself." Experimenters instructed these counselors to have a smooth and pleasant discussion and to "establish a rapport" between themselves and their clients. Discussions following such a strategy, peer counselors learned, were often very effective.

Finally, experimenters gave no special motivational instructions to peer counselors in the basic condition. Like the other peer counselors, participants in this condition understood that peer counselors sometimes have expectations of their clients and that these expectations "can be helpful in guiding the discussions."

Independent of these functional instructions, peer counselors received information designed to establish a particular expectation about their clients. Experimenters informed peer counselors that their discussions would be facilitated with some "background information" about their clients and gave counselors a folder that contained material about their clients. From a Client Personality Information Sheet, the counselor read the client's name and a written synopsis of three personality tests ostensibly completed by the client. Although the actual names of clients were provided, the personality information was randomly assigned to each counselor. In the extrovert condition, counselors read that although their clients may not always act this way, our personality tests indicate that s/he is outgoing, socially skilled and characteristically extroverted. However, like many people with this type of personality, s/he has a tendency to discuss things that others feel may be too personal for "casual" conversation.

In the introvert condition, counselors read that although their clients "may not always act this way, our personality tests indicate that s/he is quiet, reserved, and characteristically introverted. Like many people with this type of personality, s/he has a tendency to be too impersonal and withdrawn during 'casual' conversation."

Upon presenting this information, experimenters probed counselors for questions regarding procedure and then left the room to give counselors time to prepare for the discussion. Approximately 5 minutes after leaving the room, a different experimenter introduced the client to the counselor and informed them that the discussion would last approximately 15 minutes. At that time, the counselor and client would again be separated and asked to complete some final questionnaires.

Discussions were videotaped through a one-way mirror. For consistency in subsequent coding of tapes, counselors always sat on one side of the $6' \times 6'$ discussion table in the middle of the room (right side of the picture) and clients always sat on the other (left side of the picture). When the allotted time had elapsed, the second experimenter returned to escort the client to a different room and debriefed the client.

Counselors then completed material used to assess the extent to which they perceived clients in an expectation-confirming light (i.e., perceptual confirmation). Counselors indicated their impressions of clients on a number of 7-point bipolar adjective scales with one trait at each endpoint. This measure presented 10 pairs of traits related to the experimentally delivered expectations (extroverted–introverted; talkative–quiet; revealing–concealing; outgoing–reserved; involved–apathetic; personal–impersonal; enthusiastic–unenthusiastic; exciting–dull; warm–cold; socially skilled–socially unskilled) and 10 pairs of additional traits believed to be irrelevant to the expectations (weak willed–strong willed; happy–sad; intelligent–unintelligent; high self-esteem–low self-esteem; awkward–poised; flexible–rigid; kind–unkind; well adjusted–poorly adjusted; stable–unstable; trustworthy–untrustworthy).

Counselors also completed self-perception measures indicating how much effort they gave to accomplish a number of different discussion objectives. Each objective received a rating on a 7-point Likert-type scale that ranged from 1 (*I did not try very hard*) to 7 (*I tried very hard*). The following eight questions assessed the counselors' diagnostic self-perceptions: To what extent did you try to arrive at a diagnosis of your client? To what extent did you try to get a clear idea of who your client is? To what extent did you try to check out your first impressions of your client? To what extent did you try to imagine what your client would be like in other situations outside the discussion? To what extent did you try to ask a lot of questions? To what extent did you try to ask questions about your client's personality? To what extent did you try to find out if your first impressions of your client were correct? To what extent did the questions you asked test hunches that you had about your client? The following eight questions assessed the counselors' rapport-building self-perceptions: To what extent did you try to get along with your client? To what extent did you try to establish rapport with your client? To what extent did you try to be compatible with your client? To what extent did you try to say things that you thought your client would like? To what extent did you talk about things that you thought your client would be interested in talking about? To what extent did you try to avoid topics that you thought your partner might not want to talk about? To what extent did you try to ask questions related to positive topics? To what extent did you try to be very friendly? Upon completion of their ratings, counselors were debriefed.

Coding of Videotapes

To assess the extent to which clients actually behaved in expectation-consistent ways (i.e., the extent of behavioral confirmation), two judges, blind to experimental conditions, viewed the videotapes. Because counselor–client discussions occurred face-to-face and because only a single camera was used to record the conversations, a sheet of black construction paper was placed on the video screen so that judges could see only the client. Although counselors' voices could still be heard, judges were instructed to focus solely on the clients. Judges then rated clients on adjective scales similar to those used by counselors but with only five pairs of expectation-irrelevant traits.

A second set of two judges viewed the counselors. Again, a sheet of black construction paper was placed on the video screen so that judges could see only the counselor. Judges then indicated on 7-point Likert-type scales (ranging from 1 to 7) how much effort counselors expended at various discussion tasks; higher ratings indicated greater effort. The following five questions assessed the counselors' diagnostic efforts: To what extent did the counselor ask questions? To what extent did the counselor spend time talking? To what extent did the counselor initiate conversation? How inquisitive was the counselor? To what extent did the counselor get to know the client? The following five questions assessed the counselors' efforts at establishing rapport with the clients: To what extent did the counselor get along with the client? To what extent did the counselor spend time listening to the client? To what extent did the counselor spend time responding to the client's probes? How friendly was the counselor? How interested was the counselor in the client?

Results

Perceptual Confirmation

To assess the extent to which counselors formed expectation-confirming impressions of their clients, we analyzed counselors' responses to the 20 pairs of trait ratings. First, we formed a composite score based on counselors' responses to the 10 pairs of expectation-relevant traits. However, because of the low reliability of the scale based on all 10 items, 3 items (exciting–dull, enthusiastic–unenthusiastic, warm–cold) were discarded, yielding a scale whose internal consistency was more acceptable (Cronbach's alpha = .85) and whose scores could range from 7 to 49 (higher scores indicated more extroverted impressions of the clients). Then, we formed a second composite score by summing their ratings on each of the 10 pairs of expectation-irrelevant traits. Scores on this composite could range from 10 to 70, and higher scores indicated a more positive overall impression. The internal consistency of this scale was acceptable, producing a Cronbach's alpha of .80. Finally, we performed a linear transformation on the expectation-irrelevant composite scores to give them a range equal to that of the expectation-relevant composite scores (i.e., 7 to 49).

The two sets of composite scores were entered as the dependent variables in a $2 \times 3 \times 2 \times 2$ (Expectation $\times$ Function $\times$ Sex $\times$ Composite)

MANOVA with repeated measures on the last factor. This analysis revealed a significant effect for sex: Female peer counselors produced higher ratings overall ($M = 33.5$, $SD = 3.5$) than did male counselors ($M = 32.8$, $SD = 3.9$), $F(1, 46) = 4.64$, $p < .05$. There was also a significant main effect for the repeated measure, with higher scores overall on the expectation-relevant composite ($M = 33.9$, $SD = 7.9$) than on the expectation-irrelevant composite ($M = 31.2$, $SD = 3.4$).

This main effect was qualified, however, by a significant Expectation × Function × Composite interaction, $F(2, 46) = 5.07$, $p < .05$. Follow-up univariate ANOVAs on each of the composite scales indicated that although there were no significant differences in the expectation-irrelevant composite scores as a function of expectation, function, or sex (all $Fs < 1.621$, ns), there were differences on the expectation-relevant composite. First, the main effect for sex obtained, $F(1, 46) = 4.791$, $p < .05$; female counselors formed more extroverted impressions of their clients ($M = 35.8$, $SD = 2.5$) than did their male counterparts ($M = 31.8$, $SD = 3.3$). Second, the analysis also yielded a significant Expectation × Function interaction, $F(2, 46) = 4.331$, $p < .05$. Means and standard deviations for the six conditions are provided in Table 16.1.

Simple effects analyses indicated that counselors in the diagnosis condition demonstrated perceptual confirmation. In this condition, counselors given an extrovert expectation formed more extroverted impressions of their clients than counselors given an introvert expectation, $F(1, 46) = 5.309$, $p < .05$. However, counselors in the basic and rapport conditions formed impressions that, although not statistically significant, were more consistent with perceptual disconfirmation, $Fs < 2.510$, ns. In these conditions, ostensibly intro-

TABLE 16.1. Peer Counselors' Expectancy-Relevant Composite Means (and Standard Deviations)

Expectation	Functional condition		
	Basic	Diagnosis	Rapport
Extrovert	32.7 (7.2)	34.9 (4.6)	33.7 (9.2)
Introvert	36.4 (8.7)	27.9 (6.8)	37.8 (8.5)

Note. Composite mean ratings could range from 7 to 49; higher numbers indicate more extroverted impressions of clients.

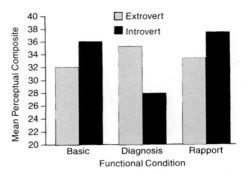

FIGURE 16.1 ■ Peer counselors' expectancy-relevant impressions of clients.

verted clients were seen by counselors as more extroverted than the ostensibly extroverted clients. This interaction is presented in Figure 16.1.

Behavioral Confirmation

To assess the extent to which clients actually behaved in expectation-confirming ways, we analyzed judges' impression ratings of clients. First, we formed a composite index of expectation-relevant traits by summing judges' ratings on the 10 expectation-relevant adjective pairs. Interrater reliability of this composite, as indexed by the correlation between judges' ratings across these traits, was good ($r = .89$) and the internal consistency of this scale was acceptable (Cronbach's alpha = .85). Composite scores could range from 10 to 70, and higher scores indicated relatively more extroverted client behavior. Next, we formed a similar composite of expectation-irrelevant traits by summing judges' ratings on the five expectation-irrelevant adjective pairs. Again, interrater reliability was good ($r = .82$) and the internal consistency of this composite was also acceptable (Cronbach's alpha = .79). Scores on this composite could range from 5 to 35, and higher scores indicated relatively more socially desirable behavior. Finally, to equate the range of scores for both scales, a linear transformation was performed on the expectation-relevant composite.

The two composite scores were then entered as the dependent variables in a 2 × 3 × 2 × 2 (Expectation × Function × Sex × Composite) MANOVA with repeated measures on the last factor. A marginally significant Expectation × Function × Composite interaction obtained, $F(2, 46) = 2.587$, $p =$

.08. A follow-up univariate ANOVA on the expectation-irrelevant composite yielded no significant differences as a function of any of the experimental variables or subject sex, $Fs < 1.00$, ns. A follow-up univariate ANOVA on the expectation-relevant composite did result in a significant Expectation × Function interaction, $F(2, 46) = 5.205$, $p < .01$ (see Figure 16.2).

Simple effects analyses revealed that behavioral confirmation occurred in the diagnosis condition, $F(1, 46) = 7.143$, $p < .05$. In this condition, clients whose counselors were given an extrovert expectation exhibited more extroverted behavior than clients whose counselors were given an introvert expectation. In the other two functional conditions, however, although not statistically significant, the results were more consistent with a pattern of behavioral disconfirmation. In both the basic and rapport conditions, ostensibly introverted clients were seen by judges as behaving in a more extroverted manner than ostensibly extroverted clients. Composite means and standard deviations for all six conditions are presented in Table 16.2.

Counselors' (Perceivers') Behavior and Self-Perceptions

To examine counselors' self-perceptions regarding their interview behavior, we analyzed their responses on the 16 self-perception questions. Because counselors' responses to the eight diagnosis and eight rapport questions demonstrated a good degree of consistency (Cronbach's alphas of .86 and .85, respectively), these responses were summed to create two indexes that served as our manipulation checks. Scores on each of these in-

TABLE 16.2. Clients' Expectancy-Relevant Composite Behavior Means (and Standard Deviations)

Expectation	Functional condition		
	Basic	Diagnosis	Rapport
Extrovert	22.9	24.4	23.0
	(1.7)	(1.4)	(2.0)
Introvert	23.8	22.1	24.4
	(2.4)	(2.6)	(1.5)

Note. Composite behavior means could range from 10 to 70; higher numbers indicate more extroverted client behavior.

dexes could range from 8 (indicating little effort toward the objective) to 56 (indicating a great deal of effort toward the objective). A modest correlation between the two scales, $r(57) = .35$, $p < .01$, indicated that, to some extent, counselors did not see diagnosis and rapport as independent objectives in their discussions.

Because we wanted to know whether our diagnosis and rapport instructions affected counselors' perceptions of these objectives during the discussions, we performed a contrast analysis (Rosenthal & Rosnow, 1985) on counselors' scores for each scale. First, we compared diagnosis scores for counselors in the diagnosis condition ($M = 40.9$, $SD = 8.5$) with the diagnosis scores of counselors in the rapport ($M = 38.1$, $SD = 7.8$) and basic ($M = 34.8$, $SD = 9.1$) conditions pooled together. Although marginally significant, results indicated that counselors in the diagnosis condition reported greater effort toward achieving a diagnosis of their clients than counselors in the rapport or basic conditions, $t(54) = 1.894$, $p = .06$.[3] Pairwise comparisons using Turkey's HSD criterion revealed that counselors in both the diagnosis condition and the rapport condition reported greater diagnosis efforts than counselors in the basic condition, $p < .05$. Counselors in the diagnosis and rapport conditions, however, did not significantly differ from each other in their diagnostic effort reports.

A second contrast analysis compared the rapport scores of counselors in the rapport condition ($M = 39.7$, $SD = 7.6$) with the rapport scores of counselors in the diagnosis ($M = 39.9$, $SD = 6.7$) and basic ($M = 36.4$, $SD = 7.0$) conditions. Results indicated that counselors in the rapport condition did not report significantly greater effort at establishing rapport with their clients than counselors in the other two conditions, $t(54) = .77$, ns.

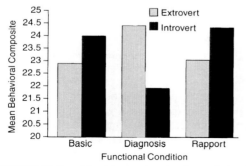

FIGURE 16.2 ■ Clients' expectancy-relevant behavior.

However, Turkey HSD pairwise comparisons indicated that counselors in the rapport condition did report significantly greater rapport-building effort than counselors in the basic condition, $p < .05$. Thus, although we were effective in getting counselors to differentially attend to issues of diagnosis in the manner we had hoped, counselors in the rapport condition were not the most concerned with issues of rapport.

One important limitation of these self-report measures is that they may only reflect counselors' subjective beliefs about what they think is generally important in therapeutic situations, irrespective of our functional instructions. Counselors' implicit notions of these settings may have emphasized rapport building regardless of our attempts to systematically vary its importance. Additionally, these measures may not reflect actual differences in counselors' efforts at diagnosis and rapport. Therefore, we examined peer counselors' behavior toward their clients during the discussions to see whether there were any reliable patterns related to the confirmation effects.

For these analyses, we constructed two composite indexes from judges' ratings of counselors' behavior. One composite assessed the extent to which counselors engaged in diagnostic behaviors and the other composite assessed the extent to which counselors engaged in rapport-building behaviors (see Method section for specific items for each scale). Interrater reliabilities and internal consistencies for both scales were good (interrater rs = .78 and .83, respectively; alpha coefficients = .82 and .79, respectively). Scores on each scale could range from 5 to 35, and higher scores reflected relatively more of a particular type of counselor behavior. Scores on these two scales were not significantly related to each other, $r(56) = -.057$, ns.

Each set of composite scores was then entered as the dependent variable in a 2 × 3 × 2 (Expectation × Function × Sex) ANOVA. Analysis of counselors' rapport-building behavior yielded no significant main effects or interactions, Fs < 1.706, ps > .19.[4] Analysis of counselors' diagnostic behaviors, however, produced two significant effects. First, a main effect for expectation obtained, $F(1, 46) = 4.378$, $p < .05$, such that counselors engaged in more diagnostic behaviors when they believed their clients were extroverted ($M = 22.8$, $SD = 2.4$) than when they believed their clients were introverted ($M = 21.6$, $SD = 3.0$). Additionally, a significant main effect for function obtained, $F(2, 46) = 7.527$, $p < .01$. Turkey HSD comparisons indicated that counselors engaged in more diagnostic behaviors in the diagnosis condition ($M = 23.7$, $SD = 2.2$) than in either the rapport condition ($M = 21.5$, $SD = 2.4$) or the basic condition ($M = 21.4$, $SD = 3.0$), $p < .05$. Counselors in the basic and rapport conditions did not differ, however, in their levels of diagnostic behavior.

To examine the mediating role of diagnostic and rapport behaviors in effecting behavioral confirmation across the three functional conditions, we first transformed scores on clients' expectancy-relevant behavioral composite (the composite used to assess behavioral confirmation). In this transformation, we first subtracted the overall composite mean from each individual composite score. Differences were then keyed so that positive scores indicated expectancy-confirming behavior from targets and negative scores indicated expectancy-disconfirming behavior from targets. We then correlated both counselors' diagnostic and rapport behavioral composites with the transformed composite. Here, significant correlations would suggest that a given type of behavior (diagnosis or rapport) was related to the tendency for behavioral confirmation to occur. Results indicated that although rapport-building behavior was not significantly related to behavioral confirmation, $r = -.057$, $p > .75$, increases in counselors' diagnostic behaviors were related to increases in behavioral confirmation from targets, $r = .422$, $p < .01$. Thus, regardless of their specific functional instructions, counselors who engaged in greater amounts of diagnostic behaviors were significantly more likely to elicit expectation-consistent behavior from their clients than counselors who did not exert such diagnostic efforts. As counselors directed greater efforts toward discovering and understanding the personalities of their clients, they were also more likely to constrain their clients to a range of expectation-confirming behaviors.

Additionally, the expectancy-relevant behavioral composite was entered as the dependent variable in two 2 × 3 × 2 (Expectation × Function × Sex) ANCOVAs, one using counselors' diagnosis behavioral composite as a covariate and the second using counselors' rapport behavioral composite as a covariate. Results of the analysis using the diagnosis composite as the covariate suggested that counselors' diagnosis behaviors mediated the tendency for behavioral confirmation to occur, as the Expectation × Function interaction term was no longer significant, $F(2, 45) = 1.221$, ns. However, no evidence was found to indicate that counselors' rapport-building behavior mediated expectation confirmation, as the Expectation × Function interaction remained statistically significant, $F(2, 45) = 5.065$, $p < .01$.

Discussion

Do counselors' motivations moderate behavioral confirmation? To answer this question, we identified two functional objectives likely to be served through counselors' interview behaviors—diagnosis and rapport building. We then began with a minimally defined interview setting and systematically added elements to this situation designed to engage motivations related to diagnosis or rapport-building functions. As a result, student-counselors concerned with diagnosis questioned their clients more and took more of a lead in discussions with their clients than student-counselors instructed to establish rapport with clients or student-counselors who received no specific functional instructions. In turn, student-counselors whose behaviors served this diagnostic function effected behavioral confirmation from their clients, whereas other student-counselors did not. Additionally, although not statistically significant, clients in the two nondiagnosis functional conditions may have behaved in an expectation-disconfirming manner.

These results do not suggest that counselors will invariably engage in expectation-confirming interactions with their clients. First, we randomly assigned college undergraduates to the role of peer-counselor, and it is still an open question as to whether professional counselors, with their years of training, would effect similar results. Additionally, our data indicate that confirmation occurs only when certain motivations are aroused. In the current study, counselors preoccupied specifically with diagnosing their clients were likely to engage in the kinds of behaviors that, ironically, prohibited clients from expressing themselves. Instead, counselors constrained the behavioral opportunities of clients, pursuing hypotheses that, although erroneous, produced behavioral confirmation. That is, although some of the clients labeled as introverts were likely to be extroverted, their diagnosis-motivated counselors elicited relatively more quiet and reserved behavior from them. Additionally, although some of the clients labeled as extroverts were likely to be introverted, their diagnosis-motivated counselors "brought them out of their shell," getting them engaged in the conversation and appearing extroverted. Indeed, as our analyses indicated, it was the diagnostic behaviors of counselors, across the functional conditions manipulated in the study, that mediated the behavioral confirmation outcomes. Once counselor diagnostic behaviors were controlled for, the previously reliable interaction between expectation and function diminished.

Similar functional concerns with "discovering" the personality of a target have been linked to behavioral confirmation in nonpsychotherapeutic settings. Employing a *getting acquainted* paradigm similar to that of Snyder et al. (1977), Snyder and Haugen (in press) found that perceivers whose behaviors served a knowledge function, in the service of forming stable, predictable impressions of targets, were likely to elicit behavioral confirmation. In contrast, perceivers whose behaviors served an adjustive function, maintaining a smooth and pleasant social interaction, did not effect such confirmatory outcomes. Additionally, Copeland (in press) found that perceivers motivated to learn more about the personalities of potential game partners (a knowledge function) were more likely to confirm their expectations of those potential partners than perceivers who were not so motivated. In the current investigation, counselors' diagnostic strategies resembled perceivers' knowledge-function behaviors, employed in the service of understanding and revealing the personalities of their clients. Likewise, counselors' rapport strategies resembled perceivers' adjustive strategies, trying to get along well with their clients and to let their clients feel at ease during the discussion.

These data suggest that forming this kind of stable, predictable, diagnostic impression of a target is not necessarily identical to forming an accurate impression. As Neuberg (1989) demonstrated, perceivers with accuracy goals can produce behavioral outcomes markedly different from those produced with the impression-formation goals of counselors in the current study. In his study, perceivers received either a negative belief about the person they were interviewing or no belief. Orthogonal to the expectation, half the perceivers were instructed to form accurate impressions of their partners, whereas the other half were not so instructed. Neuberg found that perceivers with accuracy goals did not elicit behavioral confirmation from targets, whereas those perceivers not operating under such accuracy goals did effect behavioral confirmation from their targets.

As they do not produce the same social outcomes, it appears that the diagnostic motivations of counselors in our investigation are not functionally equivalent to perceivers' accuracy goals in Neuberg's (1989) study. Instead, our diagnosis manipulation focused counselors' efforts on assessing their clients' personality traits and forming stable, predictable impressions through that assessment. Similar results were found by Harris and Rosenthal (1986), who also employed a counseling analog situation but focused on individual difference variables as predictors of expectation confirmation. In their study, student peer counselors who scored high on a measure of dogmatism were more likely to confirm their expectations of clients than student peer counselors who obtained a low score on the measure. Harris and Rosenthal speculated that this pattern of results was due to the more well-defined client schema formed by dogmatic counselors (from the expectation) and the greater adherence to that schema during the interaction with their clients. We would argue that such behavior allows dogmatic counselors a greater sense of stability in and prediction of client behaviors and, therefore, that dogmatic counselor behavior served a function similar to the diagnosis function in our study.

Generally, such stability and predictability concerns may not promote the kind of information-seeking strategies that accuracy goals engender. This distinction between stability and predictability of beliefs and their accuracy parallels Swann's (1984) distinction between circumscribed and global accuracy. Circumscribed accuracy involves specific beliefs about another person in specific situations and resembles counselors' predictive beliefs that allow for further behavioral confirmation from the same clients in future interactions. Global accuracy, however, involves widely generalizable beliefs about another person, and if counselors correctly inferred clients' personalities, this would allow for accurate predictions about the clients' behavior in myriad settings and with other interaction partners.

Both counselors' ratings and behavior indicate that we were unsuccessful in getting counselors to differentially attend to rapport-building issues in their discussions. Counselors in the rapport condition did not expend greater rapport-building effort than counselors in either of the two functional conditions, as indexed by judges' ratings. Additionally, counselors in the rapport condition reported only significantly greater efforts at establishing rapport than counselors in the basic condition. Although problematic in terms of interpreting the functional role of rapport as a potential moderator of behavioral confirmation, our data nonetheless suggest that variation in rapport-building behavior did not mediate the tendency for behavioral confirmation to occur. Additionally, our results indicate that variation in motives other than those dealing with the establishment of rapport can effect behavioral confirmation. Specifically, although counselors' rapport behavior did not differ significantly between conditions and was not related to behavioral confirmation across conditions, behavioral confirmation did occur but only when counselors set out to diagnose their clients.

We should also mention that although this study sheds light on the motivational moderators of behavioral confirmation in a counseling setting, that light is shed on only half the therapeutic relationship. These data speak to the ways in which counselors' functional concerns help to bring about behavioral confirmation, but they do not address clients' motivational moderators. For purposes of experimental control, all clients received identical instructions—information regarding their forthcoming discussions and their role as clients in those discussions. These instructions may have contributed to the activation of particular functional concerns—concerns associated with being a client.

A good deal of research on clients suggests that they have expectations that can affect the course and outcome of therapy (Higginbotham, West, & Forsyth, 1988). Clients often expect therapists to display a set of well-defined role behaviors, such as nurturance, inquisitiveness, commitment, and friendliness. Furthermore, the agreement of counselor and client role expectations as well as clients' prognostic expectations significantly affect the duration, length, and success of intervention. Higginbotham (1977) proposed that these behavioral effects are mediated by clients' positive affect and cognitive elaboration on the intervention produced when their role expectations are met. From this perspective, clients may succumb to counselors' testing of incorrect hypotheses because clients expect counselors to probe for such information, such behavior being consistent with a counselor's role. Clients accede to these probes because doing so serves a sort of therapeutic function for them.

Indirect empirical support for the moderating role of clients' motivations comes from studies conducted in nonclinical settings. In a study by Haugen and Snyder (1992), targets motivated by adjustive concerns—whose behavior functioned to keep the discussion smooth and pleasant—confirmed their perceivers' expectations. In contrast, targets motivated by knowledge concerns—whose discussion behavior functioned to get to know their perceivers—did not provide behavioral confirmation of their perceivers' expectations. Additionally, Copeland (in press) demonstrated that an imbalance of power between perceiver and target, like the imbalance that exists between a counselor and a client, promotes target motives that lead to confirmatory outcomes. Together, these data suggest that clients, as targets in the behavioral confirmation paradigm, also play an important role in determining when confirmation occurs.

In conclusion, our focus on counselors' motivations provides some answers to the question of when behavioral confirmation in therapeutic settings is likely to occur. This work adds to the growing body of work focusing on the motivational underpinnings of expectation confirmation (Hilton & Darley, 1991; Neuberg, 1989; Snyder, 1992). Additionally, our use of the functional approach compliments similar efforts in other domains of social phenomena, including attitudes (e.g., Herek, 1987; Shavitt, 1990; Snyder & DeBono, 1987), stereotypes (e.g., Snyder & Miene, in press), and helping behavior (Omoto & Snyder, 1990; Snyder, 1993). Such motivational approaches, and functional analyses in particular, hold the promise of illuminating further a wide variety of individuals' cognitive, affective, behavioral, and interpersonal processes.

NOTES

Authors' Note: This research was funded by grants from the National Science Foundation (BNS 87-18558 and DBC 91-20973) to Mark Snyder. We would like to thank Joyce Miskoweic, Catherine Peterson, Karyn Gunderson, Brenda Coushman, and Cindy Hegstrom for their valuable assistance in collecting and coding data, and Arie Kruglanski and three anonymous reviewers for their valuable comments on an earlier version of this article.

1. This design, then, does not allow for examining mixed-sex dyads. Same-sex dyads were chosen to lessen participants' anxieties regarding the discussion. Harris and Rosenthal (1986) reported results of a counseling analog employing same-sex and mixed-sex dyads.
2. The terms *counselor* and *client* are used throughout this article to denote the perceiver and target, respectively. These terms were also used in the instructions to participants to increase the experimental realism for them. Although this is consistent with the rich tradition of such analog studies in social psychology, we should note that the question of the generalizability of our results to actual clinical settings, with trained therapists, remains to be answered.
3. Because we did not have an equal number of participants in each condition, we conducted unweighted means analyses (Winer, Brown, & Michels, 1991) for all analyses comparing group means.
4. One possible explanation for the lack of reliable variation in counselors' rapport indexes (both self-report and behavioral) is that our manipulation of rapport may involve two independent and competing functions. That is, in addition to the smooth and pleasant interaction between counselors and clients implied by rapport, there may also be an extent to which counselor rapport encourage clients to "be themselves" and express aspects of their personalities. Counselor behaviors serving such an *other-expressive* function may be qualitatively different than behaviors serving a function of interaction facilitation and may have pulled our counselors in different directions. To test this possibility, the rapport indexes completed both by our perceiver-counselors and our independent judges were separated into two indexes whose items appeared to tap the two types of rapport-building functions. The resulting subscales were highly correlated ($r = .85$ for counselors' self-reports and $r = .89$ for judges' behavior ratings) and did not produce different patterns of effects when run through $2 \times 3 \times 2 \times 2$ (Expectation × Function × Sex × Composite) MANOVAs (with repeated measures on the last factor).

REFERENCES

Asch, S. E. (1946). Forming impressions of personality. *Journal of Abnormal and Social Psychology, 41*, 258–290.

Berman, J. S. (1979, August). *Therapeutic expectancies and treatment outcome: A quantitative review.* Paper presented at the annual meetings of the American Psychological Association, New York.

Berman, J. S., & Wenzlaff, R. M. (1983, August). *The impact of therapist expectancies on the outcome of psychotherapy.* Paper presented at the annual meetings of the American Psychological Association, Anaheim, CA.

Bruner, J., & Tagiuri, R. (1954). The perception of people. In G. Lindzey (Ed.), *Handbook of social psychology* (Vol. 2, pp. 634–654). Cambridge, MA: Addison-Wesley.

Burke, J. F. (1989). *Contemporary approaches to psychotherapy and counseling: The self-regulation and maturity model*. Pacific Grove, CA: Brooks/Cole.

Copeland, J. T. (in press). Prophecies of power: Motivational implications of social power for behavioral confirmation. *Journal of Personality and Social Psychology*.

Gauron, E. G., & Dickinson, J. K. (1966). Diagnostic decision-making in psychiatry: 1. Information usage. *Archives of General Psychiatry, 14*, 225–232.

Gauron, E. G., & Dickinson, J. K. (1969). The influence of seeing the patient first on diagnostic decision-making in psychiatry. *American Journal of Psychiatry, 126*, 199–205.

Harris, M. J., & Rosenthal, R. (1986). Counselor and client personality as determinants of counselor expectancy effects. *Journal of Personality and Social Psychology, 50*, 362–369.

Haugen, J. A., & Snyder, M. (1992, June). *A functional analysis of the target's role in behavioral confirmation*. Paper presented at the annual meetings of the American Psychological Society, San Diego, CA.

Herek, G. M. (1987). Can functions be measured? A new perspective on the functional approach to attitudes. *Social Psychology Quarterly, 50*, 285–303.

Higginbotham, H. N. (1977). Culture and the role of client expectancy in psychotherapy. *Topics in Culture Learning, 5*, 107–124.

Higginbotham, H. N., West, S. G., & Forsyth, D. R. (1988). *Psychotherapy and behavior change: Social, cultural and methodological perspectives*. New York: Pergamon.

Hilton, J. L., & Darley, J. M. (1991). The effects of interaction goals on person perception. In M. P. Zanna (Ed.), *Advances in experimental social psychology* (Vol. 24, pp. 235–267). San Diego, CA: Academic Press.

Jussim, L. (1986). Self-fulfilling prophecies: A theoretical and integrative review. *Psychological Review, 93*, 429–445.

Jussim, L. (1991). Social perception and social reality: A reflection-construction model. *Psychological Review, 98*, 54–73.

Leary, M. R., & Miller, R. S. (1986). *Social psychology and dysfunctional behavior: Origins, diagnosis and treatment*. New York: Springer-Verlag.

MacKinnon, R. A., & Yudofsky, S. C. (1991). *Principles of the psychiatric evaluation*. Philadelphia: J. B. Lippincott.

Meehl, P. E. (1960). The cognitive activity of the clinician. *American Psychologist, 15*, 19–27.

Miller, D. T., & Turnbull, W. (1986). Expectancies and interpersonal processes. In M. R. Rosenzweig & L. W. Porter (Eds.), *Annual review of psychology* (Vol. 37, 233–256). Palo Alto, CA: Annual Reviews, Inc.

Murray, J., & Abramson, P. R. (Eds.). (1983). *Bias in psychotherapy*. New York: Praeger.

Neuberg, S. L. (1989). The goal of forming accurate impressions during social interactions: Attenuating the impact of negative expectancies. *Journal of Personality and Social Psychology, 56*, 374–386.

Omoto, A. M., & Snyder, M. (1990). Basic research in action: Volunteerism and society's response to AIDS. *Personality and Social Psychology Bulletin, 16*, 152–166.

Rosenthal, R. (1974). *On the social psychology of the self-fulfilling prophecy: Further evidence for Pygmalion effects and their mediating mechanisms*. New York: M. S. S. Inf. Corp. Modular Publications.

Rosenthal, R., & Rosnow, R. L. (1985). *Contrast analysis: Focused comparisons in the analysis of variance*. New York: Cambridge University Press.

Rubin, M., & Shontz, F. C. (1960). Diagnostic prototypes and diagnostic processes of clinical psychologists. *Journal of Consulting Psychology, 24*, 234–239.

Shavitt, S. (1990). The role of attitude objects in attitude functions. *Journal of Experimental Social Psychology, 26*, 124–148.

Snyder, M. (1984). When belief creates reality. In L. Berkowitz (Ed.), *Advances in experimental social psychology* (Vol. 18, pp. 248–305). San Diego, CA: Academic Press.

Snyder, M. (1992). Motivational foundations of behavioral confirmation. In M. P. Zanna (Ed.), *Advances in experimental social psychology* (Vol. 25, pp. 67–114). San Diego, CA: Academic Press.

Snyder, M. (1993). Basic research and practical problems: The promise of a "functional" personality and social psychology. *Personality and Social Psychology Bulletin, 19*, 251–264.

Snyder, M., & DeBono, K. G. (1987). A functional approach to attitudes and persuasion. In M. P. Zanna, J. M. Olson, & C. P. Herman (Eds.), *Social influence: The Ontario symposium* (Vol. 5, pp. 135–153). Hillsdale, NJ: Lawrence Erlbaum Associates.

Snyder, M., & Haugen, J. A. (in press). Why does behavioral confirmation occur? A functional perspective on the role of the perceiver. *Journal of Experimental Social Psychology*.

Snyder, M., & Miene, P. (in press). Stereotypes of the elderly: A functional approach. *British Journal of Social Psychology*.

Snyder, M., Tanke, E. D., & Berscheid, E. (1977). Social perception and interpersonal behavior: On the self-fulfilling nature of social stereotypes. *Journal of Personality and Social Psychology, 35*, 656–666.

Snyder, M., & Thomsen, C. J. (1988). Interactions between therapists and clients: Hypothesis testing and behavioral confirmation. In D. C. Turk & P. Salovey (Eds.), *Reasoning, inference and judgment in clinical psychology* (pp. 124–152). New York: Free Press.

Strohmer, D. C., & Chiodo, A. L. (1984). Counselor hypothesis testing strategies: The role of initial impressions and self-schema. *Journal of Counseling Psychology, 31*, 510–519.

Strohmer, D. C., & Newman, L. J. (1983). Counselor hypothesis-testing strategies. *Journal of Counseling Psychology, 30*, 557–565.

Swann, W. B., Jr. (1984). Quest for accuracy in person perception: A matter of pragmatics. *Psychological Review, 91*, 451–477.

Wilson Dallas, M. E., & Baron, R. S. (1985). Do psychotherapists use a confirmatory strategy during interviewing? *Journal of Social and Clinical Psychology, 3*, 106–122.

Winer, B. J., Brown, D. R., & Michels, K. M. (1991). *Statistical principles in experimental design* (3rd ed.). New York: McGraw-Hill.

Discussion Questions

1. When behavioral confirmation occurs during counseling and psychotherapy, do you think that the effects are generally beneficial or detrimental for the client?
2. What steps can be taken to reduce the incidence of behavioral confirmation in clinical settings?
3. Come up with two situations in which you may have inadvertently created behavior in another person that confirmed your initial but incorrect impression of him or her.

Suggested Readings

Harris, M. J., & Rosenthal, R. (1986). Counselor and client personality as determinants of counselor expectancy effects. *Journal of Personality and Social Psychology, 50,* 362–369. This research examines characteristics of both the counselor and client that are related to the degree to which clients behaviorally confirm a counselor's impressions.

Snyder, M. (1992). Motivational foundations of behavioral confirmation. *Advances in experimental social psychology, 25,* 6–114. This chapter reviews the literature on behavioral confirmation and examines why it occurs.

Snyder, M., Tanke, E. D., & Berscheid, E. (1977). Social perception and interpersonal behavior: On the self-fulfilling nature of social stereotypes. *Journal of Personality and Social Psychology, 35,* 656–666. This classic article reports the first detailed examination of behavioral confirmation.

Wilson Dallas, M. E., & Baron, R. S. (1985). Do psychotherapists use a confirmatory strategy during interviewing? *Journal of Social and Clinical Psychology, 3,* 106–122. This study demonstrated that therapists search for information about clients in ways that confirm their initial perceptions.

READING 17

The Mythology of Psychopathology: A Social Cognitive View of Deviance, Difference, and Disorder

James E. Maddux • George Mason University

Editors' Introduction

At its heart, the job of a clinical psychologist involves forming impressions of other people (clients), using those impressions to draw inferences about the person's problems, then making informed decisions regarding treatments that will improve the quality of the client's life. Unfortunately, because clinicians fall victim to the same information-processing biases that affect us all, their inferences about clients—their diagnoses regarding the client's problem—are sometimes incorrect. Furthermore, the implicit assumptions that many clinicians hold about mental disorders and how they should be classified do not always lead them to draw accurate inferences about their clients.

James E. Maddux, a clinical psychologist and leading figure in the field of social-clinical psychology, addresses these issues from a social-cognitive view of clinical judgment and decision making. He organizes this article around what he believes are three false assumptions that are held by many clinical psychologists. The first assumption is the myth of abnormality. People who endorse this myth believe that there are clear criteria for deciding what is normal and what is abnormal, but Maddux suggests that this is not the case. He argues that classifying behavior or people as

240

normal versus abnormal represents a false dichotomy, ignoring the fact that the processes that underlie normal behavior also underlie abnormal behavior. In addition, he suggests that mental disorders are not scientific constructs in the sense that there are no clear and universally agreed upon criteria for deciding what is normal and what is abnormal. Maddux also notes that definitions of normality and abnormality have been unfairly influenced by gender. Men have been used as the standard for judging normalcy, in comparison to which women are sometimes seen as abnormal or aberrant.

The second assumption that Maddux tackles is the myth of categories. This myth assumes that a classification system that distinguishes the normal from the abnormal and that differentiates various problems of abnormality from one another is useful for diagnosing maladjustment. In fact, the prevailing diagnostic system, the *Diagnostic and Statistical Manual of Mental Disorders* (*DSM*) adopts this perspective. However, Maddux points out that classification systems, although sometimes useful for assigning names and labels, do not provide explanations for particular difficulties or recommend ways to treat these disorders. What are needed are systems that are based on solid theory and empirical research. Along these lines, Maddux discusses three such systems: the dimensional approach, the interpersonal approach, and the individual case-formulation approach.

The third myth is the myth of the superiority of clinical judgment. This myth assumes that clinical psychologists are more skilled at person perception (i.e., perceiving other people and drawing inferences about them) than other people. Thus, they are less likely to fall victim to the errors in information processing and decision making that plague the rest of us. Through a discussion of the dispositional attributional bias, confirmatory bias in hypothesis-testing, behavioral confirmation of expectancies, and the overconfidence effect, Maddux points out the flawed nature of this assumption. In fact, clinicians are as likely as other people to make mistakes in the perceptions and judgments they make about others.

The take-home message of this article is that clinicians (and other mental health professionals) need to think critically about how they perceive and evaluate their clients. They should think carefully about how they define abnormality, the classification system that they use to diagnose psychological problems, and the processing biases that may creep into their professional evaluations.

George Orwell once said that "The restatement of the obvious is the first duty of intelligent men." With that in mind, I want to discuss some concerns and problems regarding the way clinical psychologists think about the people they call clients or patients and the problems clients or patients present. Clinical psychologists are in the business of thinking about, forming impressions of, and making decisions about other people—impressions and decisions that can change the lives of others for better or worse. A practicing clinician who understands and can think critically about how he or she perceives, thinks about, and makes judgements about clients will be a more effective clinician. In addition, a broadly defined social cognitive framework provides a useful perspective for understanding and thinking critically about perceiving and judging in the clinical situation.

I want to discuss three assumptions that many clinical psychologists seem to hold when thinking about their clients and their clients' problems. *Because they are mistaken assumptions that seem to be part of the traditional "clinical lore" that is passed along from the trainers to the trainees, we might call them myths.* They are assumptions about which many clinicians seem only dimly aware and that are too rarely questioned or challenged.

The first myth is that we have clear and objective criteria for defining and distinguishing between normal and abnormal psychological and behavioral functioning (sometimes referred to as psychopathology)—that we know what normal and healthy functioning is and therefore know what abnormal and unhealthy functioning is.

The second myth is that the most logical, scientific, and constructive way to think about problems in adaptation and adjustment is to try to place people and their problems in categories—that such categories offer the best way to think about people and their problems in a manner that facilitates the development of effective methods for enhancing adjustment.

The third myth is that trained clinicians are more accurate, less error-prone, and less biased in the way they go about gathering information about and forming impressions of other people than are people who have not had the benefit of clinical training.

Each myth by itself can result in serious problems and errors in clinical judgment and decision making. Taken together, however, they have a synergistic and self-perpetuating detrimental effect on clinical judgment, an idea that I present briefly near the end of this article.

What follows is not an exhaustive and critical review of the literature on classification, clinical judgment, and the definition of psychological normality and pathology. Instead, what follows is an attempt to sort out for myself some ideas and questions that have evolved during the past 12 years of teaching abnormal and clinical psychology to both undergraduates and clinical psychology doctoral students—ideas that I have attempted to convey to students with varying degress of success. These ideas probably are not original and they certainly are not fully developed; they are still evolving. For that reason, comments and criticism are welcome.

As critical as this article will sound to some, finding fault with clinical psychologists is not my primary goal. I *am* a clinical psychologist, and I have great respect for clinical researchers and clinical practitioners. However, I have long been bothered by the *seemingly unquestioning acceptance* of certain assumptions and ideas by many involved in clinical practice and training. My goal, therefore, is to encourage clinical psychologists to develop a healthy level of skepticism toward their discipline and their clinical activities, because I believe that this skepticism is the first step toward change.

The Social Cognitive Perspective

This discussion is guided primarily by a social cognitive view. Used here, the term refers both to the field of social cognition and to what has become known as social cognitive theory. The field of social cognition has been defined by Fiske and Taylor (1991) as "the study of how people make sense of other people and themselves.... How ordinary people *think* about people and how they *think they think* about people" (p. 1). Social cognitive theory, as described by Bandura (1986), is a more cohesive general theory of human adaptation and adjustment that proposes that people are self-reflective and self-regulating; that behavior, cognition, affect, and environmental events are interactive and mutually influential; and that an understanding of human behavior can only be achieved by an analysis of the interaction of all of these influences as they occur in specific situations. As Bandura demonstrated in his book the *Social Foundations of Thought and Action* (1986), virtually all theory and research in the field of social cognition can find a home in social cognitive theory.

The social cognitive principle most relevant here is that adaptation and adjustment can be understood only by understanding the interaction of behavior, cognition, affect, and environmental events as they occur in specific situations. Some corollaries of this principle are important here. First, adaptiveness is a property not of people nor of behavior but of this complex interaction of person and situation. Second, there is continuity between so-called normal and abnormal or between adaptive and maladaptive psychological functioning; that adaptive and maladaptive behaviors differ in degree, not kind; and that the traditional division of clinical versus nonclinical problems and populations is a false and misleading dichotomy.

Third, we should be concerned not with normality and abnormality per se but with behavioral, cognitive, and emotional effectiveness and ineffectiveness in specific situations. The areas of social cognition of most concern here are person perception and impression formation—the study of how we gather information about other people and how we form impressions of and make judgments about other people. Of particular concern is research of the errors and biases that influence person perception and impression formation.

Myth One: The Myth of Abnormality

The first important myth is that we have clear criteria for defining and distinguishing between normal and abnormal or between healthy and unhealthy psychological functioning. At least four lines of arguments can be proposed to counter this myth.

1. The distinction between normal and abnormal or between healthy and pathological psychological functioning is a false dichotomy.
2. The concept of psychopathology or mental disorder is not a scientific concept.
3. Our informal and official definitions of psychological normality and health are gender biased and, therefore, unworkable.
4. We have made the concept of psychopathology or mental disorder meaningless by pathologizing too many common problems in living.

Normal Versus Abnormal: The False Dichotomy

Clinicians often seem to diagnose by location by assuming that the presence of a person in a clinical setting is sufficient reason for assuming the existence of abnormality or pathology—that because this person is here in this clinical setting, he or she must have a so-called "clinical" problem that differs in significant ways from normal problems in living. This assumption is questionable for at least three reasons.

First, the assumption ignores the thousands of essentially healthy people who have the good sense to seek professional help before problems get out of hand (and who have good health insurance coverage) and the thousands of people with severe emotional and behavioral problems who never make it to clinical settings, either because they cannot afford it, do not believe it will work, or somehow muddle through life with the help from friends, family, clergy, or Oprah.

Second, the assumption of a normal versus abnormal dichotomy runs counter to the assumption made by virtually every major theory of personality and psychological adjustment that adaptive and maladaptive psychological phenomena differ not in kind but in degree and that continuity exists between normal and abnormal and between adaptive and maladaptive. Even Freud assumed that psychopathology is characterized not by the presence of underlying unconscious conflicts and defense mechanisms, but by the degree with which such conflicts and defenses interfere with functioning in everyday life (Maddux, Stoltenberg, Rosewein, & Leary, 1987).

Third, this assumption runs counter to the assumption made by most contemporary theorists and researchers in personality, social, and clinical psychology that the processes that explain adaptive behavior also explain maladaptive behavior. No one has yet demonstrated that the psychological processes that explain the problems of people who present themselves to mental health professionals—so-called clinical populations—differ from the processes that explain the problems of people whose problems may not be severe enough to warrant consultation with a certified professional—so-called nonclinical populations. In other words, no one has demonstrated that the problems of people who seek professional help differ in kind from the problems of people who do not seek help, rather than simply differing in degree, frequency, or severity.

For these reasons, we should strongly suspect that, except for the most blatant cases, the distinction between normality and abnormality, between clinical and nonclinical populations and problems, and between problems in living and "mental disorders" is essentially an arbitrary distinction that does not accurately reflect reality, however convenient and comforting we find this distinction. For example, we may find it convenient and useful to define "mental retardation" as a measured level of intelligence that is two standard deviations or greater below the mean, but we cannot then assume that this line represents an actual discontinuity and separates people into two distinct groups, the intellectually sufficient and the intellectually deficient.[1]

"Mental Disorder" is not a Scientific Concept

The social cognitive view defines psychological dysfunction and pathology as behavioral, cognitive, and emotional ineffectiveness (Maddux, in press). Effectiveness is situation dependent and dependent on the social norms, expectations, and values relevant to that situation. For example, in his recent *American Psychologist* article "The Concept of Mental Disorder," Wakefield (1992) reviews and critiques six different conceptualizations of mental disorder. He finds logical problems with each of them and offers a definition of disorder as *harmful dysfunction*. He says that a disorder exists "when the failure of a person's internal mechanisms to perform their function as designed by nature impinges harmfully on the person's well-being as defined by social values and meanings" (p. 373).

Although this definition is an improvement over previous ones, defining "harmful" in terms of social values and meanings leaves a lot of room for subjectivity, disagreement, and social and cultural relativity. Sociocultural values and meanings themselves are by nature vague and in a constant state of flux, especially in a multicultural society such as ours. Whose cultural values are we talking about? Who defines them? As Wakefield suggests, we may agree on certain facts about a condition or problem but not agree on whether or not it is a "disorder" because of our differences in values, such as what goals are desirable for individuals.

In addition, Wakefield points out that the term "disorder," to be meaningful, must serve as an explanation for the pattern or condition of concern. However, the official definition of "mental disorder" found in the most recent edition of the *Diagnostic and Statistical Manual of Mental Disorders* (*DSM–III–R*, 1987)[2] is merely descriptive, not explanatory. In addition, the vast majority of the specific diagnostic labels in the *DSM–III–R* are simply shorthand terms for a list of vaguely described "symptoms" and explain nothing at all. Of course, the *DSM* is nonexplanatory *on purpose* and says so, but this admission does not eliminate the problem.

The concept "mental disorder" and the notions of normality, abnormality, and psychopathology are so heavily value laden that they may be more accurately viewed as moral, legal, and ethical concepts rather than scientific ones. This is not to say that clinical psychology is an inherently unscientific field or that scientific methods have no place in clinical practice. For example, designing and testing techniques for enhancing adjustment by changing behavior, cognition, and emotion can be a scientific enterprise, as indicated by the hundreds of good published studies on the effectiveness (or lack of effectiveness) of psychological interventions (e.g., Garfield & Bergin, 1986). However, it does mean that, although questions of *how* to effectively and efficiently facilitate change are scientific questions that can be answered by scientific methods, questions of *what* behaviors should be changed are primarily questions of value, not of science. Questions of what is adaptive or maladaptive are questions about social goals and social values, and, like it or not, in the realm of values, ethics, morality, legality, and social policy, scientists, including psychologists, have no special expertise (e.g., Kimble, 1989; Maddux, 1993). Values can be the topic of research, but values cannot be chosen or proven correct through research.

Gender Bias in Definitions of Psychological Normality and Health

More women than men present themselves to mental health professionals for help with problems of adjustment (e.g., Gove & Tudor, 1973; Rohrbaugh, 1979). One explanation frequently offered for this fact is that the criteria mental health professionals use for determining psychological health and illness are biased against women—that women are more often viewed as psychologically dysfunctional than men because mental health professionals tend to view typical male sex role behavior as healthy and typical female sex role behavior as maladaptive (e.g., Kaplan, 1983). Indeed, research on mental health professionals' working definitions of healthy and unhealthy psychological functioning indicates that therapists and counselors tend to equate healthy *adult* functioning with healthy *male* functioning but have different criteria for healthy *female* functioning (Broverman, Broverman, Clarkson, Rosenkrantz, & Vogel,

1970; Sherman, 1980). In addition, in her critique of the *DSM–III*, Kaplan (1983) has argued that "masculine-based assumptions about what behavior are healthy and what behaviors are crazy are codified in diagnostic criteria" (p. 786). This argument has not gone unchallenged (e.g., Williams & Spitzer, 1983), yet it has not been successfully refuted.

The most thorough recent treatment of this issue is found in social psychologist Carol Tavris's book *The Mismeasure of Woman* (1992). Tavris presents a convincing case that "male behavior [and] male psychology continue to be the standard of normalcy against which women are measured and found wanting" (p. 17). Tavris presents compelling evidence that the mental health professions take the male norm for granted and see women's behavior "as something to be explained in relation to the male norm" (p. 28). She also states that the mental health professions "are used to . . . thinking of women as being different from men, and to regarding women's differences from men as deficiencies and weaknesses" (p. 40). For example, Tavris points out that studies of self-esteem and self-confidence, including those conducted by women, usually conclude that women have lower self-esteem and less self-confidence than men, rather than concluding that men are more conceited than women. She also cites the "manufacture" of "premenstrual syndrome," "codependency," and the new "self-defeating personality disorder" as evidence of the pathologizing of behavior and experience that, although different from that of most men, is normal for a large number of women.

Tavris argues further that "if the qualities and experiences associated with the female role were regarded as the norm . . . our interpretations and treatments of 'mental disorders' would be different" (pp. 204–205). She states that mental health professionals would be worried about the national epidemic of narcissism, that thousands of support groups would develop to help men who are too independent and too unresponsive to the needs of others, and that we would stop confusing role obligations with mental illness.

The point here is that if our informal and official concepts of normality and abnormality and psychological adjustment and maladjustment are as strongly based on male norms as Tavris concludes (and she presents an excellent case that they are), then we need to question seriously the validity of those concepts. We need to question seriously our assumptions about what we think we know about our ability to define and identify health and unhealthy psychological functioning for either gender.

The Pathologizing of Problems in Living

As Tavris (1992) pointed out, the official system for classifying psychological is called "The Diagnostic and Statistical Manual of Mental Disorders," not "The Diagnostic and Statistical Manual of Mental Disorders and a Whole Bunch of Everyday Problems." Yet, as the *DSM* has gone from its first edition in 1952, to the second edition in 1968, to the third edition in 1980, and to the revised third edition in 1987 (the fourth edition will be here soon), not only has the number of mental disorders increased greatly—from 60 to over 300—but the definition and scope of "mental disorder" also have broadened greatly. Mental health professionals have not been content to concern themselves with labeling as "mental disorders" obviously and blatantly dysfunctional patterns of behaving, thinking, and feeling. Instead, they have insisted on pathologizing almost every problem in living experienced by human beings and turning them into "mental disorders." This trend is evident in both the official nomenclature and the lay literature on psychological dysfunction and treatment.

For example, premenstrual emotional changes became premenstrual syndrome and is now *late luteal phase dysphoric disorder* in *DSM–III–R*. Smoking too much became the mental disorder *nicotine dependency*, a mental disorder that afflicts over 50 million Americans (Moss, 1979). If you drink a lot of coffee, you may develop the mental disorder *caffeine intoxication*. Not wanting sex often enough became *hypoactive sexual desire disorder*. Not wanting sex at all became *sexual aversion disorder*. Wanting sex so much you get in trouble trying to get it is now called by some *compulsive sexual behavior disorder*. Erotic and emotional obsessions that lead one to commit crimes are now referred to by some as *Clerambault–Kandkinsy syndrome* (Money, 1992). These latter two conditions are not yet in the *DSM*, but only time will tell. Masturbation used to be considered a symptom of mental disorder (Gilman, 1988). Maybe in *DSM–IV* not masturbating often enough will be a mental disorder (e.g., "maturbatory aversion disorder" or "autoerotic aversion disorder").

In *DSM–III*, children's academic problems became the mental disorders *developmental disabilities*. Tantruming toddlers have *oppositional defiant disorder*. *Sibling rivalry disorder* is now in the official nomenclature of the World Health Organization's counterpart to the *DSM* (Carter & Volkmar, 1992). Children and adults who have difficulty interpreting nonverbal social cues and communicating nonverbally are now said to have *dyssemia*, and people who have dyssemia are called dyssemics (Nowicki & Duke, 1992). "Dyssemic disorder" is not yet in the *DSM*, but stay tuned.

People who inadvertently aid and abet a substance abuser with whom they are in some kind of relationship became *codependent* in the lay psychological literature. Codependency has become so broadly defined by some codpendency experts that almost anyone, especially a woman, in almost any kind of relationship meets the criteria for a codepencency disorder (Tavris, 1992).

The trend is clear. We first see a pattern of behaving, thinking, feeling, or desiring that deviates from some fictional norm or ideal, or we identify a common complaint that, as expected, is displayed with greater frequency or severity by some people than others. We then give the pattern a medical-sounding name (preferably with Greek or Latin roots) and, as a result, it becomes a diagnosable and classifiable mental disorder. Once it has an official-sounding name, it takes on a life of its own and becomes a entity, like a disease, and people begin thinking they have it, and medical and mental health professionals begin diagnosing and treating it; and, of course, it qualifies for third-party payments. Alan Ross (1976) referred to this process as the *reification* of the disorder. However, in light of the awe with which clinicians view their diagnositc terms and the power such terms exert over clinician and client, a better term for this process may be the *deification* of the disorder.

Lest people think that I do not take seriously the pain and suffering people experience trying to adjust to life's challenges and traumas, I need to make it clear that my targets here are not sufferers but the overpathologizing phrase makers. I am not denying that some people are miserably unhappy with their sex lives. I am aware that there are many people who are interpersonally very awkward and uncomfortable, some excruciatingly so. I agree that smoking is stupidly self-destructive but hard to give up. And I am sure that if I had premenstrual syndrome, I'd wish I didn't. I am not trying to trivialize human suffering and misery. What I am arguing against, in fact, is trivialization of true human suffering and misery that take place as we continue to expand the definition of mental disorder. What I question is the honesty and utility of pretending that we know what normal is and the rampant practice of turning so many common problems in living into "mental disorders" that soon everything that human beings do, think, and feel, and desire that is not perfectly logical, adaptive, or efficient will be labeled a mental disorder, especially if you are female. When everything becomes a disorder, the term will become meaningless. We are rapidly approaching that point.

Myth Two: The Myth of Categories

The essence of the second myth is that a system of categories that distinguishes abnormal or unhealthy functioning from normal or healthy functioning and that distinguishes adjustment problems from each other is the most accurate and a useful way of conceptualizing and understanding problems of adaptation and adjustment.

I begin with the first belief—that dividing psychological disorders into categories is an accurate way to conceptualize or organize our thinking and knowledge about problems of adjustment. Most proponents of traditional classification of psychological disorders justify their efforts with the assumption that "classification is the heart of any science" (Barlow, 1991, p. 243). We need to begin by questioning this assumption—that science begins with the classification of things into categories. Compared to Eastern thinkers, Western thinkers have always expended a lot of energy and ingenuity trying to fit the world of things into discrete categories, viewing the world in either-or and black-or-white dichotomies, and dividing the world into sets of separate things. What we often forget is that all systems of classification are arbitrary and none accurately captures reality. As Alan Watts (1966) said, "However much we divide, count, sort, or classify [the world] into particular things and events, this is no more than a way of thinking about the world. It is never *actually* divided" (p. 54). Too many of us, however, come to see these divisions as real and confuse our classification with the real world. Just as children may see the lines of latitude and longitude or the borders between states and nations on a map or globe and wonder why they cannot see them on the ground, we become confused when the world does not fit our categories, such as when our clients and their problems do not fit our system of disorders.

In addition, we too often confuse classifying with understanding and labeling with explaining (Ross, 1980). We often forget that being able to agree on what to name something and then being able to match things with their names does *not* guarantee that one understands or can explain the thing one is naming.

The second part of this myth is the assumption that sorting people and their problems into diagnostic categories is a useful way to think about adaptation and adjustment. Because our ways of organizing and classifying the real world can never really capture the real world, we can only assess the "correctness" of a system of representing reality by determining its utility—by asking "What do we want to accomplish, and how well does this system help us accomplish it?" To borrow again from Alan Watts (1961): Is it more correct or accurate to classify rabbits based on differences in the fur or differences in their meat? The answer depends on whether you're a furrier or a butcher. In other words, it depends on what you want to *do* with them; it depends on your purpose or goal.

In organizing and understanding problems of adjustment, the ultimate goal is developing theories and methods for enhancing adjustment. Therefore, we need to ask how well the official system for organizing and understanding problems of adjustment provides us with insight and understanding that helps us design effective ways to enhance adjustment. We need to ask to what extent the current classification system serves this purpose. Because effective interventions must be guided by theories and concepts, diagnostic categories, such as those in the *DSM*, will be most useful if they provide theories and conceptualizations of people and their problems that lead to suggestions for interventions. The *DSM* is atheoretical by design, and so by design does not provide theory-based conceptualizations of adjustment problems that lead to intervention strategies. The *DSM* may help us decide what needs to be changed, but it does not help us decide how to help people change.

In addition to questioning the utility of the present system of categories, we need to consider alternative ways of conceptualizing human adjustment that may be more useful than a system of categories. Although the jury is still out on the practical utility of DSM, some psychologists are exploring promising alternatives. Three worth mentioning briefly are the *dimensional* approach, the *interpersonal* approach, and the *individual case-formulation* approach, each of which is consistent with a social cognitive perspective.

The *dimensional* approach (e.g., Millon, 1991; Persons, 1986; Livesley, Jackson, & Schroeder, 1992; Trull, 1992) starts with the assumption that normality and abnormality, as well as effective and ineffective psychological functioning, lie along a continuum; that adaptive and maladaptive differ in degree, not kind; and that so-called psychological disorders are not discontinuous with ordinary problems in living but instead are extreme variants of normal psychological phenomena. In the dimensional approach, what are classified are *not* people or disorders but human characteristics and psychological phenomena, such as emotion, mood, intelligence, and personality styles. Tremendous individual differences on the dimensions of interest are *expected*, just as we expect a certain percentage of people to score above 130 or below 70 on an standardized intelligence test. Any divisions made between normal and abnormal are arbitrary and done for convenience or efficiency but are *not* viewed as indicative of true discontinuity.

The definition of mental disorder offered in the *DSM–III–R* does include that notion that "[t]here is no assumption that each mental disorder is a discrete entity with sharp boundaries (discontinuity) between it and other mental disorder, or between it and no mental disorder" (p. xxii). Thus, the authors of the official nomenclature present it as at least not inconsistent with a dimensional approach to understanding adjustment and maladjustment. However, by devoting the rest of the entire volume to the presentation of categories, the authors undermine the credibility of their belief in the assumption that mental disorders are discontinuous with nonclinical problems in living.

Several studies have examined the utility of a dimensional approach to understanding so-called "personality disorders" (e.g., Livesley, et al, 1992; Trull, 1992). For example, a recent factor-analytic study of personality among the general population and a population with "personality disorders" demonstrated striking similarity between the two groups. In addition, the factor structure revealed in both populations did *not* support the *DSM* system of classifying so-called personality disorders into discrete categories. Essentially, the findings were inconsistent with the notion that personality disorders are discontinuous with personality patterns or styles found in "nonclinical" populations.

In addition, research on the varieties of normal emotional experiences (e.g., Oatley & Jenkins, 1992) is inconsistent with the notion that "clinical" emotional disorders are discrete classes of emotional experience discontinuous with everyday emotional experiences and "nonclinical" emotional upsets and problems.

Research on children's problems also supports the dimensional approach. For example, recent research on the evaluation of children's reading disabilities indicates that "dyslexia" is not an all-or-none condition that children either have or do not have, but occurs in degrees without a natural break between "dyslexic" and "nondyslexic" children (Shaywitz, Escobar, Shaywitz, Fletcher, & Makuch, 1992). In addition, the work conducted by Achenbach and his colleagues over the past decade-and-a-half on empirically based assessment of childhood problems indicates that a dimensional approach not only reflects reality more accurately than a categorical approach but also has greater clinical utility (Achenbach & McConaughy, 1987).

The *interpersonal* approach (e.g., Carson, 1969; Leary, 1957; Kiesler, 1991, Strong, 1987) "focuses on human interactions, not on the behavior of individuals [but] the behavior of persons relating to and interacting in a system with other persons" (Kiesler, 1982, p. 5). An interpersonal approach to adjustment begins with the assumption that "maladjusted behavior resides in a person's recurrent transactions with others . . . [and] results from . . . an individual's failure to attend to and correct the self-defeating, interpersonally unsuccessful aspects of his or her interpersonal acts" (Kiesler, 1991, pp. 443–444). The success of interpersonal acts must be defined and determined in the contexts of specific situations (Duke & Nowicki, 1982). In addition, research has shown that "self-defeating" behaviors are extremely common and are not by themselves signs of abnormality or symptoms of "disorders" (Baumeister & Scher, 1988).

Interpersonal taxonomies have been developed for the assessment of interpersonal adjustment and maladjustment, but such taxonomies are concerned with types of interpersonal actions and transactions that vary in intensity or extremeness, rather than with normal types versus abnormal types of actions and transactions (Kiesler, 1991). This approach is a stark contrast to *DSM–III–R*'s assumption that a mental disorders is a "dysfunction in the person" (p. xxii).

The *individual case-formulation approach* (e.g., Hayes, Nelson, & Jarrett, 1987; Persons, 1986, 1989, 1991; Turkat, 1985) proposes that individualized assessment of behaviors, cognition, emotion, and situations, *not* diagnosis by symptoms clusters and categories, is the most clinically useful way to evaluate problems in adjustment and design interventions. Consistent with a social cognitive view, Persons (1986) argues that we should be studying psychological phenomena, not psychiatric diagnosis—in other words, dimensions of individual difference in behavior, cognition, and affect, not psychological disorders. The advantage of this approach is that identification of specific behavioral, cognitive, and affective patterns and the situations in which they occur allows for interventions tailored for the individual client and his or her specific adjustment difficulties. Classification by clusters of symptoms does not lead to theory-guided intervention strategies.

Alan Ross (1980) stated that a true scientific understanding of behavior consists of being able to specify the conditions under which the behavior occurs. This is the kind of understanding that leads to practical suggestions for changing behavior and enhancing adjustment. The interpersonal and case formulation approaches are consistent with this principle and with the social cognitive principle that problems in adjustment can be understood only by identifying *specific* aspects of behavioral, cognitive, and affective adaptiveness and maladaptiveness and the specific situations and conditions in which they occur (Maddux, in press). These approaches and the general social cognitive approach are concerned not with what the person *is* or what the person *has* but with what the person *does*—and under what conditions he or she does it.

Perhaps we should stop asking "How can we

devise better categories and more precise criteria for mental disorders and the people who have them?" and begin asking "What are some more useful ways of conceptualizing human adaptation and adjustment and problems in adaptation and adjustment?" We need to question not only our categories of psychological disorders but also our need to categorize psychological disorders. Diagnostic labels, such as those in the *DSM*, can help us communicate with each other more efficiently, if we can agree on their definitions, but we need to realize that diagnostic labels are not inert or innocuous terms but can have a powerful impact on the way the clinicians view their clients and the way clients view themselves (Farina & Fisher, 1982; Kayne & Alloy, 1988; Leary & Miller, 1986; Wright, 1991).

Myth Three: The Myth of the Superiority of Clinical Judgment

The third major myth is that clinical psychologists and other trained professional helpers are more skillful than untrained people in perceiving other people and are more immune or invulnerable to the errors and biases that are so common in everyday social interactions. Brehm and Smith (1986) stated that clinical judgments are interpersonal judgments "cloaked in the respectable garments of supposed scientific objectivity" (1986, p. 74). However, research suggests that these respectable garments are as transparent as the emperor's new clothes. What research reveals is that the judgments made by clinical psychologists may differ in *content* from those made by most of us in everyday social interactions but do not differ in *process* (Brehm & Smith, 1986) and that the clinical situation is more similar to than different from everyday social interactions. Research indicates that clinicians use the same shortcuts, make the same mistakes, are biased in the same directions, and as unaware of their own processes of perceiving and thinking about other people as we are in the course of everyday life—and as unjustifiably confident about their judgment.

As do all of us, clinicians in clinical situations make errors in *covariation assessment*, the degree to which one event seems to occur more often in the presence of than in the absence of the other event (Alloy & Tabachnik, 1984; Kayne & Alloy, 1988). In our attempts to assess covariation, we always bring to a situation expectations and preconceptions based on experience in other similar situations. A cognitive dilemma arises when the covariations suggested by our expectation conflict with the covariations suggested by information in the current situation. Research has shown time and time again that when faced with this dilemma, people usually make covariation assessments that are biased in the direction of their initial expectations or theories or causal schema and that the stronger our initial beliefs or expectations, the more strongly we adhere to our theories, the less accurate will be our assessments of covariation (Alloy & Tabachnik, 1984).

At least three well-documented phenomena that plague everyday person perception also color clinicians' perceptions of clients and lead to errors in covariation assessment: (1) the dispositional attributional bias, or the tendency to conclude that behavior reflects personality; (2) the use of confirmatory hypothesis-testing strategies; and (3) behavioral confirmation of expectancies about other people.

The Dispositional Attributional Bias

In explaining our own behavior, we typically invoke situational attributions and argue that we behaved the way we did because of situational demands or restrictions—not because of who we are. However, in explaining the behavior other people, we typically invoke dispositional attributions and conclude that *he* behaved the way *he* did because of *who he is*—and that it's *just like him* to behave that way. We also underestimate the role of situational factors in explaining the behavior of others. This bias is so basic and pervasive that it has been called the "fundamental attributional error" (Ross, 1977).

Not only are clinicians not immune to this attributional bias, but the tendency of clinicians to assume that behavior reflects personality increases as the behavior of the observed person becomes more deviant (Harari & Hosey, 1981). In addition, this bias seems related to the clinician's theoretical orientation. For example, it has been shown to be stronger among psychodynamic clinicians than among behavioral clinicians (Snyder, 1977).

Of greater concern is the possibility that the clinical situation may be more vulnerable than most situations to the operation of dipositional biases. The vulnerability of the clinical situation may be greater for several reasons. First, the most widely used traditional clinical assessment techniques are designed more for assessment of personality and dispositions than assessment of situations (Miller & Porter, 1988). Second, we are more likely to make dispositional attributions if we are interacting with a person rather than simply observing the person (Miller & Porter, 1988); the clinician is both an interactant and an observer of the client. Third, we are more likely to make dispositional attributions if we expect to interact with the person in the future (Miller & Porter, 1988), an expectation that certainly characterizes psychotherapy.

Fourth, research suggests that we usually underestimate the influence of role-guided behavior in explaining the behaviors of others in specific situations (Miller & Porter, 1988). We tend not to take into account the rules implicit in the person's role when explaining his or her behavior, although the person *in* the role usually is aware of role constraints. Of course, the client in a clinical situation is in the role of one in need and seeking help, and the clinician needs to consider how much of the client's presentation of pathology may be due to the client's role-based assumption that presenting pathology is expected. Fifth, because we usually think our behavior only has the effects we intend it to have, we usually underestimate the influence of our own behavior on the behavior of others (Miller & Porter, 1988). Clinicians, of course, intend to be objective, nonjudgmental, and empathic and certainly do not intend to encourage their clients to present information selectively or misleadingly. Because clinicians usually have such good intentions, they may fail to pay sufficient attention to the possible unintended effects of their behavior. For all of these reasons, clinicians should begin to seriously question their tendency to assume that the problem that brought the client to the clinic and the behavior the client is displaying in the clinical setting are indicative of enduring personality traits.

Confirmatory Bias in Hypothesis Testing

Research on how we go about gathering information about people has demonstrated repeatedly that we rarely do so objectively and systematically and that this is true of clinicians as well as laypersons. What research indicates is that we have a strong confirmatory bias in the way we gather information about people and test our hypotheses about people. We enter into evaluative situations with others with preconceptions, expectations, and hypotheses, and we tend to gather information from and about other people in a way that helps us support our preconceptions and expectancies (Kayne & Alloy, 1988; Snyder, 1984; Leary & Miller, 1986). We attend more closely to information that is consistent with our preconceptions than to information that is inconsistent with our preconceptions. We actively seek evidence for our hypotheses by asking people for instances when they behaved in ways consistent with our hypotheses about what kind of people they are, but we tend not to ask them for instances when they behaved contrary to our hypotheses. In other words, we ask questions about occurrences but not about nonoccurrences (Kayne & Alloy, 1988). In particular, clinicians are typically trained to ask for examples of ineffective functioning more so than examples of effective functioning.

The sequence of presentation of information about a client also may influence the impact of that information. The earlier a clinician is presented with seemingly pathological information about a person, the more disturbed the clinician is likely to view the person and the less likely the clinician is to see him or her as improved in treatment than if the information were presented later (Friedlander & Phillips, 1984; Friedlander & Stockman, 1983). Even when forced to pay attention to expectancy-disconfirming information, we are likely to discount the credibility of that information by viewing the sample on which it is based as too small or biased (Kayne & Alloy, 1988). Not only do we gather information in a way that helps us confirm our preconceptions, expectancies, and hypotheses, we also selectively remember information about people depending on whether it is consistent or inconsistent with our preconceptions (Kayne & Alloy, 1988) and thus provide ourselves with evidence that we are indeed perceptive.

We also tend to make dispositional attributions for expectancy-confirming behavior and tend to attribute expectancy-disconfirming behavior to the pressure of the situation (Snyder, 1984). At least one study found that the use of a confirmatory strategy *increases* with clinical experience (Hirsch & Stone, 1983).

A confirmatory strategy particularly important in clinical setting is the *illusory correlation*, perceiving or discovering a correlation or association between two events when no such correlation or association actually exists. The phenomenon of concern in clinical situations is illusory correlations between psychological test data and personality traits or psychological disorders, especially data from projective tests based on psychodynamic theory (Kayne & Alloy, 1988). Studies have shown that clinicians will "discover" a correlation between psychological test responses and thematically related psychological traits despite the absence of a true statistical relationship—for example, associating large eyes in a drawing of a person with paranoid tendencies or a highly masculine drawing with homosexuality (Kayne & Alloy, 1988).

The illusory correlation phenomenon is difficult to reduce or eliminate with training. Even when clinicians are warned against it, it persists (Kurtz & Garfield, 1978). In addition, evidence suggests that the tendency to see illusory correlations may increase as the decision-making demands on the clinician increase—for example, as the amount of information about a client increases or as the number of clients increases (Lueger & Petzel, 1979).

Because clinician confidence in his or her judgment also increases along with the amount of clinical information (Oskamp, 1965), errors in judgment may increase as confidence in one's judgment increases. In light of this, the illusory correlation phenomenon may explain why clinicians continue to use assessment instruments, especially projective tests, whose validity has not been supported empirically.

The confirmatory bias also may influence the clinician's assessment of the effectiveness of his or her clinical interventions. Clinicians naturally want very much to believe that their interventions lead to change and improvement in their clients. We want to believe that we are positive and constructive agents of change. Therefore, we may perceive change and improvement when it is not there, exaggerate the extent of change and improvement, or assume that change was caused by our interventions. Not surprisingly, research suggests that clinicians are not accurate and unbiased evaluators of the effectiveness of their own interventions, but are influenced by their expectations and theories (p. 297). For example, Kayne and Alloy (1988) examined 31 studies of psychotherapy outcome and found that, consistent with the research on judgment bias, as the objectivity of the measures of therapy outcome *increased*, the likelihood of finding a difference between therapies *decreased*. In addition, they found that researchers with a clear theoretical preference or bias usually found their favored intervention to be more effective than the other intervention. Kayne and Alloy suggest that clinicians' expectations bias their assessment of theory outcome as much as they bias client assessment or diagnosis and may be as difficult to eliminate.

Return for a moment to the first myth concerning our ability to accurately distinguish between normal and abnormal behavior. Our vague and ambiguous criteria for normality, abnormality, health, and pathology may contribute to the difficulty clinicians encounter in accurately assessing client improvement. Such vague and imprecise criteria make it easier for clinicians to see their clients as dysfunctional and abnormal to begin with and easier to see them later as improved. Also, the clinician can use the belief that the client has improved and is now functioning more effectively to bolster his or her belief that the client was abnormal or pathological to begin with. In this way, each bias or distortion increases the probability of the other.

Behavioral Confirmation of Expectancies

Research has shown consistently that the expectancies and preconceptions we bring to interactions with others and the initial impressions we quickly form can lead us to behave in ways toward others that elicit from them the behavior we expect. This *self-fulfilling prophecy* was first identified in 1948 by Merton and has been investigated by a number of researchers, Mark Snyder most prominently.

Research indicates that when we first meet other people, among the first things we notice are highly visible and distinctive features such as gender, race, physical attractiveness, and clothing style, and that although we may struggle against the influence of these superficial characteristics, our first impressions are strongly influenced by them and by the assumptions we make about the kinds of personalities suggested by these characteristics (Snyder, 1984).

Most of us assume, for example, that a physically attractive person will be friendly and outgoing and that an unattractive person will be shy, and our behavior toward them can shape their behavior toward us. We are warm and friendly toward the attractive person, who is likely to respond in kind, and we are distant toward the unattractive person, who also is likely to respond in kind. Our treatment of them leads them to provide us with behavioral confirmation that our expectations were correct.

The gender of the parties involved seems to be important in behavioral confirmation. Men may be more likely than women to elicit behavioral confirmation from other people, and women may be more likely than men to provide it (Christensen & Rosenthal, 1982). This tendency may be exacerbated when the man is in a position of power and the woman is in a subordinate position, such as female job applicant being interviewed by a male (e.g., von Baeyer, Sherk, & Zanna, 1981). These findings suggest that a common clinical situation—a male clinician and a female client (who is in distress and seeking help and is therefore subordinate)—almost guarantees that the clinician's expectations, preconceptions, and first impressions will elicit from the client expectancy-confirming behavior. Recent research on "therapist-induced memories" even indicates that, through the power of probing that becomes suggestion, therapists can cause clients to "remember" events that never happened, including sexual abuse and past lives (Spanos et al., 1991).

The effect of behavioral confirmation goes beyond your perception of me; it also influences my perception of myself. Because I develop beliefs about who I am by observing my own behavior (Markus & Wurf, 1987), when I provide behavioral confirmation for your expectations, I may come to incorporate the new behavior into my own self-concept. This internalization and perseveration of expectancy-confirming behavior is likely to occur in situations that encourage people to view their new behaviors as indicative of traits and dispositions, and is likely to occur when the target person interacts consistently and regularly with the observer (Snyder, 1984). Snyder concludes that under these conditions "People will literally become the people they are thought to be, and their behaviors will reflect the cross-situational consistency and temporal stability that are the defining features of personality traits and dispositions" (1984, p. 257). Because clinicians tend to make dispositional attributions based on client behavior, because clients tend to accept dispositional feedback from clinicians, because clinicians tend to view client acceptance of feedback as evidence of its correctness, and because clients interact regularly and consistently with their therapists, psychotherapy may be especially vulnerable to the operation of behavioral confirmation of expectancies.

Overconfidence Effect

People are generally unaware of their own errors and biases in person perception and impression formation, including trained mental health professionals. We usually think we are doing just fine because we "discover" or create so much evidence that we are objective and accurate perceivers and information gatherers. This illusion of accuracy helps produce another bias that further compounds the problem, an exaggerated sense of one's own abilities—what we might call the overconfidence effect.

Research has demonstrated consistently that confidence in one's abilities, or a strong sense of self-efficacy (Bandura, 1986), is essential for effective performance in almost any endeavor, including the activities of a professional clinician. Thus, overconfidence within limits is healthy and adaptive because it encourages us to try things we might not otherwise try (Taylor & Brown, 1988). However, when your job is to gather information about and to form impressions of another person—impressions that may have a profound influence on that person's life—confidence that exceeds accuracy can be dangerous. An awareness of the most common errors and biases in perception and judgment and a realistic sense of one's ability to perceive others accurately—a healthy skepticism—are probably useful for the clinician and in the client's best interest.

Unfortunately, research suggests that for the layperson and the trained professional helper, confidence in one's perception and judgment of others typically outstrips and accuracy of one's perception and judgment of others. One of the common myths that clinicians seem to hold dear is that the accuracy of their understanding and judgment about a client will increase as the amount of information about the client increases—the more information I have about the client's history and the more data I have from psychological tests, the more I can be sure that I know this person well and that my impressions will be valid. This belief seems implicit in the textbooks and courses of psychological assessment that usually stress extensive history taking and intensive psychological testing. However, research suggests, instead, that as the amount of information about a client increases, the accuracy of clinical judgments and predictions quickly peaks and plateaus but confidence continues to increase (Oskamp, 1965). This confidence may be bolstered by the client's belief that because the clinician "knows" a lot about him, because he or she is an expert, has good intentions, and bases his or her pronouncements on valid-appearing psychological tests, the clinician must be right (e.g., Snyder, Shenkel, & Lowery, 1977).

Implications

As I suggested near the beginning of this article, each of these myths by itself is seriously problematic for the clinical situation because they can lead to errors in judgment and decision making. Taken together, however, these three myths or mistaken implicit assumptions create a self-perpetuating system of error and distortion—a vicious circle—that consists of the following steps.

First, the clinician holds as true the false dichotomy between normal and abnormal psychological functioning—between so-called clinical and nonclinical populations or clinical and nonclinical problems—and believes that because this person is here in this clinical setting, he or she must be a member of the clinical population and have a clinically significant disorder.

Second, our criteria for defining normality and abnormality (or health and pathology) are so vague that they provide fertile ground for, and almost guarantee, the overwhelming influence of subjectivity and the most common and insidious errors and biases in perception and judgment, as indicated by the considerable research on decision making under uncertainty (e.g., Tversky & Kahnemann, 1974). Third, our assumptions that adjustment problems can be sorted into categories of so-called psychological disorders and that sorting people and their problems into categories is the most useful way to think about problems of adjustment and our acceptance of the present system for sorting, the *Diagnostic and Statistical Manual of Mental Disorders* or *'DSM* (American Psychiatric Association, 1987), provides a set of expectations and preconceptions that further increases the probability that errors and biases in clinical perception and judgment will occur.

Fourth, the subsequent errors and biases that occur in the clinical situation that result from ambiguity and preconceptions lead to the gathering of information and the formation of impressions that, although not highly accurate, provide the clinician with a false sense of confidence in his or her own abilities in social perception and social judgment, in the notion the he or she *knows* pathology when he or she sees it, and in the notion that people do indeed *fit* the categories we have devised for them. Because clients readily agree with the clinician's assessments and pronouncements (Snyder, Shenkel, & Lowery, 1977), the clinician's confidence may be bolstered by this "evidence" that he or she is correct.

Fifth, the result of this false feedback and subsequent false sense of accuracy and overconfidence is that, over time, the clinician may become increasingly confident yet increasingly error-prone, as suggested by research showing a positive correlation between clinician experience and error and bias in perceiving and thinking about clients (e.g., Wills, 1978; Leary & Miller, 1986).

In summary, the vicious circle begins with our ambiguous notions of health and pathology and our rigid system for categorizing so-called psychological disorders, both of which make clinicians vulnerable to insidious errors and biases in the way they perceive and form impressions of clients, errors and biases that usually go undetected and that lead the clinician to develop an unwarranted sense of confidence in his or her clinical acumen, which leads the clinician to blindly plunge headlong into the next clinical encounter, only to begin the process again.

This may seem to some an unusually harsh and critical portrayal of the clinical process, and I would not insist that it describes behavior typical of the clinical situation, but I believe it is more characteristic and more common than most of us would like to believe. Also, I present this portrayal as a hypothesis (or set of hypotheses) that is supported in part by research but which has not been investigated as a whole. I think it is sufficiently plausible, however, to make clinical psychologists think twice about what they do and what they train others to do.

What is the solution to these problems? Briefly, clinical psychologists need to think more critically about how they think about their clients. We need to more critically examine our definitions of psychological normality and health and abandon the false dichotomy we seem to hold between normal and abnormal psychological functioning. We need to question seriously the utility of diagnostic categories and explore seriously alternative ways of conceptualizing psychological adaptation and adjustment, such as the interpersonal, dimensional, and individual case formulation approaches.

We need to educate ourselves about what psychology knows about everyday and clinical person perception, impression formation, and decision making. We also need to keep in mind that professional training and clinical experience do not guarantee that error and bias in perception and judgment will be eliminated or even reduced. We need to encourage, support, and heed the research on these issues. Those of us who train clinical psychologists need to instill in our students the need to question basic assumptions and to examine more critically their own work. It is not enough to convince students of the importance of thinking critically and scientifically about their clients. We also must convince them of the importance of thinking the same way about themselves and their profession—and we need to teach them how by doing so ourselves.

NOTES

A slightly different version of this article was presented as an invited address through Division 1 at the annual meeting of the American Psychological Association, 1992 (August), in Washington, DC.

The author is grateful to Alan Boneau for his helpful comments on an earlier version of this article and for waiting patiently for this article following its mysterious disappearance in February from the author's computer disk. The author also thanks John Hogan, Division 1 Program Chair for the 1992 APA meeting, for the invitation to give this talk.

[1] I am aware that intelligence as measured by a standard intelligence test is no longer the sole criterion for defining mental retardation. I am merely using this as an example.

[2] "[A] clinically significant behavioral or psychological syndrome or pattern that occurs in a person and that is associated with present distress (a painful symptom) or disability (impairment in one or more important areas of functioning) or with a significantly increased risk of suffering death, pain, or disability, or an important loss of freedom" (p. xxii).

REFERENCES

Achenbach, T. M., & McConaughy, S. H. (1987). *Empirically based assessment of child and adolescent psychopathology*. Newbury Park, CA: Sage.

Alloy, L. B., & Tabachnik, N. (1984). Assessment of covariation by humans and animals: The joint influence of prior expectations and current situational information. *Psychological Review, 91*, 112–149.

American Psychiatric Association. (1952). *Diagnostic and statistical manual of mental disorders*. Washington, DC: APA.

———. (1968). *Diagnostic and statistical manual of mental disorders* (2nd ed.). Washington, DC: APA.

———. (1980). *Diagnostic and statistical manual of mental disorders* (3rd ed.). Washington, DC: APA.

———. (1987). *Diagnostic and statistical manual of mental disorders* (3rd ed., rev.). Washington, DC: APA.

Bandura, A. (1986). *Social foundations of thought and action: A social cognitive theory*. Englewood Cliffs, NJ: Prentice Hall.

Bandura, A. (1978). On paradigms and recycled ideologies. *Cognitive Therapy and Research, 2*, 79–103.

Barlow, D. H. (1991). Introduction to the special issue on diagnosis, dimensions, and DSM-IV: The science of classification. *Journal of Abnormal Psychology, 100*, 243–244.

Baumeister, R. F., & Scher, S. J. (1988). Self-defeating behavior patterns among normal individuals: Review and analysis of common self-destructuve tendencies. *Psychological Bulletin, 104*, 3–22.

Brehm, S. S., & Smith, T. W. (1986). Social psychological approaches to psychotherapy and behavior change. In S. L. Garfield & A. E. Bergin (Eds.), *Handbook of psychotherapy and behavior change* (3rd ed., pp. 69–116). New York: Wiley.

Broverman, I. D., Broverman, D. M., Clarkson, F. E., Rosenkrantz, P. S., & Vogel, S. R. (1970). Sex-role stereotypes and clinical judgments of mental health. *Journal of Consulting and Clinical Psychology, 34*, 1–7.

Carson, R. C. (1969). *Interaction concepts of personality*. Chicago: Aldine.

Carter, A. S., & Volkmar, F. R. (1992). Sibling rivalry: Diagnostic category or focus of treatment? In B. B. Lahey & A. E. Kazdin (Eds.), *Advances in clinical child psychology* (Vol. 14). New York: Plenum.

Cervone, D., & Williams, S. L. (1992). Social cognitive theory and personality. In G. V. Caprara & G. L. Van Heck (Eds.), *Modern personality psychology: Critical reviews and new directions* (pp. 200–252). New York: Harvester-Wheatsheaf.

Christensen, D., & Rosenthal, R. (1982). Gender and nonverbal decoding skill as determinants of interpersonal expectancy effects. *Journal of Personality and Social Psychology, 42*, 75–87.

Cohen, H., Sargent, M. M., & Sechrest, L. B. (1986). Use of

psychotherapy research by professional psychologists. *American Psychologist, 41*, 198–206.

Duke, M. P., & Nowicki, S., Jr. (1982). A social learning theory analysis of interactional theory concepts and a multidimensional model of human interaction constellations. In J. C. Anchin & D. J. Kielser (Eds.), *Handbook of interpersonal psychotherapy* (pp. 78–94). Elmsford, NY: Pergamon.

Farina, A., & Fisher, J. D. (1982). Beliefs about mental disorder: Findings and implications. In G. Weary & H. L. Mirels (Eds.), *Integrations of social and clinical psychology* (pp. 48–71). New York: Oxford University Press.

Fiske, S. T., & Taylor, S. E. (1991). *Social cognition* (2nd ed.). New York: McGraw-Hill.

Frances, A. J., Widiger, T. A., & Sabshin, M. (1991). Psychiatric diagnosis and normality. In D. Offer & M. Sabshin (Eds.), *The diversity of normal behavior* (pp. 3–38). New York: Basic Books.

Friedlander, M. L., & Phillips, S. D. (1984). Preventing anchoring effects in clinical judgment. *Journal of Consulting and Clinical Psychology, 52*, 366–371.

Friedlander, M. L., & Stockman, S. J. (1983). Anchoring and publicity effects in clinical judgment. *Journal of Clinical Psychology, 39*, 637–643.

Garfield, S. L., & Bergin, A. E. (Eds.). (1986). *Handbook of psychotherapy and behavior change* (3rd. ed.). New York: Wiley.

Gilbert, S. L. (1988). *Disease and representation: Images of illness from madness to AIDS.* Ithaca, NY: Cornell University Press.

Griffin, D. W., & Ross, L. (1991). Subjective construal, social inference, and human understanding. In L. Berkowitz (Ed.), *Advances in experimental social psychology* (Vol. 24, pp. 319–359). New York: Academic Press.

Harari, O., & Hosey, K. R. (1981). Attributional biases among clinicians and nonclinicians. *Journal of Clinical Psychology, 37*, 445–450.

Hayes, S. C., Nelson, R. O., & Jarrett, R. B. (1987). The treatment utility of assessment: A functional approach to evaluating assessment quality. *American Psychologist, 42*, 963–974.

Hilton, J. L., & Darley, J. M. (1991). The effects of interaction goals on person perception. In L. Berkowitz (Ed.), *Advances in experimental social psychology* (Vol. 24, pp. 235–269). New York: Academic Press.

Hirsch, P. A., & Stone, G. L. (1983). Cognitive strategies and the client conceptualization process. *Journal of Counseling Psychology, 30*, 566–572.

Kaplan, M. (1983). A woman's view of DSM-III. *American Psychologist, 38*, 786–792.

Kayne, N. T., & Alloy, L. B. (1988). Clinician and patient as aberrant actuaries: Expectation-based distortions in assessment of covariation. In L. Y. Abramson (Ed.), *Social cognition and clinical psychology: A synthesis* (pp. 295–365). New York: Guilford.

Kielser, D. J. (1982). Interpersonal theory for personality and psychotherapy. In. J. C. Anchin & D. J. Kiesler (Eds.), *Handbook of interpersonal psychotherapy.* Elmsford, NY: Pergamon.

Kiesler, D. J. (1991). Interpersonal methods of assessment and diagnosis. In C. R. Snyder & D. R. Forsyth (Eds.), *Handbook of social and clinical psychology* (pp. 438–468). New York: Pergamon.

Kimble, G. A. (1989). Psychology from the standpoint of a generalist. *American Psychologist, 44*, 491–499.

Kurtz, R. M., & Garfield, S. L. (1978). Illusory correlation: A further exploration of Chapman's paradigm. *Journal of Consulting and Clinical Psychology, 46*, 1009–1015

Leary, T. (1957). *Interpersonal diagnosis of personality.* New York: Ronald Press.

Leary, M. R., & Maddux, J. E. (1987). Toward a viable interface between social and clinical/counseling psychology. *American Psychologist, 42*, 904–911.

Leary, M. R., & Miller, R. S. (1986). *Social psychology and dysfunctional behavior.* New York: Springer-Verlag.

Langer, E. J., & Abelson, R. P. (1974). A patient by any other name . . . : Clinician groups difference in labeling bias. *Journal of Consulting and Clinical Psychology, 42*, 4–9.

Lueger, R. J., & Petzel, T. P. (1979). Illusory correlation in clinical judgment: Effects of amount of information to be processed. *Journal of Consulting and Clinical Psychology, 47*, 1120–1121.

Livesley, W. J., Jackson, D. N., & Schroeder, M. L. (1992). Factorial structure of traits delineating personality disorders in clinical and general populations samples. *Journal of Abnormal Psychology, 101*, 432–440.

Maddux, J. E. (1993). Social science, social policy, and the limits of scientific research. *American Psychologist, 48*, 689–691.

Maddux, J. E. (in press). Self-efficacy and adjustment: Basic principles and issues. In J. E. Maddux (Ed.), *Self-efficacy, adaptation, and adjustment: Theory, research, and practice.* New York: Plenum.

Maddux, J. E., Stoltenberg, C. D., Rosenwein, R., & Leary, M. R. (Eds.). (1987). Social processes in clinical and counseling psychology: Introduction and orienting assumptions. In J. E. Maddux, C. D. Stoltenberg, & R. Rosenwein (Eds.), *Social processes in clinical and counseling psychology* (pp. 1–13). New York: Springer-Verlag.

Markus, H., & Wurf, E. (1987). The dynamic self-concept. *Annual Review of Psychology, 38*, 299–338.

Merton, R. K. (1948). The self-fulfilling prophecy. *Antioch Review, 8*, 193–210.

Miller, D. T., & Porter, C. A. (1988). Errors and biases in the attribution process. In L. Y. Abramson (Ed.), *Social cognition and clinical psychology* (pp. 3–32). New York: Guilford.

Millon, T. (1991). Classification in psychopathology: Rationale, alternatives, and standards. *Journal of Abnormal Psychology, 100*, 245–261.

Money, J. (1992). Four tutorials in pediatric sexology. In M. E. Perry (Ed.), *Childhood and adolescent sexology. Handbook of sexology, Vol. 7* (pp. 137–168). New York: Elsevier Science.

Moss, A. J. (1979). Changes in cigarette smoking and current smoking practices among adults: United States, 1978. *Advance Data from NCHS, 52*, 1–19.

Nowicki, S., & Duke, M. (1992). *Helping the child who doesn't fit in.* Atlanta, GA: Peachtree.

Oatley, K., & Jenkins, J. M. (1992). Human emotion: Function and dysfunction. *Annual Review of Psychology, 43*, 55–86.

Oskamp, S. (1965). Overconfidence in case-study judgments. *Journal of Consulting Psychology, 29*, 261–265.

Persons, J. (1986). The advantages of studying psychological phenomena rather than psychiatric diagnosis. *American Psychologist, 41,* 1252–1260.

Persons, J. B. (1989). *Cognitive therapy in practice: A case formulation approach.* New York: Norton.

Persons, J. B. (1991). Psychotherapy outcome studies do not accurately represent current models of psychotherapy: A proposed remedy. *American Psychologist, 46,* 99–106.

Ross, A. O. (1980). *Psychological disorders of children: A behavioral approach to theory, research, and therapy* (2nd ed.). New York: McGraw-Hill.

Ross, L. (1977). The intuitive psychologist and his shortcomings: Distortions in the attribution process. In. L. Berkowitz (Ed.), *Advances in experimental social psychology* (Vol. 10, pp. 173–220). New York: Academic Press.

Shaywitz, S. E., Escobar, M. D., Shaywitz, B. A., Fletcher, J. M., & Makuch, R. (1992). Evidence that dyslexia may represent the lower tail of a normal distribution of reading ability. *New England Journal of Medicine, 326,* 145–150.

Sherman, J. A. (1980). Therapist attitudes and sex-role stereo-typing. In A. M. Brodksy & R. T. Hare-Msutin (Eds.), *Women and psychotherapy: An assessment of research and practice.* New York: Guilford.

Snyder C. R. (1977). "A patient by any other name" revisited: Maladjustment or attributional locus of problem? *Journal of Consulting and Clinical Psychology, 45,* 101–103.

Snyder, C. R., Shenkel, R. J., & Lowery, C. (1977). Acceptance of personality interpretations: The "Barnum effect" and beyond. *Journal of Consulting and Clinical Psychology, 45,* 104–114.

Snyder, M. (1984). When belief creates reality. In L. Berkowitz (Ed.), *Advances in experimental social psychology* (Vol. 18, 247–305). San Diego, CA: Academic Press.

Spanos, N. P., Menary, E., Gabora, N. J., DuBreuil, S. C., & Dewhirst, B. (1991). Secondary identity enactments during hypnotic past-life regression: A sociocognitive perspective. *Journal of Personality and Social Psychology, 61,* 308–320.

Strong, S. R. (1987). Interpersonal change processes in therapeutic interactions. In J. E. Maddux, C. D. Stoltenberg, & R. Rosenwein (Eds.), *Social processes in clinical and counseling psychology* (pp. 68–82). New York: Springer-Verlag.

Tavris, C. (1992). *The mismeasure of woman.* New York: Simon and Schuster.

Taylor, S. E., & Brown, J. (1988). Illusion and well-being: A social psychological perspective on mental health. *Psychological Bulletin, 103,* 193–210.

Trull, T. (1992). DSM–III–R personality disorders and the five-factor model of personality: An empirical comparison. *Journal of Abnormal Psychology, 101,* 553–560.

Turkat, I. D. (1985). *Behavioral case formulation.* New York: Plenum.

Tversky, A., & Kahneman, D. (1974). Judgment under uncertainty: Heuristics and biases. *Science, 185,* 1124–1131.

von Baeyer, C. L., Sherk, D. L., & Zanna, M. P. (1981). Impression management in the job interview: When the female applicant meets the male (chauvinist) interviewer. *Personality and Social Psychology Bulletin, 7,* 45–52.

Wakefield, J. C. (1992). The concept of mental disorder: On the boundary between biological facts and social values. *American Psychologist, 47,* 373–388.

Watts, A. (1951). *The wisdom of insecurity.* New York: Vintage Books.

Watts, A. (1966). *The book: On the taboo against knowing who you are.* New York: Vintage Books.

Williams, J. B. W., & Spitzer, R. L. (1983). The issue of sex bias in DSM–III. *American Psychologist, 38,* 793–798.

Wills, T. A. (1978). Perceptions of clients by professional helpers. *Psychological Bulletin, 85,* 968–1000.

Wright, B. A. (1991). Labeling: The need for greater person-environment individuation. In C. R. Snyder & D. R. Forsyth (Eds.), *Handbook of social and clinical psychology* (pp. 469–487). New York: Pergamon.

Discussion Questions

1. Maddux discusses three alternative ways of conceptualizing human adjustment: the dimensional approach, the interpersonal approach, and the individual case-formulation approach. Which of these approaches do you see as most valid and useful? Why?
2. Are there any of the myths that Maddux discusses with which you disagree? Why or why not?
3. How can training programs in clinical and counseling psychology help to dispel the myths that surround the practice of psychology?

Suggested Readings

American Psychiatric Association. (1994). *Diagnostic and statistical manual of mental disorders* (4th ed.). Washington, DC: American Psychiatric Association. This manual contains the classification system for psychological disorders that is used most frequently by psychiatrists and clinical psychologists.

Broverman, I. D., Broverman, D. M., Clarkson, F. E., Rosenkrantz, P. S., & Vogel, S. R. (1970). Sex-role stereotypes and clinical judgments of mental health. *Journal of Consulting and Clinical Psychology, 34,* 1–7. This study found that clinicians' ratings of a healthy adult paralleled their ratings of a healthy adult male but not a healthy adult female, suggesting that the clinicians were using men as the standard for judging psychological well-being.

Cantor, N. (1982). "Everyday" versus normative models of clinical and social judgment. In G. Weary & H. L. Mirels (Eds.), *Integrations of clinical and social psychology* (pp. 27–47). New York: Oxford University Press. This chapter examines particular aspects of clinical judgment that have parallels in everyday social judgment.

Meehl, P. E. (1954). *Clinical versus statistical prediction: A theoretical analysis and a review of the evidence.* Minneapolis: University of Minneapolis Press. This classic book examines the relative reliability and validity of clinical judgment versus statistically based predictions in making diagnoses, and concludes that statistical prediction is superior to clinical judgment.

READING 18

Lessons from Social Psychology on Discrediting Psychiatric Stigma

Patrick W. Corrigan • University of Chicago
David L. Penn • Louisiana State University

Editors' Introduction

Stereotypes are cognitive ways of organizing information that allow people to process information about other individuals quickly and efficiently. For example, people have stereotypes about various groups of people based on characteristics such as their gender, race, ethnicity, and profession. Although stereotypes of other people are not always negative, they frequently are, and when people act on their negative stereotypic beliefs, discrimination results. A large body of research in social psychology focuses on stereotyping, prejudice, and discrimination, particularly as they relate to race and gender. In the following article, Corrigan and Penn apply this research to examine the stigma associated with mental illness.

Corrigan and Penn observe that mental disorders are surrounded by negative stereotypes. If you imagine in your mind a "mentally ill person," your stereotype is likely to lead you to assume that the person is violent, childlike, or out of control, which may not be the case. The stigma surrounding mental illness tends to be more negative than that surrounding physical disabilities because people think that mental illness, unlike physical illness, is under a certain amount of control. As a result, people are assumed to be more responsible for psychological problems than they are for physical disabilities. In addition, people who show evidence of serious psychological problems elicit fear and avoidance in those who interact with them.

Not only is the stigma associated with mental illness often ill-founded, but it can have devastating effects on those who are targeted. People who are stigmatized experience lowered self-esteem, ostracism, and difficulty finding employment. In addition, people who are stigmatized by others often self-stigmatize as well, convincing themselves that they are undesirable and ineffective.

In an attempt to reduce the stigma of mental illness, advocacy groups have typically adopted three strategies—protest, education, and contact—but, until recently, little empirical evidence regarding the effectiveness of these programs was available. Corrigan and Penn provide this evidence, relying heavily on theory and research in social psychology. Protest refers to the actions taken by advocacy groups to counter negative information about psychological disorders in the eyes of the public. Although protest efforts have met with some success, social psychological research on thought suppression suggests that trying to make people suppress stigmatizing thoughts may actually make those thoughts more accessible. Education refers to providing information to dispel myths about mental illness and promoting positive attitudes toward those with psychological problems. Empirical evidence supports the effectiveness of education in reducing stereotypes about those with psychological problems. Finally, contact refers to bringing people into contact with members of the stigmatized group. As long as certain conditions are met, contact between majority and minority group members seems to help reduce negative attitudes toward mental illness.

Abstract

Advocacy, government, and public-service groups rely on a variety of strategies to diminish the impact of stigma on persons with severe mental illness. These strategies include protest, education, and promoting contact between the general public and persons with these disorders. The authors argue that social psychological research on ethnic minority and other group stereotypes should be considered when implementing these strategies. Such research indicates that (a) attempts to suppress stereotypes through protest can result in a rebound effect; (b) education programs may be limited because many stereotypes are resilient to change; and (c) contact is enhanced by a variety of factors, including equal status, cooperative interaction, and institutional support. Future directions for research and practice to reduce stigma toward persons with severe mental illness are discussed.

Severe mental illnesses like schizophrenia strike with a two-edged sword (Corrigan & Penn, 1997). On one side, the biological and psychosocial factors that affect the course of schizophrenia lead to psychotic symptoms, diminished social functioning, and depleted support networks. On the other, the stigma of severe mental illness leads to prejudice and discrimination. Stigmas are negative and erroneous attitudes about these persons. Unfortunately, stigma's impact on a person's life may be as harmful as the direct effects of the disease. As a result, various advocacy, government, and community-service groups believe that expunging stigma from societal discourse—replacing these negative stereotypes with accurate and more hopeful views of mental illness—will significantly enhance the quality of life of people with these disorders. These advocates promote a variety of strategies, including *protest*, which seeks to suppress stigmatizing attitudes of mental illness and behaviors that promote these attitudes; *education*, which replaces stigma with accurate conceptions about the disorders; and *contact*, which challenges public attitudes about mental illness through direct interactions with persons who have these disorders.

Although these stigma-reduction strategies may hold promise in improving the lives of persons with severe mental illness, such interventions should not be accepted on faith. Rather, the theoretical assumptions and empirical support for these strategies should be closely examined. Social psychology and the study of social cognition, in particular, have generated useful models for understanding the functions of stereotypes and discrimination in ethnic and other minority groups. These models may help explain the stigma experienced by persons with severe mental illness as well as further the effectiveness of strategies that attempt to reduce it.

In this article, we argue that efforts to reduce stigmatization of persons with severe mental illness will be strengthened by the use of theory and findings from the social psychology literature on stigma reduction for persons of ethnic minorities and other "out-groups." This argument is reminiscent of an earlier appeal in this journal to better integrate the fields of social and clinical psychology (Leary & Maddux, 1987). We begin by providing an overview of the stigma associated with severe mental illness, followed by a review of public efforts to reduce stigma toward persons with these disorders. Then, we describe three strategies used to reduce stigma toward persons with severe mental illness: protest, education, and contact. For each strategy, we summarize existing research conducted on changing stigma toward persons with severe mental illness and follow each summary with a discussion of the social psychological literature in this area. The article concludes with a discussion of future directions for both the practice of, and the research in, stigma reduction for those with severe mental illness.

Stigma and Stereotype Defined

Stereotypes per se are not necessarily pernicious. Social psychologists view stereotypes as knowledge structures that are learned by most members of a social group (Augoustinos & Ahrens, 1994; Esses, Haddock, & Zanna, 1994; Hilton & von Hippel, 1996; Judd & Park, 1993; Krueger, 1996; Mullen, Rozell, & Johnson, 1996). Stereotypes are especially efficient means of categorizing information about social groups. Stereotypes are considered social because they represent collectively agreed-on notions of groups of persons. They are efficient because people can quickly generate impressions and expectations of individuals who belong to a stereotyped group (Hamilton & Sherman, 1994).

Just because most people have knowledge of a set of stereotypes does not imply that they will endorse these stereotypes, use them to generate negative judgments, or act on them in a discriminatory manner (Jussim, Nelson, Manis, & Soffin, 1995). People who are prejudiced endorse these negative stereotypes and act against minority groups accordingly (Devine, 1988, 1989, 1995; Hilton & von Hippel, 1996; Krueger, 1996). *Stigma* is another term for prejudice or negative stereotyping. In terms of mental illness, stigmas represent invalidating and poorly justified knowledge structures that lead to discrimination.

The Stigma of Severe Mental Illness

Stigmas about mental illness seem to be widely endorsed by the general public.[1] Citizens have negative stereotypes that are not warranted and are overgeneralized. Studies have shown that many citizens in the United States (Link, 1987; Rabkin, 1974; Roman & Floyd, 1981) and in most Western nations (Bhugra, 1989; Brockington, Hall, Levings, & Murphy, 1993; Greenley, 1984; Hamre, Dahl, & Malt, 1994; Madianos, Madianou, Vlachonikolis, & Stefanis, 1987) endorse stigmatizing attitudes about mental illness. Stigmatizing views about mental illness are not limited to uninformed members of the general public. Research has also shown that well-trained professionals from most mental health disciplines subscribe to stereotypes about mental illness (Keane, 1990; Lyons & Ziviani, 1995; Mirabi, Weinman, Magnetti, &

Keppler, 1985; Page, 1980; Scott & Philip, 1985).

Several themes recur in stigmatizing attitudes. Media analyses of film and print representations of mental illness have identified three common misconceptions: People with mental illness are homicidal maniacs who need to be feared, they have childlike perceptions of the world that should be marveled at, or they are rebellious, free spirits (Farina, 1998; Gabbard & Gabbard, 1992; Hyler, Gabbard, & Schneider, 1991; Mayer & Barry, 1992; Monahan, 1992; Wahl, 1995). Similarly, results of two independent factor analyses of the survey responses of more than 2,000 English and American citizens yielded three factors (Brockington et al., 1993; Taylor & Dear, 1980). The first factor is *fear and exclusion:* Persons with severe mental illness should be feared and, therefore, should be kept out of most communities. The second factor is *authoritarianism:* Persons with severe mental illness are irresponsible, and their life decisions should be made by others. The third factor is *benevolence:* Persons with severe mental illness are childlike and need to be cared for.

Stigmatizing attitudes are not limited to mental illness. Persons with physical illness and disabilities are also the object of disparaging opinions. However, the general public seems to disapprove of persons with severe mental illness significantly more than of persons with physical disabilities like Alzheimer's disease, blindness, or paraplegia (Corrigan, River, Lundin, Wasowski, et al., 1998; Piner & Kahle, 1984; Socall & Holtgraves, 1992; Weiner, Perry, & Magnusson, 1988). Severe mental illness has been viewed as similar to drug addiction, prostitution, and criminality (Albrecht, Walker, & Levy, 1982; Skinner, Berry, Griffith, & Byers, 1995). Unlike physical disabilities, persons with mental illness are perceived to be in control of their illness and responsible for causing it (Weiner et al., 1988). Furthermore, research respondents were less likely to pity persons with mental illness, instead reacting to psychiatric disability with anger and believing that help is not deserved (Socall & Holtgraves, 1992; Weiner et al., 1988).

Negative attitudes like these have a significant impact on the disabilities associated with mental illness. First-person accounts in *Schizophrenia Bulletin* repeatedly describe the pain of stigma and discrimination. The results from more carefully sampled survey research support these accounts; one study found that 75% of family members believed stigma decreased their children's self-esteem, hindered their ability to make friends, and undermined their success in obtaining employment (Wahl & Harman, 1989). Persons with severe mental illness living in New York City viewed stigma with similar concern (Link, Cullen, Struening, Shrout, & Dohrenwend, 1989). They believed the public would be likely to exclude them from close friendships or competitive jobs because of their mental illness. The impact of stigma is not limited to the individual diagnosed with mental illness. Families also report lowered self-esteem and strained relationships with other family members because of stigma (Lefley, 1992; Wahl & Harman, 1989) and may be the victims of a "courtesy-stigma" (i.e., being stigmatized because of their association with someone with a severe mental illness; Goffman, 1963).

Despite these findings, some researchers have argued that stigma is a societal illusion. They cite data that suggest the public does not endorse negative attitudes about mental illness (Crocetti, Spiro, & Siassi, 1971; Lindsay, 1982) or that the public does not always act on these attitudes with rejecting behaviors (Farina, 1981; Huffine & Clausen, 1979; Weinstein, 1983). Link and colleagues (Link & Cullen, 1983; Link, Cullen, Mirotznik, & Struening, 1992) responded to these assertions by noting that just because people publicly renounce stigma does not mean stigma is absent from Western culture or that it does not lead to discrimination. There are cultural benefits for citizens who deny endorsement of stereotypes in public, yet still are likely to prejudge in private. Hence, persons may say they do not agree with stigma but, in fact, discriminate when private opportunities present themselves (Gaertner & Dovidio, 1986).

Several studies have documented the behavior (i.e., discrimination) that results from stigma. Citizens are less likely to hire persons who are labeled mentally ill (Bordieri & Drehmer, 1986; Farina & Felner, 1973; Link, 1987; Olshansky, Grob, & Ekdahl, 1960), are less likely to lease them apartments (Page, 1977, 1983, 1995), and are more likely to falsely press charges against them for violent crimes (Sosowsky, 1980; Steadman, 1981). The detrimental impact of stigma is not limited to discrimination by others. Some persons with severe mental illness also endorse stigmatizing attitudes about psychiatric disability and hence about themselves. These persons may experience diminished self-esteem, which correlates with a lower quality of life (Mechanic, McAlpine, Rosenfield, & Davis, 1994). Moreover, persons who self-stigmatize are less likely to be successful in work, housing, and relationships (Link et al., 1989). These individuals seem to convince themselves that socially endorsed stigmas are correct and that they are incapable of independent living.

Public Efforts to Reduce Stigma Toward Severe Mental Illness

Advocacy and other groups have targeted stigma in a deliberate attempt to improve the lot of persons with severe mental illness. For example, the National Alliance for the Mentally Ill (NAMI), a grass-roots group of family members and persons with severe mental illness, has made combating stigma a top priority for its 172,000 members (Flynn, 1987; NAMI E-news, 1998). They launched the "Campaign to End Discrimination" in 1995 as a concerted effort to diminish stigma. The National Mental Health Association, a mental health advocacy group, has been educating the public about mental illness for more than 90 years. Furthermore, nationwide consumer groups have examined the loss of personal power that results from stigma and have developed corresponding education and advocacy programs. The National Stigma Clearinghouse, for example, aggressively responds to negative images of mental illness, raises public consciousness about psychiatric disabilities, and communicates with the media about positive images of mental illness (Arnold, 1993).

Government agencies have also joined the fray. The Center for Mental Health Services has an intramural office on consumer empowerment and funds extramural projects that attempt to discount stigma. Many state departments of mental health hire consumer advocates whose job, in part, requires vigilance to misrepresentations of mental health issues. Service groups made up of private citizens have also shown their concern about stigma. In 1996, Rotary International inaugurated "Erase the Stigma," a campaign to educate American business leaders about the truths and misconceptions of severe mental illness.

Three types of strategies—protest, education, and contact—make up the stigma-reduction armamentarium. Advocacy groups protest inaccurate and hostile representations of mental illness as a way to challenge the stigmas they represent. These efforts send two messages: To the media, they say stop reporting inaccurate representations of mental illness; to the public, they say stop believing negative views about mental illness. Protest is a reactive strategy; it diminishes negative attitudes about mental illness but fails to promote more positive attitudes that are supported by facts. Education provides information so that the public can make more informed decisions about mental illness. Education strategies are augmented by face-to-face contact. Stigma is diminished when members of the general public meet persons with schizophrenia who are able to hold down jobs or live as good neighbors in the community.

It should be noted that these stigma-reduction strategies are not always conducted in isolation from one another (Holmes, Corrigan, Williams, Canar, & Kubiak, in press). For example, an advocate might educate media groups while protesting a stigmatizing image of mental illness. A consumer group might recruit a person with mental illness (contact) to present an education program. Hence, we must also consider the combined impact of two or three of these stigma-reduction strategies.

Protesting Prejudice About Mental Illness

One way to diminish the impact of stereotypes and stigma is to protest situations where these experiences occur. The news media is replete with examples of minority groups protesting messages of the Ku Klux Klan or the American Nazi Party. In a like manner, advocacy and service groups have embraced protest as a means of diminishing mental illness stigma. NAMI, for example, has passed out "media watch kits" to local affiliates for monitoring newspapers, television, and periodicals in their area (Flynn, 1987). These kinds of efforts seek to change representations of mental illness. For example, newspaper and poster ads for a film titled *Crazy People* were patently offensive; they included a picture of a cracked egg with hands and arms and the caption, "Warning: Crazy people are coming" (Wahl, 1995). Paramount Pictures changed marketing strategies after a discussion with representatives from several advocacy groups. The new ad had pictures of the film's stars, Dudley Moore and Daryl Hannah, with the revised header, "You wanna laugh tonight?" A Philadelphia newspaper was promoting the Paramount picture by offering free admission to persons who could prove they were "crazy." Members of local advocacy groups wrote letters, marched outside newspaper offices, and met with the paper's publisher until this marketing scheme stopped.

Examples like these suggest that protest reduces the frequency of publicly endorsed stereotypes. Citizens may be encountering far fewer sanctioned examples of stigma and stereotypes because of protest efforts (Wahl, 1995). There is, however, little empirical research on the psychological impact of protest campaigns on people's prejudice about mental illness. Researchers do not know, for example, whether a "just say no to negative stereotypes" effort actually leads to more enlightened views of mental illness. Social psychological research on suppression of prejudice against minority groups has yielded some interesting findings that may answer questions about the short-term impact of protest. Suppression occurs with the controlled inhibition of unwanted stereotypic thoughts and is evinced when persons either no longer endorse prejudice or fail to recall specific stereotypes (Devine, 1989; Macrae, Bodenhausen, Milne, & Wheeler, 1996). Suppression is frequently brought about by public protest (e.g., one product of the 1960s civil rights crusade was the message that it was not socially permissible to endorse stereotypes about racial minorities).

Unfortunately, there are limits to suppression. Wegner and Erber (1992) expressed these limits when noting the irony of attitude suppression: "It seems that the very attempt to keep unwanted thoughts out of mind makes them all the more insistent" (p. 903). Wegner, Schneider, Carter, and White (1987) demonstrated this effect in their white bear experiment. Research participants who were instructed to *not* think about a white bear were initially successful by distracting themselves. However, white bear thoughts eventually returned, demonstrating the difficulty of effective thought suppression. Subsequent research showed that the suppression of targeted ideas leads to the same psychophysiological reactions as active thought about these ideas (Wegner, Shortt, Blake, & Page, 1990). Research participants instructed not to think about sex showed the same elevations in sympathetic arousal as participants who concentrated on the topic.

Macrae, Bodenhausen, Milne, and Jetten (1994) demonstrated the relevance of this rebound effect to suppressing minority group stereotypes in three studies. Participants who were instructed to avoid thinking about a White male skinhead in a stereotypic fashion were more likely to write a negatively stereotypic life story about the person, more quickly identified stigmatizing descriptors from an adjective checklist, and physically distanced themselves from skinheads, relative to participants who were not asked to suppress stereotypic beliefs. Extrapolating these findings to mental illness stigma, this research suggests that members of the general public who attempt to suppress negative stereotypes about psychiatric disability may actually be priming these stereotypes.

Rebound occurs because suppression is fundamentally an effortful cognitive process (Macrae, Bodenhausen, et al., 1994; Macrae et al., 1996). Persons must actively keep stereotypes out of consciousness by attending to other social events or recalling irrelevant information. Unfortunately, the cognitive capacity needed to keep a stereotype out of consciousness depletes limited capacity reserves that might be used for other purposes. Persons have difficulty processing other social information, including information that might disconfirm the stereotype, when suppressing these attitudes (Bargh, 1989; Hasher & Zacks, 1979; Macrae et al., 1996). Thus, persons are not able to learn information that might contradict the stereotypes (Hewstone, Macrae, Griffiths, & Milne, 1994; Macrae, Bodenhausen, & Milne, 1995). For example, citizens trying to suppress dangerousness stereotypes about a patient from a nearby psychiatric hospital may fail to notice that the patient is actually friendly and engaging, information that would disconfirm the dangerousness stigma.

Research on stereotype suppression and rebound suggests some compelling limitations to protest efforts. However, most of this research examined short-term effects on attitude change. Research needs to examine how extended protest affects attitudes over the long term. Perhaps stereotype rebound does not occur when citizens encounter repeated instructions to suppress a stereotype. Research should also examine protest effects on behavior, because the ultimate goal of suppression is on behavioral, not attitude, changes. Wahl (1995) has suggested that efforts to suppress the behavior of media groups (i.e., in their portrayal of persons with severe mental illness) may lead to fewer negative portrayals of persons with mental illness on television and in the movies. Thus, changes in media behavior may lead to improved attitudes and behaviors of the average citizen over time.

Public Education About Mental Illness

A second way to impact stereotypes and prejudice is by providing information that contradicts them. Education and information programs that address minority-group stereotypes have used books, videos, slides, and other audiovisual aids to highlight false assumptions about groups (e.g., that all persons with severe mental illness are extremely violent) and to provide facts that counter these assumptions (Bookbinder, 1978; Pate, 1988; Shapiro & Margolis, 1988; Smith, 1990). Such didactic formats are frequently augmented by discussions (Lynch, 1987; Quicke, Beasley, & Morrison, 1990); participants are more likely to reject false assumptions and remember accurate information when they discuss the material with teachers and peers. Participants may also obtain information through simulations (e.g., negotiating a wheelchair through an obstacle course to understand ambulatory disabilities or participating in "Simon says" games where up–down and left–right are reversed to experience spatial disorientation). Simulations were developed by members of the disability community to help persons who are not disabled understand their trials (Kiger, 1992). Patricia Deegan and the National Empowerment Center have devised a simulation for mental illness. In this exercise, participants experience the intrusive nature of auditory hallucinations by trying to complete simple work tasks while listening to an audiotape of irrelevant and mixed-up voices.

Several groups have developed and implemented education programs. NAMI developed and distributed their "science and treatment kit" for informing the public about mental illness and corresponding treatment. The National Mental Health Association has developed education programs for children. The popular media has produced films and television shows that disseminate stigma-countering information. For example, NAMI worked with CBS to produce the *Marie Balter Story*, a movie about the struggle and successes of a woman who had been institutionalized for more than a decade. CBS and Hallmark Cards aired a 1986 film, *Promise*, in which James Woods and James Garner depicted the real-life interactions of a man with schizophrenia and his brother. Media efforts are promising because they can reach a large audience.

Several studies have examined the effects of education on mental illness stigma. Research indicates that persons who have a better understanding of mental illness are less likely to endorse stigma and discrimination (Brockington et al., 1993; Link & Cullen, 1986; Link, Cullen, Frank, & Wozniak, 1987; Roman & Floyd, 1981). Several studies have also shown that participation in brief courses on mental illness and treatment lead to improved attitudes about persons with mental illness (Keane, 1990, 1991; Morrison, 1976, 1977, 1980; Morrison, Becker, & Bourgeois, 1979; Morrison, Cocozza, & Vanderwyst, 1980; Morrison & Teta, 1977, 1978, 1979, 1980). These programs are effective for a wide variety of participants, including psychology graduate students, adolescents, nursing students, community residents, persons with mental illness, and medical students.

Penn et al. (1994) examined the effect of education in a study that controlled the kinds of information presented to participants. Some participants received information about the target individual's acute symptoms, whereas others were informed about his after-care plan. Although the investigators believed this information would allay negative responses toward the target, results were mixed. Information about posttreatment living arrangements reduced negative judgments about the target person. However, participants who were given information about psychotic symptoms showed a significant increase in negative attitudes about schizophrenia. In a subsequent study, Penn, Kommana, Mansfield, and Link (in press) assumed that stigmatizing views about schizophrenia stem from concerns about dangerousness and targeted these beliefs in various information segments. Results showed that participants who learned the base rates of violence in persons with mental illness (relative to other disorders) were less likely to stigmatize than a no-information control group.

A brief education effort by Thornton and Wahl

(1996) seemed to diminish stigmatizing attitudes about mental illness. They appended an article that discussed misconceptions about mental illness to a popular press item about the tragic death of an innocent victim at the hands of a mentally ill patient. Persons who read the appended article endorsed fewer stigmatizing attitudes. Sometimes, however, brief programs like these fail; other studies have shown that brief informational segments attached to media presentations about mental illness seem to have no effect on viewer attitudes (Domino, 1983; Wahl & Lefkowits, 1989).

Providing sufficient information to counter stigma regarding symptoms is difficult in brief programs like these. Holmes et al. (in press) examined the effects of a semester-long education program on the stigmatizing attitudes of community college students. Participants improved their attitudes about benevolence and fear, although the size of these effects was limited and attitude change affected by education interacted with the research participants' preeducation knowledge. Students with more knowledge about severe mental illness prior to participating in an education program were less likely to endorse stigmatizing attitudes after completing the program. This finding is generally consistent with what's known about propaganda-related efforts to change attitudes and beliefs toward minority groups: They tend to reach those who already agree with the message (Devine, 1995).

Stereotypes' Resilience to Disconfirmation

These general findings parallel the mixed results of education programs that target race and other minority group stereotypes (Devine, 1995; Pruegger & Rogers, 1994). On the one hand, attitudes (and hence stereotypes) seem to be relatively plastic phenomena, which can be modified through planned change techniques (Rothbart & Lewis, 1988). Fields like advertising and marketing are dedicated to the belief that personal opinion can be influenced by appropriately formatted information. On the other hand, social psychological researchers have documented several resilient characteristics of stereotypes, suggesting that these knowledge structures are extremely difficult to disconfirm once developed (Fyock & Stangor, 1994; Rothbart & John, 1993). These characteristics explain why the effects of education on psychiatric stigma may be limited.

Researchers have suggested that activation of well-learned and often-used stereotypes, as opposed to newly acquired attitudes, is an automatic cognitive process (Devine, 1989; Hilton & von Hippel, 1996; Macrae, Milne, & Bodenhausen, 1994). For example, people spontaneously become aware of stereotypes after encountering a minority group member to which the stereotypes correspond. Well-learned and preexisting stereotypes serve as templates that encode subsequent information that might counter these stereotypes. As a result, stereotypes produce a consistency effect that undermines disconfirmation (i.e., social information is recalled in a manner that is consistent with the preexisting stereotypes). This phenomenon has been supported in two independent meta-analyses of 80 studies (Fyock & Stangor, 1994; Stangor & McMillan, 1992).

The consistency effect is evident even in situations where research participants are explicitly directed to suppress a stereotype (Fyock & Stangor, 1994). This effect tends to be most pronounced in situations that demand high cognitive load (Macrae, Hewstone, & Griffiths, 1993; Stangor & Duan, 1991). Persons are likely to be most sensitive to stereotype-confirming information when they are distracted by other cognitive tasks or when cognitive capacity is diminished by psychophysiological arousal.

The consistency–confirmation effect is not limited to passive influences on the recollection of information; it also affects active processes related to information seeking. There is a tendency to seek out information about minority group members that confirms stereotypes about those groups (Bodenhausen & Wyer, 1985; Pendry & Macrae, 1994; Skov & Sherman, 1986). Moreover, stereotypes have been perceived to be confirmed even when confirming evidence is absent (Bodenhausen & Wyer, 1985). Finally, stereotypes seem to override information that would discount a prejudicial judgment (Krueger & Rothbart, 1988; Macrae et al., 1995). For example, criminal justice research has shown that minority group stereotypes may outweigh factual case evidence in a jury's decision about guilt (Bodenhausen & Lichtenstein, 1987). These findings suggest that participants in an education program may easily recall information that confirms mental illness stigma about dangerousness and may ignore information that challenges these stigmas, such as information that the acute symptoms associated with violent behavior, may remit.

Limits to Resilience

Despite these findings, there are limits to the resilience of stereotypes. First, just because most people have knowledge of a set of stereotypes does not imply that they will endorse these stereotypes, use them to generate stigmatizing judgments, or act on them in a discriminatory manner (Jussim et al., 1995). For example, persons can recall stereotypes about a racial group in America but do not necessarily agree that the stereotypes are valid. According to Devine (1995), negative stereotypes may be automatically activated by environmental factors, but individuals low in prejudice may inhibit these stereotypes by using more cognitively controlled personal beliefs (e.g., that it is unfair to stereotype on the basis of ethnic group or gender). People who are prejudiced endorse these negative stereotypes and act against minority groups accordingly (Devine, 1989, 1995; Hilton & von Hippel, 1996; Krueger, 1996).

Second, the stereotype-consistency effect does not alter the processing of all information. It is most pronounced when persons are asked to consider whether minority group members' traits, rather than their behaviors, are consistent with a stereotype (Fyock & Stangor, 1994). Research has shown that persons are more likely to relate traits (e.g., members of that group are aloof and unfriendly) to stereotype labels rather than behaviors (e.g., those group members will not be helpful in a time of need). Therefore, behavioral expectations about minority groups may be more amenable to education than trait characteristics. Thus, if we intend to improve housing opportunities for persons with severe mental illness, then the target of education should be prospective landlords' beliefs about the likelihood of physical violence (behavior) among persons with severe mental illness rather than on whether persons are irritable or unpredictable (traits).

This finding suggests that education programs might lead to diminished discrimination even if dramatic changes in stereotypes and stigma are not observed. Unfortunately, researchers have not examined the impact of education programs on behavior change. Moreover, researchers have examined the immediate impact of education on attitudes (Corrigan, River, Lundin, Penn, et al., 1998; Holmes et al., in press; Keane, 1990, 1991; Penn et al., 1994, in press) but generally have not followed up on its long-term impact. Researchers need to examine how education facilitates attitude and behavior change over the long term.

Contact With Persons With Severe Mental Illness

Contact with minority group members may augment the effects of education on reducing stigma. Researchers have shown that members of the majority who have met persons representing a minority or other group are more likely to disconfirm stereotypes describing that group (Gaertner, Rust, Dovidio, Bachman, & Anastasio, 1996). Hence, contact may be an important strategy for decreasing stereotypes and mental health stigma.

One important variable that mediates contact is opportunity; members of the majority must have opportunities to interact with minority group members if stigma is to change (Sigelman & Welch, 1993). Hence, persons with severe mental illness must have formal opportunities to contact and interact with the general public. Many state departments of mental health have developed offices of consumer affairs to, in part, foster contact. For example, the State of Connecticut Department of Mental Health and Addiction Services is promoting a program called "Disclosure" to further this cause. They believe disclosing the breadth of psychiatric disability in Connecticut and revealing recovery stories will significantly reduce stigma and discrimination. The states of New York (Blanch, Fisher, Tucker, Walsh, & Chassman, 1993; Knight & Blanch, 1993a, 1993b), Florida (Loder & Glover, 1992), and Illinois (Corrigan, Lickey, Schmook, Virgil, & Juricek, in press) have expanded on this effort by arranging formal dialogues between persons with mental illness and mental health care professionals. These dialogues provided a forum for consumers and health care professionals to exchange perspectives about mental illness and challenge latent stigmatizing attitudes.

Researchers have examined the effect of contact on psychiatric stigma. A recent meta-analysis revealed that providing contact with persons with mental illness is associated with improved attitudes, with the findings strongest when contact was provided in the context of general undergraduate training (Kolodziej & Johnson, 1996). The positive effects of contact on attitudes toward persons with mental illness has also been demonstrated outside of student and employee training. Specifically, there is an inverse relationship between self-reported previous contact with persons with mental illness and psychiatric stigma (Holmes et al., in press; Link & Cullen, 1986; Penn et al., 1994, in press). In a laboratory study, Desforges et al. (1991) carefully examined the effects of strategic contact in a study with 95 undergraduates in a randomized controlled trial. After students who were initially prejudiced participated in a cooperative task with a person described as recently released from a mental institution, these students endorsed more positive attitudes about the mentally ill person and showed greater acceptance toward mental illness in general.

This study by Desforges et al. (1991) echoes the results of numerous studies that have shown that contact improves attitudes about minority and other groups (for reviews, see Gaertner et al., 1996; Hamburger, 1994; Rothbart & John, 1985; Stephan, 1987). Additional research has identified factors that augment the effects of interpersonal contact, including equal status among participants (Cook, 1985; Riordan, 1978), cooperative interaction (Johnson, Johnson, & Maruyama, 1984; Worchel, 1986), institutional support for contact (Adlerfer, 1982; Williams, 1977), frequent contact with individuals who mildly disconfirm the stereotype (Johnston & Hewstone, 1992; Weber & Crocker, 1983), a high level of intimacy (Amir, 1976; Brown & Turner, 1981; Ellison & Powers, 1994), and real-world opportunities to interact with minority group members outside of contrived situations (Sigelman & Welch, 1993). These factors have several implications for programs that facilitate contact between members of the general public and persons with severe mental illness.

Contact programs for mental illness will be more successful when all participants have equal status. Hence, persons with mental illness need to be presented as one of many citizens attending a program rather than as the "token mentally ill patient." Equal status is facilitated when persons with mental illness are cooperating with others on a work task. In this way, citizens with mental illness are viewed as competent and bring needed skills and energy to the chore. Status is also facilitated when contact provides opportunities for friendly and intimate interaction among participants. Rather than limiting the engagement to businesslike exchanges, stereotype and stigma are diminished when members of the public have mutual and informal conversations with persons with mental illness. Finally, the goals of contact are facilitated when the institution formally acknowledges the effort. For example, a contact program in a school will be more effective when the principal publicly approves the effort.

Contact seems to affect stigmatizing knowledge structures through cognitive individuation (i.e., a person's natural stereotype of a minority group member is superseded by another, more positive image when that person contacts a member of that group; Horwitz & Rabbie, 1989; Rothbart & John, 1985), although recategorization of the minority group member is also possible (i.e., changes in the classification from "them" to "us"; Gaertner, Mann, Dovidio, Murrell, & Pomare, 1990). For example, encountering an equal-status person with severe mental illness during a mutually cooperative task (e.g., working with a mentally ill woman on a church social) might suppress negative images about the person being dangerous or incompetent. Instead, members of the general public engaged in this interaction are likely to view the person as friendly and capable.

The strength of individuation effects varies with the level of disconfirmation engendered by the contacted group member (Kunda & Oleson, 1995). Experiences with persons who grossly vary with stereotypes about a minority group are likely to have little effect on those stereotypes. For example, members of the general public who viewed the "church social" woman with severe mental illness as friendly, capable, and hardworking may show little change in stigma about mental illness and continue to view persons with mental illness as dangerous and incompetent. Experiences with markedly "atypical" group members may not only fail to discredit stigma (Hamburger, 1994; Rothbart & Lewis, 1988; Weber & Crocker, 1983) but may actually lead to a boomerang effect where stereotypes become more extreme (Kunda & Oleson, 1997). The woman with mental illness in our church social example is atypical because she is not disheveled or dangerous. Rather than using information about her to discount mental illness stigmas, she may be subtyped as unusual and not representative of mental illness as a whole. Subtyping in essence insulates the broader stereotype (Kunda & Oleson, 1995).

Inhibitions to stigma change caused by atypical persons are limited to individuals who are extremely dissimilar to stereotypes. Experience with contacted group members who mildly or moderately disconfirm a stereotype seems to change stigma (Kunda & Oleson, 1995, 1997). Individuals who are similar to stereotypes in most ways but vary on one or two key dimensions can also change attitudes about those perspectives. Hence, a good contact might be a person who is struggling with residual symptoms and seems socially anxious but who is earning a living wage through a job as a bagger at a local market. Citizens who meet this person may change their attitudes about mental illness hindering people from working and living independently.

Conclusions

Reducing stigma is essential for improving the quality of life of people with severe mental illness. Decreasing stereotypes and prejudices about severe mental illness could potentially diminish the discrimination experienced by persons with these disorders. Advocacy groups, governmental organizations, and public service agencies have embraced stigma-reduction strategies like protest, education, and contact as essential ways to challenge negative stereotypes and stop discrimination. Researchers who have examined the social psychology of minority group stereotypes have highlighted some of the cognitive mechanisms that reduce stigma, the limitations of these strategies, and some factors that moderate their effects.

Extrapolating research based on minority and other group stereotypes to the injustice of psychiatric disability has its problems. For example, persons who are subjected to racial stereotypes exemplify a "discredited" stigma because the characteristics identifying the minority group (e.g., skin color) are readily apparent to others (Goffman, 1963). Persons with severe mental illness may represent individuals who are both discredited (i.e.,

they may manifest psychotic symptoms in public) and "discreditable" (i.e., *if in remission, they may* be able to hide their mental illness from others). For persons with discredited stigma (i.e., acute symptoms), stigma-reduction efforts might need to focus on making accomodations for them and building community tolerance and compassion for their disorder. For persons with a discreditable stigma (i.e., their symptoms are in remission), efforts should be focused on dispelling myths about severe mental illness and trying to change negative stereotypes (e.g., once a person has had a mental illness, they'll always be unpredictable). Therefore, researchers need to consider the discredited–discreditable dimension when developing specific interventions to reduce stigmatization toward persons with severe mental illness.

The research reviewed in this article points to a number of future directions in the practice and research of eliminating psychiatric stigma. For example, the integration of research in social and clinical psychology leads to the following hypotheses:

1. Protest and suppression of mental illness stigma may lead to short-term rebound effects. Namely, members of the general public will more likely recall negative information about individuals with severe mental illness when they are instructed to suppress stereotypes about them. Moreover, members of the general public who are instructed to suppress stigma will learn less factual information about mental illness during educational programs than will peers who do not receive those instructions.
2. Active forms of education that combine formal instruction with discussion and simulations will lead to greater reduction in stigma than formal lectures alone. Program success will depend, however, on providing information that presents the symptoms and deficits of mental illness in a hopeful light. Education programs should have more positive effects on expectations about the behavior of a person with mental illness, whereas views about the person's traits should remain static.
3. Contact with persons with mental illness should diminish psychiatric stigma. Contact effects should improve when there is equal status among participants, cooperative tasks define the

interaction, there is institutional support for contact, there are high levels of intimacy, and the person with severe mental illness does not greatly differ from the stereotype.

Stigma-changing efforts should not be limited to changing attitudes only. For example, in a recent meta-analysis, Krauss (1995) found that the mean association between attitudes and future behavior is approximately .39, suggesting that changing attitudes does not assure change in behavior. This association is strengthened if attitudes are accessible, stable, formed as a result of direct experience, and personally relevant (Krauss, 1995; Petty, 1995). Moreover, individual differences in responding to stigma-reduction strategies should be explored. This may be especially appropriate for factors such as gender; although men and women have similar attitudes toward persons with mental illness, women's behavior tends to be kinder (Farina, 1981). Such individual difference variables may represent rate-limiting factors in the effectiveness of various stigma-reduction strategies.

Research reviewed in this article has focused on strategies for changing public attitudes about and behavior toward persons with severe mental illness. Persons with mental illness need not, however, be passive agents in this process, awaiting society to become more accepting of them and their mental illness. There are a variety of strategies that persons with severe mental illness might select to cope with the impact of stigma (Corrigan, 1998; Farina, 1998). Specific strategies include selective disclosure of one's mental health history (River & Holmes, in press); those that foster empowerment like mutual help groups (Kurtz & Chambon, 1987), psychosocial clubhouses (Beard, Propst, & Malamud, 1994), and Fairweather lodges (Fairweather, 1969); and hiring consumers of mental health services to provide these services (Mowbray, Moxley, Jasper, & Howell, 1997). These strategies may counteract the loss of self-esteem and self-efficacy experienced by persons with severe mental illness because of societal stigma. Future research needs to examine the impact of stigma on self-coping and empowerment.

These investigations only begin to define a research program that will significantly enhance stigma-reduction efforts. Information from this program will sharpen activist efforts to diminish negative stereotypes and discrimination aimed at persons with severe mental illness. With diminished stigma, these persons will have greater opportunities to live independent lives and successfully address their personal goals.

ACKNOWLEDGMENTS

We thank Leonard Newman for reviewing a draft of this article.

NOTES

1. We define mental illness as the categories of schizophrenia and other psychotic disorders, mood disorders, anxiety disorders, and personality disorders listed in the *Diagnostic and Statistical Manual of Mental Disorders* (4th ed.; *DSM–IV*; American Psychiatric Association, 1994). Stigma researchers typically distinguish the stigma of mental illnesses like these from other *DSM–IV* groups such as developmental disabilities and substance abuse disorders.

REFERENCES

Adlerfer, C. P. (1982). Problems of changing white males' behavior and beliefs concerning race relations. In P. Goodman (Ed.), *Change in organizations* (pp. 122–165). San Francisco, CA: Jossey-Bass.

Albrecht, G. L., Walker, V. G., & Levy, J. A. (1982). Social distance from the stigmatized: A test of two theories. *Social Science & Medicine, 16,* 1319–1327.

American Psychiatric Association. (1994). *Diagnostic and statistical manual of mental disorders* (4th ed.). Washington, DC: Author.

Amir, Y. (1976). Contact hypothesis in ethnic relations. *Psychological Bulletin, 71,* 319–342.

Arnold, J. (1993). A clearinghouse mobilizes against stigma. *Journal of the California Alliance for the Mentally Ill, 4,* 50–51.

Augoustinos, M., & Ahrens, C. (1994). Stereotypes and prejudice: The Australian experience. *British Journal of Social Psychology, 33,* 125–141.

Bargh, J. A. (1989). Conditional automaticity: Varieties of automatic influence in social perception and cognition. In J. S. Uleman & J. A. Bargh (Eds.), *Unintended thought* (pp. 3–51). New York: Guilford Press.

Beard, J. H., Propst, R. N., & Malamud, T. J. (1994). The Fountain House model of psychiatric rehabilitation. In *An introduction to psychiatric rehabilitation* (pp. 42–52). Columbia, MD: International Association of Psychosocial Rehabilitation Services.

Bhugra, D. (1989). Attitudes toward mental illness: A review of the literature. *Acta Psychiatrica Scandinavica, 80,* 1–12.

Blanch, A., Fisher, D., Tucker, W., Walsh, D., & Chassman, J. (1993). Consumer-practitioners and psychiatrists share insights about recovery and coping. *Disability Studies Quarterly, 13,* 17–20.

Bodenhausen, G. V., & Lichtenstein, M. (1987). Social stereotypes and information-processing strategies: The impact of task complexity. *Journal of Personality and Social Psychology, 52*, 871–880.

Bodenhausen, G. V., & Wyer, R. S. (1985). Effects of stereotypes on decision making and information processing. *Journal of Personality and Social Psychology, 48*, 267–282.

Bookbinder, S. R. (1978). *Mainstreaming—What every child needs to know about disabilities*. Providence, RI: Rhode Island Easter Seal Society.

Bordieri, J., & Drehmer, D. (1986). Hiring decisions for disabled workers: Looking at the cause. *Journal of Applied Social Psychology, 16*, 197–208.

Brockington, I., Hall, P., Levings, J., & Murphy, C. (1993). The community's tolerance of the mentally ill. *British Journal of Psychiatry, 162*, 93–99.

Brown, R. J., & Turner, J. C. (1981). Interpersonal and intergroup behavior. In J. Turner & H. Giles (Eds.), *Intergroup behavior* (pp. 33–65). Chicago: University of Chicago Press.

Cook, S. W. (1985). Experimenting on social issues: The case of school desegregation. *American Psychologist, 40*, 452–460.

Corrigan, P. W. (1998). The impact of stigma on severe mental illness. *Cognitive and Behavioral Practice, 5*, 201–222.

Corrigan, P. W., Lickey, S., Schmook, A., Virgil, L., & Juricek, M. (in press). Dialogue among stakeholders of severe mental illness. *Psychiatric Rehabilitation Journal*.

Corrigan, P. W., & Penn, D. L. (1997). Disease and discrimination: Two paradigms that describe severe mental illness. *Journal of Mental Health, 6*, 355–366.

Corrigan, P. W., River, L. P., Lundin, R. K., Penn, D. L., Wasowski, K. U., Campion, J., Mathisen, J., Gagnon, C., Bergman, M., Goldstein, H., & Kubiak, M. A. (1998). *Three strategies for changing attributions about severe mental illness*. Manuscript submitted for publication.

Corrigan, P. W., River, L. P., Lundin, R. K., Wasowski, K. U., Campion, J., Mathisen, J., Goldstein, H., Bergman, M., Gagnon, C., & Kubiak, M. A. (1998). *Stigmatizing attributions about mental illness*. Manuscript submitted for publication.

Crocetti, G., Spiro, H. R., & Siassi, I. (1971). Are the ranks closed? Attitudinal social distance and mental illness. *American Journal of Psychiatry, 127*, 1121–1127.

Desforges, D. M., Lord, C. G., Ramsey, S. L., Mason, J. A., Van Leeuwen, M. D., West, S. C., & Lepper, M. R. (1991). Effects of structured cooperative contact on changing negative attitudes toward stigmatized social groups. *Journal of Personality and Social Psychology, 60*, 531–544.

Devine, P. G. (1988). *Stereotype assessment: Theoretical and methodological issues*. Unpublished manuscript, University of Wisconsin–Madison.

Devine, P. G. (1989). Stereotypes and prejudice: Their automatic and controlled components. *Journal of Personality and Social Psychology, 56*, 5–18.

Devine, P. G. (1995). Prejudice and out-group perception. In A. Tesser (Ed.), *Advanced social psychology* (pp. 467–524). New York: McGraw-Hill.

Domino, G. (1983). Impact of the film, One Flew Over the Cuckoo's Nest, on attitudes towards mental illness. *Psychological Reports, 53*, 179–182.

Ellison, C. G., & Powers, D. A. (1994). The contact hypothesis and racial attitudes among Black Americans. *Social Science Quarterly, 75*, 385–400.

Esses, V. M., Haddock, G., & Zanna, M. P. (1994). The role of mood in the expression of intergroup stereotypes. In M. P. Zanna & J. M. Olson (Eds.), *The psychology of prejudice: The Ontario experience* (Vol. 7, pp. 77–101). Hillsdale, NJ: Lawrence Erlbaum Associates.

Fairweather, G. W. (1969). *Community life for the mentally ill: An alternative to institutional care*. Chicago: Aldine.

Farina, A. (1981). Are women nicer people than men? Sex and the stigma of mental illness. *Clinical Psychology Review, 1*, 223–243.

Farina, A. (1998). Stigma. In K. T. Mueser & N. Tarrier (Eds.), *Handbook of social functioning in schizophrenia* (pp. 247–279). Boston: Allyn & Bacon.

Farina, A., & Felner, R. D. (1973). Employment interviewer reactions to former mental patients. *Journal of Abnormal Psychology, 82*, 268–272.

Flynn, L. M. (1987). The stigma of mental illness. In A. B. Hatfield (Ed.), *Families of the mentally ill: Meeting the challenges* (pp. 53–60). San Francisco: Jossey-Bass.

Fyock, J., & Stangor, C. (1994). The role of memory biases in stereotype maintenance. *British Journal of Social Psychology, 33*, 331–343.

Gabbard, G. O., & Gabbard, K. (1992). Cinematic stereotypes contributing to the stigmatization of psychiatrists. In P. J. Fink & A. Tasman (Eds.), *Stigma and mental illness* (pp. 113–126). Washington, DC: American Psychiatric Press.

Gaertner, S. L., & Dovidio, J. F. (1986). The aversive form of racism. In J. F. Dovidio & S. L. Gaertner (Eds.), *Prejudice, discrimination, and racism* (pp. 61–89). San Diego: Academic Press.

Gaertner, S. L., Mann, J., Dovidio, J. F., Murrell, F., & Pomare, M. (1990). How does cooperation reduce intergroup bias? *Journal of Personality and Social Psychology, 59*, 692–704.

Gaertner, S. L., Rust, M. C., Dovidio, J. F., Bachman, B. A., & Anastasio, P. A. (1996). The contact hypothesis: The role of a common ingroup identity on reducing intergroup bias among majority and minority group members. In J. L. Nye & A. M. Brower (Eds.), *What's social about social cognition?* (pp. 230–260). Thousand Oaks, CA: Sage.

Goffman, E. (1963). *Stigma: Notes on the management of spoiled identity*. Englewood Cliffs, NJ: Prentice Hall.

Greenley, J. (1984). Social factors, mental illness, and psychiatric care: Recent advances from a sociological perspective. *Hospital and Community Psychiatry, 35*, 813–820.

Hamburger, Y. (1994). The contact hypothesis reconsidered: Effects of the atypical outgroup member on the outgroup stereotype. *Basic and Applied Social Psychology, 15*, 339–358.

Hamilton, D. L., & Sherman, J. W. (1994). Stereotypes. In R. S. Wyer & T. K. Srull (Eds.), *Handbook of social cognition* (2nd ed., Vol. 2, pp. 1–68). Hillsdale, NJ: Lawrence Erlbaum Associates.

Hamre, P., Dahl, A., & Malt, U. (1994). Public attitudes to the quality of psychiatric treatment, psychiatric patients, and prevalence of mental disorders. *Nordic Journal of Psychiatry, 4*, 275–281.

Hasher, L., & Zacks, R. T. (1979). Automatic and effortful processes in memory. *Journal of Experimental Psychology: General, 108*, 356–385.

Hewstone, M., Macrae, C. N., Griffiths, R., & Milne, A. B. (1994). Cognitive models of stereotype change: 5. Measurement, development, and consequences of subtyping. *Journal of Experimental Social Psychology, 30*, 505–526.

Hilton, J. L., & von Hippel, W. (1996). Stereotypes. *Annual Review of Psychology, 47*, 237–271.
Holmes, P., Corrigan, P. W., Williams, P., Canar, J., & Kubiak, M. (in press). The relation of knowledge and attitudes about persons with a severe mental illness. *Schizophrenia Bulletin.*
Horwitz, M., & Rabbie, J. M. (1989). Stereotypes of groups, group members, and individuals in categories: A differential analysis. In D. Bar-Tal, C. F. Graumann, A. W. Kruglanski, & W. Stroebe (Eds.), *Stereotyping and prejudice: Changing conceptions* (pp. 105–129). New York: Springer-Verlag.
Huffine, C. L., & Clausen, J. A. (1979). Madness and work: Short- and long-term effects of mental illness on occupational careers. *Social Forces, 57*, 1049–1062.
Hyler, S. E., Gabbard, G. O., & Schneider, I. (1991). Homicidal maniacs and narcissistic parasites: Stigmatization of mentally ill persons in the movies. *Hospital and Community Psychiatry, 42*, 1044–1048.
Johnson, D. W., Johnson, R., & Maruyama, G. (1984). Goal interdependence and interpersonal attraction in heterogeneous classrooms. In N. Miller & M. B. Brewer (Eds.), *Groups in contact* (pp. 187–213). New York: Academic Press.
Johnston, L., & Hewstone, M. (1992). Cognitive models of stereotype change: 3. Subtyping and the perceived typicality of disconfirming group members. *Journal of Experimental Social Psychology, 28*, 360–386.
Judd, C. M., & Park, B. (1993). Definition and assessment of accuracy in social stereotypes. *Psychological Review, 100*, 109–128.
Jussim, L., Nelson, T. E., Manis, M., & Soffin, S. (1995). Prejudice, stereotypes, and labeling effects: Sources of bias in person perception. *Journal of Personality and Social Psychology, 68*, 228–246.
Keane, M. (1990). Contemporary beliefs about mental illness among medical students: Implications for education and practice. *Academic Psychiatry, 14*, 172–177.
Keane, M. (1991). Acceptance vs. rejection: Nursing students' attitudes about mental illness. *Perspectives in Psychiatric Care, 27*, 13–18.
Kiger, G. (1992). Disability simulations: Logical, methodological and ethical issues. *Disability, Handicap & Society, 7*, 71–78.
Knight, E., & Blanch, A. (1993a). *A dialogue on recovery: An experiment in progress.* Albany, NY: New York State Office of Mental Health.
Knight, E., & Blanch, A. (1993b). *A dialogue on recovery: Tips for structuring a recipient dialogue.* Albany, NY: New York State Office of Mental Health.
Kolodziej, M. E., & Johnson, B. T. (1996). Interpersonal contact and acceptance of persons with psychiatric disorders: A research synthesis. *Journal of Consulting and Clinical Psychology, 64*, 1387–1396.
Krauss, S. J. (1995). Attitudes and the prediction of behavior: A meta-analysis of the empirical literature. *Personality and Social Psychology Bulletin, 21*, 58–75.
Krueger, J. (1996). Personal beliefs and cultural stereotypes about racial characteristics. *Journal of Personality and Social Psychology, 71*, 536–548.
Krueger, J., & Rothbart, M. (1988). Use of categorical and individuating information in making inferences about personality. *Journal of Personality and Social Psychology, 55*, 187–195.

Kunda, Z., & Oleson, K. C. (1995). Maintaining stereotypes in the face of disconfirmation: Constructing grounds for subtyping deviants. *Journal of Personality and Social Psychology, 68*, 565–579.
Kunda, Z., & Oleson, K. C. (1997). When exceptions prove the rule: How extremity of deviance determines the impact of deviant examples on stereotypes. *Journal of Personality and Social Psychology, 72*, 965–979.
Kurtz, L. F., & Chambon, A. (1987). Comparison of self-help groups for mental health. *Health and Social Work, 12*, 275–283.
Leary, M. R., & Maddux, J. E. (1987). Progress towards a viable interface between social and clinical psychology. *American Psychologist, 42*, 904–911.
Lefley, H. P. (1992). The stigmatized family. In P. J. Fink & A. Tasman (Eds.), *Stigma and mental illness* (pp. 127–138). Washington, DC: American Psychiatric Press.
Lindsay, W. R. (1982). The effects of labeling: Blind and nonblind ratings of social skills in schizophrenic and nonschizophrenic control subjects. *American Journal of Psychiatry, 139*, 216–219.
Link, B. G. (1987). Understanding labeling effects in the area of mental disorders: An assessment of the effects of expectations of rejection. *American Sociological Review, 52*, 96–112.
Link, B. G., & Cullen, F. T. (1983). Reconsidering the social rejection of ex-mental patients: Levels of attitudinal response. *American Journal of Community Psychology, 11*, 261–273.
Link, B. G., & Cullen, F. T. (1986). Contact with the mentally ill and perceptions of how dangerous they are. *Journal of Health and Social Behavior, 27*, 289–303.
Link, B. G., Cullen, F. T., Frank, J., & Wozniak, J. F. (1987). The social rejection of former mental patients: Understanding why labels matter. *American Journal of Sociology, 92*, 1461–1500.
Link, B. G., Cullen, F. T., Mirotznik, J., & Struening, E. (1992). The consequences of stigma for persons with mental illness: Evidence from the social sciences. In P. J. Fink & A. Tasman (Eds.), *Stigma and mental illness* (pp. 87–96). Washington, DC: American Psychiatric Press.
Link, B. G., Cullen, F. T., Struening, E. L., Shrout, P. E., & Dohrenwend, B. P. (1989). A modified labeling theory approach to mental disorders: An empirical assessment. *American Sociological Review, 54*, 400–423.
Loder, A., & Glover, R. (1992). *New frontiers: Pioneer dialogue between consumers/survivors and commissioners.* Fort Lauderdale, FL: Peer Center.
Lynch, J. (1987). *Prejudice reduction and the schools.* London: Cassell.
Lyons, M., & Ziviani, J. (1995). Stereotypes, stigma and mental illness: Learning from fieldwork experiences. *American Journal of Occupational Therapy, 49*, 1002–1008.
Macrae, C. N., Bodenhausen, G. V., & Milne, A. B. (1995). The dissection of selection in person perception: Inhibitory processes in social stereotyping. *Journal of Personality and Social Psychology, 69*, 397–407.
Macrae, C. N., Bodenhausen, G. V., Milne, A. B., & Jetten, J. (1994). Out of mind but back in sight: Stereotypes on the rebound. *Journal of Personality and Social Psychology, 67*, 808–817.
Macrae, C. N., Bodenhausen, G. V., Milne, A. B., & Wheeler, V. (1996). On resisting the temptation for simplification:

Counterintentional effects of stereotype suppression on social memory. *Social Cognition, 14,* 1–20.

Macrae, C. N., Hewstone, M., & Griffiths, R. J. (1993). Processing load and memory for stereotype-based information. *European Journal of Social Psychology, 23,* 77–87.

Macrae, C. N., Milne, A. B., & Bodenhausen, G. V. (1994). Stereotypes as energy-saving devices: A peek inside the cognitive toolbox. *Journal of Personality and Social Psychology, 66,* 37–47.

Madianos, M. G., Madianou, D. G., Vlachonikolis, J., & Stefanis, C. N. (1987). Attitudes toward mental illness in the Athens area: Implications for community mental health intervention. *Acta Psychiatrica Scandinavica, 75,* 158–165.

Mayer, A., & Barry, D. D. (1992). Working with the media to destigmatize mental illness. *Hospital and Community Psychiatry, 43,* 77–78.

Mechanic, D., McAlpine, D., Rosenfield, S., & Davis, D. (1994). Effects of illness attribution and depression on the quality of life among persons with serious mental illness. *Social Science & Medicine, 39,* 155–164.

Mirabi, M., Weinman, M. L., Magnetti, S. M., & Keppler, K. N. (1985). Professional attitudes toward the chronic mentally ill. *Hospital and Community Psychology, 36,* 404–405.

Monahan, J. (1992). Mental disorder and violent behavior: Perceptions and evidence. *American Psychologist, 47,* 511–521.

Morrison, J. K. (1976). Demythologizing mental patients' attitudes toward mental illness: An empirical study. *Journal of Community Psychology, 4,* 181–185.

Morrison, J. K. (1977). Changing negative attributions to mental patients by means of demythologizing seminars. *Journal of Clinical Psychology, 33,* 549–551.

Morrison, J. K. (1980). The public's current beliefs about mental illness: Serious obstacle to effective community psychology. *American Journal of Community Psychology, 8,* 697–707.

Morrison, J. K., Becker, R. E., & Bourgeois, C. A. (1979). Decreasing adolescents' fear of mental patients by means of demythologizing. *Psychological Reports, 44,* 855–859.

Morrison, J. K., Cocozza, J. J., & Vanderwyst, D. (1980). An attempt to change the negative, stigmatizing image of mental patients through brief reeducation. *Psychological Reports, 47,* 334.

Morrison, J. K., & Teta, D. C. (1977). Increase of positive self-attributions by means of demythologizing seminars. *Journal of Clinical Psychology, 33,* 1128–1131.

Morrison, J. K., & Teta, D. C. (1978). Effect of demythologizing seminars on attributions to mental health professionals. *Psychological Reports, 43,* 493–494.

Morrison, J. K., & Teta, D. C. (1979). Impact of a humanistic approach on students' attitudes, attributions, and ethical conflicts. *Psychological Reports, 45,* 863–866.

Morrison, J. K., & Teta, D. C. (1980). Reducing students' fear of mental illness by means of seminar-induced belief change. *Journal of Clinical Psychology, 36,* 275–276.

Mowbray, C. T., Moxley, D. P., Jasper, C. A., & Howell, L. L. (Eds.). (1997). *Consumers as providers in psychiatric rehabilitation.* Columbia, MD: International Association of Psychosocial Rehabilitation Services.

Mullen, B., Rozell, D., & Johnson, C. (1996). The phenomenology of being in a group: Complexity approaches to operationalizing cognitive representation. In J. L. Nye & A. M. Brower (Eds.), *What's social about social cognition?* (pp. 205–229). Thousand Oaks, CA: Sage.

NAMI E-news. (1998). *State parity update* [Online]. Retrieved August 8, 1998, from the World Wide Web: http://www.nami.org.

Olshansky, S., Grob, S., & Ekdahl, M. (1960). Survey of employment experience of patients discharged from three mental hospitals during the period 1951–1953. *Mental Hygiene, 44,* 510–521.

Page, S. (1977). Effects of the mental illness label in attempts to obtain accommodation. *Canadian Journal of Behavioral Sciences, 9,* 85–90.

Page, S. (1980). Social responsiveness toward mental patients: The general public and others. *Canadian Journal of Psychiatry, 25,* 242–246.

Page, S. (1983). Psychiatric stigma: Two studies of behavior when the chips are down. *Canadian Journal of Community Mental Health, 2,* 13–19.

Page, S. (1995). Effects of the mental illness label in 1993: Acceptance and rejection in the community. *Journal of Health and Social Policy, 7,* 61–68.

Pate, G. S. (1988). Research on reducing prejudice. *Social Education, 52,* 287–289.

Pendry, L. F., & Macrae, C. N. (1994). Stereotypes and mental life: The case of the motivated but thwarted tactician. *Journal of Experimental Social Psychology, 30,* 303–325.

Penn, D. L., Guynan, K., Daily, T., Spaulding, W. D., Garbin, C. P., & Sullivan, M. (1994). Dispelling the stigma of schizophrenia: What sort of information is best? *Schizophrenia Bulletin, 20,* 567–577.

Penn, D. L., Kommana, S., Mansfield, M., & Link, B. G. (in press). Dispelling the stigma of schizophrenia: II. The impact of information on dangerousness. *Schizophrenia Bulletin.*

Petty, R. E. (1995). Attitude change. In A. Tesser (Ed.), *Advanced social psychology* (pp. 195–249). New York: McGraw-Hill.

Piner, K., & Kahle, L. (1984). Adapting to the stigmatizing label of mental illness: Forgone but not forgotten. *Journal of Personality and Social Psychology, 47,* 805–811.

Pruegger, V. J., & Rogers, T. B. (1994). Cross-cultural sensitivity training: Methods and assessment. *Journal of Intercultural Relations, 18,* 369–387.

Quicke, J., Beasley, K., & Morrison, C. (1990). *Challenging prejudice through education: The story of a mental handicap awareness curriculum project.* Bristol, PA: Falmer Press.

Rabkin, J. G. (1974). Public attitudes toward mental illness: A review of the literature. *Psychological Bulletin, 10,* 9–33.

Riordan, C. (1978). Equal-status interracial contact: A review and revision of the concept. *International Journal of Intercultural Relations, 2,* 161–185.

River, P., & Holmes, E. P. (in press). Individual strategies for coping with stigma. *Cognitive and Behavioral Practice.*

Roman, P. M., & Floyd, H. H., Jr. (1981). Social acceptance of psychiatric illness and psychiatric treatment. *Social Psychiatry, 16,* 16–21.

Rothbart, M., & John, O. P. (1985). Social categorization and behavioral episodes: A cognitive analysis of the effect of intergroup contact. *Journal of Social Issues, 41,* 81–104.

Rothbart, M., & John, O. P. (1993). Intergroup relations and stereotype change: A social-cognitive analysis and some longitudinal findings. In P. M. Sniderman, P. E. Tetlock, & E. G. Carmines (Eds.), *Prejudice, politics, and the American dilemma* (pp. 32–59). Stanford, CA: Stanford University Press.

Rothbart, M., & Lewis, S. (1988). Inferring category attributes from exemplar attributes: Geometric shapes and social categories. *Journal of Personality and Social Psychology, 55*, 861–872.

Scott, D. J., & Philip, A. E. (1985). Attitudes of psychiatric nurses to treatment and patients. *British Journal of Medical Psychology, 58*, 169–173.

Shapiro, A., & Margolis, H. (1988). Changing negative peer attitudes toward students with learning disabilities. *Reading, Writing, and Learning Disabilities, 4*, 133–146.

Sigelman, L., & Welch, S. (1993). The contact hypothesis revisited: Black-White interaction and positive racial attitudes. *Social Forces, 71*, 781–795.

Skinner, L. J., Berry, K. K., Griffith, S. E., & Byers, B. (1995). Generalizability and specificity of the stigma associated with the mental illness label: A reconsideration twenty-five years later. *Journal of Community Psychology, 23*, 3–17.

Skov, R. B., & Sherman, S. J. (1986). Information-gathering processes: Diagnosticity, hypothesis-confirmatory strategies, and perceived hypothesis confirmation. *Journal of Experimental Social Psychology, 22*, 93–121.

Smith, A. (1990). Social influence and antiprejudice training programs. In J. Edwards, R. S. Tindale, L. Heath, & E. J. Posavac (Eds.), *Social influence processes and prevention* (pp. 183–196). New York: Plenum.

Socall, D. W., & Holtgraves, T. (1992). Attitudes toward the mentally ill: The effects of label and beliefs. *Sociological Quarterly, 33*, 435–445.

Sosowsky, L. (1980). Explaining the increased arrest rate among mental patients: A cautionary note. *American Journal of Psychiatry, 137*, 1602–1604.

Stangor, C., & Duan, C. (1991). Effects of multiple task demands upon memory for information about social groups. *Journal of Experimental Social Psychology, 27*, 357–378.

Stangor, C., & McMillan, D. (1992). Memory for expectancy-congruent and expectancy-incongruent information: A review of the social and social developmental literatures. *Psychological Bulletin, 111*, 42–61.

Steadman, H. J. (1981). Critically reassessing the accuracy of public perceptions of the dangerousness of the mentally ill. *Journal of Health and Social Behavior, 22*, 310–316.

Stephan, W. G. (1987). The contact hypothesis in intergroup relations. In C. Hendrick (Ed.), *Group processes and intergroup relations* (pp. 13–40). Beverly Hills, CA: Sage.

Taylor, S. M., & Dear, M. J. (1980). Scaling community attitudes toward the mentally ill. *Schizophrenia Bulletin, 7*, 225–240.

Thornton, J. A., & Wahl, O. F. (1996). Impact of a newspaper article on attitudes toward mental illness. *Journal of Community Psychology, 24*, 17–24.

Wahl, O. F. (1995). *Media madness: Public images of mental illness*. New Brunswick, NJ: Rutgers University Press.

Wahl, O., & Harman, C. (1989). Family views of stigma. *Schizophrenia Bulletin, 15*, 131–139.

Wahl, O. F., & Lefkowits, J. Y. (1989). Impact of a television film on attitudes about mental illness. *American Journal of Community Psychology, 17*, 521–528.

Weber, R., & Crocker, J. (1983). Cognitive processes in the revision of stereotypic beliefs. *Journal of Personality and Social Psychology, 45*, 961–977.

Wegner, D. M., & Erber, R. (1992). The hyperaccessibility of suppressed thoughts. *Journal of Personality and Social Psychology, 63*, 903–912.

Wegner, D. M., Schneider, D. J., Carter, S. R., & White, T. L. (1987). Paradoxical effects of thought suppression. *Journal of Personality and Social Psychology, 53*, 5–13.

Wegner, D. M., Shortt, J. W., Blake, A. W., & Page, M. S. (1990). The suppression of exciting thoughts. *Journal of Personality and Social Psychology, 58*, 409–418.

Weiner, B., Perry, R. P., & Magnusson, J. (1988). An attributional analysis of reactions to stigmas. *Journal of Personality and Social Psychology, 55*, 738–748.

Weinstein, R. M. (1983). Labeling theory and the attitudes of mental patients: A review. *Journal of Health and Social Behavior, 24*, 70–84.

Williams, R. M., Jr. (1977). *Mutual accommodation: Ethnic conflict and cooperation*. Minneapolis, MN: University of Minnesota Press.

Worchel, S. (1986). The role of cooperation in reducing intergroup conflict. In S. Worchel & W. G. Austin (Eds.), *Psychology of intergroup relations* (pp. 116–143). Chicago: Nelson-Hall.

Discussion Questions

1. In what ways do you think negative stereotypes about the mentally ill manifest themselves?
2. What factors determine whether or not a person's negative attitudes toward members of stigmatized groups, such as those with psychological problems, would lead to actual discrimination against those groups?
3. Corrigan and Penn discuss the rebound effect that often occurs when people attempt to suppress unwanted or undesired thoughts. Why does this effect occur? Given that it occurs, how can we get people to stop thinking negative thoughts about other people?

4. In the long run, how successful do you think advocacy groups will be in changing people's attitudes toward those who have psychological problems? How successful have such groups been in changing people's attitudes toward members of other minority groups?
5. How likely is it that psychiatrists and psychologists also hold stigmatizing attitudes toward people who have psychological problems? If you think that they do, what effects do you think those stereotypes have on the clients, and what would you recommend as a way of reducing those stereotypes among mental health professionals?

Suggested Readings

Brown, K., & Bradley, L. J. (2002). Reducing the stigma of mental illness. *Journal of Mental Health Counseling, 24,* 81–87. This article discusses the stigma of mental illness and how that stigma leads many people to avoid seeking treatment for their psychological problems.

Corrigan, P. W., & Watson, A. C. (2002). The paradox of self-stigma and mental illness. *Clinical Psychology: Science and Practice, 9,* 35–53. This article discusses individual differences in the effects of the stigma of mental illness on the person's self-esteem.

Flynn, L. M. (1987). The stigma of mental illness. *New Directions for Mental Health Services, 34,* 53–60. This article discusses the impact of the stigma of mental illness on the mentally ill.

Kolodziej, M. E., & Johnson, B. T. (1996). Interpersonal contact and acceptance of persons with psychiatric disorders: A research synthesis. *Journal of Consulting and Clinical Psychology, 64,* 1387–1396. This meta-analysis suggests that personal contact with people with psychological problems is useful in altering people's attitudes toward them.

PART 4

Social Psychological Processes in Clinical Treatment and Psychological Change

READING 19

American Psychotherapy in Perspective (Excerpt from *Persuasion and Healing*)

Jerome Frank

Editors' Introduction

Jerome Frank was among the first writers to suggest explicitly that basic social psychological processes underlie the psychological changes that occur during psychotherapy. (Ironically, Frank was neither a social nor a clinical psychologist, but rather a psychiatrist.) In his book *Persuasion and Healing*, first published in 1961, Frank argued that all psychological change results from the same social psychological processes. This is true, according to Frank, not only in the case of the changes that occur during psychotherapy but also for changes that arise from faith healing, brainwashing, placebo effects in medicine, and religious conversion. During and after World War II, social psychologists devoted a great deal of attention to the processes that lead people to change their attitudes, beliefs, and behavior, and Frank drew upon this extensive research literature to identify the factors that underlie psychological change. He urged mental health professionals to pay greater attention to basic processes of social influence in order to help their clients change more effectively.

 In this selection from *Persuasion and Healing*, Frank discusses the common characteristic of all people who seek psychotherapy and the common features of all types of psychotherapy. In his view, all positive effects of psychotherapy can be traced to basic social psychological processes that involve the relationship between the therapist and client, the nature of the social setting in which therapy occurs, the client's adoption of a particular explanation or "myth" that accounts for his or her problem, and the use of therapeutic techniques that the client is led to believe will help. Whatever a psychotherapist's particular theoretical orientation or therapeutic approach, all effective psychological treatments rely on the same interpersonal processes.

Human beings spend most of their lives interacting with each other. In the process they influence one another powerfully for good or ill. This book has singled out for study one particular class of influencing procedures—the psychotherapy of adults. This is a help-giving process in which a professionally trained person, sometimes with the aid of a group, tries to relieve certain types of distress by facilitating changes in attitudes. As a relationship in which one person tries to induce changes in another, psychotherapy has much in common with child-rearing, education, and various forms of leadership. Its closest affinities, however, are with time-limited interactions between a sufferer and specially trained persons that stress either healing or attitude change. The former include therapeutic rituals in primitive societies and healing religious shrines in our own; the latter include religious revivalism and Communist thought reform. This chapter considers the nature of psychotherapy in the light of our survey and then proceeds to review certain implications for psychotherapy in America today.

Demoralization—The Common Characteristic of Persons in Psychotherapy

At this point it becomes necessary to ask in what sense it is legitimate to refer to psychotherapy as a single entity, rather than to different psychotherapies. At first glance the question seems to answer itself. The number of schools of psychotherapy exceeds the tens and continues to increase. The conditions which psychotherapies purport to treat also cover an enormous range. They include the whole gamut of neurotic and psychotic reactions, personality disorders, disturbances of sexual functions, addiction, school phobias, marital discord—the list could be continued indefinitely.

On closer inspection, however, certain aspects of the psychotherapeutic scene strongly suggest that the features shared by psychotherapies far outweigh their differences. Practitioners of all schools claim to be able to treat persons with a wide variety of diagnostic labels, and each can report success with patients who had failed to respond to the methods of another. Since all can do this, however, the claims cancel each other. That is, therapists using method A cure some patients whom method B failed to help, but method B also succeeds after method A has failed.

In view of this state of affairs, it is not surprising that all therapeutic schools persist. Despite vigorous and prolonged polemics, no school has yet succeeded in driving a rival from the field. The obvious conclusion is that all must do some good but that none has produced results clearly superior to the results of any other.

There is one exception to this statement. Phobias seem to respond more promptly to brief behavioral techniques than to evocative interview therapies, and emotional flooding may prove superior to systematic desensitization in the treatment of agoraphobics. Findings such as these justify continued searching for differential effects of different procedures for different conditions. Since phobic patients comprise less than 3% of persons seeking psychotherapy, however, this may be the exception that proves the rule.

To put the issue in terms of an analogy, two apparently very different psychotherapies, such as psychoanalysis and systematic desensitization, might be analogous to penicillin and digitalis—totally different pharmacological agents suitable for completely different conditions. On the other hand, the active ingredient of both may be the same, analogous to two compounds, marketed under different names, both of which contain aspirin. I believe the second alternative is closer to the mark. In this connection, it is intriguing that the company that initially put aspirin on the market now advertises that its product is "pure" aspirin, implying that other agents reduce its effectiveness. This is uncannily similar to Freud's comment about diluting the "pure gold" of psychoanalysis with the dross of suggestion.

To forestall misunderstanding, let me remind the reader that aspirin is not a placebo. It has powerful pharmacological effects, among them inhibition of the synthesis of prostaglandins. These substances play a part in inflammation. By reason of its pharmacological action, aspirin reduces fever and alleviates aches and pains almost regardless of the specific illness with which they are associated.

Pursuing the analogy one step further, we must ask: Is there a state common to all persons seeking psychotherapy that this treatment alleviates, just as aspirin relieves aches and pains? I believe that there is such a state, which may be termed "demoralization."

Dictionaries define "to demoralize" as "to deprive a person of spirit, courage, to dishearten, bewilder, to throw him into disorder or confusion." These terms well describe the state of candidates for psychotherapy, whatever their diagnostic label. They are conscious of having failed to meet their own expectations or those of others, or of being unable to cope with some pressing problem. They feel powerless to change the situation or themselves. In severe cases they fear that they cannot even control their own feelings, giving rise to the fear of going crazy which is so characteristic of those seeking psychotherapeutic help. Their life space is constricted both in space and time. Thus they cling to a small round of habitual activities, avoid novelty and challenge, and are reluctant to make long-term plans. It is as if psychologically they are cowering in a spatio-temporal corner. In other terms, to various degrees the demoralized person feels isolated, hopeless, and helpless, and is preoccupied with merely trying to survive.

Having lost confidence in his ability to defend himself against a threatening world, the demoralized person is prey to anxiety and depression (the two most common complaints of persons seeking psychotherapy) as well as to resentment, anger, and other dysphoric emotions. Persons with certain personality structures manage to use symptoms to conceal these feelings. Their presence just under the surface is shown by the fact that the feelings erupt into consciousness if the symptom is removed while the patient is still demoralized. The hypnotic removal of a hysterical paralysis, for example, has been known to precipitate suicidal depression.

Although some demoralized patients fight helpgivers because they are so mistrustful, most actively seek help and respond readily to a helper; that is, they are in a state of heightened suggestibility. Usually they find help in their own circle. The psychotherapist sees only those who have failed in this attempt.[1]

At their first meeting the therapist examines the patient and gives him a diagnostic label. The patient abets him in this by presenting a specific complaint as his reason for coming. More often than not, however, this is merely his admission ticket—the basis for his claim on the therapist's attention. It may be a direct expression of his demoralization such as depression, an unsuccessful attempt to overcome it such as excessive drinking, or even be irrelevant such as a circumscribed phobia. The psychotherapist's orientation leads him to accept the complaint presented as the real reason the patient has come to him and proceeds to make its relief the object of treatment.

But most persons do not seek therapy because they hallucinate or fear snakes or enjoy a few drinks too many, much less because they have obsessional, hysterical, or passive-aggressive personalities. The community is full of people with these and other psychopathological conditions going about their daily business. In fact, most persons who are entitled to psychiatric diagnoses probably never come to the psychotherapist's attention. University researchers on psychotherapy, for example, by giving a class a fear survey schedule, can always unearth sufficient numbers of students with phobias who never thought of seeking treatment until the researcher offered it.

Morale can be restored by removal of crippling symptoms, and different psychotherapeutic procedures may be differentially effective for some of these. Conversely, insofar as the patient's symptoms are expressions of his demoralized state, restoration of his self-esteem by whatever means causes them to subside. Not infrequently, successful psychotherapy enables a patient to function more successfully in the face of persisting symptoms.[2] Examples are the paranoid patient whose delusions are unchanged but who has become able to keep them to himself, or the patient who no longer avoids the phobic situation although he still has the same physiological symptoms of anxiety in its presence.

In most general terms, a person becomes demoralized when he finds that he cannot meet the demands placed on him by his environment, and cannot extricate himself from his predicament. This situation has been conceptualized as "crisis" if acute and "the social breakdown syndrome" if chronic.[3] Although demoralization depends on the interaction between factors in the person and in the environment, it is convenient to consider them separately.

Environmental stresses may overtax a person's adaptive capacities for reasons beyond his control. As wartime experiences have shown, everyone has a breaking point. In peace, as in war, environmental stress sets limits to what psychotherapy can accomplish. No amount of treatment will abolish stresses created by a brutal, unpredictable alcoholic parent, a spouse with a slowly fatal illness, or those impinging on a child whose parents are a militant atheist and a devout Catholic. Limits to psychotherapeutic benefit are also set by poverty, unemployment, and other forms of social oppression. Since a person's attitudes and behavior affect his environment, however, demoralization may aggravate crisis. Psychotherapy, by bolstering the patient's morale and enabling him to modify his perceptions and behavior, can sometimes help to break the resulting vicious circle.

From the standpoint of the person, adaptive capacity can be limited by constitutional defects or vulnerabilities. By "constitutional" is meant that they are built into his structure, either because they are genetic or because they are the after-effects of trauma occurring early enough to affect the subsequent development of his nervous system. Sometimes constitutional factors wax and wane periodically—and with them the patient's capacity to cope—as in manic-depressive disorders. Problems that seem overwhelming to a patient when he is depressed shrink to trivialities when his mood brightens. Constitutional sources of weakness in coping capacity cannot be directly treated by psychotherapy, but some may be helped by drugs. Psychotherapy, however, can help such persons to maintain their morale despite their handicaps.

Two other personal sources of demoralization do respond to psychotherapy. One may be termed "learned incapacity." That is, through unfortunate past experiences, a person may have learned faulty ways of perceiving and dealing with life's stresses. As a result, he may fall short in his ability to perform and to develop satisfying relationships with others, leading to feelings of failure and alienation. His symptoms are self-defeating, self-perpetuating maneuvers to deal with these feelings. Most American schools of psychotherapy subscribe to this view of the cause of psychopathological symptoms insofar as they are not based on constitutional flaws. Psychoanalytically oriented interview therapies try to overcome these symptoms by unearthing their initial causes. Behavioral therapies seek the same end by teaching the patient to identify and combat features of his present environment that perpetuate his inappropriate responses.

The other personal source of demoralization has been characterized by such terms as ontological anxiety or existential despair. The philosopher Santayana characterized life as a predicament. We have many defenses against recognizing this demoralizing fact, such as religious faith or membership in organized groups with high morale. Both these sources of support are weak in today's society, which may partly account for the large numbers of persons, especially among the young, who seek psychotherapy for what is best described by the German word "Weltschmerz"—world pain. Existentialist and mystical therapies strive to combat this source of psychopathology.

Later in this chapter we review features shared by all forms of psychotherapy that combat demoralization. First, however, let us attempt to place mental illness and psychotherapy in their cultural perspective.

Mental Illness, Psychotherapy, and Society

Mental illnesses are results or expressions of disharmonies within a person and between him and his society. Because a person's patterns of perceiving and relating to others reflect his internal psychic state, and affect it in turn, these are two sides of the same coin. Moreover, the cause–effect sequence runs both ways. A person's internal harmony or conflict affects his relationships with others, and his interpersonal experiences influence his internal state. They may disorganize him, as seen in the primitive who dies from a witch's curse, or help him to reintegrate himself, as in religious conversion.

Cultural factors determine to a large extent which conditions are singled out as targets of psychotherapy and how they manifest themselves. The same phenomena may be viewed as signs of mental illness in one society, of demoniacal possession in another, and as eccentricities to be ignored in a third. Moreover, the behavior of the afflicted person is greatly influenced by culturally determined expectations of how persons so defined should behave.

It has been suggested that psychotherapies flourish in eras such as ours when cultural values and social norms break down. At such times, organized religion and other traditional institutions for maintaining a sense of ontological security and of community lose their effectiveness and psychotherapy seems to be one substitute for them.[4] In complex societies, the difficulties leading a person to seek or be offered psychotherapy, and the type he receives, depend to some extent on his geographical location and class position. Psychotherapists and their patients congregate in cities, perhaps because city dwellers suffer especially from alienation and insecurity. Furthermore, knowledge of the availability of psychotherapy is related to educational level, and the density of city populations assures sufficient numbers of the well-educated. Educated, middle- or upper-class urbanites seek or are brought to psychotherapy for less severe or vaguer complaints than poorly educated, lower-class farmers, and are more apt to receive evocative individual or group therapies, as contrasted with directive approaches or those that rely heavily on medication.

Since the therapist's power over the patient rests in part on his role and function as a mediator between the patient and the larger society and may even extend to power to incarcerate the patient if his behavior is socially unacceptable, he inevitably functions as an agent of social integration. This is explicit in preindustrialized societies, in which illness is thought to be punishment for transgression and recovery involves atonement and reacceptance by the group under the guidance of the shaman.[5] In the past the democratic ethos has obscured this aspect of the psychotherapist's function in the West. Recently, it has surfaced with a vengeance.

The issue of the psychotherapist as an agent of social control directly concerns psychiatrists because of their power to lock people up in mental hospitals, "for care and treatment." It is not always clear whether a patient is committed for his own benefit or to relieve others of his irritating, frightening, or embarrassing presence.[6]

Although this issue presents itself in more subtle form to nonmedical psychotherapists, they too cannot escape it. Symptoms and behavior hitherto regarded as signs of mental illness, we are told, may be appropriate responses to oppression by society or the patient's family. Should the psychotherapist use his power to help the patient submit more gracefully or to encourage him to resist? If the therapist throws his weight on the side of conformity, is he helping to perpetuate social evil?

Consistent with this line of thought, Black militants are abjured to avoid psychotherapy, lest it destroy their revolutionary zeal by convincing them that their distress is caused by internal conflicts rather than social oppression. Some writers even suggest that to be truly effective the psychotherapist must be a revolutionary himself.[7]

Most therapists would regard this position as extreme, for it is clear that the psychotherapist lacks power to correct culturally induced stresses. The best he can do is strengthen the patient's ability to deal with them; their correction lies in the hands of the political and economic elite. Sometimes the psychotherapist may have a marginal ameliorating effect on social oppression by offering insights that help shape the aims and guide the activities of a society's leaders, but this is prevention, not treatment.[8]

Since the distress and disability for which persons seek psychotherapy, however, is almost always related to friction with their surroundings, past or present, and since improvement therefore necessarily involves achieving greater harmony with the larger group or finding the courage to rebel more effectively against it, the issue of the political implications of psychotherapy is a real and important one. It is also complex and controversial, and to pursue it further would lead too far afield.

In any case, American psychotherapy is colored by certain interrelated features of American society, notably its diversity, the high value it places on democracy and science, and the methods of training psychotherapists. The diversity of American society permits the coexistence of various therapies based on differing conceptual schemes representing the value systems of different subcultures. This may have certain virtues. A patient whose outlook is at variance with one group may find acceptance in another. If after therapy he can no longer find support from his former group, he may be able to get it from a new one. Group support need not be expressed as liking. What really counts is whether the patient's new self or behavior achieves recognition and respect. Psychotherapy may help him to gain increased group support by enabling him to embody the group's values more successfully, or, in line with our democratic values, by becoming able to think and act more independently. In any case, he can more readily maintain changes induced by therapy to the extent that they enable him to feel less derogated and isolated.

Moreover, the pluralism of American society enables the psychotherapist to represent attitudes and values differing from those of the patient. If the differences are not too great, this may help him to gain some new and useful perspectives on his problems. On the other hand, differences in worldview of psychotherapist and patient, based on differences in their backgrounds, may impede communication between them. In addition, the absence of a single, all-embracing world view shared by the patient, the therapist, and the larger society limits the amount of pressure the therapist can mobilize to help the patient change his attitudes. No form of American psychotherapy can approximate the influencing power of primitive healing or thought reform in this respect, though perhaps an ideal therapeutic community, which completely immersed the patient in a culture expressing a self-consistent assumptive world, could approach it.

Almost all segments of American society place a high value on democracy and science. The democratic ideal assigns high worth to individual self-fulfillment. It regards behavior that is apparently self-directed as more admirable than behavior apparently caused by external pressures. Thus it values independence of thought and action within limits, and the rebel or deviate, if not too extreme, may continue to count on group tolerance and even respect. The concept of the therapeutic community, with its view of the hospital inmate as a responsible person entitled to kindness, understanding, and respect, is an expression of the democratic worldview.

The scientific ideal reinforces the democratic one by valuing lack of dogmatism. In addition, its emphasis on objectivity and experimentation provides a congenial intellectual atmosphere for behavior therapies and is also a powerful source of their appeal in the West. Being ostensibly based on rigorous animal experimentation, these therapies have impeccable scientific credentials, and they follow scientific canons in claiming to be concerned only with objectively measurable behavior. They also conceptualize therapy in terms of the formulation of hypotheses whose validity is determined by verification of predictions based on them. To be sure, they may achieve conceptual rigor by excluding much of what goes on in psychotherapy, and in actuality many behavior therapies deal primarily with fantasy rather than behavior, but they can more plausibly assume the mantle of science than can interview therapies.

Scientific values of objectivity and intellectual comprehension are not entirely unmixed blessings. Even in interview therapy, they tend to foster an overvaluation of the cognitive aspects of the treatment. "Insight" in the sense of ability to verbalize self-understanding may be mistaken for genuine attitude change, and the therapist may place undue stress on interpretations. The scientific attitude also justifies avoidance of "unscientific," emotion-arousing procedures such as group rituals and dramatic activities, even though there is universal agreement that in order to succeed, psychotherapy must involve the patient's emotions.

Both democratic and scientific ideals tend to cause many American therapists to underestimate the extent to which psychotherapy is a process of persuasion. Members of a democracy do not like to see themselves as exercising power over someone else, and the scientist observes—he does not influence. In this connection, evocative therapies are often termed permissive, reflecting the reluctance of practitioners of these methods to recognize the extent of their influence on patients. Even many behavior therapists formulate their activities in terms of placing themselves under the patient's control rather than manipulating him. That is, their role, as they see it, is to help the patient to discover the environmental contingencies that are sustaining his maladaptive behavior and then to help him change them. In short, reflecting this cultural setting, most psychotherapies in America claim to be both scientific and democratic, although in many respects they are neither.

Common Features of Psychotherapy

At this point, let us return to our main quest, which is to tease out features of psychotherapy common to all societies and cultures as they have emerged in our survey of the field. In approaching this topic, one should keep in mind that demoralization, the common property of the conditions that psychotherapy attempts to relieve, involves all aspects of personal functioning. Although the locus of the major disturbance may differ considerably in the different types of distress with which we have been concerned, biological, psychological, and social components are always involved to some degree. Thus successful psychotherapy, whatever its major focus, affects all three.

Four shared features of all psychotherapies seem distinguishable. The first is a particular type of relationship between the patient and a help-giver, sometimes in the context of a group. The essential ingredient of this relationship is that the patient has confidence in the therapist's competence and in his desire to be of help. That is, the patient must feel that the therapist genuinely cares about his welfare.

Caring in this sense does not necessarily imply approval, but rather a determination to persist in trying to help no matter how desperate the patient's condition or how outrageous his behavior. Thus the therapeutic relationship always implies genuine acceptance of the sufferer, if not for what he is, then for what he can become, as well as the therapist's belief that the patient can master his problems.

The therapist's acceptance, based on empathic understanding, validates the patient's personal outlook on life. The patient's sense that he is understood and accepted by someone he respects is a strong antidote to feelings of alienation and is a potent enhancer of morale. Caring and empathy imply some emotional investment by the therapist, which, as already indicated, can be conveyed by such qualities as active participation, warmth, empathy, and enthusiasm. Some stern and harsh therapists, however, also succeed in conveying that they care. In any case, the patient's discovery that someone has enough faith in him to make a big effort to help is in itself a powerful boost to morale, especially since most patients reach the psychotherapist only after they have failed to gain help from others.

The patient's faith in the therapist's competence is enhanced by the latter's socially sanctioned role as a help-giver, evidenced by the fact that he has had special training and, in therapy, by his mastery of a special technique. The success of relatively untrained therapists, however, is evidence that this is not always necessary.

A second common feature of all psychotherapies is that their locales are designated by society as places of healing. Thus the setting itself arouses the patient's expectation of help. Furthermore, it is a temporary refuge from the demands and distractions of daily life. It also is sanctioned by the value system of its society. Thus, in preindustrialized societies, healing rituals are typically conducted in sacred buildings such as temples. If the setting is the sufferer's home, this is transformed into a sacred place by purification rituals. Some personal growth centers, newcomers to the American scene, also have an ambience with religious overtones. In industrialized societies, however, therapy is typically conducted in the therapist's office, a hospital, or a university health clinic, all of which have the aura of scientific healing.

In any case, the setting is sharply distinguished from the rest of the patient's environment by its special qualities, including clearly delineated temporal and spatial boundaries. Protected by the setting, the patient can concentrate on the prescribed therapeutic activities. He can participate in complex, emotionally charged rituals, suspend his critical faculties, freely express his emotions, indulge in leisurely self-exploration, daydream, or do whatever else the therapy prescribes, secure in the knowledge that no harm will come to him during the session and that he will not be held accountable in his daily life for whatever he says or does during it. By thus freeing him to experiment, the combination of healer and setting creates favorable conditions for change.

Third, all psychotherapies are based on a rationale or myth that includes an explanation of illness and health, deviancy, and normality. If the rationale is to combat the patient's demoralization, it must obviously imply an optimistic philosophy of human nature. This is clearly true of the rationales underlying most American psychotherapies, which assume that aggression, cruelty, and other unattractive forms of human behavior result from past hurts and frustrations and that, as the person progressively frees himself from these and achieves fuller self-awareness, leading him to feel more secure, he will become kinder, more loving, more open to others, and more able to reach his full potential.

Those psychotherapies imported from Europe, notably psychoanalysis and the existential psychotherapies, although more pessimistic about human nature, still place their therapies in an optimistic context. The Freudian view of human nature, which sees the human psyche as a battleground between the instincts of Life and Death, with the latter winning in the end, could hardly be called cheerful, but it is redeemed by the faith that, to use a religious phrase, the truth shall make you free. Truth was Freud's god, and psychoanalysis, as the scientific search for it, enabled humans, by gaining control of the base impulses of the Unconscious, to free more energy for the life-instinctual goals of love and work.

The most pessimistic of the philosophies on which psychotherapies are based are those existentialist ones that stress the essential meaninglessness of human existence. They manage to give this outlook a heroic twist, however, by maintaining that the human, although he cannot control his fate, does have the potential ability to wrest a sense of meaning and purpose out of life.

Within a broad, often not fully articulated philosophy of life, the rationale of each school of psychotherapy explains the cause of the sufferer's distress, specifies desirable goals for him, and prescribes procedures for attaining them. To be effective, the therapeutic myth must be compatible with the cultural world view shared by patient and therapist. The hypothesis that all mental illnesses, insofar as they respond to psychological treatment, are products of damaging early life experiences underlies almost all Western psychotherapies, including behavioral approaches. Psychotherapies based on it, however, may be ineffective for patients in cultures that attribute mental illness to, for example, spirit possession.

The provocative word "myth" has been used to emphasize that although the rationales of many Western psychotherapies do not invoke supernatural forces, they resemble the myths of primitive ones in that they cannot be shaken by therapeutic failures. That is, they are not subject to disproof. The infallibility of the rationale protects the therapist's self-esteem, thereby strengthening the patient's confidence in him. In addition, for both patient and therapist, it provides the powerful emotional support of a like-minded group, whose members may gain further ego support by viewing themselves as a select few, superior in some respects to ordinary mortals. Thus the conceptual scheme combats the patient's sense of alienation.

The therapeutic rationale, finally, enables the patient to make sense of his symptoms. Since he often views them as inexplicable, which increases their ominousness, being able to name and explain them in terms of an overarching conceptual scheme is in itself powerfully reassuring. The first step in gaining control of any phenomenon is to give it a name.

The fourth ingredient of all forms of psychotherapy is the task or procedure prescribed by the theory. Some therapeutic procedures closely guide the sufferer's activities, others impel him to take the initiative; but all share certain characteristics. The procedure is the means by which the sufferer is brought to see the error of his ways and correct them, thereby gaining relief. It also affords the patients a face-saving device for relinquishing his symptoms when he is prepared to do so. The procedure demands some effort or sacrifice on the patient's part, ranging all the way from collaborating in hypnosis to undergoing repeated painful shocks. Since it requires active participation of both patient and therapist and is typically repetitive, it serves as the vehicle for maintaining the therapeutic relationship and transmitting the therapist's influence. It also enhances the therapist's self-confidence by enabling him to demonstrate mastery of a special set of skills. Procedures such as hypnosis, relaxation, or emotional flooding in which the therapist alters the patient's subjective state are especially convincing demonstrations of the therapist's competence. Any procedure that can alter one's state of consciousness must be powerful indeed.

The central point is that the therapeutic efficacy of rationales and techniques may lie not in their specific contents, which differ, but in their functions, which are the same. The therapeutic relationship, setting, rationale, and task in conjunction influence patients in five interrelated ways that seem necessary to produce attitude change and therapeutic benefit. First, they provide him with new opportunities for learning at both cognitive and experiential levels. Cognitively the therapist may help the patient to clarify sources of his difficulties in his past life, or the contingencies in his environment that maintain his distress. The therapist and other members of a group in group therapy also serve as models of alternative ways of handling problems. But the most important learning in therapy is probably experiential and is provided by confronting the patient with discrepancies or contradictions between his assumptive world and actuality. Insight-oriented therapies confront him with discrepancies between his self-image and his own hidden feelings; group methods face him with discrepancies between his assumptions about others and their actual feelings or between the impression he thinks he is making and his actual effect. Awareness of these dissonances creates a powerful incentive to change in directions suggested by the cognitive insights the patient is gaining simultaneously.

Second, all therapies enhance the patient's hope of relief. This hope rests in part on the patient's faith in the therapist and the treatment method. Experienced therapists in early interviews explicitly try to strengthen the patient's favorable expectations and to tailor them to the therapeutic procedure.

A more enduring source of hope deserves a heading of its own because it includes other components. This is, third, the provision of success experiences which enhance the sufferer's sense of mastery, interpersonal competence, or capability. The detailed structure of behavior therapies, the objective measures of progress, and the emphasis on the patient's active participation virtually assure that he will experience successes as treatment progresses.

Unstructured, open-ended procedures like psychoanalysis also provide success experiences. These therapies seem ideally suited for intelligent, verbally adept patients who rely heavily on words to cope with life's problems. The patient experiences a feeling of mastery when he gains a new insight or becomes aware of a hitherto unconscious thought or feeling. The therapist enhances the patient's sense of achievement by maintaining that all progress is due to the patient's own efforts. Thus all successful therapies implicitly or explicitly change the patient's image of himself as a person who is overwhelmed by his symptoms and problems to that of one who can master them.

Fourth, all forms of psychotherapy help the patient to overcome his demoralizing sense of alienation from his fellows. Through his interactions with the therapist and the group (if there is one) within the framework of a shared conceptual scheme, he discovers that his problems are not unique and that others can understand him and do care about his welfare.

Finally, all forms of psychotherapy, when successful, arouse the patient emotionally. The role of emotional arousal in facilitating or causing psychotherapeutic change is unclear. One can only note that it seems to be a prerequisite to all attitudinal and behavioral change. It accompanies all confrontations and success experiences, and production of intense arousal is the central aim of emotional flooding techniques.

In short, when successful, all forms of psychotherapy relieve dysphoric feelings, rekindle the patient's hopes, increase his sense of mastery over himself and his environment, and in general restore his morale. As a result, he becomes able to tackle the problems he had been avoiding and to experiment with new, better ways of handling them. These new capabilities decrease the chance that he will become demoralized again and, with good fortune, enable him to continue to make gains after psychotherapy has ended.

Implications for Research

As this book has made evident, though there is an abundance of clinical lore, the amount of experimentally verified knowledge about psychotherapeutic processes is meager, though not through want of trying. Psychotherapy has absorbed the attention of many able investigators,[9] and while this is not the place for detailed consideration of research aspects of psychotherapy, a brief attempt to make explicit some of the major areas of difficulty and the most promising directions of progress seems appropriate.

One set of problems arises from the fact that psychotherapists have a vested interest in their methods. Each has become expert in a particular mode of psychotherapy as the result of long and arduous training. His self-esteem, status, and financial security are linked to its effectiveness. Under these circumstances he can hardly be expected to be an impartial student of his own method, and any data he reports cannot escape the suspicion of bias. Theoretically there is an easy solution to this dilemma, which is to separate the roles of researcher and therapist. The therapist would permit himself to be observed by trained researchers through a one-way vision screen or by means of sound films and tape recordings of interviews. Psychiatrists have resisted this on the ostensible grounds that it infringes on the confidentiality of the patient-physician relationship, but they have been progressively yielding to the blandishments of researchers and the good example set by their psychologist colleagues. Since the self-esteem of psychologists rests on research ability as well as therapeutic skill, most psychotherapy that has been the object of research has been conducted by them.

There is no denying that research poses threats to the therapist. He may discover that what he actually does differs considerably from what he thinks he does, that changes in patients are not caused by the maneuvers he thinks causes them, and that his results are no better than those obtained by practitioners of other methods. All in all, he can hardly be blamed for subscribing to a bit of wisdom attributed to Confucius: "A wise man does not examine the source of his well-being." This understandable prudence, however, has forced researchers to rely too often on therapists in training, especially graduate students in psychology, in which case the results obtained are open to criticism on the grounds of the therapists' lack of experience.

Furthermore, human beings can be disciplined only to a certain point, so unless the subjects of research are students whose grades depend on their participation, carrying through a research design in psychotherapy is far from easy. Therapists chafe at the restrictions imposed by research requirements and are tempted to circumvent them on the grounds that they interfere with treatment. Captive patients in hospitals can be fairly easily controlled. In contrast with them, outpatients break appointments, drop out of treatment without warning, and take vacations at the wrong times.

Research in psychotherapy bears a painfully close resemblance to the nightmarish game of croquet in *Alice in Wonderland*, in which the mallets were flamingos, the balls hedgehogs, and the wickets soldiers. Since the flamingo would not keep its head down, the hedgehogs kept unrolling themselves, and the soldiers were always wandering to other parts of the field, "Alice soon came to the conclusion that it was a very difficult game indeed."

If the subjects of psychotherapy create special problems, so does its subject matter. Being concerned with all levels of human functioning from the biological to the social, psychotherapy raises all the issues concerned with human nature and the communication process. The range and complexity of this material create difficulties of conceptualization. Some formulations try to encompass all its aspects. Many of these have been immensely insightful and stimulating and have illuminated many fields of knowledge. To achieve all-inclusiveness, however, they have resorted to metaphor, have left major ambiguities unresolved, and have formulated their hypotheses in terms that cannot be subjected to experimental test.

The opposite approach has been to try to conceptualize small segments of the field with sufficient precision to permit experimental test of the hypotheses, but these formulations run the risk of achieving rigor at the expense of significance. The researcher is faced with the problem of delimiting an aspect of psychotherapy that is amenable to experimental study and at the same time includes the major determinants of the problem under consideration. He finds himself in the predicament of the Norse god Thor who tried to drain a small goblet only to discover that it was connected with the sea. Under these circumstances there is an inevitable tendency to guide the choice of research problems more by the ease with which they can be investigated than by their importance. One is reminded of the familiar story of the drunkard who lost his keys in a dark alley but looked for them under the lamp post because the light was better there.

A persistent, nontrivial research problem is that of definition and measurement of improvement.[10] Patients seek psychotherapy for a wide variety of complaints, ranging from something as vague as spiritual malaise to a specific disability like stage fright. Since only the patient knows how badly he feels, measures of improvement must include self-reports, but these may be distorted by the impression the patient wishes to make on the interviewer as well as by other extraneous factors.

The measurement of change in a circumscribed symptom presents little problem, especially if it involves a specific bit of behavior that can be observed, but the complaints of most patients include multiple miseries. One way of dealing with this diversity, which, although not completely satisfactory, has led to research progress, is to devise scales that include the major types of unpleasant feelings and use changes in average scores as measures of improvement; another is to use a great number of measures and define improvement in terms of positive change in most of them.

Evaluations of social behavior can be more objective but they must also include a subjective component, since what is improvement for one patient may represent a worsening for another, depending on his attitudes toward the situation. A good example would be divorce, which may be a healthy step or a tragedy for different people. As the research reviewed in this book shows, however, scales of subjective distress and social behavior have been devised that yield usable results.

A more difficult problem with respect to improvement is determining how much of it is actually due to therapy. The psychotherapeutic session represents only a tiny fraction of the patient's encounters with others, so results attributed to psychotherapy may really be due to concurrent life events, including the patient's seeking help from someone other than the therapist.[11] Therapy may be given credit for improvement really due to a change in the patient's living pattern such as getting married, or its potentially beneficial effects may be wiped out by a personal catastrophe. To complicate matters further, improvement in the patient started by therapy may lead him to enter into new personal transactions which he had been avoiding. Because of the reciprocal nature of social behavior, this may produce favorable changes in the attitudes of others. Therapy may have given him the courage to ask his girl to marry him, affording her the opportunity to accept him. Questions of this type loom especially large with respect to the evaluation of long-term treatment, which requires some way of determining whether the patient handles stress subsequent to undergoing therapy more confortably and effectively than before.

In any case, it is important to distinguish conceptually between influences that produce therapeutic benefit and those that maintain it. If a therapeutic method does not produce any beneficial change, then it is of no interest. If therapy does produce some benefit, whether it is maintained or not may depend primarily on factors that are beyond the control of the therapist.

Every experienced psychotherapist has treated cases in which therapy seemed to have far-reaching and permanent effects, enabling the patient to reach a level of comfort and effectiveness that he would have been most unlikely to attain without treatment. By and large, however, the effect of successful psychotherapy seems to be to accelerate or facilitate healing processes that would have gone on more slowly in its absence. This is, of course, the function of most medical treatment. If psychotherapists did no more than reduce duration of suffering and disability, this would be well worth their efforts.

It seems that many patients come to psychotherapy when they are under internal or external pressures to modify their feelings and behavior, and the psychotherapist assists in the process much as a midwife might at the birth of a baby. What he does may make a lot of difference in how smoothly or rapidly the process occurs, but the extent to which he causes it is uncertain.

Among the therapeutic features of all psychotherapies, four that seem to afford especially promising areas for research have beem emphasized in this book. The first concerns determinants and transmitters of the therapist's influence. The other three are the determinants of the patient's emotional states, his expectation of help, and his sense of mastery.

Especially pertinent to psychotherapy has been the experimental demonstration that evaluation apprehension, as experienced by most patients, makes them highly sensitive to the therapist's influence, which can be transmitted through cues so subtle that the therapist may not notice them. In fact, it seems plausible that one mode of transmission of the therapist's influence may be telepathy. Research into this phenomenon presents many inherent difficulties, as indicated earlier, but the major obstacle is probably that it lacks scientific respectability. In any case, recent studies have shown that rigorous research into telepathy is possible.

Studies of transmission of the therapist's influence, in addition to illuminating an important aspect of psychotherapy, are reminders of the need for caution in evaluating patients' productions. If the therapist has a hypothesis in mind—and he could not do research without one—he may unwittingly convey it to the patient, who may oblige by producing supportive material. Obviously, this type of confirmation is of dubious value. Until the personal and situation conditions determining the influence of the therapist's expectancies on the patient's productions, and the kinds of material most susceptible and most resistant to this type of influence are better understood, hypotheses about human nature supported solely by patients' productions in psychotherapy must be regarded as unproven.

Improved methods of monitoring, evoking, and modifying emotional states are opening up new vistas for research.[12] These methods may help to define the personal and situational factors arousing patients' anxieties on the one hand and hopes on the other, as well as personal differences in emotional responsivity, which have formed the basis of personality classifications since the days of Hippocrates. Some patients are too phlegmatic, others too excitable, and the optimal degrees of therapeutically useful tension for them may be quite different.

Monitoring emotional states during psychotherapy can also cast light on the difficult question of the relationship between a patient's self-reports and his actual emotional state. Thus it has been found that a patient's report that he feels relaxed may not be confirmed by actual reduction of autonomic tension. Modern advances in telemetry now make possible unobtrusive, continuous monitoring of a person's autonomic functions as he goes about his daily affairs, overcoming a serious obstacle to the evaluation of therapeutic improvement.

Of more potential therapeutic significance is the experimental production of emotional arousal to facilitate therapeutic change. The use of agents such as ether, adrenaline, and especially LSD, which can be brought under some degree of experimental control, represents a potentially important research advance. The most exciting prospect, however, has been created by the demonstration that through operant conditioning techniques patients can be taught to control their own visceral functions.[13] This opens up new vistas for the study and treatment of bodily symptoms of anxiety and depression, as well as psychosomatic disorders such as high blood pressure, peptic ulcer, and asthma.

A third promising research area deals with the determinants and effects of the patient's favorable expectations. An experimental approach to this problem has been investigation of conditions determining responses of psychiatric patients to inert medications whose therapeutic properties lie in their symbolization of the physician's role. The placebo response proves to be quite a complex matter involving the interaction of personality characteristics, attitudes toward physicians and medication, and properties of the therapeutic situation. A simple experimental approach that deserves further exploration has been the mobilization and intensification of patients' positive expectations through preparatory interviews.

The fourth promising research area, an unexpected by-product of experiments in behavior therapy, lies in investigation of ways of heightening the patient's sense of mastery over his symptoms and his environment through providing him with success experiences in therapy, an area that has barely been tapped.

In conclusion, mention should be made of features of therapy that may actually be the most important determinants of outcome but that have received practically no research attention because they seem to defy conceptualization in terms of the scientific worldview. One is the therapist's healing power. This seems to transcend such qualities as warmth, acceptance, enthusiasm, and the like, and may depend in part on telepathy.

Nor do we understand nearly enough about the determinants of *kairos*, the auspicious moment.[14] A great variety of psychological states in combination with certain external circumstances may be followed by abrupt, large, enduring changes in a person's outlook, values, and behavior. Examples of *kairos* range from an alcoholic's "hitting bottom" and other experiences of extreme demoralization, to ecstatic peak experiences. Sometimes it occurs in psychotherapy—every experienced psychotherapist has seen profound changes in a patient following a single interview.[15] Perhaps *kairos* can be commanded by drugs like LSD or the production of emotional flooding. Perhaps the resulting changes involve the same principles as the gradual ones occurring typically in psychotherapy; perhaps they are quite different. It may be that all the principles of psychotherapy we have explored produce only minor changes in patients' personalities; major ones may always depend on *kairos*. Unfortunately, the research genius who can encompass such phenomena as healing power and *kairos* has not yet revealed himself.

NOTES

1. Kadushin (1969).
2. Sifneos (1972).
3. For the first term, see Caplan (1964) and Rusk (1971); for the second term, see Gruenberg (1967).
4. May (1968); Masserman (1971).
5. Cawte (forthcoming).
6. Szasz (1963).
7. Halleck (1971).
8. Examples are Group for the Advancement of Psychiatry (1957); Frank (1967).
9. For recent reviews of the experimental literature on psychotherapy see Meltzoff and Kornreich (1970); Bergin and Garfield (1971).
10. Parloff et al. (1954); Group for the Advancement of Psychiatry (1966); Frank (1968).
11. See discussion of "spontaneous" improvement in Bergin (1971), pp. 239–246.
12. Lang (1971).
13. Barber et al. (1971).
14. Kelman (1969).
15. For a case report, see pp. 226–228 above.

Discussion Questions

1. What does Frank mean when he suggests that all psychotherapy clients are characterized by "demoralization?" What interpersonal processes may be involved in demoralization?
2. Discuss how demoralization may be involved in: (a) depression, (b) test anxiety, (c) marital problems, and (d) severe loneliness.
3. Critique Frank's statement that "Symptoms and behavior hitherto regarded as signs of mental illness . . . may be appropriate responses to oppression by society or the patient's family." If this is the case, should the patient be considered "mentally ill" or normal? Should a psychotherapist help the patient "submit more gracefully" to this mistreatment by others (by not showing normal symptoms of abuse)?
4. Do you agree with Frank's conclusion that psychotherapy is essentially a process of persuasion?
5. In what ways are the four common features of all psychotherapy identified by Frank social psychological in nature?

Suggested Readings

Derlega, V., Hendrick, S. S., Winstead, B. A., & Berg, J. H. (1992). Psychotherapy as a personal relationship: A social psychological perspective. *Psychotherapy, 29*, 331–335. Two social psychologists, a counseling psychologist, and a clinical psychologist collaborate on a discussion of the social psychology of counseling and psychotherapy.

Mallinckrodt, B. (1996). Change in working alliance, social support, and psychological symptoms in brief therapy. *Journal of Counseling Psychology, 43*, 448–455. This is one of many research studies that have examined the processes that underlie therapeutic change.

Strong, S. (1968). Counseling: An interpersonal influence process. *Journal of Counseling Psychology, 15*, 215–224. This influential early article echoed Frank's claims about the role of social psychological processes in counseling.

READING 20

The Scientific Study of Counseling and Psychotherapy: A Unificationist View

Donelson R. Forsyth and Stanley R. Strong • Viriginia Commonwealth University

Editors' Introduction

Since the end of World War II, the *science* and *practice* of psychology have developed along two somewhat different paths. Even though efforts have been made to assure that the practice of psychotherapy is rooted firmly in scientific theory and research, clinical and counseling psychologists have often been as indifferent to the findings of basic psychological researchers as basic researchers have been to the practice of psychotherapy. Practicing psychologists often dismiss basic research on counseling and psychotherapy as artificial and useless for understanding treatment, and scientific psychologists often regard research on psychotherapeutic processes as somehow nonscientific.

In this article, Donelson Forsyth (a social psychologist) and Stanley Strong (a counseling psychologist) argue for a unified approach to research about counseling and psychotherapy. They suggest that research on counseling and psychotherapy is as scientific as research dealing with any other facet of human behavior (providing, of course, that it adheres to the fundamental requirements of science). In fact, they suggest that psychotherapy research is a critical aspect of a unified attempt to understand human behavior. Understanding the conditions under which behavior changes provides insights for the practice of psychology as well as for a deeper understanding of psychological processes more generally.

For many practicing psychologists, the most controversial aspect of this article may be Forsyth and Strong's suggestion that behavioral scientists should use all approaches at their disposal to understand psychotherapy, including a broad mix of laboratory and field investigations. Many practitioners have assumed that highly controlled laboratory experiments have nothing to contribute to our understanding of counseling and psychotherapy. For many clinical and counseling psychologists, only field research that is conducted during real, ongoing counseling or psychotherapy can tell us about psychological treatment. Forsyth and Strong strongly disagree.

Controlled experiments permit a close and careful look at particular processes that may be impossible to study in the stewing cauldron of real-life psychotherapy. Furthermore, contrary to what many assume, studies conducted during actual psychotherapy are not necessarily more generalizable to the "real world" than those conducted in laboratories. The goal of research is not to generalize the results of a particular study but rather to test theoretical ideas about how and why treatment is effective, then apply those theoretical insights to psychological practice. As Forsyth and Strong note, the ability to generalize a theory to psychological practice depends more on the quality of the theory than on the specific results of particular studies that support it.

Abstract

Three propositions underlying a unificationist view of research in counseling and clinical psychology are tentatively offered: (a) Psychotherapy research is science; (b) psychotherapy research is part of a unified attempt to understand human behavior; and (c) all scientific tools are acceptable in the effort to understand the process of psychotherapy. These propositions advocate the integration of basic and applied research, theory, and practice and of laboratory-experimental and field-correlational methods, and offer potential answers to questions concerning the practical value of basic research, "fact-finding" research, laboratory studies, theory, and technological research. Last, the unificationist view suggests that (a) fuller development of the theoretical side of psychological science and (b) the integration of theory with research and application are needed in the scientific study of counseling and psychotherapy.

Although psychologists have been investigating the process of counseling and psychotherapy for many years, a number of critical methodological issues remain unresolved: Should research in counseling and clinical psychology be directly relevant to psychotherapy? Are findings obtained in other fields of psychology—such as social or developmental psychology—relevant to psychotherapy? Can studies conducted in laboratory settings have any bearing on psychotherapy? Should correlational findings based on nonexperimental designs be taken seriously? Are subjective conclusions reached during the course of psychotherapy scientifically sound data? What is the role of theory in guiding psychotherapy research?

These complex issues undoubtedly arise from a number of interrelated sources. However, Kuhn's (1962) approach to science suggests that these issues remain unanswered because psychologists disagree about the goals of science, psychology, and clinical and counseling (or, more simply, psychotherapy) research. We lack a *disciplinary matrix*, or *paradigm* (Kuhn, 1970)—a shared set of fundamental beliefs, exemplars, and symbolic generalizations. Therefore, disagreements about what makes for good research and what should be done to advance the field are inevitable.

Kuhn's concept of paradigm suggests that one path to the resolution of the current methodological and epistemological debate requires a careful and open examination of psychology's undergirding, if implicit, paradigmatic assumptions. As a first step toward this goal, we wish to nominate three propositions about psychotherapy research and science as candidates for psychology's paradigm. The three potential shared beliefs are: (a) Psychotherapy research is science; (b) psychotherapy research is part of a larger effort aimed at understanding human behavior; and (c) all scientific tools are acceptable in the drive to better understand the process of psychotherapy. Although we strive to defend these three statements, it must be stressed that—in the logical and rhetorical sense—they remain propositions: statements or arguments that can be accepted, doubted, or rejected. Thus, we admit from the outset that these statements must be treated as propositions (conjectures, suppositions, or assumptions), rather than as taken-for-granted givens, axioms, or truths. After examining these three propositions, a number of contemporary questions concerning research in psychotherapy are then raised, and possible answers suggested by the three propositions are offered. Again, the issues involved are complex and highly debatable, so our proposition-based conclusions should be viewed as stimulating suggestions rather than solutions to long-debated questions. Last, the three propositions are used to derive possible guidelines for improving psychological research.

Three Propositions

Psychotherapy Research Is Science

Philosophers of science often note that basic science is not the same thing as applied science (e.g., Bunge, 1974; Ziman, 1974). For example, Bunge (1974) emphasized their divergent goals; he noted that systematic knowledge is the essential goal of basic researchers, whereas the applied scientist seeks information that will increase knowledge while also proving itself to be relevant to some particular problem. Bunge also proposed that research questions originate from different sources in basic and applied research. The basic researcher, according to Bunge, is interested in investigating some puzzle or problem that is suggested by theory. He or she asks, "Let's compare 'what is' with 'what should be' to see if the theory is adequate." In applied science, the research may spring from practical concerns as much as from theoretically relevant hypotheses. In essence, the applied researcher asks, "Let's understand the nature of this problem so we can do something to resolve it."

Although similar distinctions between basic and applied research have also been noted in the psychological literature (e.g., Azrin, 1977; Bevan, 1980; Fishman & Neigher, 1982; Morell, 1979), our first proposition suggests that basic and applied research are more similar than different, for both are science rather than technology. Both accept the long-term goal of increasing knowledge and understanding. Both involve relating observations back to theoretical constructs that provide the framework for interpreting data and generating predictions. Both insist that the test of theory lies in objective, empirical methods rather than logical claims or subjective feelings. Both involve a striving for consensus among members of the discipline concerning acceptable, unacceptable, and to-be-evaluated explanations of empirical observations.

Our first proposition states that psychotherapy research, although characterized by both basic and applied concerns, is science rather than "technology," "social engineering," or "developmental research." Problems relevant to the therapeutic process are the initial source of research questions, but these applied concerns are ultimately placed into a theoretical context, and the long-term goal of such research includes testing the adequacy of assumptions and hypotheses that make up the theory. The theory is therefore not solely used to develop some product, such as a diagnostic instrument that can be sold for profit, an intake procedure that will satisfy the needs of some treatment agency, or a cost-effective structured training workshop. Rather, the theory is examined by gathering information relevant to predictions derived from that theory. Furthermore, the adequacy of the theory—and the value of any products or practical, useful information that are obtained through psychotherapy research—must be determined by methods recognized as acceptable by other researchers in the field. With technological research, the employer is sometimes the only regulator of methods and evaluator of conclusions. Finally, psychotherapy research involves a free exchange of information and findings among researchers in the hope of finding answers to key questions with psychotherapeutic relevance. The consumers of the products created by researchers are not just clients or employers, but other researchers as well.

Psychotherapy Research Is Part of a Larger Effort to Understand Human Behavior

Just as our first proposition argued for the scientific unity of basic and applied research, our second proposition recommends the unification of psychotherapy research and other branches of psychology. Although the unique characteristics of psychotherapeutic settings pose special problems for researchers, the unification perspective argues that psychotherapy researchers and investigators in other areas of psychology share the superordinate goal of increasing our understanding of human behavior.

In contrast to a unificationist viewpoint, other investigators have advocated a *dualistic* approach to psychotherapy research. Due to their circumscribed interest in (a) the psychotherapy process and/or (b) problems related to psychological adjustment and functioning, proponents of dualism suggest that psychotherapy is so unique that its processes cannot be explained using principles of human behavior derived from other branches of psychology. One proponent of this view stated that, "as counseling researchers we are interested in developing principles of human behavior only inasmuch as they tap principles of counseling" (Gelso, 1979, p. 14). According to this perspective, Gelso stated that investigators must keep "actual counseling in central focus" (p. 14) with methodologies that closely approximate ongoing psychotherapy. To the staunch dualist, basing explanations of psychotherapeutic processes on theoretical propositions drawn from other areas of psychology (or on conclusions drawn from studies specifically designed to test psychotherapy-relevant theories but conducted in nontherapy settings) is misguided (cf. Garfield, 1979, 1980; Gibbs, 1979; see Bandura, 1978, for a discussion of the dualistic approach).

In arguing against dualism, the second proposition emphasizes the shared goal of psychological scientists: to develop and test generalizable principles of human behavior. If these "laws" of behavior make reference to specific settings, then the inevitable changes in these settings that take place over time and across situations undermine the generalizability of the laws themselves. For example, a proposition such as "Black clients respond best when given tangible rewards rather than verbal rewards" may fade in importance when racial differences in socialization and socioeconomic status are erased in 30 years time. However, the more general the statement—for example, "The impact of verbal rewards as reinforcers is directly related to socioeconomic background" (Zigler & Kanzer, 1962)—the more likely it is that the hypothesis will stand the test of time. Similarly, a proposition such as "Gestalt group therapy is more effective than sensitivity training" seems trivial in a time when few therapists use unstructured group methods, but a more lawlike statement such as "Groups with centralized rather than decentralized communication networks stimulate more rapid member change" is less temporally limited.

Because researchers should strive to explain clients' actions in terms of general statements that hold across many situations and times, findings obtained in other branches of psychology that bear on these general statements are necessarily relevant in evaluating the adequacy of these propositions. For example, if a therapist suggests that behavior modification represents an effective means of dealing with social skills deficits, he or she can buttress this argument by drawing on supporting evidence for operant conditioning obtained in experimental research settings. If, however, basic researchers discovered that the law of effect does not hold for the acquisition of social behaviors, then this finding would warn the therapist that the behavior modification of social skills may fail. Evidence concerning the adequacy of a general principle of human behavior should be drawn from all available sources, including both basic research and applied research within and outside clinical and counseling psychology. As Merton (1949) noted long ago, applied researchers cannot afford to adopt a myopic, single-discipline focus because practical problems often involve variables that do not fall within the scope of any particular subfield of psychology. From this perspective, psychotherapy research must draw on the findings of other fields to be successful.

All Scientific Tools Are Acceptable in the Effort to Understand the Process of Psychotherapy

Homans emphasized the importance of empirical evidence when judging sciences. To Homans (1967), "When the test of truth of a relationship lies finally in the data themselves, and the data are not wholly manufactured—when nature, however stretched out on the rack, still has a chance to say 'no!'—then the subject is a science" (p. 4). This viewpoint, although a simplification of science, nonetheless underscores the importance of some type of data in scientific research. In addition, the proposition also suggests that—like eclectic therapists who integrate many theories of psychological functioning when interacting with clients—psychological scientists must also remain eclectic by drawing on findings generated in fields other than their own. That is, researchers should use any and all scientific means possible to gather information concerning the theoretical system under investigation. Whether experimental, correlational, field, laboratory, role-play, or analog, no opportunity to further our understanding of psychotherapy should be bypassed. As Hilgard (1971) noted, in order to "satisfy the criteria of 'good science'" the researcher "must cover the whole spectrum of basic and applied science by doing sound (and conclusive) work all along the line" (p. 4).

Implications

The three propositions form the foundation for what can be termed a *unificationist* view of psychological science. To the unificationist, researchers working in the many and varied subfields of psychology are united in their professional identity (they are all scientists), their goals (they seek to extend our understanding of behavior), and their empirical outlook (they all strive to collect data relevant to the research questions at hand). In consequence, unificationism (which is an admittedly prescriptive viewpoint arguing how psychology *should be*) advocates the integration and synthesis of theory and research dealing with psychological topics. The position also offers potential answers to the currently debated methodological issues in psychotherapy research examined later.

Applied Versus Basic Science

Glasser (1982) and Sommer (1982) each commented on the problematic consequences of separating applied and basic research. According to Glasser, as early as 1900 John Dewey recommended unificationism in the study of learning—that is, linking theory and educational practice with each pursuit stimulating the other. However, for many decades experimental learning theorists worked on their own questions in psychology departments, whereas educational researchers examined practical problems from positions in education programs. Glasser suggested that the slow progress of educational psychology stemmed from this artificial separation and recommended integration under the rubric "instructional psychology."

Sommer (1982) focused on basic research gone awry in his analysis of historical trends in Prisoner's Dilemma (PD) research. As he noted, the laboratory simulations became further and further removed from the original questions concerning bargaining and negotiation. In consequence, "PD research has tended to be drawn from previous PD research, thus creating a hermetic laboratory system without the validity checks and enrichment of experimental conditions that could come from the study of actual cases" (Sommer, 1982, p. 531). Sommer therefore stated that "a blending of laboratory and field methods rather than an exclusive preoccupation with either will be of most value to both psychological science and to society" (p. 531).

Supporting Glasser and Sommer, the unificationist view suggests that psychotherapy research should be as basic as it is applied. Basic research provides the initial evidence concerning theoretical propositions and hence represents the first hurdle that any explanation of human action must pass. The second hurdle, however, is the successful application of the theory to psychotherapy. As in medicine, basic research should be inextricably linked with applied research to guard against the limitations of each pursuit. If too applied, research can become theoretically simplistic, situationally restricted, and technologically oriented. In contrast, basic researchers sometimes develop elaborate theoretical conceptualizations that have little relationship to reality or lose sight of the social value of their findings. As Lewin (1951) stated long ago, psychologists can reach their goal of helping others only if applied researchers make use of theories *and* basic researchers develop theories that can be applied to important social problems.

Fact Finding

Science is based on the accumulation of evidence and fact, but such an accumulation is not the only goal of science. Facts are used to spin theoretical systems or support existing frameworks, but because of their mutability and situational specificity, facts are of little long-lasting value in science. Unfortunately, many psychotherapy researchers consider themselves to be finders of facts, striving to answer such questions as: What impact does extensive eye contact have on client behavior? Is therapist effectiveness related to client race? Does therapy X work better than therapy Y? Is an elevated score on a certain subscale of the Minnesota Multiphasic Personality Inventory (MMPI) an indicator of psychopathology? Are therapists' religious values related to their clinical style? Although all raise important issues, such studies cannot advance our understanding of psychotherapy unless the obtained findings are relevant to transituational statements dealing with behavior. Specific facts—or, as in this case, empirical findings—are not themselves generalizable, but the hypotheses they either support or disconfirm are. For example, the investigator who finds that therapists who maintain eye contact 60% of the time are more effective than therapists who maintain eye contact 30% of the time may be tempted to tell practitioners to maintain a good deal of eye contact. Unfortunately, the specifics of the setting—the attractiveness of the therapists, the type of clients, the content of the therapists' statements during eye contact—all limit the generalizability of the "fact" that high eye contact makes counselors and clinicians more effective. If, however, the researcher had been studying a higher order theoretical proposition—such as (a) the greater the client's trust in the therapist, the more effective the therapy, (b) ceteris paribus, eye contact implies honesty and openness, and therefore (c) eye contact will create greater client–therapist trust and facilitate therapy—then the study has implications beyond the obtained data. In this case the researcher would be scientifically justified in suggesting that therapists establish a deep level of trust with clients and that this trust can be created by appropriate nonverbal behaviors.

Although the three propositions advocate the development of higher order hypotheses to guide and summarize research, the researcher must always remember Hempel's (1966) requirement of testability: "The statements constituting a scientific explanation must be capable of empirical test" (p. 49). Seeking broad, generalizable explanations of behavior is a laudable goal, but these explanations must not be so general that they are untestable or so empirically bound that they are merely accidental generalizations (Goodman, 1973). The investigator must therefore strike a balance between generality and specificity in his or her theoretical thinking. (For a philosophical discussion of the difference between generalizable, lawlike statements and accidental generalizations see Goodman's [1973] theory of "projectability.")

The Generalizability Quandary

The question "Do laboratory findings have any relevance for understanding 'real' behavior?" has been a topic of recent debate in many areas of psychology (e.g., Berkowitz & Donnerstein, 1982; Bronfenbrenner, 1977; Dipboye & Flanagan, 1978; Gelso, 1979; Gibbs, 1979; Harré & Secord, 1972; Herrnstein, 1977; Jenkins, 1974; McCall, 1977; McGuire, 1973; Mook, 1983; Rakover, 1980). In terms of application to psychotherapy research, several discussants have suggested that laboratory studies that simulate psychotherapy or examine only one particular aspect of the psychotherapeutic setting in detail are only tangentially relevant to clinical and counseling practices (e.g., Gibbs, 1979; Goldman, 1978). They suggest that the nature of clinical and counseling psychology requires field studies conducted in real therapy settings, with real clients and real therapists, and that only findings that can be easily generalized to real-life psychotherapy are data worth discussing.

Although the issues are complex and defy any simple solution, the second and third propositions of a unificationist position advocate an empirical eclecticism that is inconsistent with the wholesale rejection of any research method or theory. To elaborate, a unificationist approach argues that the generalizability question (a) should be settled empirically and (b) may be a moot issue from an epistemological perspective. Focusing first on the empiricism argument, the third assumption suggests that the context must be thought of as only one more variable or dimension that must be interpreted within the larger theoretical scheme. Kazdin (1978) stated,

> Research in psychotherapy and behavior therapy can differ from clinical application of treatment along several dimensions such as the target problem, the clients and the manner in which they are recruited, the therapists, the selection treatment, the client's set, and the setting in which treatment is conducted. (p. 684)

However, Kazdin argued that increasing the "similarity of an investigation to the clinical situation . . . does not necessarily argue for greater generality of the results" (p. 684). In essence, the importance of the setting must be established empirically (Bass & Firestone, 1980; Berkowitz & Donnerstein, 1982; Flanagan & Dipboye, 1980).

Second, as Mook (1983) and Rakover (1980) have noted recently, many laboratory studies certainly involve highly artificial situations. However, they may still be relevant to practical problems if they examine theoretical generalizations that are relevant to these applied problems (Stone, 1984). For example, say a therapist is asked to choose between two therapies. The first, therapy X, has never been applied to a clinical population, but in over two dozen laboratory studies the theory has perfectly predicted behavior change. Therapy Y, in contrast, has never been tested in the laboratory, but in one study conducted with clients at a Veterans Administration hospital several of the curative factors emphasized in the approach were positively correlated with improvement. Which therapy should be used?

To many psychotherapists, therapy Y may seem to be the more appropriate choice because it was supported by field research. However, what if the therapist's clients are verbally skilled female teenagers, and the subjects in the study of therapy Y were World War II combat veterans with only limited verbal abilities? In contrast, what if the laboratory studies examined the effects of dietary factors on behavior and found that the behavior the therapist wished to increase could be reliably obtained by modifying the client's diet?

The generalizability of a theory from one situation to another depends more on the theory than on the results that support it. Although therapy Y was corroborated in a field setting, if its theoretical structure cannot explain what effect gender, age, and verbal skill have on the therapy outcome, then it does not generalize to the new situation. If, however, therapy X is based on a physiological explanation of behavior that applies to a wide range of individuals, then its generalizability is far greater. In sum, generalizability is determined more by the structure of the theory—its scope, specificity, and universality—than by location of the supporting research.

The Value of Theory

Implicit in all three propositions making up the unificationist view is the belief that science depends upon theory as much as it depends upon data. Although the role of theory in psychotherapy research and practice has been questioned by some (e.g., Rogers, 1973; see Sarason, 1981; Strupp, 1975; Wachtel, 1980), theory provides the organizing framework for conceptualizing problems, organizing knowledge, and suggesting solutions. Supporting this view, when decision makers in mental health fields (federal and state administrators of psychological services programs) were asked "What makes research useful?" (Weiss & Weiss, 1981), the most frequently mentioned attribute was the theoretical conceptualization of the problem.

This implication contrasts sharply with the recommendation to avoid theory because it biases the researcher's observations. In contrast to this argument, a protheory perspective suggests that research is always guided by some assumptions and that theories are the means by which these assumptions can be clearly articulated and explicitly determined. According to Jacob (1977),

The scientific process does not consist simply in observing, in collecting data, and in deducing from them a theory. One can watch an object for years and never produce any observation of scientific interest. To produce a valuable observation, one has first to have an idea of what to observe, a preconception of what is possible. (p. 1161)

These theoretical propositions need not be the formal, elegant models once prescribed by deductive-nomological approaches to science (e.g., Hempel, 1966), but at minimum some theoretical ideas are required to structure our knowledge and provide direction for future efforts. According to Sidman (1960), "Observations must be brought into some kind of order before they can be said to contribute to a science of behavior" (p. 12).

The Value of Information Obtained During Practice

Although we hold that basic and applied research share scientific unity, wholly problem-solving activities are best described as technology rather than science. Even though the distinction is not always clear, attempts to solve a specific problem in a specific situation without concern for increasing our general understanding of human behavior are more akin to technological research or social engineering than to science. Technological researchers may borrow the theories of science to guide their problem solving, but their efforts are not designed to test generalizable propositions derived from these theories. Technological research may generate information that is useful in science—such as providing an indication of what variables are important in a given setting, stimulating research, or refining methodological tools and innovations—but the research is so problem and situation specific that generalizations to other settings are limited.

Another distinction between science and technology has been noted by Ziman (1974). Although he prefaced his analysis by stating that the two areas are "now so intimately mingled that the distinction can become rather pedantic" (p. 24), he pointed out that scientists strive for a "consensus of rational opinion over the widest possible field" (p. 11). Technology, Ziman continued, does not attempt to gain this consensus, for it is focused on solving a specific problem; it provides the "means to do a definite job—bridge this river, cure this disease, make better beer" (p. 23). In consequence, the technological researcher owes primary responsibility to his or her employer rather than peers.

Although the actual practice of psychotherapy may involve a "scientific attitude," it is not science per se. However, the close correspondence between science and practice cannot be overstated. For example, although a good theory of psychological adjustment may state that increases in factors A, B, and C will benefit clients with D, E, and F characteristics, technological research may be needed to determine the optimal levels of A, B, and C, techniques to use in varying these factors, and ways to assess D, E, and F. Few theories in psychology are so precise that they yield mathematical statements describing the magnitude of important variables, so practitioners must be prepared to turn to situation-specific and client-specific research to obtain the precision they require.

Beyond the Three Propositions

The three propositions suggest that the scientific study of psychotherapy cannot succeed without an interweaving of theory and research. The widespread outcry over the apparent sterility and lack of relevance of research to practice (Goldman, 1976; 1978) as well as the current controversy over the generalizability of research results (Gelso, 1979; Osipow, Walsh, & Tosi, 1980; Strong, 1971) are inevitable consequences of inadequate attention to the role of theory in scientific endeavors. Graduate training in clinical and counseling psychology focuses on the technology of collecting and analyzing data, with a special emphasis on applying findings to therapy, whereas the vital and creative steps of generating transsituational propositions from observed relationships are bypassed. The result is the reduction of the scientific study of psychotherapy to technological inquiry. Technicians are being trained rather than scientists, and the products of their situationally limited work are of little value to practitioners.

A solution to these limitations of training and research lies in more fully developing the theoretical side of psychological science and integrating research and theory. Although the logic and methods of science can be described in many ways (e.g., Hempel, 1966; Lakatos & Musgrave, 1970; Manicas & Secord, 1983; Platt, 1964; Popper, 1959), descriptions of the scientific inference process often make reference to the dual importance of theory construction and theory testing. Unfortunately, researchers tend to be so preoccupied with theory testing that they overlook the critical role played by theory construction. Granted, investigators are highly proficient in finding hypotheses to test, operationalizing concepts in the specific settings examined in the study, determining the statistical significance of the results, and even relating the evidence back to the initial hypotheses, but too often researchers fail to go the additional steps needed to develop strong, applicable theoretical systems. In consequence, very few theories capable of explaining psychotherapeutic processes possess many of the characteristics of good theories: simplicity, interpretability, usefulness, generality, testability, disconfirmability, and logical internal consistency.

As to integrating theory and research, how often do researchers conduct research programs that facilitate "strong inference" (Platt, 1964, p. 347) by devising alternative hypotheses, pitting rival hypotheses against one another in carefully designed studies, and refining the theory through the development of subhypotheses? Likewise, how many researchers follow the scientific steps recommended by Popper's "sophisticated methodological falsifictionism" (Lakatos & Musgrave, 1970; Popper, 1959) approach to science by focusing more on unexpected, disconfirming findings rather than on confirming evidence? Although we are often more gratified by supporting rather than disconfirming evidence, failures to corroborate hypotheses invite us to abandon our preconceived notions and creatively reconstruct our perspective to better account for observed relationships. Popper and other philosophers of science suggest that the greatest advances in science occur when researchers focus on unexpected irregularities in their data, seemingly trivial observations, and even subjective impressions that are inconsistent with the best theories they can construct. From these disconfirmations the scientist artfully reconstructs a broader, more all-encompassing system that not only accounts for findings that supported the previous theory but also explains the newly obtained disconfirming data. Granted, such research practices may require creativity, the abandonment of firmly held beliefs, a propensity toward risk taking, speculation, and commitment to goals of research, but the growth of knowledge requires theoretical refinements and revolutions as much as it requires empiricism.

At core, the major roadblock to advancement in the scientific study of psychotherapy is inadequate attention to discovery (McGuire, 1973; Wachtel, 1980). Concern for directly applicable research has short-circuited the scientific process and inhibited rather than encouraged the creative use of evidence from both field and laboratory settings. According to Stone (1984), this obsession with "relevance" has led to a "knee-jerk mentality" in research consumers who "automatically dismiss meaningful research solely on artificiality grounds" (p. 108). Rather than focusing exclusively on application, we should also take care to generate theoretical statements that link together therapeutic and interpersonal variables. Instead of being concerned about how similar a specific time/space event of a study is to a specific time/space event of therapy, we should creatively reconstruct how the relations among events differ in various settings and induce transituational statements about these differences. Rather than limiting our focus to only therapeutic settings, we should generate theories of such wide scope that they apply to a host of interpersonal situations.

Psychotherapy will not be better understood by overvaluing generalizability of settings, but by the energetic application of the scientific model to generate a theory of biological, social, interpersonal, and psychological relationships that specifies how the dynamics of therapeutic and nontherapeutic settings differ (Sarason, 1981). In addition, increased effectiveness of psychotherapy will not come from direct application of research results to practice, but from the application of theory to practice (Shakow, 1976; Strupp, 1975). Events generated for research purposes are applications of theories to a specific time and place, just as psychotherapy is an application of a theory to a particular client with a particular therapist in a specific treatment location. Theories that explain psychotherapeutic outcomes must, in many ways, be capable of explaining outcomes in many other types of interpersonal settings.

ACKNOWLEDGMENT

The helpful comments of Nancy Forsyth, Pam Knox, Doug Tuthill, and several anonymous reviewers of earlier drafts of this article are gratefully acknowledged.

REFERENCES

Azrin, N. H. (1977). A strategy for applied research: Learning based but outcome oriented. *American Psychologist, 32*, 140–149.

Bandura, A. (1978). On paradigms and recycled ideologies. *Cognitive Therapy and Research, 2*, 79–103.

Bass, A. R., & Firestone, I. J. (1980). Implications of representativeness for generalizability of field and laboratory research findings. *American Psychologist, 35*, 463–464.

Berkowitz, L., & Donnerstein, E. (1982). External validity is more than skin deep. *American Psychologist, 37*, 245–257.

Bevan, W. (1980). On getting in bed with a lion. *American Psychologist, 35*, 779–789.

Bronfenbrenner, U. (1977). Toward an experimental ecology of human development. *American Psychologist, 32*, 513–531.

Bunge, M. (1974). Towards a philosophy of technology. In A. C. Michalos (Ed.), *Philosophical problems of science and technology* (pp. 28–46). Boston: Allyn & Bacon.

Dipboye, R. L., & Flanagan, M. R. (1978). Research settings in industrial and organizational psychology: Are findings in the field more generalizable than in the laboratory? *American Psychologist, 34*, 141–150.

Fishman, D. B., & Neigher, W. D. (1982). American psychology in the eighties: Who will buy? *American Psychologist, 37*, 533–546.

Flanagan, M. R., & Dipboye, R. L. (1980). Representativeness does have implications for the generalizability of laboratory and field research findings. *American Psychologist, 35*, 464–466.

Garfield, S. L. (1979). Editorial. *Journal of Consulting and Clinical Psychology, 47*, 1–4.

Garfield, S. L. (1980). *Psychotherapy: An eclectic approach.* New York: Wiley.

Gelso, C. J. (1979). Research in counseling: Methodological and professional issues. *Counseling Psychologist, 8*, 7–36.

Gibbs, J. C. (1979). The meaning of ecologically oriented inquiry in contemporary psychology. *American Psychologist, 34*, 127–140.

Glasser, R. (1982). Instructional psychology. *American Psychologist, 37*, 292–305.

Goldman, L. (1976). A revolution in counseling research. *Journal of Counseling Psychology, 23*, 543–552.

Goldman, L. (Ed.). (1978). *Research methods for counselors.* New York: Wiley.

Goodman, N. (1973). *Fact, fiction, and forecast* (3rd ed.). New York: Bobbs-Merrill.

Harré, R., & Secord, P. F. (1972). *The explanation of social behavior.* Oxford, England: Blackwell.

Hempel, C. G. (1966). *Philosophy of natural science.* Englewood Cliffs, NJ: Prentice Hall.

Herrnstein, R. J. (1977). The evolution of behaviorism. *American Psychologist, 32*, 593–603.

Hilgard, E. R. (1971). Toward a responsible social science. *Journal of Applied Social Psychology, 1*, 1–6.

Homans, G. C. (1967). *The nature of social science.* New York: Harcourt, Brace, & World.

Jacob, F. (1977). Evolution and tinkering. *Science, 196*, 1161–1167.

Jenkins, J. J. (1974). Remember that old theory of memory? Well, forget it! *American Psychologist, 29*, 785–795.

Kazdin, D. E. (1978). Evaluating the generality of findings in analogue therapy research. *Journal of Consulting and Clinical Psychology, 46*, 673–686.

Kuhn, T. S. (1962). *The structure of scientific revolutions.* Chicago: University of Chicago Press.

Kuhn, T. S. (1970). *The structure of scientific revolutions* (2nd ed.). Chicago: University of Chicago Press.

Lakatos, I., & Musgrave, A. (Eds.). (1970). *Criticism and the growth of knowledge.* New York: Cambridge University Press.

Lewin, K. (1951). *Field theory in social science.* New York: Harper.

Manicas, P. T., & Secord, P. F. (1983). Implications for psychology of the new philosophy of science. *American Psychologist, 38*, 399–413.

McCall, R. B. (1977). Challenges to a science of developmental psychology. *Child Development, 48*, 333–344.

McGuire, W. J. (1973). The yin and yang of progress in social psychology: Seven koan. *Journal of Personality and Social Psychology, 26*, 446–456.

Merton, R. K. (1949). *Social theory and social structure.* Glencoe, IL: Free Press.

Mook, D. G. (1983). In defense of external invalidity. *American Psychologist, 38*, 379–387.

Morell, J. A. (1979). *Program evaluation in social research.* New York: Pergamon.

Osipow, S. H., Walsh, W. B., & Tosi, D. J. (1980). *A survey of counseling methods.* Homewood, IL: Dorsey Press.

Platt, J. R. (1964). Strong inference. *Science, 146*, 347–353.

Popper, K. R. (1959). *The logic of scientific discovery.* New York: Basic Books.

Rakover, S. S. (1980). Generalization from analogue therapy to the clinical situation: The paradox and the dilemma of generality. *Journal of Consulting and Clinical Psychology, 48*, 770–771.

Rogers, C. R. (1973). Some new challenges. *American Psychologist, 28*, 379–387.

Sarason, S. B. (1981). An asocial psychology and a misdirected clinical psychology. *American Psychologist, 36*, 827–836.

Shakow, D. (1976). What is clinical psychology? *American Psychologist, 31*, 553–360.

Sidman, M. (1960). *Tactics of scientific research.* New York: Basic Books.

Sommer, R. (1982). The district attorney's dilemma: Experimental games and the real world of plea bargaining. *American Psychologist, 37*, 526–532.

Stone, G. L. (1984). Reaction: In defense of the "artificial." *Journal of Counseling Psychology, 31*, 108–110.

Strong, S. R. (1971). Experimental laboratory research in counseling. *Journal of Counseling Psychology, 18*, 106–110.

Strupp, H. H. (1975). Clinical psychology, irrationalism, and the erosion of excellence. *American Psychologist, 31*, 561–571.

Wachtel, P. J. (1980). Investigation and its discontents: Some constraints on progress in psychological research. *American Psychologist, 35,* 399–408.

Weiss, J. A., & Weiss, C. H. (1981). Social scientists and decision makers look at the usefulness of mental health research. *American Psychologist, 36,* 837–847.

Zigler, E., & Kanzer, P. (1962). The effectiveness of two classes of verbal reinforcers on the performance of middle- and lower-class children. *Journal of Personality, 30,* 157–163.

Ziman, J. (1974). What is science? In A. C. Michalos (Ed.), *Philosophical problems of science and technology* (pp. 5–27). Boston: Allyn & Bacon.

Discussion Questions

1. Do you agree with Forsyth and Strong's unificationist approach to psychotherapy research? Why or why not?
2. Imagine that you are trying to persuade a practicing psychologist that basic research from social psychology can help us to understand and improve counseling and psychotherapy. What arguments would you offer?
3. Given the points made in this article, what changes should be made in how psychologists are trained with respect to their attitudes toward research?
4. Traditionally, social psychology has had a greater effect on clinical psychology than clinical psychology has had on social psychology. Discuss three ways that the science of social psychology would benefit from paying greater attention to the practice of clinical and counseling psychology.

Suggested Readings

Forsyth, D. R., & Leary, M. R. (1991). Metatheoretical and epistemological issues. In C. R. Snyder & D. R. Forsyth (Eds.), *Handbook of social and clinical psychology: The health perspective* (pp. 757–773). New York: Pergamon. This chapter examines how social and clinical psychologists differ in their beliefs about human beings and in their assumptions regarding how knowledge about human behavior should be obtained.

Harari, H. (1983). Social psychology of clinical practice and in clinical practice. *Journal of Social and Clinical Psychology, 1,* 173–192. Harari offers ideas for improving the controversies between social and clinical psychology.

Kowalski, R. M., & Leary, M. R. (1999). Interfaces of social and clinical psychology: Where we have been, where we are. In R. M. Kowalski & M. R. Leary (Eds.), *The social psychology of emotional and behavioral problems* (pp. 7–33). Washington, DC: American Psychological Association.

Maddux, J. E., & Stoltenberg, C. D. (1983). Clinical social psychology and social clinical psychology: A proposal for a peaceful coexistence. *Journal of Social and Clinical Psychology, 1,* 289–299. Maddux and Stoltenberg address tensions that exist between social, clinical, and counseling psychology, and offer solutions for their resolution.

READING 21

Disclosure of Traumas and Immune Function: Health Implications for Psychotherapy

James W. Pennebaker • Southern Methodist University
Janice K. Kiecolt-Glaser • Department of Psychiatry and Comprehensive Cancer Center, Ohio State University College of Medicine
Ronald Glaser • Department of Medical Microbiology and Immunology and Comprehensive Cancer Center, Ohio State University College of Medicine

Editors' Introduction

When people think about the benefits of counseling and psychotherapy, they usually think of reducing clients' feelings of distress, anxiety, and depression, or perhaps helping them to solve marital difficulties or other life problems. Research evidence suggests, however, that psychotherapy not only helps people deal with their psychological and social difficulties but can contribute to improved physical health as well. For example, studies have shown that people who received psychotherapy used medical services less often and had fewer days of hospitalization than people who had not received psychotherapy. However, this research left unanswered the question of why psychotherapy improves physical health.

Research on stress and illness provides one possible answer. Given that stress can undermine good health, then reducing stress and emotional distress, whatever their source, should help to improve health. One common source of stress involves failing to confront traumatic experiences in one's life. When people try not to think and talk about a traumatic event or serious problem, they do not resolve the troublesome issue in their own mind, so they continue to ruminate about it. In addition, trying not to think about the trauma creates stress in its own right. Thus, merely confronting the traumas or stressors in one's life may help to lower stress and improve health. In support of this idea, Pennebaker and Beall (1986) found that people who wrote about the facts and emotions surrounding a traumatic event showed improved physical health relative to people who did not write about the trauma in the same way. The researchers suggested that people who disclose traumatic information no longer ruminate about that trauma in their minds to the same degree. In addition, by writing about the trauma, people are sometimes able to find some meaning in the event.

Most studies that examined the relationship between disclosure and physical health relied on self-reports of physical health symptoms or on accounts of visits to physicians, and few of them tried to understand the factors responsible for the relationship between disclosure and health. The following study by Pennebaker, Kiecolt-Glaser, and Glaser dealt with these issues by examining the relationship between disclosing traumatic events and immunological functioning. Participants wrote about either traumatic events or trivial topics for 20 minutes a day for four consecutive days. Blood samples were drawn the day before writing, the last day of writing, and 6 weeks after writing to provide an index of immunological functioning. Results of the study indicated that people who wrote about traumatic experiences showed improved immunological functioning compared to those who wrote about trivial topics. Furthermore, the greatest health improvements occurred in participants who had never disclosed information about their traumatic experience before. These results support the hypothesis that holding back thoughts, feelings, and emotions related to a stressful experience taxes the immune system, thereby compromising health. Letting go of the inhibition and confronting the trauma, therefore, improves the functioning of the immune system.

Abstract

Can psychotherapy reduce the incidence of health problems? A general model of psychosomatics assumes that inhibiting or holding back one's thoughts, feelings, and behaviors is associated with long-term stress and disease. Actively confronting upsetting experiences—through writing or talking—is hypothesized to reduce the negative effects of inhibition. Fifty healthy undergraduates were assigned to write about either traumatic experiences or superficial topics for four consecutive days. Two measures of cellular immune-system function and health center visits suggested that confronting traumatic experiences was physically beneficial. The implications for psychotherapy as a preventive treatment for health problems are discussed.

There is little doubt that psychotherapy reduces subjective distress and yields positive behavioral outcomes. In recent years, a small group of researchers has sought to learn whether psychotherapy can also reduce health problems. Two promising reviews have indicated that the use of mental health services is associated with fewer medical visits, fewer days of hospitalization, and lower overall medical costs. In a summary of 15 studies published between 1965 and 1980, Mumford, Schlesinger, and Glass (1981) found that individuals who underwent psychotherapy evidenced a 13% decrease in medical utilization relative to nonpsychotherapy control subjects. Similarly, in a review of 13 studies of mental health services that were introduced into organizations, Jones and Vischi (1980) found that psychotherapy was associated with a 20% drop in medical utilization.

Although promising, these findings leave open the question of why medical use drops following psychotherapy. Kiesler (1983), for example, urged caution in blindly accepting a causal interpretation because we do not know if these effects generalize across practitioners and sites. Furthermore, individuals who seek psychotherapy in an organized health system, such as a health maintenance organization (HMO), tend to be some of the highest users of the medical system (see also Tessler, Mechanic, & Diamond, 1976). Finally, these studies have not distinguished between actual health problems and unnecessary medical visits.

Ironically, in the fields of psychosomatics and health psychology, researchers have long known that psychological disturbance can lead to health problems. Alexander (1950), Selye (1976), and other pioneers have provided overwhelming evidence that psychological conflict, anxiety, and stress can cause or exacerbate disease processes. It follows that the reduction of conflict or stress should reduce illness.

An important predictor of illness is the way in which individuals cope with traumatic experiences. It has been well documented that individuals who have suffered a major upheaval, such as the death of a spouse or a divorce, are more vulnerable to a variety of major and minor illnesses. However, the adverse effects of stress can be buffered by such things as a social support network (e.g., Cohen & Syme, 1985; Swann & Pridmore, 1985) and by a predisposition toward hardiness (Kobasa, 1982).

A common theme in the psychotherapy literature is that individuals tend to deal with trauma most effectively if they can understand and assimilate it. Indeed, Breuer and Freud (1895/1966), in their development of the cathartic method, emphasized the value of talking about the thoughts and feelings associated with upsetting events in the reduction of hysterical symptoms. To examine the links between confronting traumatic events and long-term health, Pennebaker and Beall (1986) asked healthy college students to write about either personally traumatic experiences or trivial topics for 4 consecutive days. Subjects who wrote about traumatic events were required to discuss either the relevant facts (trauma-fact condition), their feelings about the events (trauma-emotion), or both their thoughts and feelings (trauma-combination). In the months following the study, subjects in the trauma-combination condition visited the student health center for illness significantly less often than people in any of the other conditions.

Confronting a trauma may be beneficial from at least two perspectives. First, individuals no longer need to actively inhibit or hold back their thoughts and feelings from others. Indeed, several studies have indicated that actively inhibiting ongoing behavior is associated with both short-term autonomic activity (cf. Fowles, 1980; Gray, 1975) and long-term stress-related disease (Pennebaker & Susman, in press). Confronting a trauma, then, may reduce the long-term work of inhibition. Second, by confronting the trauma, individuals may assimilate, reframe, or find meaning in the event (Horowitz, 1976; Meichenbaum, 1977; Silver, Boon, & Stones, 1983).

A major problem in evaluating the health effects of confronting a trauma is that most measures are relatively subjective or are susceptible to demand characteristics, such as self-reported symptoms or physician visits. Furthermore, studies such as these fail to identify the underlying mechanisms that influence health. Recent research in psychoneuroimmunology has indicated that the central nervous system can directly influence the functioning of the immune system. For example, the psychological stress associated with exams, loneliness, and divorce can lead to adverse immunological changes (e.g., Bartrop, Luckhurst, Lazarus, Kiloh, & Penny, 1977; F. Cohen, 1980; Kiecolt-Glaser, Garner, Speicher, Penn, & Glaser, 1984; Kiecolt-Glaser et al., 1987). Similarly, relaxation interventions can enhance some aspects of immunocompetence (Kiecolt-Glaser et al., 1985).

Although there is no single, general measure of immune function, many psychoimmunological studies have examined the lymphocyte (white blood cell) response to stimulation by substances foreign to the body, called *mitogens*. *Blastogenesis*, the measurement of the proliferation of lymphocytes in response to stimulation, is thought to provide an in vitro model of the body's response to challenge by infectious agents, such as bacteria or viruses. Because different mitogens stimulate different subpopulations of lymphocytes, two types of mitogens—phytohemagglutinin (PHA) and concanavalin A (ConA)—were used. Both PHA and ConA stimulate the proliferation of T-lymphocytes. PHA stimulates the proliferation of helper cells, whereas ConA stimulates both helper and suppressor T-cells (e.g., Ader, 1981; Glaser et al., 1985; Reinherz & Schlossman, 1980).

The present project examined the effects of writing about a traumatic experience on immunological function and on other measures of distress. We predicted that individuals assigned to write about traumatic experience would demonstrate a heightened proliferative response to PHA and ConA assays relative to control subjects who merely wrote about superficial topics.

Method

Overview

Fifty healthy undergraduates were randomly assigned to write about either personal traumatic events or trivial topics for 20 minutes on each of four consecutive days. Lymphocytes, which were prepared from blood samples obtained the day before, the last day, and 6 weeks after writing, were assayed for their blastogenic response to PHA and ConA. Health center illness records, self-reports, autonomic measures, and individual difference measures were collected before and during the experiment.

Subjects

Thirty-six women and 14 men who were enrolled in undergraduate psychology courses participated as part of an extra-credit class option. Prior to agreeing to participate, all subjects were told that the experiment might require that they write about extremely personal material and that they would have their blood drawn. All subjects participated in the pretest and in the four writing days. Two subjects missed the 6-week follow-up blood draw. Two subjects' immunological data were excluded from the analyses: one for taking cortisone, the other for pregnancy. In addition, three blood samples for the second draw and one for the third draw were lost during the assaying process.

Procedure

The day prior to the actual writing, subjects met as a group and completed a battery of questionnaires. During the session and after sitting quietly for at least 10 minutes, subjects' blood pressure levels, heart rates, and skin conductance levels were measured. At assigned times, subjects were escorted to the adjacent Student Health Center building where blood was drawn by the nursing staff. After the blood was drawn and all questionnaires were completed, subjects met individually with the first experimenter, who randomly assigned them to conditions with the provision that an equal ratio of men to women be in each of the two conditions. All subjects were told that they would be required to write about specific topics on each of the following four days. Subjects in the trauma condition were informed as follows:

> During each of the four writing days, I want you to write about the most traumatic and upsetting experiences of your entire life. You can write on different topics each day or on the same topic for all four days. The important thing is that you write about your deepest thoughts and feelings. Ideally, whatever you write about should deal with an event or experience that you have not talked with others about in detail.

Those in the no-trauma condition were informed that they would be asked to write on an assigned topic during each of the four writing days. The experimenter emphasized that subjects were to describe specific objects or events in detail without discussing their own thoughts or feelings.

On each of the four writing days, subjects first met individually with the first experimenter, who reiterated the instructions. For subjects in the no-trauma cell, the specific writing topic was assigned. Depending on the day of the study, subjects were variously asked to describe their activities during the day, the most recent social event that they attended, the shoes they were wearing, or their plans for the remainder of the day. Each day, subjects were escorted to individual private rooms by an experimenter blind to condition, where they were given 20 minutes to write on their assigned topics. Immediately before and after writing, subjects completed a brief questionnaire that assessed their moods and physical symptoms. After writing only, subjects evaluated their day's essay. The questionnaires and writing samples were stapled and deposited in a large box by the subjects as they left.

After writing on the fourth day, blood pressure, heart rate, and skin conductance were measured before subjects went to the health center for the second blood draw. After the draw, subjects completed a brief questionnaire. Six weeks later, subjects returned to the health center, where autonomic levels and blood samples were collected for a third time. Subjects completed a postexperimental questionnaire and were extensively debriefed about the experiment.

At the conclusion of the study, the health center provided data regarding the number of visits each student had made for illness for the 5 months prior to the study and for the 6 weeks of the study. Approximately 3 months after the writing phase of the study, all subjects were mailed a final questionnaire in order to assess the possible long-term effects of the experiment. The long-term follow-up questionnaire included items assessing subjective distress and daily habits (e.g., smoking and exercise patterns) that had been completed earlier in the study. Of the 50 subjects, 2 did not receive the questionnaire (due to incorrectly listed mailing addresses) and 4 failed to return the questionnaire. All subjects were mailed a follow-up letter that provided the study's outcome their own immune data, and an interpretation of these data. All essays, physiological data, and self-reports included only subject numbers. Immune assays were collected, performed, and analyzed blind to condition.

Immune Assays

In the study, each subject's blood was drawn at the same time each day to control for possible diurnal variations. For each blood draw, whole blood treated with ethylenediamine tetraacetic acid (EDTA) to prevent clotting was collected from each subject. The blood samples were sent to the laboratory the following morning and assayed for their ability to respond to PHA and ConA (Kiecolt-Glaser et al., 1984). Lymphocytes were separated from whole blood samples on Hypaque-Ficoll gradients.

The PHA and ConA were used at three different concentrations: 5, 10, and 20 mg/ml for PHA and 2, 5, and 10 mg/ml for ConA. Each assay was performed in triplicate. Complete medium was used for baseline controls. One-tenth milliliter of mitogen was added to 1×10^6 lymphocytes (in 0.1 ml medium) in 96-well plates and was incubated at 37°C for 48 h. Fifty microliters of tritiated thymidine (10 mCi/ml, specific activity 82 Ci/mmol) were added to each well and the plates were incubated at 37°C for 4 h. Cells were harvested onto GF11A filters. Radioactivity was measured using a Beckman LS7000 scintillation counter. The mean stimulation value (expressed in counts per minute) was subtracted from the control value and transformed to log (base 10).

Results

Three general classes of data were collected: evaluations of and responses to the essays, long-term effects of the experiment, and individual differences mediating responses to the essays. Each is discussed separately.

Parameters of Essay Writing

Subjects disclosed highly personal and upsetting experiences in the trauma condition. Overall, the primary topics of the essays were coming to college (19%), with 10% focusing on the loss and loneliness associated with leaving home; conflicts associated with members of the opposite sex (15%); parental problems (14%), including divorce (6%), family quarrels (6%), and family violence (2%); death (13%) of either a relative (6%), friend (4%), or pet (3%); injury or illness (12%), including eating disorders (4%), car accidents (4%), alcohol/drug abuse (2%), or other causes; sexual abuse (9%) by family member (4%) or stranger (5%); serious thoughts of suicide (6%); public humiliation (5%), such as learning that others suspected the subject of homosexuality; and miscellaneous concerns about religion (4%) and the meaning of life (3%).

Two independent judges rated each essay for

the degree to which the content was personal, using a 7-point unipolar scale on which 7 = *personal*. Interjudge correlations across essays averaged .89. In addition, objective parameters of each essay were tabulated, including the total number of words, number of self-references (I, me, my, mine), and number of emotion words. An overall multivariate analysis of variance (MANOVA) was initially computed on the objective and self-ratings of the essays. As expected, a highly significant condition effect was obtained, $F(9, 40) = 72.31$, $p < .01$. As can be seen in Table 21.1, simple one-way analyses of variance (ANOVAs) indicated that trauma subjects' essays were rated as more personal than those of control subjects, $F(1, 48) = 215.94$, $p < .01$. Finally, relative to control subjects, trauma subjects wrote more words and included more self-references and more emotion words (all $ps \leq .01$) on each essay.

After completing each writing session, subjects rated how personal they considered their essay to be, the degree to which they revealed emotions in their essay, and the degree to which they had previously held back telling others about the subject covered in their essay. Subjects rated each question along a 7-point unipolar scale on which 7 = *a great deal*. Averaging across the four days of writing, subjects in the trauma group considered their essays to be far more personal, $F(1, 48) = 279.89$, $p < .01$, and revealing of their emotions, $F(1, 48) = 266.73$, $p < .01$, than those in the control group. As depicted in Table 21.1, subjects in the trauma group wrote about topics that they had previously held back from telling others relative to those in the control group, $F(1, 48) = 73.80$, $p < .01$.

Each day, immediately before and after writing, subjects completed a brief questionnaire assessing the degree to which they felt each of eight common physical symptoms (e.g., headache, pounding heart, tense muscles) and six negative moods (e.g., frustrated, guilty, depressed). The self-report items were summed to yield separate physical symptom and mood scales. The two scales were subjected to separate 2 × 2 × 4 (Condition × Time [before vs. after writing] × Day) repeated-measures ANOVAs. Contrary to a simplistic catharsis or venting view, subjects in the trauma group reported higher levels of physical symptoms and negative moods following the writing compared with the control subjects. Significant Condition × Time interactions emerged for both symptoms, $F(1, 48) = 37.21$, $p < .001$, and negative moods, $F(1, 48) = 61.27$, $p < .001$. Although significant main effects for condition and time for the negative moods were obtained (both $ps < .01$), these effects were attributable to the interaction. No other effects attained significance.

TABLE 21.1. Parameters and Responses to Essays

	Condition	
	Trauma	Control
Variable	($n = 25$)	($n = 25$)
Essay parameter		
Number of words/essay	465.8	388.8
Number of self-references/essay	46.8	30.2
Number of emotion words/essay	11.7	0.6
Personal rating	4.69	1.08
Self-report essay rating		
Personal	5.87	2.14
Revealing of emotions	5.18	1.34
Previously held back	4.58	1.52
Response to essay		
Physical symptoms		
Before writing	12.3	12.2
After writing	15.4	11.4
Negative moods		
Before writing	13.4	13.1
After writing	17.8	11.4

Note. Means for the two groups were all significantly different ($p < .01$) except for ratings of symptoms and moods before writing.

Long-Term Effects of Essay Writing

Four types of data assessed the long-term effects of disclosing traumatic experiences: mitogen responses, health center visits, self-reports of subjective distress, and autonomic changes. The immune, subjective distress, and autonomic data were collected the day before the experiment began (and before assignment to condition was made), approximately 1 h after the final writing sample was collected, and 6 weeks after the conclusion of the writing portion of the study.

Immunological data. The blastogenic data for PHA and ConA stimulation were analyzed separately. A 2 × 3 × 3 (Condition × Day × Concentration [of mitogen; 5, 10, and 20 mg/ml]) repeated-measures ANOVA was computed on the PHA data. Significant effects emerged for day, $F(2, 80) = 79.10$, $p < .001$, concentration, $F(2, 80) = 29.94$, $p < .001$, and Concentration × Day interaction,

TABLE 21.2. Mean Lymphocyte Response to PHA Stimulation Over Sample Points in Counts per Minute, $\log_{10}$

Group	5 mg/culture	10 mg/culture	20 mg/culture
Trauma ($n = 20$)			
Before writing	4.93	4.99	4.90
After writing	4.96	5.00	4.94
6-Week follow-up	5.43	5.42	5.34
Control ($n = 22$)			
Before writing	5.01	5.07	4.97
After writing	4.82	4.88	4.81
6-Week follow-up	5.37	5.39	5.30

Note. PHA = phytohemagglutinin. Higher numbers reflect greater lymphocyte response. The writing period took place during the first week of February. Average standard deviation within mitogen concentration levels was .260 for the trauma group and .262 for the control group.

$F(4, 160) = 5.25, p = .001$. Most important, however, was the emergence of the Condition × Day interaction, $F(2, 80) = 3.36, p = .04$, indicating that trauma subjects demonstrated an overall higher mitogen response following baseline in comparison with control subjects (Table 21.2).

The writing phase of the experiment took place during the first week of February immediately prior to midterm exams. According to annual health center records, this period is marked by one of the highest illness rates of the entire school year. The follow-up blood draw, 6 weeks later, took place 4 days before the school's spring break vacation, a time when the incidence of illness visits is much lower. In short, the highly significant increase in immune response for the follow-up period may reflect, in part, both normal seasonal variation and normal fluctuations in the mitogen stimulation assays.

The ConA data, which were only available from the first two blood draws (due to a problem with the ConA preparation), were subjected to a 2 × 2 × 3 (Condition × Day × Concentration [mitogen stimulation level]) ANOVA. As with the PHA findings, significant day, concentration, and Day × Concentration effects emerged (all $ps \leq .01$). Although it occurred in the same direction as the PHA means, the Condition × Day interaction did not attain significance, $F(1, 43) = 2.03, p = .16$. No other effects approached significance.

Health center data. The number of health center visits for illness were tabulated by the student health center over two time periods: from the beginning of the school year until the beginning of the study (covering a 4-month interval) and from the beginning of the study until the debriefing period (a 6-week interval). The number of health center visits was adjusted to reflect visits per month and was subjected to a 2 × 2 (Condition × Time) ANOVA.

Consistent with the Pennebaker and Beall (1986) findings, a significant Condition × Time interaction emerged for health center visits for illness, $F(1, 48) = 4.20, p < .05$. As depicted in Figure 21.1, trauma subjects evidenced a drop in visits relative to control subjects. No other effects attained significance. As with the immune data, it is important to note that the apparent increase in illness visits for the control group probably reflects normal seasonal illness rates during the month of February.

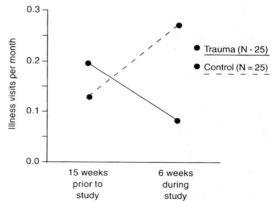

FIGURE 21.1 ■ Mean health center illness visits for the periods before and during the experiment. (Note that the standard deviation for visits per month ranged from .12 to .40, averaging .26 over the four observations.)

Subjective distress. Questionnaires pertaining to the effects of the experiment were completed 1 h after the last writing session, 6 weeks later prior to the final blood draw, and again at the end of the semester approximately 3 months after the writing phase of the study. Two general types of information were included on the questionnaires. The first included subject general attitudes about the experiment. The second focused on the health-related behaviors that had changed since the experiment.

Although the experiment was associated initially with some negative feelings among the trauma subjects, they were significantly happier than control subjects at the 3-month follow-up, $t(42) = 2.09$, $p < .05$. In response to the question "Looking back on this experiment, to what degree has this experiment been valuable or meaningful for you?," trauma subjects were far more positive than control subjects, $t(42) = 4.50$, $p < .001$ (on a 7-point scale on which $7 = $ *a great deal*, trauma mean = 4.35, control mean = 2.33). Although subjects in the trauma group reported feeling more depressed than control subjects on the last day of writing, $t(48) = 2.81$, $p < .01$ (trauma mean = 3.80, control mean = 2.68), this difference disappeared by the follow-up questionnaire, $t = .09$ (trauma mean = 2.70, control mean = 2.67). No other simple effects attained significance.

A series of repeated-measures ANOVAs was computed on questions assessing the following health-related behaviors: cigarettes smoked per day, caffeinated and alcoholic beverages consumed per day, aspirin and sleeping pill use, and hours of strenuous exercise per week. No significant main effects or interactions approached significance. In short, the experiment did not appear to influence long-term behavior.

Other relevant data. Resting levels of systolic and diastolic blood pressure, heart rate, and skin conductance level were measured approximately 1 h prior to each of the three blood draws. Repeated-measures ANOVAs on each autonomic index yielded no significant effects.

Finally, simple correlations were computed between changes in immune response and changes in health center visits and autonomic levels from the first to the final day of the study. Although PHA and ConA changes over the first 5 days of the study were correlated with each other, $r(43) = .88$, $p < .01$, changes in PHA and ConA were unrelated to all other variables. Similarly, changes in illness visits were unrelated to autonomic levels.

Who Benefits Most: Exploring Individual Differences

Do all individuals who write about a traumatic experience benefit equally? We have argued here and elsewhere (cf. Pennebaker, Hughes, & O'Heeron, 1987) that the failure to confront traumatic experience is stressful. A significant form of stress is associated with the work of inhibiting or actively holding back the disclosure of important traumas. All participants in the present study rated the degree to which they had written about an event that they had "actively held back in discussing with others" after each writing session. According to our conception, those individuals in the trauma condition who had addressed issues that they had previously held back should have benefited most.

To test this idea, subjects in the trauma condition were split at the median into two groups based on their mean response to the actively-holding-back question. Those who reported that they had written about topics that they had previously held back were labeled high disclosers ($n = 11$) and the remainder were labeled low disclosers ($n = 14$). A series of ANOVAs was computed on the primary variables of interest using the three groups (trauma, high discloser; trauma, low discloser; control) as the between-subjects factor. Contrasts using the mean square error term compared high versus low disclosers.

Overall, high disclosers wrote significantly more words, $t(48) = 3.53$, $p < .01$ (high mean = 505.3, low mean = 435.5) on each essay than low disclosers. Although high disclosers reported that their essays were more personal than low disclosers, $t(48) = 2.94$, $p < .05$ ($Ms = 6.13$ vs. 5.68, respectively), independent judges rated the two groups equivalently, $t < 1.0$. No other significant essay characteristics emerged that separated high and low disclosers.

More interesting were the physiological correlates of disclosure. Analyses of the immune data indicated that, overall, high disclosers had a marginally higher response to PHA stimulation than low disclosers, $t(39) = 1.96$, $p = .06$ (high mean = 5.18, low mean = 5.00). An ANOVA on the ConA data, on the other hand, yielded a significant Condition × Day × Concentration interaction, $F(4, 84) = 2.99, p = .02$. As can be seen in Figure 21.2; high disclosures demonstrated an improved mitogen response across all mitogen concentrations relative to low disclosers and control subjects from before the study to the last day of writing (recall that follow-up ConA data were lost). No other interactions with the discloser variable attained significance for either PHA or ConA.

Although there were no initial differences in autonomic levels as a function of type of discloser or condition prior to the study, repeated-measures ANOVAs yielded Condition × Day effects for systolic blood pressure, $F(4, 84) = 2.68, p < .05$, and a marginal effect for heart rate, $F(4, 84) = 1.97, p = .10$. Indeed, from the beginning of the study to follow-up, high disclosers showed a greater decline than low disclosers in both systolic blood pressure, $t(44) = 3.42, p < .01$ (change from before study to follow-up: high disclosers = −5.5 mm Hg, low disclosers = 8.7 mm Hg), and diastolic blood pressure, $t(44) = 2.50, p < .05$ (high disclosers = −5.8 mm Hg, low disclosers = 1.0 mm Hg). Similar nonsignificant trends were found for heart rate (high disclosers = −1.2 beats per minute, low disclosers = 1.1) and skin conductance (high disclosers = −2.6 mmhos, low disclosers = 0.3).

Discussion

The results indicate that writing about traumatic experience has positive effects on the blastogenic response of T-lymphocytes to two mitogens, on autonomic levels, on health center use, and on subjective distress. The results are important in (a) supporting an inhibitory model of psychosomatics, (b) pointing to the effectiveness of using writing as a general preventive therapy, and (c) promoting an awareness that psychotherapy can bring about direct and cost-effective improvements in health.

Within psychology, it has been generally accepted that stress can increase the incidence of illness. We have proposed that one form of stress is associated with the failure to confront traumatic experience. Specifically, the inhibition or active holding back of thoughts, emotions, or behaviors is associated with physical work that, over time, can become manifested in disease. The present study supports this idea. Individuals who are forced to confront upsetting experiences in their lives show improvements in physical health relative to control subjects. More important, in our study the individuals who showed the greatest health improvements were those who wrote about topics that they had actively held back from telling others.

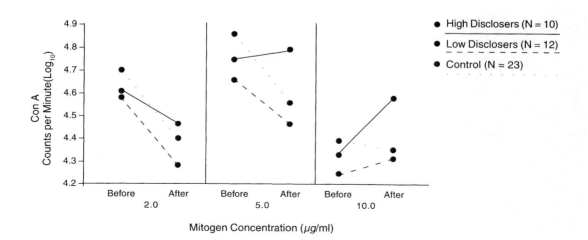

FIGURE 21.2 ■ Lymphocyte response to three levels of concanavalin A (Con A) stimulation before and after the writing sessions.

One important remaining question concerns the specific dimensions of writing that actively promote health. Based on previous work (e.g., Pennebaker & O'Heeron, 1984; Wegner, in press), we believe that the failure to confront a trauma forces the person to live with it in an unresolved manner. Indeed, not disclosing a recent trauma such as the death of a spouse is associated with increased obsessions about the spouse. It follows then, that actively confronting a trauma allows for the understanding and assimilation of that trauma.

In the present study, for example, several subjects who wrote about the same traumas day after day gradually changed then perspectives. One woman, who had been molested at the age of 9 years by a boy 3 years older, initially emphasized her feelings of embarrassment and guilt. By the third day of writing, she expressed anger at the boy who had victimized her. By the last day, she had begun to put it in perspective. On the follow-up survey 6 weeks after the experiment, she reported, "Before when I thought about it, I'd lie to myself. . . . Now, I don't feel like I even have to think about it because I got it off my chest. I finally admitted that it happened. . . . I really know the truth and won't have to lie to myself anymore."

Clinical psychologists within the cognitive and psychodynamic traditions are currently addressing some of the processes underlying this confrontational strategy (Horowitz, 1976, Meichenbaum, 1977). Through writing or talking about an upsetting experience, the person can come to understand the causes and effects of the trauma better, which may ultimately eliminate the need for inhibition.

Although some therapists have asserted the value of writing about one's problems, such as in bibliotherapy (cf. Lazarus, 1984), very little systematic work has been done on it. Within the context of the present study, psychologically healthy individuals were initially upset about disclosing personal and upsetting experiences. That is, immediately after writing, trauma subjects reported more physical symptoms and negative moods. Writing about traumas, then, appears to be painful in the short run. Indeed, in a recent study by Lamnin and Murray (1987) comparing a writing therapy with a client-centered approach, clients were found to be more depressed immediately after each writing session than after a live therapy session.

There are clear disadvantages as well as advantages to writing versus talking with another person about traumas. Writing about intensely personal experiences does not allow for an objective outside opinion, support from others, or objective coping information. Alternatively, writing is tremendously cost-effective, allows people to confront traumas at their own rates, and encourages them to devise their own meaning and solutions to their problems. Above all, writing may provide an alternative form of preventive therapy that can be valuable for individuals who otherwise would not enter therapy.

Previous archival studies have indicated that medical use decreases once psychotherapy begins (e.g., Mumford et al., 1981). Although encouraging, meta-analyses such as these have not been able to pinpoint the direct causal mechanisms. The present study offers experimental evidence linking the confronting of traumas with health improvement. Obviously, we have only examined the responses of a psychologically healthy population. Nevertheless, the present findings, along with those from conceptually similar experiments (e.g., Pennebaker & Beall, 1986), suggest that the disclosure of traumas is simultaneously associated with improvement in certain aspects of immune function and physical health.

ACKNOWLEDGMENTS

We are indebted to Sondra Brumbelow, Steve Gordon, Jean Czajka, Kathleen Ferrara, Holly Williams, Hema Patel, Brad Richards, David Alexander, Richard Cole, and John Tiebout (at Southern Methodist University) and to Paula Ogrocki (at Ohio State University) for their help in conducting the research. Thanks are extended to Jonathon Brown and David Watson for comments on the manuscript.

Portions of this research were funded by National Science Foundation Grant BNS 8606764 and National Institutes of Health Grant HL32547 to James W. Pennebaker and by National Institute of Mental Health Grant MH40787 to Janice K. Kiecolt-Glaser and Ronald Glaser.

REFERENCES

Ader, R. (1981). *Psychoneuroimmunology*. New York: Academic Press.

Alexander, F. (1950). *Psychosomatic medicine*. New York: Norton.

Bartrop, R. W., Luckhurst, E., Lazarus, L., Kiloh, L. G., & Penny, R. (1977). Depressed lymphocyte function after bereavement. *Lancet, 214,* 834–836.

Breuer, J., & Freud, S. (1966). *Studies on hysteria*. New York: Avon. (Original work published 1895).

Cohen, F. (1980). Personality, stress, and the development of physical illness. In G. C. Stone, F. Cohen, & N. E. Adler (Eds.), *Health psychology* (pp. 77–111). San Francisco: Jossey-Bass.

Cohen, S., & Syme, S. (Eds.). (1985). *Social support and health*. Orlando, FL: Academic Press.

Fowles, D. C. (1980). The three arousal model: Implications of Gray's two-factor theory for heart rate, electrodermal activity, and psychopathy. *Psychophysiology, 17*, 87–104.

Glaser, R., Kiecolt-Glaser, J. K., Stout, J. C., Tarr, K. L., Speicher, C. E., & Holliday, J. E. (1985). Stress-related impairments in cellular immunity. *Psychiatric Research, 16*, 233–239.

Gray, J. (1975). *Elements of a two-process theory of learning*. New York: Academic Press.

Horowitz, M. J. (1976). *Stress response syndromes*. New York: Jacob Aronson.

Jones, K., & Vischi, T. (1980). Impact of alcohol, drug abuse and mental health treatment on medical care utilization: A review of the literature. *Medical Care, 17* (Suppl. 2), 1–82.

Kiecolt-Glaser, J. K., Fisher, L., Ogrocki, P., Stout, J. C., Speicher, C. E., & Glaser, R. (1987). Marital quality, marital disruption, and immune function. *Psychosomatic Medicine, 49*, 13–34.

Kiecolt-Glaser, J. K., Garner, W., Speicher, C., Penn, G., & Glaser, R. (1984). Psychosocial modifiers of immunocompetence in medical students. *Psychosomatic Medicine, 46*, 7–14.

Kiecolt-Glaser, J. K., Glaser, R., Williger, D., Stout, J., Messick, G., Sheppard, S., Ricker, D., Romisher, S. C., Briner, W., Bonnell, G., & Donnerberg, R. (1985). Psychosocial enhancement of immunocompetence in a geriatric population. *Health Psychology, 4*, 25–41.

Kiesler, C. A. (1983). Psychology and mental health policy. In M. Hersen, A. E., Kazdin, & A. S. Bellack (Eds.), *The clinical psychology handbook* (pp. 63–82). New York: Pergamon Press.

Kobasa, S. (1982). The hardy personality: Toward a social psychology of stress and health. In G. S. Sanders & J. Suls (Eds.), *Social psychology of health and illness* (pp. 3–32). Hillsdale, NJ: Lawrence Erlbaum Associates.

Lamnin, A. D., & Murray, E. (1987). *Catharsis versus psychotherapy*. Unpublished manuscript, University of Miami.

Lazarus, A. A. (1984). Multimodal therapy. In R. J. Corsini (Ed.), *Current psychotherapies* (3rd ed., pp. 491–530). Itasca, IL: Peacock.

Meichenbaum, D. H. (1977). *Cognitive-behavior modification: An integrative approach*. New York: Plenum Press.

Mumford, E., Schlesinger, H. J., & Glass, G. V. (1981). Reducing medical costs through mental health treatment: Research problems and recommendations. In A. Broskowski, E., Marks, & S. H. Budman (Eds.), *Linking health and mental health* (pp. 257–273). Beverly Hills, CA: Sage.

Pennebaker, J. W., & Beall, S. (1986). Confronting a traumatic event: Toward an understanding of inhibition and disease. *Journal of Abnormal Psychology, 95*, 274–281.

Pennebaker, J. W., Hughes, C., & O'Heeron, R. C. (1987). The psychophysiology of confession: Linking inhibitory and psychosomatic processes. *Journal of Personality and Social Psychology, 52*, 781–793.

Pennebaker, J. W., & O'Heeron, R. C. (1984). Confiding in others and illness rate among spouses of suicide and accidental death victims. *Journal of Abnormal Psychology 93*, 473–476.

Pennebaker, J. W., & Susman, J. R. (in press). Disclosure of traumas and psychosomatic processes. *Social Science and Medicine*.

Reinherz, E. L., & Schlossman, S. F. (1980). Current concepts in immunology: Regulation of the immune response—Inducer and suppressor T-lymphocyte subsets in human beings. *New England Journal of Medicine, 303*, 370–373.

Selye, H. (1976). *The stress of life*. New York: McGraw-Hill.

Silver, R. L., Boon, C., & Stones, M. H. (1983). Searching for meaning in misfortune: Making sense of incest. *Journal of Social Issues, 39*, 81–102.

Swann, W. B., & Pridmore, S. C. (1985). Intimates as agents of social support: Sources of consolation or despair? *Journal of Personality and Social Psychology, 49*, 1609–1617.

Tessler, R., Mechanic, D., & Diamond, M. (1976). The effect of psychological distress on physician utilization. *Journal of Health and Social Behavior, 17*, 353–364.

Wegner, D. M. (in press). Stress and mental control. In S. Fisher & J. Reason (Eds.), *Handbook of life stress, cognition, and health*. London: Wiley.

Discussion Questions

1. Pennebaker et al. suggested two mechanisms by which disclosures of traumatic events may have their impact—release of inhibition and helping people to find meaning in stressful events. Can you think of any other reasons why such disclosures might be physically and psychologically beneficial?
2. What implications do the results of this study have for keeping a journal (sometimes called "journaling") as a therapeutic technique?
3. Do you think that there are any potential negative effects associated with writing or talking about traumatic events?
4. Do you think that everyone benefits from disclosing traumatic events to the same degree? Or, do you think that some personality variables might moderate who shows improved immunological functioning following disclosures of traumatic events?

Suggested Readings

Kennedy-Moore, E., & Watson, J. C. (1999). *Expressing emotion: Myths, realities, and therapeutic strategies.* New York: Guilford. This book examines emotional expression and how therapists can learn to examine and treat problems related to emotional expression.

Pennebaker, J. W. (1990). *Opening up.* New York: Guilford. This interesting book summarizes much of the research that Pennebaker has conducted examining the health benefits of self-disclosure.

Pennebaker, J. W. (Ed.). (1995). *Emotion, disclosure, and health.* Washington, DC: American Psychological Association. This edited volume covers many issues related to psychotherapy, including an examination of why disclosure can be beneficial to one's health.

Pennebaker, J. W., & Beall, S. (1986). Confronting a traumatic event: Toward an understanding of inhibition and disease. *Journal of Abnormal Psychology, 95,* 274–281. This study shows the long-term health benefits of disclosing traumatic events.

READING 22

Cognitive Dissonance and Psychotherapy: The Role of Effort Justification in Inducing Weight Loss

Danny Axsom and Joel Cooper • Princeton University

Editors' Introduction

Successful psychotherapy requires effort on the part of the client. Clients must first decide to seek professional help. They then call to make an appointment, drive to the therapy session, give up some of their valuable time and money, and devote effort and emotional energy wrestling with troubling issues and struggling to change how they think, feel, and behave. Believing that asking clients to expend too much effort might make therapy less appealing and lead clients to quit prematurely, many therapists have tried to minimize the effort required. They have tried to accommodate the schedules of the clients and decrease the draining nature of the sessions themselves.

Social psychological research suggests, however, that requiring clients to work hard in therapy may, in fact, make therapy more attractive to the client and more beneficial in the long run. Experimental studies have shown that the more effort people put into something, the more they come to value the results of their efforts (within limits, of course). Generalizing this basic research to counseling and psychotherapy suggests that the more effort a client puts into therapy, the more beneficial the results may be.

313

One mechanism that may contribute to this effect involves effort justification. This explanation, which is based on cognitive dissonance theory, suggests that people experience dissonance, an unpleasant state of cognitive tension, when they devote effort to a task that may prove not to be worth the effort after all. In order to justify all of the effort that they have put into the task, and thereby reduce dissonance, people come to evaluate the effortful task more positively. To say it differently, people are bothered by the possibility that they may have worked hard for no good reason and thus conclude that effortful and difficult tasks are worthwhile. Applied to psychotherapy, this suggests that people should come to view psychotherapy as more appealing and more effective the more effort they expend.

In an ingenious test of this hypothesis, Axsom and Cooper recruited overweight women to participate in a weight-loss program. Participants attended five sessions over a 3-week period. During the first four of these sessions, women in both conditions completed perceptual and cognitive tasks. These tasks, such as discriminating lines on a tachistoscope, had nothing to do with weight loss itself, but were intended purely to create differences in the amount of effort the women in the high- and low-effort conditions exerted during their "therapy." The tasks for women in the high-effort condition were more difficult and of longer duration than those completed by women in the low-effort condition.

The results of the study supported the idea that effort increased both the attractiveness and effectiveness of the weight loss program. Women in the high-effort group lost more weight over the 3-week period of the experiment than women in the low-effort group. Even more interesting, a 6-month follow-up revealed that women in the high-effort group had lost even more weight following the last session of the program, whereas the weight for women in the low-effort group remained relatively unchanged. Thus, not only did effort increase the efficacy of the attempted weight loss, but it helped to sustain and increase that weight loss over time. Axsom and Cooper explained these findings by saying that women in the high-effort group justified their effort as a means of reducing dissonance by increasing the attractiveness of losing weight.

Although Axsom and Cooper used cognitive dissonance as the theoretical foundation of their research, other theoretical explanations can also be offered. Among these are self-perception theory and impression management theory. Self-perception theory suggests that people infer their attitudes by observing their behavior. Applied to the results of the Axsom and Cooper study, women in the high-effort group inferred that they must have really wanted to lose weight given the amount of effort that they exerted in the program. Alternatively, a self-presentational explanation may explain that participants who freely engaged in the effortful tasks as part of the weight-loss program may have felt pressure to make sure the program worked in order to control the impressions that other people or the experimenter may have formed of them, fearing that they would look foolish for working hard on a worthless task. In any case, this article provides interesting insights into the role of effort in counseling and psychotherapy.

Abstract

The role of effort justification in psychotherapy was examined. It was hypothesized that the effort involved in therapy, plus the conscious decision to undergo that effort, lead to positive therapeutic changes through the reduction of cognitive dissonance. An experiment was conducted in which overweight subjects attempted to lose weight through one of two forms of "effort therapy." These therapies were bogus in that they were based solely on the expenditure of effort on a series of cognitive tasks that were unrelated to any existing techniques or theory addressing weight loss. One of the therapies called for a high degree of effort whereas the degree of effort in the second therapy was low. A no-treatment control group was also included. It was predicted that greater weight loss would occur for high-effort than low-effort or control subjects, and that this weight loss would be maintained or increased over time. Results supported these predictions. Over an initial 3-week period, high-effort subjects lost slightly more weight than low-effort subjects or controls. A 6-month follow-up revealed that the effects of effort on weight loss had increased and were highly significant. Reliable differences remained even 1 year after the initial experimental sessions. Possible mechanisms mediating the dissonance effect were discussed, as were several alternative explanations.

Several theorists have noted that psychotherapy is potentially a fertile arena for the application of social psychological principles (Brehm, 1976; Frank, 1961; Goldstein, Heller, & Sechrest, 1966; Strong, 1978; Weary & Mirels, 1982). Frank (1961), for example, has characterized therapy as a relationship between a sufferer and a socially sanctioned authority who attempts to produce certain changes in the emotions, attitudes, and behaviors of the sufferer. Clearly this implies the importance of social psychological processes dealing with attitude change and social influence. These would seem to have an important bearing on the interpersonal influence setting we call psychotherapy.

Recent evidence suggests that one approach applied to the study of attitude change—the concept of effort justification derived from cognitive dissonance theory (Festinger, 1957)—might be at the base of much psychotherapeutic change (Cooper, 1980; Cooper & Axsom, 1982). Effort justification concerns the consequences of engaging in an effortful activity in order to obtain some goal. The fact that one has engaged in an effortful event is discrepant from the notion that one does not usually engage in such effort. And for what purpose? In the typical effort justification sequence, either the goal or the means of achieving that goal is not attractive initially. In the classic experiment by Aronson and Mills (1959), subjects in a high-effort condition were made to undergo an event that was difficult and embarrassing. Their goal was to join a sexual discussion group that was, in reality, dull, boring, and a general waste of time. Yet subjects who underwent the highly effortful procedure came to indicate that the group and its members were generally interesting and enjoyable. The reason given by Aronson and Mills was based upon the tension state of dissonance that was created by the voluntary expenditure of effort. "Why did I undergo such embarrassment and effort?" a subject may have questioned. "Because I really did like the discussion group," might be the reply. In other words, the goal was elevated in attractiveness as a way of justifying the expenditure of effort.

Similarly, psychotherapy typically involves a patient volunteering for an effortful and sometimes emotionally draining process. A client may fear certain objects, find relationships with others unpleasant, or find it noxious to behave in certain socially adaptable ways. Yet in any of the myriad of procedures generically called psychotherapy, clients often make changes in their attitudes, emotions, and behaviors. The goals—be they increased interaction with phobic objects, better interpersonal relations, or more socially adaptable behavior—become more acceptable or attractive. At least part of this change may result from an attempt to justify the expenditure of effort, just as in Aronson and Mills's study the discussion group became more attractive.

Cooper (1980) conducted a pair of experiments to test the role of effort justification in psychotherapy. He reasoned that if generic effort influenced therapy outcomes, then any form of effort, regardless of whether it is tied to a conventional form of psychotherapy, should have the potential to be effective. He constructed a bogus therapy made up of physical exercises (jumping rope, running in place, etc.) and presented it to subjects who were either fearful of snakes (Study 1) or unassertive (Study 2). In each case the effort therapy was compared to a more conventional therapy—implosion (Stampfl & Levis, 1967) in Study 1 and behavior rehearsal (Salter, 1949) in Study 2—that had been rated in pretesting to be of equal effort as the exercise therapy. A second variable, decision freedom to engage or not engage in the studies, was also varied. According to dissonance theory, the effort justification sequence should be invoked only under conditions of an informed choice (Linder, Cooper, & Wicklund, 1968). Results in both studies supported a dissonance interpretation. The bogus, effort therapy was as successful as the conventional therapies with which it was compared, but only when decision freedom was high; when decision freedom was low neither the effort therapy nor the conventional therapies were successful.

The conclusion from Cooper's experiments is that the voluntary expenditure of effort is at least one of the effective ingredients in psychotherapy, regardless of whether that effort forms part of a traditional therapy or whether it is improvised in a series of physical exercises. Exercise therapies or traditional therapies may be effective in promoting change, as long as they are engaged in voluntarily. However, several important questions remain unanswered. First, the notion that effort leads to positive changes in psychotherapy has yet to receive a direct test. This is because neither of Cooper's experiments used *variations* in effort as an independent variable. To the extent that effort justification is involved in psychotherapy, it should be shown that variations in the degree of effort will lead to variations in the degree of change that ensues.

Equally important is the question of duration of change that occurs as a result of effort justification. Both of Cooper's experiments involved single-session therapies with change measured immediately after the session. Although this is a typical procedure in laboratory experiments involving attitude change, it is not parallel to the desired outcome of psychotherapy. Change as a result of therapy is anticipated to be more long lasting, and an assessment of the effort justification procedure should be based not so much on an immediate assessment as by its long-term consequence. There are only a few reports in the dissonance literature of cognitive changes lasting well beyond the experimental session (e.g., Freedman, 1965). So the question of duration of consequences takes on enormous significance in assessing the appropriateness of the conceptual analysis that is based upon the psychology of effort justification.

The focus of the present experiment was weight loss. This problem offers unique advantages for an experimental study of effort justification procedures. First, there are objective and nonreactive measurements available for body weight that can be easily and repeatedly sampled. Second, the dependent measure thoroughly defines the criterion of a successful therapy, since weight loss represents the specific goal of treatment (Wollersheim, 1970). It was predicted that subjects freely choosing to undergo highly effortful sessions would produce the greatest weight loss, relative to those in a lower effort therapy and a control group. In addition, weight loss resulting from highly effortful sessions was expected to be maintained or even increased over time. This is because effort justification is assumed to enhance the goal of therapy (i.e, increase the attractiveness of the goal of weight loss), a change that should endure beyond the initial sessions and continue to influence weight change.

Method

Subjects

Subjects were recruited via newspaper advertisements for an "Experiment concerning possible methods of weight reduction." They were contacted by phone for scheduling and were assured that the procedure would be safe and would not include any medication. Because initial response to the advertisements was overwhelmingly by women, only females formed the final subject pool.

Also, to increase subjects' homogeneity, only those 18 and older who were between 10 and 20% above "desirable body weight" according to the Metropolitan Life Insurance Company statistics (1959) were solicited. No one receiving therapy or medication for their weight was included. Finally, only subjects who lived within 20 minutes traveling time to the laboratory were included, since extraordinary distances could affect the manipulation of effort.

Sixty-eight subjects who fulfilled these requirements began the experiment. They were randomly assigned to conditions. Each was paid at the rate of $1 per session. Fifteen subjects were lost through attrition. Chi-square analyses failed to reveal any relationship between experimental conditions and the decision to terminate ($\chi^2(4) = 1.64$, n.s.).[1] In addition, data from one subject were omitted when she arrived at two consecutive sessions too late to complete the full procedure. Fifty-two subjects comprised the final sample.

Procedure

General overview. A 2 (Level of Effort) × 2 (Level of Choice) between-subjects design with an external control group was utilized. Subjects attended five sessions over a 3-week period. They attended two sessions during each of the first 2 weeks and one during the final week. To minimize extraneous influences on weight change, sessions for each subject were scheduled at the same time of day and the same days of the week throughout. Six months after the experimental sessions were completed, a final weighing session was conducted.

The choice variable. Subjects in the four experimental conditions were met by a female first experimenter who measured and recorded their weight.[2] She then administered the choice variable. Subjects in the high-choice conditions were told: "I have been instructed to advise you that although the procedures you will follow are perfectly safe and harmless, they may also be effortful and anxiety producing. If you like, you can stop the experiment now and you will be paid for this session. Would like to continue?"

A Princeton University Informed Consent form was then given to be read and signed. This stated, in part, "I may withdraw my consent and discontinue participation in the project at any time." As the form was being read, the weigher emphasized, "As you notice on the form, you may withdraw your consent and stop at any time . . . you still have the prerogative to stop participation later."

Subjects in the low-choice condition were not asked whether they wanted to continue. Subjects were merely warned about the potential effort and anxiety, then told, "We'll go ahead and begin."

The second experimenter introduced himself and administered a "Life Pattern Questionnaire" concerning everyday eating and exercising patterns and other activities that might be useful in interpreting weight change data. It was also administered to increase the perceived legitimacy of the procedure. All subjects were then given a small booklet in which to monitor their eating over the 3-week period. This, too, was partly to increase the perceived legitimacy of the procedure.

The second experimenter explained the rationale for the study by noting that psychologists have frequently found strong correlations between heightened neurophysiological arousal and increased emotional sensitivity. The present researchers, he added, had been able to take advantage of this by presenting subjects with various tasks designed specifically to increase this neurophysiological arousal and thereby to enhance emotional sensitivity in a way that helped lead to weight reduction. He then explained that although the procedure had been very successful in the preliminary investigations, the precise reasons for the weight loss obtained were still uncertain and that the present study was to make the process clearer.

The tasks were described as requiring much concentration and consequently as being neurophysiologically arousing and sometimes stressful. The subject was assured that this arousal and stress would be brief and not last beyond any session. In keeping with the cover story, all subjects were attached to a galvanic skin response (GSR) apparatus (ostensibly to measure their level of arousal) while performing the tasks described next.

The effort variable. Effort in the present experiment was manipulated by varying the difficulty and duration of a variety of cognitive tasks, the tasks and parameters chosen being established through pretesting. Subjects in the high-effort conditions worked for 20 min at a three-channel tachistoscope. Their task was to discriminate which of several near-vertical lines presented sequentially was most vertical. Each line was visible for only

350 ms. Those in the low-effort condition worked for 3 min and were given a full 1 s to view each line.

Subjects then moved to a delayed auditory feedback (DAF) apparatus. High-effort subjects were given 30 min of recitation in which they attempted to recite nursery rhymes, read a short story, and recite the U.S. Pledge of Allegiance with their own voice reflected back to them via earphones at a delay of 316 ms. The delay was similar to that used by Zimbardo (1965) in his manipulation of high effort. In addition, the voice of a woman attempting similar tasks during pretesting was overlayed onto the recorder so that the subject had to contend not only with the delay, but also with yet another voice. Low-effort subjects worked for only 10 min and the auditory delay was cut in half (158 ms). This reduced delay, accomplished by increasing tape speed, also rendered the voice distraction incomprehensible and therefore less disruptive (Mackworth, 1970).

To avoid the potential confounding of session length with level of effort, subjects in the low-effort condition, after completing the tachistoscope task, returned to the waiting room to relax for 40 min before finishing the session. This procedure, which is similar to that used by Wicklund, Cooper, and Linder (1967), was explained to low-effort subjects as being necessary to allow the arousal due to the tachistoscope task to dissipate before beginning the next task.

Upon finishing the final task, the subject completed a brief questionnaire concerning her impression of the session. Most importantly, she was asked, "In general, how effortful would you describe the hour as a whole?" This was followed by a 7-point response scale labeled *very little* and *very much* at the end points. The subject then returned to the weighing room for the final choice manipulation. For high-choice subjects, the first experimenter stated, "I'll remind you again that you can still stop the experiment and be paid for what you've done so far. Would you like to continue?" When the subject acknowledged that she wished to continue, she was given an appointment card containing the time and date of the next session. Low-choice subjects were merely given the appointment card without any mention of a new decision.

Sessions 2–4. The following three sessions were similar to the first. The Life Pattern Questionnaire was not administered during these sessions and the cover story was not repeated. The sessions contained tachistoscope and DAF tasks that were of the same durations as those of Session 1, although the content of the visual discriminations and DAF reading tasks were altered to relieve possible boredom. High-choice subjects resigned the consent form and were reminded of their choice at the end of each session.

The final experimental session. Session 5 contained the final assessment of weight change during the experimental period. The effort tasks were not given. The second experimenter, still unaware of the subject's choice condition, weighed the subject and then informed her that her participation in the study was completed. He asked the subject to fill out at questionnaire that covered various weight-related topics and the subject's perceptions of the study. Crucial were two final manipulation checks: "How effortful would you describe the experiment as a whole?" (1 = *very little*; 9 = *very much*); and "How free did you feel *not* to continue with the experiment at any time?" (1 = *not free to choose*; 9 = *very free to choose*). Next the Life Patterns Questionnaire was readministered. Finally, the subject was carefully questioned about any suspicions she may have had about the purpose of the study, fully debriefed, and paid for her participation. The need for deception and the importance and possible implications of the study were discussed at length.

Control group. To provide a baseline indication of normal weight fluctuation among subjects in our sample, 10 subjects from those who responded to the advertisement were randomly assigned to a control condition. When contacted to begin, they were told that they would be unable to participate as originally planned due to a change in the procedure that meant using fewer participants. They were then asked to engage in a project "to determine normal female weight fluctuation over time." Control subjects also participated in five sessions, scheduled in a similar fashion as the experimental subjects. They were simply greeted and weighed during each session. The Life Patterns Questionnaire was administered at the first and fifth sessions. A shortened verson of the final questionnaire was also administered at the fifth session. It was emphasized that this was not a weight reduction study, and that subjects should therefore simply carry on their normal daily activities. Dieting was left to their discretion.

The final assessment. Six months after the fifth session was completed, participants were contacted for a follow-up weighing. The subjects were unaware that they would be recontacted. Forty-two of the 52 subjects were able to return; 9 had since moved from the area or were unable to be reached; 1 had become pregnant. At this follow-up, subjects were given a copy of the results from the original experiment.

Results

Checks on the manipulations. The amount of effort involved in the subjects' participation was assessed in two ways. First, at the end of each of the first four experimental sessions, subjects were asked to rate the effortfulness of the preceding hour (1 = *very little*; 7 = *very much*).[3] A 2 (Choice) × 2 (Effort) × 4 (Sessions) repeated-measures analysis of variance showed a significant main effect for effort (M high = 4.31 vs. M low = 3.14), $F(1, 37) = 10.21$, $p < .005$. In addition, during the final session all subjects, including the control group, rated the effortfulness of the experiment as a whole (1 = *very little*; 9 = *very much*).[4] This also indicated a main effect for effort, with high-effort subjects ($M = 5.00$) rating the study as more effortful than low-effort subjects ($M = 3.62$) or controls ($M = 2.78$), $F(1, 45) = 7.99$, $p < .01$.

Results from the perceived choice manipulation checks revealed that, because of an apparent ceiling effect, the manipulation of this variable was not effective. For example, at the final session, the subject was asked how free she felt not to continue with the experiment at any time. Of the 41 subjects in the experimental groups who responded to this question, 56% marked the highest level of choice. In fact, even 40% of the low-choice subjects responded this way. In retrospect, the problem with the manipulation of choice could have been expected. Subjects came to the university from various locations in the community. They returned for several sessions. Attempting to convince low-choice subjects that they were not at all free to discontinue the experiment would have strained ethical considerations as well as credibility. Rather, we remained silent about choice considerations to low-choice subjects and instead emphasized the high degree of decision freedom to those subjects assigned to the high-choice conditions. Since freedom was apparently already assumed to be high by the participants, our manipulation had little differential impact. Because perceived choice was high in all conditions, subsequent analyses are collapsed over the choice variable.

Weight loss: Data from session 5.[5,6] Since perceived choice was high in all groups, the effort justification hypothesis predicts that subjects in the high-effort condition would lose more weight than those in the low-effort or control conditions. Weight change at the immediate conclusion of the experimental sessions can be seen in the first column of Table 22.1.[7] Consistent with dissonance predictions, high-effort subjects produced the greatest weight loss. A contrast of this condition with low-effort and control subjects was statistically reliable, $F(1, 49) = 5.96$, $p < .02$. Also, t-tests, adjusted for the number of possible comparisons, revealed that only in the high-effort condition was weight deviation significantly different from zero, $t(20) = 4.11$, $p < .02$. Although the pattern of these results is statistically reliable and in the predicted direction, it is obvious from examining the means that a dramatic shift in weight did not occur over the five sessions. An important question, then, concerns the magnitude and duration of weight change over a longer period.

Weight loss: The final measure. Encouraged by the direction if not the magnitude of the results, we proceeded with the final dependent measure: the 6-month follow-up. As Table 22.1 indicates, dramatic differences had developed over the 6-month period. High-effort subjects were now over 8 pounds lighter than their initial weight, whereas low-effort and control subjects had changed little. A contrast of high-effort with low-effort and control conditions was highly significant, $F(1, 39) = 25.56$, $p < .001$. Fifteen of the 16 high-effort subjects who reported for the final measure had lost

TABLE 22.1. **Mean Weight Change (in Pounds)**

	Time of measurement		
Effort condition	After 3 weeks	After 6 months	After 1 year
High	−1.76 (21)	−8.55 (16)	−6.78 (20)
Low	− .82 (21)	− .07 (18)	− .44 (21)
Control	+ .18 (10)	+ .94 (8)	−1.86 (9)

Note. N's per cell are in parentheses.

weight, compared to only 7 of 18 low-effort and 4 of 8 control subjects, $\chi^2(2) = 12.74$, $p < .01$.

Weight loss: One more time. One year from the date of the initial experimental session, subjects were contacted once again. By this time, many had either moved or otherwise changed situations so that they could no longer return in person for the weighing. These subjects weighed themselves at home and reported their weight by phone. As a result, data were obtained for 50 of the 52 original subjects. Analyses using only those subjects who returned to be weighed in person were similar to findings based on the full subject pool, so only the latter are reported. As Table 22.1 indicates, weight loss remained largest in the high-effort condition, and a contrast of this group with low-effort and control subjects was highly significant, $F(1, 47) = 6.67$, $p < .02$. One full year after participating in the experimental sessions, 90% of high-effort subjects were below their initial weight, versus only 48% of low-effort and 56% of control subjects.

Trend analysis. Another way of examining weight change over time is to focus only on those 41 subjects for whom data are available at all measurement points: initially, after 3 weeks (end of five sessions), after 6 months, and after 1 year. A 3 (Effort) × 4 (Time) repeated measures analysis of variance revealed a significant Effort × Time interaction, $F(6, 114) = 4.29$, $p < .001$. This interaction can be partitioned into several orthogonal components. The effort justification hypothesis would predict that high-effort subjects would lose weight at a faster rate than subjects in the remaining groups. The specific test of this prediction—that the contrast between high effort and the remaining two conditions will interact with the linear component of time—is significant, $F(1, 114) = 8.16$, $p < .01$.[8] The pattern of weight change indicated by this interaction is shown graphically in Figure 22.1.

Discussion

The weight loss observed in the high-effort cells was both substantial and consistent. Since subjects were initially an average of 17 pounds overweight, high-effort subjects—who lost an average of 8.55 pounds over the first follow-up—were able to achieve a 50% reduction in excess weight. The chief issue to be addressed, then, is not whether positive therapeutic change occurred, but rather whether effort justification processes can account for this change.

The results offer clear support for the role of effort in instigating the weight reduction. But the

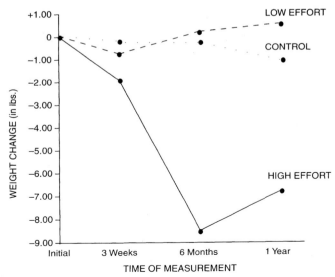

FIGURE 22.1 ■ Weight change for subjects providing data at all four measurement points. Note: *N*'s for high effort, low effort, and control are 16, 18, and 7, respectively.

weakness of the choice manipulation makes a final interpretation less clear than would be desired. The notion of effort justification predicts weight loss for participants who engaged in a high degree of effort and who perceived their freedom to participate to be high. Since an overwhelming proportion of subjects perceived their freedom to be high, the effects found for the effort variable are consistent with the effort justification approach.

The dramatic amount of weight change that occurred during the 6-month period following the experimental session stands in marked contrast to the marginal degree of weight change that occurred immediately after the experiment. Of course, weight change takes time and it is not surprising that only a few pounds could be changed during the 3 weeks of the sessions. But this weight loss was not only maintained over the half-year period, it was markedly increased by those subjects in the high-effort conditions. Why should this have happened? Long-term changes as a function of laboratory intervention are not commonplace in the literature.

Our supposition, based upon the concept of effort justification, is that dissonance processes operated to increase the attractiveness of the goal of weight loss. Just as Aronson and Mills's (1959) subjects who underwent effort viewed the goal of belonging to the discussion group with greater attractiveness, so too do we believe our subjects came to view the goal of losing weight with more zeal and fervor. As a result, subjects in the high-effort conditions pursued that goal regardless of how successful they might have been during the five experimental sessions.

It is always difficult to gain direct evidence of dissonance processes, but it may be possible to examine some alternative explanations of the results. For example, it could be argued that subjects who saw they were able to lose a little weight at the end of five sessions gained a feeling of mastery, which, in turn, enabled them to accelerate their weight loss after 6 months. The data are not consistent with this explanation, however. The data show little relationship between weight loss during the initial experimental sessions and weight loss over the first follow-up (for the high-effort group, $r(14) = .07$). High-effort subjects showed consistent weight loss after 6 months *regardless* of whether they had lost weight by the end of the experimental sessions. Similarly, low-effort subjects' weight loss could not be predicted from their weight loss at the end of the five sessions.

A related alternative explanation for the data is that high-effort subjects may have formed differentially higher expectations about the therapy's potential outcome. These high expectations may have led to stricter adherence to some self-prescribed regimen that resulted in weight loss. Those who initially lost weight might have formed what Ross, Lepper, and Hubbard (1975) have referred to as antecedent–consequent explanations for why they were losing weight. However, it is difficult for an expectation-based hypothesis to explain why those initially showing little or no weight loss would later lose. As we have already mentioned, the data reveal that high-effort subjects lost weight during the 6-month period regardless of whether they had initially lost or gained. This factor is more consistent with the effort justification hypothesis for it appears to be the goal of weight loss which becomes more attractive.

An additional consideration revolves around the initial debriefing. Of course, ethical considerations demanded that subjects be debriefed after the initial experimental sessions. Otherwise, subjects unable to be contacted 6 months later would never have been debriefed. Moreover, all subjects would have gone 6 months without knowing the essential features of the experiment. However, because subjects were partially debriefed (they were not informed that a follow-up was to occur), if subjects in the two effort conditions were treated differently at that session, then later weight changes might have reflected this. It might be argued that subjects in the high-effort conditions, having found themselves in a condition in which weight loss was expected, proceeded to lose weight via some self-fulfilling prophecy. Though possible, this explanation seems unlikely when the debriefing is examined more closely. If subjects lost more weight over the follow-up only after having learned that they had been expected to lose, then only high-effort, high-choice subjects should have continued to lose. High-effort, low-choice subjects would realize that they had not been expected to lose weight. At the time of the debriefing, we were not aware that subjects assigned to the low-choice condition had perceived high decision freedom. Nonetheless, high-effort subjects in *both* choice conditions lost weight over the follow-up period, an effect that is inconsistent with a self-fulfilling prophecy explanation.

Of course, one direction for future research will be to collect more direct evidence on the presumed attitudinal and behavioral mediators of therapeutic change. The present experiment, however, in conjunction with the two experiments reported by Cooper (1980), adds to the confidence with which the concept of effort justification can be applied to psychotherapy. In the present experiment, the concept of effort was expanded to include cognitive tasks and the data showed that variations in this type of effort led to systematic differences in the amount of weight which participants lost. Although the findings were of a small magnitude at the conclusion of the five experimental sessions, the amount of weight lost after a 6-month period by subjects who had undergone a highly effortful procedure was considerable. The extension over time adds important new dimensions to research in effort justification, particularly as it pertains to research on psychotherapeutic outcomes.

ACKNOWLEDGMENT

This research was supported by a grant from the National Science Foundation, BNS76-19384.

NOTES

1. Reported reasons for dropping included loss of interest, outside interference such as sudden job changes, and unexpected transportation problems which prevented participation. Attrition rate by condition: high effort, high choice (HEHC) = 29%; high effort, low choice (HELC) = 27%; LEHC = 27%; LELC = 23%; control = 9%.
2. Subjects were weighed in indoor clothing and without shoes.
3. One subject provided effort ratings at only 3 of 4 sessions.
4. Two subjects left this question blank.
5. Subjects' initial weight did not differ by experimental conditions (in pounds: high effort = 149.85, low effort = 149.30, control = 148.90; $F < 1$).
6. Since the duration of this portion of the experiment was short and weight changes were expected to be small, data on each subject's menstrual cycle were also collected (during the fifth session). This was to ensure against any spurious weight change effects resulting from water retention (congestive dysmenorrheà) coinciding with menstruation. Analyses of the menstrual data showed that only a small number of subjects had either started or finished their sessions around menstruation and that these subjects were equally distributed across conditions.
7. For clarity of presentation, weight change analyses reported are based on difference scores. The crucial assumptions behind the use of difference scores, namely, that within-group regression coefficients relating initial to final weight are homogeneous and equal to 1.00, are both satisfied (bs for high effort, low effort, and the control were, respectively, .97, 1.01, and 1.01).
8. Also reliable, largely because the high-effort group gains slightly from the first to second follow-up, is the high-effort versus low-effort/control contrast and the cubic component of Time, $F(1, 114) = 13.60, p < .001$.

REFERENCES

Aronson, E., & Mills, J. (1959). The effects of severity of initiation on liking for a group. *Journal of Abnormal and Social Psychology, 59,* 177–181.

Brehm, S. S. (1976). *The application of social psychology to clinical practice.* Washington, DC: Hemisphere.

Cooper, J. (1980). Reducing fears and increasing assertiveness: The role of dissonance reduction. *Journal of Experimental Social Psychology, 16,* 199–213.

Cooper, J., & Axsom, D. (1982). Effort justification in psychotherapy. In G. Weary & H. Mirels (Eds.), *Integrations of clinical and social psychology* (pp. 214–230). New York: Oxford University Press.

Festinger, L. (1957). *A theory of cognitive dissonance.* Stanford, CA: Stanford University Press.

Frank, J. D. (1961). *Persuasion and healing.* Baltimore, MD: Johns Hopkins Press.

Freedman, J. L. (1965). Long-term behavioral effects of cognitive dissonance. *Journal of Experimental Social Psychology, 1,* 145–155.

Goldstein, A. P., Heller, K., & Sechrest, L. B. (1966). *Psychotherapy and the psychology of behavior change.* New York: Wiley.

Linder, D. E., Cooper, J., & Wicklund, R. A. (1968). Pre-exposure persuasion as a result of commitment to pre-exposure effort. *Journal of Experimental Social Psychology, 4,* 470–482.

Mackworth, J. F. (1970). *Vigilance and attention: A signal detection approach.* Harmondsworth: Penguin.

Metropolitan Life Insurance Co., New York. (1959). New weight standards for men and women. *Statistical Bulletin, 40.*

Ross, L., Lepper, M. R., & Hubbard, M. (1975). Perseverance in self-perception and social perception: Biased attributional processes in the debriefing paradigm. *Journal of Personality and Social Psychology, 32,* 880–892.

Salter, A. (1949). *Conditioned reflex therapy: The direct approach to the reconstruction of personality.* New York: Creative Age Press.

Stampfl, T., & Levis, D. (1967). Essentials of implosive therapy: A learning theory based psychodynamic behavioral therapy. *Journal of Abnormal Psychology, 72,* 496.

Strong, S. R. (1978). Social psychological approach to psychotherapy research. In S. Garfield & A. Bergin (Eds.), *Handbook of psychotherapy and behavior change.* New York: Wiley.

Weary, G., & Mirels, H. L. (Eds.). (1982). *Integrations of clinical and social psychology.* New York: Oxford.

Wicklund, R. A., Cooper, J., & Linder, D. E. (1967). Effects of expected effort on attitude change prior to exposure. *Journal of Experimental Social Psychology, 3,* 416–428.

Wollersheim, J. (1970). Effectiveness of group therapy based upon learning principles on the treatment of overweight women. *Journal of Abnormal Psychology, 76,* 462–474.

Zimbardo, P. G. (1965). The effect of effort and improvisation on self-persuasion produced by role playing. *Journal of Experimental Social Psychology, 1,* 103–120.

Discussion Questions

1. If people are more attracted to therapies that require more effort, is there a ceiling effect where the effort expended might backfire in terms of client perceptions of the attractiveness of therapy? In other words, can too much effort be required?
2. Could the findings of the Axsom and Cooper study be applied to personal relationships? Specifically, would an individual find a dating partner more attractive when more effort was required to secure a date with that person?
3. Are some people more likely to put forth effort in therapy than others? If so, what personality characteristics might distinguish such individuals from those who are less willing to put forth any effort?
4. How could hazing and initiations used by fraternities and sororities be justified using the findings of Axsom and Cooper?

Suggested Readings

Aronson, E., & Mills, J. (1959). The effects of severity of initiation on liking for a group. *Journal of Abnormal and Social Psychology, 59,* 177–181. This interesting study shows the role that effort can play in increasing the favorable evaluations people assign to a task.

Cooper, J. (1980). Reducing fears and increasing assertiveness: The role of dissonance reduction. *Journal of Experimental Social Psychology, 16,* 199–213. This research showed that a nonsensical "effort therapy" was as effective as real clinical treatments as long as clients freely exerted sufficient effort.

Cooper, J., & Axsom, D. (1982). Effort justification in psychotherapy. In G. Weary & H. Mirels (Eds.), *Integrations of clinical and social psychology* (pp. 214–230). New York: Oxford University Press. In this article, the authors suggest that effort is essential to effective psychotherapy.

READING 23

Reconceptualizing Social Influence in Counseling: The Elaboration Likelihood Model

Brian W. McNeill • Department of Counseling Psychology, University of Kansas
Cal D. Stoltenberg • Department of Educational Psychology, University of Oklahoma

Editors' Introduction

Starting in the 1960s, many theorists and researchers began to think about counseling and psychotherapy in terms of social psychological processes. Indeed, Strong (1968, p. 101), one of the early proponents of this view, stated that "psychotherapy can be viewed as a branch of applied social psychology." Given that psychotherapy usually involves an interaction between two or more individuals, whatever happens during therapy—for good or for bad—is largely due to the interpersonal dynamics between therapist and client.

In his social influence model of counseling, Strong (1968) likened a counselor trying to change a client's attitudes to a speaker trying to change the attitudes of a listener. He and others used the pioneering research on attitude change by Hovland, Janis, and Kelley (1953) to identify characteristics of the source (counselor), message (therapy), and receiver (client) that would increase a counselor's success in changing the attitudes of a client. However, precisely when and how characteristics of the source, message, and receiver exerted their influence was unclear. For example, sometimes the expertise of the counselor was found to increase persuasion and sometimes it decreased persuasion.

To bring order to the diverse and inconsistent findings in the literature, a new theoretical model was introduced, the Elaboration Likelihood Model of Persuasion (ELM; Petty & Cacioppo, 1981). According to the ELM, attitude change following a persuasive communication can occur via either the central route or the peripheral route. Central-route processing occurs when individuals are motivated to attend to the persuasive communication and are able to consider the merits of the communication. Peripheral-route processing occurs when people are either unmotivated to attend to the communication or lack the cognitive resources to process the message fully. In these instances, attitude change occurs in response to extraneous factors, such as the credibility of the speaker or the number of arguments presented in the communication, rather than to the merits of the message itself. The advantage of central-route processing over peripheral-route processing is that attitude change tends to last longer and the resulting attitudes predict behavior more closely.

In this article, McNeill and Stoltenberg discuss empirical evidence involving the ELM, both in general and as applied to counseling. They describe the results of various studies and discuss ways in which the results of ELM studies that focus on counseling differ from basic social psychological research on the ELM. McNeill and Stoltenberg discuss the fact that independent and dependent variables are often operationalized differently in analog studies of counseling than in basic social psychological research. A review of the ELM as it applies to psychotherapy by Cacioppo, Claiborn, Petty, and Heesacker (1991) suggests ways in which methodological problems such as those discussed in this article can be handled so that greater consistency across analogue and basic studies can be realized.

Abstract

Previous investigations of attitude change in counseling based on Strong's (1968) social influence model have yielded mixed and inconclusive results. Such findings resemble the state of attitude change research that until recently existed in social psychology. In this article we introduce a model of attitude change from social psychology, the Elaboration Likelihood Model (ELM) of persuasion, which has served to unify some of the conflicting results in social psychology. The ELM may potentially account for the inconsistent findings within counseling psychology, providing a reconceptualization of the social influence process that builds upon Strong's (1968) theory and subsequent research. We also provide guidelines for the integration of recent social and counseling literatures in regard to the interpersonal influence process as represented by the ELM.

Twenty years ago, Strong (1968) characterized counseling as an interpersonal influence process and suggested a two-stage model of counseling. In the first stage counselors enhance their perceived expertness, attractiveness, and trustworthiness, which serves to increase clients' involvement in counseling. In the second stage, counselors make maximum use of their influence to precipitate attitude behavior change in clients. The processes by which such client change is presumed to occur were explicated by Strong and Matross (1973). In this conceptualization the authors conceive of the ability to influence clients as *therapist power*. Therapist power (P) is a function of the congruence ($\cong$) between the clients' perception of the therapist's resources (R) and the clients' perception of their needs (N) and can be symbolized as $P = F(R \cong N)$. Therefore, in counseling, the therapist's influence potential arises from the client's perception that the therapist possesses resources that could help the client (e.g., expertise) and the client's perception that he or she needs the help (Strong, 1968).

The heuristic value of Strong's (1968) seminal formulation has been demonstrated by the fact that the area of social influence in counseling has come to be regarded as a primary recurrent research theme within counseling psychology (Wampold & White, 1985) and continues to generate research and theoretical interest (see Dorn, 1986, for a collection of articles on the topic). Indeed, numerous investigations have addressed the role of the counselor source characteristics of expertness, attractiveness, and trustworthiness in the counseling process (see reviews by Corrigan, Dell, Lewis, & Schmidt, 1980; Heppner & Dixon, 1981). In brief, the results of these investigations have documented the capacity of various cues associated with counselor behavior (e.g., verbal and nonverbal), reputation (e.g., background, accomplishments), and other characteristics (e.g., attire, office decor) to affect ratings of the perceived expertness, attractiveness, and trustworthiness of a counselor (Corrigan et al., 1980; Heppner & Dixon, 1981). However, as these reviews point out, the function of these client perceptions remains unclear.

Despite the large volume of research devoted to the study of the interpersonal influence process, studies in counseling indicate a lack of clarity regarding when and how perceived counselor source characteristics will in fact influence client attitudes and behavior. For example, some studies have found that expert counselors produce more attitude and behavior change than nonexperts (e.g., Friedenberg & Gillis, 1977; Heppner & Dixon, 1978; Strong & Schmidt, 1970), whereas others have found that both kinds of counselors produce about the same amount of change (e.g., R. P. Greenberg, 1969; Sprafkin, 1970). These inconclusive findings are similar to the state of research that, until recently, existed within social psychology wherein expert sources have also been shown to occasionally produce less agreement than less credible sources (Petty, Cacioppo, & Heesacker, 1984; Sternthal, Dholakia, & Leavitt, 1978; Stoltenberg & Davis, 1988).

The purpose of this article is to introduce a model of attitude change that has served to explain and unify the diverse findings in the social psychological literature and may similarly account for the inconsistent findings within the counseling psychology literature. Thus, a conceptualization of the social influence process in counseling is provided that may serve to expand on Strong's (1968) original theory and subsequent research. We argue that counselor expertness, attractiveness, and trustworthiness conceptualized by Strong as the basis of counselor influence rely heavily on peripheral-route processing. This approach to persuasion as delineated by Petty and Cacioppo's (1981, 1986a) Elaboration Likelihood Model (ELM) tends to work best for issues low in perceived relevance and to produce only temporary attitude change with little effect on subsequent behavior. We go on to argue that central-route processing, which elicits more stable attitude change and is predictive of subsequent behavior, is the desired approach for counselors.

Thus, our intent in this article is twofold. First, we hope to make another step toward the needed integration of recent social and counseling literatures in regard to the interpersonal influence process. Second, we hope that this article will serve as a stimulus for future research investigating the model we present. Possible directions as well as guidelines for such research are provided.

Elaboration Likelihood Model and Strong's Interpersonal Influence Model

Recent work in social psychology includes a number of studies that have indicated that the effect of communicator characteristics may be more predictable when the quality of the message given by the communicator and the subject's motivation and ability to process the message are taken into account (Petty & Cacioppo, 1979a, 1979b). Petty and Cacioppo (1981, 1986a) introduced a framework of persuasion, the ELM, in which these variables represent various approaches to persuasion that can be thought of as emphasizing two distinct routes that form the poles of a continuum to attitude change.

If a person lacks the motivation (high issue involvement or perceived personal relevance) or ability (cognitive capacity and environmental distractions) to think about a message, attitudes may be affected by positive and negative cues in the persuasion context, or the person may use a simple decision rule to evaluate a persuasive message. These cues or inferences may stem from characteristics of the source (e.g., expertise, attractiveness) or the message (e.g., number of arguments in the absence of more simple cues such as source credibility). Such attention to cues and decision rules may shape attitudes or allow a person to decide what attitudinal position to adopt without the need for engaging in any extensive cognitive work relevant to the issue under consideration. This process constitutes the peripheral route to persuasion and is characteristic of Strong's (1968) description of the counselor's interpersonal influence base.

Another approach called the central route views attitude change as resulting from a diligent consideration of information that is central to what people believe are the true merits of an advocated position. Thus, a person must be able to think about and be motivated to scrutinize the merits of an advocacy (e.g., cognitive ability and high issue involvement) as this is posited to be the most direct determinant of the direction and amount of persuasion produced. Two important advantages of the central route are that attitudinal changes tend to persist longer and are more predictive of behavior than changes induced through the peripheral route (see reviews by Cialdini, Petty, & Cacioppo, 1981; Petty & Cacioppo, 1986a).

Strong's (1968) model of interpersonal influence with its two-stage model of counselor influence can be accommodated within the ELM. Counselors' focus on enhancing their perceived expertness, attractiveness, and trustworthiness for subsequent increases in influence over clients' attitudes and behaviors reflects a process similar to using peripheral cues to enhance persuasion in ELM terms. This process would have different results, however, depending upon the motivation (and ability) of the clients regarding the issues addressed in counseling.

For example, under conditions of low involvement, enhancing the counselor cues of expertness, attractiveness, and trustworthiness would serve to elicit transitory attitude change in clients but, unfortunately, would usually result in limited behavioral compliance. In essence, such an approach may work against behavior change (through the central route) as it increases the likelihood of peripheral route processing and can inhibit a thoughtful consideration of the issues. At best, we might hope that this approach would elicit compliance with minor behavioral tasks (such as limited homework assignments) that may then lead to an increased perception of the personal relevance of the issues for the client. Indeed, initial research by Pierce and Stoltenberg (1988) suggests such an approach may be helpful in enhancing compliance through initial behavior tasks designed to increase the clients' perception of the personal relevance of subsequent treatment programs and behavior change and increase the clients' ability to centrally process relevant information regarding the key issues dealt with in counseling.

Under conditions of high perceived personal relevance, the ELM suggests that counselor cues become less important, although they may retain a limited ability to elicit increased attention by clients to what counselors are saying. For these situations, the intervention is the powerful base of interpersonal influence. The clients are primed for central route processing and will carefully evaluate the counselors' conceptualization of the problem, interpretations, and treatment plans.

Another aspect of the ELM that has been identified as an important factor in determining the type of information processing likely to occur concerns whether the recommendation made by a source is proattitudinal (i.e., one with which the recipient is already in agreement) or counterattitudinal (contrary to the recipients' initial attitude). For example, evidence suggests that subjects are less likely to engage in central-route processing when the recommendation from a source is proattitudinal, particularly if it relates to an issue for which the subject has only a moderate level of personal involvement (Petty & Cacioppo, 1979a, 1979b). In this situation, the subjects appear to perceive little need for a careful consideration of the message when they already agree with the recommendation and the source is perceived as an expert. However, the persuasive advantage may actually shift to a source of less credibility if the message presents strong arguments and the issue is not viewed as personally relevant (Stoltenberg & Davis, 1988). Thus, under certain conditions, more persuasion can result in response to a moderately credible source than a highly credible source due to more attention being paid to the message. This effect was not anticipated by Strong (1968) or Strong and Matross (1973) in their earlier interpersonal influence models but is consistent with studies in the counseling literature reporting similar amounts of attitude change in response to both nonexpert and expert counselors (e.g., R. P. Greenberg, 1969; Sprafkin, 1970).

The ELM also notes that the processing of information may occur in a biased manner. Petty and Cacioppo (1986a) hypothesized that under certain circumstances where personal interests are so intense, as when an issue is intimately associated with central values (i.e., overinvolvement), processing will either terminate in the interest of self-protection or will become biased in the service of a person's own ego. Thus, bias results from a person's initial attitude or prior knowledge becoming a more important cognitive schema in guiding processing (Petty & Cacioppo, 1986a). This is conceptually similar to Strong and Matross's (1973) notion of client oppositional forces. Specifically, the issue of the centrality of an attitude or behavior makes it increasingly resistant to change in counseling and may elicit psychological defensiveness in resisting persuasive attempts. Other variables that may elicit biased processing include forewarning of persuasive intent by the communicator and affective level on the part of the subject (Petty & Cacioppo, 1986a; Stoltenberg, 1986).

According to Strong and Matross (1973), client resistance refers to the clients' refusal to consider change because of the low perceived utility of alternative beliefs or behaviors in comparison with currently held ones. The clients' values may also be consistent with current attitudes and behaviors or inconsistent with perceived alternative attitudes and behaviors. Additionally, important referent or social support groups may perceive issues in ways similar to the client and different from the counselor. Under the rubric of the ELM, high-quality messages by counselors may be determined by adequately addressing these issues in the view of the clients (e.g., if they present relevant evidence regarding the benefits of change, address values, and challenge the validity of perceptions of referent groups; Stoltenberg & McNeill, 1987).

It is important to understand that issues of high personal relevance for clients will often be characterized by a relatively elaborate schema of attitudes and a considerable store of supportive arguments. Consequently, interpretations or interventions implemented by counselors will often be perceived as a threat to this attitudinal framework and will meet with resistance. This can result in active resistance through strong disagreement with counselors, passive resistance through simply ignoring what counselors say, or passive-aggressive resistance through verbally agreeing with counselors but not behaving as such (Stoltenberg, Leach, & Bratt, 1988). Again, the quality of the counselors' message will be of primary importance in such situations. When resistance is likely, counselors may assist clients in examining all of the reasons why change should not occur (i.e., examining the clients' arguments in support of maintaining current attitudes and behaviors) and subsequently assist the clients in evaluating the persuasiveness of these reasons in comparison with alternatives either offered by the counselor or generated by the clients.

The ELM suggests that for issues of low perceived personal relevance for the clients, the initial focus of counseling should be on increasing issue involvement rather than working to enhance perceived counselor expertness, attractiveness, and trustworthiness. For example, most counselors have worked with clients who come seeking help with issues for which limited involvement is apparent. Consider the college student who needs to decide upon a major but has limited investment in the process of career exploration. Such a client is likely to already perceive the counselor as a credible source and may readily agree with recommendations for completing career assessment batteries but will balk at counselor recommendations to commit time and effort toward investigating various career options. With low issue involvement, the client may prefer that the counselor identify the appropriate career and related major without wishing to make an effort to evaluate the information provided and the options available (peripheral route processing). With increased issue involvement, the client will pay more attention to the counselor's recommendations, leading to greater effort and evaluation of available options (central route processing).

Laboratory Evidence for the Elaboration Likelihood Model

A number of studies have tested and provided support for the assumptions posited by the ELM. A seminal investigation by Petty, Cacioppo, and Goldman (1981) examined the two routes as a function of issue involvement (which serves as a measure of motivation). College students were exposed to a communication advocating that seniors be required to take comprehensive exams in their major prior to graduation. This counterattitudinal advocacy contained either strong or weak arguments emanating from a source of high or low expertise. For some subjects, the advocacy possessed high personal relevance (i.e., the policy would begin the next year), whereas for others the advocacy possessed low personal relevance (i.e., the policy would take effect in 10 years). As predicted by the model, highly involved subjects were primarily influenced by the quality of the arguments (as the expertise of the source had no significant effect). In contrast, under low-involvement conditions, subjects' attitudes were primarily influenced by the expertise of the source and were unaffected by the quality of the arguments. Thus, under high relevance or involvement, factors central to the issue become more important; under low relevance or involvement, peripheral factors became more important.

In the preceding study, attitudes in response to high-involvement communications were primarily affected by message factors, and attitudes in response to low-involvement communications were affected primarily by source factors. Cacioppo, Petty, and Stoltenberg (1985), however, noted that the central–peripheral distinction is not just a difference between message and source factors (i.e., either source or message factors can serve as peripheral cues). In Petty et al. (1981) the source of the message served as a peripheral cue under low-involvement conditions. In another study (Petty & Cacioppo, 1984), the simple number of arguments presented in support of a recommendation of low personal relevance to the subjects served as a peripheral cue in the absence of more simple cues (e.g., source expertise, attractiveness). Attitudes reported by the subjects toward a counterattitudinal advocacy were more positive in response to nine as opposed to three supportive arguments. In contrast, when the recommendation was of high personal relevance, attitudes were affected by the quality of the message arguments (central route).

In short, the basic tenet of the ELM is that under certain circumstances attitudes will be formed and changed depending primarily upon the manner in which a person understands, evaluates, and integrates the issue-relevant information presented (i.e., central route), as "elaboration likelihood" is said to be high. At other times, however, attitudes will be formed and changed with little cognitive work and based more on other peripheral cues in the persuasion setting, typifying the processes involved when elaboration likelihood is low (Petty & Cacioppo, 1981). It is also important to note that the central and peripheral routes represent positions on a continuous dimension ranging from high to low likelihood of issue-relevant thinking rather than two mutually exclusive and exhaustive "types" of message processing (Cacioppo et al., 1985). Thus, the ELM accounts for a number of both communicator and recipient variables present in the persuasion setting as well as the effects of various combinations of these variables on attitudinal and behavioral change. As a result, the ELM has served as a general unifying conceptual schema in which diverse and conflicting results in social psychological investigations of attitude change under a variety of circumstances have been integrated (Petty & Cacioppo, 1986a).

Elaboration Likelihood Model and Studies in Counseling

The variables of issue involvement, the pro- or counterattitudinal nature of an advocacy, and the quality of messages in terms of central versus peripheral processing were not included in Strong's (1968) original interpersonal influence model or the later conceptualization of therapist influence potential by Strong and Matross (1973). Thus, it may be useful to examine the role of these variables in predicting greater effectiveness for counselors demonstrating high levels of expertness, attractiveness, and trustworthiness.

In an exhaustive review of relevant counseling studies, McNeill (1985) found it difficult (in most cases) to ascertain if the messages contained in investigations of the effects of counselor expertness were pro- or counterattitudinal for the subjects or whether they were strong or weak quality messages. However, it appears that past investigations within counseling have often manipulated message quality in terms of counselor verbal behavior as an aspect of counselor expertise or attractiveness (e.g., Schied, 1976, Sprafkin, 1970; Strong & Dixon, 1971). Within the framework of the ELM, such counselor verbal behavior may be considered as more of a variable related to message quality. In contrast, evidential or reputational cues of counselor expertness would be conceptualized by the ELM as source cues and would therefore be less likely in and of themselves to elicit lasting attitude and behavior change. Also, it appears that many counseling studies have combined elements of counselor verbal behavior with various evidential and reputational cues (e.g., Childress & Gillis, 1977; Heppner & Dixon, 1978) to form a general counselor "expertness," confounding source and message factors. Thus, it is not surprising that inconsistent effects upon attitude and behavior change have resulted.

With regard to the variable of issue involvement or personal relevance, McNeill (1984/1985) again found it difficult to identify the level of involvement likely for subjects participating in counseling studies. According to the ELM, the importance of issue involvement lies in its capacity to determine the client's motivation to either centrally or peripherally process information. In counseling studies personal relevance has usually been ignored, as issues have not been determined to be personally relevant for the typically employed samples of college students used as potential clients or client surrogates (e.g., Brooks, 1974; Heppner & Pew, 1977). Some investigators appear to have assessed issue involvement through the manipulation of levels of client "perceived need" or request for help (Dixon & Claiborn, 1981; Heppner & Dixon, 1978), measurement of motivation for counseling (Heppner & Heesacker, 1982), and "commitment to change" (Dixon & Claiborn, 1981), thus far resulting in no consistent differential effects.

An investigation by Stoltenberg and McNeill (1984) examined the variables of issue involvement and source credibility in an attempt to provide an initial validation of the ELM in a counseling analogue setting. College students listened to an audiotaped proattitudinal counseling session of high message quality, consisting of a counselor working with a student whose career goals differed from those promoted by his parents. Subjects were assigned to conditions of high and low issue involvement based on their scores on the career decisiveness scale of the Career Maturity Inventory (Crites, 1973). Subjects in the low-involvement conditions were operationally defined as those who demonstrated a high degree of career decisiveness and consequently engaged in less issue-relevant thinking while listening to a counseling session dealing with a career decision-making problem. Conversely, subjects in high-involvement conditions were those who were lower in career decisiveness and therefore were expected to be more motivated to attend to a discussion on choosing a career. The variable of counselor expertise was manipulated by a presession introduction of a counselor of high or moderate credibility.

With high-quality proattitudinal messages, the ELM predicts that source or counselor expertise serves to increase or decrease the amount of thinking or cognitive effort a client is willing to engage in concerning a given issue depending upon the personal relevance for the individual. Three hypotheses were partially supported. First, under conditions of high involvement, subjects' attitudes toward the way the counseling session was conducted were more favorable when exposed to a highly credible (i.e., expert) counselor than a moderately credible counselor. Second, subjects under low-involvement conditions were more influenced by the moderately credible counselor. Third, subjects under high-involvement conditions were influenced more by the high-quality message than subjects under low-involvement conditions.

The findings of Stoltenberg and McNeill (1984), however, were limited in that only subjects' global attitudes towards the counseling session were assessed. In an effort to replicate and extend their previous results, McNeill and Stoltenberg (1988) attempted to further test the validity of the ELM in a counseling analogue setting. Independent variable conditions were similar to the 1984 study for conditions of issue involvement and counselor expertise except that message quality was also manipulated. In the high-quality condition, the counselor's verbal interactions with the client reflected an empathic, understanding manner. In the low-quality condition, the counselor was generally less understanding and not as empathic. In both conditions, the counselor made two distinct, similar recommendations for further career exploration. Consequently, more refined dependent measures directly assessing subjects' specific attitudes toward the recommendations made by the counselor were utilized.

We expected that under conditions of high involvement, subjects' attitudes would be primarily influenced by the quality of the message (central route), whereas under conditions of low involvement, subjects would be influenced more by the credibility of the source (peripheral route). In contrast to the findings of Stoltenberg and McNeill (1984), McNeill and Stoltenberg (1988) found that subjects' cognitions, attitudes, and behavioral intention toward the counselor's recommendations appeared to be influenced only by the quality of the message, regardless of source credibility or subject's involvement level. This finding indicated that subjects were engaged primarily in central route processing.

Similar hypotheses were investigated and parallel conclusions reached by Heesacker (1986) in his investigation of pretreatment attitudes toward participation in social skills or career counseling groups within the context of the ELM. Subjects were designated as high, moderate, or low "ego-involved" based on their level of personal concern with vocational and career/social skills and dating problems. They were then exposed to either high- or low-quality arguments emanating from a source of high or low credibility. Similar to the findings of McNeill and Stoltenberg (1988), subjects' cognitions, attitudes, and behavioral intentions were consistently affected by high-quality messages. Although highly involved subjects' attitudes toward counseling were more favorable than those of subjects who were less involved, Heesacker found none of the expected interactive effects for the personal involvement of the subjects. Like Stoltenberg and McNeill (1984), however, Heesacker found subjects to be more persuaded by low-credibility sources under high message quality conditions. Additionally, Heesacker (1986) hypothesized that the effects he obtained may have been due to a lack of clear differences in subjects' level of involvement. That is, all subjects may have more accurately reflected only moderate levels of involvement.

The investigations of Stoltenberg and McNeill (1984), McNeill and Stoltenberg (1988), and Heesacker (1986) have not replicated all of the predicted ELM effects evidenced in previous social psychological studies. Nonetheless, these counseling-related studies are suggestive of the utility of the ELM in explaining previous equivocal findings regarding the effects of source expertise on attitude and behavior change. For example, the influence of the quality of the message on subjects' attitudes in the studies by Heesacker (1986) and McNeill and Stoltenberg (1988) indicates that subjects were engaged primarily in central route processing, which, in turn, overwhelms any effects of a simple peripheral cue such as source credibility.

These findings suggest that potential clients' judgments of the quality or effectiveness of treatments presented verbally by counselors may be more influential in affecting attitude change than descriptions of credentials, status, and experience. These implications support the conclusions of others (e.g., Corrigan et al., 1980; Heppner & Dixon, 1981) who posit that social influence in counseling is more complex than originally suggested by Strong's (1968) two-stage model. In other words, the influential base of counselor expertness hypothesized by Strong to affect attitude and behavior change may be severely limited in situations where it is defined primarily in terms of peripheral cues (e.g., credentials). As a result, the ELM provides an alternative hypothesis suggesting that the lack of a central–peripheral distinction in the operationalization of counselor expertise apparent in numerous investigations of Strong's model may be a factor responsible for the conflicting findings in the literature.

Thus, we believe that the ELM, with its emphasis on the central–peripheral continuum in conceptualizing cues of counselor credibility and in-session behaviors, the role of varying levels of involvement (and ability), and accounting for the influence of the pro- or counterattitudinal recommendations, further builds upon and enhances the important work of Strong and his colleagues. In addition, the ELM addresses the concerns of others (e.g., Heesacker, 1986; Heppner, Menne, & Rosenberg, 1986) by evaluating a wider range of variables, including the reciprocal interaction between counselor and client characteristics in the interpersonal influence process (see Figure 23.1).

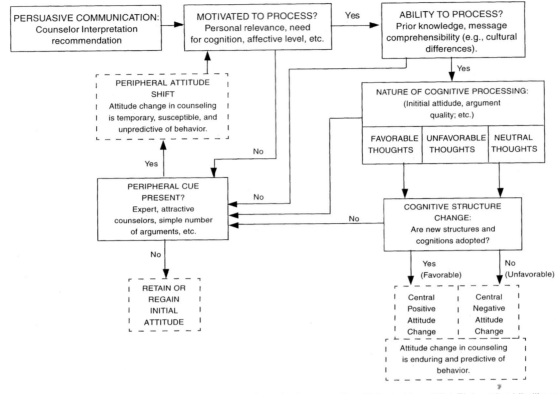

FIGURE 23.1 ■ Central and peripheral routes to persuasion in counseling. (Adapted from "The Elaboration Likelihood Model of Persuasion," by R. E. Petty and J. T. Cacioppo, 1986, in L. Berkowitz, *Advances in Experimental Social Psychology* [Vol. 19, pp. 123–205], New York: Academic Press. Copyright 1982 by Academic Press. Adapted by permission.)

Directions for Future Research

Cacioppo et al. (1985) guarded against the assumption that social psychological research will necessarily generalize in a simple manner to counseling settings and relationships. As we have acknowledged, previous studies in counseling are difficult to conceptualize under the rubric of the ELM. However, the recent work discussed here represents the initial programmatic attempts to operationalize and test the constructs associated with the ELM within the context of the counseling setting. In the Stoltenberg and McNeill (1984), McNeill and Stoltenberg (1988), and Heesacker (1986) studies, the effects of simple source cues were mediated by either message quality or issue involvement. Consequently, although these studies are suggestive of the relevance of the ELM to counseling, they are also demonstrative of the difficulties inherent in attempting to test the validity of a well-established theory in a new domain (i.e., producing the necessary conditions to properly test the theory yet retaining a degree of external validity relevant to the setting of application; see McGlynn, 1987, for a discussion of this problem).

For example, the operationalizations of issue involvement in the studies mentioned previously represent attempts to generalize this variable to the counseling setting, with differences in levels of involvement verified by manipulation checks. However, as noted by Heesacker (1986) and McNeill and Stoltenberg (1988), these operationalizations differed from past social psychological studies (e.g., Petty et al., 1981) in which subjects under high-involvement conditions would likely have had direct, externally imposed personal consequences, whereas subjects in low-involvement conditions would have been led to believe that issues had few personal consequences. Thus, the involvement levels in these studies may not have reflected the degrees of high and low involvement previously utilized in tests of the ELM, underscoring the importance of accurately operationalizing a variable such as issue involvement to reflect levels found in counseling. Different operationalizations of the variables important to the ELM may lead to different effects, especially as applied to the counseling domain. Because of the preliminary nature of this work, the relevance of the ELM for counseling has yet to be adequately tested. Much work remains to be done before we can unequivocally conclude that the ELM unifies the conflicting findings regarding the social influence process in counseling. Thus, we now turn to some considerations and guidelines for those future studies attempting to apply the concepts of the ELM to the counseling domain.

Source factors. Within the framework of the ELM, evidential cues of expertness, attractiveness, and trustworthiness (e.g., diplomas, credentials) are conceptualized as source cues and thus should not be confounded with variables related to message quality such as counselor verbal behavior. As indicated by previous counseling studies, evidential source or counselor characteristics may be defined in any number of ways (see Corrigan et al., 1980; Heppner & Dixon, 1981). Although such cues are typically attended to most in peripheral route processing and are more likely to result in only temporary shifts of attitude change without lasting behavioral change, they may still have potential in eliciting initial attitude change until conditions for more central route processing are created (Cacioppo et al., 1985).

Message factors. It may prove fruitful for future investigations of the interpersonal-influence process in counseling to redefine counselor verbal as well as nonverbal behavior as a component of message quality. In the typical social psychological lab study, message quality involves the manner of the presentation of an advocacy (e.g., the use of logical arguments and accompanying statistics and graphs in strong conditions versus illogical arguments and anecdotal information in weak conditions). Operationalizations of message quality with more generalizability to the counseling setting may be accomplished by employing strong versus weak arguments as utilized by Heesacker (1986) or components of empathy and understanding as in studies by Stoltenberg and McNeill (1984) and McNeill and Stoltenberg (1988). Additionally, differences in the quality of messages might be defined through the use of therapeutic jargon (Barak, Patkin, & Dell, 1982), style of interpretation (e.g., Claiborn, 1979), or perhaps counseling orientation (Stoltenberg, Maddux, & Pace, 1986), method of presenting evidence, or even self-efficacy (Bandura, 1977).

It appears that within the typical counseling setting, recommendations made by the counselor are equally likely to be either pro- or counterattitudinal in nature (Stoltenberg, 1986). That is, as often as clients may be initially resistant to the recommendations, interpretations, or conceptualizations of their counselors, they will often initially and quite readily agree with their counselors.

As demonstrated by the studies investigating the ELM in counseling, effects consistent with high and low levels of involvement were difficult to obtain. The ELM suggests that issue involvement is directly tied to topic specificity. That is, a subject's level of involvement is a function of prior knowledge or interest in the topic of discussion. However, many issues in counseling may lack some type of direct, externally imposed consequence or personal threat to clients. Higher levels of involvement consistent with previous social psychological research might be produced by emphasizing the negative or positive consequences associated with an individual's maladaptive or adaptive behavior, respectively. For example, Rogers (1984) used fear appeals to increase subjects' motivation to give up cigarette smoking. This approach highlights the negative consequences of current behavior to increase motivation to consider ways to change and adopt alternative behaviors.

On the other hand, involvement may occur very differently in the counseling setting. For example, Barber and Stoltenberg (1988) found that different operationalizations of personal involvement yielded differential effects in the alleviation of depression and loneliness. Investigations might also emphasize personal consequences through the use of homework assignments in which clients report back to a counselor or (as suggested by Corrigan et al., 1980) explore the level of client involvement in the counseling relationship. It is important to note, however, that due to the topic-specific nature of issue involvement, a client's level of *involvement* may change and shift throughout a single counseling session, as topics of discussion between client and counselor vary (Stoltenberg & McNeill, 1987).

Recipient characteristics. Additional factors that influence a client's motivation to process information through either the central or peripheral routes include characteristics of the client or recipient. Such characteristics will interact with the message to influence the type and degree of information processing that occurs. Social psychological research has identified "need for cognition" (Cacioppo & Petty, 1984) and field dependence/field independence (Heesacker, Petty, & Cacioppo, 1983) as recipient factors that influence a person's propensity for either central- or peripheral-route processing. An investigation by Stoltenberg et al. (1986) indicated that the cognitive style of clients as measured by the Myers–Briggs Type Indicator may affect their perceptions of the viability of various counseling approaches as well as the attitudes toward the counselor. The authors found that "thinking" type subjects rated higher the quality of a counseling session that used a rational-emotive counseling approach than did subjects identified as "feeling" types. Thinking type subjects also rated their counselors as more credible than the feeling types did and reported that they were more likely to consider seeking out such counselors in the future, should they need counseling.

The role of client affective level has only begun to be investigated in the context of the ELM. Preliminary studies by Bratt and Stoltenberg (1987) and Stoltenberg et al. (1988) have suggested that low levels of depression may actually increase central-route processing in comparison to an elated mood, when the issue is mood congruent (i.e., counterattitudinal for a dysphoric mood). It also seems likely that extreme levels of affect may inhibit central-route processing. The client's ability to process information must be considered in eliciting enduring attitude change and related behaviors. For example, "psychological mindedness" or client level of intelligence may be relevant to communicating in counseling (Stoltenberg & McNeill, 1987). Research in cross-cultural counseling (see review by Casas, 1984) suggests that client–counselor cultural differences may also result in ineffective communication due to difficulties in message comprehensibility and subsequent processing.

Measuring attitudes and cognitions. A number of techniques may be applied in measuring and quantifying the ELM variables. For example, Petty and Cacioppo (1986a) defined high- and low-quality messages as those that are persuasive or not persuasive, respectively. In determining the high or low quality of a message or advocacy, semantic differential or Likert-type items assessing subjects' favorable or unfavorable attitudes toward the message have been frequently employed. Thought listing techniques applied immediately following the presentation of an advocacy have also been found to be an unobtrusive, valid method of directly assessing subjects' attitudes and cognitions regarding a message (Cacioppo & Petty, 1981). As such, thought listing procedures have the added advantage of providing information with regard to the content and meaning of the subjects' cognitive processing. These measures may be utilized both in piloting and operationalizing the ELM variables and in assessing degree of attitude change following independent variable manipulations. The initial pro- or counterattitudinal nature of advocacies made by sources may also be similarly assessed through these methods prior to any manipulations of independent variables.

In piloting and verifying manipulations of source cues, the Counselor Rating Form (LaCrosse & Barak, 1976) or its abbreviated version (Corrigan & Schmidt, 1983) provide a reliable, valid measure of counselor expertness, attractiveness, and trustworthiness. Level or degree of subject involvement may be verified through items assessing subjects' perceptions of involvement in the topic of discussion or personal relevance of the issue at hand. In addition, measures are also available for assessing the recipient characteristics of need for cognition (Cacioppo & Petty, 1984) and field dependence–independence (Heesacker et al., 1983). Finally, behavioral intentions as a result of attitude change have been quantified through items assessing the likelihood of going to a counselor (McNeill & Stoltenberg, 1988) or signing up for dating or social skill groups (Heesacker, 1986).

Design considerations. The primary consideration in the design of future studies investigating the application of the ELM to counseling is the proper operationalization of the variables. Consistent with other researchers (e.g., Gelso, 1979; Munley, 1974), we would urge that future investigations use independent variable manipulations that reflect a reasonable degree of external generalizability to the counseling setting. This recommendation is especially relevant when applied to the operationalization of the counselor source characteristics, as well as the other variables stressed by the ELM.

It also seems likely that the frequently used analogue design of using subjects in the role of judging a counseling interaction may be limited in assessing effects associated with level of issue involvement and attitude-behavior relationships (e.g., subject participation as an observer may limit levels of subject involvement). Therefore, the employment of alternative designs in both the laboratory and field (e.g., in which subjects take the client role, or in which actual clients are used) is recommended for future investigations of the ELM. Due to the ELM's focus on attitude change as a result of the client-counselor interaction, methodological strategies focusing on the assessment of in-session behaviors such as "task analysis" (L. S. Greenberg, 1984) and the "discovery oriented approach" proposed by Elliot (1984) may be useful.

Summary and Conclusions

The strength of the ELM lies in its ability to conceptualize and account for the interactive effects of source or counselor characteristics, client or recipient characteristics, cues in the persuasion situation, and aspects of the message. Although some may find the model overly complicated, we believe that the ELM provides an alternative to earlier thinking regarding social influence in counseling suggesting a more complex interaction of a number of factors present in the persuasion setting.

The ELM has served to unify the diverse and conflicting findings regarding the interpersonal influence process in social psychology. Thus, we believe that this model may also serve to clarify the inconsistent results apparent in investigations of the social influence process in counseling, thus warranting further investigation by building upon the earlier work of Strong (1968) and others. We concur with Strong and Claiborn (1982) that the greatest potential for the social influence model of the counseling process lies in its value as a metatheory explaining the attitude and behavior change process across theoretical orientations. However, the ELM also shows promise for prescribing more effective ways to increase change in clients through central processing (see Stoltenberg, 1986; Stoltenberg & McNeill, 1987). For instance, Pierce and Stoltenberg (1988) were able to increase clients' compliance with a behavioral weight loss program by increasing the personal relevance of weight loss to the clients and by presenting counterarguments when the clients were tempted to stray from the diet plan.

In our view, it is unfortunate that empirical investigations of the process of social influence in counseling have recently lost some momentum due perhaps in part to misconceptions of the process. For example, Patterson (1986) appeared to equate social influence variables with "nonspecific variables" or placebos in counseling, as well as with unethical practice. By outlining the parameters of the ELM in this article, we hope to add momentum to the investigation of the interpersonal influence process so that future studies may test and clarify the potential for this model in further explaining the attitude and behavior change process in counseling.

ACKNOWLEDGMENT

We thank Martin Heesacker for his helpful comments on an earlier draft of the manuscript.

REFERENCES

Bandura, A. (1977). Self-efficacy: Toward a unifying theory of behavioral change. *Psychological Review, 84,* 191–215.

Barak, A., Patkin, J., & Dell, D. M. (1982). Effects of certain counselor behaviors on perceived expertness and attractiveness. *Journal of Counseling Psychology, 29,* 261–267.

Barber, L. C., & Stoltenberg, C. D. (1988). *The effects of emotional locus of control and personal relevance on self-efficacy for counseling approaches.* Unpublished manuscript, Texas Tech University, Lubbock.

Bratt, A., & Stoltenberg, C. D. (1987). *The Elaboration Likelihood Model and the role of affect.* Unpublished manuscript, University of Oklahoma, Norman.

Brooks, L. (1974). Interactive effects of sex and status on self-disclosure. *Journal of Counseling Psychology, 21,* 269–474.

Cacioppo, J. T., & Petty, R. E. (1981). Social psychological procedures for cognitive assessment: The thought listing technique. In T. Merluzzi, C. R. Glass, & M. Genest (Eds.), *Cognitive assessment* (pp. 309–342). New York: Guilford Press.

Cacioppo, J. T., & Petty, R. E. (1984). The need for cognition: Relationship to attitudinal processes. In R. P. McGlynn, J. E. Maddux, C. D. Stoltenberg, & J. H. Harvey (Eds.), *Social perception in clinical and counseling psychology* (pp. 113–139). Lubbock: Texas Tech Press.

Cacioppo, J. T., Petty, R. E., & Stoltenberg, C. D. (1985). Processes of social influence: The elaboration likelihood model of persuasion. In P. Kendall (Ed.), *Advances in cognitive-behavioral research and practice* (Vol. 4, pp. 215–274). New York: Academic Press.

Casas, J. M. (1984). Policy, training, and research in counseling psychology: The racial/ethnic minority perspective. In S. D. Brown & R. W. Lent (Eds.), *Handbook of counseling psychology* (pp. 785–831). New York: Wiley.

Childress, R., & Gillis, J. S. (1977). A study of pretherapy role induction as an influence process. *Journal of Clinical Psychology, 33*, 540–544.

Cialdini, B. R., Petty, R. E., & Cacioppo, J. T. (1981). Attitudes and attitude change. *Annual Review of Psychology, 32*, 357–404.

Claiborn, C. D. (1979). Counselor verbal intervention, nonverbal behavior, and social power. *Journal of Counseling Psychology, 26*, 378–383.

Corrigan, J. D., Dell, D. M., Lewis, K. N., & Schmidt, L. D. (1980). Counseling as a social influence process: A review. *Journal of Counseling Psychology, 27*, 395–441.

Corrigan, J. D., & Schmidt, L. D. (1983). Development and validation of revisions in the Counselor Rating Form. *Journal of Counseling Psychology, 30*, 64–75.

Crites, J. O. (1973). *Career Maturity Inventory*. Monterey, CA: CTB/McGraw-Hill.

Dixon, D. N., & Claiborn, C. D. (1981). Effects of need and commitment on career exploration behaviors. *Journal of Counseling Psychology, 28*, 411–415.

Dorn, F. J. (Ed.). (1986). *The social influence process in counseling and psychotherapy*. Springfield, IL: Charles C. Thomas.

Elliot, R. (1984). A discovery-oriented approach to significant change events in psychotherapy: Interpersonal process recall and comprehensive process analysis. In L. N. Rice & L. S. Greenberg (Eds.), *Patterns of change: Intensive analysis of psychotherapy process* (pp. 249–286). New York: Guilford Press.

Friedenberg, W. P., & Gillis, J. S. (1977). An experimental study of the effectiveness of attitude change techniques for enhancing self-esteem. *Journal of Clinical Psychology, 33*, 1120–1124.

Gelso, C. J. (1979). Research in counseling: Methodological and professional issues. *Counseling Psychologist, 8*, 7–35.

Greenberg, L. S. (1984). Task analysis: The general approach. In L. N. Rice & L. S. Greenberg (Eds.), *Patterns of change: Intensive analysis of psychotherapy process* (pp. 124–148). New York: Guilford Press.

Greenberg, R. P. (1969). Effects of presession information on perception of the therapist and receptivity to influence in a psychotherapy analogue. *Journal of Consulting and Clinical Psychology, 33*, 425–429.

Heesacker, M. H. (1986). Counseling pretreatment and the Elaboration Likelihood Model of attitude change. *Journal of Counseling Psychology, 33*, 107–114.

Heesacker, M., Petty, R. E., & Cacioppo, J. T. (1983). Field dependence and attitude change: Source credibility can alter persuasion by affecting message-relevant thinking. *Journal of Personality, 51*, 653–666.

Heppner, P. P., & Dixon, D. N. (1978). The effects of client perceived need and counselor role on client's behaviors. *Journal of Counseling Psychology, 25*, 514–519.

Heppner, P. P., & Dixon, D. N. (1981). Review of the interpersonal influence process in counseling. *Personnel and Guidance Journal, 40*, 542–550.

Heppner, P. P., & Heesacker, M. (1982). Interpersonal influence process in real life counseling: Investigating client perceptions, counselor experience level, and counselor power over time. *Journal of Counseling Psychology, 29*, 215–233.

Heppner, P. P., Menne, M. M., & Rosenberg, J. I. (1986). Some reflections on the interpersonal influence process in counseling. In F. J. Dorn (Ed.), *The social influence process in counseling and psychotherapy* (pp. 137–146). Springfield, IL: Charles C. Thomas.

Heppner, P. P., & Pew, S. (1977). Effects of diplomas, awards, and counselor sex on perceived expertness. *Journal of Counseling Psychology, 24*, 147–149.

LaCrosse, M. B., & Barak, A. (1976). Differential perception of counselor behavior. *Journal of Counseling Psychology, 23*, 170–172.

McGlynn, R. P. (1987). Research issues at the social, clinical, and counseling psychology interface. In J. E. Maddux, C. D. Stoltenberg, & R. Rosenwein (Eds.), *Social processes in clinical and counseling psychology* (pp. 14–22). New York: Springer-Verlag.

McNeill, B. W. (1985). Social influence in the counseling setting: Effects of source credibility, issue involvement, and message quality (Doctoral dissertation, Texas Tech University, 1984). *Dissertation Abstracts International, 45*, 314.

McNeill, B. W., & Stoltenberg, C. D. (1988). A test of the elaboration likelihood model for therapy. *Cognitive Therapy and Research, 12*, 69–80.

Munley, P. H. (1974). A review of counseling analogue research methods. *Journal of Counseling Psychology, 21*, 320–330.

Patterson, C. H. (1986). *Theories of counseling and psychotherapy*. New York: Harper & Row.

Petty, R. E., & Cacioppo, J. T. (1979a). Effects of forewarning of persuasive intent and involvement on cognitive responses and persuasion. *Personality and Social Psychology Bulletin, 5*, 173–176.

Petty, R. E., & Cacioppo, J. T. (1979b). Issue involvement can increase or decrease persuasion by enhancing message-relevant cognitive responses. *Journal of Personality and Social Psychology, 37*, 1915–1926.

Petty, R. E., & Cacioppo, J. T. (1981). *Attitudes and persuasion: Classic and contemporary approaches*. Dubuque, IA: William C. Brown.

Petty, R. E., & Cacioppo, J. T. (1984). The effects of involvement on responses to argument quantity and quality: Central and peripheral routes to persuasion. *Journal of Personality and Social Psychology, 46*, 69–81.

Petty, R. E., & Cacioppo, J. T. (1986a). *Communication and persuasion: Central and peripheral routes to attitude change*. New York: Springer-Verlag.

Petty, R. E., & Cacioppo, J. T. (1986b). The elaboration likelihood model of persuasion. In L. Berkowitz (Ed.), *Ad-*

vances in experimental social psychology (Vol. 19, pp. 123–205). New York: Academic Press.

Petty, R. E., Cacioppo, J. T., & Goldman, R. (1981). Personal involvement as a determinant of argument-based persuasion. *Journal of Personality and Social Psychology, 41*, 847–855.

Petty, R. E., Cacioppo, J. T., & Heesacker, M. (1984). Central and peripheral routes to persuasion: Application to counseling. In R. P. McGlynn, J. E. Maddux, C. D. Stoltenberg, & J. H. Harvey (Eds.), *Social perception in clinical and counseling psychology* (pp. 59–89). Lubbock: Texas Tech Press.

Pierce, R. P., & Stoltenberg, C. D. (1988). *Cognitive self-persuasion and persistence in a weight loss program.* Unpublished manuscript, Texas Tech University, Lubbock.

Rogers, R. W. (1984). Changing health-related attitudes and behaviors: An interface of social and clinical psychology. In R. P. McGlynn, J. E. Maddux, C. D. Stoltenberg, & J. H. Harvey (Eds.), *Social perception in clinical and counseling psychology* (pp. 91–112). Lubbock: Texas Tech Press.

Scheid, A. B. (1976). Clients' perception of the counselor: The influence of counselor introduction and behavior. *Journal of Counseling Psychology, 23*, 503–508.

Sprafkin, R. P. (1970). Communicator expertness and changes in word meaning in psychological treatment. *Journal of Counseling Psychology, 17*, 117–121.

Sternthal, B., Dholakia, R., & Leavitt, C. (1978). The persuasive effect of source credibility: A test of cognitive response analysis. *Journal of Consumer Research, 4*, 252–260.

Stoltenberg, C. D. (1986). Elaboration likelihood and the counseling process. In F. J. Dorn (Ed.), *The social influence process in counseling and psychotherapy* (pp. 55–64). Springfield, IL: Charles C. Thomas.

Stoltenberg, C. D., & Davis, C. (1988). Career and study skills information: Who says what can alter message processing. *Journal of Social and Clinical Psychology, 6*, 38–52.

Stoltenberg, C. D., Leach, M. M., & Bratt, A. (1988). *Effects of depression and elation on information processing.* Manuscript submitted for publication.

Stoltenberg, C. D., Maddux, J. E., & Pace, T. (1986). Client cognitive style and counselor credibility: Effects on client endorsement of rational emotive therapy. *Cognitive Therapy and Research, 10*, 237–243.

Stoltenberg, C. D., & McNeill, B. W. (1984). Effects of expertise and issue involvement on perceptions of counseling. *Journal of Social and Clinical Psychology, 2*, 314–325.

Stoltenberg, C. D., & McNeill, B. W. (1987). Counseling and persuasion: Extrapolating the elaboration likelihood model. In J. E. Maddux, C. D. Stoltenberg, & R. Rosenwein (Eds.), *Social processes in clinical and counseling psychology* (pp. 56–67). New York: Springer-Verlag.

Strong, S. R. (1968). Counseling: An interpersonal influence process. *Journal of Counseling Psychology, 15*, 215–224.

Strong, S. R., & Claiborn, C. D. (1982). *Change through interaction: Social psychological process of counseling and psychotherapy.* New York: Wiley.

Strong, S. R., & Dixon, D. N. (1971). Expertness, attractiveness, and influence in counseling. *Journal of Counseling Psychology, 18*, 562–570.

Strong, S. R., & Matross, R. P. (1973). Change process in counseling and psychotherapy. *Journal of Counseling Psychology, 20*, 25–37.

Strong, S. R., & Schmidt, L. D. (1970). Expertness and influence in counseling. *Journal of Counseling Psychology, 20*, 25–37.

Wampold, B. E., & White, T. B. (1985). Research themes in counseling psychology: A cluster analysis of citation in the process and outcomes section of the *Journal of Counseling Psychology*. *Journal of Counseling Psychology, 32*, 123–126.

Discussion Questions

1. How do you typically process persuasive communications? Do you think you are more of a central processor or a peripheral processor?
2. Why would attitude change via the central route produce more lasting attitude changes (and attitudes that are more predictive of behavior) than attitude change via the peripheral route?
3. How do you think issue involvement should be conceptualized in an analog counseling study? Would issue involvement as defined in an analog study generalize to issue involvement in an actual therapy setting?
4. The degree to which people enjoy thinking and engaging in cognitive activities can be measured by the Need for Cognition Scale. People who score high on this scale enjoy engaging in cognitive activities and thinking about issues. How would people's scores on the Need for Cognition Scale relate to whether they were likely to process a persuasive communication centrally versus peripherally?

Suggested Readings

Cacioppo, J. T., Claiborn, C. D., Petty, R. E., & Heesacker, M (1991). General framework for the study of attitude change in psychotherapy. In C. R. Snyder & D.R. Forsyth (Eds.), *Handbook of social and clinical psychology: The health perspective* (pp. 523–539). New York: Pergamon. This chapter reviews the literature on attitude change and applies research in that area to psychotherapy.

Petty, R. E., & Cacioppo, J. T. (1986). The elaboration likelihood model of persuasion. *Advances in Experimental Social Psychology, 19,* 123–205. This chapter presents a thorough presentation of the elaboration likelihood model of persuasion.

Strong, S. R. (1968). Counseling: An interpersonal influence process. *Journal of Counseling Psychology, 15,* 215–224. This seminal article was one of the early writings examining counseling as a social influence process.

Strong, S. R. (1991). Social influence and change in therapeutic relationships. In C. R. Snyder & D. R. Forsyth (Eds.), *Handbook of social and clinical psychology: The health perspective* (pp. 540–562). New York: Pergamon. In this chapter, Strong applies the principles of social influence to the therapeutic process.

READING 24

The Effects of Choice and Enhanced Personal Responsibility for the Aged: A Field Experiment in an Institutional Setting

Ellen J. Langer • Graduate Center, City University of New York
Judith Rodin • Yale University

Editors' Introduction

Many theorists have suggested that having personal control over one's life contributes to psychological well-being. For example, Adler (1930) believed that the need to control aspects of one's life is "an intrinsic necessity of life itself" (p. 398). Having control is important because it allows people to achieve desired outcomes and to avoid undesired outcomes. In addition, it is rewarding simply to perceive that one has control. Furthermore, people who believe they have control experience positive psychological effects such as lower anxiety (Stotland & Blumenthal, 1964) and greater confidence (Langer, 1975). Alternatively, the failure to exercise control over one's environment has been associated with an increase in the number of physical symptoms experienced (Pennebaker, Burnam, Schaeffer, & Harper, 1977).

The relationship between perceived control and both psychological and physical well-being suggests that enhancing people's perceptions of control may have beneficial effects. This may be particularly true among people who feel that they do not have much control over their lives, such as the elderly. With old age generally comes increasing physical infirmity and, concomitantly, decreased feelings of control and responsibility. These physical and psychological changes often lead to a lowered sense of self-esteem and compromised physical and psychological health.

Langer and Rodin designed this study to determine whether increasing the degree to which elderly people feel they have control leads to improved physical and psychological health outcomes. Ninety-one individuals living in a nursing home served as participants. Some residents were assigned to a responsibility-induced group (high perceived control), in which their own personal responsibility and freedom to make daily choices was emphasized. The other residents were assigned to the comparison group (low perceived control), in which it was stressed that the staff was responsible for the resident's well-being. In fact, residents in both groups were treated in the same way, and the choices that were provided to the responsibility-induced group had been available to them prior to the study. Three weeks later, those residents for whom personal responsibility and choice were emphasized reported being more active and alert, happier, and more involved in activities at the facility. Ratings by the nursing staff confirmed the improved physical and psychological status of these individuals, indicating that they were more interested, sociable, and active than other individuals at the facility. Although 93% of the participants in the responsibility-induced group showed improvement, 71% of the residents in the comparison group showed debilitation over the 3-week period. A follow-up study by Rodin and Langer (1977) even suggested that residents who felt greater control lived longer than those who did not. Clearly, the perception of control exerted a powerful effect on the health of residents in the nursing home facility.

Abstract

A field experiment was conducted to assess the effects of enhanced personal responsibility and choice on a group of nursing home residents. It was expected that the debilitated condition of many of the aged residing in institutional settings is, at least in part, a result of living in a virtually decision-free environment and consequently is potentially reversible. Residents who were in the experimental group were given a communication emphasizing their responsibility for themselves, whereas the communication given to a second group stressed the staff's responsibility for them. In addition, to bolster the communication, the former group was given the freedom to make choices and the responsibility of caring for a plant rather than having decisions made and the plant taken care of for them by the staff, as was the case for the latter group. Questionnaire ratings and behavioral measures showed a significant improvement for the experimental group over the comparison group on alertness, active participation, and a general sense of well-being.

The transition from adulthood to old age is often perceived as a process of loss, physiologically and psychologically (Birren, 1958; Gould, 1972). However, it is as yet unclear just how much of this change is biologically determined and how much is a function of the environment. The ability to sustain a sense of personal control in old age may be greatly influenced by societal factors, and this in turn may affect one's physical well-being.

Typically the life situation does change in old age. There is some loss of roles, norms, and reference groups, events that negatively influence one's perceived competence and feeling of responsibility (Bengston, 1973). Perception of these changes in addition to actual physical decrements may enhance a sense of aging and lower self-esteem (Lehr & Puschner, Reference Note 1). In response to internal developmental changes, the aging individual may come to see himself in a position of lessened mastery relative to the rest of the world, as a passive object manipulated by the environment (Neugarten & Gutman, 1958). Questioning whether these factors can be counteracted, some studies have suggested that more successful aging—measured by decreased mortality, morbidity, and psychological disability—occurs when an individual feels a sense of usefulness and purpose (Bengston, 1973; Butler, 1967; Leaf, 1973; Lieberman, 1965).

The notion of competence is indeed central to much of human behavior. Adler (1930) has described the need to control one's personal environment as "an intrinsic necessity of life itself" (p. 398). deCharms (1968) has stated that "man's primary motivation propensity is to be effective in producing changes in his environment. Man strives to be a causal agent, to be the primary locus of, causation for, or the origin of, his behavior; he strives for personal causation" (p. 269).

Several laboratory studies have demonstrated that reduced control over aversive outcomes increases physiological distress and anxiety (Geer, Davison, & Gatchel, 1970; Pervin, 1963) and even a nonveridical perception of control over an impending event reduces the aversiveness of that event (Bowers, 1968; Glass & Singer, 1972; Kanfer & Seidner, 1973). Langer, Janis, and Wolfer (1975) found that by inducing the perception of control over stress in hospital patients by means of a communication that emphasized potential cognitive control, subjects requested fewer pain relievers and sedatives and were seen by nurses as evidencing less anxiety.

Choice is also a crucial variable in enhancing an induced sense of control. Stotland and Blumenthal (1964) studied the effects of choice on anxiety reduction. They told subjects that they were going to take a number of important ability tests. Half of the subjects were allowed to choose the order in which they wanted to take the tests, and half were told that the order was fixed. All subjects were informed that the order of the tests would have no bearing on their scores. They found that subjects not given the choice were more anxious, as measured by palmar sweating. In another study of the effects of choice, Corah and Boffa (1970) told their subjects that there were two conditions in the experiment, each of which would be signaled by a different light. In one condition they were given the choice of whether or not to press a button to escape from an aversive noise, and in the other one they were not given the option of escaping. They found that the choice instructions decreased the aversiveness of the threatening stimulus, apparently by increasing perceived control. Although using a very different paradigm, Langer (1975) also demonstrated the importance of choice. In that study it was found that the exercise of choice in a chance situation, where choice was objectively inconsequential, nevertheless had psychological consequences manifested in increased confidence and risk taking.

Lefcourt (1973) best summed up the essence of this research in a brief review article dealing with the perception of control in man and animals when he concluded that "the sense of control, the illusion that one can exercise personal choice, has a definite and a positive role in sustaining life" (p. 424). It is not surprising, then, that these important psychological factors should be linked to health and survival. In a series retrospective studies, Schmale and his associates (Adamson & Schmale, 1965; Schmale, 1958; Schmale & Iker, 1966) found that ulcerative colitis, leukemia, cervical cancer, and heart disease were linked with a feeling of helplessness and loss of hope experienced by the patient prior to the onset of the disease. Seligman and his coworkers have systematically investigated the learning of helplessness and related it to the clinical syndrome of depression (see Seligman, 1975). Even death is apparently related to control-relevant variables. McMahon and Rhudick (1964) found a relationship between decision or hopelessness and death. The most graphic description of this association comes from Bettelheim (1943), who in his analysis of the "Muselmanner," the walking corpses in the concentration camps, described them as:

Prisoners who came to believe the repeated statements of the guards—that there was no hope for them, that they would never leave the camp except as a corpse—who came to feel that the environment was one over which they could exercise no influence whatsoever. . . . Once his own life and the environment were viewed as totally beyond his ability to influence them, the only logical conclusion was to pay no attention to them whatsoever. Only then, all conscious awareness of stimuli coming from the outside was blocked out, and with it all response to anything but inner stimuli.

Death swiftly followed and, according to Bettelheim,

[survival] depended on one's ability to arrange to preserve some areas of independent action and keep control of some important aspects of one's life despite an environment that seemed overwhelming and total.

Bettelheim's description reminds us of Richter's (1957) rats, who also "gave up hope" of controlling their environment and subsequently died.

The implications of these studies for research in the area of aging are clear: objective helplessness as well as feelings of helplessness and hopelessness—both enhanced by the environment and by intrinsic changes that occur with increasing old age—may contribute to psychological withdrawal, physical disease, and death. In contrast, objective control and feelings of mastery may very well contribute to physical health and personal efficacy.

In a study conceived to explore the effects of dissonance, Ferrare (1962; cited in Seligman, 1975; Zimbardo & Ruch, 1975) presented data concerning the effects of the ability of geriatric patients to control their place of residence. Of 17 subjects who answered that they did not have any other alternative but to move to a specific old age home, 8 died after 4 weeks of residence and 16 after 10 weeks of residence. By comparison, among the residents who died during the initial period, only one person had answered that she had the freedom to choose her alternatives. All of these deaths were classified as unexpected because "not even significant disturbances had actually given warning of the impending disaster."

As Zimbardo (Zimbardo & Ruch, 1975) suggested, the implications of Ferrare's data are striking and merit further study of old age home settings. There is already evidence that perceived personal control in one's residential environment is important for younger and noninstitutional populations. Rodin (in press), using children as subjects, demonstrated that diminished feelings of control produced by chronic crowding at home led to fewer attempts to control self-reinforcement in the laboratory and to greater likelihood of giving up in the face of failure.

The present study attempted to assess directly the effects of enhanced personal responsibility and choice in a group of nursing home patients. In addition to examining previous results from the control-helplessness literature in a field setting, the present study extended the domain of this conception by considering new response variables. Specifically, if increased control has generalized beneficial effects, then physical and mental alertness, activity, general level of satisfaction, and sociability should all be affected. Also, the manipulation of the independent variables, assigning greater responsibility and decision freedom for relevant behavior, allowed subjects real choices that were not directed toward a single behavior or stimulus condition. This manipulation tested the ability of the subjects to generalize from specific choices enumerated for them to other aspects of their lives, and thus tested the generalizability of feelings of control over certain elements of the situation to more broadly based behavior and attitudes.

Method

Subjects

The study was conducted in a nursing home, which was rated by the state of Connecticut as being among the finest care units and offering quality medical, recreational, and residential facilities. The home was large and modern in design, appearing cheerful and comfortable as well as clean and efficient. Of the four floors in the home, two were selected for study because of similarity in the residents' physical and psychological health and prior socioeconomic status, as determined from evaluations made by the home's director, head nurses, and social worker. Residents were assigned to a particular floor and room simply on the basis of availability, and, on the average, residents on the two floors had been at the home about the same length of time. Rather than randomly assigning subjects to experimental treatment, a different floor was randomly selected for each treatment. Since there was not a great deal of communication between floors, this procedure was followed in order to decrease the likelihood that the treatment effects would be contaminated. There were 8 males and 39 females in the responsibility-induced condition (all fourth-floor residents) and 9 males and 35 females in the comparison group (all second-floor residents). Residents who were either completely bedridden or judged by the nursing home staff to be completely noncommunicative (11 on the experimental floor and 9 on the comparison floor) were omitted from the sample. Also omitted was one woman on each floor, one 40 years old and the other 26 years old, due to their age. Thus, 91 ambulatory adults, ranging in age from 65 to 90, served as subjects.

Procedure

To introduce the experimental treatment, the nursing home administrator, an outgoing and friendly 33-year-old male who interacts with the residents daily, called a meeting in the lounge of each floor. He delivered one of the following two communications at that time:

> [*Responsibility-induced group*] I brought you together today to give you some information about Arden House. I was surprised to learn that many of you don't know about the things that are available to you and more important, that many of you don't realize the influence you have over your own lives here. Take a minute to think of the decisions you can and should be making.
>
> For example, you have the responsibility of caring for yourselves, of deciding whether or not you want to make this a home you can be proud of and happy in. You should be deciding how you want your rooms to be arranged—whether you want it to be as it is or whether you want the staff to help you rearrange the furniture. You should be deciding how you want to spend your time, for example, whether you want to be visiting your friends who live on this floor or on other floors, whether you want to visit in your room or your friends' room, in the lounge, the dining room, etc., or whether you want to be watching television, listening to the radio, writing, reading, or planning social events. In other words, it's your life and you can make of it whatever you want.
>
> This brings me to another point. If you are unsatisfied with anything here, you have the influence to change it. It's your responsibility to make your complaints known, to tell us what you would like to change, to tell us what you would like. These are just a few of the things you could and should be deciding and thinking about now and from time to time everyday. You made these decisions before you came here and you can and should be making them now.
>
> We're thinking of instituting some way for airing complaints, suggestions, etc. Let [nurse's name] know if you think this is a good idea and how you think we should go about doing it. In any case let her know what your complaints or suggestions are.
>
> Also, I wanted to take this opportunity to give you each a present from the Arden House. [A box of small plants was passed around, and patients were given two decisions to make: first, whether or not they wanted a plant at all, and second, to choose which one they wanted. All residents did select a plant.] The plants are yours to keep and take care of as you'd like.
>
> One last thing, I wanted to tell you that we're showing a movie two nights next week, Thursday and Friday. You should decide which night you'd like to go, if you choose to see it at all.
>
> [*Comparison group*] I brought you together today to give you some information about the Arden House. I was surprised to learn that many of you don't know about the things that are available to you; that many of you don't realize all you're allowed to do here. Take a minute to think of all the options that we've provided for you in order for your life to be fuller and more interesting. For example, you're permitted to visit people on the other floors and to use the lounge on this floor for visiting as well as the dining room or your own rooms. We want your rooms to be as nice as they can be, and we've tried to make them that way for you. We want you to be happy here. We feel that it's our responsibility to make this a home you can be proud of and happy in, and we want to do all can to help you.
>
> This brings me to another point. If you have any complaints or suggestions about anything, let [nurse's name] know what they are. Let us know how we can best help you. You should feel that you have free access to anyone on the staff and we will do the best we can to provide individualized attention and time for you.
>
> Also, I wanted to take this opportunity to give you each a present from the Arden House. [The nurse walked around with a box of plants and each patient was handed one.] The plants are yours to

keep. The nurses will water and care for them for you.

One last thing, I wanted to tell you that we're showing a movie next week on Thursday and Friday. We'll let you know later which day you're scheduled to see it.

The major difference between the two communications was that on one floor, the emphasis was on the residents' responsibility for themselves, whereas on the other floor, the communication stressed the staff's responsibility for them. In addition, several other differences bolstered this treatment: Residence in the responsibility-induced group were asked to give their opinion of the means by which complaints were handled rather than just being told that any complaints would be handled by staff members; they were given the opportunity to select their own plant and to care for it themselves, rather than being given a plant to be taken care of by someone else; and they were given their choice a movie night, rather than being assigned a particular night, as was typically the case in the old age home. However, there was no difference in the amount of attention paid to the two groups.

Three days after these communications had been delivered, the director visited all of the residents in their rooms or in the corridor and reiterated part of the previous message. To those in the responsibility-induced group he said, "Remember what I said last Thursday. We want you to be happy. Treat this like your own home and make all the decisions you used to make. How's your plant coming along?" To the residents of the comparison floor, he said the same thing omitting the statement about decision making.

Dependent Variables

Questionnaires. Two types of questionnaire designed to assess the effects of induced responsibility. Each was administered 1 week prior to and 3 weeks after the communication. The first was administered directly to the residents by a female research assistant who was unaware of the experimental hypotheses or of the specific experimental treatment. The questions dealt with how much control they felt over general events in their lives and how happy and active they felt. Questions were responded to along 8-point scales ranging from 1 (none) to 8 (total). After completing each interview, the research assistant rated the resident on an 8-point scale for alertness.

The second questionnaire was responded to by the nurses, who staffed the experimental and comparison floors and who were unaware of the experimental treatments. Nurses on two different shifts completed the questionnaires in order to obtain two ratings for each subject. There were nine 10-point scales that asked for ratings of how happy, alert, dependent, sociable, and active the residents were as well as questions about their eating and sleeping habits. There were also questions evaluating the proportion of weekly time the patient spent engaged in a variety of activities. These included reading, watching television, visiting other patients, visiting outside guests, watching the staff, talking to the staff, sitting alone doing nothing, and others.

Behavioral measures. Since perceived personal control is enhanced by a sense of choice over relevant behaviors, the option to choose which night the experimental group wished to see the movie was expected to have measurable effects on active participation. Attendance records were kept by the occupational therapist, who was unaware that an experiment was being conducted.

Another measure of involvement was obtained by holding a competition in which all participants had to guess the number of jelly beans in a large jar. Each patient wishing to enter the contest simply wrote his or her name and estimate on a piece of paper and deposited it in a box that was next to the jar.[1]

Finally, an unobtrusive measure of activity was taken. The tenth night after the experimental treatment, the right wheels of the wheelchairs belonging to a randomly selected subsample of each patient group were covered with 2 inches (.05 m) of white adhesive tape. The following night, the tape was removed from the chairs and placed on index cards for later evaluation of amount of activity, as indicated by the amount of discoloration.

Results

Questionnaires. Before examining whether or not the experimental treatment was effective, the pretest ratings made by the subjects, the nurses, and the interviewer were compared for both groups. None of the differences approached significance, which indicates comparability between groups prior to the start of the investigation.

The means for responses to the various questionnaires are summarized in Table 24.1. Statistical tests compared the posttest minus pretest scores of the experimental and comparison groups.

In response to direct questions about how happy they currently were, residents in the responsibility-induced group reported significantly greater increases in happiness after the experimental treatment than did the comparison group, $t(43) = 1.96$, $p < .05$.[2] Although the comparison group heard a communication that had specifically stressed the home's commitment to making them happy, only 25% of them reported feeling happier by the time of the second interview, whereas 48% of the experimental group did so.

The responsibility-induced group reported themselves to be significantly more active on the second interview than the comparison group, $t(43) = 2.67, p < .01$. The interviewer's ratings of alertness also showed significantly greater increase for the experimental group, $t(43) = 2.40, p < .025$. However, the questions that were relevant to perceived control showed no significant changes for the experimental group. Since over 20% of the patients indicated that they were unable to understand what we meant by control, these questions were obviously not adequate to discriminate between groups.

The second questionnaire measured nurses' ratings of each patient. The correlation between the two nurses' ratings of the same patient was .68 and .61 ($ps < .005$) on the comparison and responsibility-induced floors, respectively.[3] For each patient, a score was calculated by averaging the two nurses' ratings for each question, summing across questions, and subtracting the total pretreatment score from the total posttreatment score.[4] This yielded a positive average total change score of 3.97 for the responsibility-induced group as compared with an average negative total change of -2.37 for the comparison group. The difference between these means is highly significant, $t(50) = 5.18, p < .005$. If one looks at the percentage of people who were judged improved rather than at the amount of judged improvement, the same pattern emerges: 93% of the experimental group (all but one subject) were considered improved, whereas only 21% (6 subjects) of the comparison group showed this positive change ($\chi^2 = 19.23$, $p < .005$).

The nurses' evaluation of the proportion of time subjects spent engaged in various interactive and noninteractive activities was analyzed by comparing the average change scores (post–precommunication) for all of the nurses for both groups of subjects on each activity. Several significant differences were found. The experimental group showed increases in the proportion of

Table 24.1. Mean Scores for Self-Report, Interviewer Ratings, and Nurses' Ratings for Experimental and Comparison Groups

Questionnaire responses	Responsibility induced ($n = 24$)			Comparison ($n = 28$)			Comparison of change scores ($p <$)
	Pre	Post	Change: post–pre	Pre	Post	Change: post–pre	
Self-report							
Happy	5.16	5.44	.28	4.90	4.78	−.12	.05
Active	4.07	4.27	.20	3.90	2.62	−1.28	.01
Perceived control							
Have	3.26	3.42	.16	3.62	4.03	.41	—
Want	3.85	3.80	−.05	4.40	4.57	.17	—
Interviewer rating							
Alertness	5.02	5.31	.29	5.75	5.38	−.37	.025
Nurses' ratings							
General improvement	41.67	45.64	3.97	42.69	40.32	-2.39	.005
Time spent							
Visiting patients	13.03	19.81	6.78	7.94	4.65	−3.30	.005
Visiting others	11.50	13.75	2.14	12.38	8.21	−4.16	.05
Talking to staff	8.21	16.43	8.21	9.11	10.71	1.61	.01
Watching staff	6.78	4.64	−2.14	6.96	11.60	4.64	.05

time spent visiting with other patients (for the experimental group, $\bar{X} = 12.86$ vs. -6.61 for the comparison group, $t(50) = 3.83$, $p < .005$; visiting people from outside of the nursing home (for the experimental group, $\bar{X} = 4.28$ vs. -7.61 for the comparison group, $t(50) = 2.30$, $p < .05$, and talking to the staff (for the experimental group, $\bar{X} = 8.21$ vs. 1.61 for the comparison group), $t(50) = 2.98$, $p < .05$.[5] In addition, they spent less time passively watching the staff (for the experimental group, $\bar{X} = -4$ vs. 9.68 for the comparison group), $t(50) = 2.60$, $p < .05$. Thus, it appears that the treatment increased active, interpersonal activity but not passive activity such as watching television or reading.

Behavioral measures. As in the case of the questionnaires, the behavioral measures showed a pattern of differences between groups that was generally consistent with the predicted effects of increased responsibility. The movie attendance was significantly high in the responsibility-induced group than in the control group after the experimental treatment ($z = 1.71$, $p < .05$, one-tailed), although a similar attendance check taken one month before the communications revealed no group differences.[6]

In the jelly-bean-guessing contest, 10 subjects (21%) in the responsibility-induced group and only 1 subject (2%) from the comparison group participated ($\chi^2 = 7.72$, $p < .01$). Finally, very little dirt was found on the tape taken from any of the patients' wheelchairs, and there was no significant difference between the two groups.

Discussion

It appears that inducing a greater sense of personal responsibility in people who may have virtually relinquished decision making, either by choice or necessity, produces improvement. In the present investigation, patients in the comparison group were given a communication stressing the staff's desire to make them happy and were otherwise treated in the sympathetic manner characteristic of this high-quality nursing home. Despite the care provided for these people, 71% were rated as having become more debilitated over a period of time as short as 3 weeks. In contrast with this group, 93% of the people who were encouraged to make decisions for themselves, given decisions to make, and given responsibility for something outside of themselves actually showed overall improvement. Based on their own judgments and by the judgments of the nurses with whom they interacted on a daily basis, they became more active and felt happier. Perhaps more important was the judged improvement in their mental alertness and increased behavioral involvement in many different kinds of activities.

The behavioral measures showed greater active participation and involvement for the experimental group. Whether this directly resulted from an increase in perceived choice and decision-making responsibility or from the increase in general activity and happiness occurring after the treatment cannot be assessed from the present results. It should also be clearly noted that although there were significant differences in active involvement, the overall level of participation in the activities that comprised the behavioral measures was low. Perhaps a much more powerful treatment would be one that is individually administered and repeated on several occasions. That so weak a manipulation had any effect suggests how important increased control is for these people, for whom decision making is virtually nonexistent.

The practical implications of this experimental demonstration are straightforward. Mechanisms can and should be established for changing situational factors that reduce real or perceived responsibility in the elderly. Furthermore, this study adds to the body of literature (Bengston, 1973; Butler, 1967; Leaf, 1973; Lieberman, 1965) suggesting that senility and diminished alertness are not an almost inevitable result of aging. In fact, it suggests that some of the negative consequences of aging may be retarded, reversed, or possibly prevented by returning to the aged the right to make decisions and a feeling of competence.

ACKNOWLEDGMENT

The authors would like to express sincere thanks to Thomas Tolisano and the members of his staff at the Arden House in Hamden, Connecticut, for their thoughtful assistance in conducting this research.

NOTES

1. We also intended to measure the number of complaints that patients voiced. Since one often does not complain after becoming psychologically helpless, complaints in this

context were expected to be a positive indication of perceived personal control. This measure was discarded, however, since the nurses failed to keep a systematic written record.
2. All of the statistics for the self-report data and the interviewers' ratings are based on 45 subjects (25 in the responsibility-induced group and 20 in the comparison group), since these were the only subjects available at the time of the interview.
3. There was also significant agreement between the interviewer's and nurses' ratings of alertness ($r = .65$).
4. Since one nurse on the day shift and one nurse on the night shift gave the ratings, responses to questions regarding sleeping and eating habits were not included in the total score. Also, in order to reduce rater bias, patients for whom there were ratings by a nurse on only one shift were excluded from this calculation. This left 24 residents from the experimental group and 28 from the comparison group.
5. This statistic is based only on the responses nurse on duty in the evening.
6. Frequencies were transformed into arcsines analyzed using the method that is essentially the same as that described by Langer and Abelson (1972).

REFERENCE NOTE

1. Lehr, K., & Puschner, I. *Studies in the awareness of aging.* Paper presented at the 6th International Congress on Gerontology, Copenhagen, 1963.

REFERENCES

Adamson, J., & Schmale, A. (1965). Object loss, giving up, and the onset of psychiatric disease. *Psychosomatic Medicine, 27,* 557–576.
Adler, A. (1930). Individual psychology. In C. Murchinson (Ed.), *Psychologies of 1930.* Worcester, MA: Clark University Press.
Bengston, V. L. (1973). Self determination: A social and psychological perspective on helping the aged. *Geriatrics.*
Bettelheim, B. (1943). Individual and mass behavior in extreme situations. *Journal of Abnormal and Social Psychology, 38,* 417–452.
Birren, J. (1958). Aging and psychological adjustment. *Review of Educational Research, 28,* 475–490.
Bowers, K. (1968). Pain, anxiety, and perceived control. *Journal of Consulting and Clinical Psychology, 32,* 596–602.
Butler, R. (1967). Aspects of survival and adaptation in human aging. *American Journal of Psychiatry, 123,* 1233–1243.
Corah, N., & Boffa, J. (1970). Perceived control, self-observation, and response to aversive stimulation. *Journal of Personality and Social Psychology, 16,* 1–4.
de Charms, R. (1968). *Personal causation.* New York: Academic Press.

Geer, J., Davison, G., & Gatchel, R. (1970). Reduction of stress in humans through nonveridical perceived control of aversive stimulation. *Journal of Personality and Social Psychology, 16,* 731–738.
Glass, D., & Singer, J. (1972). *Urban stress.* New York: Academic Press.
Gould, R. (1972). The phases of adult life: A study in developmental psychology. *American Journal of Psychiatry, 129,* 521–531.
Kanfer, R., & Seidner, M. (1973). Self-control: Factors enhancing tolerance of noxious stimulation. *Journal of Personality and Social Psychology, 25,* 381–389.
Langer, E. J. (1975). The illusion of control. *Journal of Personality and Social Psychology, 32,* 311–328.
Langer, E. J., & Abelson, R. P. (1972). The semantics of asking a favor: How to succeed in getting help without really dying. *Journal of Personality and Social Psychology, 24,* 26–32.
Langer, E. J., Janis, I. L., & Wolfer, J. A. (1975). Reduction of psychological stress in surgical patients. *Journal of Experimental Social Psychology, 11,* 155–165.
Leaf, A. (1973). Threescore and forty. *Hospital Practice, 34,* 70–71.
Lefcourt, H. (1973). The function of the illusion of control and freedom. *American Psychologist, 28,* 417–425.
Lieberman, M. (1965). Psychological correlates of impending death: Some preliminary observations. *Journal of Gerontology, 20,* 181–190.
McMahon, A., & Rhudick, P. (1964). Reminiscing, adaptational significance in the aged. *Archives of General Psychiatry, 10,* 292–298.
Neugarten, B., & Gutman, D. (1958). Age-sex roles and personality in middle age: A thematic apperception study. *Psychological Monographs, 72*(17; Whole No. 470).
Pervin, L. (1963). The need to predict and control under conditions of threat. *Journal of Personality, 31,* 570–585.
Richter, C. (1957). On the phenomenon of sudden death in animals and man. *Psychosomatic Medicine, 19,* 191–198.
Rodin, J. (in press). Crowding, perceived choice, and response to controllable and uncontrollable outcomes. *Journal of Experimental Social Psychology.*
Schmale, A. (1958). Relationships of separation and depression to disease. I.: A report on a hospitalized medical population. *Psychosomatic Medicine, 20,* 259–277.
Schmale, A., & Iker, H. (1966). The psychological setting uterine cervical cancer. *Annals of the New York Academy of Sciences, 125,* 807–813.
Seligman, M. E. P. (1975). *Helplessness.* San Francisco: Freeman.
Stotland, E., & Blumenthal, A. (1964). The reduction of anxiety as a result of the expectation of making a choice. *Canadian Review of Psychology, 18,* 139–145.
Zimbardo, P. G., & Ruch, F. L. (1975). *Psychology and life* (9th ed.). Glenview, IL: Scott, Foresman.

Discussion Questions

1. Would the positive relationship between perceived control and psychological well-being differ for people who are low versus high in their overall need for control?
2. Why do you think it is primarily the perception of control that is important as opposed to actually having control?
3. In your own life, what factors undermine your sense of control over your environment? What do you do to restore a sense of control?
4. Imagine that you are a therapist. A client who is experiencing learned helplessness and who feels completely out of control in every aspect of his life comes to you for assistance. What do you say to this client?
5. Can you think of ways in which the medical profession has tried to increase patients' sense of control to decrease the aversiveness of medical procedures?

Suggested Readings

Janoff-Bulman, R., & Marshall, G. (1982). Mortality, well-being, and control: A study of a population of institutionalized aged. *Personality and Social Psychology Bulletin, 8,* 691–698. This study examined predictors of well-being among the elderly. Control was found to be a significant predictor.

Lefcourt, H. M., & Davidson-Katz, K. (1991). Locus of control and health. In C. R. Snyder & D. R. Forsyth (Eds.), *Handbook of social and clinical psychology: The health perspective* (pp. 246–266). New York: Pergamon. This chapter reviews the literature on control and its relationship with health outcomes.

Rodin, J., & Langer, E. J. (1977). Long-term effects of a control-relevant intervention with institutionalized aged. *Journal of Personality and Social Psychology, 35,* 897–902. This is the follow-up study to the article you just read, which examined the long-term benefits of perceived control.

Schulz, R. (1976). The effects of control and predictability on the psychological and physical well-being of the institutionalized aged. *Journal of Personality and Social Psychology, 33,* 563–573. This study provides another illustration of the role of control in influencing the physical and psychological health of the aged.

READING 25

The Trouble With Change: Self-Verification and Allegiance to the Self

William B. Swann, Jr. • University of Texas at Austin

Editors' Introduction

The ultimate goal of all counseling and psychotherapy is psychological change. Clients seek professional help because they want relief from some problem, and the job of the practicing psychologist is to help the client to modify his or her problematic thoughts, emotions, or behaviors in a desired direction. Thus, researchers have been interested in understanding factors that facilitate and interfere with therapeutic change. What stumbling blocks lie in the client's way on the road to psychological well-being? William Swann, Jr., suggests that one such stumbling block involves the motive to self-verify. According to Swann's self-verification theory, people are motivated to maintain their existing views of themselves. People's perceptions of who they are and what they are like play an important role in their lives. Their self-perceptions guide their decisions and behavior, allow them to predict other people's reactions to them, and help to organize their perceptions of reality. Because their self-perceptions are important to functioning in everyday life, changes in people's self-views may make them feel uncertain and anxious, and lead them to behave less effectively. For this reason, people try to maintain their existing views of themselves, and they may do so even when those self-views are outdated, inaccurate, or a source of personal distress.

Research by Swann and others has documented the ways in which people strive to maintain consistent self-views. For example, people prefer to interact with those who see them as they see themselves, and they work harder to maintain close relationships with romantic partners who verify their self-views. When people receive information that threatens to discredit their self-perceptions, they may misinterpret or misremember it to be more consistent with their self-image than it really is. Perhaps most surprisingly, people who see themselves negatively may seek out negative information and misinterpret positive information about themselves in order to verify their existing negative self-images.

In this article, Swann applies self-verification theory to psychotherapy. As he points out, therapy often involves trying to get clients to adopt new views of themselves. Particularly when the client's self-image is part of his or her problem, as in the case of depression, eating disorders, and feeling unloved, the therapist understandably wants to modify the client's self-beliefs in a positive direction. Yet, according to self-verification theory, the therapist's efforts will often run up against the client's desire to maintain his or her existing image. Recognizing this, an effective therapist must work within the framework of the client's self-concept, even if it is negative. In fact, research suggests that clients with negative self-views may benefit most if therapists validate the clients' shortcomings rather than try to provide positive feedback that is inconsistent with their self-concepts. Self-verification theory offers many suggestions for how to provide clients with feedback in a way that pushes their self-images in a desired direction.

Abstract

Past approaches to the self have emphasized people's desire for positive evaluations. I suggest that this emphasis overlooks another powerful and important motive, the desire for evaluations that verify self-views. Among people with negative self-views, this desire for self-verification can override the desire for positive evaluations. For example, people with negative self-views seek relationship partners who view them negatively, elicit unfavorable evaluations from partners, and "see" more negativity in the reactions of others than is actually there. Although these self-verification processes ordinarily impede progress in therapy, awareness of these processes can allow therapists to either circumvent them or actually use them in the service of fostering self-concept change.

For Ms. W, suffering and victimization were in some respects preferable to kindness and concern. Ms. W not only misperceived that Mr. S was unfaithful but also resisted any information that contradicted her misperception and actively sought verification that he was unfaithful. The better he treated her, the more depressed and pessimistic she became [for] she was threatened by a caring and loving partner. She accepted her past abuse as an appropriate reflection of her worth. A challenge to this self-image was a challenge to how she adapted and coped with her victimization. (Widiger, 1988, p. 821)

The responses of Ms. W seem paradoxical because they defy the widespread conviction that all people possess a deep-seated need for praise and adulation. It turns out that although people with negative self-views do at some level desire praise and adoration, they also want *self-verification* in the form of evaluations that confirm and validate their self-views. This desire for self-confirmation appears to be an exceedingly general one, one that shapes the lives of all of us, whether we have high or low self-esteem. In fact, it does not matter whether people's self-views are positive or negative, well-founded or misplaced, or based on something that happened during the previous year or in the distant past: Once people become confident of their self-views, they rely on these self-views to predict the reactions of others, to guide behavior, and to organize their conceptions of reality (e.g., Mead, 1934). Because self-views must be stable to serve these vital functions, people work to verify and confirm them (e.g., Aronson, 1968; Secord & Backman, 1965; Swann, 1983, 1996). These self-verification strivings may operate consciously or nonconsciously and may take several distinct forms.

Forms of Self-Verification

An especially important form of self-verification occurs when people choose partners who see them as they see themselves, thereby creating social environments that are likely to support their self-views. In one study, for example, we asked people with positive and negative self-views whether they would prefer to interact with evaluators who had favorable or unfavorable impressions of them. As can be seen in Figure 25.1, people with positive self-views preferred favorable partners, and people with negative self-views preferred unfavorable partners (e.g., Swann, Stein-Seroussi, & Giesler, 1992).

More than a dozen replications in different laboratories using diverse methodologies have left little doubt that people with negative self-views seek unfavorable feedback and partners (e.g., Hixon & Swann, 1993; Robinson & Smith-Lovin, 1992; Swann, Hixon, Stein-Seroussi, & Gilbert, 1990; Swann, Pelham, & Krull, 1989; Swann, Wenzlaff, Krull, & Pelham, 1992). Males and females display this propensity to an equal degree, regardless of the degree to which the self-views are changeable or whether they are associated with specific qualities (intelligence, sociability, dominance) or global self-worth (self-esteem, depression). Similarly, people prefer to interact with self-verifying partners even if presented with the alternative of participating in a different experiment (Swann,

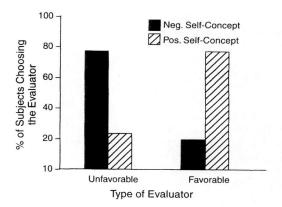

FIGURE 25.1 ■ Preferences for favorable versus unfavorable interaction partners among people with positive (pos.) versus negative (neg.) self-concepts. The data on which this figure is based are from Swann, Stein-Seroussi, and Giesler (1992).

Wenzlaff, & Tafarodi, 1992). Finally, people are particularly likely to seek self-verifying evaluations if their self-views are extreme and firmly held (e.g., Pelham & Swann, 1994; Swann, Pelham, & Chidester, 1988; Swann & Ely, 1984). Clinically depressed persons, for example, are more likely to seek negative evaluations than people with low self-esteem, presumably because depressives are thoroughly convinced that they are worthless (Giesler, Josephs, & Swann, 1996).

People's efforts to verify their negative self-views should not be confused with masochism. For example, rather than savoring unfavorable evaluations (as one might expect masochists to do), people with negative self-views are intensely ambivalent about such evaluations. In choosing a negative evaluator in one study (Swann, Stein-Seroussi, & Giesler, 1992), one person with low esteem noted:

> I like the [favorable] evaluation but I am not sure that it is, ah, correct, maybe. It *sounds* good, but [the unfavorable evaluator] . . . seems to know more about me. So, I'll choose [the unfavorable evaluator].

The thoughts that give rise to such ambivalence emerge sequentially. Upon receiving and categorizing positive feedback, people are immediately drawn to it, regardless of their self-views. A preference for self-confirming feedback emerges later when people access their self-views and compare these self-views to feedback (for a further discussion of the mechanisms that seem to underlie self-verification effects, see Swann, 1996, pp. 55–69).

The foregoing analysis implies that any procedure that prevents people from engaging in the comparison process that gives rise to self-verification strivings should cause people with negative self-views to prefer favorable appraisals. In support of this proposition, when my colleagues and I (Swann et al., 1990) had some people choose an interaction partner while they were deprived of cognitive resources (by rushing their decision or having them rehearse a phone number), we found that people with negative self-views were less inclined to self-verify (i.e., choose a partner who appraised them unfavorably). Furthermore, after participants were no longer deprived of cognitive resources, they repudiated their earlier choices in favor of self-verifying ones. Such findings suggest that when people with negative self-views choose unfavorable feedback over favorable feedback, it is because their desire for self-verifying unfavorable feedback overrides their desire for favorable feedback.[1]

Recent work indicates that if, despite their attempts to acquire self-verifying feedback, people receive doses of self-discrepant feedback that cannot be readily dismissed, they become anxious (Pinel & Swann, 1996). In extreme cases, people may experience what Kohut (1984) referred to as disintegration anxiety, a sinking feeling that something is terribly wrong accompanied by severe disorientation and a sense of emptiness, incoherence, and worthlessness.

In light of the obvious aversiveness of disintegration anxiety, it is not surprising that people who receive disconfirming feedback take steps to counter it. For example, when people suspect that others perceive them as being more or less likable than they perceive themselves to be, they strive to bring the partners' evaluations into harmony with their self-views, even if (in the case of people with low self-esteem) this means lowering the partners' evaluations (e.g., Swann & Read, 1981, Study 2). Such compensatory activity, in turn, stabilizes people's self-views against self-discrepant feedback. In one study, for instance, people who had an opportunity to resist a challenge to their self-views by "setting the evaluator straight" were less likely to experience change in their self-views than those who had no opportunity to correct the evaluator (e.g., Swann & Hill, 1982).

Should the foregoing strategies fail to produce self-confirming social worlds, people may withdraw from the relationships in which they are receiving disconfirming feedback. For example, if people wind up in marriages in which their spouses perceive them more (or less) favorably than they perceive themselves, they become less intimate with those spouses (Ritts & Stein, 1995; Swann, De La Ronde, & Hixon, 1994).

If self-discrepant feedback is unavoidable, people may construct the illusion of self-confirming worlds by "seeing" more support for their self-views than actually exists. For example, just as people with positive self-views spend the longest time scrutinizing what someone says about them when they expect the remarks will be favorable, those with negative self-views spend the longest time scrutinizing when they expect the remarks will be unfavorable (e.g., Swann & Read, 1981, Study 1). A parallel phenomenon emerges when researchers examine what people remember about the evaluations they receive: Just as people with positive self-views remember more favorable than unfavorable statements that have been made about them, people with negative self-views remember more unfavorable than favorable statements (e.g., Swann & Read, 1981, Study 3).

And if these attentional and memorial processes are not enough to insulate people against evaluations that challenge their self-views, people may nullify discrepant evaluations by selectively dismissing incongruent feedback. For example, people express more confidence in the perceptiveness of evaluators whose appraisals confirm their self-conceptions (e.g., Shrauger & Lund, 1975).

In conjunction with the processes already outlined, such selective dismissal of challenging feedback may systematically skew people's perceptions of reality, encouraging them to conclude that their social worlds are far more supportive of their self-views than is warranted. Although these processes may stabilize people's self-views and foster feelings of coherence and predictability, they are also likely to impede positive psychological change.

Implications of Self-verification Processes for Therapy

Imagine a woman who seeks therapy in the hope of removing the self-doubt that has plagued her since her youth. Although the therapist may succeed in bringing her to acknowledge and derive a feeling of pride from her strengths, she may also discover that these positive self-views are undone when she returns home to a husband who is contemptuous of her. Such a scenario is not just hypothetical. In one study, Predmore and I invited couples to the laboratory and seated partners in a room together. Some intimates perceived their partner congruently and some perceived their partner less congruently. At a key point in the procedure, we gave one member of each couple incongruent feedback. When we later measured how much people's self-views changed in the direction of the feedback, we found that participants were relatively impervious to the feedback if they were sitting with an intimate who saw them congruently. This tendency for congruent relationship partners to insulate one another against challenging feedback was equally apparent whether their self-views were positive or negative (Swann & Predmore, 1985).

Such evidence suggests an important addendum to Mark Twain's adage "A man cannot be comfortable without his own approval." To establish and sustain positive self-views, people must not only gain their own approval, they must also gain the approval and support of certain key interaction partners, including friends, coworkers, lovers, and relatives. In this sense, self-views are not merely psychological structures that exist inside people, as their hearts, lungs, or livers do; rather, through people's interactions, their self-views become externalized into the social worlds that they construct around themselves. As a result, when patients enter therapy in the hope of improving their self-views, their therapists' efforts to convince them that they are lovable and competent may be undone when they return home to lovers or family members who dismiss them. And if therapists do manage to instill a sense of self-worth that is resilient against challenges, patients' partners may respond by encouraging the patients to revert back to their former selves, withdraw from therapy, or both (e.g., Kerr, 1981; Wachtel & Wachtel, 1986).

But intimates who have unfavorable impressions of their partners may do more than stabilize their partners' negative self-views. Because intimates tend to assume that their partners' shortcomings reflect on *them*, they may be highly intolerant of such shortcomings and actively reject partners whom they perceive to suffer from such shortcomings (e.g., Swann et al., 1994). This means that when people with negative self-views choose intimates who see them as they see themselves, they increase the chance that their intimates will reject them in a general way. Such rejecting intimates may even go so far as to verbally and physically abuse them: Women with low self-esteem seem to be particularly apt to marry men who are high in negative instrumentality (i.e., who are hostile, egotistical, dictatorial, arrogant). Women involved with such men are especially apt to report being physically abused (Buckner & Swann, 1995).

The therapeutic context may provide one way out of this conundrum. Because therapists do not feel that the shortcomings of their patients reflect on them, therapists are in a good position to validate their patients' shortcomings (i.e., provide negative feedback) in a supportive and accepting context. When administered in such a context, negative feedback may actually be beneficial. Finn and Tonsager (1992), for example, established warm and supportive relationships with patients and then gave those patients feedback that confirmed their self-views. Two weeks later, patients who had received congruent feedback displayed better psychological functioning and higher self-esteem than a no-feedback control group—despite the fact that the congruent feedback was sometimes decidedly negative (e.g., "you are depressed, thought disordered, angry, obsessional"). Patients seemed to benefit enormously from the perception that "you seem to know all my shortcomings but still like me."[2]

Why are confirming, negative evaluations beneficial? One reason is that congruent feedback may increase people's perceptions that they are competent in at least one sphere: knowing themselves. This realization may foster a feeling of psycho-epistemological competence, a sense of mastery, and heightened perceptions of predictability and control—perceptions that may reduce anxiety. In addition, being understood by a therapist may reduce feelings of alienation, for it tells patients that someone thought enough of them to learn who they are. For these and related reasons, when provided in a supportive context, self-verifying feedback may have beneficial effects, even when it is negative (see also Linehan, in press).

Another approach that therapists may use is to employ the self-verification strivings of patients in the service of changing their self-views. In one study, for instance, my colleagues and I capitalized on the tendency for people to resist feedback that disconfirms their self-views. We asked people questions that were so conservative (e.g., "Why do you think men always make better bosses than women?") that even staunch conservatives resisted the premises inherent in the questions. Upon observing themselves take a somewhat liberal position, these conservative participants adjusted their attitudes in a liberal direction (Swann et al., 1988). This effect is conceptually related to *paradoxical* techniques in which therapists impute to patients qualities that are more extreme than the patients' actual qualities (e.g., characterizing an unassertive person as a complete doormat) in the hope that the patients will behaviorally resist the innuendo (e.g., become more assertive) and adopt corresponding self-views (e.g., Watzlawick, Weakland, & Fisch, 1974).

There are, of course, additional strategies that may be exploited in attempting to change people's self-views. The more general point here, however, is that therapists who are interested in changing self-views should recognize that people's desire for positive evaluations may sometimes be overridden by a desire for self-verification. The desire for self-verification may compel people to work to maintain their positive—and negative—self-views by embracing confirming feedback, eschewing disconfirming feedback, and surrounding themselves with friends, intimates, and associates who act as accomplices in maintaining their self-views. Research on the nature, underpinnings, and boundary conditions of such self-verification strivings may thus provide insight into the widely reported phenomenon of *resistance*—the tendency for patients in therapy to resist positive change. In so doing, such research may pave the way for the development of intervention strategies that accommodate or exploit self-verification strivings rather than being sabotaged by them.

ACKNOWLEDGMENTS

I am grateful to Stephen Finn, Mike Gill, Liz Pinel, and Stephanie Rude for commenting on an earlier version of this article. This project was supported by a grant from the National Science Foundation (SBR-9319570).

NOTES

1. The second stage that gives rise to self-verification strivings may later be overridden during a third stage in which people's responses are based on a cost-benefit analysis of characteristics of the feedback, their self-views, and the social context. Hence, there appear to be at least three distinct phases in people's reactions to feedback: an initial phase characterized by a preference for positive feedback, a second phase characterized by a preference for congruent feedback, and a final phase during which people systematically analyze the options available to them and behave so as to maximize their benefits and minimize their costs. For a further discussion, see Swann and Schroeder (1995).
2. Although such comments seem to suggest that people with negative self-views want others to verify their specific shortcomings but accept them in general, it could be that this desire for global acceptance is characteristic only of those people with negative self-views who seek therapy. Alternately, a desire for global acceptance may manifest itself only after people receive such acceptance. More research on this issue is needed.

REFERENCES

Aronson, E. (1968). A theory of cognitive dissonance: A current perspective. In L. Berkowitz (Ed.), *Advances in experimental social psychology* (Vol. 4, pp. 1–34). New York: Academic Press.

Buckner, C. E., & Swann, W. B., Jr. (1995, August). *Physical abuse in close relationships: The dynamic interplay of couple characteristics*. Paper presented at the annual meeting of the American Psychological Association, Washington, DC.

Finn, S. E., & Tonsager, M. E. (1992). Therapeutic impact of providing MMPI-2 feedback to college students awaiting therapy. *Journal of Psychological Assessment, 4*, 278–287.

Giesler, R. B., Josephs, R. A., & Swann, W. B., Jr. (1996). Self-verification in clinical depression: The desire for negative evaluation. *Journal of Abnormal Psychology, 105*, 358–368.

Hixon, J. G., & Swann, W. B., Jr. (1993). When does introspection bear fruit? Self-reflection, self-insight, and interpersonal choices. *Journal of Personality and Social Psychology, 64*, 35–43.

Kerr, M. E. (1981). Family systems theory and therapy. In A. S. Gurman & D. P. Kiskern (Eds.), *Handbook of family therapy* (pp. 226–264). New York: Brunner/Mazel.

Kohut, H. (1984). *How does analysis cure?* (A. Goldberg & P.E. Stepansky, Eds.). Chicago: University of Chicago Press.

Linehan, M. M. (in press). Validation and psychotherapy. In A. C. Bohart & L. S. Greenberg (Eds.), *Empathy reconsidered: New directions in psychotherapy*. Washington, DC: American Psychological Association.

Mead, G. H. (1934). *Mind, self and society*. Chicago: University of Chicago Press.

Pelham, B. W., & Swann, W. B., Jr. (1994). The juncture of intrapersonal and interpersonal knowledge: Self-certainty and interpersonal congruence. *Personality and Social Psychology Bulletin, 20,* 349–357.

Pinel, E. C., & Swann, W. B., Jr. (1996). *The cognitive-affective crossfire revisited: Affective reactions to self-discrepant evaluations.* Manuscript submitted for publication.

Ritts, V., & Stein, J. R. (1995). Verification and commitment in marital relationships: An exploration of self-verification theory in community college students. *Psychological Reports, 76,* 383–386.

Robinson, D. T., & Smith-Lovin, L. (1992). Selective interaction as a strategy for identity maintenance: An affect control model. *Social Psychology Quarterly, 55,* 12–28.

Secord, P. F., & Backman, C. W. (1965). An interpersonal approach to personality. In B. Maher (Ed.), *Progress in experimental personality research* (Vol. 2, pp. 91–125). New York: Academic Press.

Shrauger, J. S., & Lund, A. (1975). Self-evaluation and reactions to evaluations from others. *Journal of Personality, 43,* 94–108.

Swann, W. B., Jr. (1983). Self-verification: Bringing social reality into harmony with the self. In J. Suls & A. G. Greenwald (Eds.), *Social Psychological perspectives on the self* (Vol. 2, pp. 33–66). Hillsdale, NJ: Erlbaum.

Swann, W. B., Jr. (1996). *Self-traps: The elusive quest for higher self-esteem.* New York: Freeman.

Swann, W. B., Jr., De La Ronde, C., & Hixon, G. (1994). Authenticity and positivity strivings in marriage and courtship. *Journal of Personality and Social Psychology, 66,* 857–869.

Swann, W. B., Jr., & Ely, R. J. (1984). A battle of wills: Self-verification versus behavioral confirmation. *Journal of Personality and Social Psychology, 46,* 1287–1302.

Swann, W. B., Jr., & Hill, C. A. (1982). When our identities are mistaken: Reaffirming self-conceptions through social interaction. *Journal of Personality and Social Psychology, 43,* 59–66.

Swann, W. B., Jr., Hixon, J. G., Stein-Seroussi, A., & Gilbert, D. T. (1990). The fleeting gleam of praise: Behavioral reactions to self-relevant feedback. *Journal of Personality and Social Psychology, 59,* 17–26.

Swann, W. B., Jr., Pelham, B. W., & Chidester, T. (1988). Change through paradox: Using self-verification to alter beliefs. *Journal of Personality and Social Psychology, 54,* 268–273.

Swann, W. B., Jr., Pelham, B. W., & Krull, D. S. (1989). Agreeable fancy or disagreeable truth? How people reconcile their self-enhancement and self-verification needs. *Journal of Personality and Social Psychology, 57,* 782–791.

Swann, W. B., Jr., & Predmore, S. C. (1985). Intimates as agents of social support: Sources of consolation or despair? *Journal of Personality and Social Psychology, 49,* 1609–1617.

Swann, W. B., Jr., & Read, S. J. (1981). Self-verification processes: How we sustain our self-conceptions. *Journal of Experimental Social Psychology, 17,* 351–372.

Swann, W. B., Jr., & Schroeder, D. G. (1995). The search for beauty and truth: A framework for understanding reactions to evaluations. *Personality and Social Psychology Bulletin, 21,* 1307–1318.

Swann, W. B., Jr., Stein-Seroussi, A., & Giesler, B. (1992). Why people self-verify. *Journal of Personality and Social Psychology, 62,* 392–401.

Swann, W. B., Jr., Wenzlaff, R. M., Krull, D. S., & Pelham, B. W. (1992). The allure of negative feedback: Self-verification strivings among depressed persons. *Journal of Abnormal Psychology, 101,* 293–306.

Swann, W. B., Jr., Wenzlaff, R. M., & Tafarodi, R. W. (1992). Depression and the search for negative evaluations: More evidence of the role of self-verification strivings. *Journal of Abnormal Psychology, 101,* 314–371.

Wachtel, E. F., & Wachtel, P. L. (1986). *Family dynamics in individual psychotherapy: A guide to clinical strategies.* New York: Guilford Press.

Watzlawick, P., Weakland, J. H., & Fisch, R. (1974). *Change: Principles of problem formation and problem resolution.* New York: Norton.

Widiger, T. A. (1988). Treating self-defeating personality disorder. *Hospital and Community Psychiatry, 39,* 819–821.

Discussion Questions

1. People are motivated not only to self-verify (that is, to maintain a consistent self-image) but also to self-enhance (to maintain a positive self image). For people who see themselves positively, these motives work in concert; verifying self-images are also self-enhancing. But for people with negative self-images, these motives may conflict because self-enhancing images are not self-verifying. Discuss how people may deal with this tension between the desire to self-verify and the desire to self-enhance.
2. Imagine that you are a counseling psychologist who is trying to change an adolescent girl's negative self-image. According to this article, what's the best way to approach this task?

3. Research suggests that the desire to self-verify may maintain certain psychological problems such as depression (because depressed individuals resist positive information about themselves that would help alleviate their depression). Speculate regarding at least five emotional or behavioral problems that may be difficult to treat because of self-verification.

Suggested Readings

Giesler, R. B., Josephs, R. A., & Swann, W. B., Jr. (1996). Self-verification in clinical depression: The desire for negative evaluation. *Journal of Abnormal Psychology, 105,* 358–368. This study showed that when given the choice, clinically depressed individuals tend to choose unfavorable rather than favorable feedback about themselves.

Linehan, M. M. (1997). Self-verification and drug abusers: Implications for treatment. *Psychological Science, 8,* 181–183. This commentary discusses implications of self-verification theory for psychotherapy.

Swann, W. B., Stein-Seroussi, A., & Giesler, R. B. (1992). Why people self-verify. *Journal of Personality and Social Psychology, 62,* 392–401. This article describes two studies that examined the question of why people try to maintain consistent images of themselves.

Appendix: How to Read a Journal Article in Social Psychology

Christian H. Jordan and Mark P. Zanna • University of Waterloo

When approaching a journal article for the first time, and often on subsequent occasions, most people try to digest it as they would any piece of prose. They start at the beginning and read word for word, until eventually they arrive at the end, perhaps a little bewildered, but with a vague sense of relief. This is not an altogether terrible strategy; journal articles do have a logical structure that lends itself to this sort of reading. There are, however, more efficient approaches—approaches that enable you, a student of social psychology, to cut through peripheral details, avoid sophisticated statistics with which you may not be familiar, and focus on the central ideas in an article. Arming yourself with a little foreknowledge of what is contained in journal articles, as well as some practical advice on how to read them, should help you read journal articles more effectively. If this sounds tempting, read on.

Journal articles offer a window into the inner workings of social psychology. They document how social psychologists formulate hypotheses, design empirical studies, analyze the observations they collect, and interpret their results. Journal articles also serve an invaluable archival function: They contain the full store of common and cumulative knowledge of social psychology. Having documentation of past research allows researchers to build on past findings and advance our understanding of social behavior, without pursuing avenues of investigation that have already been explored. Perhaps most importantly, a research study is never complete until its results have been shared with others, colleagues and students alike. Journal articles are a primary means of communicating research findings. As such, they can be genuinely exciting and interesting to read.

That last claim may have caught you off guard. For beginning readers, journal articles may seem anything but interesting and exciting. They may, on the contrary, appear daunting and esoteric, laden with jargon and obscured by menacing statistics. Recognizing this fact, we hope to arm you, through this chapter, with the basic information you will need to read journal articles with a greater sense of comfort and perspective.

Social psychologists study many fascinating topics, ranging from prejudice and discrimination, to culture, persuasion, liking and love, conformity and obedience, aggression, and the self. In our daily lives, these are issues we often struggle to understand. Social psychologists present systematic observations of, as well as a wealth of ideas about, such issues in journal articles. It would be a shame if the fascination and intrigue these *topics have were lost in their translation* into journal publications. We don't think they are, and by the end of this chapter, we hope you won't either.

Journal articles come in a variety of forms, including research reports, review articles, and theoretical articles. Put briefly, a *research report* is a formal presentation of an original research study, or series of studies. A *review article* is an evaluative survey of previously published work, usually organized by a guiding theory or point of view. The author of a review article summarizes previous investigations of a circumscribed problem, comments on what progress has been made toward its resolution, and suggests areas of the problem that require further study. A *theoretical article* also evaluates past research, but focuses on the development of theories used to explain empirical findings. Here, the author may present a new theory to explain a set of findings, or may compare and contrast a set of competing theories, suggesting why one theory might be the superior one.

This chapter focuses primarily on how to read research reports, for several reasons. First, the bulk of published literature in social psychology consists of research reports. Second, the summaries presented in review articles, and the ideas set forth in theoretical articles, are built on findings presented in research reports. To get a deep understanding of how research is done in social psychology, fluency in reading original research reports is essential. Moreover, theoretical articles frequently report new studies that pit one theory against another, or test a novel prediction derived from a new theory. In order to appraise the validity of such theoretical contentions, a grounded understanding of basic findings is invaluable. Finally, most research reports are written in a standard format that is likely unfamiliar to new readers. The format of review and theoretical articles is less standardized, and more like that of textbooks and other scholarly writings, with which most readers are familiar. This is not to suggest that such articles are easier to read and comprehend than research reports; they can be quite challenging indeed. It is simply the case that because more rules apply to the writing of research reports, more guidelines can be offered on how to read them.

The Anatomy of Research Reports

Most research reports in social psychology, and in psychology in general, are written in a standard format prescribed by the American Psychological Association (1994). This is a great boon to both readers and writers. It allows writers to present their ideas and findings in a clear, systematic manner. Consequently, as a reader, once you understand this format, you will not be on completely foreign ground when you approach a new research report—regardless of its specific content. You will know where in the paper particular information is found, making it easier to locate. No matter what your reasons for reading a research report, a firm understanding of the format in which they are written will ease your task. We discuss the format of research reports next, with some practical suggestions on how to read them. Later, we discuss how this format reflects the process of scientific investigation, illustrating how research reports have a coherent narrative structure.

Title and Abstract

Alhough you can't judge a book by its cover, you can learn a lot about a research report simply by reading its title. The title presents a concise statement of the theoretical issues investigated, and/or the variables that were studied. For example, the following title was taken almost at random from a prestigious journal in social psychology: "Sad and Guilty? Affective Influences on the Explanation of Conflict in Close Relationships" (Forgas, 1994, p. 56). Just by reading the title, it can be inferred that the study investigated how emotional states change the way people explain conflict in close relationships. The title also suggests that when feeling sad, people accept more personal blame for such conflicts (i.e., feel more guilty).

The abstract is also an invaluable source of information. It is a brief synopsis of the study, and packs a lot of information into 150 words or less. The abstract contains information about the problem that was investigated, how it was investigated, the major findings of the study, and hints at the theoretical and practical implications of the findings. Thus, the abstract is a useful summary of the research that provides the gist of the investigation. Reading this outline first can be very helpful, because it tells you where the report is going and gives you a useful framework for organizing information contained in the article.

The title and abstract of a research report are like a movie preview. A movie preview highlights the important aspects of a movie's plot, and provides just enough information for one to decide whether to watch the whole movie. Just so with titles and abstracts: They highlight the key features of a research report to allow you to decide if you want to read the whole paper. And just as with movie previews, they do not give the whole story. Reading just the title and abstract is never enough to fully understand a research report.

Introduction

A research report has four main sections: introduction, method, results, and discussion. Though it is not explicitly labeled, the introduction begins the main body of a research report. Here, the researchers set the stage for the study. They present the problem under investigation, and state why it was important to study. By providing a brief review of past research and theory relevant to the central issue of investigation, the researchers place the study in an historical context and suggest how the study advances knowledge of the problem. Beginning with broad theoretical and practical considerations, the researchers delineate the rationale that led them to the specific set of hypotheses tested in the study. They also describe how they decided on their research strategy (e.g., why they chose an experiment or a correlational study).

The introduction generally begins with a broad consideration of the problem investigated. Here, the researchers want to illustrate that the problem they studied is a real problem about which people should care. If the researchers are studying prejudice, they may cite statistics that suggest discrimination is prevalent, or describe specific cases of discrimination. Such information helps illustrate why the research is both practically and theoretically meaningful, and why you should bother reading about it. Such discussions are often quite interesting and useful. They can help you decide for yourself if the research has merit. But they may not be essential for understanding the study at hand. Read the introduction carefully, but choose judiciously what to focus on and remember. To understand a study, what you really need to understand is what the researchers' hypotheses were, and how they were derived from theory, informal observation, or intuition. Other background information may be intriguing, but may not be critical to understand what the researchers did and why they did it.

While reading the introduction, try answering these questions: What problem was studied, and why? How does this study relate to, and go beyond, past investigations of the problem? How did the researchers derive their hypotheses? What questions do the researchers hope to answer with this study?

Method

In the method section, the researchers translate their hypotheses into a set of specific, testable questions. Here, the researchers introduce the main characters of the study—the subjects or participants—describing their characteristics (gender, age, etc.) and how many of them were involved. Then they describe the materials (or apparatus), such as any questionnaires or special equipment, used in the study. Finally, they describe chronologically the procedures of the study—that is, how the study was conducted. Often, an overview of the research design will begin the method section. This overview provides a broad outline of the design, alerting you to what you should attend.

The method is presented in great detail so that other researchers can recreate the study to confirm (or question) its results. This degree of detail is normally not necessary to understand a study, so don't get bogged down trying to memorize the particulars of the procedures. Focus on how the independent variables were manipulated (or measured) and how the dependent variables were measured.

Measuring variables adequately is not always an easy matter. Many of the variables psychologists are interested in cannot be directly observed, so they must be inferred from participants' behavior. Happiness, for example, cannot be directly observed. Thus, researchers interested in how being happy influences people's judgments must infer happiness (or its absence) from their behavior—perhaps by asking people how happy they are, and judging their degree of happiness from their responses; perhaps by studying people's facial expressions for signs of happiness, such as smiling. Think about the measures researchers use while reading the method section. Do they adequately reflect or capture the concepts they are meant to measure? If a measure seems odd, consider carefully how the researchers justify its use.

Often in social psychology, getting there is half the fun. In other words, how a result is obtained can be just as interesting as the result itself. Social psychologists often strive to have participants behave in a natural, spontaneous manner, while controlling enough of their environment to pinpoint the causes of their behavior. Sometimes the major contribution of a research report is its presentation of a novel method of investigation. When this is the case, the method will be discussed in some detail in the introduction.

Participants in social psychology studies are intelligent and inquisitive people who are responsive to what happens around them. Because of this, they are not always initially told the true purpose of a study. If they were told, they might not act naturally. Thus, researchers frequently need to be creative, presenting a credible rationale for complying with procedures, without revealing the study's purpose. This rationale is known as a *cover story,* and is often an elaborate scenario. While reading the method section, try putting yourself in the shoes of a participant in the study, and ask yourself if the instructions given to participants seem sensible, realistic, and engaging. Imagining what it was like to be in the study will also help you remember the study's procedure and will aid you in interpreting the study's results.

While reading the method section, try answering these questions: How were the hypotheses translated into testable questions? How were the variables of interest manipulated and/or measured? Did the measures used adequately reflect the variables of interest? For example, is self-reported income an adequate measure of social class? Why or why not?

Results

The results section describes how the observations collected were analyzed to determine whether the original hypotheses were supported. Here, the data (observations of behavior) are described, and statistical tests are presented. Because of this, the results section is often intimidating to readers who have little or no training in statistics. Wading through complex and unfamiliar statistical analyses is understandably confusing and frustrating. As a result, many students are tempted to skip over reading this section. We advise you not to do so. Empirical findings are the foundation of any science and results sections are where such findings are presented.

Take heart. Even the most prestigious researchers were once in your shoes and sympathize with you. Though space in psychology journals is limited, researchers try to strike a balance between the need to be clear and the need to be brief in describing their results. In an influential paper on how to write good research reports, Bem (1987) offered this advice to researchers:

> No matter how technical or abstruse your article is in its particulars, intelligent nonpsychologists with no expertise in statistics or experimental design should be able to comprehend the broad outlines of what you did and why. They should understand in general terms what was learned. (p. 74)

Generally speaking, social psychologists try to practice this advice.

Most statistical analyses presented in research reports test specific hypotheses. Often, each analysis presented is preceded by a reminder of the hypothesis it is meant to test. After an analysis is presented, researchers usually provide a narrative description of the result in plain English. When the hypothesis tested by a statistical analysis is not explicitly stated, you can usually determine the hypothesis that was tested by reading this narrative description of the result, and referring back to the introduction to locate an hypothesis that corresponds to that result. After even the most complex statistical analysis, there will be a written description of what the result means conceptually. Turn your attention to these descriptions. Focus on the conceptual meaning of research findings, not on the mechanics of how they were obtained (unless you're comfortable with statistics).

Aside from statistical tests and narrative descriptions of results, results sections also frequently contain tables and graphs. These are efficient summaries of data. Even if you are not familiar with statistics, look closely at tables and graphs, and pay attention to the means or correlations presented in them. Researchers always include written descriptions of the pertinent aspects of tables and graphs. While reading these descriptions, check the tables and graphs to make sure what the researchers say accurately reflects their data. If they say there was a difference between two groups on a particular dependent measure, look at the means in the table that correspond to those two groups, and see if the means do differ as described. Occasionally, results seem to become stronger in their narrative description than an examination of the data would warrant.

Statistics *can* be misused. When they are, results are difficult to interpret. Having said this, a lack of statistical knowledge should not make you overly cautious while reading results sections. Though not a perfect antidote, journal articles undergo extensive review by professional researchers before publication. Thus, most misapplications of statistics are caught and corrected before an article is published. So, if you are unfamiliar with statistics, you can be reasonably confident that findings are accurately reported.

While reading the results section, try answering these questions: Did the researchers provide evidence that any independent variable manipulations were effective? For example, if testing for behavioral differences between happy and sad participants, did the researchers demonstrate that one group was in fact happier than the other? What were the major findings of the study? Were the researchers' original hypotheses supported by their observations? If not, look in the discussion section for how the researchers explain the findings that were obtained.

Discussion

The discussion section frequently opens with a summary of what the study found, and an evaluation of whether the findings supported the original hypotheses. Here, the researchers evaluate the theoretical and practical implications of their results. This can be particularly interesting when the results did not work out exactly as the researchers anticipated. When such is the case, consider the researchers' explanations carefully, and see if they seem plausible to you. Often, researchers will also report any aspects of their study that limit their interpretation of its results, and suggest further research that could overcome these limitations to provide a better understanding of the problem under investigation.

Some readers find it useful to read the first few paragraphs of the discussion section before reading any other part of a research report. Like the abstract, these few paragraphs usually contain all of the main ideas of a research report: what the hypotheses were, the major findings and whether they supported the original hypotheses, and how the findings relate to past research and theory. Having this information before reading a research report can guide your reading, allowing you to focus on the specific details you need to complete your understanding of a study. The description of the results, for example, will alert you to the major variables that were studied. If they are unfamiliar to you, you can pay special attention to how they are defined in the introduction, and how they are operationalized in the method section.

After you have finished reading an article, it can also be helpful to reread the first few paragraphs of the discussion and the abstract. As noted, these two passages present highly distilled summaries of the major ideas in a research report. Just as they can help guide your reading of a report, they can also help you consolidate your understanding of a report once you have finished reading it. They provide a check on whether you have understood the main points of a report, and offer a succinct digest of the research in the authors' own words.

While reading the discussion section, try answering these questions: What conclusions can be drawn from the study? What new information does the study provide about the problem under investigation? Does the study help resolve the problem? What are the practical and theoretical implications of the study's findings? Did the results contradict past research findings? If so, how do the researchers explain this discrepancy?

Some Notes on Reports of Multiple Studies

Up to this point, we have implicitly assumed that a research report describes just one study. It is also quite common, however, for a research report to describe a series of studies of the same problem in a single article. When such is the case, each study reported will have the same basic structure (introduction, method, results, and discussion sections) that we have outlined, with the notable exception that sometimes the results and discussion section for each study are combined. Combined "results and discussion" sections contain the same information that separate results and discussion sections normally contain. Sometimes the authors present all their results first, and only then discuss the implications of these results, just as they would in separate results and discussion sections. At other times, however, the authors alternate between describing results and discussing their implications, as each result is presented. In either case, you should be on the lookout for the same information, as already outlined in our consideration of separate results and discussion sections.

Reports including multiple studies also differ from single study reports in that they include more general introduction and discussion sections. The general introduction, which begins the main body of a research report, is similar in essence to the introduction of a single study report. In both cases, the researchers describe the problem investigated and its practical and theoretical significance. They also demonstrate how they derived their hypotheses, and explain how their research relates to past investigations of the problem. In contrast, the separate introductions to each individual study in reports of multiple studies are usually quite brief, and focus more specifically on the logic and rationale of each particular study presented. Such introductions generally describe the methods used in the particular study, outlining how they answer questions that have not been adequately addressed by past research, including studies reported earlier in the same article.

General discussion sections parallel discussions of single studies, except on a somewhat grander scale. They present all of the information contained in discussions of single studies, but consider the implications of all the studies presented together. A general discussion section brings the main ideas of a research program into bold relief. It typically begins with a concise summary of a research program's main findings, their relation to the original hypotheses, and their practical and theoretical implications. Thus, the summaries that begin general discussion sections are counterparts of the summaries that begin discussion sections of single study reports. Each presents a digest of the research presented in an article that can serve as both an organizing framework (when read first), and as a check on how well you have understood the main points of an article (when read last).

Research Reporting as Storytelling

A research report tells the story of how a researcher or group of researchers investigated a specific problem. Thus, a research report has a linear, narrative structure with a beginning, middle, and end. In his paper on writing research reports, Bem (1987) noted that a research report "is shaped like an hourglass. It begins with broad general statements, progressively narrows down to the specifics of [the] study, and then broadens out again to more general considerations" (p. 175). This format roughly mirrors the process of scientific investigation, wherein researchers do the following: (1) start with a broad idea from which they formulate a narrower set of hypotheses, informed by past empirical findings (introduction); (2) design a specific set of concrete operations to test these hypotheses (method); (3) analyze the observations collected in this way, and decide if they support the original hypotheses (results); and (4) explore the broader theoretical and practical implications of the findings, and consider how they contribute to an understanding of the problem under investigation (discussion). Although these stages are somewhat arbitrary distinctions—research actually proceeds in a number of different ways—they help elucidate the inner logic of research reports.

While reading a research report, keep this linear structure in mind. Although it is difficult to remember a series of seemingly disjointed facts, when these facts are joined together in a logical, narrative structure, they become easier to comprehend and recall. Thus, always remember that a research report tells a story. It will help you to organize the information you read and to remember it later.

Describing research reports as stories is not just a convenient metaphor. Research reports *are* stories. Stories can be said to consist of two components: a telling of what happened, and an explanation of why it happened. It is tempting to view science as an endeavor that simply catalogues facts, but nothing is further from the truth. The goal of science, social psychology included, is to *explain* facts, to explain *why* what happened happened. Social psychology is built on the dynamic interplay of discovery and justification, the dialogue between systematic observation of relations and their theoretical explanation. Although research reports do present novel facts based on systematic observation, these facts are presented in the service of ideas. Facts in isolation are trivia. Facts tied together by an explanatory theory are science. Therein lies the story. To really understand what researchers have to say, you need consider how their explanations relate to their findings.

The Rest of the Story

"There is really no such thing as research. There is only search, more search, keep on searching" (Bowering, 1988, p. 95). Once you have read through a research report, and understand the researchers' findings and their explanations of them, the story does not end there. There is more than one interpretation for any set of findings. Different researchers often explain the same set of facts in different ways.

Let's take a moment to dispel a nasty rumor. The rumor is this: Researchers present their studies in a dispassionate manner, intending only to inform readers of their findings and their interpretation of those findings. In truth, researchers aim not only to inform readers, but also to *persuade* them (Sternberg, 1995). Researchers want to convince you their ideas are right. There is never only one explanation for a set of findings. Certainly, some explanations are better than others; some fit the available data better, are more parsimonious, or require fewer questionable assumptions. The point here is that researchers are very passionate about their ideas, and want you to believe them. It's up to you to decide if you want to buy their ideas or not.

Let's compare social psychologists to sales clerks. Both social psychologists and sales clerks want to sell you something: either their ideas: or their wares. You need to decide if you want to buy what they're selling or not—and there are potentially negative consequences for either decision. If you let a sales clerk dazzle you with a sales pitch, without thinking about it carefully, you might end up buying a substandard product that you don't really need. After having done this a few times, people tend to become cynical, steeling themselves against any and all sales pitches. This too is dangerous. If you are overly critical of sales pitches, you could end up foregoing genuinely useful products. Thus, by analogy, when you are too critical in your reading of research reports, you might dismiss, out of hand, some genuinely useful ideas—ideas that can help shed light on why people behave the way they do.

This discussion raises the important question of how critical one should be while reading a research report. In part, this will depend on why one is reading the report. If you are reading it simply to learn what the researchers have to say about a particular issue, for example, then there is usually no need to be overly critical. If you want to use the research as a basis for planning a new study, then you should be more critical. As you develop an understanding of psychological theory and research methods, you will also develop an ability to criticize research on many different levels. And *any* piece of research can be criticized at some level. As Jacob Cohen (1990) put it, "A successful piece of research doesn't conclusively settle an issue, it just makes some theoretical proposition to some degree more likely" (p. 1311). Thus, as a consumer of research reports, you have to strike a delicate balance between being overly critical and overly accepting.

While reading a research report, at least initially, try to suspend your disbelief. Try to understand the researchers' story; that is, try to understand the facts—the findings and how they were obtained—and the suggested explanation of those facts—the researchers' interpretation of the findings and what they mean. Take the research to task only after you feel you understand what the authors are trying to say.

Research reports serve not only an important archival function, documenting research and its findings, but also an invaluable stimulus function. They can excite other researchers to join the investigation of a particular issue, or to apply new methods or theory to a different, perhaps novel, issue. It is this stimulus function that Elliot Aronson, an eminent social psychologist, referred to when he admitted that in publishing a study he hopes his colleagues will "look at it, be stimulated by it, be provoked by it, annoyed by it, and then go ahead and do it better. . . . That's the exciting thing about science; it progresses by people taking off on one another's work" (1995, p. 5). Science is indeed a cumulative enterprise, and each new study builds on what has (or, sometimes, has not) gone before it. In this way, research articles keep social psychology vibrant.

A study can inspire new research in a number of different ways, such as: (1) It can lead one to conduct a better test of the hypotheses, trying to rule out alternative explanations of the findings; (2) it can lead one to explore the limits of the findings, to see how widely applicable they are, perhaps exploring situations to which they do not apply; (3) it can lead one to test the implications of the findings, furthering scientific investigation of the phenomenon; (4) it can inspire one to apply the findings, or a novel methodology, to a different area of investigation; and (5) it can provoke one to test the findings in the context of a specific real-world problem, to see if they can shed light on it. All of these are excellent extensions of the original research, and there are, undoubtedly, other ways that research findings can spur new investigations.

The problem with being too critical, too soon, while reading research reports is that the only further research one may be willing to attempt is research of the first type: redoing a study better. Sometimes this is desirable, particularly in the early stages of investigating a particular issue, when the findings are novel and perhaps unexpected. But redoing a reasonably compelling study, without extending it in any way, does little to advance our understanding of human behavior. Although the new study might be "better," it will not be "perfect," so *it* would have to be run again, and again, likely never reaching a stage where it is beyond criticism. At some point, researchers have to decide that the evidence is compelling enough to warrant investigation of the last four types. It is these types of studies that most advance our knowledge of social behavior. As you read more research reports, you will become more comfortable deciding when a study is "good enough" to move beyond it. This is a somewhat subjective judgment, and should be made carefully.

When social psychologists write up a research report for publication, it is because they believe they have something new and exciting to communicate about social behavior. Most research reports that are submitted for publication are rejected. Thus, the reports that are eventually published are deemed pertinent not only by the researchers who wrote them, but also by the reviewers and editors of the journals in which they are published. These people, at least, believe the research reports they write and publish have something important and interesting to say. Sometimes, you'll disagree; not all journal articles are created equal, after all. But we recommend that you, at least initially, give these well-meaning social psychologists the benefit of the doubt. Look for what they're excited about. Try to understand the authors' story, and see where it leads you.

ACKNOWLEDGMENTS

Preparation of this paper was facilitated by a Natural Sciences and Engineering Research Council of Canada doctoral fellowship to Christian H. Jordan. Thanks to Roy Baumeister, Arie Kruglanski, Ziva Kunda, John Levine, Geoff MacDonald, Richard Moreland, Ian Newby-Clark, Steve Spencer, and Adam Zanna for their insightful comments on, and appraisals of, various drafts of this chapter. Thanks also to Arie Kruglanski and four anonymous editors of volumes in the series *Key Readings in Social Psychology* for their helpful critiques of an initial outline of this paper.

REFERENCES

American Psychological Association. (1994). *Publication manual* (4th ed.). Washington, DC: Author.

Aronson, E. (1995). Research in social psychology as a leap of faith. In E. Aronson (Ed.), *Readings about the social animal* (7th ed., pp. 3–9). New York: W. H. Freeman.

Bem, D. J. (1987). Writing the empirical journal article. In M. P. Zanna & J. M. Darley (Eds.), *The compleat academic: A practical guide for the beginning social scientist* (pp. 171–201). New York: Random House.

Bowering, G. (1988). *Errata*. Red Deer, Alberta.: Red Deer College Press.

Cohen, J. (1990). Things I have learned (so far). *American Psychologist, 45,* 1304–1312.

Forgas, J. P. (1994). Sad and guilty? Affective influences on the explanation of conflict in close relationships. *Journal of Personality and Social Psychology, 66,* 56–68.

Sternberg, R. J. (1995). *The psychologist's companion: A guide to scientific writing for students and researchers* (3rd ed.). Cambridge: Cambridge University Press.

References

Abramson, L. Y., Seligman, M. E. P., & Teasdale, J. D. (1978). Learned helplessness in humans: Critique and reformulation. *Journal of Abnormal Psychology, 87,* 49–74.

Adler, A. (1930). Individual psychology. In C. Murchinson (Ed.), *Psychologies of 1930* (pp. 395-405). Worcester, MA: Clark University Press.

American Psychiatric Association. (1994). *Diagnostic and statistical manual of mental disorders* (4th ed.). Washington, DC: Author.

Ayduk, O., Downey, G., Testa, A., Yen, Y., & Shoda, Y. (1999). Does rejection elicit hostility in high rejection sensitive women? *Social Cognition, 17,* 245–271.

Beach, S. R. H., Sandeen, E., & O'Leary, K. D. (1990). *Depression in marriage.* New York: Guilford Press.

Braginsky, B., Grosse, M., & Ring, K. (1966). Controlling outcomes through impression-management: An experimental study of the manipulative tactics of mental patients. *Journal of Consulting Psychology, 30,* 295–300.

Burns, M. O., & Seligman, M. E. P. (1991). Explanatory style, helplessness, and depression. In C. R. Snyder & D. R. Forsyth (Eds.), *Handbook of social and clinical psychology: The health perspective* (pp. 267–284). New York: Pergamon.

Cacioppo, J. T., Claiborn, C. D., Petty, R. E., & Heesacker, M. (1991). General framework for the study of attitude change in psychotherapy. In C. R. Snyder & D. R. Forsyth (Eds.), *Handbook of social and clinical psychology: The health perspective* (pp. 523–539). New York: Pergamon.

Coyne, J. C. (1976). Depression and the response of others. *Journal of Abnormal Psychology, 85,* 186–193.

Coyne, J. C. (1976). Toward an interactional description of depression. *Psychiatry, 39,* 28–40.

Downey, G., Feldman, S., & Ayduk, O. (2000). Rejection sensitivity and male violence in romantic relationships. *Personal Relationships, 7,* 45–61.

Downey, G., Lebolt, A., Rincon, C., & Freitas, A. L. (1998). Rejection sensitivity and children's interpersonal difficulties. *Child Development, 69,* 1072–1089.

Frank, J. D. (1961). *Persuasion and healing.* Baltimore, MD: Johns Hopkins University Press.

Harvey, J. H. (1987). Attributions in close relationships: Research and theoretical developments. *Journal of Social and Clinical Psychology, 5,* 420–434.

Hovland, C. I., Janis, I. L., & Kelley, H. H. (1953). *Communication and persuasion.* New Haven, CT: Yale University Press.

Ickes, W. (1988). Attributional styles and the self-concept. In L. Y. Abramson (Ed.), *Social cognition and clinical psychology* (pp. 66–97). New York: Guilford Press.

Janoff-Bulman, R. (1979). Characterological versus behavioral self-blame: Inquiries into depression and rape. *Journal of Personality and Social Psychology, 31,* 1798–1809.

Jones, E. E., Kanouse, D. E., Kelley, H. H., Nisbett, R. E., Valins, S., & Weiner, B. (Eds.). (1976). *Attribution: Perceiving the causes of behavior.* Morristown, NJ: General Learning Press.

Kelley, H. H. (1950). The warm-cold variable in first impressions of persons. *Journal of Personality, 18,* 431–439.

Langer, E. J. (1975). The illusion of control. *Journal of Personality and Social Psychology, 32,* 311–328.

Leary, M. R., & Miller, R. S. (1986). *Social psychology and dysfunctional behavior.* New York: Springer-Verlag.

Millon, T. (1975). Reflections on Rosenhan's "On being sane in insane places." *Journal of Abnormal Psychology, 84,* 456–461.

Pennebaker, J. W., & Beall, S. (1986). Confronting a traumatic event: Toward an understanding of inhibition and disease. *Journal of Abnormal Psychology, 95,* 274–281.

Pennebaker, J. W., Burnam, M. A., Schaeffer, M. A., & Harper, D. C. (1977). Lack of control as a determinant of perceived physical symptoms. *Journal of Personality and Social Psychology, 35,* 167–174.

Petty, R. E., & Cacioppo, J. T. (1981). *Attitudes and persuasion: Classic and contemporary approaches.* Dubuque, IA: Wm. C. Brown.

Rappaport, J., & Cleary, C. P. (1980). Labeling theory and the social psychology of experts and helpers. In M. Gibbs, J. Lachenmeyer, & J. Sigal (Eds.), *Community psychology: Theoretical and empirical approaches* (pp. 71–96). New York: Gardner Press.

Robins, C. J. (1988). Attributions and depression: Why is the literature so inconsistent? *Journal of Personality and Social Psychology, 54,* 880–889.

Rodin, J., & Langer, E. J. (1977). Long-term effects of a control-relevant intervention with institutionalized aged. *Journal of Personality and Social Psychology, 35,* 897–902.

Spitzer, R. L. (1975). On pseudoscience in science, logic in remission, and psychiatric diagnosis: A critique of Rosenhan's "On being sane in insane places." *Journal of Abnormal Psychology, 84,* 442–452.

Stotland, E., & Blumenthal, A. (1964). The reduction of anxiety as a result of the expectation of making a choice. *Canadian Review of Psychology, 18,* 139–145.

Strong, S. R. (1968). Counseling: An interpersonal influence process. *Journal of Counseling Psychology, 15,* 215–224.

Temerlin, M. K. (1968). Suggestion effects in psychiatric diagnosis. *Journal of Nervous and Mental Disease, 147,* 349–359.

Terman, L. M., & Oden, M. H. (1947). *Genetic studies of genius: IV. The gifted child grows up: Twenty-five years follow-up of a superior group.* Stanford, CA: Stanford University Press.

Valins, S., & Nisbett, R. E. (1972). Attribution processes in the development and treatment of emotional disorders. In E. E. Jones, D. E. Kanouse, H. H. Kelley, R. E. Nisbett, S. Valins, & B. Weiner (Eds.), *Attribution: Perceiving the causes of behavior* (pp. 137–150). Morristown, NJ: General Learning Press.

Vanfossen, B. E. (1986). Sex differences in depression: The role of spouse support. In S. E. Hobfoll (Ed.), *Stress, social support, and women* (pp. 78–89). Washington, DC: Hemisphere.

Weiner, B. (1975). "On being sane in insane places": A process (attributional) analysis and critique. *Journal of Abnormal Psychology, 84,* 433–441.

Author Index

Abelson, R., 40, 217
Abramson, L., 27, 28, 35, 44, 45, 46, 71
Abramson, P., 227
Achenbach, T., 248
Acksen, B., 89
Adamson, J., 341
Ader, R., 304
Adler, A., 339, 341
Adlerfer, C., 267
Ahrens, A., 46
Ahrens, C., 260
Ainsworth, M., 186
Albrecht, G., 261
Aldwin, C., 164
Alexander, C., 155
Alexander, F., 303
Alloy, L., 46, 249, 250, 251
Ambady, N., 53, 62
American Psychiatric Association (APA), 17, 106, 194, 203, 221, 253, 269
American Psychological Association, 32, 358
Amir, Y., 267
Anastasio, P., 266
Anderson, C., 28, 29, 30, 31, 32, 33, 35, 37, 38, 39, 40
Anderson, E., 61, 170
Anderson, K., 30, 45, 71
Apospori, E., 121
Appelman, A., 65
Arbuckle, J., 47
Arieti, S., 80
Arizmendi, T., 102
Arnold, J., 262
Arnoult, L., 29, 35
Aronson, E., 315, 316, 321, 351, 364–65
Artiss, K., 80
Asch, S., 206, 218, 227
Asher, S., 119, 120
Atkinson, J., 87
Augoustinos, M., 260
Averill, J., 119
Axsom, D., 314, 315
Ayduk, O., 174
Azrin, N., 292

Bachman, B., 266
Back, K., 100, 113

Backman, C., 351
Bagley, C., 121
Bailey, S., 30, 45, 71
Baker, E., 121
Baker, G., 165
Bandura, A., 53, 122, 176, 178, 242, 252, 293, 333
Barak, A., 333, 334
Barash, D., 119
Barber, L., 333
Bargh, J., 176, 263
Barke, C., 19
Barlow, D., 246
Barnett, P., 150, 158
Baron, R., 226, 227
Barry, D., 261
Barton, R., 154
Bartrop, R., 303
Bass, A., 296
Battle, J., 119, 120
Baucom, D., 131, 133, 135, 177
Baumeister, R., 51, 52, 53, 54, 55, 58, 62, 63, 65, 117, 118, 119, 120, 121, 123, 124, 173, 174, 175, 248
Bazerman, M., 65
Beach, S., 130, 131, 132, 135, 143, 177
Beall, S., 302, 303, 307, 310
Beamesderfer, A., 134
Beard, J., 269
Beasley, K., 264
Beauvais, F., 122
Beck, A., 34, 35, 47, 134, 137, 149, 150, 163, 164, 166, 169, 170
Beck, R., 35, 150, 166
Becker, E., 80
Becker, R., 264
Bednar, R., 117, 120
Behar-Mitrani, V., 31
Bell, C., 124
Bellak, C., 80
Bem, D., 361, 363
Benedict, R., 202
Bengston, V., 341, 346
Benjamin, L., 18
Bennett, W., 101
Bergbower, K., 46, 72
Bergin, A., **244**
Berglas, S., 85, 86, 88
Berkowitz, L., 57, 61, 295, 296

Berland, D., 124
Berman, J., 20, 228
Berry, K., 261
Berscheid, E., 180, 190, 194, 227
Bettelheim, B., 341–42
Betz, N., 123
Beutler, L., 102
Bevan, W., 292
Bhugra, D., 260
Billings, A., 158
Bing, L., 61
Birren, J., 340
Black, S., 106
Blake, A., 263
Blalock, S., 46
Blampied, N., 132
Blanch, A., 266
Blaney, P., 164
Blankstein, K., 31
Blehar, M., 186
Block, J., 54
Blotcky, M., 124
Bloxom, B., 164
Blumberg, S., 158, 165
Blumenthal, A., 339, 341
Bodenhausen, G., 263, 265
Boffa, J., 341
Boniecki, K., 65
Bonner, T., 164
Bookbinder, S., 264
Boon, C., 303
Bordieri, J., 261
Boskind-Lodahl, M., 100
Bossio, L., 49, 71
Botvin, F., 121
Botvin, G., 121
Bourgeois, C., 264
Bowering, G., 364
Bowers, K., 341
Bowlby, J., 119, 120, 175, 176
Bradbury, T., 130, 131, 132, 133, 135, 137, 140, 141, 142, 177, 180, 185, 187
Braginsky, B., 78, 79, 80, 218
Braginsky, D., 78, 79, 218
Brannon, A., 46
Bratt, A., 328, 334
Brehm, J., 13
Brehm, S., 15, 17, 18, 249, 315
Brennan, K., 186
Bretherton, I., 175
Breuer, J., 303
Brickman, P., 87
Brockington, I., 260, 261, 264
Brockner, J., 62
Bronfenbrenner, U., 295
Brooks, L., 330
Broverman, D., 244
Broverman, I., 244
Brown, G., 119, 149, 153, 158
Brown, J., 118, 252
Brown, R., 267
Browning, J., 194

Bruner, J., 227
Buchanan, G., 46
Buckner, C., 353
Buehlman, K., 194
Bullock, J., 122
Bunge, M., 292
Burawoy, M., 57
Burdick, C., 46
Burke, J., 228
Burnam, M., 339
Burnett, C., 133
Burns, M., 70
Burroughs, J., 101
Bushman, B., 60
Buss, A., 184, 186
Butler, A., 194
Butler, R., 341, 346
Butler, S., 121
Byers, B., 261

Cacioppo, J., 325, 326, 327, 328, 329, 332, 333, 334
Canar, J., 262
Cantril, P., 103
Cantwell, P., 102
Carnelley, K., 177
Carr, J., 61
Carson, R., 13, 14, 248
Carter, A., 246
Carter, J., 63
Carter, S., 263
Carver, C., 30, 31, 46, 53, 58, 133, 135, 137, 140
Casas, J., 334
Cassidy, J., 175
Castellon, C., 72
Catano, V., 46
Center for Mental Health Services, 262
Chambon, A., 269
Chang, E., 48
Chaplin, W., 154
Chartier, G., 133
Chassman, J., 266
Cheek, J., 184, 186
Cheek, P., 41
Chidester, T., 351
Childress, R., 330
Chiodo, A., 228
Christensen, D., 252
Cialdini, B., 327
Claiborn, C., 14, 17, 46, 325, 330, 333, 335
Clark, L., 120
Clarkson, F., 244
Clausen, J., 261
Clayton, P., 158
Clayton, S., 121
Cleary, C., 216
Cleveland, S., 218
Cochran, S., 46
Cocozza, J., 264
Cohen, F., 303
Cohen, J., 190, 364
Cohen, L., 19

Cohen, M., 165
Cohen, P., 190
Cohen, R., 165
Cohen, S., 119, 149, 303
Cohn, D., 194
Coie, J., 122, 175
Collins, N., 177, 187
Conlon, E., 62
Cook, S., 267
Cookson, H., 121
Coombs, R., 122
Cooper, H., 60–61
Cooper, J., 314, 315, 316, 318, 322
Coopersmith, S., 120
Copeland, J., 225, 226, 235, 237
Corah, N., 341
Corrigan, J., 326, 331, 333, 334
Corrigan, P., 258, 259, 261, 262, 266, 269
Costanzo, P., 89
Costello, C., 169
Covi, L., 151
Covington, M., 46
Coyne, J., 147, 149, 153, 158, 162, 164, 165, 166, 167, 169, 170, 171, 175, 194
Crago, M., 102, 103, 123
Cramer, L., 131
Crandall, C., 99, 100, 101
Crick, N., 176
Crites, J., 330
Crocetti, G., 261
Crockenberg, S., 121
Crocker, J., 267
Cronbach, L., 47, 73, 167
Crossman, R., 122
Crowther, J., 134
Cullen, F., 261, 264, 267
Culp, A., 122
Culp, R., 122
Currie, E., 61
Cutrona, C., 35, 120
Cvetkovich, G., 121
Czechowicz, D., 121

Dahl, A., 260
Darley, J., 237
Daston, S., 106
Davis, C., 326, 328
Davis, D., 262
Davis, K., 89, 186
Davison, G., 341
Dear, M., 261
DeBono, K., 237
deCharms, R., 341
Deegan, Patricia, 264
De La Ronde, C., 352
Dell, D., 326, 333
deMayo, R., 150
DePaola, S., 124
Depue, R., 133
Derogatis, L., 151, 181, 185
Desforges, D., 267

Deuser, W., 30, 40
Deux, K., 97
DeVellis, B., 46
Devine, P., 260, 263, 265, 266
Dewey, John, 294
Dholakia, R., 326
Diamond, M., 303
Dickinson, J., 227
DiClemente, C., 55
Dill, J., 28
Dipboye, R., 295, 296
Dixon, D., 326, 330, 331, 333
Doctora, J., 46
Dodder, L., 118
Dodge, K., 122, 175, 176, 177
Doherty, W., 132, 133
Dohrenwend, B., 261
Domino, G., 265
Donnerstein, E., 295, 296
Dorn, F., 326
Douglass, F., 121
Dovidio, J., 261, 266, 267
Dowd, E., 46
Doweiko, H., 62
Downey, A., 180
Downey, G., 173, 174, 175, 176, 184, 185, 194
Downs, D., 118, 119
Downs, W., 123
Drehmer, D., 261
Duan, C., 265
Duhe, A., 135
Duke, M., 246, 248
Dunn, O., 101
Dunn, P., 123
Dusek, J., 118
Dusenbury, L., 121
Dutton, D., 194
Dweck, C., 176
Dwyer, J., 101
Dykema, J., 72
Dykema, K., 46, 47

Eagly, A., 89
Egeland, B., 194
Eisler, R., 62
Ekdahl, M., 261
Elliot, R., 335
Elliott, R., 19
Ellis, A., 124
Ellison, C., 267
Ely, R., 351
Emmons, R., 53
Endicott, J., 150, 151, 152
Epstein, N., 131, 177
Erbaugh, J., 34
Erber, R., 263
Erikson, E., 175
Escobar, M., 248
Eskilson, A., 118
Esses, V., 260
Evans, E., 121

Eysenck, H., 72, 186
Eysenck, S., 186

Fairweather, G., 269
Falk, J., 101
Farber, P., 121
Farina, A., 249, 261, 269
Farris, E., 97
Fashimpar, G., 123, 124
Fauber, R., 175
Fazio, R., 131
Feather, N., 31, 35
Feeney, J., 177, 187
Feldman, J., 101
Feldman, S., 173, 174, 175, 176, 184, 185, 194
Felner, R., 261
Felson, R., 61
Ferguson, L., 218
Festinger, L., 87, 100, 103, 104, 107, 108, 110, 315
Fierman, L., 80
Fincham, F., 130, 131, 132, 133, 135, 137, 140, 141, 142, 143, 177, 180, 185, 187, 190
Finison, L., 80
Finn, S., 353
Firestone, I., 296
Fisch, R., 354
Fischer, K., 41
Fisher, D., 266
Fisher, J., 97, 249
Fishman, D., 292
Fiske, S., 242
Fitness, J., 132
Fitzpatrick, M., 133
Flanagan, M., 295, 296
Fleiss, J., 152
Fleming, B., 177
Fletcher, G., 131, 132, 141
Fletcher, J., 248
Fletcher, P., 194
Flett, G., 31
Flippo, J., 153
Floyd, H., Jr., 260, 264
Flynn, L., 262
Folkman, S., 170
Forehand, R., 120, 175
Forgas, J., 358
Forsyth, D., 21, 123, 236, 290, 291
Fowles, D., 303
Frame, C., 120
Frank, J., 13, 14, 17, 264, 277, 315
Franklin, J., 150
Frazier, P., 31
Freedman, J., 316
Freedman, L., 80
Freitas, A., 174
French, D., 122
French, J., 120
French, R., 31, 32
Freud, S., 16, 113, 243, 279, 284, 303
Friedenberg, W., 326
Friedlander, M., 250

Friedman, H., 72, 75
Friedman, L., 55
Friedman, S., 175
Friedrich, G., 169
Friend, R., 184, 185
Frieze, I., 97
Fritz, J., 122
Fromm-Reichmann, F., 165
Funder, D., 54
Fyock, J., 265, 266

Gabbard, G., 261
Gabbard, K., 261
Gaertner, S., 261, 266, 267
Galassi, J., 31
Gallagher, E., 80
Galvin, K., 18
Gandour, M., 100, 101
Ganellen, R., 31, 133
Garber, J., 119, 142
Garbin, M., 134
Garfield, S., 244, 251, 293
Garfinkel, P., 101, 102, 103, 112
Garner, D., 101, 102, 103, 112
Garner, W., 303
Garrow, J., 101
Gasiewski, E., 122
Gatchel, R., 341
Gauron, E., 227
Geer, J., 341
Gelso, C., 293, 295, 297, 335
Gerstein, L., 19, 20
Gibbs, J., 293, 295
Giesler, B., 351
Gillham, J., 49
Gillis, J., 326, 330
Ginter, E., 120
Giuliano, T., 65
Glaser, R., 302, 303, 304
Glass, D., 55, 341
Glass, G., 303
Glasser, R., 294
Glover, R., 266
Glueck, E., 122
Glueck, S., 122
Goffman, E., 79, 80, 212, 261, 268
Gold, R., 122
Goldman, L., 295, 297
Goldman, R., 329
Goldner, V., 194
Goldstein, A., 13, 14, 315
Goldstein, D., 122
Goldwyn, R., 175
Goodman, L., 295
Gormally, J., 106
Gotlib, I., 133, 141, 143, 149, 150, 158, 159
Gottfredson, M., 54, 57
Gottman, J., 142, 193, 194
Gouaux, C., 169
Gould, R., 340
Grauer, L., 165

Gray, J., 303
Greenberg, J., 125n1
Greenberg, L., 335
Greenberg, R., 326, 328
Greenley, J., 260
Griffin-Shelley, E., 121
Griffith, S., 261
Griffiths, R., 263, 265
Grob, S., 261
Gross, J., 123
Grosscup, S., 149
Grosse, M., 80
Grote, B., 121
Guenther, R., 133
Gurin, J., 101
Gutman, D., 341

Haaga, D., 46
Haddock, G., 260
Haefner, P., 133
Hagman, L., 102
Haines, D., 120
Hall, P., 260
Halmi, K., 101, 123
Hamburger, Y., 267
Hamilton, D., 260
Hammen, C., 46, 119, 149, 150, 164
Hamre, P., 260
Hannah, Daryl, 263
Hanson, P., 218
Hanusa, B., 97
Harari, O., 249
Harman, C., 261
Harper, D., 101, 339
Harper, R., 124
Harpster, L., 57
Harré, R., 295
Harris, L., 123, 124
Harris, M., 227, 228, 236
Harris, T., 119, 149, 153, 158
Harter, S., 118
Harvey, J., 15, 18, 129, 131, 164
Hasher, L., 263
Hatch, R., 122
Haugen, J., 229, 235, 237
Haupt, A., 116
Hayes, S., 248
Hazan, C., 175, 177, 186, 187
Hazler, R., 122
Heatherton, T., 52, 53, 57, 62, 65
Heckhausen, H., 62
Hedeen, C., 150
Heesacker, M., 325, 326, 330, 331, 332, 333, 334
Heider, F., 87
Heller, K., 315
Hempel, C., 295, 297, 298
Hendrick, C., 20
Hendrick, S., 20
Heppner, P., 326, 330, 331, 333
Herd, J., 20
Herek, G., 237

Herman, C., 64, 104
Heron, N., 131
Herrnstein, R., 295
Herz, E., 122
Herzberger, S., 31, 48
Hewitt, J., 170
Hewstone, M., 263, 265, 267
Heyman, R., 131, 135
Higginbotham, H., 236
Higgins, E., 53, 176
Hildebrandt, K., 31
Hilgard, E., 294
Hill, C., 352
Hill, J., 220
Hilton, J., 237, 260, 265, 266
Hirsch, P., 251
Hirschfield, R., 158
Hirschi, T., 54, 57
Hixon, G., 352
Hixon, J., 351
Hokanson, J., 148, 150, 154, 158, 159, 164, 165, 194
Hollis, J., 41
Hollon, S., 142, 149
Holmbeck, G., 122
Holmes, E., 269
Holmes, J., 131, 132
Holmes, P., 262, 265, 266, 267
Holowaty, L., 31
Holroyd, K., 171
Holtgraves, T., 261
Holtzworth-Munroe, A., 177, 194
Holzberg, J., 80
Homans, G., 294
Homlish, J., 124
Hooley, J., 141, 143
Hoover, J., 122
Horney, K., 120, 174, 175, 185, 193
Horowitz, L., 31, 32, 175
Horowitz, M., 303, 310
Horwitz, M., 267
Hosey, K., 249
Hovland, C., 324
Howard, K., 220
Howell, L., 269
Howes, M., 150, 154, 158, 164
Hubbard, M., 321
Hudson, J., 101, 102
Huffine, C., 261
Hughes, C., 308
Huguenard, T., 218
Hull, J., 46, 53, 121
Hulson, R., 122
Hurlbert, D., 122
Hutchinson, G., 194
Hyler, S., 261
Hyman, C., 175
Hymel, S., 119, 122

Ickes, W., 132, 133
Iker, H., 341
Izard, C., 119

Jackson, D., 247
Jacob, F., 296
Jacobs, C., 101
Jacobson, E., 165, 170
Jacobson, N., 177
Jacobvitz, D., 194
Jaffe, K., 177
James, W., 55
Janis, I., 104, 107, 324, 341
Jankowski, M., 61
Janoff-Bulman, R., 28, 29, 30, 31, 32, 37, 39, 41
Jarratt, L., 119
Jarrett, R., 248
Jasper, C., 269
Jaycox, L., 49
Jenkins, E., 124
Jenkins, J., 248, 295
Jenkins, T., 18
Jennings, D., 29
Jessor, R., 112
Jessor, S., 112
Jetten, J., 263
John, O., 265, 267
Johnson, B., 267
Johnson, C., 102, 104, 260
Johnson, D., 218, 267
Johnson, R., 267
Johnston, L., 267
Joint Commission on Mental Illness and Health, 80
Jones, E., 85, 86, 88, 89
Jones, K., 303
Jones, S., 89
Jones, W., 120
Josephs, R., 58, 351
Joshi, P., 119, 120
Judd, C., 260
Juricek, M., 266
Jussim, L., 227, 260, 266

Kahle, L., 261
Kahnemann, D., 253
Kandel, D., 121
Kanfer, F., 18, 19, 53
Kanfer, R., 341
Kanzer, P., 293
Kao, B., 194
Kaplan, K., 175
Kaplan, M., 244, 245
Karniol, R., 56
Karoly, P., 53
Kasian, M., 189
Katz, L., 194
Katzman, M., 123
Kayne, N., 249, 250, 251
Kazdin, D., 296
Keane, M., 260, 264, 266
Keller, M., 159
Kelley, H., 29, 87, 216, 218, 324
Kendall, P., 149, 151
Keppler, K., 261
Kerckhoff, A., 113

Kerr, M., 353
Khavari, K., 121
Khuri, J., 175
Kiecolt-Glaser, J., 48, 302, 303, 305
Kiesler, C., 303
Kiesler, D., 248
Kiger, G., 264
Kiloh, L., 303
Kim, C., 48
Kimble, G., 244
King, L., 53
Kirschenbaum, D., 53, 55
Klerman, G., 158
Knight, E., 266
Kobak, R., 175, 177, 187
Kobasa, S., 303
Kohut, H., 352
Koivumaki, J., 133
Kolodziej, M., 267
Kommana, S., 264
Kowalski, R., 20, 120
Krasner, L., 14
Krauss, S., 269
Kraxberger, B., 123
Krokoff, L., 142
Krueger, J., 260, 265, 266
Kruglanski, A., 176
Krull, D., 351
Kubiak, M., 262
Kuhn, T., 291, 292
Kunda, Z., 267, 268
Kupersmidt, J., 119
Kurtz, L., 269
Kurtz, R., 251

Lacrosse, M., 334
LaForge, R., 153
Lai, J., 48
Lakatos, I., 298
Lamberth, J., 169
Lamnin, A., 310
Landrum, G., 165
Landsverk, J., 122
Langer, E., 217, 339, 340, 341
Larson, D., 150
Latane, B., 104
Latkin, C., 123
Lawson, A., 65
Layden, M., 133
Lazarus, A., 310
Lazarus, L., 303
Lazarus, R., 164, 170
Leach, M., 328
Leaf, A., 341, 346
Leary, M., 11–12, 15, 16, 17, 18, 19, 20, 116, 117, 118, 119, 123, 129, 173, 174, 175, 180, 184, 186, 227, 243, 248, 249, 250, 253, 260
Leary, T., 153
Leavitt, C., 326
Lebolt, A., 174, 176, 180
Lees, C., 121

Lefcourt, H., 132, 341
Lefkowits, J., 265
Lefkowitz, M., 175
Lefley, H., 261
Leggett, E., 176
Lehr, K., 341
Leichner, P., 101
LeMare, L., 122
Lepper, M., 321
Letts, D., 122
Levine, J., 104
Levings, J., 260
Levinson, D., 80
Levis, D., 316
Levy, J., 261
Levy, M., 186
Lewin, K., 295
Lewis, C., 102
Lewis, K., 326
Lewis, S., 265, 267
Lewisohn, P., 149, 150, 153, 154, 158, 159, 164, 165, 170
Libet, J., 164, 165, 170
Lichtenstein, M., 265
Lickey, S., 266
Liddle, C., 194
Lieberman, M., 341, 346
Liebowitz, M., 185
Linder, D., 316, 318
Lindsay, W., 261
Linehan, M., 353
Link, B., 260, 262, 264, 267
Link, G., 261
Lipman, R., 151
Litovsky, V., 118
Livesley, W., 247
Lochman, J., 175
Locke, H., 134, 137
Loder, A., 266
Loewenstein, D., 150, 158
Lofland, L., 120
Lorr, M., 81
Lowenstein, L., 122
Lowery, C., 253
Lubin, B., 166
Luckhurst, E., 303
Lueger, R., 251
Lund, A., 352
Lundin, R., 261, 266
Lynch, J., 264
Lynd-Stevenson, R., 46
Lyons, M., 260

MacCallum, R., 48
Maccoby, E., 175
Macdonald, D., 121
Mace, W., 164
Mack, D., 64
MacKinnon, R., 228
Mackworth, J., 318
MacPhillamy, D., 155
Macrae, C., 263

Macrae, M., 265
Maddux, J., 11–12, 15, 18, 20, 240–41, 243, 244, 248, 260, 333
Madianos, M., 260
Madianou, D., 260
Magnetti, S., 260
Magnusson, J., 261
Maguire, T., 123
Maier, S., 45, 46, 75
Main, M., 175
Major, B., 31
Makuch, R., 248
Malamud, T., 269
Malt, U., 260
Manicas, P., 298
Manis, M., 260
Mann, J., 267
Mansfield, M., 264
Marecek, J., 88
Margolis, H., 264
Marks, T., 150
Markus, H., 252
Marlatt, G., 59, 64, 65
Martin, J., 175
Martin, L., 75
Maruyama, G., 267
Maslow, A., 120, 174
Matarazzo, J., 20
Matross, R., 325, 328, 329
Mayer, A., 261
Mayer, J., 101
Mayol, A., 150
McAlpine, D., 262
McCabe, S., 133
McCall, R., 295
McClelland, D., 87, 174
McConaughy, S., 248
McGlynn, R., 15, 332
McGuire, W., 15, 103, 295, 298
McHugh, M., 97
McKean, K., 46
McKirnan, D., 119, 120
McLean, P., 165
McLemore, C., 17
McMahon, A., 341
McMillan, D., 265
McNeill, B., 325, 328, 329, 330, 331, 332, 333, 334, 335
Mead, G., 351
Mecca, A., 117, 125n2
Mechanic, D., 262, 303
Meehl, P., 227
Meichenbaum, D., 303, 310
Mendolia, M., 46
Menne, M., 331
Mermelstein, R., 155
Merton, R., 251, 294
Metalsky, G., 46
Mettee, D., 88
Meuhlhauer, G., 118
Meyer, C., 31
Michela, J., 29
Miene, P., 237

Miller, D., 40, 56, 227, 250
Miller, N., 20
Miller, P., 132
Miller, R., 15, 16, 17, 20, 28, 120, 129, 227, 249, 250, 253
Millon, T., 202, 247
Mills, J., 315, 316, 321
Milne, A., 263, 265
Milne, C., 46
Mintz, L., 123
Mirabi, M., 260
Mirels, H., 15, 315
Mirotznik, J., 261
Mischel, W., 53, 54, 56, 62, 154, 176, 192, 207
Mock, J., 34
Monahan, J., 261
Money, J., 245
Monroe, S., 133, 149
Mook, D., 295, 296
Moore, Dudley, 263
Moore, E., 121
Moos, R., 158
Moreland, R., 104
Morell, J., 292
Morell, W., 101
Morgan, C., 57
Morrison, C., 264
Morrison, J., 264
Morrow-Bradley, C., 19
Morvitz, E., 118
Moss, A., 245
Motta, R., 118
Mowbray, C., 269
Moxley, D., 269
Mueller, P., 31
Mullen, B., 260
Mumford, E., 303, 310
Munley, P., 335
Munoz, C., 122
Murphy, C., 260
Murray, E., 164, 310
Murray, J., 227
Murrell, F., 267
Musgrave, A., 298

NAMI-E news, 262
Nathanson, S., 62
National Alliance for the Mentally Ill (NAMI), 262, 264
National Empowerment Center, 264
National Mental Health Association, 262, 264
National Stigma Clearinghouse, 262
Neigher, W., 292
Nelson, G., 135
Nelson, R., 248
Nelson, T., 260
Neuberg, S., 235–36, 237
Neugarten, B., 341
Newcomb, T., 113
Newman, J., 101
Newman, L., 228
Nisbett, K., 27
Nisbett, R., 61, 101

Nolen-Hoeksema, S., 193
Noller, P., 133, 177, 187
Norton, N., 20
Norusis, M., 47
Notarius, C., 133
Nowicki, S., 246
Nowicki, S., Jr., 248

Oatley, K., 248
Oden, M., 71, 72
Ogston, K., 165
O'Heeron, R., 308, 310
O'Leary, K., 130, 132
Oleson, K., 267, 268
Olshansky, G., 261
Olson, J., 131, 176
Omelich, C., 46
Omoto, A., 180, 237
Ondercin, P., 101, 123
Orbach, S., 101
Orford, J., 112, 113
Orlinsky, D., 220
Orwell, G., 241
O'Shea, K., 180
Osipow, S., 297
Oskamp, S., 251, 253

Pace, T., 333
Padawer-Singer, A., 103
Page, M., 263
Page, S., 261
Painter, S., 189
Panak, W., 119
Park, B., 260
Parkel, D., 80
Parkhurst, J., 119
Pate, G., 264
Patkin, J., 333
Patterson, C., 119, 194, 335
Paulson, M., 122
Paykel, E., 170
Pazda, S., 123
Peake, P., 54
Pelham, B., 351
Pendry, L., 265
Penn, D., 258, 259, 264, 266, 267
Penn, G., 303
Penn, P., 194
Pennebaker, J., 302, 303, 307, 308, 310, 339
Penny, R., 303
Peplau, L., 35, 120
Perlman, D., 120
Perry, R., 261
Persons, J., 247, 248
Pervin, L., 341
Peters, S., 164
Peterson, C., 31, 32, 33, 44, 45, 46, 48, 49, 71, 72, 75
Peterson, S., 117
Petty, R., 269, 325, 326, 327, 328, 329, 332, 334
Petzel, T., 251

Pew, S., 330
Philip, A., 261
Phillips, J., 207
Phillips, S., 65, 250
Pierce, R., 327, 335
Pietromonaco, P., 177
Pinel, E., 352
Piner, K., 261
Platt, B., 165, 170
Platt, J., 298
Plotnik, R., 121
Plummer, D., 122
Polivy, J., 53, 65, 104
Pomare, M., 267
Pope, H., 101, 102
Popper, K., 298
Porter, C., 250
Powers, D., 267
Precht, D., 119
Predmore, S., 353
Prentice, D., 40
Pretzer, J., 177
Pridmore, S., 303
Prince, M., 19
Printz, A., 101
Prochaska, J., 55
Propst, R., 269
Pruegger, V., 265
PsycLit, 32
Puschner, I., 341
Pyszcynski, T., 125n1

Quellet, R., 119, 120
Quicke, L., 264
Quinton, D., 194

Rabbie, J., 267
Rabkin, J., 260
Rachlin, H., 58
Radant, S., 101
Rakover, S., 295, 296
Rakusin, J., 80
Rapp, D., 218
Rappaport, J., 216
Rardin, D., 106
Raupp, C., 101
Rawson, H., 119, 120
Read, S., 177, 187, 352
Redl, F., 112
Redlich, F., 80
Reich, J., 133
Reinherz, E., 304
Reis, J., 122
Reivich, K., 48
Reivich, M., 49
Rempel, J., 131
Resnick, P., 124
Rezek, P., 123
Rholes, W., 46
Rhudick, P., 341

Rial, W., 47
Richman, A., 123
Richter, C., 342
Rickels, K., 47
Ridgeway, D., 175
Ridgood, B., 123
Rigby, K., 122
Riger, A., 28, 30
Riggio, R., 124
Rincon, C., 174, 176
Ring, K., 80, 218
Riordan, C., 267
Riskind, J., 46
Ritts, V., 352
River, L., 261, 266
River, P., 269
Robbins, B., 164, 165
Robertson, J., 123
Robins, C., 130, 132
Robins, E., 151
Robinson, D., 351
Robinson, L., 158
Robinson-Whelen, S., 48
Rodin, J., 100, 101, 102, 123, 175, 340, 342
Rodriguez, M., 56
Roese, N., 176
Rogers, C., 120, 124, 174, 296
Rogers, R., 333
Rogers, T., 265
Rohner, R., 175
Roman, P., 260, 264
Rose, J., 120
Rose, M., 104
Rosen, J., 123
Rosenbaum, A., 122
Rosenberg, J., 331
Rosenberg, M., 107, 134, 186
Rosenfield, S., 262
Rosenhan, D., 201–2, 218
Rosenkrantz, P., 244
Rosenthal, R., 40, 227, 228, 233, 236, 252
Rosenwein, R., 15, 243
Rosenzweig, M., 101, 111
Rosnow, R., 233
Ross, A., 246, 247, 248
Ross, L., 143, 249, 321
Ross, M., 131
Rotary International, 262
Rothaus, P., 218
Rothbart, M., 265, 267
Rothery, M., 123
Rozell, D., 260
Rubin, J., 62
Rubin, K., 122
Rubin, M., 227
Rubin, Z., 131
Ruch, F., 342
Rush, A., 163
Russell, D., 35, 120
Russell, R., 122
Rust, M., 266
Rutter, M., 194

Sacco, W., 165
Sager, E., 218
Saleh, W., 132
Salkin, B., 101
Salovey, P., 175
Salter, A., 316
Sandeen, E., 130, 132
Sandler, K., 121
Sansone, C., 57
Sarason, I., 14
Sarason, S., 296, 298
Sargent, M., 19
Sayers, S., 131, 135
Scalise, J., 120
Sceery, A., 175
Schachter, S., 55, 56, 100, 103
Schaeffer, M., 339
Scheff, T., 119
Scheier, M., 30, 46, 53, 58
Scher, S., 248
Schied, A., 330
Schlenker, B., 65, 120, 184
Schlenker, D., 65
Schlesier-Stropp, B., 100
Schlesinger, H., 303
Schlossman, S., 304
Schmale, A., 341
Schmidt, L., 326, 334
Schmook, A., 266
Schneider, D., 63, 263
Schneider, I., 261
Schoeneman, T., 41
Schooler, C., 80
Schreindorfer, L., 116
Schroeder, M., 247
Schulman, P., 72
Schwartz, D., 101
Schwartz, E., 101
Schwartz, S., 32
Scott, D., 261
Searles, H., 80
Sechrest, L., 19, 315
Secord, P., 295, 298, 351
Sedikides, C., 28
Seidner, M., 341
Seligman, C., 131
Seligman, M., 27, 32, 35, 44, 45, 46, 49, 70, 71, 72, 75, 88, 169, 341
Selye, H., 303
Semmel, A., 35
Shakow, D., 298
Shapiro, A., 264
Shaver, K., 132
Shaver, P., 175, 177, 186, 187
Shavitt, S., 237
Shaywitz, B., 248
Shaywitz, S., 248
Sheinberg, M., 194
Shenkel, R., 253
Sheppard, J., 18
Sher, T., 131
Sherif, M., 103

Sherk, D., 252
Sherman, J., 245, 260
Sherman, S., 265
Shilts, R., 63
Shisslak, C., 123
Shoben, E., 14
Shoda, V., 174
Shoda, Y., 54, 56, 176, 192
Shontz, F., 227
Shortt, J., 263
Shrauger, J., 352
Shrout, P., 261
Shute, R., 121
Siassi, I., 261
Sidman, M., 297
Sigelman, L., 266, 267
Silber, E., 135
Silberstein, L., 100, 101, 123
Sillars, A., 132
Silver, R., 303
Simons, R., 123
Simpson, J., 177, 187, 194
Singer, J., 55, 341
Sinoway, C., 101
Sirlin, J., 100
Sjostrom, L., 105
Skinner, L., 261
Skinner, M., 122
Skov, R., 265
Slee, P., 122
Smart, R., 119
Smelser, N., 117
Smit, S., 119
Smith, A., 264
Smith, T., 15, 17, 18, 249
Smith-Lovin, L., 351
Snyder, C., 120, 249, 253
Snyder, M., 164, 180, 225, 226, 227, 228, 229, 235, 237, 250, 251, 252
Soby, B., 121
Socall, D., 261
Society for the Advancement of Social Psychology, 21
Soffin, S., 260
Solano, C., 120
Solomon, S., 125n1
Solursh, D., 121
Solursh, L., 121
Somberg, D., 175, 177
Sommer, R., 294
Sosowsky, L., 261
Soulis, J., 122
Southwick, L., 53, 61
Spanier, G., 188
Spanos, N., 252
Speicher, C., 303
Spiro, H., 261
Spitzer, R., 150, 151, 152, 202, 245
Sprafkin, R., 326, 328, 330
Spruill, J., 101, 111
Squire, S., 102, 104, 112
Srikameswaran, S., 101
Sroufe, L., 194

Staats, A., 13
Stampfl, T., 316
Stangor, C., 265, 266
State of Connecticut Department of Mental Health and Addiction Services, 266
Staw, B., 62, 65
Steadman, H., 261
Steele, C., 53, 58, 61
Steer, R., 134
Stefanis, C., 260
Stein, J., 352
Steiner, S., 149
Steinmetz, J., 150
Stein-Seroussi, A., 351
Sternberg, R., 364
Sternthal, B., 326
Stevens, V., 41
Stewart, M., 122
Stillwell, A., 57, 62
Stockman, S., 250
Stokes, J., 119, 120
Stokes, R., 170
Stoltenberg, C., 15, 20, 243, 325, 326, 327, 328, 329, 330, 331, 332, 333, 334, 335
Stoltz, R., 31
Stone, G., 251, 296, 298
Stones, M., 303
Stotland, E., 339, 341
Strack, S., 158, 163, 164
Strang, H., 62
Strangler, R., 101
Strauss, C., 120
Striegel-Moore, R., 100, 101, 102, 104, 123
Strober, M., 101
Strohmer, D., 228
Strong, S., 14, 15, 17, 18, 21, 248, 290, 291, 297, 315, 324, 325, 326, 327, 328, 329, 330, 331, 335
Struening, E., 261
Strupp, H., 18, 296, 298
Suczek, R., 153
Sullivan, H., 174, 175
Sullivan, M., 46
Summers, K., 193
Susman, J., 303
Swann, W., 236, 303
Swann, W., Jr., 349, 350, 351, 352, 353, 354
Sweeney, P., 30, 45, 47, 71
Syme, S., 303
Szasz, T., 80

Tabachnik, N., 249
Tafarodi, R., 351
Tagiuri, R., 227
Tambor, E., 118
Tan, E., 61
Tanke, E., 227
Tashakkori, A., 121
Tavris, C., 61, 62, 245, 246
Taylor, S., 31, 133, 242, 252, 261
Tchividjian, L., 123
Teasdale, J., 27, 44, 45, 71

Tedeschi, J., 61
Teger, A., 65
Temerlin, M., 217, 218, 219
Tennant-Clark, C., 122
Tennen, H., 31, 48
Terdal, S., 118
Terman, L., 71, 72
Terry, R., 175
Tesiny, E., 175
Tessler, R., 303
Testa, A., 174
Teta, D., 264
Thompson, M., 101
Thompson, V., 121
Thomsen, C., 227
Thorton, J., 264
Throckmorton, B., 124
Tice, D., 53, 62, 119, 120
Tiggemann, M., 35
Tippett, J., 135
Toch, H., 122
Tonsager, M., 353
Tosi, D., 297
Towbin, A., 80
Tripp, D., 46
Trope, Y., 87
Trull, T., 247
Tucker, W., 266
Tuma, N., 73
Turkat, I., 248
Turnbull, W., 227
Turner, J., 267
Tutty, L., 123
Tversky, A., 253
Twain, Mark, 353
Tyler, L., 15

Ullman, L., 14
U.S. Department of Health and Human Services, 73

Vaidya, R., 44, 45
Valins, S., 27
Vallacher, R., 58
Valle, V., 97
Vanderwyst, D., 264
Vanfossen, B., 130, 133
Van Hook, E., 53
Vasconcellos, J., 117
Vaux, A., 120
Vega, W., 121
Vigil, J., 122, 123
Villanova, P., 46
Virgil, L., 266
Vischi, T., 303
Vlachonikolis, J., 260
Vogel, S., 244
Volkmar, F., 246
von Baeyer, C., 35, 252
von Hippel, W., 260, 265, 266

Author Index

Waas, G., 122
Wachtel, E., 353
Wachtel, P., 164, 296, 298, 353
Wagner, S., 123
Wahl, O., 261, 262, 263, 264, 265
Wakefield, J., 244
Walker, G., 194
Walker, L., 193, 194
Walker, V., 261
Wall, S., 186
Wallace, K., 134, 137
Walsh, D., 266
Walsh, G., 119
Walsh, W., 297
Walters, R., 122
Wampold, B., 326
Wandrei, M., 122
Ward, C., 34, 62
Ware, E., 132
Warheit, G., 121
Wasowski, K., 261
Waters, E., 186
Watson, D., 120
Watson, P., 184, 185
Watts, A., 246, 247
Watzlawick, P., 354
Weakland, J., 354
Weary, G., 15, 315
Weber, R., 267
Wegner, D., 56, 58, 63, 263, 310
Weigert, E., 165
Weiner, B., 29, 87, 202, 261
Weinman, M., 260
Weinstein, H., 123
Weinstein, R., 261
Weir, C., 57
Weiss, C., 296
Weiss, J., 296
Weiss, R., 131, 135, 193
Weiss, S., 20
Weissman, M., 170
Welch, S., 266, 267
Wells, M., 117
Wenzlaff, R., 228, 351
West, S., 236
Wheeler, B., 122
Wheeler, L., 112, 113
Wheeler, V., 263
White, M., 19
White, T., 63, 263, 326
Whittaker, K., 122
Wicklund, R., 316, 318

Widiger, T., 350
Wierson, M., 175
Wiggins, J., 153
Wiley, M., 118
Williams, G., 119
Williams, J., 120, 245
Williams, N., 121
Williams, P., 262
Williams, R., 267
Wills, T., 119, 149, 253
Wilson Dallas, M., 226, 227
Wine, J., 65
Winer, D., 164
Witt, T., 89
Wolchik, S., 123
Wolf, G., 62
Wolf, S., 104
Wolfer, J., 341
Wollersheim, J., 316
Wood, S., 122
Worchel, S., 267
World Health Organization, 246
Wortman, C., 89
Wotman, S., 62
Wozniak, J., 264
Wright, B., 249
Wright, J., 62
Wurf, E., 252
Wuzhacher, K., 121
Wyer, R., 265

Yarkin, K., 164
Yates, A., 102, 218, 219
Yen, Y., 174
Young, L., 121
Youngren, M., 149, 155, 159, 165, 170
Yudofsky, S., 228
Yurko, K., 120

Zacks, R., 263
Zajonc, R., 170
Zanna, M., 131, 176, 252, 260
Zautra, A., 133
Zeiss, A., 155
Zigler, E., 207, 293
Ziman, J., 292, 297
Zimbardo, P., 318, 342
Zimmerman, R., 121
Ziviani, J., 260
Zuckerman, M., 166

Subject Index

Index note: page references listed with an *f* or a *t* indicate a figure and/or table.

abnormality
  assumptions and myths about, 243–44
  diagnostic categories of, 246–49, 253
abstinence violation effect, 64
achievement motivation, self-handicapping strategies and, 87
acquiescence, 58–61, 66
Actavil, 89–94, 95
adjustment, role of social support in, 17
Adult Attachment Style Questionnaire, 186
Affects Balance Scale, 181
aggression, level of self-esteem and, 122
aging, effects of personal control on, 339–45, 345*t*, 346–48
AIDS epidemic, self-regulation and, 64
alcohol
  lapse-activated response theory of, 64
  self-esteem and use of, 121
  self-handicapping behaviors using, 87–88
  self-regulation and, 57–58, 59
alcohol myopia, 58
Alice in Wonderland, 286
American Nazi Party, 262
American Psychologist, 244
AMOS, 47, 48, 48*t*
anxiety, level of self-esteem as predictor of, 120
APA Diagnostic Nomenclature for Psychiatric Disorders, 221
attributional style
  defined, 29–30
  depression and, 27–43
  direct rating method of, 31
  effects of, 29–33
  external circumstances and, 33
  forced choice method of, 32
  goals and methods of, 33–34, 34*t*, 35–36
  open-ended coding method of, 31, 31*t*, 32
  research and studies of, 32–33, 36, 36*t*, 37, 37*t*, 38, 38*t*, 39–40
Attributional Style Assessment Test (ASAT-III), 35
Attributional Style Questionnaire (ASQ), 35, 46, 47, 48*t*
attributional theory, 16, 17
attributions, marital satisfaction and, 129–36, 136*t*, 137, 137*t*, 138, 138*t*, 139, 139*t*, 140, 140*t*, 141–46

Balanced Attributional Style Questionnaire, 35
Beck Depression Inventory (BDI)
  in studies of attributional style, 34, 35
  in studies of explanatory style, 47, 48*t*
  in study of binge eating, 107
  in study of depression and marital satisfaction, 134, 136*t*, 137, 137*t*, 138*t*, 139*t*, 140*t*
  in study of interpersonal factors in depression, 150, 152
Beck Depression Inventory-Short Form (BDI-SF), 150, 151, 152, 166
behavioral confirmation effect, 227, 228, 229, 251–52
bias
  in clinical judgment, 250–51, 253
  in defining normality vs abnormality, 244–46
  dispositional attributional bias, 249–50, 253
  labeling bias by clinicians, 216–21, 221*t*, 222–24
  type 2 error of, 205, 212
binge eating
  in college sororities, 99–106, 106*t*, 107–8, 108*t*, 109, 109*t*, 110–11, 111*t*, 112–15
  contagion coefficient of, 109, 110
  Monte Carlo study of, 109, 110, 113–14*n*6
  patterns of popularity in, 105–6, 106*t*
  risk factors and epidemiological approach of, 102
  self-regulation and, 59
  as social norm, 100, 101
  social pressure in, 102–5, 108–9, 109*t*, 110, 111–13
  social psychological factors in, 102, 111, 111*t*
  study of dieting and, 99–106, 106*t*, 107–8, 108*t*, 109, 109*t*, 110–11, 111*t*, 112–15
  theories of, 101–5
Binge Eating Scale (BES), 106, 109
blastogenesis, 304, 305–6, 309
body mass index (BMI), 105, 106*t*
Brief Symptom Inventory (BSI), 150, 151, 152
bulimia. *See* binge eating

California Task Force to Promote Self-Esteem and Personal and
  Social Responsibility, 125*n*2
Career Maturity Inventory, 330
catastrophizing and untimely death, 70–74, 74*f*/*t*, 75–77

381

choking, 63
classification systems of psychiatric diagnoses, 247–49, 253
  See also Diagnostic and Statistical Manual of Mental Disorders (DSM)
Clerambault-Kandkinsy syndrome, 245
Client Personality Information Sheet, 230
clinical and nonclinical populations, 243–44
clinical judgment
  assumptions about normal vs. abnormal, 15–16, 201–9, 209t, 210–15, 243–44, 246–49
  behavioral confirmation effect in, 225–32, 232f/t, 233, 233f/t, 234–39, 251–52
  classification systems of psychiatric diagnoses, 246–49, 253
  confirmatory bias in hypothesis testing in, 250–51, 253
  content and process of, 249
  covariation assessment in, 249
  diagnostic experiences of pseudopatients, 203–9, 209t, 210–15
  dispositional attributional bias in, 249–50, 253
  expectation confirmation in, 225–32, 232f/t, 233, 233f/t, 234–39
  illusory correlation in, 251
  labeling of psychiatric patients and, 201–9, 209t, 210–15
  myths about psychopathology in, 240–56
  perception and evaluation of patients in, 216–21, 221t, 222–24
  professional bias with, 216–21, 221t, 222–24
  superiority and overconfidence effect in, 252–53
codependent, 246
cognitive dissonance, 16, 314, 315–19, 319t, 320, 320f, 321–23
compulsive behavior disorder, 245
concanavalin A (ConA), 304, 305, 306, 307, 308, 309, 309f
content analysis of verbatim explanations (CAVE), technique of, 72
counseling
  barriers to and recommendations for, 20–21
  Elaboration Likelihood Model (ELM) of Persuasion in, 325–32, 332f, 333–38
  health improvement and physical benefits with, 301–6, 306t, 307, 307f/t, 308–9, 309f, 310–12
  history of, 13–23
  rapprochement of, 14–15
  study of expectation confirmation in, 225–32, 232f/t, 233, 233f/t, 234–39
  unificationist view of, 290–300
Counselor Rating Form, 334
counterregulatory eating, 64
covariation assessment, 249
Cox approach/Cox model, 73, 74

deification of disorder, 246
delayed auditory feedback (DAF), 318
depersonalization of patients, 210–12
depression
  antecedent hypothesis of, 147, 148, 149, 156–57, 157t, 158
  attributional role in marital distress, 132–33, 136, 136t, 137, 137t, 138, 138t, 139, 139t, 140, 140t, 141

attributional style in, 27–43
concomitant hypothesis of, 147, 148, 149, 155–56, 156t
explanatory style and, 44, 45–48, 48f/t, 49–50, 71
interpersonal factors in, 147–56, 156t, 157, 157t, 158–61
low self-esteem associated with, 119–20
role in eating disorders, 101–2
study of college students with, 147–56, 156t, 157, 157t, 158–61
study of social responses to dysphoria in, 162–67, 167t, 168, 168t, 169, 169t, 170–72
"success depression" in, 88
developmental disabilities, 246
Diagnostic and Statistical Manual of Mental Disorders (DSM), 203, 248, 249, 253
  (DSM-III), 106, 245, 246, 247
  (DSM-III-R), 244, 247, 248
  (DSM-IV), 17, 269
dieting
  counterregulatory eating and, 64
  self-regulation and, 56, 60
dimensional approach, classification system of, 247
disclaimers, 170
drugs/drug addiction
  lapse-activated response theory of, 64
  self-esteem and use of, 121
  as self-handicapping strategy, 85–93, 93t, 94–95, 95t, 96–98
Dyadic Adjustment Scale, 188
dysphoric emotions
  low self-esteem associated with, 119–20
  study of social responses to, 162–67, 167t, 168, 168t, 169, 169t, 170–72
dyssemia, 246

eating disorders
  self-esteem and, 123
  study of dieting in, 99–106, 106t, 107–8, 108t, 109, 109t, 110–11, 111t, 112–15
  See also binge eating
effort justification, 313–19, 319t, 320, 320f, 321–23
Elaboration Likelihood Model (ELM) of Persuasion, 325–32, 332f, 333–38
emotion regulation, self-regulation and, 56–57
enhanced personal responsibility, impact on the aged, 339–45, 345t, 346–48
essay writing, confronting trauma with, 305–6, 306t, 307–10
ethylenediamine tetraacetic acid (EDTA), 305
exercise, self-regulation and, 55
existential despair, 280
explanatory style
  defined, 71
  expectations and depressive symptoms of, 44, 45–48, 48f/t, 49–50
  globality of, 73–74, 74f, 75
  research methods of, 46–47
  role in catastrophizing and untimely death, 70–74, 74f/t, 75–77
  studies of, 46–48, 48f/t, 49

Eysenck Personality Inventory (EPI), 107, 186

fatigue hypothesis, 55

galvanic skin response (GSR), 317
gambling, self-regulation and, 59
gender, bias in defining normality vs abnormality, 244–46
globality, in explanatory style, 71
Gompertz model, 73, 74t

helper cells, 304
hypoactive sexual desire disorder, 245

illusory correlation, 251
immune function, effects of psychotherapy on, 301, 302, 303–4, 305, 306–7, 307f/t, 308, 309, 309f
impulse, 53, 66n1
individual case-formulation approach, classification system of, 247
insanity, distinguishing the sane from, 201–9, 209t, 210–15
Interaction Anxiousness Scale, 186
internality, in explanatory style, 71
International Classification of Diseases, 73
interpersonal approach, classification system of, 247, 248
Interpersonal Checklist (ICL), 153, 158
Interpersonal Events Schedule (IES), 155, 158
Interpersonal Events Schedule-Target (IES-Target), 155–56, 158
Interpersonal Sensitivity Scale (IPS), 185, 187

Journal of Personality and Social Psychology, 21
Journal of Social and Clinical Psychology, 15, 21

kairos, 288, 289
Ku Klux Klan, 262

labeling
    of psychiatric patients, 201–9, 209t, 210–15
        studies of labeling bias by clinicians, 216–21, 221t, 222–24
lapses/relapses, breakdown of self-regulation in, 64–66
late luteal phase dysphoric disorder (DSM-III-R), 245
learned helplessness
    catastrophizing and untimely death with, 70–74, 74f/t, 75–77
    explanatory style and, 44, 45–48, 48f/t, 49–50
    role in self-handicapping, 88
    theory of, 27–28
Life Orientation Test (LOT), 46, 47
LOGIST, 73, 74f
loneliness, self-esteem and, 120
Loneliness Scale, Revised UCLA, 35
Lorr scale, 81, 82
lymphocytes, 304, 305, 306, 307, 307t, 309

Marital Adjustment Test (MAT), 134, 136t, 137, 138t
marriage, attributions to satisfaction in, 129–36, 136t, 137, 137t, 138, 138t, 139, 139t, 140, 140t, 141–46
mental illness
    activism against public stigma of, 259, 260, 262–69
    authoritarianism toward persons with, 261
    benevolence toward persons with, 261
    effects of labeling psychiatric patients, 201–9, 209t, 210–15
    fear and exclusion of, 261
    public education about, 264–66, 268
    stereotypes and stigma of, 258–74
"mental patient," label of, 218
"mental retardation," defining, 243–44
mental status induction, 81
Minnesota Multiphasic Personality Inventory (MMPI), 295
misregulation, self-regulation and, 52, 61–64, 66
mitogens, 304, 305, 306, 309, 309f
Multiple Affect Adjective Check List Today Form (MAACL), 166, 167t
"Muselmanner," 341–42
Myers-Briggs Type Indicator, 334

nicotine dependency, 245
"normal," 15–16
    criteria for defining, 242
    gender bias in definitions of, 244–46
    judgment and labeling of psychiatric patients, 201–9, 209t, 210–15
    myth of diagnostic categories of, 246–49, 253
    normal vs. abnormal dichotomy of, 243–44
    staff recognition of, 201–9, 209t, 210–15

ontological anxiety, 280
open-ended coding method, 31, 31t, 32
oppositional defiant disorder, 246
Outward Bound, 123–24

Pandocrin, 89–94, 95, 96, 97
personal control, effects in the aged, 339–45, 345t, 346–48
Persuasion and Healing (Frank), 14, 277
pessimistic explanatory style, 71
phytohemagglutinin (PHA), 304, 305, 306, 307, 308, 309
Pleasant Events Schedule (PES), 155
premenstrual syndrome, 245
Prisoner's Dilemma (PD), 165, 294
procrastination, self-regulation and, 59, 63
psychiatric stigma, 258–74
    activism for reducing and preventing of, 259, 260, 262–69
    self-stigmatizing and, 258–74
psychological change, self-verification and, 349–51, 351f, 352–56
"psychopathology of everyday life," 16
psychotherapy
    American practices of, 277–89
    benefits of confronting a trauma, 301–6, 306t, 307, 307f/t, 308–9, 309f, 310–12
    characteristics of patients in, 278–80

psychotherapy (*continued*)
  cognitive dissonance and, 314
  common features of, 283–85
  demoralized patients in, 210–12, 279–80
  Elaboration Likelihood Model (ELM) of Persuasion in, 325–32, 332*f*, 333–38
  health improvement and physical benefits with, 301–6, 306*t*, 307, 307*f*/*t*, 308–9, 309*f*, 310–12
  patient work and effort justification in, 313–19, 319*t*, 320, 320*f*, 321–23
  research of and changes in, 285–89
  social control associated with, 280–83
  as a social encounter, 16–17
  unificationist view of, 290–300
  value of theory in, 296–97

rapport, *behavioral confirmation* effect on, 228–32, 232*f*/*t*, 233, 233*f*/*t*, 234–37, 251–52
reactance theory, 16
reification of disorder, 246
rejection sensitivity
  behaviors associated with, 189–90, 190*f*, 191, 191*f*
  impact on intimate relationships, 176–77, 192
  self-reported mood change with, 182–83, 183*f*/*t*
  studies of, 173–79, 179*t*, 180–83, 183*f*/*t*, 184–87, 187*t*, 188–90, 190*f*, 191, 191*f*, 192–98
  theories of, 175
Rejection Sensitivity Questionnaire (RSQ), 173, 174, 177, 178, 179, 179*t*, 180, 182, 183, 184, 185, 186, 187, 187*t*, 188, 189, 191
relapse prevention, therapy with, 64
Relationship Attribution Scale, 185
Research and Diagnostic Criteria (RDC), 150, 151, 152
"research consumerism," 20–21
Revised UCLA Loneliness Scale, 35
Rosenberg Self-Esteem Scale (RSE), 107, 110, 134–35, 136*t*, 137*t*, 138*t*, 139*t*, 140*t*
Rubin's Liking Scale, 131
Rubin's Love Scale, 131

sanity, distinguishing the insane from, 201–9, 209*t*, 210–15
Schedule for Affective Disorders and Schizophrenia (SADS), 150, 151, 152, 156
schizophrenia
  labeling of patients with, 202, 204–5
  manipulative behavior in, 78–82, 82*t*, 83–84
  study of patients in psychiatric interview, 78–82, 82*t*, 83–84
SCL-90, 151
self-blame, attributional style and, 27–43
self-defeating behaviors, strategies of, 85–93, 93*t*, 94–95, 95*t*, 96–98
self-efficacy models, of fear and avoidance, 17
self-esteem
  aggression and level of, 122
  attributional role in marital distress, 132–33, 136, 136*t*, 137, 137*t*, 138, 138*t*, 139, 139*t*, 140, 140*t*, 141
  clinical implications of, 123–24
  depression associated with level of, 119–20
  dysfunctional attempts of, 17
  dysphoric emotions associated with level of, 119–20
  eating disorders and, 123
  emotional/behavioral problems and, 116–28
  membership in socially deviant groups and, 122
  role of social rejection in, 118–19
  sexual behavior and level of, 117, 121–22
  sociometer model of, 118–19
  state and *trait* model of, 118
  substance abuse and, 121
self-handicapping
  contingency manipulation in, 90
  defined, 87
  drug choice as, 85–93, 93*t*, 94–95, 95*t*, 96–98
  gender differences in, 95–97
  publicity manipulation in, 90–91
  victims of noncontingent success and, 88–89
self-presentational model, of social anxiety, 17
self-regulation
  abstinence violation effect and, 64
  acquiescence and overriding in, 58–61, 66
  consummatory responses with, 63–64
  cultural factors and, 60, 66
  delayed gratification and, 56
  emotion regulation and, 56–57
  failure of, 51–69
  false assumptions and, 62
  fatigue hypothesis and, 55
  features of, 53–66
  feedback-loop models of, 53–54
  impulse in, 53, 58, 66*n*1
  individual differences and, 56
  inertia and attention in, 55–56, 66
  lapse-activated responses and, 64–66
  misregulation and, 52, 53, 61–64, 66
  monitoring of, 53
  procrastination and, 59, 63
  resisting temptation and, 59–60
  short-term depletion of, 54–55
  situational factors and, 56
  standards of, 53
  strength model of, 54–55, 66
  task performance and, 57, 59
  transcendence and, 56–58, 66
  underregulation and, 52, 53, 54, 66
  zero-tolerance beliefs and, 65
self verification, 349–51, 351*f*, 352–56
sexual aversion disorder, 245
sexual behavior, self-esteem and, 117, 121–22
sibling rivalry disorder, 246
smoking, 245
  lapse-activated response theory of, 64
  self-regulation and, 58–59
social and clinical-counseling psychology, 12, 17–21
Social Avoidance and Distress Scale (SADS), 185, 186, 187
social cognitive principle, 242–43
social-diagnostic psychology, 12, 17–18
social-dysgenic psychology, 12, 17
socially deviant groups, self-esteem of members in, 122–23
social psychology
  history of, 13–23
  impact of social and clinical-counseling psychology on, 19–20

reading journal articles and research reports of, 357–66
schism with clinical counseling, 13–15
social rejection, 117, 118–19
social-therapeutic psychology, 12, 18
Spielberger Trait Anxiety Scale, 107
stability, 12, 71
stereotypes, psychiatric stigma as, 258–74
stigma, psychiatric, 258–74
Strange Situation Test, 186
strategy of addition, 229
"street school," 124
structural equation modeling (SEM), 45, 46, 47, 48, 48*t*
substance abuse, self-esteem and, 117
success depression, 88
Symptom Distress Checklist (SCL-90-R), 185

task performance, self-regulation and, 57, 59
temptation, self-regulation and, 59–60
Terman Life-Cycle Study, 71, 72, 75, 76
terror management theory, 125*n*1
thought suppression, 63
transcendence, self-regulation and, 56–58, 66

trauma, benefits of confronting, 301–6, 306*t*, 307, 307*f/t*, 308–9, 309*f*, 310–12
type 2 error, bias of, 205, 212

underregulation, 52, 53, 54, 66
unification view of counseling and psychotherapy, 291–300
Unpleasant Events Schedule (UES), 155*f*, 157, 158
untimely death, 70–74, 74*f/t*, 75–77

Veterans Administration, 14, 296
violence, theory and self-regulation of, 57, 60, 61, 66

weight loss, effort justification in program of, 313–19, 319*t*, 320, 320*f*, 321–23
World War II, 14
writing, confronting trauma with, 305–6, 306*t*, 307–10

Zeigarnik effect, 55
zero-tolerance beliefs, 65